Failure to Pursue

# Failure to Pursue

*How the Escape
of Defeated Forces
Prolonged the Civil War*

DAVID FREY

McFarland & Company, Inc., Publishers
*Jefferson, North Carolina*

LIBRARY OF CONGRESS CATALOGUING-IN-PUBLICATION DATA

Names: Frey, David, 1939– author.
Title: Failure to pursue : how the escape of defeated forces prolonged the Civil War / David Frey.
Description: Jefferson, North Carolina : McFarland & Company, Inc., Publishers, 2016. | Includes bibliographical references and index.
Identifiers: LCCN 2016039927 | ISBN 9781476666693 (softcover : acid free paper) ∞
Subjects: LCSH: United States—History—Civil War, 1861–1865—Campaigns. | Command of troops—United States—History—19th century.
Classification: LCC E470 .F79 2016 | DDC 973.7/3—dc23
LC record available at https://lccn.loc.gov/2016039927

BRITISH LIBRARY CATALOGUING DATA ARE AVAILABLE

**ISBN (print) 978-1-4766-6669-3**
**ISBN (ebook) 978-1-4766-2713-7**

© 2016 David Frey. All rights reserved

*No part of this book may be reproduced or transmitted in any form or by any means, electronic or mechanical, including photocopying or recording, or by any information storage and retrieval system, without permission in writing from the publisher.*

Front cover illustrations of General Frémont's Army (top) and Sheridan's Ride (bottom) © 2016 iStock

Printed in the United States of America

*McFarland & Company, Inc., Publishers*
*Box 611, Jefferson, North Carolina 28640*
*www.mcfarlandpub.com*

# Acknowledgments

This effort has taken much longer than I ever envisioned, in large part because I quickly discovered that the more I learned through my research the more I still had to learn. As the finish line neared and I struggled to complete a final draft I realized how indebted I am for the help and encouragement of my wife, Janey Luchs Smith, who has acted as an invaluable sounding board. I am also grateful to my step-daughter, Julie Barikman-Smith, for helping correct a terrible technical glitch that almost destroyed part of my earlier drafts. Some fellow members of our local Civil War round-table, Jim Fuller, John Murray, and most especially Don Stout, with his sharp eye for critical details, served as readers of original drafts and provided valuable critiques. Todd Bastin of our county library and Rich Purdy as well as Curt Holsapple have helped to obtain hard-to-find books. I'm also thankful for the sustained support and encouragement for two friends, Sally Welch and John Aylesworth.

I freely acknowledge the debt that I owe to all the many authors, writers, and other historians upon whose shoulders I humbly stand. But I also owe much appreciation to a long-time friend and Civil War authority, the Honorable Lawrence Taylor of Gettysburg, for his feedback and tremendous encouragement as I began to wonder whether the end result was ever going to be worth the effort. Thanks to all!

"It is never too late to be what you might have been."
—George Eliot (1819–1890)

# Table of Contents

| | |
|---|---:|
| *Acknowledgments* | v |
| *Introduction* | 1 |

## Western Theater

| | |
|---|---:|
| 1. Overview—Antebellum Influences | 7 |
| 2. Grant at Shiloh—April 6–7, 1862 | 17 |
| 3. Buell vs. Bragg in Kentucky—1862 | 27 |
| 4. Iuka and Corinth II—September and October 1862 | 43 |
| 5. Rosecrans Replaces Buell—October 1862–October 1863 | 57 |
| 6. Turnaround at Chattanooga—October and November 1863 | 82 |
| 7. Sherman's Atlanta Campaign—1864 | 92 |
| 8. Thomas After Nashville—December 1864 | 120 |

## Eastern Theater

| | |
|---|---:|
| 9. First Bull Run—July 21, 1861 | 149 |
| 10. Stonewall in the Valley—Spring 1862 | 156 |
| 11. Lee's Pursuit of Seven Days—June 25–July 1, 1862 | 173 |
| 12. Second Bull Run—August 29–30, 1862 | 196 |
| 13. Chantilly, a.k.a. Ox Hill—September 1, 1862 | 209 |
| 14. McClellan After Antietam—September–October 1862 | 218 |
| 15. Eastern Horse Soldiers | 236 |
| 16. Gathering at Getttysburg—June–July 1863 | 250 |
| 17. Lee and Meade After Gettysburg—July 4–14, 1863 | 271 |
| 18. Little Phil Comes East—1864 | 300 |
| 19. Grant's Ultimate Pursuit—April 1865 | 328 |
| 20. Conclusions | 348 |

| | |
|---|---:|
| *Chapter Notes* | 359 |
| *Bibliography* | 393 |
| *Index* | 397 |

# Introduction

The Civil War was, and continues to be, one of the most powerfully and substantively defining events in America's heritage. Not to ignore its self-evident importance in helping to free four million slaves while also preserving the Union, the monumental struggle also came at an immense cost that still staggers the imagination. Those costs in lost lives and debilitating injuries remained for decades with families that lost loved ones and communities that were left without leaders and other prominent citizen-soldiers. In many other instances, communities near the battlefields were almost completely destroyed and had to be rebuilt with their economies resuscitated and resurrected, incurring tangible and intangible costs practically impossible to measure.

No issue was as perplexing or frustrating to Federal civilian leaders, especially Abraham Lincoln, as the failure of the Union's commanding generals to accomplish decisive victories (meaning the enemy army's annihilation or surrender) following their all-too-rare battlefield victories. As Commander in Chief, Lincoln was often exasperated that regardless of battlefield results, Southern armies always seemed to survive to fight another day. Even before his generals realized this, Lincoln understood battles alone were not decisive unless the enemy was captured or annihilated, and unable to resume combat at a later time. As a result of not achieving decisive victories, Lincoln fired several generals, including Don Carlos Buell, John Charles Frémont, and George Brinton McClellan, and was tempted to dismiss George Gordon Meade even after Meade's great victory at Gettysburg. And why Meade? Because Lincoln's initial reaction—one that he later moderated but never completely set aside—was that Meade's failure to aggressively pursue and "bag" Robert E. Lee's army before it could re-cross the Potomac River meant that a potentially great, strategically important victory had unnecessarily and tragically slipped through the Union's grasp.

Several factors, such as poor strategies and/or battlefield tactics, inept, or at least incompetent, commanders, more lethal weapons, or even poor camp hygiene, are often cited as reasons why there were so many casualties. But these discussions seem to accept the premise the war was destined to last more than four years, no matter what. Therefore it seems significant and relevant to ask whether effective, successful pursuits might have enabled one side to more quickly vanquish the other, thus mitigating the immediate and long-term suffering as well as other societal losses.

The purpose of this book is to examine the extent to which the lack of successful pursuits contributed to any unnecessary length, and consequently the inordinate casualties and economic costs, of the Civil War. It does not try to cover every major battle—even some of those with the longest butchers' bill—but instead tries to identify battles with aftermaths that were, or might have been, opportunities for decisive results typically lacking after the overwhelming majority of Civil War battles. In retrospect it almost goes without saying that the war was bound to continue almost forever without decisive results following battles.

This book is not about abstract military theories or doctrines. Nevertheless it is important to develop some doctrinal context within which battles were approached and fought, and how such doctrines, specifically the philosophy of soft war (based largely upon maneuver to gain occupation of strategic places with limited objectives) influenced an essential unwillingness to follow up in meaningful ways after battles were fought, especially in the war's early years. I begin with a review of some of the rudiments about retreats and pursuits. We will see the limits of tactical options possibly continued to impede the desired results even after the philosophies of war changed. We will also try to identify other obstacles to successful pursuits, including the soldiers' stamina or endurance, insufficient logistics, the lack of necessary assets, particularly cavalry, as well as terrain and weather conditions.

We will quickly see that any pursuit, whether successful or not, was almost easier said than done. Christopher J. Einolf, in his book *George Thomas: Virginian for the Union* (2007), observes that "there were very few examples of pursuits after victory in *any* theater of the Civil War" (emphasis added) citing an early study by Thomas Van Horne, a 19th century military historian. Not only were some pursuits attempted but failed, there were other instances when commanders probably ignored or overlooked legitimate opportunities for successful pursuits to the probable detriment of their missions, and, more importantly, possibly extending the end of the war.

On the other hand, the almost classic pursuit in 1865 by Ulysses Simpson Grant, with a huge assist from Philip H. Sheridan, after they forced Lee's army out of its trenches at Petersburg and Richmond decisively hastened the end of the Confederate resistance, bringing the end of the war that much closer, almost to the extent that many people still equate Lee's subsequent surrender at Appomattox Court House to have ended the war. What then were the different circumstances and factors that had precluded successful pursuits or conversely led to decisive victories?

Upon my first of several visits to Gettysburg I had the same question as did Lincoln, as I suspect have hundreds of other visitors to that national treasure: Why didn't Meade's Northerners immediately take after Lee's retreating, and presumably shattered, virtually defenseless Southerners? I asked similar questions repeatedly as I visited and/or toured other battlefields—Antietam quickly comes to mind. Also as I started reading about other battles and various commanders the same nagging question kept repeating itself in a variety of forms: Why didn't Grant pursue after Shiloh? What, if anything, was restraining Buell after Perryville? And Rosecrans after Stones' River? Is the criticism of McClellan for dragging his feet after Antietam justified?

On the other hand, the premise of my curiosity became muddled after reading about John Bell Hood in November and December of 1864 when he chased Yankees desperately retreating toward Franklin, Tennessee, and soon afterwards toward Nashville. Maybe, I began to realize, pursuits were not always a simple maneuver guaranteed to bring success to the pursuer and ignominious defeat to the retreating army.

Nevertheless it still seemed to me our Civil War lasted too long with too many casualties than were absolutely necessary. As I reviewed battlefield descriptions I began to suspect battles alone, while generating ample fodder for untold numbers of writings and even movies, and while helping to create numerous legendary figures (as well as a plentiful number of goats) actually did not go very far in determining the war's eventual closure. My underlying thesis—which I attempt to investigate and test—evolved that our Civil War was not won or lost by the terrible carnage mutually inflicted on the battlefields but instead was decided in large part after battles when one side could have pursued, but didn't pursue, a fleeing enemy to render that enemy *hors de combat.*

It should be noted that most, but not all, of this evaluation will be upon and from the Union perspective. Lincoln, with virtually no military experience, constantly urged his commanders to be more aggressive; he even took punitive measures when he felt commanders had failed to seize the day. On the other hand, the Confederate President, Jefferson Davis, a West Point graduate and a veteran of the Mexican-American War as well as a former Secretary of War with considerably more military experience than Lincoln, tried to adopt a national objective—which Lee ostensibly observed in form but not always in practice—to conduct a defensive war in hopes that Northern resolve would eventually fade and dissipate if the Confederacy could not quickly be conquered. In other words, as Davis viewed the war for the most part, it was not necessary to conquer the Union and its armies. Instead he believed the Confederacy would eventually prevail when the Union gave up after being prevented from winning. Thus the potential nature, especially benefits, of decisive victories played a much greater part in Lincoln's concept of national strategy than it did for Davis's. Accordingly it seems more pertinent to focus in this book upon the Federal issues with pursuits but some attention will also be given to how the Confederates likewise handled (or mishandled) their opportunities to achieve decisive victories.

We should also realize that nothing, no amount of reading, or any number of battlefield visits or tours, or any number of seminars or lectures, will begin to approximate the fog of war or the harsh, vicious, often bewildering dynamics of actual combat. We now have the advantage of 20/20 hindsight, and are often armed with information, such as the enemy's remaining strength and/or resources, frequently not available to battlefield commanders 150 or so years ago. We have the advantage of making analyses under no particular pressure or discomfort, but during the Civil War field commanders could have been suffering from fatigue in the aftermath of an adrenaline-sapping, life-or-death battle. For instance, during one extended period Lee, 56 years of age, never enjoyed more than two consecutive hours of sleep each night, all the while apparently suffering preliminary symptoms of the heart ailment that eventually took his life. Often, especially after the bloodiest of battles, commanders may have seen long-time colleagues, even friends killed, mortally wounded, or maimed, certainly emotionally wrenching, judgment challenging experiences. And dawdling or dithering could be one of the worst mistakes commanders could make. With or without sufficient information they still had to, or should have acted quickly or else any opportunity might, and often did, simply evaporate. They didn't have the opportunity to partake in a nice meal with families, to enjoy quiet before-dinner drinks (and not to suggest all commanders themselves were always abstinent), take comfort in a good night's sleep, all before arising the next morning to re-check all relevant factors, including modern resources of the local library or even the internet.

Keeping these circumstances in mind, my intent is not to be unjustifiably judgmental. Instead I try to review pertinent factors and to understand whether more could have, or in some cases should have, been done, or conversely, what probably contributed to successful retreats. Admittedly the line between being analytical or being judgmental is sometimes thin and fuzzy; nevertheless my objective remains of trying to better understand what happened, and perhaps why.

As reflected by my previous reference to Christopher J. Einolf, I do not hesitate to draw upon, or cite, the analyses and conclusions of historians, either renowned or otherwise. But it is also fair to say that I have often exercised my prerogative to respectfully disagree in instances where dissent seems warranted. Actually other writings have not widely covered pursuits or the corollary of retreats. Thus there is good opportunity to forge ahead with fresh perspectives about issues related to pursuits: Why they didn't happen more often, and if their absence had any material impact upon the war's outcome?

Because of its eventual importance toward achieving decisive victories, I have given considerable attention to the evolution of cavalry throughout the Civil War. In the beginning Federal cavalry was a virtual non-entity, at least in comparison to Confederate cavalry or for that matter in comparison to earlier European armies. Various chapters in this book, particularly chapters 5 and 16, about cavalry, will outline how the ridership and mettle of Federal cavalry, together with its horses, equipment, firepower, and tactics, gradually improved and eventually surpassed the Gray horse riders. More importantly, a few commanders developed cavalry into mobile and lethal strike forces, especially when deployed in conjunction with infantry. However, some authorities in high places continued to ignore, even resist, advancements in ideas about pursuits almost to the very end of the war.

To facilitate easier reading I often deviate from practices of many other Civil War books. For instance I do not include an overwhelming number of subordinate unit designations or the names of their commanders. Almost without exception battlefield commanders rather than their subordinates made the end-of-battle decisions to either retreat, to pursue, or to stay put, although to be sure we will learn an occasional pursuit was undone by subordinates who will be appropriately identified. My endnotes list several books that are available to provide enormous details not necessarily pertinent to these purposes. I'm simply trying to avoid losing sight of the proverbial forest for the trees while still providing sufficient facts—outlined in a different if not unique perspective—to support an analysis or informed opinion.

But for all the discussion about strategy and tactics, and about military units, individual actions were imperative. In competitive affairs such as mid–19th century warfare it is often said you win with people. Accordingly we will track the careers of important Civil War generals, a few who have already been mentioned, who planned for successful, or at least better, pursuits, or conversely failed to seek decisive victories with pursuits. For instance we read how Little Phil Sheridan, a bandy-legged former quartermaster who once might have been in over his head as a cavalry commander, eventually emerged as one of the most significant Union generals, a reputation built largely upon his pursuits. Conversely we watch as two highly regarded commanders, Don Carlos Buell and George Brinton McClellan, saw their military careers come undone because they were reluctant, if not outright unwilling, to aggressively seek decisive victories by pursuits. On the other side of the coin, we will also review the records of those commanders, such as Stonewall Jackson, who were particularly adroit in managing retreats to stymie pursuits.

One final feature is that I conclude battle chapters with sections titled "Dénouements and Precursors." Sometimes when I read other books I wonder what may have happened after specific battles; what, if any, were the consequences—either strategic or political—of the actions? What happened to some of the main actors mentioned in the descriptions of the battles? One of the things that makes an Ed Bearrs tour so delightful is that he can regale with so many back stories and other anecdotes. My Dénouements and Precursors are mainly modest ways of trying to connect some dots but admittedly there are also times when I mention oddities and curiosities simply because I find them to be interesting. Hopefully none of these distract from my main purpose of looking at pursuit opportunities. History cannot change what has already happened. But the study of history can, and should, help to better understand what happened, and why it happened. More importantly having a better understanding of history, and of the individuals who made it happen, should give us a deeper appreciation of those at various Civil War command levels who made decisions that for better or worse decided the fates of millions of others, including those living today. While asking did it have to happen in the way that it did, this book seeks to add to the vast accumulation of what we know, or think we know, about one of the most important, most influential episodes of America's heritage.

# WESTERN THEATER

## 1

# Overview—Antebellum Influences

Combat objectives and operations changed dramatically during the course of the Civil War. The military historian Bevin Alexander, in his book *How Great Generals Win* (1993), states, "Few soldiers and fewer politicians recognized that the conditions of warfare changed fundamentally between the end of the Napoleonic Wars in 1815 and the outbreak of the American Civil War in 1861."[1] The American Civil War has been called the first modern war but especially in its beginning the Civil War could have also been called the last of the traditional, Napoleonic wars.[2] The means of conducting warfare, for instance the weapons and ammunition as well as the utilization of fortifications, changed the way the war was fought but equally as significantly commanders were forced to adopt new strategic objectives.

At the onset of the hostilities the political leaders of both sides assumed that a quick battlefield victory would bring an early end to the war.[3] From the Union's standpoint, this quick victory would be accomplished by capturing Richmond, Virginia, the new capital of the Confederate States of America. Additionally Richmond was the location of extensive munitions factories as well as being a strategically important rail center. Under the strategic objectives of the Napoleon era—Jomini had stated, "All capitals are strategic points, for the double reason that they are not only centers of communications, but also the seats of power and government"[4]—capture of Richmond would have been a prime objective, and if successful presumably meant a quick end of the Rebellion.

Although one side, specifically the North, had advantages in manpower, technology, and materiel,[5] the other side, meaning the South, had partially compensating advantages such as strategic interior lines, shorter lines of communications, and fighting on terrain that often was a significant impairment for the invaders. Additionally, technical and mechanical advancements meant the foes would be more evenly matched, meaning that it had almost become impossible for either side to score a fast, easy, and decisive triumph. For instance, the availability and use of railroads meant that either side often could rapidly move large number of soldiers over considerable distances to reinforce or to exploit as the case might be.

Finally neither side would enjoy a significant military leadership advantage since both sides were drawing many of their generals and colonels with similar educations and experiences. As a result there was significant—albeit not perfect—military parity between the opposing sides. Yet very few of those in high office—Winfield Scott perhaps being an exception[6]—could foresee how these changes would affect the manner in which the war would be conducted.

As the war advanced certain leaders of both sides, most notably Lincoln and George H. Thomas, began to realize the traditional objective of capturing places was misplaced; even if the enemy were driven from the battlefield, the traditional measure of determining which side had won a battle, little was accomplished if the "defeated" or "vanquished" enemy retreated to a safe, well-protected position, refitted and regrouped, and be ready to fight another day, sometimes surprisingly sooner rather than later.

Instead the more insightful leaders started to conclude the more realistic objective should be to defeat the enemy's fighting force, whether by capture, by destruction, or even by complete and total annihilation. Eventually the newer philosophy of "hard war" took another step, that being to take the war to the enemy's populace in order to break the will and capacity of the citizenry; this of course most often and dramatically manifested itself as the scorched earth strategy, leaving wide spread plunder and devastation.

The relatively new philosophy of trying to conquer the adversary's army, as opposed to capturing places or simply chasing personal fame and glory, was difficult for many senior commanders who—as military commanders are sometimes wont to do—stubbornly continued to fight the last war instead of adjusting to new and different circumstances. Moreover, the limited military education gained by Regular Army officers tended to reflect the chessboard philosophy—sometimes called soft war—of maneuvering to force surrender rather than fierce fighting intended to annihilate.

## *Sources of Officers*

American commanders on either side came from all walks of life. Some had been career Regular Army officers, some of whom—most famously Robert E. Lee—resigned or were expelled before accepting commissions with the Confederacy. In late 1860 the Regular Army had 1,080 officers, approximately three-fourths being graduates of the U.S. Military Academy ("West Point") where despite its name cadets had received scant education in large unit tactics and strategy.

Essentially the antebellum West Point was a civil engineering school,[7] perhaps the best in the nation at that time. Its curriculum for the first two years of instruction was basically that of a modern liberal arts college, emphasizing history, literature and even drawing classes. Third year students received instruction in mathematics and science classes. Although they had had ample training at close order drill and other fundamentals of soldiering, including riding and field fortifications, cadets were not exposed to military strategy until the fourth year of their instruction.

Some former Regular Army officers resigned several years prior to the onset of hostilities; two of the most famous examples of this pattern were Ulysses S. Grant and William T. Sherman. But political influence played a major part in these appointments, regardless of the officer's prior military experience or lack thereof. Some officers had no prior military experience but had been selected as lieutenants or captains by the members of their companies or regiments. Men who had been lawyers, shop keepers, school teachers and professors, politicians, or factory owners were in charge of units such as regiments or brigades.

Both sides needed bodies and the bodies needed leaders, several times more than could be provided from the Old Army. Additionally the public generally distrusted professionalism in all occupations, including the military. Antebellum standards for admission to professions such as the practice of law were still lax as were the requirements for practicing medicine or dentistry.[8] The Radical Republicans, who dominated Congress, did not trust the presumably professional officer corps, most of who compounded their sins by being Democrats.[9] Furthermore there was a commonly accepted notion that a leader in one field, or community, could easily transfer his leadership characteristics to any other field, especially the military. After all, what could be so difficult about riding a horse at the head of a column into a battleground?

Regular Army veterans were not always acceptable leaders because, in a counterintuitive manner, duty in the Regular Army tended to stifle rather than expand upon the skills of officers. Garrison duty lacked stimulation and there were few funds, and little motivation, for field exercises. Even officers in horse mounted companies garrisoned in the Western territories gained little experience that would be useful in infantry command. For instance Richard Stoddart Ewell was a horse mounted officer before accepting a Confederate commission. He lamented that frontier service taught him little of the requirements of an infantry-oriented campaign except how to command a single company, approximately 50 men, of dragoons.[10] To illustrate, one of the major management problems of battlefield command at First Bull Run was that commanders on both sides tended to behave as company commanders rather than as regimental, brigade or even army commanders, old habits difficult to change on such short notice.[11] After First Bull Run, and especially by 1862 as the sizes of the armies increased, some Regular Army junior officers who once might have commanded a company of fifty soldiers found themselves in charge of brigades with perhaps hundred times that number.

In fairness to the graduates of West Point, it should also be noted that they—along with considerable assists from civilian administrators such Secretary of War Edwin Stanton and Secretary of Navy Gideon Wells—provided organizational and operational capacities by which both sides existed. That both belligerents were able to create, organize and train such large armies in such short periods was a testament to the proficiencies of the professional corps of officers mostly educated by West Point.

Aside from Indian fighting, the Mexican War (1846–1848) provided the only combat experience for a select few American officers. This war was fought with relatively well-trained soldiers armed for the most part with smoothbore muskets. Although the Minié ball had been developed in 1843, it was not widely available during the Mexican War.[12] And although the commanding general, Winfield Scott, was generally adverse to wide spread employment of frontal assaults, that tactic was still used with enough success to give Scott's junior officers ambivalent attitudes about frontal assaults.

## *Retreat Doctrine*

It is difficult to study pursuits without understanding retreats, for which there was little theory or doctrine. Carl von Clausewitz[13] discussed retreats only within the context of a "lost battle" when "the power of an Army is broken, the moral [sic] to a greater degree than the physical."[14] Clausewitz also said, "According to the usual course the retreat is continued up to the point where the equilibrium of force is restored, either by reinforcements, or by the protection of strong fortresses, or by great defensive positions afforded by the country, or by a separation of the enemy's force."[15] In other words the retreating side would continue its retrograde movement until it could reach safe harbor.

Contrary to the leading European military theorists, the early odds weighed heavily in favor of retreating Civil War armies. Antonie-Henri Jomini[16] claimed, "Retreats are certainly the most difficult operations in the war" and the "…it is not hard to understand why the most experienced generals have hesitated to attempt such operations."[17] Jomini's observations, published shortly after Fort Sumter, were hardly validated during the Civil War when numerous retreats grossly outnumbered successful pursuits. Instead of being hesitant to "attempt such operations," Civil War generals retreated in all number of circumstances, including when repositioning for better tactical advantage; when realizing that although not defeated his command was outnumbered and outgunned and thus would be threatened if it had remained on the battleground; when hoping to lure the enemy into an ambush; and of course when the general's command had suffered significant losses on the battlefield, of which there were numerous examples.

And finally, despite Clausewitz's assertions, in some instances the morale of the retreating army remained high, the soldiers being convinced they had not been defeated but, for instance, simply had run out of ammunition and intended to return to the arena. Thus Clausewitz's definition, while useful, is hardly all-encompassing, at least within the context of our War Between the States.

Assuming defenders were not driven from the battlefield in disorder, or even in an every-man-for-himself skedaddle, the process of extracting units from the battle lines was closely tied to the order of march, perhaps the most critical aspect of a retreat. The army leaving the field was probably at its highest risk during such extrication. Its intentions were susceptible to discovery at the same time when its capacity to defend itself was severely compromised. Obviously it could be catastrophic if an army were attacked as it was midway through reconfiguring from battle lines to marching columns with its artillery awkwardly positioned. Nevertheless such transformation had to be made with efficiency rather than as hasty as possible.

Given the numbers of men, animals, wagons and ambulances, and artillery pieces it would be necessary to commence the retrograde movement even before all units were withdrawn from their battle positions. Optimistically, a retreat could begin its march undetected and unmolested with enough lead-time to gain its safe haven. But once underway it would be important that the pace not be terribly rapid or helter-skelter but instead be measured and controlled. Clausewitz said. "In order to keep the morale as high as possible it is absolutely necessary to make a slow fighting retreat, boldly confronting the pursuer whenever he tries to make too much of an advantage." Clausewitz also warned that a pace that was too rapid tended to be difficult to control, especially if unit cohesion starts to dissolve or if units become separated. Any retreat that allowed gaps to form between units would become ripe for relatively easy pickings by pursuing cavalry.

But in fact march discipline became important whether an army was in retreat, in pursuit, or merely maneuvering for whatever reason. Almost any marching column would, and still will, stretch or lengthen so that the soldiers in the rear lag further and further behind the soldiers in the front of the column. If this stretching became too prominent soldiers in the rear would complain that the march had already resumed by the time the rear units halted for a rest. Lagging and straggling could never be completely eliminated but company level officers and sergeants were responsible to promote good march discipline by maintaining proper spacing among ranks.

The retreating army's rear guard was almost always its most important element. This unit could be comprised of either infantry, or cavalry, or a mix of these two branches. Occasionally some artillery would also be added to the mix to discourage, or surprise, a reckless pursuit. A rear guard normally was not expected to repulse the entire pursuing army but rather should slow the pursuing army's pace while the rest of the retreating army gained as much distance as possible. Not only would the rear guard skirmish with the pursuer's advance party but an innovative rear guard might erect a series of obstacles, cut trees across the roads, dig ditches across the roads, burn or otherwise destroy bridges, create ruses such as erecting Quaker guns,[18] or even alter road signs, as various ways of slowing the pursuer's progress,[19] or start fires so that the smoke would obscure the pursuer's vision.

Retreats, seldom if ever, resulted in victories, decisive or otherwise, for the army in retreat. Nevertheless they were an essential component in any commanding general's repertoire of command and leadership skills, if only to assure the preservation of his army to be able to fight again another day. Remarkably during the four years of the Civil War, notwithstanding the difficulty and numerous challenges in initiating and accomplishing retreats there were few significant failures of such maneuvers; however the question remains whether this was because of good military skills on the part of retreating armies, or was it because of the even greater challenges and/or deficiencies of the pursuing armies and their commanders?

## Pursuit Challenges

There were myriad reasons for the lack of successful, even properly initiated but ultimately failed, pursuits. Often after a battle there was only a slight difference between the combatants' respective capacities for further combat. This point was not always comprehended or appreciated by civilian authorities who could not understand why battlefield winners did not immediately begin to try to "bag" the army in retreat. Sometimes tactical winners of the battles were forced to withdraw for lack of supplies or ammunition, not because they had been tactically defeated. In these instances the side that remained on the battleground would hardly be in any shape to do much except to declare victory, lick their wounds and be glad the other side was gone.[20]

It would almost seem axiomatic that a commanding general would be anxious to decisively defeat his battlefield enemy but too many generals were simply content to have won the battleground. Sometimes this was a simple matter of settling the honor of individual glory, especially if the adversaries were personally acquainted, but other times it was more general adherence to the philosophy of soft war. Sometimes the commanding general rationalized his decision either to not pursue or to significantly delay the start of a pursuit on the basis that his soldiers were tired, a rationalization that would be overlooking the probability that the soldiers in the retreating army were equally as fatigued if not more so. Commanding generals had to possess mind sets that were not, and would not, be bothered by such negative factors.

Clausewitz considered difficult terrain as a factor that would hamper an effective pursuit to prevent a decisive victory.[21] Weather, especially heavy rains, also played a heavy part in determining the success of a pursuit. One important key for a successful retreat was to be able to get to the retreating army's flank or flanks in order to eventually get into position to form a blocking force. This meant that potential blocking forces, normally cavalry, had to leave roads to cut across fields or other open areas. But in at least a couple instances heavy rains saturated the soil in the fields to the extent that they were virtually impassable. In these instances the commander could do little except to try to find ways to circumvent the obstacles. Furthermore, swollen streams or rivers capable of subduing an aggressive pursuit were sometimes the retreating army's best friends.

## Command Skills Applied to Pursuits

Overwhelmingly the root cause of such early failures rested at the feet of commanders who did not view decisive victories as being essential. Much of the lack of command enthusiasm for pursuits was found in the attitude that taking and controlling locations was more important than eliminating the enemy's army. Until our Civil War, wars commonly had been won by capturing the enemy's capital as had happened in 1848 when Winfield Scott led American forces in the capture of Mexico City. Both Clausewitz and Jomini, the leading military theorists of the day, treated pursuits as afterthoughts. Furthermore most of the military leaders in the Civil War were engineers whose training and experience had oriented them to conservative measures intended to avoid defeat rather than taking risks that would be necessary to eliminate an enemy.

Pursuits that tended to be successful were almost always initiated soon after the battle was decided, usually defined when one of the belligerents withdrew from the field. Between the daunting tasks of trying quickly to assess the post-battle situation, including the enemy's residual strength and intentions,[22] and to orchestrate large units for pursuits while adjusting to new objectives, many, if not most, battlefield commanders simply did not possess the managerial skills, most importantly decisiveness, or let alone the derring-do needed to initiate pursuits. Accordingly, a pursuit, requiring an unexpected, quickly formed, and fast-moving maneuver of inexperienced officers and soldiers over unfamiliar terrain immediately after the pell-mell of battle, would not, in these circumstances be a tactic to be undertaken on an improvised basis by the faint of heart or by a neophyte commander unable to decide whether to, or how to, undertake such step.

The demands of a successful pursuit would test the whole range of capabilities, including management as well as leadership of almost all generals, especially under the pressure of time, and having only reduced resources including adequate intelligence. Accordingly many commanders, especially in the beginning of the war when many were relatively inexperienced, were too conservative, too timid, or too unimaginative to see beyond the immediate field of battle. Instead many early generals were unable to improvise plans of pursuit but were content to allow the defeated foe simply to withdraw to fight another day.

Furthermore too many military commanders in the early part of the war viewed the conflict in limited terms that seldom incorporated pursuits as viable tactics. Or even if they saw the war in a broader manner, they did not have the management skills described by

Brian Reid to implement and manage successful pursuits. Since planning and preparation for effective pursuits had to begin as early as possible, certainly before too much time had lapsed after a defeated enemy began its retreat, prolonged indecisiveness or dithering at the end of battles often meant important decisions were made by command indecision resulting in lost opportunities for decisive victories.

## Factors Encouraging Pursuits

It should almost go without saying that a successful pursuit required management, including planning and preparation, by the commander of the prevailing main army.[23] Pursuits could hardly be initiated by the soldiers alone; if pursuits were started by the troops it is likely that they would have resembled the mobs described so disdainfully by General Helmuth von Moltke, the Prussian Chief of Staff, as merely "two armed mobs, chasing each other around the country, from which nothing could be learned."[24] This statement of course reflected an observation about the armies' lack of preparedness, soldiers who lacked sufficient training, and the relative parity between the sides that tended to resort to orthodox, and similar, strategies and tactics.

On the other hand, and frankly the more likely scenario, most soldiers were reluctant to leave the relative security of their fortifications. In order to begin a pursuit battle-weary soldiers had to be brought out of their entrenchments, had their food and ammunition replenished, re-formed into march columns, and pushed to the further limits of their endurance. In all probability the pursuer's order of battle required repair if not extensive reconstitution. Commanding officers of units on the move had to arrange coordinated movements among infantry, cavalry, and artillery; the wrong order of march—for instance artillery positioned ahead of infantry—could seriously impede how fast an army could move. All these arrangements had to be swiftly and effectively communicated to, and understood by, subordinate commanders.

Although pursuit attempts might be rapid developing and fast moving they still required broad planning and preparation. Obviously it would never be easy or simple to efficiently move an army of 50,000 or so men, even with the advantage of articulation.[25] This was especially true if the army had just been involved in a ferocious, debilitating battle that inflicted numerous casualties, not only among the rank-and-file but also among the officers and non-commissioned officers who were responsible to manage the details of the pursuit. Naturally a commander would prefer to embark upon a pursuit with familiar subordinates but such lack of familiarity alone should never be sufficient reason for failing to pursue. Since a pursuit could not be unduly delayed without losing its effectiveness, much of the planning and preparation would have to occur before the precipitating battle was over.[26]

Moreover, a major task of any commanding general was not just to assign missions but to assure that the subordinate commanders fully understood the need to operate with verve and resolve to implement the commander's plans. In reality a pursuit could be only as effective as its weakest component or link. Each subordinate commander had to understand that a lukewarm effort by any one unit would probably negate the efforts of the rest of the command. The plan and its objectives should not only be known to subordinate commanders but had to be promulgated to staff officers who might have responsibilities for preparing the details of the plan. The very astute Confederate artillerist, General Edward Porter Alexander, emphasized that generals in command needed an abundance of competent staff officers, stating, "An army is like a great machine, and in putting it into battle it is not enough for its commander to merely issue the necessary orders. He should have a staff ample to supervise the execution of each step, & to properly report any difficulty or misunderstanding."[27]

Finally the commander of a fast moving pursuit could not ignore his logistics. Not only would consideration be given to providing supplies of food and ammunition, both of which might be distributed before commencing a pursuit, but other ordinary but essential items such as shoes might have to be replaced. A unit commander had to assure wounded from the battle were being tended and treated.[28] Medical triage had become standard operating procedure not requiring new detailed orders for every maneuver or campaign; nevertheless pursuits could not be launched without assuring that some degree of medical care could be provided if fighting should erupt between retreating forces and their pursuers. Moreover, prisoners taken during the battle had to be processed, sometimes paroled.

In the absence of a conveniently located railroad to transport infantry ahead of a retreating army, or alternatively in the absence of units fortuitously located to head off or to block a retreating, mobility of horses would be needed to get ahead of a retreating army and create a blocking, or at least a delaying, party. Without some means to stop or at least seriously delay a retreating army the vanquished were able to survive to fight another day thereby prolonging the conflict. Foot soldiers simply did not have the necessary speed or mobility to flank or to interdict a retreating army. Accordingly cavalry was slowly but uncertainly emerging as an essential if not indispensable component for successful pursuits to help shorten the war.

## *Cavalry's Early Status*

There once was a time, extending into the early decades of the 19th century, when cavalry was the elite, dominating military arm. The prototypical, and well chronicled, tactic was to keep cavalry in reserve while lines of foot soldiers struggled with one another, often hand-to-hand, and then in at a propitious time to unleash the horsemen to create panic, chase after, break up and scatter formations, and try to kill, capture or seriously wound routed infantry soldiers fleeing on foot.[29]

Mounted soldiers, especially *en masse*, had several distinct advantages over foot soldiers. These advantages included the physical leverage of being higher off the ground, giving the mounted soldiers a clear advantage of swinging a sword downward; having the weight and strength of the horse to bump and perhaps trample those on foot; the mobility and speed of the horse, enabling the cavalry to move into and out of battle quickly, thus minimizing risks to the riders.

But by the beginning of the Civil War in 1861 the role of mounted troops had been significantly diminished, primarily because of three important factors. The first factor was the costs of training, equipping, and maintaining cavalry units were considerably higher than were the costs for comparable infantry units.[30] Furthermore, it simply took longer to train cavalry units to be battle-ready than it would take to make infantry units likewise battle-ready. Because the leaders of both sides assumed the War of Rebellion would be quickly decided, they—especially Federal leaders—could not foresee the need to recruit, outfit and train additional cavalry units. The assumption was that the war would be concluded before new cavalry could be ready to take to the field, so why bother?

Not only did authorities assume the Rebellion would be suppressed in relatively short order, they, at that time, also assumed an army of 90-day volunteers to supplement the Regular Army of 17,000, including existing horse soldiers, would suffice for the task of suppressing the Rebellion. At the outbreak of the Civil War, five regiments of horse soldiers existed, at least on paper. Of these five regiments, two were designated as dragoons, one was comprised of mounted infantrymen, and only two, both created in 1855, were designated as traditional cavalry units.[31]

The second major factor was the development of better and more reliable firepower over several decades. The development of the Minié ball, together with the wide use of the rifled musket, which increased the effective range of musket fire from 100 yards to 400 yards, was a major factor diminishing cavalry as the preeminent force on the field of battle. Prior to the increase of firepower cavalry could, at a walk or slow trot, approach infantry lines to within a couple hundred yards without incurring heavy casualties from musket fire; at that point cavalry would charge at a gallop and be upon the infantry lines before infantry soldiers could reload. However the extended lethal range available to infantry with rifled muskets using Minié balls for ammunition meant that cavalry should expect to take much heavier casualties from reasonably trained and seasoned infantry. Although not universally recognized by all military commanders, especially those with long experience as cavalrymen, the days of being able to turn the tide of battle by cavalry charges against infantry were quickly drawing to a close during the Civil War, that is if not already closed.

Increased use and development of field fortifications was a third factor contributing to the altered deployment of cavalry. At the beginning of the Civil War commanders discouraged the use of field fortifications but as the war continued various typed of fortifications were developed and hastily erected by infantry soldiers, with or without their commanders' orders. Obviously infantry riflemen fighting on open ground were more vulnerable than were those protected behind trenches, abitis, and other devises that could and did impede the movements of attackers, including those astride horses.

## Cavalry Commanders

All military units require good commissioned and noncommissioned officers in order to be effective fighting machines, but no more so than for cavalry units. The difficulty of executing cavalry maneuvers, the challenges of maintaining contact and communications under free flowing, quickly changing circumstances, and the speed of movement over longer distances meant that cavalry commanders encountered challenges never encountered by their infantry counterparts. Adding to the challenges of cavalry commanders was that cavalry troopers were not the most disciplined soldiers in the armed forces. Excessive drunkenness was often one particular problem, but those who rode horses, including the commanders of the mounted soldiers, frequently craved independent duty under terms and conditions of their own making.

From the very beginning of the conflict, the Confederacy was blessed with several quite capable cavalry commanders who were typically "bold and full of stratagems." At least two such officers, James Ewell Brown ("Jeb") Stuart and Nathan Bedford Forrest, rode well above almost anyone else on either side of the belligerency. On the other hand, the two most successful Federal cavalry commanders, Philip Sheridan and James Wilson, did not become full time cavalry officers until the last year of the war.

## *Riders and Horses*

Many young men probably joined cavalry units on the assumption that cavalry service would be more glamorous and easier duty than that of their rifle-toting brethren on foot.[32] However, that would turn out to be a naïve, mistaken assumption. First, many younger soldiers had to learn to ride, often on horses that were yet to be broken for riding. Once basic horse riding skills were mastered the troopers began learning and training for cavalry basics, the riding and care—grooming, watering, and feeding—of horses, with endless drilling of cavalry tactics that was arduous and difficult.[33] In essence cavalry did double duty since the horse soldiers were also required to learn and prepare for all infantry responsibilities.[34] Beyond the training periods, cavalry, because of its versatility, was often used non-stop, frequently being on twenty-four hour patrol or picket duty while the infantry and artillery soldiers were all but idle in camp.

During the early period of the Civil War the Gray riders enjoyed a decided edge over Union cavalry. However, the Union's materiel and manpower superiority began to manifest themselves in cavalry as it did in other arms including infantry and artillery, and not to ignore navy. The Rebel horse soldiers had to supply and outfit their own mounts. If a Confederate trooper lost his horse, the trooper had to use his own resources to find a replacement mount; those resources might include another horse from home but more likely as not any replacements could include using the horse of a fallen comrade, capturing a horse of a Union rider after a battle, or confiscating an animal from an unfortunate farmer. On the other hand the Federals began systemically to procure and outfit vast numbers of horses, even in some instances retreading or remounting horses that had become jaded or lame. During the first two years of the war, the Federal government purchased almost 250,000 horses for cavalry duty. However the system was rife with corruption, many of the horses simply not fit for service, some barely able to walk.

Obviously as the war continued beyond the original, naively shortsighted projection of ninety days, cavalry needed to assume a more significant role that would have to change from its glory days of charges against infantry if either side was going to achieve decisive victories to win the conflict.

# 2

# Grant at Shiloh[1]
*April 6–7, 1862*

## Western Strategic Background

The Eastern campaigns have almost always drawn more attention and scrutiny in Civil War history than those west of the Appalachians. The respective capital cities were in the East, only 110 miles apart; likewise major Northern cities, such as Baltimore and Philadelphia, often seemed vulnerable to threats from Lee's Army of Northern Virginia. The two largest armies of either side, the Union's Army of the Potomac, and the Confederate's Army of Northern Virginia, campaigned and frequently fought epic battles against one another in the East. Most newspaper coverage came from Eastern cities, thereby tending to reflect disproportionate attention to the eastern campaigns from the very start of the conflict.

But there were also important strategic issues in the West. From the very beginning, Winfield Scott had envisioned the importance of seizing the Mississippi River as well as coastal seaports such as New Orleans and Mobile as major components of his strategy to choke off the Confederacy's capacity to feed, supply, and otherwise sustain its rebellion.[2] On the other side of the same coin, Jefferson Davis was committed from the very beginning to try to protect all territory in the newly formed Confederate States of America, including most improbably the vast, sparsely populated areas west of the Appalachians.[3]

And while Eastern campaigns, especially those involving Lee's Army of Northern Virginia, were fought within relatively compact areas, Western campaigns could stretch over much more extended territories. One of the cornerstones of Federal strategy envisioned a thrust from Nashville in Middle Tennessee all the way to Atlanta in central Georgia and from there continuing to the Atlantic seaboard. After its singular victory at Mill Springs, Kentucky, January 19–20, 1862,[4] Union command continued to develop its strategy, but one designed primarily to capture important places and facilities, sometimes called "strategic places."

Henry W. Halleck remained the overall commander of the region west of the Cumberland River.[5] Undoubtedly Halleck seemed to be one of the brighter, more knowledgeable Americans to wear the uniform. While still on active duty in 1846, Halleck wrote *Elements of Military Art and Science*, one of the reasons, apart from his balding, bug-eyed appearance, why he was known as "Old Brains." After resigning as a captain from the Regular Army in 1854, he became a senior partner in a prominent law firm in California; he also found time to publish two books on mining law. Halleck returned to active service in August 1861, receiving a major general's commission. Old Brains possessed considerable political skills that enabled him to gain the trust and confidence of a wide range of players, including legislators as well as those in uniform. Halleck was good at organizing and administrating but the question remained whether as a prototypical desk general he would be an enthusiastic, bold battlefield leader.

Ulysses S. ("Sam") Grant, 39, Halleck's second-in-command, was Halleck's *de facto* field, or tactical, commander with operational control of the combat units. After seeing valuable service during the Mexican War,[6] Grant served until 1854 when he resigned as a captain, perhaps because of allegations of excessive drinking.[7] In contrast to Halleck—Grant's West Point classmate—Grant did not succeed as a civilian, once in 1859 trying to sell firewood along the road near St. Louis.[8] When the war broke out Grant received a recommendation from his congressman for an appointment as a full colonel, even with his abysmal failures in his civilian pursuits; but the Union needed officers for its vastly expanded army, especially since one third of its Regular Army officers resigned to join the C.S.A. Thus Grant, as were scores of other previously resigned officers, was brought back on active duty with much higher rank than when he had left active service seven years earlier.[9]

Given everything about his adult life, both in and out of the military, there was little reason to expect much from Grant once he returned to active duty. It is unlikely he had gained any significant improvement in his military acumen; inexplicably, however, he was different from the scores of other citizens who had obtained commissions but quickly proved unworthy of the responsibilities of their new ranks. In contrast, Grant quickly exhibited an aptitude for command and actually managed to accomplish objectives, mainly because he was not hesitant to engage in battle (sometimes even impetuously), he was decisive (although not always very thorough or meticulous in his planning), and perhaps most importantly during the heat and turmoil of battle he remained calm, cool, and collected. Furthermore it never hurt his advancement that he never complained about a lack of resources or quarreled with the objectives of his superiors.

One of Grant's division commanders was BGen. William Tecumseh Sherman, 42, who had resigned from the Regular Army in 1853 but also experienced an unsettled, checkered civilian career. Eventually with the help of some army friends, in 1859 he became superintendent of the Louisiana Military Seminary, now Louisiana State University, where he enjoyed one of the most satisfying periods of his life. Upon the outbreak of the Civil war, he was conflicted but through the influence of his brother, John, a U.S. Senator from Ohio, he accepted a commission as a colonel in the Regular Army (as opposed to a volunteer unit). Within a couple months he was named commanding officer of a volunteer brigade that, while not spectacular, performed in a solid, steady manner at First Bull Run.

In recognition of Sherman's command performance, Lincoln appointed him as the second-in-command to BGen. Robert Anderson, the commander of the then named Department of Cumberland, consisting of Kentucky and Tennessee. (The names of these departments or armies, changed constantly in the early periods of the Civil War.) When Anderson, the Union hero of Fort Sumter, was overcome with the pressure of his command, Sherman was elevated to a command that frankly he did not desire.

Unfortunately Sherman's nerves also succumbed to the same pressures, causing him to among other things to exaggerate and to openly predict the imminent Rebel conquest of the border states. When Sherman demanded to be relieved, Lincoln complied by sending BGen. Don Carlos Buell to succeed Sherman. Eventually Sherman was sent his hometown of Lancaster, Ohio, to rest and to recuperate. After recovering sufficiently he became associated with Grant, whom Sherman had known from his army days.

Union Western strategy focused upon taking control of rivers and railroads, two major means of transportation of troops and supplies. Additionally the Federals were quickly developing an inland fleet of gunboats that from time to time would render invaluable support afloat on various rivers to infantry and field artillery. Under Grant's opportunistic leadership, Union forces had captured several important locations, including two strategic locations in northern Tennessee: Fort Henry on the Tennessee River (February 6, 1862) and Fort Donelson on the Cumberland River (February 15, 1862). Not only did the capture of these forts—together with the Mill Springs rout—force the Rebels to pull back from Kentucky but control of these rivers greatly enhanced Federal access into the heart of Tennessee.

Other Confederate setbacks in the Western theater included their evacuation from Columbus, Kentucky, Buell's takeover of Nashville, Tennessee, after he decided to not exploit the Mill Springs victory by moving into East Tennessee, and a major defeat at Pea Ridge, Arkansas. In the early months of 1862 MGen. Earl ("Buck") Van Dorn, 42, was put in charge of Confederate operations in Missouri with orders to clear the region of Federal forces. By March 1862, at Pea Ridge, Van Dorn—while leading 17,000 soldiers against only 11,000 Federals—suffered a crushing defeat, losing a couple Confederate able generals, James McIntosh and Ben McCulloch, recently one of the most popular men in Texas.[10] Van Dorn's withdrawal from Pea Ridge helped to assure Missouri would remain in the Union—albeit as a neutral state—for the balance of the war.[11]

Halleck and Buell—the respective commanders of the two largest departments in the Western theater—failed to develop a cooperative relationship. In response to several requests by Halleck to be given complete command of the Western theater, Lincoln, in early March 1862, appointed Halleck as commanding general of the Department of Mississippi, encompassing all territory west of the Alleghenies. Furthermore, Halleck would answer directly to the President, meaning he could bypass George McClellan, general in chief of all Union forces.

Halleck's next strategic objectives were the capture of the Confederate's railroad centers in Mississippi at Jackson, Humbolt, and Corinth, and to destroy a critical railroad bridge across Big Bear Creek east of Iuka, also in Mississippi. Taking these objectives would help to further starve the Confederacy by severing the Confederates' rail connections between the Mississippi River and East Tennessee as well as those to Atlanta, Georgia, further to the east.

The Union hierarchy determined it made sense to use the Tennessee River as egress for a southward movement. Accordingly Halleck ordered five divisions to head south toward Corinth. Once combined, these divisions became the Army of the Mississippi[12] under Grant's field command.[13] Additionally Halleck directed the 18,000-man Army of the Ohio, Buell commanding, to leave Nashville and to join Grant on his way to Corinth. Halleck intended to take field command of these two armies once they converged at Pittsburg Landing on the Tennessee River.[14]

In Corinth the Confederates also divined the importance of their railroads. By March 1862 the Confederates in the West were under the command of Gen. Albert Sidney Johnston, 59, considered by many as the most skillful Confederate general, outranked in seniority only by Samuel Cooper, 66, who because of his age and administrative abilities, was desk bound in Richmond making Sidney Johnston the most senior Rebel commander in the field.

Johnston graduated from West Point two years ahead of Jefferson Davis who was a great admirer of Johnston's command abilities. Johnston resigned his Regular Army commission in 1834 only to join the Texas army as a private before catching the eye of President Sam Houston who jumped Johnston to the rank of major. Although Johnston saw service in the Mexican War he was not able to regain a commission in the Regular Army until December 1849 when newly elected Zachary Taylor offered Johnston an army commission along with a position as paymaster. In 1855 then-Secretary of War Davis named Johnston as the commander of the newly formed 2nd U.S. Cavalry with Robert E. Lee as his second in command.[15] When the Civil War broke out, Winfield Scott ordered that Johnston return to Washington; instead Johnston enlisted as a private in a pro–Confederate regiment from California that started making its way east. Shortly thereafter Davis appointed Johnston as commander of the Confederates' western defenses.[16] Johnston's second-in-command at Shiloh was the ubiquitous Gen. P.T.G. ("The Cajun") Beauregard, 44, whose egocentric, grandiose personality had worn out his welcome in the East notwithstanding his hero status from his successes at Fort Sumter and First Bull Run before being sent to the Western theater.[17]

Johnston and Beauregard knew Buell had left Nashville to join Grant on the way to Corinth. They also realized Confederate defenders would be seriously outnumbered once these two Union armies converged. Therefore the Confederates planned to march north 26 miles where they had learned Grant's army was garrisoned at and around Pittsburg Landing. Making a preemptory strike upon Grant before Buell could meet and reinforce him was the linchpin of the Confederate plan.

One of the five Union divisions, commanded by MGen. Lew Wallace, 35, was encamped around Crump Landing, six miles downstream (north) of Pittsburg Landing. The other four Federal divisions, including Sherman's, bivouacked in a random manner near and around the Shiloh Methodist Church, south of Pittsburg Landing, were hardly expecting an attack. Because they were so nonchalant, even disdainful, about the possibility of an attack, the Pittsburg Landing divisions established their camps mainly for convenience and comfort rather than for defense. Grant, their overall commander, was not even in camp, instead staying in relative comfort of a hotel in Savannah, Tennessee,[18] eight miles downstream.

The marches of both Johnston's 40,000 Confederates, coming north, as well as Buell's Army of the Ohio, coming south, were encountering unforeseen delays, mostly caused by virtually impassable roads from rainy weather. Still both armies pressed on to their designated destinations. By Saturday evening, April 5, 1862, a day later than planned, the Confederates approached to within a couple hundred yards of Federal pickets near the Shiloh church.

## The Battle Begins

During the early morning of April 6, 1862, the first day of the battle of Shiloh, Southerners overran Northerners having their breakfasts, driving many northward to cower along the banks of the Tennessee River. Later Buell reported that upon arriving at Pittsburg Landing the morning of the 6th he observed "…the banks swarmed with confused mass of men of various regiments. The number could not have been less than 4,000 or 5,000, and later in the day it became much larger."[19] Although Sherman, commander of the southern-most division, and Grant both denied the Union army had been surprised there is much evidence to belie such denials.[20] For one thing, Sherman's division was enjoying a leisurely breakfast with arms stacked; these troops were not entrenched or otherwise fortified although that alone was not unusual at that phase of the war.[21]

Notwithstanding their early success against these scrambling Yankees, in the rush to feed regiments onto the rugged, heavily wooded battleground the Confederates had difficulty realigning their column formations into a cohesive line of battle. The Confederate plan looked good on paper but the implementation of the plan was left to officers and men who had never fought before.[22] Additionally divisions led by Sherman and MGen. John A. McClernand, 50, on the Union right provided the stiffest resistance, delaying the Confederates long enough for Grant to organize a last line of defense.[23] As a result Southern regiments became disorganized losing their cohesion making field command all the more confused and jumbled.

The Rebel attack devolved into a series of local piecemeal assaults by brigades—some becoming intermingled—with only minimal control by division leaders.[24] Since the Confederates were the numerically weaker side these disjointed assaults eventually dissipated the fighting power directed at the decisive point.[25] On the other hand the Federals successfully improvised a series of defensive points, perhaps the most famous being the Hornets Nest commanded by BGen. Benjamin Prentiss, 43, with a division that refused to withdraw until eventually forced to surrender. The Confederates, under the command of MGen. Braxton Bragg, 45, missed an opportunity to advance further by outflanking Prentiss' division; instead Bragg harangued his exhausted soldiers to continue the attack upon Prentiss. Although 2,000 men in the Union division became prisoners, their stand bought precious time for Grant until he was able to consolidate his defenses.[26] Furthermore Johnston—in the manner of a company or regimental commander—attempted to manage his offensive from the front where he unknowingly took one or more shell fragments in his leg. Without realizing the extent of his blood loss Johnston continued to direct troops before an aide could attempt first aid. However this attempt was too late and the Rebels lost their leader on the field of battle at a most critical time. Beauregard now assumed command.

By the end of the first day's fighting the sides suffered unprecedented number of casualties. Beauregard, with his characteristic bravado, told a staff officer, "Tonight we will water our horses in the Tennessee River."[27] And rather than ordering one last assault while the North's defenses were still weak and vulnerable, The Cajun ordered his lines to withdraw approximately one-half mile, presumably in order to reorganize.[28] Meanwhile Grant, knowing that Buell's arrival was imminent, remained composed, that evening telling Sherman, "We'll lick 'em tomorrow, though."[29]

With Buell's army arrival—as well at last of Lew Wallace's division—that evening and night,[30] Grant could reform new lines of battle, including the massing of 36 pieces of artillery. A midnight thunderstorm together with shelling from Federal gunboats made for a miserable night. Nevertheless many of the Rebel soldiers made themselves comfortable in the abandoned Union campsites while freely looting "all the tea, coffee, sugar, cheese, hardtack and bacon they could want."[31] Ironically even though the Rebel high command was aware that Buell's Army of the Ohio was advancing southward, those same generals were surprised, even disbelieving, when cavalry scouts reported their sightings of crossings of steamboats carrying Federal reinforcements.[32]

Buell—whose army filled in the left two-thirds of the Blue lines—began his attack the next morning at 5:00 a.m. and continued as more regiments arrived.[33] Although the Confederates launched several counterattacks against the advancing Yanks, the fighting of the second day lacked the ferocity of the first day.[34] The lines surged back and forth but that afternoon the Confederates, licking their wounds, and learning reinforcements with Van Dorn would not be forthcoming, by noon began a disorganized withdrawal back to their original fortifications at Corinth.[35] One estimate had the Confederates having no more than 20,000 effectives remaining while the combined Union armies had at least 35,000 effectives at their disposal.[36] The Confederates suffered 1,728 killed at Shiloh, 8,012 wounded, and 959 missing.[37] Bruce Catton flatly states: "In all American history, no more amazing battle was ever fought than [Shiloh]"[38]

## *The Pursuit*

Shiloh was an early example of command lack of enthusiasm about pursuits. William G. Stevenson described a fascinating account of the beginning of the Rebel retreat. Stevenson was a transplanted Yankee living in Arkansas who avoided lynching by joining Jeff Davis' Invincibles. By the time of Shiloh, Stevenson had become a trusted aide-de-camp to C.S.A. BGen. John C. Breckinridge, 40,[39] commander of the Reserve Corps at Shiloh.

Stevenson was seriously wounded during Shiloh's second day but after recovering he escaped to Federal territory where he wrote a book, *Thirteen Months in the Rebel Army*, as a means of trying to convince Northerners of his true allegiance. Stevenson tells of the Confederate vulnerability by 5:00 p.m., or two hours after Beauregard had ordered the retreat. According to Stevenson:

> Up to this time the pursuit seemed feeble, and the Confederates were surprised that the victorious Federals made no more of their advantage. Nor is it yet understood why the pursuit was not pressed. A rapid and persistent pursuit would have created a complete rout of the now broken, weary, and dispirited Rebels. Two more hours of such fighting as Buell's fresh men could have made, would have demoralized and destroyed Beauregard's army. For some reason this was not done, and night closed the battle.[40]

Grant failed to initiate an immediate pursuit despite having some momentum as a result of his second day counterattack, and despite nearly impassible, extremely muddy roads that turned the retreat into a nightmare for Beauregard. Although hardly a full-fledged pursuit, on April 8,[41] the day after the Confederate army withdrew from the battlefield, Grant sent two of Sherman's infantry brigades, accompanied by a cavalry regiment as an advance guard, southward on a reconnaissance mission. What must Grant have expected from this deployment? Since they had been in the thick of battle for two days, Sherman's troops hardly would have been fresh or eager for more fighting. But more importantly two brigades were of insufficient size to accomplish much against any army still of at least 20,000 effectives except perhaps to capture and retrieve some Rebel stragglers. If indeed reconnaissance were the true objective then a sufficiently sized cavalry unit alone should have been able to accomplish that mission.

At Falling Timbers, six miles south of Shiloh, the Federals encountered one of the serious perils of engaging the rear guard of a retreating army.[42] As they headed south, the Confederates felled trees that not only slowed the Federal progress but also caused Union troops to break formation in order to clear trees from their path. As the Yanks broke ranks to clear these obstacles, the Rebel rear guard, comprised of cavalry led by Nathan Bedford Forrest, 42, thought it saw an opportunity to strike. Forrest definitely was not a graduate of West Point, and for that matter was not a graduate of any level of formal education beyond six months. Instead Forrest was a self-taught military tactician whose mantra was simply to "get there firstus with the mostest"[43] and who less than two months earlier had escaped from Fort Donelson the night before its surrender. Forrest's cavalry immediately charged through and dispersed the Federal cavalry and continued to charge, cutting and slashing, until repulsed by the Union's main body of infantry.

But somehow after the repulse of his troops Forrest found himself remaining isolated in the midst of Yanks. Bluecoats were rushing at him from all sides screaming. "Shoot that man! Knock him off his horse!" His horse was shot twice; Forrest was severely wounded when a Union soldier shot Forrest point blank in his left side with the bullet ripping through Forrest's hip before lodging against his spine. Somehow remaining upright in his saddle, Forrest fought his way through the mass of Union soldiers, and was able to round up his troopers before making a hasty retreat.[44] Forrest not only recovered from the shooting but would continue to bedevil Federal cavalry, garrisons, and lines of communication for most of the next three years. Sherman led his group back to camp that night,[45] reflecting several years later "…we had had quite enough of their society for two whole days, and were only too glad to be rid of them on any terms."[46]

If successful, a pursuit would have gone a long way toward ending the western conflict. Grant's explanation for not pursuing might not seem to make much sense, but at least he was forthright. In his memoirs Grant offers a two-pronged explanation: (1) His troops were too exhausted after the battle to be forced to chase after the retreating Confederates, and (2) he—Grant—felt he did not have sufficient seniority over Buell to order Buell's army to give chase.[47] O. Edward Cunningham, in his seminal work *Shiloh and the Western Campaign of 1862*, as edited by Gary D. Joiner and Timothy B. Smith, concludes that "Grant's argument remains a little shakey."[48] Frank Varney is even more critical of Grant's explanation, noting that Buell said his army was available and willing, albeit tired, but that Grant never consulted with his about the possibility of pursuing the Rebels.[49]

Furthermore, in fairness to Grant, the Federal soldiers had been engaged in non-stop fighting and/or marching for two days, diminishing their physical and psychological conditions for the demands of a pursuit.[50] The Federals suffered grievously from 1,754 killed, 8,408 wounded, and 2,885 missing.[51] Grant's artillery lost 36 guns.[52] Grant's order of battle was badly damaged with the loss of two division commanders, and any pursuit would have to transverse roads that were becoming all the more impassable by the Confederate retreat. Nevertheless, one cannot help but ponder whether the Grant of 1864 or of 1865 would have been as passive, considerate and as deferential about seniority as was the Grant of early 1862. After all the rail lines running through Corinth continued as the strategic objective, and remained to be taken. Further the combined Union forces greatly outnumbered the beaten Confederates in retreat!

Although the benefits accruing from a successful pursuit are almost self-apparent the critical question was whether the armies were even capable of a successful pursuit. Not only were the generals still inexperienced with managing large sized units on suddenly started, fast paced movements but at this point in the war pursuits were little more than footraces, essentially soldiers slogging through mud that sometimes was knee deep. More mobility would be required for a pursuing force to succeed in overcoming a retreating army and such mobility could only be found with cavalry that was superior to the cavalry of the retreating army. At Shiloh the Union battalion sized cavalry was scattered among the infantry divisions, hardly organized to support an army in pursuit.

## *Dénouements and Precursors*

The death of Albert Sidney Johnston is sometimes a part of the Myth of the Lost Cause, the contention being that the Confederates would have won the Battle at Shiloh if not for Johnston's untimely death.[53] On the other hand the poor tactical deployment of Southern troops at Shiloh tends to belie Johnston's reputation as anything other than a mediocre military combat commander.

After Shiloh, Halleck—who seemed to have a passive-aggressive attitude towards Grant—seized upon the possibility that Grant may have been surprised by the attack at Shiloh to insert himself as field commander of the Union army.[54] Upon arriving at Pittsburg Landing on April 11,[55] Halleck began to reinforce, refit, and reorganize the available Federal forces that would exceed 100,000 soldiers.[56] After being reinforced by the Army of the Mississippi, commanded by John Pope, Halleck shuffled divisions among the three armies before forming three wings with Pope on the left, Buell in the center, and George Thomas commanding the right wing.[57] Grant was "promoted" to become Halleck's second-in-command, an unhappy assignment since it was a virtually useless position[58]; Grant complained it was worse than being in jail and contemplated leaving the army again.[59] The day before Grant was scheduled to leave Corinth, presumably to prepare his exit from the army, he was visited by Sherman who persuaded Grant to stay in the army a little while longer.[60]

After earlier surrenders of four Confederate forts downstream from New Orleans, on April 27, 1862, a Union naval fleet under Flag Officer David Farragut seized New Orleans at the mouth of the Mississippi River. Within a few days MGen. Ben Butler, 44, a renowned political general,[61] arrived with his troops to begin his management of the city. Capture of New Orleans, and controlling the mouth of the Mississippi River, was a major step in implementing the Federals' Anaconda strategy designed to starve the South.

On April 29—more than three weeks after the battle was over—Halleck's reorganized force headed south for Corinth. If pursuit means "chase," this movement was anything but a chase. On May 3 Halleck telegraphed Secretary of War Stanton that; "I leave here tomorrow, and our army will be before Corinth tomorrow night."[62] Instead Halleck proceeded with an abundance of caution, advancing no more than two miles per day before stopping to entrench each night.[63] Steven Woodworth has noted that Halleck's purpose was not to secure a decisive victory by annihilating the Southern army. Instead the capture of Corinth was Halleck's object.[64]

Some armies could easily cover the twenty-six miles to Corinth in two or three days.[65] In contrast, by May 25 Halleck reached the outskirts of Corinth. Halleck's slow, safe pace was consistent with his primary objective of seizing Corinth's important railroad junction. Beauregard, in the face of what he perceived to be overwhelming odds against his army, had time to abandon Corinth to retreat fifty miles south.

As he approached Corinth, Halleck ordered a cavalry raid that included Philip H. ("Little Phil") Sheridan, 31, who had recently been promoted to full colonel and given command of a cavalry regiment.[66] For eight years prior to the beginning of the Civil War Sheridan had been a shave tail lieutenant serving with dragoons in the Western territories. His biographer, Roy Morris, Jr., noted that during that period Sheridan "had 'seen the elephant,' as the phrase then had it, from the Rio Grande to the Pacific Northwest, commanded small numbers of men in battle, gotten himself wounded and a few of his subordinates killed for his trouble, taken some Indian losses in return, and learned how an officer of the army ought to conduct himself."[67] As a captain Sheridan had seen service at Pea Ridge where he became acquainted, and formed a lifetime friendship, with BGen. Glenville Dodge, 32. During the battle of Shiloh Captain Sheridan was a roving quartermaster assigned to buy horses in Chicago; most recently during the march south from Shiloh Sheridan was Halleck's most efficient and valuable quartermaster.[68]

During the night of May 27, Sheridan's new cavalry command, along with another cavalry regiment, both carrying only sugar, coffee, and salt, set out for Booneville, Mississippi,[69] a village sitting astride the Mobile & Ohio R.R., approximately 22 miles south of Corinth. On May 30 his troopers reached Booneville where they seized and/or destroyed vast amounts of Rebel ordinance and miles of rail track while capturing 2,000 Confederate soldiers.

Meanwhile Halleck had carefully and cautiously approached Corinth with his expanded army of 110,000 while preparing his heavy guns for a siege.[70] Beauregard reasonably determined that the odds were seriously weighed against his army of 66,000—he had recently been reinforced at last by Van Dorn—and having to contend with an epidemic of typhoid and/or dysentery, decided to withdraw without giving battle. Thus during the night of May 29–30, 1862, Beauregard abandoned his defenses at Corinth to retreat to a new defense line along the Tuscumbia River, further south in Mississippi.[71]

On the day after returning to Halleck's command Sheridan and the rest of the cavalry brigade were riding again, this time in support of Pope's army in pursuit of Beauregard.[72] On Wednesday, June 11, 1862, Halleck halted Pope's pursuit, being fearful of the potentially crippling effect of summer swamp fever upon his army. Halleck may have also been concerned with the challenges of providing logistical support when there was but one vulnerable railroad from Corinth to Tupelo for the transportation of necessary supplies. Arguably Halleck could have also eliminated, or at least drastically reduced, any threats against his lines of communications if he had committed sufficient resources to eliminate what was left of Beauregard's army. In any event the Rebels were able to complete their retreat "…unmolested, except for whatever desultory damage Sheridan and the cavalry had managed to inflict upon the sick, the lame, and the laggard."[73]

Larry J. Daniel, author of *Days of Glory: The Army of the Cumberland, 1861–1865*[74] says that on several occasions he had "heard historian Edwin C. Bearrs declare Halleck's failure to pursue as one of the great lost opportunities of the war—the General should have 'pushed them into the swamp.'" Daniel also notes that James Lee McDonough in *War in Kentucky: From Shiloh to Perryville* (1994) has expressed sympathy with Halleck's decision not to pursue; however Daniels says he still agrees with Bearrs. Brian Holder Reid concludes, "A great Union strategic opportunity had been squandered."[75] To underscore why Shiloh was not a decisive battle, Reid observes the Rebel army remained intact with unbroken discipline and cohesion, and its commanders still had ambitious plans.[76]

From his new base in Tupelo, 50 miles south of Corinth, Beauregard pronounced his evacuation of pestilential Corinth as "equivalent to a great victory," an assessment not shared by Jeff Davis who was aghast a strategically critical rail line terminus was surrendered without giving battle. Beauregard then went on sick leave, turning his command temporarily (he thought) over to Braxton Bragg. Thereafter Beauregard did not see any further significant action until early 1864 when he defeated Benjamin Butler at Drewry's Bluff in Virginia.[77]

However, Sheridan's cavalry remained on patrol even after Pope's pursuit was cancelled. On July 1, 1862, Sheridan was still scouting at Booneville when he was attacked by Confederate cavalry four or five times his number. Against these odds, and with authorization to withdraw, Sheridan divided his regiment into two groups—one armed with carbines and rifled muskets, and engaging the enemy's front while the other group, armed only with sabers and pistols, worked its way around the Rebels' flank enabling the Yanks to launch a surprise attack against the Confederate rear, causing a rout of the much larger force. In the process Sheridan was also able to gather important intelligence about the Rebel forces in the area. As a result Sheridan was promoted to brigadier general after five generals endorsed his promotion with the comment, "He is worth his weight in gold."[78] By the following September Pope was transferred East to be replaced by MGen. William S. Rosecrans as army commander while Sheridan was given command of an infantry division in Rosecrans' new command.

As a result of their shared experiences at Shiloh, Grant and Sherman began a closer working association that would endure at least for the remainder of the war. However, shortly after Shiloh Sherman served a stint as military commander of Memphis after it fell into Federal control. During that period Sherman had to fight Rebel guerrillas instead of Confederate regulars, an experience that made Sherman realize the war was between two societies. This was a lesson Sherman would remember for two more years. Grant's lesson from Shiloh was that the war would not be won by one titanic battle but could be won only after a long, drawn out process relying upon rapid movement to destroy the enemy army rather than cautious marches to occupy places.

On July 11, 1862, one month after Halleck had concluded the post–Corinth pursuit, Lincoln appointed Halleck to the vacant position of General-in-Chief of the Union army. For several months after relieving McClellan as General-in-Chief Lincoln, with considerable help from Stanton, had attempted to serve as actual Commander-in-Chief as well as in title. Relatively soon Lincoln concluded the position needed someone with more expertise and experience than either he or Stanton possessed. Furthermore as President, Lincoln had numerous other responsibilities requiring his attention. On the surface, at least, Halleck, with his background and credentials, seemed like a good, solid choice, especially since he had no known political ambitions.

Back in Richmond, Samuel Cooper, who knew Davis when Davis was the Federal Secretary of War, remained as the C.S.A.'s Adjutant-General and Inspector General throughout the war; Cooper accompanied Davis when Davis was escaping from Richmond in April 1865.

# 3

# Buell vs. Bragg in Kentucky
## 1862

## Preliminary Maneuvering

Northern cities in the West such as Cincinnati, Ohio, and Louisville, Kentucky, both along the banks of the Ohio River, would be invaluable prizes if any were to fall to and become occupied by Rebel armies. Although technically and ostensibly Kentucky was a neutral state, Lincoln once famously said, "To lose Kentucky is nearly to lose the whole game."[1] Reflecting that importance, the high tide of Confederate influence in the West occurred one hot, dry day when two opposing armies, both seeking water, met almost by accident near a small central Kentucky town. It may be no accident to claim that this battle—as were the preceding maneuvers—was as confusing and as bizarre as any fought during the Civil War. But at the same time, while the Rebels retreated from the battlefield, the failure of the Union commander to pursue as ordered was the straw that eventually cost him his command.

Ever since November 1861, when Lincoln appointed Henry W. ("Old Brains") Halleck to succeed John C. Frémont as commander of the Missouri Department, including the subordinate departments, or districts, of Ohio, Kansas, Kentucky, and Tennessee, Halleck had been the organizer and administrator of most of the major military efforts in the West. However, his performance as a field commander—on those rare occasions when he deigned to leave the office and take to the field—was mediocre and tepid at best. Most of the significant military successes, such as Fort Henry, Fort Donelson, and Shiloh, were accomplished when Halleck had relinquished field command to his principle subordinate, Sam Grant, whom Old Brains did not always entirely trust.

Ostensibly hoping a lighter load of responsibilities would enable George McClellan to focus upon his duties as commander of the Army of the Potomac, on March 11, 1862, Lincoln relieved McClellan as General in Chief of all Federal forces. The position remained vacant as Lincoln and Secretary of War Edwin Stanton attempted to discharge those duties, mostly without any particular success, especially in the Shenandoah Valley where Stonewall Jackson was running amok against three independent and uncoordinated Federal armies, including ironically one commanded by Frémont. On July 11, 1862, when the Federal administration realized it needed an actual General in Chief, Halleck was summoned to Washington to take McClellan's place as commander over all Union armies.[2]

Upon Halleck's departure from the West his old unified command of most of the region between the Appalachians and the Mississippi River reverted into two new, reconfigured departments or commands. Grant was reinstated into command of his former District of West Tennessee that had been expanded to include the Districts of Cairo and Mississippi. This meant Grant was now in charge of all Union military operations between the Tennessee and Mississippi Rivers and the Ohio River.

The remaining part of Halleck's old command was given to Don Carlos Buell, commanding the reconstituted Department of Ohio that included a portion of Tennessee as well as those portions of Alabama and Georgia that happened to be under Federal control. As far as Washington was concerned, Grant's and Buell's commands were independent of the other with each answering directly to Halleck in Washington.

George H. Thomas, 46, the most prominent Southern born officer—other than the by-then retired Winfield Scott—remaining with the Union army, became Buell's principle subordinate. Buell outranked Thomas only because the promotion of The Virginian[3] to major general had not been back dated to the rout at Mills Springs, as would have been common under similar circumstances.

Buell possessed many of McClellan's characteristics such as being an excellent disciplinarian, having a robust physique as well as being a hardworking, round-the-clock fastidious administrator. On the other hand, Buell did not share any of McClellan's charm, glamour, or charisma.[4] Indeed the placid Buell had been described as being the most reserved, distant, and unsociable general in the army. To compound the notion of being distant from much of the Union mainstream, Buell continued to own slaves and was a brother-in-law to C.S.A. General David Twiggs, who in February 1861 as the Federal commander of various departments in the South, surrendered all Union forces and supplies in Texas to the Texas Rangers.[5] As an inexperienced field commander Buell was cautious to a fault, which led many to believe he lacked sufficient devotion to either the war or to its cause. One volunteer officer compared Buell to having a "dancing-master policy: 'By your leave, my dear sir, we will have a fight; that is if your are sufficiently fortified; no hurry; take your time.'"

The Confederates also had independent commands in the West. The largest and most prominent of the western Confederate armies was commanded by MGen. Braxton Bragg, 45, a Mexican War veteran who in June 1862 relieved P.G.T. Beauregard following the latter's unauthorized sick leave after Corinth. While Beauregard tended to be grandiose and impracticable, Bragg enjoyed a reputation for being a capable administrator and for battlefield bravery. As a lieutenant of artillery Bragg served in the Seminole War as well as in the Mexican-American War where he had formed a close relationship with Jefferson Davis, but also earned a reputation as "the most cantankerous man in the army."[6] At Shiloh Bragg led one of the flanks of the Rebel assaults but felt there was an enormous lack of discipline on both sides of the battle. Accordingly Bragg held a low opinion of volunteer troops, an attitude that led to a legendary abuse of troops in an attempt to instill discipline. As a result of his unbending commitment to rigorous discipline along with an untrusting dyspeptic outlook on life[7] his soldiers feared and despised Bragg while his officers often viewed him as a pettifogging despot. Bragg had several other personality traits that diminished his effectiveness as a commander; among other things he was a workaholic[8] (he served as his own chief of staff) obsessed with detail and minutia that often impaired any strategic vision. Worst of all, he lacked self-confidence and had difficulty making decisions; perhaps he was bipolar. Despite his subordinates' hostility toward him, Bragg was disposed to call frequent councils of war, presenting even more opportunities for quarrels and command friction.

MGen. Simon B. Buckner, 39, another Mexican War veteran who had also taught at West Point, was one of Bragg's division commanders. Prior to accepting a Confederate commission Buckner, a native of Munfordville, Kentucky, was offered a similar commission from the Federal administration. He had also been left "holding the bag" at Fort Donelson when Gen. John B. Floyd and BGen. Gideon J. Pillow turned over their command to Bucker before escaping from the inevitable surrender to Grant.[9] After Floyd and Pillow departed Buckner had no alternative except to accept Grant's demand for unconditional surrender. Buckner was stunned when Grant, Buckner's friend from West Point who had accepted a loan from Buckner in order to return home when he (Grant) had resigned, refused to follow the custom of negotiating terms of surrender.

Bragg's Army of Tennessee had a couple other highly regarded generals. One such general was MGen. William J. Hardee, 47, who had served in the Seminole and Mexican Wars, who had studied at the French cavalry academy, and who had served as commandant of cadets at West Point where he wrote the standard manual on tactics used by both sides in the Civil War.[10] Hardee served as a corps commander for Bragg.

MGen. Leonidas Polk, 56, served as Bragg's other corps commander as well as being his second-in-command. Polk's pre-war military credentials were slim but he was well connected, being distantly related to former President James Polk as well as being close friend and West Point classmate of Jefferson Davis. He had also been the late Albert S. Johnston's roommate. Although a West Point graduate, Polk resigned after six months of active duty and eventually became an ordained Episcopal Bishop. Early in the war Polk violated Kentucky's neutrality when he occupied Columbus, Kentucky, giving the Federals, under Grant, the excuse to launch their own invasion of Kentucky, thereby vitiating Kentucky's neutral stance. Polk had commanded the C.S.A. right at Shiloh, personally leading four charges.

The next most important Rebel army in the west was commanded by MGen. E. Kirby Smith, 37, also a veteran of the Mexican War. After graduating from West Point, Smith, nine years younger than Bragg, also fought in the Mexican-American War before serving on the frontier to fight Indians.[11] After resigning from the Regular Army to join the Confederacy, Smith was seriously wounded—having been shot through the neck—at First Bull Run, but while recovering he met and married his wife. In March 1862 he was sent to Knoxville, Tennessee, to take independent command of the Confederate Department of East Tennessee. Any Confederate commander in that region would likely have his hands full because of the presence of so many Union sympathizers. However Smith had proven equal to the task but also saw opportunity for moving north into Kentucky. Another independent C.S.A. command was led by yet another veteran of the Mexican and Seminole Wars, MGen. Earl ("Buck") Van Dorn, who we recall had not arrived in time to help at Shiloh.

Starting in August of 1862 the opposing armies engaged in a contest of maneuvering. To the west, Bragg, with Buell cautiously following, continued his massive flanking movement from Tupelo to Mobile.[12] From Mobile Bragg transported his army by rail to Chattanooga where he flanked both Grant and more importantly Buell in Nashville. In Chattanooga Bragg and Smith conferred about their joint plans for invading Kentucky, hopefully all the way to Louisville.[13] Trying to work in concert with Smith, Bragg temporarily transferred two brigades commanded by the Irish born Patrick Cleburne to Smith. Nevertheless Bragg still did not have enough logistical support to keep his men and horses fed and nourished for any extended period.

Meanwhile Smith advanced toward and into Eastern Kentucky without significant opposition. On Saturday, August 30, 1862, Smith overran the Federal garrison of mostly raw recruits at Richmond, Kentucky,[14] scoring the most lopsided Confederate victory in the Civil War. Before being struck by a bullet in his left cheek and two teeth in his lower jaw, Cleburne organized and coordinated a counterattack winning the day for the Confederates.[15] The Federals suffered approximately 83 percent casualties while also losing stockpiles of supplies, their wagons, their artillery, and one of their commanders. Within another week Smith advanced to ten miles of Cincinnati, Ohio, before the Ohio governor managed to muster 20,000 volunteers to defuse that threat. This victory left Smith virtually unopposed in Eastern Kentucky but he then became content enjoying the autumn bounty of the Bluegrass country around Lexington, Kentucky.

Buell, as always concerned about maintaining his substantial supply lines, was averse to taking any chances, including engaging in battle, that might threaten his supply lines. Furthermore Buell was handicapped by weak intelligence, having only five widely scattered cavalry regiments.[16] Without being able to determine Bragg's movements, Buell's orders to his subordinate commanders were hesitant and indecisive. Furthermore Buell and his subordinate commanders were in constant disagreement about how to deploy the corps in Buell's army.

In a controversial move that was not supported by Thomas, among others, Buell—apparently believing Nashville was Bragg's objective—withdrew back westward to Nashville, in effect giving Bragg unimpeded access to Kentucky and beyond.[17] Buell claimed "dwindling rations" were the reason for his move, a rationale that practically no one else believed.[18] By the 10th of September Bragg's entire army had crossed the Cumberland River. Buell also started moving five of his eight divisions northward toward Bowling Green, leaving Thomas with three divisions in Nashville.[19]

The enemy armies avoided any hostile contact until Friday, September 12, 1862, when Bragg marched into Glasgow, Kentucky, where the four Rebel divisions had rested for two days, their first break since leaving Chattanooga seventeen days earlier.[20] At Glasgow Bragg was located between Smith, to the east, and Buell, thirty miles to the west. From this point if Buell and Bragg continued to move at the same pace in parallel lines Bragg would come between Buell and Louisville. Bragg decided to merge with Smith to hit Louisville.[21] From Glasgow Bragg sent an infantry brigade forward fourteen miles to Cave City, Kentucky, to cut the Louisville & Nashville rail line and to capture available supplies. (Coincidentally this was one day prior to the discovery of a lost copy of Lee's Special Order 191 near Frederick, Maryland.)

## Turmoil in Louisville

At that time the entire Kentucky region was under the command of BGen. Charles C. Gilbert, 40, a Mexican War veteran who once taught at West Point. Gilbert's efforts were making Louisville almost impregnable at least against an army the size of Bragg's; meanwhile

Kirby Smith remained in Lexington still showing no inclination to join Bragg, ostensibly Smith's senior in rank. Furthermore, were Bragg to assault Louisville, presumably he would also have to contend with Buell coming up on the attacking Rebels' rear. Accordingly on September 30 Bragg made a logical but controversial and unpopular decision to veer away from Louisville, instead trekking eastward toward Frankfort, Kentucky's capital in the center of the state. Bragg's critics, and to be sure there were plenty, contended Bragg had wasted an excellent opportunity to win Kentucky for the Confederacy. But Bragg intended instead to take a political tact by installing a new Confederate governor for Kentucky.

When Buell learned Bragg had swung toward Frankfort, Buell—by then reinforced by Thomas with two more divisions—moved directly toward Louisville. (Although Buell's movement from Nashville is commonly called a "pursuit," mainly because he was more or less following Bragg, such movement was not a pursuit in the sense that it was intended to capture or annihilate Bragg's army. Indeed it is difficult to fathom Buell's purpose except perhaps that he was merely reacting to Bragg's movements.) Buell's men were also unhappy with their latest turn of events figuring their long marches and many deprivations had accomplished little. Essentially after a year's effort Buell was returning the Army of the Ohio to its place of origin without accomplishing much of strategic importance.[22] From within his own army as well as from the entire Federal nation, pressure was building on Buell to drive the Rebels out of Kentucky.

Once Bragg was no longer in his front, Buell force-marched his army the rest of the way Louisville, his lead elements arriving September 25, 1862. When Buell arrived by river boat two days later, he found himself in an uproar over his command. Not only was his military command skills in question but his political views were held in disdain from a variety of sources, Republican as well as Democratic.[23] The discord among some high ranking generals of his command suggested a possible coup.[24]

On Monday, September 29, 1862, Washington sent a telegram directing George H. Thomas to replace Buell as commander, but to almost everyone's surprise and amazement Thomas refused, claiming it would be improper for him to take command on such short notice before the army was to start its march south toward Bragg.[25] It is also possible that Thomas was aware of how much the Kentucky elements in the army were upset by the sudden, and for them the tragic, turn of events, and did not want to inherit a command in chaos. Later documentation also revealed that whatever Thomas' motivation may have been he certainly was not a loyal supporter of Buell. Thomas later admitted that he would have accepted command if the Administration had pressed the issue.[26] Whatever, under the circumstances, the Administration had no choice except to reinstate the commander it had just tried to fire.[27]

Within the short time between his reinstatement as army commander and departing Louisville, Buell had to reorganize his command structure by replacing and appointing new subordinate commanders. First, in a manner similar to Halleck's "promotion" of Grant after Shiloh, Buell made Thomas second-in-command but without field command of any division or wing. (Throughout Thomas had previously been serving as a division commander.) As Daniel notes this assignment meant that Thomas became Buell's *de facto* aide.[28]

Buell's army of nine divisions was organized into three wings, commanded from left to right by MGen. Alexander McD. McCook, 31—who considered himself the rightful successor to Buell—BGen. C.C. Gilbert, whose recent promotion to brigadier had yet to be confirmed, and MGen. Thomas Crittenden. (Wings and corps were interchangeable terms, especially in the early years of the war. Corps commands required Congressional approval and in lieu of such authorizations army commanders would organize their divisions into "wings" in order to streamline their chains of command.) To a large extent these appointments reflected serious hostilities among elements under Buell's command. Regiments from Indiana were strongly opposed to Buell while regiments from Kentucky still favored his leadership. And since almost every general in the army outranked Gilbert—in reality a captain as confirmed—there was much discontent and suspicion about his appointment, especially in light of his apparent lack of command skills for such an important position. Many considered Gilbert to be a silly martinet with the advantage of having influential personal connections. Gilbert's fondness for strict discipline had been effective with regular army soldiers but was counterproductive with volunteer soldiers.

BGen. Phil Sheridan was one officer who loudly complained about Buell's reorganized command structure. Sheridan, who only a few weeks previously had been a captain commanding a cavalry regiment, was unhappy that as a brigadier he was relegated to brigade command while, as he stated, "...men who had no commission at all[29] were being made chiefs of corps." In order to settle that controversy, Buell reassigned one division commander to stay in Louisville to organize and train a new division so that Sheridan could have the newly vacated division command, incidentally under Gilbert's command. And so Sheridan's meteoric rise continued.

But Sheridan's inexperience as division commander was not unique within the Army of the Ohio. Including Sheridan, seven of Buell's nine division commanders had no command experience at that level. Furthermore none of the three wing commanders had credentials commensurate with the demands of those commands. Both Alex McCook[30]—described as an overgrown schoolboy, his troops nicknamed him "Gut" because of his stout physique— and Gilbert were unreliable while Crittenden's value was based upon his political connections, being another son of John J. Crittenden, a U.S. Senator from Kentucky; Crittenden's military acumen was akin to that of a country lawyer.

## *The Frankfort Ruse*

On October 2, 1862, Buell, departed Louisville with 70,000 men, including two divisions of raw, undisciplined recruits, together with a 1,700 wagon train that occupied seventeen miles of road.[31] Buell's army also included three brigades of cavalry, two of which initially remained in the rear to guard wagons and railroads. The third cavalry brigade led the march but one of the lead regiments was mostly armed only with pistols.

Buell planned to split his army into three columns before converging at Bardstown, Kentucky, hopefully to force Bragg either to fight or to retreat toward the Kentucky River. Buell also sent 20,000 troops, two reinforced divisions under the combined command of BGen. Joshua W. Sill, 31, in a feint toward Frankfort, northeast of Bardstown, to keep Smith from reinforcing Bragg. Buell intended to engage and defeat an unreinforced Bragg after which Buell could eliminate Smith's much smaller army.

But despite all his travails, including a dysfunctional command structure, untested recruits, and low morale with divided loyalties among junior officers and the rank-and-file, Buell's situation was much better than was Bragg's who still was unable to link up with Smith whose army remained in the Lexington area, sixty miles away from Bardstown. (In true cavalier spirit, each C.S.A. command was independent of the other, Richmond never designating an overall commander for the entire invasion.) Furthermore by veering away from his original path to Louisville Bragg allowed Buell to flank him and essentially get to his (Bragg's) rear. Accordingly what began as an invasion designed to establish a Confederate presence along the Ohio River now became a giant raid.[32] Once Buell refitted and established new supply lines from Louisville, he could at last initiate a pursuit toward Bragg with an objective, albeit somewhat amorphous, to either capture or destroy Bragg's army. The tables having been turned, Bragg could not determine Buell's intentions. In essence, simply by marching south toward Bragg, Buell seized the initiative, almost always a significant advantage, while Bragg was set back on his heels.

Initially Bragg thought he could crush Buell at Bardstown, and thus deployed both his corps there. However, Bragg continued to show signs of doubt and hesitation so that on October 2—Buell was still leaving Louisville—Bragg ordered Hardee and Polk to leave Bardstown to accomplish a concentration of forces at Harrodsburg, south of Frankfort. By October 4, the Rebels left Bardstown but instead of moving directly to Harrodsburg, approximately thirty miles due east, Hardee detoured through Perryville to try to find badly needed water.

Because of Buell's ruse in the form of cannon fire aimed at Frankfort, approximately thirty-five miles from Bardstown, Bragg was erroneously convinced that Kentucky's state capital was Buell's intended point of concentration. Polk warned Bragg that Frankfort was not Buell's real target but Bragg's shortage of cavalry prevented as much scouting as would have been desired or effective. Now misled by Buell's ruse, Bragg ordered Polk to move toward Frankfort. But Polk ascertained Buell's actual deployment and moved to Harrodsburg instead of following Bragg's order.

On October 6, the day before twenty-one subordinate officers were signing a petition demanding Buell's removal from command, Bragg met personally with Smith in Harrodsburg. Bragg wanted to consolidate those two Southern armies but ultimately Smith was not able to set aside his own ambitions.[33] Instead he insisted his army remain in the relative comfort of the Blue Grass region, arguing they could concentrate their armies if need be. At this point the Confederates were split 25 miles apart with 20,000 soldiers in Perryville and 22,000 under Smith in Versailles.[34] Unfortunately since neither Bragg nor Smith had much accurate information about the disposition of Buell's army they had no idea when or where they might be required to converge, nor for that matter how long it would take to merge their armies, if need be.

## The Battle at Perryville

Throughout much of the campaign Kentucky was suffering from a severe, prolonged drought. What little water was available in ponds, pools, or creek beds was usually filthy, often polluted or contaminated causing widespread dysentery among soldiers on both sides.

Both sides learned that good water could be available at the hamlet of Perryville, in central Kentucky about sixteen miles southwest of Harrodsburg and approximately twenty-five miles southeast of Bardstown. Buell's columns—having bypassed Bardstown after it was evacuated by Bragg[35]—were still advancing in roughly parallel columns as many as twenty miles apart flank to flank, were ordered to converge at Perryville on October 7, 1862. Not only could water possibly be found at Perryville—which straddles the Chaplin River—but Buell also believed Bragg's and Smith's entire armies were at Perryville, thus enabling Buell to accomplish his primary objective of retrieving Kentucky from Confederate domination.

Buell's three columns marching southward were spread too far apart to remain abreast of one another. Gilbert's corps was the first to arrive—having taken the most direct route from Bardstown—with Sheridan's division in the lead, advancing almost due west of Perryville to the high ground overlooking the west bank of Doctor's Creek, a tributary of the Chaplin River. At the end of their respective marches on October 7, another miserably hot day, McCook stopped eight miles short of Perryville while Crittenden—who, looking for water elsewhere, had taken a circuitous route—was ten miles away. During the course of the day Buell—now riding with Gilbert's column—was chastising some soldiers who had broken ranks to forage. One of the soldiers grabbed the bridle of Buell's horse causing the animal to spook and fall backward over Buell.[36] Buell's injuries were serious enough to confine him to an ambulance or his headquarters at the Dorsey house, four miles from the front, for the next several days, grossly impairing his mobility and ability to command from the saddle.

Upon the deployment of his Federals, Buell had eight divisions—two divisions remained to divert Smith in Frankfort—with a total of 52,000 men. (Due to several factors, including too much whiskey consumed at Louisville, the poor conditioning of the new recruits, sunstrokes caused by the hot weather, and dysentery from foul water, Buell's army suffered 6,000 casualties, including deaths and stragglers, *en route*.) On the other side, when Bragg learned Federal columns were moving toward Perryville, he continued to fall for the ruse Frankfort was still Buell's primary objective and that only a fraction of Buell's army was headed for Perryville. Despite Hardee's recommendation that Bragg not split his army between Perryville and Frankfort, Bragg did just that sending one of the Polk's divisions from Harrodsburg to Frankfort to reinforce Smith while sending Polk along with his other division to buttress Hardee at Perryville.

Buell intended to launch his attack with all three corps beginning at 7 o'clock on the morning of Wednesday, October 8, 1862.[37] But neither of his flanking corps had reported; thus Gilbert was ordered to reschedule his attack to 10:00 a.m. when presumably all units would be in line. But Gilbert earlier discovered two of Sheridan's brigades had already advanced toward the creek. Gilbert—claiming he was to avoid a general engagement until Buell's entire army was available—then ordered Sheridan to disengage and withdraw.[38]

By now McCook's corps had arrived at a position northwest of Perryville and approximately three quarters of a mile north, or left, of Gilbert. But nothing had yet been heard from Thomas or Crittenden, even though the previous evening Buell had sent a message to Thomas to report to Buell as soon as he, Thomas, arrived. Since Buell had no intentions to launch an overall attack until all three corps were in place, Buell's Army of the Ohio stood still merely marking time but without making any precautionary measures such as entrenching for their security. When Crittenden arrived mid-morning he positioned his corps astride Lebanon and Brumfield Station Roads right of Gilbert three miles southeast of Perryville creating a crescent shaped front of five or six miles for the entire army. Claiming he was preoccupied by the Rebel skirmishers, Thomas neglected to report to Buell.[39]

Consistent with the strange layering of confusing events that occurred throughout the entire campaign, at this juncture both army commanders were confused about the strength and composition of the other.[40] Both Buell and Bragg mistakenly believed the other side's main body was at Frankfort!

Since Buell did not know whether Crittenden's corps had arrived he contemplated postponing his attack until the next day. It was almost as though he was validating his dancing-master characteristic of giving the enemy sufficient time to prepare for battle. Throughout the early afternoon of October 8 the opposing artillery batteries exchanged sporadic fire while some of McCook's brigades advanced in uncoordinated movements. Polk, with seniority over Hardee, soon realized numbers were not in the Confederates' favor, and was hesitant to start an attack. However Bragg—who had ridden frantically in from Harrodsburg that morning—insisted that attacks should commence immediately. Accordingly at approximately 2:30 p.m. the Rebels launched a frontal attack along the entire length of McCook's front catching the unsuspecting Bluecoats almost completely off guard. McCook's left, composed mostly by the new, untried recruits, quickly found itself in dire straits, in danger of being routed, which would precipitate an entire collapse of the Union defense. Before Union reinforcements could arrive, the Confederate attack pushed the Union left flank back about a mile while also capturing fifteen Federal guns.

Shortly thereafter McCook's right also came under attack with a couple more Union brigades being driven back toward the rear. Alexander McCook had directed ammunition be preserved for "close work"[41] while Gilbert's corps, to McCook's immediate right, initially failed to commit any reserves to help, even though Gilbert's left flank was only four hundred yards from the point of attack.[42] Sheridan's division was the closest of Gilbert's corps next to McCook's and as such was most available to render assistance to McCook but also had to be preparing for an attack against its own position. Sheridan's artillery turned its guns to the left upon advancing Rebels but soon had to turn back to the front to be able to fire against any charging Rebels. Sheridan's division would have been in much more effective position to assist McCook had it been allowed to maintain the forward position its brigades had gained earlier that morning. Otherwise Gilbert rendered little assistance to McCook. Only the decisive, impulsive orders of BGen. Lovell H. Rousseau, 42, a Mexican War veteran as well as Louisville's leading criminal defense lawyer, but then a division commander in McCook's 1st Corps, saved the day by countering McCook's direction to save ammunition. But Rousseau's actions were not without their costs; his division suffered almost two thirds of the casualties incurred by McCook's entire corps.

The battle of Perryville unfolded from north to south, in other words the three Confederate divisions first against McCook's corps and then toward Gilbert's. It is also noteworthy that whether by design or otherwise the Confederates had managed to concentrate all three available divisions against McCook's two, thus explaining in part why a Rebel force one-third the size of the Federal army was able to gain so much success during the afternoon of the 8th. Cheatham's division, arrayed against McCook, bore the brunt of the Rebels' fighting but Cleburne's brigade, to the south, drove furthest into the Federal lines. Again Cleburne was injured, this time[43] when his horse was killed before falling upon Cleburne.

Not only was Gilbert—who was visiting with Buell at the Dorsey House—oblivious to the threat on his left, McCook was sluggish in his reaction to the circumstances on either of his flanks. McCook was dilatory in asking for reinforcements but more importantly failed to apprise the immobilized Buell of the unfavorable, even potentially disastrous situation. That McCook's left flank was in danger of collapsing of course meant Buell's entire left flank was likewise threatened to collapse. In his report Buell blamed Alex McCook for stubbornly believing he could handle the situation by himself.[44]

Again—as it had at Iuka (described in Chapter 4)—acoustic shadowing was a key impediment in communications, which often depended upon the sounds of battle, especially cannon fire. Often Civil War commanders would—without further orders—rush their units toward the sound of gunfire. But on October 8 artillery fire simply could not be heard from a few miles away, apparently muffled by the terrain of the battlefield's rolling hills as well as by atmospheric conditions. Buell, at the Dorsey House, heard only occasional artillery rumbling, at one point sending word to Sheridan to quit wasting gun powder. Remarkably Buell did not learn of the battle that he had been anticipating for months, especially after leaving Louisville, until at 4:00 p.m. when a courier from McCook apprised Buell and Gilbert that McCook's corps was being mauled while being driven back. Later Buell admitted that he "was astonished" by the news.[45] Earl Hess has noted, "If Buell had been willing to ride out, even if it were inside an ambulance, to inspect his army firsthand, or if Gilbert had been more energetic and imaginative, the Army of Ohio might have taken advantage of its overwhelming numerical advantage to crush Bragg that afternoon."[46] For that matter Crittenden with his corps of 20,000 men was in an excellent position to flank Bragg's army and to force it to withdraw or else be captured. Is it any wonder that James McPherson characterizes the battle at Perryville as "…a battle that set a new record for confusion among the top brass on both sides."[47]

Several questions arose about the initial lack of assistance from Gilbert's corps; eventually an investigative commission placed the blame upon Gilbert and his lack of initiative. On the other hand, Shelby Foote gives Gilbert much more credit, stating that Gilbert, "…detach[ed] first one brigade, then another, to go to McCook's assistance."[48] (When Gilbert and Buell received word of the Rebel advance an order was issued to send a couple brigades from Gilbert's corps to help McCook; it is unclear whether that order came from Buell or from Gilbert.) Daniel also directs criticism at Thomas for his failure to report to Buell at 1:30 p.m. on the 8th with the implication that had Thomas reported as ordered he would have been in position to have taken effective command, or at least closer management, of the whole affair.[49]

By dark the Confederate attack lost its cohesion, exhausting itself and its ammunition, grinding to a halt opposite the badly bruised and battered brigades in McCook's corps. Late in the evening Sheridan pushed a Rebel brigade back into Perryville. Earlier Buell attempted to deploy Crittenden's 2nd Corps by sending an order to Thomas to attack from the right, an order that did not reach Thomas until after dusk. Thomas, convinced that Crittenden was being opposed by a full Confederate army—when in reality it was merely a cavalry brigade—refused to launch a night attack; instead he said he would "advance in the morning with first sound on the left."

In frustration Buell ordered Thomas to tell Crittenden to "be prepared to attack at daylight in the morning." At 1:30 a.m. on Friday, the 9th of October, Thomas told Crittenden to "Have your different divisions ready to attack at daylight." When Buell had heard no sounds or other reports of combat from Crittenden's area by 8:00 a.m., three hours after daylight, Buell sent his chief-of-staff to learn why no attack had been launched. Crittenden's response was that his orders had been to be ready to attack, which he was. Since he had received no orders to actually attack, no attack had been launched![50] Now completely exasperated, Buell ordered Crittenden to attack immediately, which Crittenden did only to discover Bragg was gone, having withdrawn from the lines prior to beginning to retreat during the night.

The previous evening Bragg had convened a council of war during which he learned of the full extent and locations of the Union forces deployed against him. Throughout much of the campaign, probably starting shortly before Munfordville, several of Bragg's mental shortcomings and emotional instabilities were emerging and continuing to affect his command capabilities. He was frequently indecisive, agitated, vacillating from one position to the next despondent and in despair, and perhaps most important unable to focus upon his strategic objectives. Given the lack of support from Kentucky citizens and given further his isolated position to gain reinforcements and additional supplies, that night after realizing during a council of war that his battered force was grossly outnumbered[51] Bragg decided to "redeploy"—rather than "retreat"—to Harrodsburg where he intended to join forces with Kirby Smith. Bragg still had enough sense to realize Buell was in position, if he acted fast enough, to deny a retreat through the Cumberland Gap where the western tip of Virginia meets the border between Kentucky and Tennessee.[52]

Although by midnight the Confederates had begun to retire from the field—one of the traditional markers of which side won or lost of the battle—it was hardly a Federal victory. Bragg's much smaller Rebel army had inflicted terrible carnage against McCook's corp. Out of 36,940 effectives the Federals lost 4,211 (845 killed, 2,852 wounded, and 515 missing.) Of 16,000 effectives the Confederates lost 3,396 (510 killed, 2,635 wounded and 251 missing). But the tactical reality was that the Confederates had suffered approximately 20 percent casualties while the Federals had two more corps that hardly had been engaged in the battle of October 8. Both Gilbert and Crittenden had virtually clear paths into Perryville which would either put the Rebels into the jaws of a vice or at least cut off the Rebels' best route for a retreat. Despite Buell's command shortcomings, he—or perhaps more accurately his rank-and-file—had managed to compel Bragg's army to resume its retreat from Kentucky.

## Retreat and Pursuit

When Buell determined that Bragg was moving his forces toward Harrodsburg, Buell planned to cut off Bragg's retreat to the Cumberland Gap. On October 10, a day after learning of Bragg's withdrawal, Buell ordered Gilbert to follow Bragg directly northeast to Harrodsburg while Crittenden would march east toward Danville, hopefully to head off Bragg's retreat.[53] Buell decided upon the two prong advance because he was uncertain about Bragg's whereabouts and because he, Buell, did not want to risk the possibility of an attack against the flank of a single column. Otherwise a quick movement directly to Danville might have been the most effective maneuver. Sill was ordered to leave Frankfort to reinforce McCook's corps that remained in Perryville for a short period of badly needed recuperation, repair and rest.

By Saturday, October 11, 1862, Union scouts reported Confederates were in a line of battle three miles south of Harrodsburg where Smith adamantly had urged Bragg to take a stand to fight. But Bragg's mindset was continuing to deteriorate.[54] Once he learned the Union column was moving toward Danville Bragg realized his escape route via the Cumberland Gap, together with all the supplies and foodstuffs he had collected,[55] would be jeopardized by lingering too long at Harrodsburg. To facilitate his retreat from Kentucky Bragg designated Col. Joseph Wheeler, 26, as commander of all cavalry units in both armies,[56] to screen the retreat route from Danville across the Dick's River to Lancaster, ten miles southeast of Camp Dick Robinson.

Soon thereafter Blue-coated cavalry discovered the Rebels had vacated the lines at Harrodsburg, abandoning twelve hundred sick and wounded. The Confederates had gotten across Dick's (or Dix) River before also burning all the bridges over the Salt River. Meanwhile Crittenden's corps continued to plod toward Danville, only to find the Confederates had already fled after confiscating everything of any value from the town and surrounding countryside.

By October 12 the Rebels, Smith as well as Bragg, crossed Dick's River to form a new line of battle near Camp Dick Robinson, a position Buell considered to be virtually impregnable.[57] To counteract the Confederate advantage of position Buell planned a southward flanking movement to try to get to the Confederate rear, conceivably interdicting any retreat.

However, instead of starting Buell's flanking movement to the Rebel rear in a timely and expeditious manner on the evening of October 12, as originally planned, the Federal march was postponed until the next morning, October 13. Even at that Buell took all day supervising careful and cautious movements only to learn that Bragg—upon learning of the Federals' approaching columns—had stolen another march by leaving for the Cumberland Gap at 1:00 that morning, leaving Smith's army as a rear guard at Lancaster.[58] Nevertheless, the thousands of wagons filled with 20,000 muskets Bragg had brought to arm recruits that never emerged slowed the retreat to a crawl.[59] Wheeler's gray cavalry was widely deployed to protect the enormous droves of livestock being herded by cowboys recruited from Texas regiments.[60]

At Lancaster the Confederates separated again into two columns with Bragg marching from Lancaster to Crab Orchard and from there southeast toward the Cumberland Gap. Meanwhile Kirby Smith, along with twenty miles of wagon train—including four hundred brand new Union wagons captured at Richmond[61]—and herds of confiscated livestock moved toward Big Hill before proceeding to Barboursville to follow Bragg toward the Cumberland Gap. Had Gilbert, leading the Federal column headed toward Lancaster, departed and proceeded at a reasonable rate of march he should have been able attack the extended and vulnerable Confederate column. But even when part of the Rebel train was spotted ahead, Gilbert ordered his lead brigade to retract rather than attack; Gilbert's feeble rationalization was there was no water ahead![62]

Kirby Smith, protected by Wheeler's cavalry that was engaged in continuous rear guard skirmishes, fighting no less than twenty-six separate engagements,[63] retraced the route of his original invasion; on October 16 Smith finally crossed the crest of Big Hill, along a dirt road on a sixteen-hundred-foot slope. Cleburne took personal charge of the train, employing 1,500 men borrowed from Henry Heth's division to haul the wagons by hand[64] up the slope and over the crest. Crossing Big Hill gave Bragg's column a measure of safety from Buell's pursuit.[65]

Bragg remained a day's march ahead of Buell. For instance Bragg entered Crab Orchard on Monday, October 13; Buell entered the same town on October 14, the same day when Bragg made it to Mount Vernon, less than five miles further down the Wilderness Road. On October 15, Bragg's Confederates crossed Rockcastle River where they encountered hostile civilians with Unionist leanings.

By October 15 the dual pursuits against Bragg's column were also over for all intents and purposes. Four miles from Mount Vernon two of Crittenden's divisions entered a deep gorge in which the retreating Rebels had felled several trees, making the gorge impassible.[66] Although Buell and Thomas probably knew at that point the Confederates' adroit use of the mountainous topography meant further pursuit would be futile, on October 16, after cutting a new road, the pursuit resumed, only to encounter more blocked passages and skirmishers from the Rebel rear guard. This pattern continued through Sunday, October 19. And although the Federals captured some stragglers and wagons, the main body of Confederates was beyond reach, especially after Bragg's army passed through Cumberland Gap on October 20,[67] followed by Smith's army two days later.

Gilbert's lame refusal to try to strike against the Confederate trains near Lancaster probably forfeited the Union's best, and certainly last, chance to score any success of pursuit against the retreating Rebels. Without sufficient mobility to get in front of either of the retreating Rebel armies, the best the pursuing Union forces could hope to accomplish was to hassle either rear guard unit, seldom a successful tactic in pursuit. Once the Rebel columns left Bluegrass country the topography of Appalachian foothills tilted the odds further in the Confederates' favor. But much more than anything else, the command structure and command mentalities of the Army of the Ohio simply were not well suited, or even inclined, to plan and prepare for the rapid, aggressive but coordinated movement necessary to capture and/or destroy an enemy. Buell's attitude, which permeated downward throughout much of his chain of command, was too cautious, too risk adverse, too concerned about protecting his supply trains, and too willing to accept the consequences of letting an adversary escape to be able to fight another day. In two weeks Buell's pursuit had progressed a mere sixty-five miles![68]

When Buell received a report that C.S.A. forces were beginning to concentrate for an attack against Nashville, he, on October 19, revealed his true inclinations when following a litany of excuses he notified General in Chief Henry Halleck in Washington that he intended to "...direct my main force by the most direct route to Nashville."[69] For the next several days Halleck, speaking for Lincoln and the rest of the Federal administration, and Buell continued to exchange a series of telegrams. Halleck kept directing Buell to proceed toward Knoxville, at one point for instance wiring, "*I am directed by the President* to say to you that your army must enter East Tennessee this fall..." (emphasis added). Buell consistently and stubbornly replied with his litany of reasons why he shouldn't, couldn't and/or wouldn't. Washington had long held aspirations of retaking East Tennessee, a hope that had been fermenting before Thomas' rout of the Confederates at Mills Springs. On the other hand in Buell's defense there were legitimate military reasons—including hostile topography, a lack of sufficient roads and opportunity to forage, the difficulty of supply, and a sparsely populated area—why retaking East Tennessee did not seem to make much sense. Finally on October 23, after Halleck had directed Buell "to proceed to and occupy East Tennessee with all possible dispatch," in an act of rank insubordination Buell ordered that his army return to Nashville.

Neither side had much, if any, reason to feel proud of the long, difficult campaign, including the pursuit that followed Perryville. The Confederates had been on the move, much of it by foot, for months and aside from capturing a generous, badly needed amount of supplies, including livestock for food, accomplished little to show for their efforts. Men as well as horses and mules suffered terrible deprivations; significant casualties were suffered, including those wounded Rebels abandoned to the care and custody of the Federals.

But much of the same thing could be said of Union soldiers, especially those who had been with the army prior to Louisville. Neither commander had any reason to take pride in his command accomplishments; each commander was reliably able to conjure up excuses to avoid taking advantage of opportunities to inflict serious injury to the other. Essentially both sides ended approximately where they had begun with little of any strategic value being accomplished. In other words, the Confederates lost their bid to capture Kentucky but the issue of control of Tennessee had yet to be settled. Sadly, the campaign resembled what Helmuth von Moltke described as two armed mobs chasing each other around the country.

## *Dénouements and Precursors*

As if Buell's defiant rejection of Halleck's, and presumably the President's, directions to pursue into East Tennessee was not enough, especially in the light of Buell's failure to prevent the Confederate escape from Kentucky, Buell was again being subjected to scathing criticism from several quarters. McClellan's persona helped him to retain the loyalty, even devotion, of his subordinate officers and rank-and-file even after his repeated failures but Buell's personality engendered no such loyalty or devotion. When his subordinates were not quarreling with each other they were complaining about Buell; even Thomas Crittenden, once one of his supporters, opined that Buell was a "hopeless case" while Crittenden's father, John Crittenden, the U.S. Senator from Kentucky, expressed his "profound disappointment." Other politicians, including the governors of Illinois, Indiana, and Ohio, weighed in with their lack of confidence in Buell's leadership. Likewise cabinet members, most notable Secretary of War Stanton and Secretary of Treasury Chase believed Buell's pro-slavery views accounted for his lack of aggressiveness.

By some traditional measures, Buell was hardly a disaster. After all Kentucky had been saved from Confederate domination. Buell had operated under some severe handicaps, including inexperienced commanders saddled with raw recruits. Despite Bragg's shortcomings he could be an elusive adversary reluctant to give battle that might risk the destruction of his command. Likewise Buell was careful to protect his army, to see that it was decently fed and supplied, and otherwise generally performed as competently as generals had performed for decades.

But Buell was also tone deaf to political considerations, theretofore considered a military virtue. In particular Buell failed appreciate the importance of politics and political factors in a civil war where attitudes of a wide spectrum of people could be as important as were geographic gains of armies.

Furthermore it must be said that Lincoln was becoming a tough demanding Commander in Chief not satisfied by traditional battlefield and/or maneuvering victories that left the vanquished enemy still able to fight another day. Lincoln was no longer tolerant of the soft war philosophy of the old regular army, something that escaped Buell's attention: Lincoln expected that his commanders could and would extend pursuits to the fullest, especially if a pursuit was perceived as also potentially achieving important political goals.

And while George McClellan had a political constituency that was of some value to Lincoln, at least until the election in November 1862, Buell's lack of political support made him entirely dispensable without delay. The only question was who would be appointed to replace him. Buell's army career was essentially finished. An investigation commission—the so-called Buell Commission—was convened but found no basis for action against Buell. Nevertheless upon being relieved by Rosecrans, Buell awaited further orders for more than a year after which he resigned from the army.

Upon his return to Knoxville, Braxton Bragg might have expected a warm reception; he had managed to escape from a much larger army; he had returned with a huge bounty of confiscated supplies and captured materiel, including 30 artillery pieces; and his army, while damaged, would soon be able to return to engage the enemy in battle. Furthermore, Bragg's campaign had achieved strategic gains by relieving Federal pressure upon Chattanooga while reclaiming territories of Alabama and Tennessee.

And of course the latter part of Bragg's Kentucky campaign coincided with Robert Lee's raid into Maryland, a raid that culminated with Lee's retreat from Antietam. Lee's army suffered more casualties with less accomplished in material results that had Bragg's army.[70] Additionally Lee's Maryland campaign had accomplished nothing of any strategic importance for the Confederacy. Yet while Lee was being treated as a hero, Bragg was greeted with harsh criticism from a wide range of sources from within and without his army. In response to the criticisms, Bragg was summoned back to Richmond, coincidentally the same day when Buell was ordered to Indianapolis to await further orders.

After Rosecrans was appointed to command the newly named Army of Cumberland, Joshua Sill became a brigade commander but was killed December 31, 1862, at Stone's River. Phil Sheridan, Sill's West Point classmate, was one of Sill's division commanders. In 1869 Sheridan named a fort in Oklahoma for his former classmate, that facility now being the home of the U.S. Army's artillery school.

But despite all the demands for Bragg's dismissal, Confederate President Davis was not about to relieve his old Mexican War comrade. Instead Davis wanted to hear Bragg's side of the story after which Davis congratulated Bragg and sent him back to rejoin his army. Bruce Catton noted that some strategic realities, specifically the Federals' capacity to use its superior numbers to great advantage throughout all theaters, were beginning to dawn upon Davis who could no longer promise robust defenses to all governors in the C.S.A.[71] Kirby Smith had been one of Bragg's most severe critics; like Bragg, Smith was ordered back to Richmond also to consult with Davis. Promoted to lieutenant general, Smith was eventually given command of the Trans-Mississippi Department and Army. The later surrender of Vicksburg isolated Smith's command, essentially making it an independent command. In 1865, after learning of the capture of Jefferson Davis, Smith's force was the last Confederate army in the Civil War to surrender.

By war's end, Simon Buckner, by then lieutenant general and Kirby Smith's chief of staff, accepted the terms of surrender upon Smith's behalf; a week later Smith signed the formal agreement of surrender. Buckner, who had been the first to surrender a Confederate army, that occurring at Fort Donelson, had the ignominy of also arranging one of the Confederacy's final surrender.

After the war, Simon Buckner became editor of the Louisville *Courier*. His friendship with Grant resumed and he was a pallbearer at Grant's funeral. Buckner was the last surviving Confederate officer above the rank of brigadier general. Buckner's son commanded the U.S. 10th Army but was killed in Okinawa in 1945.

Although the Union victory at Antietam is often cited for discouraging, or even preventing, the possibility of European intervention in America's Civil War, likewise the outcome at Perryville, coming as it did twenty-two days after Antietam, was another contributing factor in showing that a C.S.A. victory should not be presumed. The Confederacy had planned and embarked upon a massive, seven front offensive but would never again be able to undertake such an ambitious undertaking. In many respects, Perryville represented the South's "High Tide" in the Western theater of the Civil War, especially since the Confederacy would never reach as far north to engage in battle.

# 4

# Iuka and Corinth II
## *September and October 1862*

## *Lineups of Commanders*

Upon Halleck's departure from the West, Grant's enlarged and decentralized command became collectively known as the Army of the Tennessee (named after the river and not to be confused with the C.S.A.'s Army of Tennessee named for the state). Initially Grant established his headquarters at Corinth but later to Jackson, Tennessee, to better communicate with his scattered sub-commands.

Not only were Grant's sub-commands scattered, they had a diverse lot of commanders. MGen. William S. ("Old Rosey") Rosecrans, 43, was named to replace Pope as commander of the Army of the Mississippi.[1] Rosecrans resigned from the Regular Army in 1854 when he suffered a nervous breakdown; he then had successful various careers in engineering, architecture, and refining of coal and oil. Upon his re-entry into the Federal army he served as McClellan's chief subordinate in western Virginia in 1861 when they more or less bested Robert E. Lee. Old Rosey, a big, burly man with an extensive vocabulary of profanity, was energetic and hardworking, and enjoyed staying up late at night to discuss religious issues with his staff. Because he consistently demonstrated concern for the welfare of his troops, they responded with affection and respect. Rosecrans continued to serve in western Virginia (later West Virginia) until May 1862 when he was appointed to take charge of two divisions in Pope's Army of the Mississippi.[2] A short while later in June 1862 when Pope was transferred back east Rosecrans was appointed to succeed Pope. Rosecrans inherited a "contrary lot" of subordinates including BGen. David Sloane Stanley, 34, 'capable but petulant," leading the Second Division, and MGen. Gordon Granger, 40, "testy but talented," commanding the cavalry corps.[3]

MGen. Edward O.C. Ord, 44, was another subordinate commander in Grant's army. Ord—Halleck's and Sherman's friend at West Point—had extensive military experience including action in the Seminole War as well as in the Washington territory. He was also part of the expedition to suppress John Brown at Harper's Ferry in 1859. Because of his pro-slavery attitudes as an antebellum Democrat, some Republican Congressmen demanded Ord's removal from the Army; however, Halleck and Sherman protected him. Prior to being assigned to the Army of the Mississippi, Ord commanded various artillery and infantry units in northern Virginia and around Washington; on December 20, 1861, Ord captivated the nation's attention when he defeated Jeb Stuart in a large skirmish at Dranesville, Virginia. Grant viewed Ord as a solid, if not spectacular, soldier.

Among the independent Confederate commands, none were quite as exotic as the one commanded by MGen. Earl Van Dorn. Van Dorn, Rosecrans' classmate at West Point, having been nominated by his great uncle, Andrew Jackson,[4] remained in the Regular Army, once being struck by two arrows while fighting Comanches, but he resigned from the Regular Army to join the Confederate effort when the Civil War erupted. Van Dorn was described as being "small, elegant figure, elegant person" who was "courtly, aristocratic" but "headstrong." Earlier he was, next to Jeff Davis, the favorite son of Mississippi. As a military commander Van Dorn was characterized as being aggressive enough but giving little attention to proper planning or logistics. After its catastrophic Pea Ridge defeat in March 1862, Van Dorn's command was ordered to leave Arkansas and to come across the Mississippi River, after failing to reinforce Johnston and Beauregard at Shiloh, by the late summer of 1862, Van Dorn settled his command at Holly Springs, about sixty miles west of Corinth.

Another Mexican War veteran, MGen. Sterling ("Old Pap") Price, 52 years old weighing 290 pounds, a farmer and politician—he previously served as a Congressman and as a Governor of Missouri—led another Southern command in the West.[5] Not only was Price not a West Point graduate, he once bought a newspaper notice to refute rumors that he once attended a military academy. At Wilson's Creek, Missouri, on August 10, 1861, his force combined with Ben McCulloch's to overwhelm the Federals, causing them to flee in disarray.

Later Price served under Van Dorn at Pea Ridge, where he was wounded while leading a futile charge against the Yankees. After the Pea Ridge defeat, Price reluctantly accompanied Van Dorn east across the Mississippi River. By September 1862, Price's command had split away from Van Dorn's, and was in the vicinity of Tupelo, Mississippi, approximately sixty miles south of Corinth. Price's devotion to Missouri, rather than to the entire Confederacy, prompted Jeff Davis to keep Price at arm's length.

## *Rebels Maneuver*

Both sides were relatively inactive during much of the summer of 1862 for a variety of reasons, including logistical difficulties, not the least of which was the lack of water caused by a summer of 1862 drought, plus uncertainty about strategic intentions and/or guidelines in the respective capitals. However, as described in Chapter 3, by late August 1862 military operations began to stir, especially in Kentucky.

Prior to moving to Mobile[6] Bragg detached Price with 16,000 men in the northern part of Mississippi while leaving Van Dorn with another 16,000 soldiers to guard Vicksburg. Once Bragg advanced into Middle Tennessee he directed Van Dorn and Price to accomplish three tasks: (1) hold Mississippi; (2) prevent Grant from being able to support Buell—who as previously described in Chapter 3 should have been also moving north to defend against Bragg and Smith; and (3) move their own forces into Middle Tennessee to reinforce Bragg directly. While each of these tasks was reasonable from Bragg's standpoint, Van Dorn and Price hardly had the means to accomplish all three at the same time. To complicate matters, neither Van Dorn nor Price was inclined to cooperate with the other,[7] even though Bragg had directed Van Dorn to assist Price, thus inverting their command relationship at Pea

Ridge. For that matter, neither general was particularly anxious to assist Bragg. Van Dorn—whose recent offensive initiative against Baton Rouge had been soundly repulsed—entertained grandiose aspirations of capturing Paducah, Kentucky, on the Ohio River.

## *Iuka* (October 3 and 4, 1862)

Eventually Price decided he could best contribute to Bragg's effort by attacking and hopefully capturing the Iuka supply depot, Grant's eastern most outpost, twenty miles east by southeast of Corinth.

When Halleck was still in command of the Union's western campaign he had dispersed forces to several key locations, keeping four divisions in the defenses of Corinth under Rosecrans' command. Other deployments included a force under Ord's command at Jackson, Tennessee, fifty-five miles north of Corinth. Other divisions under William Sherman and BGen. Stephen A. Hurlbut, 47, respectively, were located in Memphis and Bolivar, respectively.[8]

As soon as the Federals occupied Corinth it became apparent that maintaining a force of 100,000 soldiers would have little effectiveness against smaller, more mobile Confederate units that could strike and capture other key locations, especially those that were essential because they were astride railroads or were river or sea ports. Rebel cavalry detachments, led by a bevy of resourceful, energetic, freewheeling leaders such as Nathan Belford Forrest and John Hunt Morgan, consistently took advantage of undersized garrisons, undermanned supply depots, and exposed transportation facilities to raid, plunder, and destroy whenever possible. Accordingly in the late spring and early summer of 1862 smaller armies were formed and dispersed beyond Corinth while Federal commands became decentralized. The hamlet of Iuka, found at the eastern border of Mississippi, close to where the Memphis & Charleston Railroad bridged the Tennessee River,[9] was one such outpost.

Upon getting word that Price was moving northward Grant deduced Price was probably headed either toward Iuka or perhaps further north to reinforce Bragg. In order to solidify his defenses, Grant recalled most of his outposts to Corinth while leaving a light brigade consisting of two infantry regiments together with a cavalry regiment to protect the supply depot at Iuka.

By Saturday, September 13, Price's cavalry engaged Union pickets around Iuka, each side taking a small number of prisoners. When the outpost's commander learned that Price's main body was about a day's march away, and also learning that Rebels cut the rail line as well the telegraph line to Corinth, the local Union commander decided to burn all the supplies before withdrawing his brigade to Corinth.[10]

As soon as the Union garrison withdrew, Price's Confederates occupied the depot, saving the newly captured new guns and ammunition as well as a variety of food stuffs and liquid refreshments.[11] When Grant and Rosecrans learned of the loss of Iuka and its bonanza of supplies, Grant immediately relieved the Iuka garrison's commander. Grant also immediately began to make preparations, ordering a reconnaissance to retake Iuka.

Grant realized Van Dorn was still at least four days away, meaning that if Rosecrans moved quickly enough Grant had sufficient forces available to defeat Price in Iuka while still being able to defend Corinth. Grant accepted Rosecrans' proposal that Rosecrans would approach Iuka from the southwest with 9,000 troops while Ord, accompanied by Grant, would move his division of 6,500 men by rail to Burnsville.[12] Ord would then hit Iuka from the northwest.[13] Rosecrans' element would block Price's potential retreat routs to the south before also striking the Rebels. Ideally these separate columns would converge at the same time in a pincers movement with superior numbers upon Price.[14] However, Grant was especially anxious that these attacks be launched without delay since Rosecrans and Ord had to return quickly to Corinth lest it remain relatively vulnerable to attack from Van Dorn. Grant determined that his units should begin their march to Iuka on September 16.[15]

However, in the Civil War these tactical convergences were almost always fraught with considerable difficulties, as had been the case earlier with the coordination of Union forces trying to capture Stonewall Jackson in the Shenandoah Valley. First and foremost, communications between separated columns were always problematic, usually depending upon couriers who might or might not know the location of the other column. In the instant case the pincers movements would be made across rough, uneven terrain, much of which was still heavily forested, but sometimes through swamps, and without many secondary roads. Accordingly to overcome these difficulties it was a common technique to agree that simultaneous strikes would commence when one column fired a cannon to signal to the other that the attack should start. In this case it was agreed Rosecrans would fire his cannon to let Ord's column begin its attack.

But this plan started to go awry almost immediately. Rosecrans' rate of march was hampered by hard rains turning Rosey's route into muddy quagmires. Furthermore, a civilian guide took one of Rosecrans' divisions on a wrong turn, necessitating a countermarch, never an easy maneuver for a couple thousand soldiers with their horse drawn wagons and artillery pieces on narrow, unimproved roads. Rosecrans sent a message to Grant to advise that Rosey would not be at Iuka until between 1:00 and 2:00 p.m. on the 19th. As a result Ord, after leaving Grant at Burnsville, halted about six miles from Iuka on September 18,[16] about twenty-four hours before Rosecrans was expected to arrive. Apparently Grant changed the plans so that Rosecrans should begin his attack with Ord to join in once he heard the sounds of the battle. According to Ord, Grant made little other effort to stay in contact with Rosecrans.[17]

Moreover, because of the difficulty of traversing the roads approaching Iuka, Rosecrans decided to advance along only one road instead of two as Grant anticipated.[18] Rosecrans was also concerned that splitting his small force could make it possible for Price to defeat his Federals in detail.[19]

Sometime after 3:30 p.m. of Friday, September 19, 1862, skirmishers in Rosecrans' vanguard emerged from thickets and scrub woods to meet Price's full defensive lines, which immediately launched a full volley of fire.[20] Old Rosey had not anticipated his skirmishers would encounter Rebel defenders so soon but after some hesitation and confusion he aligned his troops to give battle. Meanwhile the Rebel defenses continued to fire with muskets as well with artillery. An intense, strenuous struggle, some of it hand-to-hand, ensued in the brush-entangled terrain with the Rebels—who engaged 3,179 men—suffering approximately 17 percent casualties with the Federals—who engaged approximately 4,500 men[21] suffering approximately 28 percent during three and half hours of fighting. By the end of the battle, Rosecrans was pushed back six hundred yards.[22]

And to complicate things further, once Rosecrans began to attack, the sound of his and Price's guns was muffled by another acoustic shadow.[23] When circumstances were right Civil War artillery could sometimes be heard about a hundred miles away. But conversely given a combination of certain terrain configurations, including the valleys and density of the forests, and atmospheric conditions, such as humidity and wind direction, artillery barrages would also not even be heard a couple miles away.

Throughout it all Grant and Ord kept waiting for Rosey's signal that the latter's attack had started; neither heard so much as a single shot from the battle raging only six miles distant. Afterwards Grant and Ord, as well as some of their subordinates, claimed the wind blew from the north all day, apparently carrying the sounds of gunfire to the south.[24] Sharp controversy still remains about the communications breakdown between Rosecrans and Grant.[25] However the record is reasonably clear that eventually late at night or early the next morning a courier from Rosecrans reached Grant who immediately ordered Ord to attack first thing in the morning.[26] Coincidentally, at Iuka Rosecrans also ordered Stanley to strike with the bayonet at sunrise that same morning.[27]

However, that morning, September 20, Stanley's soldiers found only massive bodies of dead soldiers and horses, Price's Confederates having escaped the battlefield southeastward by way of the road that Rosecrans had opted not to block during his approach to Iuka.[28] Before he went to bed after the fierce engagement of September 19, Price told his chief of staff his Confederates would resume their attack at daybreak. However his generals stirred him from his sleep to convince him that "Grant would attack with an overwhelming force."[29] When they discovered the Rebels were gone, and although he had yet to hear from Grant, Rosecrans immediately dispatched Granger's cavalry to pursue the retreating Rebels while ordering both his infantry divisions to start their march at 8:30 a.m.[30]

Ord arrived at approximately 10:0 a.m., explaining he resumed his advance toward Iuka as soon as he heard sounds of battle. When Grant arrived at noon on the 20th he ordered Ord back to Corinth, meaning that Rosecrans' pursuit force was smaller than the force they were chasing. Grant was also disappointed Price had escaped but his subsequent ride over the ground convinced Grant (at least at that time) that Rosecrans simply did not have enough troops to have covered both roads.[31]

Given a head start along narrow, easily defensible roads Price's retreat might not have been in any realistic danger of being overtaken even by a vigorous pursuit. Union cavalry did catch up to Price's rear guard on the afternoon of Saturday, September 20; however these cavalrymen were easily repulsed by Rebels waiting in ambush eight miles south of the battlefield. Although Rosecrans' soldiers had marched twenty miles the previous day, had not eaten in twenty-four hours, and had just fought a major battle, they pursued for fifteen miles on the 20th.[32] By the end of the twentieth both infantry division commanders felt further pursuit was pointless, and Grant approved Rosecrans' recommendation that his army begin to withdraw back to their starting point.[33]

Grant's larger concern for Corinth arose because Van Dorn was making moves that Grant interpreted as advances upon Corinth. On the other hand Rosecrans saw the situation as an opportunity to capture Van Dorn in detail.[34] In any event, after approaching to within seven miles of Corinth Van Dorn withdrew to Mississippi to meet Price's battered and retreating army.[35] In the meanwhile Grant returned to his Burnsville headquarters before returning to Corinth and eventually taking a train to St. Louis where he had sent his family.

Given the size and scope of several other battles during the Civil War, and despite its bloody results, Iuka by itself was not a big deal. Nevertheless, Iuka demonstrated among other things the inherent difficulties of implementing classic textbook maneuvers such as pincers, especially across the types of rugged terrain typically found in the Lower South. Pertaining to pursuits, Iuka illustrated the difficulty of extending a pursuit when the troops were tired and hungry even if the pursuit had been initiated in a timely manner. Iuka also showed the futility of trying to pursue if a commander was not enthusiastic about seeking decisive victory, or at least perceived other, more pressing priorities. Iuka also demonstrated Grant's propensity—at least at this point in the war—to change his mind about continuing a vigorous pursuit, once launched as had happened after Shiloh.

Iuka also exposed the futility of small independent Confederate infantry commands trying to operate against larger Union armies commanded by reasonably competent battlefield commanders such as Grant and Rosecrans. Although Price—with fortuitous help from atmospheric conditions—had narrowly escaped the possible destruction of his small army, he accomplished little other than the capture of a wealth of badly-needed supplies. He had not been able to reinforce Bragg; neither had Price prevented Grant from sending further reinforcements to Buell in Kentucky. After retreating from Iuka Old Pappy's only option was to join his army with Van Dorn's in Mississippi. Per a directive from Jefferson Davis, Price would again be Van Dorn's subordinate.

Although providing useful case lessons about tactics, including factors necessary for a successful pursuit, Iuka's strategic significance was to set the stage for another battle of Corinth, a battle that has been ranked among the fifty most significant battles of the Civil War.

## *Corinth II* (October 3 and 4, 1862)

Buck Van Dorn finally gave up on his impractical and risky aspirations to capture Paducah, instead now focusing upon the recapture of the much closer Corinth. In Van Dorn's view, not only was Corinth the centerpiece of the Federal's defense in that region but conversely the recapture of Corinth would give him several strategic options, including moving toward Memphis, or St. Louis, or even retaking western Tennessee.[36] Additionally any credible action against Corinth should hamper Grant's capacity to send more reinforcements to Buell.

Additionally to any strategic considerations, based upon some of their letters home, it appears that Van Dorn and Rosecrans—West Point classmates—both looked forward to engaging each other's army to prove he was the more worthy classmate. But while Van Dorn had visions of great accomplishments, Grant anticipated the Confederates might try to recapture Corinth, and envisioned an opportunity to strike a major blow against these Confederate forces.

Van Dorn planned to have Price join with him at Ripley, Mississippi, a few miles west of the Hatchie River and south of the Memphis & Charleston Railroad.[37] At that point Van Dorn and Price would have approximately 22,000 men under their combined command. Van Dorn estimated there were maybe 8,000, but not more than 15,000, Union soldiers defending Corinth, and if he and Price moved quickly enough they would have superior

## 4. Iuka and Corinth II

numbers to attack Corinth before Grant could send sufficient reinforcements. Price, who had served under Van Dorn in similar circumstances at Pea Ridge the previous March, was apprehensive about Van Dorn's plan but had little option except to go along with Buck.

Corinth was ringed with extensive fortifications, some having been built by the Confederates shortly after Shiloh, with even more fortifications built later under Halleck's direction. Grant—from his headquarters 58 miles north of Corinth in Jackson, Tennessee—ordered the construction of more redoubts armed with heavy artillery,[38] these to be built inside the earlier works, closer to Corinth itself. Subsequent to Iuka Rosecrans resumed charge of the defenses of Corinth, but contrary to Van Dorn's estimate, actually had approximately 22,000 soldiers at his disposal.

On Sunday, September 28, 1862, just barely one week after Price managed to escape from Iuka, he and Van Dorn joined their forces (and commands) at Ripley from whence they marched thirty miles north until on October 1 they reached Pocahontas, twenty miles northwest of their destination at Corinth.[39]

Van Dorn planned to feint toward the west at Pocahontas to try to make Grant believe the Rebels were heading west. Grant warned his subordinate commanders Van Dorn was headed toward Bolivar or Corinth.[40]

Instead of continuing west Van Dorn turned right at Pocahontas to head east toward Corinth. But the next day skirmishers were met by Union infantry and cavalry at Chewalla, ten miles from Corinth.[41] Although Van Dorn had intended to advance upon Corinth by surprise, encountering Federals so far from Corinth told Van Dorn he had lost any element of surprise. Nevertheless he continued to push on until the morning of Friday, October 3, and while still two miles shy of his objective, Buck's skirmishers came upon more Union soldiers in fortifications. Ironically earlier that spring while awaiting Halleck's columns cautiously advancing from Shiloh Van Dorn had helped—under Beauregard's supervision—to construct some of these extensive fortifications!

Because Grant had not yet returned from St. Louis where he had gone after Iuka, the responsibility for defending Corinth fell directly upon Rosecrans' shoulders.[42] Rosey placed four divisions in an arc running from the west—starting to the left of the Memphis & Charleston rail tracks—around to the north. Initially Rosecrans tried to defend at the outer ring of breastworks, i.e., the ones built earlier by the Confederates, but even his own troops knew the outer ring of entrenchments would be difficult to hold.

Once the Rebels began their strike, one of Rosey's divisions—outnumbered at the point of attack and outflanked—had no choice except to fall back to the newer, more compact arc of fortifications closer to Corinth. Although the Bluecoats retreated in great haste, their movement was not done in the helter skelter panic of Shiloh[43]; instead they quickly reorganized and repositioned themselves for more fighting. By the late afternoon all Northern units had reached the relative safety of the inner, more compact ring of entrenchments.

By the end of the first day, portions of the Yankee defenders were badly battered.[44] On division bore the brunt of the Confederate assaults, with all three brigade commanders being wounded, two mortally. But there would be no rest for the weary. Instead Rebel artillery began its barrage before first light the next morning of the 4th of October. After holding its fire until the light had improved for better visibility, Union artillery countered, silencing the Rebel guns within only thirty minutes.[45] For several hours further fighting was limited to light skirmishing but eventually the Confederates concentrated against a weak link in the Union defensive lines, forcing a break- through that almost reached the Union's baggage trains staged in the streets of the town. Although the Rebels gained valuable ground, they paid dearly. First the Rebel units lost their continuity becoming separated, disorganized and confused among the houses in the town of Corinth; individual soldiers were exhausted and not very capable of further fighting; plus Union artillery continued to inflict considerable casualties.

But the battle's turning point was developing on the Union's left center where the Confederates were preparing another assault. While the Confederates were assembling in near parade ground fashion, their advance across rugged, undulating ground was contested by well-placed artillery and hampered by abatis a hundred yards in front of the Union entrenchments. The first line of Rebel attackers suffered terrible losses before breaking and falling back but a second line quickly formed to resume the assault. In desperation the Yank defenders resorted to the bayonet and hand-to-hand combat as the Rebels surged forward.[46] Finally the Union commanders unloosed a small reserve that tipped the precarious balance in the defenders' favor, repulsing the attack of depleted and exhausted Rebel survivors.

Van Dorn conceded to reality at noon, pulling the last of his troops from the battlefield at 2:00 p.m.[47] At the end of this bitter, hard-fought two-day battle, the Confederates suffered between 4,000 to 5,000 casualties in comparison to 2,500 Union losses. One Rebel division, commanded by BGen. Dabney H. Maury, 40,[48] lost almost 48 percent of its men. Because of heavy losses of officers, because of the fatigue of the soldiers, and because of the difficult terrain, the Rebel's retreat began in great disorder. But once away from imminent danger the soldiers reformed into their units with military order being restored into columns for retreat. Owing to its heavy losses, Maury's division was placed in the lead where presumably it was least likely to encounter any more action. By the end of the evening, Van Dorn's army had gotten as far as Chewalla before stopping for the night.[49]

Van Dorn's venture at Corinth ended no better than had his similar attempt at Pea Ridge, seven months earlier when he had also attacked from the Federal rear thus jeopardizing his own line of retreat. Although his army had suffered tremendously, he had accomplished no strategic objective; specifically Grant's Army of the Tennessee remained in control of the region and would continue to be position to advance upon remaining Confederate strongholds, including Vicksburg. Perhaps even worse for a man as vain and as proud as Van Dorn, the popular reaction was unforgiving in its assessment of his generalship.

As usually seemed to be the case there are conflicting opinions about Rosecrans' management of the battlefield. Steven E. Woodworth offers strong criticisms, stating among other things that Rosecrans' orders were unrealistic and ignored.[50] On the other hand several reports from those at the battlefield paint another picture. For instance: "[He] ... had shown tremendous personal courage during the fight, riding from one hot spot to another, exhorting, inspiring, directing the Union defenses." Another correspondent reported Rosecrans "...dashed to the front. [He] rallied the men, by his splendid example. The men, brave when bravely led, fought again." One of his staff officers described Rosecrans as "one of the most fearless officers I ever saw in battle. He seemed to be unconscious of danger ... like the very spirit of war."[51]

Grant was becoming—as was Lincoln—less satisfied by indecisive battles whereby the enemy was merely driven from the battlefield to be able to fight another day. Instead Grant was learning from the post–Shiloh mistakes of not capturing a retreating army so now he wanted a result that would prevent the vanquished army from ever again being able to fight. Accordingly upon hearing of the battle at Corinth Grant attempted to position a blocking force that could cut off the retreating Confederates. In order to reach its safe haven at Holly Springs—approximately sixty-five miles due west of Corinth—Van Dorn's army, with its five hundred wagons, first had to swing north before heading west across poor roads; additionally, Buck's retreating army had to make a number of difficult river crossings, the first and most critical being Davis' Bridge across the Hatchie River near Pocahontas. Thus, while McClellan was still dithering after Antietam, Grant, now back at his headquarters in Jackson, and in anticipation of Van Dorn's retreat from Corinth, took two important steps to try to interdict Van Dorn's army from its retreat presumably to Holly Springs.

First, Grant ordered Hurlbut's division of 5,000 soldiers to move from Bolívar to Pocahontas, where Ord—four and half months senior to Hurlbut—would personally arrive to assume command.[52] After arising at 3:00 a.m. and marching twenty three miles, Hurlbut's division arrived within six miles of its destination by the evening of October 4.

Second, Grant also ordered four infantry regiments with some cavalry and artillery— essentially a heavy brigade commanded by BGen. James B. McPherson, 34—to move quickly from guard duty at Jackson to reinforce Rosecrans. McPherson's reinforcements arrived at Corinth after sundown on October 4 after the fighting ended.[53]

And so Grant had reason to believe he had all the pieces in place to capture or destroy Van Dorn's army by cutting off his retreat. Grant was so pleased with these developments that he telegraphed Halleck, "At this distance everything looks favorable, and I cannot see how the enemy are to escape without losing everything but their small arms."[54] But the realities of strenuous, hard fought combat, including exhausted soldiers and famished horses, together with the challenges of trying to coordinate widely separated commands, became flies in this ointment.

Instead of immediately going after Van Dorn's badly mauled army, Rosecrans ordered his soldiers—who had fought for two days with little sleep in between—to return to their camps, get some sleep, prepare five days' rations, and together with McPherson's recently arrived brigade, be ready to pursue the next morning, October 5. Rosecrans did promptly dispatch cavalry to ascertain the enemy's posture.[55] That evening Rosecrans also tasked BGen. John McArthur, 34, to use his brigade to cautiously shadow the retreating Rebels.[56] A mitigating factor in Rosey's favor was that he was almost totally exhausted from lack of sleep, including only a half hour sleep the previous night.

At the end of the first day of the Rebels' retreat, October 4, Van Dorn halted at Chewalla, four miles from the Hatchie River.[57] Buck's generals were puzzled why they stopped as close to the vital river crossing until they learned Van Dorn wanted to circle back to launch another strike against Corinth. Aghast at the irrationality of that possibility, Van Dorn's generals dissuaded him from such notion; Buck than agreed to cross the Davis Bridge next day before turning south toward Ripley.[58]

Early the next morning Sunday, October 5, Hurlbut repositioned his soldiers on high bluffs overlooking Davis Bridge, a span of sixty feet. Ord arrived at the Hatchie Sunday morning to take command of Hurlbut's reinforced division. Soon Southerners started crossing the bridge but were confronted by and driven back by Federal artillery well-placed upon the ridgeline overlooking the bridge. Later that morning a Union brigade—after struggling with fatigued and hungry troops of Maury's advance guard—seized physical possession of the bridge.[59]

But instead of being content to remain in possession of the bridge, as well as of the commanding heights west of the bridge, Ord ordered Hurlbut's Federals to cross to the eastern side of the Hatchie, an order almost immediately creating chaos and confusion.[60] Among other factors several Rebel batteries had taken positions a few hundred yards east of the Hatchie and could fire effectively upon Union soldiers as they clustered trying to cross. One Confederate gunner felt he had never seen such a wealth of targets.[61]

Ord recognized his mistake but was severely wounded attempting to cross the bridge[62]; causing command to revert to Hurlbut. Eventually sufficient Blue coated soldiers were able to assemble on the east side of the bridge but once across, there was not have enough level terrain east of the bridge to permit much maneuvering to organize a line of attack; nevertheless they took the hill where the Rebel tubes were abandoned too quickly to be spiked. Hurlbut, knowing his division would be outnumbered three to one by the remnants of Van Dorn's army, did not attempt to advance further east.[63] Additionally Hurlbut had every reason to assume Rosecrans would be advancing from the other direction to compress Van Dorn from the rear.

On the morning of October 5 Rosecrans sent two separate columns toward Pocahontas. McPherson's brigade led one column while McArthur's led the second column.[64] Rosey remained in Corinth to try to coordinate these movements and to stay in touch with Grant. However, even though Grant had urged Rosecrans to "push the enemy to the wall," once underway Rosey's columns moved at lethargic and disorganized paces. Even with an overnight rest the soldiers were still exhausted while the horses were weak from lack of forage.[65] McPherson complained about his lack of water and rations, his men were tired, and his wagons were either broken or lost. Stanley—part of McPherson's column—wrote "The heat was excessive and the men were worn out; they had narrowly escaped a most terrible defeat, and no one was anxious to crowd their late antagonists."[66] Stanley—whose own performance was less than stellar—also sent a dispatch complaining the divisions were moving too slowly—"one division poked along painfully all day"—and had become detached.[67] Thomas McKean—part of McArthur's column—inexplicably brought his division's train of wagons, one mile long, that managed to snarl two divisions. By the end of the first day only the brigades led by McPherson and McArthur had advanced far enough to be productive, getting to the east bank of the Tuscumbia River, approximately five miles west of Chewalla but still two miles away from the Davis Bridge.[68]

Most of the rest of the main body advanced only to Chewalla, where Van Dorn had stopped twenty-four hours earlier, and still eight miles from Hurlbut's blocking position at the Davis Bridge.[69] By 3:00 p.m. on October 5 Maury withdrew his lead brigade from Davis Bridge and without any bother from Hurlbut's disorganized division Maury headed south to cross six miles upstream at Crum's Bridge (essentially laid across an earthen dam) by 6:00 p.m. Without any significant pressure from Rosecrans, Van Dorn also had room to circumvent Hurlbut before turning his main army southward, eventually crossing the Hatchie on Crum's Bridge under Price's watchful eye during the early morning of October 6.[70] Once Buck's army crossed his rear guard destroyed the bridge.

## 4. Iuka and Corinth II

With the situation failing to improve the second day Rosecrans decided to take personal charge of the pursuit ordering, among other things, McKean to take his wagon train back to Corinth; Rosecrans also elevated McArthur to replace McKean as division commander.[71] Although his army's pace remained slow, Rosey became reenergized during the pursuit's second day.[72] He ordered rations and forage to be delivered, and he bivouacked five miles west of the Hatchie.[73] Rosecrans contemplated asking that Hurlbut's mission be changed so that Hurlbut could join the chase of Van Dorn; that evening he wired Grant to request further orders.

His blocking mission having ceased to be, Hurlbut complained directly to Grant about his lack of rations and his need to tend to his wounded.[74] Peter Cozzens also maintains Hurlbut was too drunk to continue.[75] Accordingly on October 6, the second day of the pursuit, Grant—over Rosey's vehement and repeated objections—ordered Hurlbut to return to Boliver.[76] By late that evening Van Dorn's army had reached Ripley, sixteen miles south by southwest of Crum's Bridge. Although the Rebels lost only thirteen wagons they also left immense quantities of debris of combat, including swollen bodies of their dead comrades, scattered food stuffs, clothing, supplies, and equipment, as well as artillery caissons and ammunition.[77] Additionally scores of hungry, demoralized Confederate soldiers, too exhausted to continue, fell out of ranks of the retreat gladly to surrender to the Federals; those who remained with the retreating masses searched far and wide for virtually anything to forage.

Van Dorn continued his retreat to Holly Springs where he briefly attained some degree of safe harbor. On the afternoon of October 7 Rosecrans telegraphed Grant to ask that Hurlbut and Sherman be ordered to join the push toward Mobile and Jackson, Mississippi, in effect proposing to convert the pursuit of Van Dorn to initiating a campaign against Vicksburg.[78] Rosecrans claimed he was about a six days march across "rich farming country" from Vicksburg.[79] Grant, for reasons that might have been specious since Hurlbut had reported to Grant that the Rebels had abandoned Holly Springs,[80] claimed it was not only futile but risky to try to dislodge Van Dorn from his safe harbor.

On October 7, 1862, when McPherson was still thirty miles from Van Dorn, Grant called off any further pursuit[81]; Rosecrans protested, arguing there was still opportunity for great victory.[82] Even Halleck seemed surprised by Grant's order inquiring of Grant: "Why order the return of our troops? Why not reinforce Rosecrans and pursue the enemy into Mississippi, supporting your army on the country?"[83] Grant responded of the possibility of disaster to his army. Shelby Foote notes, "Grant had been soundly oddly unlike himself. ... [Grant] never spoke of disaster except within the intention of inflicting it, and presently he was sounding even less so, calling urgently for reinforcements in expectation of having to fight another battle."[84] Nevertheless the campaign, and the ensuing pursuit, of Corinth II was over.

As the second battle for Corinth unfolded, Grant might have seen from 58 miles afar the opportunity to win a decisive battle, and toward that end he deployed and attempted to coordinate widely dispersed divisions. But manipulating pieces on a map can be vastly different from actual maneuvers on the ground where soldiers are tired and hungry, where water is scarce, where animals are weakened from lack of forage, and when chains of command have been fractured. Grant's theory about establishing a blocking force at the Davis Bridge was sound but Ord, sent by Grant to take command, made a serious tactical mistake by being too aggressive. The chase element of the pursuit was well managed by McPherson and McArthur but other subordinate generals failed to come reasonably close to the command level necessary to manage all the details, especially logistics, necessary to achieve a successful pursuit. The lack of maps, which Grant's staff had taken when Grant's headquarters were transferred to Jackson, did not help matters as divisions became lost and confused along the way.

Sometimes Rosecrans has been criticized for not immediately beginning his pursuit on the afternoon of October 4 as the Rebels appeared to be retreating. However given the various tactical and logistics problems encountered once the pursuit began the next morning it is difficult to envision that an immediate start would have somehow gained any significant advantage. Beyond command skills, or lack of same, the pursuit from Corinth illustrates the difficulty of sustaining a pursuit with exhausted and hungry soldiers, especially without providing food and water, as well as forage for the horses. It is also conjectural whether Rosecrans had rebounded sufficiently to gain success past the third day of his pursuit—and all evidence indicates that Van Dorn's army was ripe for the picking, especially if caught out in the open—but Grant's somewhat devious refusal to allow the pursuit to continue for more than three days reflected his own lack of commitment to Rosecrans' possible success. At the very least the manner in which the pursuit was terminated showed that Grant, as the overall commander, and Rosecrans, as the tactical commander on the ground, did not see eye-to-eye about the objectives of the pursuit nor about the respective commitments necessary to fulfill those objectives, whatever they may have been. Albert Castel and Brooks Simpson criticize both generals for acting "as much, if not more, out of personal considerations as they did strategic."[85]

William Sherman observed "[Corinth II] was, indeed, a decisive blow to the Confederate cause in our quarter, and changed to whole aspect of affairs in West Tennessee. From the timid defensive we were at once enabled to assume the bold offensive." And while Van Dorn's battered army did survive, by being pushed so far away from Corinth the army was never going to become a factor in Bragg's campaign in Kentucky. Thus to that limited degree the pursuit was successful.

## *Dénouements and Precursors*

Two days after the Rebels had skedaddled from Iuka, President Lincoln issued his Emancipation Proclamation to go into effect the following New Year's Day. Perhaps as much as any singular event the issuance of this military directive changed the meaning of the Civil War while also helping to shift the numerical odds even more in the Union's favor.

By sheer coincidence Saturday, October 4, 1862, was a day of extraordinary significance in the Civil War. Not only did Van Dorn withdraw from Corinth II to begin his retreat but Bragg's Rebels also completed their withdrawal from Bardstown on October 4. Also on the same day the Confederate attempt to install a C.S.A. appointed government in Frankfort was aborted upon hearing the distant sounds of approaching artillery. Moreover on the 4th of October Halleck telegraphed George McClellan, still north of the Potomac two and half weeks after Antietam, that, "The President directs that you cross the Potomac and give battle to the enemy or drive him south....*"* The events in Corinth served as another marker of success for Rosecrans, and by extension for Grant, while the developments in Bardstown and Frankfort appeared to show Buell was making good progress in Kentucky. And while not necessarily apparent at the time, Halleck's directive was a long piece of rope to protract McClellan's demise as an army commander as soon as the 1862 elections were over.

For reasons not clearly established Iuka marked the beginning of the deterioration of the relationship between Grant and Rosecrans. Grant's first report after Iuka was fairly complimentary of Rosecrans but thereafter each subsequent writing became more critical, even scathing, culminating with Grant's *Memoirs* published in 1886. Castel and Simpson opine that Rosecrans fumed upon learning from Ord that Grant did not even know of the Iuka attack until it was over, meaning in Rosecrans' view that Grant was a hard fighter on the battlefield but off the battlefield Grant's record was that of a careless lucky dog.[86] Frank Varney offers several reasons of what might have caused the acrimony between these generals, one plausibility being Grant became upset that Rosecrans was responsible for published reports that Grant had been drinking during Iuka.[87] After Corinth II Grant issued General Order 88, a congratulatory message that barely mentioned Rosecrans while extending extravagant praise upon Hurlbut.[88] Their hostilities continued to escalate in after action reports filed by both camps and spilled over into press accounts. After the war, one of Old Rosey's regimental commanders wrote that "...General Grant ... was not disposed to forgive it in General Rosecrans, and General Rosecrans was never disposed to forgive Grant for not forgiving it."[89]

Rosecrans' progress during the first day of his Corinth pursuit is sharply debated and might be additional fodder for Grant's negative attitude about Rosecrans. Many histories inaccurately report Rosecrans stopped at Chewalla.[90] Rosecrans—who had remained in Corinth on October 5—probably underestimated his army's overall progress and mislead Grant when he telegraphed Grant that evening that "Leading divisions arrived at Chewalla. No news from McPherson since noon." Notwithstanding Grant's attitude, Rosecrans' reputation blossomed after Corinth II and of course the Federal administration was always looking for generals who could claim successes on fields of battle. A promotion to an independent command would mean Rosecrans would no longer be Grant's troublesome subordinate[91]; thus it was little surprise Grant did nothing to retain Rosecrans' services when on October 30, 1862, Rosey was assigned independent command of the Army of the Ohio, replacing Don Carlos Buell.[92]

Ord recovered sufficiently from his severe wounds to take command of a corps during Grant's Vicksburg campaign the following summer.

Stephen Hurlbut, a lawyer with experience in the Seminole Wars, also served as a corps commander under Grant during the Vicksburg campaign. Toward the end of the war Hurlbut was charged with corruption but was allowed to resign honorably. After the war, Hurlbut, a Republican, became a party leader in Illinois politics but again ran into charges of corruption. He became the first commander in chief of the G.A.R. After a six year stint in Congress he became Minister to Peru where he became involved in an altercation with the American Minister to Chile, Judson Kilpatrick, whom we will meet as one of the prominent cavalry commanders in the Army of the Potomac.

James B. McPherson, considered one of the rising stars among Union Generals, was promoted to Major General on October 8 almost immediately as his pursuit of Van Dorn was terminated. McPherson remained in the Army of the Tennessee, first as a division commander and then as a wing commander during Grant's Vicksburg campaign.

Criticism of Earl Van Dorn began immediately after his army reached Holly Springs. Formal charges were brought and included a wide range of allegations of neglect, including failure to obtain sufficient maps and/or to properly reconnoiter, and relying entirely upon captured food from the enemy to feed his own soldiers. A court of inquiry exonerated Van Dorn of any blame for Corinth II but he still was transferred to command a cavalry unit. Unfortunately, whether justified or not, Van Dorn had developed a reputation as a drunk and fornicator. On May 8, 1863, Van Dorn was killed in his headquarters at Spring Hill, Tennessee.[93] Van Dorn's killer—a wealthy fifty-one-year-old physician who had been absent for a year while leaving a twenty-five-year-old wife at home—claimed Van Dorn had been "violating the sanctity of the [killer's] home" but Van Dorn's family and friends contended he had been shot in the back, in cold blood, for political reasons. While Van Dorn may have had some supporters within the Confederacy he also had his critics. The *Atlantic Confederacy* was among the critics, editorializing after his death: "Van Dorn has been recognized for years as a rake, a most wicked libertine—and most especially of late. If he had led a virtuous life, he would have died—unwept, unhonored, and unsung. ... The country has sustained no loss in the death of Van Dorn. It is a happy riddance."

Five months after Corinth Sterling Price was ordered to report to E. Kirby Smith's trans–Mississippi department in Little Rock, Arkansas. Price had anticipated that his soldiers from Missouri would follow but none other than his staff and a small cavalry escort made the trip across the Mississippi. In September and October of 1864 Price led a cavalry raid into Missouri with a force of 12,000 men, one third of who did not have weapons. Initially Federal resistance was light as he savaged the countryside, cutting telegraph and rail lines, ransacking towns, overrunning garrisons, burning bridges, and generally terrorizing the local populations, especially those of the Union persuasion. But as Price moved west he encountered additional Union resistance. Eventually Union forces were at Price's front and rear; instead of opting to safely retreat to the south, Price chose to attack first one Union force and then the other. Unfortunately the Confederate forces suffered a devastating defeat at Westport, Missouri, in what may have been the largest Civil War engagement west of the Mississippi.

Once driven out of Missouri Price continued to retreat to Texas before escaping to Mexico where his personal plans collapsed along with those of Maximilian's government. Price eventually returned to Missouri but by then its former governor was a broken and impoverished man.

On April 15, 1863, Jefferson Davis assigned Dabney Maury to command the Confederate department at Knoxville but two weeks later he was assigned to replace Simon Buckner as commander of the District of the Gulf, a position he held until the end of the war. After the war Maury helped create the Southern Historical Society which had a purpose of collecting and preserving the archives of the Confederacy. Maury was a prolific writer and along with Jubal Early was instrumental in formulating the Myth of the Lost Cause, based upon a collection of writings that shaped and perpetuated the Southern perspective of the Rebellion. In 1885, President Grover Cleveland appointed Maury as U.S. Minister to Columbia.

# 5

# Rosecrans Replaces Buell
## October 1862–October 1863

## A New Commander and a New Designation

Two of the most savage, bloodiest battles of the Civil War were fought at Stones River near Murfreesboro, Tennessee, and at Chickamauga near Chattanooga, Tennessee. Although each battlefield saw abundant amounts of spilled blood neither of these battles was any more decisive than most other Civil War battles. In other words, for all these battles sacrifices, the losing sides survived to fight other days. The question then becomes whether the lack of pursuits by the prevailing sides contributed to the lack of decisiveness.

After Buell's insubordination cost him his command of the Army of the Ohio, his replacement became the only remaining question. Essentially the choices narrowed down to George H. Thomas or William S. Rosecrans. Since Thomas previously refused the appointment, Rosecrans got the nod. Based upon the hard feelings between Sam Grant and Rosecrans,[1] Grant may have been the only higher ranking official with any reservations about Rosecrans; nevertheless Grant saw no reason to get in the way of a big promotion for his subordinate. Thus on Friday, October 24, 1862, the Washington administration transferred Rosecrans from the Army of the Tennessee to Nashville to assume command of the Army of the Ohio in place of Buell, effective October 30.[2]

Rosecrans' appointment reflected the inexact process of command appointments as the armies underwent unprecedented expansions of manpower and command opportunities.[3] On paper at least Rosecrans, after eighteen months of combat experience, seemed like a suitable candidate for higher command, given his successes in western Virginia under McClellan as well as recent Union victories under his command at Iuka and Corinth II as earlier described.[4]

Competent, fighting generals were at a premium, especially for the North; Old Rosey's predecessor not only had become insubordinate but at least in Washington's eyes seemed to lack initiative or eagerness to engage the enemy.[5] And so, even though Grant may have entertained some misgivings about the extent of Rosecrans' mettle as a battlefield commander, and even though McClellan had viewed Rosecrans as a "silly, fussy goose,"[6] Rosecrans seemed to be a superior alternative to Buell or almost any other available general, especially in the West.[7]

Predictably, the issue of Thomas' seniority erupted again. Under normal circumstances Thomas would have had seniority over Rosecrans, and thus should have been given priority consideration to replace Buell; but Rosecrans' commission as major general was belatedly and conveniently backdated to give Old Rosey seniority over The Virginian.[8] Upon learning of the circumstances of Rosecrans' appointment Thomas wrote to Henry Halleck, "You may hereafter put a stick over me if you chose to do so. I will take care, however, to so manage my command, whatever it may be, as not to be involved in the mistakes of the stick."[9]

Despite Thomas' anger at Halleck, he and Rosecrans had a working relationship of mutual respect and confidence. Thomas desired to have a command, as opposed to being somebody's assistant or deputy; accordingly Rosecrans appointed Thomas commander of the largest or center wing, replacing C.C. Gilbert who was reverted back to his Regular Army rank of captain and was sent away to a desk job. Moreover, Thomas doubled in brass as *de facto* chief-of-staff for Rosecrans who frequently referred to Thomas as his "chief counselor."[10] Thomas L. Crittenden and Alexander McD. McCook retained their respective wing commands but several division commands were shuffled. Phil Sheridan remained as a division commander, at thirty-two years of age being the youngest division commander in the army.

Further departmental and army reorganization was concurrent with the order naming Rosecrans as the new commander. A new department, called the Department of the Cumberland, was created and while the forces in the field would continue to be designated as the 14th Corps before becoming known as the Army of the Cumberland.[11] This change reflected more than just nomenclature; now the army's orientation was expanded from Kentucky to include and take control of Tennessee. At the same time former wings were designated as new corps.

Rosecrans made important organizational change by consolidating his cavalry under the single command of the former dragoon, David S. Stanley.[12] As was typical throughout all the theaters in that era of the Civil War, the Confederate cavalry, under the likes of Bedford Forrest and John Hunt Morgan, had been far superior to the Union horsemen. Union cavalry was poorly armed, as many as half without firearms and many who were armed had a variety of muskets. Stanley, another alcoholic, was a veteran of Indian fighting as well as the Kansas border wars, and had commanded infantry division including those at Iuka and Corinth II. Although it would still be some time before the Union cavalry would reach parity with the Rebels, Stanley's organizing of his brigades and his insistence upon extensive drilling, coupled with arming his troopers with swords, revolvers, and the latest models of carbines, meant the gap soon began to close. Nevertheless for several months Confederate cavalry would continue to plague Union forces, especially those along extended, hard-to-defend lines of communications.

Command changes were also made on the Confederate side. Beyond all the continuing turmoil surrounding Bragg's leadership, Patrick R. Cleburne was promoted to major general and made a division commander in Hardee's corps. Cleburne was twenty seven years old when the death of his father—a member of the gentry who had been a country doctor—together with the potato famine forced Cleburne to immigrate to the United States where he settled in Helena, Arkansas. Cleburne became a successful druggist, lawyer, and Democratic politician before seizing the Little Rock Arsenal. Cleburne was named as a captain when Arkansas seceded before being commissioned as a brigadier in the Confederate army. Upon becoming a major general, Cleburne became the Confederacy's highest ranking "foreigner."[13]

## *Stones River*[14] (December 30–January 3)

After Buell decided not to advance any further into East Tennessee, Bragg withdrew back to Chattanooga, Tennessee, a scruffy little industrial town but an important rail junction on the eastern bank of the Tennessee River, making it the strategic gateway to the South.[15] However by mid–November 1862, in order to block any Union advance toward Chattanooga Bragg re-advanced forward to Murfreesboro, Tennessee, thirty-five miles southeast of Nashville.

Rosecrans concentrated his army of 47,000 troops at Nashville but concluded the liberation of East Tennessee was a logistical as well as a strategic impossibility.[16] Accordingly he was not inclined to head for Eastern Tennessee as still desired by Lincoln,[17] who still clung to his aspirations to seize control of East Tennessee while also looking for more battlefield victories to influence the January session of the British Parliament.[18]

Perhaps because he no longer expected a Federal offensive, Bragg—reinforced by John Breckinridge's division—went into winter quarters in the countryside north of Murfreesboro, sitting astride the Nashville & Chattanooga R.R. as well as the Nashville Turnpike. The west fork of the Stones River, an easily fordable tributary, meandered in a north and south direction crossing the Nashville Turnpike approximately a mile and quarter northwest of the town.

On Christmas night Rosecrans—after repeated hectoring from Henry Halleck to start moving—suddenly announced the Army of the Cumberland would leave Nashville the next day to start southward along the Nashville & Chattanooga R.R. toward Chattanooga. After three days of marching by fits and starts, meeting resistance only from a series of hit-and-run cavalry attacks under recently promoted BGen. Joseph Wheeler,[19] on Sunday, December 28, Rosecrans halted his army's general movements, thus giving Bragg an extra day to consolidate and prepare his defensive alignments.[20]

By December 30, 1862, Phil Sheridan's lead elements approached to within three miles of Stones River[21] where Bragg was waiting with anywhere from 25,000 to 38,000 troops along with thirty-five guns positioned west of Murfreesboro but entrenched mostly south of the railroad and turnpike.

The two sides faced each other with remarkably similar strategies: Each army commander—of course unbeknownst to the other—intended to strike the other's right side! Rosecrans' plan depended upon two questionable variables: First that McCook could hold his position on the Federal right for three hours and, two that Bragg would passively await the Yankee attack.[22] On the other side of the lines Bragg ordered his left-most divisions to drive the Federals back like a jackknife, capture the road to Nashville, and isolate Rosecrans from the state capital.[23] The key tactical advantage would undoubtedly depend upon which side struck first, and here Bragg seized the initiative by ordering his attack to begin at dawn Wednesday, December 31, 1862; across the lines Rosecrans intended his attack to launch later at 7:00 a.m. that same morning.

At the southern end of the battle line the Confederates swung several divisions like a giant gate with the outer arc having to advance for about three miles.[24] McCook's Federals were having breakfast when suddenly the Rebels struck! Sheridan's division excepted, the surprise forced McCook's, hence the Union's, right flank to fall back in disarray.[25] Bruce Catton wrote, "All chance for a Federal offensive vanished. McCook's entire army corps was routed, and unless Rosecrans could form a new line and find men who could hold it he might lose his whole army."[26] The Union line had begun in a roughly straight line perpendicular to the turnpike but by noon its right flank was turned to become parallel to the turnpike with Thomas' 14th Corps holding the corner.

After seven hours of fierce fighting McCook's corps was in shambles with only Sheridan's division being able to conduct a fighting withdrawal[27] But after eight hours of fighting across cold ground, having no sleep the previous night, and no having anything to eat or drink, Rebel soldiers were losing their strength.[28] Consequently the Confederate attack lost its steam thereby allowing the Union right to stabilize.

By the end of the day the Federals suffered in excess of 10,000 casualties while losing 20 guns. Additionally Wheeler's cavalry captured another 150 wagons along with 700 men leaving the Federals with only one day's ammunition.[29] In comparison the Confederates suffered only 7,500 casualties. That evening Bragg telegraphed Richmond, "God had granted us a happy New Year." Previously in similar situations many armies would have been making preparations to retreat and indeed Bragg believed the Federals would be retreating the next day. However Rosecrans convened a council of war late in the evening of December 31 during which Thomas purportedly awoke from a nap to proclaim, "This army does not retreat," before falling back asleep.[30] Accordingly Rosecrans decided the better course of action was to remain in his newly consolidated position and to fight.

Little happened the next day, New Year's Day, when Lincoln signed the Emancipation Proclamation, as the armies faced each other only a few hundred yards apart.[31] But late on the afternoon of January 2, 1863—bitterly cold and cloudy—Bragg ordered Breckinridge, still on the Confederate right, to assault the Union left, now positioned on the west of the Stones River but more importantly augmented by a line of 54 to 57 pieces of field artillery of various poundage and caliber massed hub-to-hub.[32] This massive firepower, together with frantically inserted reserves, drove Breckinridge's four brigades back to their starting positions, giving the Federals a stunning victory. Larry J. Daniel, characterized this barrage as "the most decisive and stupefying use of artillery in the Western Theater during the war."[33] The next day Thomas, still operating from the Union's center corner, took the initiative to launch an attack that drove the Confederates from their entrenchments. A large sized supply train reached the Union army the same day, all of which made Bragg believe he was simply overmatched although his army had fought well enough to have gained some ground. And so that night—in a manner similar to Perryville less than three months earlier when he had also won a narrow tactical victory—Bragg began to withdraw toward Shelbyville, another thirty miles south by southeast along the Nashville & Chattanooga R.R.

Stones River was one of the bloodiest battles of the entire war. The numbers of its butchers' bill equaled Shiloh's while exceeding Shiloh's in proportional numbers.[34] The number of casualties at Stones River was exceeded only by the numbers of casualties suffered at Gettysburg and at Chickamauga. Yet for all of that bloodshed little was accomplished in terms of drawing the end of the war significantly closer.

Rosecrans moved his army into Murfreesboro, and although the Rebels were in retreat, Rosecrans made no further effort to pursue, not wanting to anger the Almighty with a Sunday march[35]; otherwise his decision is difficult to criticize severely, if only because of the logistical challenges of advancing further at that time. Additionally Bragg's army had essentially prevailed at Stones River leaving Rosecrans too wounded to attempt a *coup de grâce*.[36]

It was always difficult to roust soldiers from their defensive entrenchments and to realign them into pursuit columns. Moreover, and perhaps as important as any other factor, Rosecrans and his subordinate commanders simply were not willing to risk losing the gains made by winning the battlefield and stymieing the enemy's advance.[37]

Phil Sheridan was one general in McCook's corps who had distinguished himself at Stones River with his stalwart defense at the left of McCook's line. Although Grant was not present at the battle he enthused, "[Sheridan's fighting] showed what a great general can do even in a subordinate command; for I believe Sheridan in that battle saved Rosecrans' army."[38] To show his appreciation Rosecrans recommended Sheridan receive a second star as major general, a promotion occurring only nine months after Little Phil had been a Captain.

## *Tullahoma* (June 23–30)

The relatively bloodless Tullahoma campaign is seldom viewed as one of the major events of the Western campaigns. Nevertheless it serves to illustrate the fault line between soft wars as opposed to prosecuting battles or campaigns of annihilation. Tullahoma also points out the difficult and tenuous nature of pursuits.

Although Stones River was essentially a stalemate, Lincoln sent a letter expressing his congratulations and heart-felt appreciation to Rosecrans who suddenly emerged as a new national hero.[39] However Lincoln's notion of how the war should be conducted was that his armies should always apply constant pressure against the enemy's armies. Thus Lincoln's principle subordinates, Secretary of War Edwin Stanton and General-in-Chief Henry Halleck, soon began to urge Rosecrans to continue to advance toward Bragg's position.[40] More ominously the Washington officials were beginning to suspect they may have had another conservative, cautious Buell in command as Rosecrans developed and voiced a litany of excuses for not leaving Murfreesboro. By May 1863, or five months at Murfreesboro, Rosecrans's Cumberlanders were the only Federal army not on the offensive. In comparison, elsewhere in the Western theater Grant was taking active measures in the field in the development of his Vicksburg campaign.[41]

Although the Federal administration fretted about Rosecrans' lengthy stay in Murfreesboro, to his credit Rosecrans was attempting to make best use of that time. One particular project was to develop an entirely new massive cavalry that could be used as an offensive strike force that would spearhead the army's advance.[42] To be sure he needed more horses (and riders) for scouting the unfamiliar but rough terrain ahead but also to guard and protect the supply lines that of necessity would be stretched longer and longer, and becoming more and more vulnerable. But more significantly Rosecrans wanted to expand the cavalry's customary role, at least within the context of the Civil War, beyond mere scouting, guarding supply lines, and protecting the army's rear and flanks.[43]

Rosecrans determined that the mountainous terrain—passable only through widely separated gaps or passes—required more mobility than normally provided by typical infantry units. Thus Rosecrans permitted, over Stanley's trepidations, two of his infantry brigades to purchase horses and repeating carbines, in other words to become mounted infantry.[44] These mounted infantry brigades would not closely mimic cavalry; they would for instance not be used for scouting or be deployed to protect the infantry's flanks. Neither would they be expected to fight while mounted in traditional cavalry style. Instead they would fight dismounted in more or less dragoon style but would be able to remount and ride rapidly from location to location. The repeating carbines would of course enable the mounted infantry to deliver massive bursts of firepower. Col. John T. Wilder, 32, a former Indiana businessman, proposed the idea of these mounted infantry and was appointed to command one of these brigades, eventually to be renowned as the Lightening Brigade.[45] Reflecting his lack of appreciation or support[46] for evolving tactics, Halleck grumbled that "mounted infantry are neither good infantry nor good cavalry."[47]

Rosecrans also had a new chief of staff in the person of BGen. James Garfield, 32, a former Ohio state senator and a protégé of Salmon P. Chase. As Rosecrans' new chief of staff, Garfield's duties included acting as liaison with the War Department.[48]

Although Bragg established his headquarters at Tullahoma,[49] five miles from Shelbyville, his army was deployed in an attenuated line several miles forward of that crossroads town and rail junction; a series of mountain ridges running southwest to northeast made the gaps through the ridges, and their defenses, critical. Bragg was forced to scatter his units, especially his limited cavalry, across wide geographic areas in order to find enough food and forage to sustain his army.[50] But the barren nature of the country was such that forage and food remained scarce meaning that animals as well as men were becoming malnourished.

During the spring of 1863 Rosecrans developed a plan of attack, based upon maneuver, a plan about as complex as any devised in the Civil War. Rosecrans' planned a double fake with that column reversing itself to become the fulcrum for a right wheel movement into the middle of the Union line with Manchester being the intermediate objective.[51] In the meanwhile the two mounted infantry brigades were to advance toward the middle gaps to hold those Confederate defenders in place. Of these two gaps, Hoover Gap, being seven miles long and so narrow that wagons and batteries could hardly pass, was the more daunting.[52] It was a bold plan dependent upon deception coupled with rapid, well timed execution.

Remarkably Rosey's plan succeeded beyond his expectations but not exactly in the manner he had anticipated! Early in the morning of June 24 subordinate units were ordered to start moving in less than two hours, which was successfully accomplished, somewhat of a miracle in itself.[53] The feint to the Union right fooled Wheeler who shifted all his troopers to Bragg's left side.[54]

In the middle of the lines the two Blue brigades of mounted infantry quickly overcame and dispatched Rebel defenders who supposed they were encountering infantry whose strengths were overestimated because of the rate of fire from the repeating carbines. Rather than stand and fight to defend their assigned gaps, the Rebel cavalries decided to retreat to the southern sides of gaps where they assumed additional reinforcements would be in place and ready to assist.

Each of the Yankee commanders of mounted infantry immediately seized significant tactical advantage by moving forward as quickly as possible rather than waiting and consolidating with trailing infantry as had been contemplated by Rosecrans.[55] Rather than continue their retreats to the next set of gaps the Confederates simply dispersed and faded into the woods allowing the Federals to continue their advances more or less unimpeded until they were in possession of the two most important gaps, Liberty and Hoover's, en route to Tullahoma. When Thomas caught up to Wilder at Hoover's Gap he gleefully shook Wilder's hand and exclaimed, "You have saved the lives of a thousand men by your gallant conduct today. I didn't expect to get to this gap for three days."[56]

But while Old Rosey had planned, and his commanders had executed, a nearly perfect operation of maneuver, torrential downpours made the unpaved country roads all but impassible while troop movements that did pass only worsened the roads' conditions. Accordingly the next day most of the Army of the Cumberland was forced to simply halt and hold their positions.

Standing still—whether by choice or compelled because of circumstances—in the aftermath of a successful offensive push always risked the loss of initiative, time and time again one of the most important factors on the battlefield. Indeed only eight weeks earlier Joe Hooker had paused after early success against the Army of Northern Virginia at Chancellorsville; Hooker's hesitation enabled R.E. Lee to seize the initiative, thereby reversing the battle's momentum, which Lee never relinquished until Hooker was licked like a dog between his legs. (See Chapter 15.)

The continued downpour caused some delay, but mid-morning of June 26, 1863, Thomas resumed his march toward Rosecrans' next objective, Manchester, Tennessee, approximately ten miles northeast of Tullahoma, which would flank Bragg's position at Tullahoma.

Once Bragg realized that several of his brigades were in retreat and that he was flanked he had no reasonable choice except to order a retreat of his entire army. Accordingly on June 27, 1863, both armies were moving along parallel paths, approximately ten miles apart, in a southeasterly direction, with Wilder's mounted cavalry moving into Manchester where it captured a forty man picket post.[57] By Sunday morning, June 28, the Bluecoats, except Crittenden's 21st Corps, were occupying the area in and around Manchester while most of the Grays were found in and around Tullahoma.[58] Keeping in character, Rosecrans felt compelled to stop, regroup, and resupply at Manchester rather than continuing.[59] Meanwhile Robert Minty's Saber Brigade (the second brigade of mounted infantry) cleared Shelbyville while capturing three hundred men and three guns in a stunning triumph for the well-handled Union horsemen.[60]

On Sunday, June 28, Rosecrans sent Wilder's Lightning Brigade behind Bragg in order to create as much havoc as possible, including the possible destruction of the bridge over the swollen Elk River that would be critical for any Rebel retreat. However, Forrest blocked Wilder from reaching the bridge.

Rosecrans spent Monday, June 29, waiting for Crittenden to catch up before attacking the Rebels' entrenchments at Tullahoma. Two days later Rosecrans had all in readiness to launch frontal assaults upon Bragg's defenses; however unbeknownst to the Union commanders, Polk and Hardee had convinced Bragg that, notwithstanding numbers favorable for an entrenched defensive, further retreating was a better alternative than receiving an Union attack.[61] Steven E. Woodworth observes that "If the Army of Tennessee could not have prevailed in those circumstances [existing at Tullahoma], it might as well have given up the war and gone home."[62] Regardless a demoralized Bragg reluctantly acceded to order a retreat from the Tullahoma entrenchments starting the afternoon of June 30. When one of Thomas' civilian sources told Thomas the town was vacant he sent a brigade forward to investigate.[63]

Leaving entrenchments at Tullahoma, Bragg resumed his southeastern retreat. At several places the Rebels stopped while a demoralized Bragg and his commanders debated whether to make a stand against the oncoming Army of the Cumberland[64]; however at each juncture the Rebels resumed their retreat toward Chattanooga. Immediately upon discovering the Confederates' withdrawal from Tullahoma the Federals dispatched three infantry divisions, Sheridan's division in the van,[65] to give chase, skirmishing with the Rebels' rear guard. These divisions got as far as Elk River, about eight miles from Tullahoma, where they exchanged gunfire with Cleburne's soldiers on the other side. The problem of getting any closer arose because the Elk was swollen from the nearly unprecedented amounts of rainfall and the Confederates had destroyed the bridges necessary for crossing.

The swollen Elk could not be forded until July 3 when Sheridan was able to find the one location that could be crossed but only with extreme caution.[66] Once across Sheridan's relatively small group continued to follow the Confederates but through woods and along roads of almost bottomless mud. This effort continued until it petered out late that same day as the Yanks approached the little railroad town of Cowan where the Rebels held commanding positions; the lack of artillery support plus the lack of supplies compelled an end of any meaningful pursuit.[67] Bragg's army kept retreating, crossing the Tennessee River on July 4, 1863.[68] Finally on July 7, 1863, the Confederates had found their way to safe harbor at Chattanooga beneath the protective gaze of Lookout Mountain.

In a sense Tullahoma was a brilliant victory for Rosecrans, perhaps his finest hour, or at least so he believed.[69] He had formulated an outstanding plan, mostly of maneuver well supported with ample logistics, and his subordinate commanders had implemented the plan with near perfection, much of which was executed under severe adverse conditions of hard rains causing widespread and persistent quagmire. It was the first time in the war that a large army had been forced from entrenched positions by maneuver. As a result the Union had advanced 80 miles in 11 days, seizing considerable territory in Middle Tennessee at a relatively lost cost of casualties.[70] Additionally Port Hudson, the Southern bulwark protecting the Mississippi River 25 miles upstream from Baton Rouge, Louisiana, capitulated to a naval siege five days after Vicksburg surrendered. Coming so soon after the Confederate defeats at Vicksburg, Gettysburg, and Mobile Bay, the unexpected loss of so much territory added to the sense of despair to the Southern population living in the area.[71] Rosecrans was confident these territorial gains had vindicated his careful, deliberate, and lengthy preparations that had so frustrated Washington.

But as impressive as the territorial gains may have seemed, Braxton Bragg and his Army of Tennessee had escaped to survive and to prepare to fight another day. Although Rosecrans and his top subordinates, including especially Thomas, felt they had accomplished a noble feat in seizing so much territory at a relatively lost cost in casualties the Washington authorities did not share that assessment.[72] Rosecrans was taken back by the implication that he had not accomplished the same degree of triumph as had occurred at Vicksburg and Gettysburg. In response to Stanton's telegram urging Rosecrans promptly to get on with the task of going after Bragg, Old Rosey defiantly wired Stanton, "…I beg in behalf this army that the War Department may not overlook so great an event [as capturing Tullahoma] because it is not written in letters of blood."[73]

Second guessing always enjoys the advantage of 20/20 hindsight but Rosecrans' penchant for overcautious perfection might have caused him to miss opportunities for a successful pursuit resulting in a decisive victory at Tullahoma.[74] Granted rains had caused miserable conditions for expedient movement, but maybe, just maybe it was not necessary to remain in Manchester for three days before deploying to launch a frontal assault against Tullahoma. By the time Federal forces entered Tullahoma the Confederate retreat had almost a full day's head start. And instead of sending just a mounted brigade of 2,000 infantry men to capture the critical bridge across the Elk—at that point the only means of Rebel escape—could an additional brigade of infantry have provided enough force to have overcome Forrest as he protected the bridge?[75]

We can only conjecture what the results may have been otherwise but it is clear that Rosecrans still did not grasp the necessity of at least a couple components for a successful pursuit, the first being to create and maintain immediate and constant pressure upon a retreating army while secondly blocking or eliminating critical points of escape. Of course perhaps the larger question is whether Rosecrans still adhered to the philosophy of soft war, that is having a lukewarm, even indifferent, attitude toward the annihilation of his enemy, it being enough in his mind to capture and occupy territory. Moreover Rosecrans seemed to have a myopic view of the war's strategy, meaning that he failed to see beyond the engagement immediately before him and how the application of force in one sector could, and often did, influence, even impact, other sectors. Ironically Rosecrans' enemy was already planning and taking steps toward the destruction of Rosecrans' army with a large part of those plans involving the movement of a large number of troops from one sector to give Bragg enough soldiers to accomplish that decisive blow.

## *Chattanooga I* (August 15–September 4)

Immediately following the Tullahoma victory Washington authorities, under Lincoln's constant prodding, continued to press Rosecrans to carry his momentum even further into the Deep South.[76] In terms of strategic value, Chattanooga—with a population of 2,545 residents—loomed large if only because its convergence of two rail lines provided access to Virginia, Atlanta, northern Alabama, Corinth, as well as Nashville. Capture of Chattanooga would provide massive staging areas for further thrusts into the Deep South, particularly Atlanta.[77] However, Rosecrans remained fixated upon perpetuating the glory of battles won while carefully assuring that everything would be perfectly in place before advancing further. He and most of his subordinates remained confident their Army of the Cumberland would be able to overcome Bragg's Army of Tennessee if only given enough time to be thoroughly prepared, including being supplied with almost everything. Once Rosecrans felt he was ready he decided to replicate his recent Tullahoma campaign based upon maneuver.[78]

East Tennessee—with its robust contingent of Unionists—continued to be one of Lincoln's strategic objectives.[79] In the summer of 1863 Knoxville was occupied by a force of 5,000 Rebels led by Simon Buckner under Bragg's nominal command in Chattanooga, 100-miles to the southwest. On Sunday, August 16, 1863, Ambrose Burnside, leading the Army of the Ohio (a newly comprised army not to be confused with the predecessor to the Army of the Cumberland), was sent toward Knoxville.[80] This of course was basically the same objective assigned to Don Carlos Buell—commanding the original Army of the Ohio—a year earlier before he decided to pivot his army back to Nashville. As Burnside began to advance Bragg ordered Buckner to move closer to Chattanooga.

Meanwhile in order to keep Bragg from sending reinforcements to Buckner, Rosecrans began a "stupendous undertaking"[81] advancing toward the Tennessee River; Old Rosey's front extended 65 miles from flank to flank. His two brigades of mounted soldiers were positioned at either flank, Wilder's Lightning Brigade on the north with Minty's Saber Brigade to the south.[82]

But the mission of the mounted infantry brigades was not to screen and to protect the foot soldiers but rather was to create and act out a ruse that preparations were being made for a major crossing of the Tennessee River, especially upstream from Chattanooga.[83] Upon reaching the Tennessee River on August 21 the Lightning Brigade made as much noise as possible, cutting, sawing, and hammering, and occasionally throwing scraps of wood to float downstream as though bridges were being built.[84] At night multiple surplus campfires were lighted to exaggerate the number of troops available to cross the river.[85] Wilder even had an artillery battery, led by Eli Lilley, the former druggist from Indiana, fire shells from four 3-inch rifles into Chattanooga as though in preparation for an assault. Not only did this fusillade panic the civilian population, it also managed to sink two steamers tied to the dock.[86] LGen. Daniel Harvey Hill, 42, replacing Hardee—who had been mercifully transferred to another command—complained that there had been no warning of the Yankee approach.[87]

Bragg's defenses were stretched across an extenuated front. Bragg sent Wheeler downstream to scout and screen cover an extensive area around Bridgeport, a little more than 25 miles west by southwest as the crow flies from Chattanooga. Bridgeport consisted mainly of a partially destroyed railroad trestle that was especially important because it was the junction of the railroad from the west. Considerable perseverance would have been necessary to cover such a large area but unfortunately for Bragg, Wheeler discharged his responsibilities in a lackadaisical, careless manner.

By Tuesday, August 25, 1863, Bragg suddenly had lost track of most of the Army of Tennessee![88] Unknown to him, Rosecrans had pulled his army, except Crittenden's corps that remained visible in the Sequatchie Valley to the north, back from positions along the Tennessee River to reposition them at various downstream locations. Rosecrans started crossing at the same or near the Rebels' former locations. On August 29, 1863, the three corps of the Army of the Cumberland were separated by as many as 75 miles. But on that date Thomas crossed the river unopposed[89] using both boats and pontoon bridges while Crittenden's corps shifted southward.

Promptly upon learning from Wheeler's cavalry that Federals were crossing the river, Bragg began to concentrate his army in and around Chattanooga; this included bringing Buckner all the way back into Chattanooga. Additionally sometime around September 1, 1863, to reinforce Bragg's army, two undermanned divisions arrived from the C.S.A.'s Army of Mississippi bringing Bragg's army to more than 66,000 men.

Although bridges and boats were few and far between, meaning that several crossings had to be improvised, by Wednesday, September 2, 1863, Sheridan's division had completed all repairs to the bridge to Bridgeport.[90] That same day Burnside's Army of Ohio seized unopposed control of Knoxville.[91] On Friday, September 4 the Union's crossing operation was complete, and the entire Army of the Cumberland—including artillery pieces and support vehicles as well as supply wagons—was on the Chattanooga side of the Tennessee River.[92] In three weeks, the Army of the Cumberland had marched an incredible 300 miles, a trek that included crossing three mountain ranges as well as crossing a mighty river!

Although Bragg's army was not as large as was Rosecrans' the numbers could become almost even if Bragg were reinforced by a good sized corps from another sector. The most obvious possibility was Longstreet's corps from Lee's Army of Northern Virginia; however Lee was always reluctant to allow any meaningful decrease in his numbers from detachment and reassignment to other regions. But there seemed to be less reason to retain all his units after Lee had repositioned his army into the relative safety of the Culpeper area following his retreat from Gettysburg; Lee did not have the strength to consider another offensive thrust and Meade was acting too cautiously to create any opportunities for Lee to launch any counteroffensives. Furthermore James Longstreet, 41, Lee's "Old Warhorse," was ambitious, extremely self-confident, and anxious for command opportunity other than as Lee's principle subordinate. Thus as soon as Burnside captured Knoxville the Richmond hierarchy—Lee excepting—made plans to transport Longstreet and two of his divisions to the Western theater via a grueling, circuitous train ride west.[93]

The topography around Chattanooga presented enormous operational challenges. At least three steep mountain ranges, Sand Mountain, Lookout Mountain, and Missionary Ridge ran more or less parallel with the Tennessee River south of Chattanooga. These mountain chains created easily defended valleys and could be crossed only with enormous difficulty through shallow gaps, which could also be easily defended given enough soldiers.[94] In order to move beyond his beachhead Rosecrans had the choice of keeping his entire army together, a move that would impede his mobility and agility, or he could disperse his army into smaller units that could more easily move through the gaps. The risk of the latter option was that strength would be sacrificed while the smaller units could become vulnerable to attack from any larger Rebel units.

Rather than put all his operational eggs into one basket Rosecrans decided to dispatch his corps toward three separate directions; essentially his three corps were aligned the same way relative to one another that they had been throughout the campaign with Crittenden's 21st Corps in the north, or left; Thomas's 14th Corps in the middle with McCook's 20th Corps, along with most of the Union cavalry, on the right or southern-most column. It should also be noted that most of these corps did not remain intact but had brigades and even divisions detached and assigned or attached elsewhere.

Crittenden was sent toward Chattanooga; Thomas was sent to take several routes eastward toward and across Lookout Mountain heading for Steven's Gap, approximately 24 miles south of Crittenden's objective. Taking a daring risk by further separating his army so far apart, Rosecrans sent McCook toward Alpine, 45 miles south by southwest of Chattanooga[95]; Alpine had little significance of its own but it was only 23 miles from Rome, Georgia, not only a potential blocking position but also the place of one of the 15 private cannon factories in the South. Despite encountering little, if any, resistance the movements progressed slowly but by September 8, 1863, four days after completing the crossing of the Tennessee River, each of the corps had reached its intermediate objectives.[96]

For days several Rebel deserters were telling Union officers that Bragg was demoralized and would soon be making a hasty retreat toward Atlanta. On September 8 as Rosecrans and Thomas were looking eastward from Lookout Mountain they could see dust clouds in the valley. This sighting seemed to confirm deserters' reports of Bragg's intention to retreat; accordingly Rosecrans impulsively decided to redirect his army from its turning movement into a pursuit mode,[97] hoping to accomplish at last what he had been criticized for not doing at Tullahoma by trapping the Confederates between Chattanooga and Rome, Georgia.

Over the objections of Thomas,[98] who wanted to march and to occupy Chattanooga to regroup as originally planned,[99] Rosecrans ordered: (1) Crittenden to continue north before circling behind Bragg's retreating army, (2) Thomas to move down the eastern slope of Lookout Mountain and continue east to be in position at La Fayette[100]—15 miles southeast of Chattanooga—to hit Bragg from the side and if possible cut off Bragg's line of escape,[101] and (3) McCook to divert from his route to Alpine to establish blocking positions.[102] At first blush this appeared to be a feasible plan of pursuit albeit with units too widely scattered throughout wilderness country for effective, timely communications.

However, there was one other not-so-minor flaw in this plan: It was based upon faulty intelligence; Bragg was not retreating! To be sure Bragg realized that once again he had been outflanked by Rosecrans and that he was forced to abandon Chattanooga without a fight.[103] Accordingly he decided to relocate to La Fayette while Forrest guarded his rear.[104] From La Fayette Bragg could attack Rosecrans in detail, in other words piece by piece. Not only were the Union divisions and brigades too far apart to render mutual assistance but some of these units, especially those belonging to Thomas' command, without cavalry to scout or to screen, might be caught in terrain—e.g. valleys, gaps, or coves—in which they would be trapped without any means of escape.[105] Bragg had demonstrated his capacity at Perryville and at Stones River to create numerical superiority against isolated units or lines; now he believed he had even better opportunities.

By acting so rashly to initiate a pursuit (indeed the "deserters" had been plants) Rosecrans inadvertently endangered a good portion of his army, especially those units that could stumble into ambushes or traps. While several commanders, Rosecrans included, frequently lost pursuit opportunities by acting sluggishly if they reacted at all, in this instance Bragg's army was hardly beaten or defeated—having left Chattanooga September 7 more or less on its own accord—and thus was not susceptible to easy capitulation or destruction. While Thomas' suggestion to proceed to Chattanooga may or may not have been excessively conservative, and certainly would have been unpopular in Washington, Rosecrans' decision to pursue illustrates it was not a simple matter to decide when and how to pursue.

But if Rosecrans was operating upon false intelligence, Bragg's plan was also largely based upon guesswork.[106] Although he had general information indicating that the Federals were widely dispersed, he lacked specific information about the enemy's exact locations or maneuvers. Nevertheless, Bragg had every reason to believe that Rosecrans had been deceived by Bragg's "deserters" and that the division of MGen. James S. Negley, 37, from Thomas' corps, could be trapped at the narrow end of McLemore's Cove.[107] Accordingly he decisively ordered two Rebel divisions to strike concurrently on September 10, Simon Buckner to strike from the flank and Patrick Cleburne[108]—with probably Bragg's best division— to attack the Federals' front.[109] Bragg's plan was about as well conceived and organized as a plan could be, and should have had every reasonable chance to succeed.

But this strategy would become undone by the same bugaboo that consistently plagued the Army of Tennessee, to-wit, the abysmal lack of reasonable command effort—verging upon insubordination—by Bragg's subordinates, many who were R.E. Lee's castoffs.[110]

However rather than assiduously following Bragg's orders, the subordinates (1) quarreled with each other about which general had seniority to command the joint effort, (2) excessively and needlessly scouted the area, and (3) eventually convened councils of war that (4) voted to ignore Bragg's plan and instead to advise Bragg to attack Crittenden.

When his subordinate commanders failed to more one the first opportunity Bragg reissued similar orders for the next day. One division was commanded by MGen. Thomas C. Hindman, 35, Cleburne's former law partner and a former Congressman who had fought in the Mexican War.[111] Inexplicably by mid-afternoon Hindman decided to retreat his forces and to "retire" to his rear at La Fayette.[112] Had Hindman obeyed Bragg's orders it is reasonable to speculate that much of Thomas's corps would have been destroyed.[113] And so the ineptitude of Confederate commanders, rather than any great expertise by Rosecrans, allowed the Federals escape a potential disaster.

During the next couple days starting in the afternoon of September 11 Rosecrans realized his situation had indeed become a tactical predicament. First scouts from either flank were reporting large masses of Confederate troops, primarily at La Fayette but also five miles further north at Lee & Gordon's Mill along the eastern banks of the Chickamauga Creek. These concentrations meant the Rebels were not retreating to Atlanta; if they were not retreating it probably meant they were preparing to launch their own offensive efforts. And if that was the Rebels' intent the locations of these concentrations meant Bragg's brigades were closer to Rosecrans' brigades than the Federal brigades were to each other! Tactically this meant the Confederates still had opportunities to destroy at least portions of the Army of the Cumberland in detail. It became apparent that if Thomas had not defied Rosecrans' orders to advance, Bragg might have trapped and destroyed two Federal divisions.[114] As often happens in combat the table was quickly and unexpectedly reversed, Rosecrans' pursuit had run aground, and Rosecrans eventually realized his situation was becoming "a matter of life or death."[115] Accordingly on September 13 Rosey had no choice except to order a concentration of his army around Thomas in the area of Lee and Gordon's Mill.[116]

Rosecrans' ill-considered pursuit exposed many of the risks, especially one launched without adequate, indeed hardly any, planning and preparation. Certainly Rosecrans acted aggressively and decisively, two essential prerequisites for a successful pursuit, but in acting without better intelligence about the enemy's situation, Rosecrans also acted impulsively and recklessly thereby exposing his army, or at least major portions of it, to serious countermeasures, including an ambush. The Army of Tennessee had evacuated from Chattanooga, to be sure, but had done so without the wounds, carnage, and other damage from a battlefield defeat. Instead Bragg left to protect his lines of communications while trying to entice his unwary pursuer into a trap.

But why would Rosecrans, who after all had taken time to initiate a chase after Corinth II and who dallied before trying to catch Bragg during and after Tullahoma, now act so precipitously so as to endanger his army at Chattanooga? Two major factors seem to have converged to enable if not compel Rosey's recklessness. First, Rosecrans was sensitive to Washington's disapproving critique, which continued to be relentless in attempting to force Rosecrans to act more aggressively. Second, Rosecrans was hearing what he wanted to hear from an accumulation of bad intelligence from Crittenden as well as from the "deserters" planted by Bragg, all of which seemed to be validated by the clouds of dust. Furthermore most of the Federals' regular cavalry—which should have been acting as Rosey's eyes and ears—was deployed with McCook's corps far to the west. While pursuits might have an impromptu element they still required a basic understanding of risks versus rewards; Rosecrans was blinded by potential rewards and failed to give appropriate or sufficient heed to very real dangers.[117]

## *Chickamauga* (September 19 and 20)

Union commanders were also beginning to learn from captured prisoners that Longstreet was on his way to reinforce Bragg's army.[118] In response to these reports—Henry Halleck also wired Rosecrans that Longstreet was being detached to reinforce Bragg—Rosecrans urgently began to try to consolidate his army, ordering Crittenden and McCook to move from their respective flanking positions toward Thomas near La Fayette.[119]

However, it took McCook longer to reach Thomas' right flank than Rosecrans hoped. McCook originally thought his corps would have a relatively easy fifteen-mile march to La Fayette, where he thought he would meet Thomas, but his scouts learned that Confederates were also concentrating at La Fayette thereby forcing McCook to take an indirect route to reach Thomas north of La Fayette.[120] But once on September 17, 1863, as McCook was in position to Thomas' right, the opposing armies sought a common objective, specifically control of the routes back to Chattanooga! Isolated as they were and about to exhaust the ten days' worth of supplies they had brought across the river, the Federals' imperative was to preserve routes to Chattanooga, not only as re-supply lines but as retreat passages if necessary. Conversely the Confederates wanted to turn the Federals' left flank to block their route or routes northward to Chattanooga. And so the stage was set for one of the greatest battles of the Western theater![121]

The opposing armies began a series of complex maneuvers that mirrored each other on opposite sides of the Chickamauga Creek (actually its West Branch) with the Yankees sidling to their left while the Rebels kept adjusting their lines to their right. The Chickamauga landscape was dominated by vine covered thickets interspersed with cleared fields of small farms.[122] Although Bragg had formulated his general strategy as early as September 15 the ever changing locations kept him from implementing specific plans to attack. The cornerstone of Bragg's strategy was to seize the area north of Lee & Gordon's Mill where the two essential escape routes were only about three-quarters of a mile apart; control of that area would block the Union's paths for re-supply and/or escape.[123]

From the northern flank Minty continued to send warnings to Crittenden that Bragg was beginning to mass troops in the vicinity of Lee & Gordon's Mill, warnings that Crittenden minimized.[124] Additionally neither Rosecrans nor Crittenden believed reports that Longstreet's troops were arriving at Ringgold, approximately ten miles east of Lee & Gordon's Mill.

Bragg intended to strike the first blow on Friday, September 18, 1863, when the first three of Longstreet's brigades arrived under the command of MGen. John Bell Hood, 32, his disabled left arm in a sling.[125] Bragg intended to turn Crittenden's left at Lee & Gordon's Mill while attempting several crossings of the Chickamauga both north and south of mill.[126] Bragg reasonably envisioned that turning Crittenden's left would not only inject his Rebels between the Army of the Cumberland and Chattanooga but additionally could drive at least Crittenden into McLemore Cove where Crittenden would have no means of escape.[127]

Although his maneuvers were stalled on the 18th[128] Bragg retained his same offensive scheme for the 19th, especially since several of his brigades were in better starting positions than they had been 24 hours earlier. At the break of dawn on Saturday, September 19, 1863, Crittenden remained opposite Lee & Gordon's Mill, apparently accommodating Bragg's planned attack. However, unbeknownst to Bragg—whose cavalry and infantry pickets had failed to detect the movements across their front—Thomas' divisions had marched to Crittenden's left, positioned generally on either side of the La Fayette Road.[129] A Union reserve corps led by MGen. Gordon Granger, 41, another veteran of the Mexican War, was positioned further north about a mile and half east of Rossville, positioned to help protect the Rossville Road.[130]

That Thomas was now north, or to the left, of Crittenden was a result of Rosecrans reacting to Wilder's reports during the afternoon of the 18th that Confederates were crossing the creek north of Crittenden's position[131]; those reports were corroborated late in the afternoon of September 19 when a Union signal station observed large clouds of dust, tell-tale signs that columns of soldiers were marching from the rear toward the Chickamauga.[132] Until then Rosecrans had no idea how close he was to having his left outflanked. Rosecrans had grown over-confident, relying to his detriment upon Crittenden's hubris that the Rebels posed no significant threat.

Rosecrans then ordered a massive northward reshuffling of the divisions in his lines. Initially Crittenden was ordered to move his entire corps north of the mill but later Thomas was ordered to move most of his corps even further north to establish the new left flank of Rosecrans' army. Negley's division remained behind as a rear guard as the rest of Thomas' 14th Corps stumbled north during a difficult, confused night march.[133]

The 14th Corps' hasty overnight march had a two-fold effect: First it extended the Union's left flank beyond the Confederate's right flank meaning that Bragg would have difficulty turning Crittenden's flank and, second, the Federals were now posted on either side of the intersection of the potential escape routes, La Fayette Road and Dyer Lane. But if Bragg was not aware of Thomas' new location, neither was Thomas fully advised of the extent of Confederate positions. In response to an erroneous report that a single Rebel brigade had crossed Reed's Bridge but was stranded near Jay's Mill on the west side of the Chickamauga, Thomas dispatched a brigade, under the command of Col. John T. Croxton, a 26-year-old Kentucky lawyer, to investigate.[134] Unfortunately for Croxton he ran into Bedford Forrest on a recon patrol. Instead of trying to determine the strength of the attacking Federals, and reporting any resultant intelligence to Bragg, Forrest locked into combat thereby depriving Bragg of knowing what was happening on his right flank.[135] A pitched battle ensued as both sides "fed the fire" with reinforcements hoping to envelop the other side; thus began the Battle of Chickamauga.[136] This accidental encounter ignited confused, close-encounter savagery eventually extending for four miles along the lines.[137]

September 19, 1863, Chickamauga was a classic soldiers' battle.[138] Rugged terrain and thick brush meant commanders could only send reinforcements "to the sound of battle."

The lack of sight lines impeded coordinated, large scale attacks but these close quarter fights were hardly any less vicious for the combatants. Thick woods, tangled underbrush and scrub land, together with gunpowder smoke, obscured the visions of officers who were barely able to stay in touch with their own soldiers let alone the enemy on either side of these melees. Momentum on either side kept shifting as piecemeal reinforcements were fed into combat to give one side or the other temporary numerical superiority. Fixed lines quickly dissipated into bayonet charges before dissolving into desperate hand-to-hand, life-or-death struggles. Artillery pieces were lost, recaptured, and then abandoned because not enough horses were still alive to pull the pieces. At one point Rosecrans was forced to rely upon the Widow Glenn where Rosecrans had established his latest headquarters to tell him the source of gun fire.[139]

Longstreet with the rest of his brigades, minus artillery and wagons, arrived in the area after dark the evening of September 19.[140] Although Bragg had not provided the courtesy of sending anyone to meet Longstreet, he and his staff, after a couple hours wandering in the darkness—at one point accidentally wandering into Yankee lines—finally located Bragg's headquarters where Bragg gave Old Pete a map and informed him that he was being assigned as the commander of Bragg's newly created left wing.[141] Leonidas Polk, the next senior general, would command Bragg's right wing.[142] The creation of new wings was an impromptu reorganization that perhaps was reasonable under difficult circumstances, especially given Longstreet's seniority and stature as one of Robert E. Lee's top generals; but this quickly cobbled reorganization also created a number of other problems: First, it created another layer of command, making communications all the more cumbersome; second, it necessitated reassignments of divisions and brigades from one familiar command to another not so familiar; third, it placed some truculent or ego inflated generals, especially such as D.H. Hill, under command of generals such as Polk with whom they were at frequent odds. Finally, Bragg's reorganization meant divisions had to be physically redeployed overnight in order to be in place to implement Bragg's plans. In any event, shortly after meeting with Bragg, Longstreet went to sleep without taking the opportunity of explaining Bragg's plans to anyone.[143]

Also late that evening across the creek Rosecrans convened another council of war, this one in the cramped room of Rosecrans' headquarters in Widow Glenn's small cabin.[144] As he had during similar circumstances at Stones River, Thomas—who had been awake for more than 36 hours—dozed throughout but one time awakened to opine that he "would strengthen the left."[145] Negley's division was then ordered up from its rear guard position to start entrenching along Thomas's left flank. By the morning of the 20th the Army of the Cumberland had developed two defensive configurations: An arc comprised mostly of divisions from the 14th Corps with either end positioned on the east side of La Fayette Road and a more or less straight line—under McCook's nominal command—running south along the west side of La Fayette Road. Granger's reserve corps remained about three miles to the north of the Union left flank. Thomas, the *de facto* commander of these intermingled divisions, ordered the pioneers, or engineers, to begin constructing breastworks from felled trees and fence rails. Although the Confederates could hear the sound of chopping, nevertheless the next morning they were astonished to see the strength of these new works.[146]

Instead of the ad hoc, uncoordinated maneuvers of the previous day, for Sunday, September 20, 1863, Bragg devised an intricate operational scheme that was supposed to begin with an oblique attack with each division starting its assault 30 minutes after the division to its right had begun its attack. Although Bragg had planned and ordered the first division (former Vice President John Breckinridge's) to attack at dawn, that charge did not start until 9:30 a.m.[147] Breckinridge was eventually repulsed by the just arriving Negley who had taken advantage of the fortuitous three hour delay of the Confederate attack.[148] Cleburne's division attacked next but breastworks constructed overnight by Thomas' engineers helped keep that assault from gaining much; normally Cleburne's thorough pre-battle preparation was one of his trademarks but that morning's short notice had precluded any opportunity for the necessary scouting and issuance of detailed instructions. More significantly just when Rebel soldiers were dying in droves from their valiant efforts and when reinforcements could have tipped the scales in the Confederates' favor, Polk's subordinate commanders were quarrelling over how, and by whom, reinforcements could be sent. Woodworth claims that, "Taken as a whole, the performance of the Confederate right wing this morning had been one of the most appalling exhibitions of command incompetence of the entire Civil War."[149] The bishop-general, Polk, in charge of the Bragg's attack on the right, failed once more as he had done on several occasions but perhaps never more dearly than on September 20, 1863, at Chickamauga.

Frustrated by the failure of any rolling thunder of his oblique plan to materialize, Bragg by-passed his wing commanders to simply order his entire line to move forward in a frontal assault against heavily fortified positions, thereby foregoing his previous intention of turning the Union's left—in reality the best, if not only, chance to cut off the Federal line of retreat.

Although Thomas had managed to hold most of the northern, or left, flank against the charges by Breckinridge and later by Cleburne, he had done so in large part because he and Rosecrans continued to shuffle and realign divisions to bolster Thomas' lines. Unfortunately Thomas and Rosecrans were not in constant contact with one another; consequently neither one was always aware of all the division alignments. And so it was during the morning of Sunday, September 20, 1863, the division of MGen. John M. Brannon, 40, which had been held in reserve, already had moved forward to plug a gap along La Fayette Road as the Union lines had been sliding to their left. However, Thomas was not aware of this change.[150] Later one of Thomas' staff officers, still thinking Brannon was in reserve, ordered Brannon to move to the far left to support Baird's division, which in fact did not require support at that time. Although perplexed, Brannon started to move as directed while Thomas' staff officer rode to Rosecrans' headquarters to advise that a new gap had been created where Brannon had been.[151] Actually there was no hole because MGen. Joseph J. Reynolds, 41, who had been to Brannon's left, had on his own initiative begun to stretch his lines to cover the space that Brannon had been occupying.

Upon further reflection Brannon decided his previous decision to relocate was ill-advised; so he countermarched to resume his previous position, meaning the report to Rosecrans was incorrect since no gap existed. But by the time Rosecrans received the report his frame of mind had been worn to a frazzle from the continuous stresses and strains of command ever since his army had crossed the Tennessee River 16 days earlier. He then made a quick, almost impulsive decision to have BGen. Thomas J. Wood, 40,[152] to fill the presumed gap.[153] At that time Wood's division was on Brannon's right side. So to recap, at mid-morning on September 20 Reynolds was at the lower part of the Thomas' arc, or salient, with his right anchored on the La Fayette Road; Brannon was stationed along the La Fayette Road to the immediate right of Reynolds. Wood was also along the La Fayette Road to Brannon's right while Sheridan occupied a line a little further to the right in front of Rosecrans' headquarters at Widow Glenn's house.

Normally James Garfield, Rosecrans' chief-of-staff, would prepare the actual order implementing Rosecrans' decision but Garfield was otherwise occupied; instead an aide-de-camp wrote the order.[154] Unfortunately for the immediate fortunes of the Army of the Cumberland the written order to Wood was self-contradictory, its substance reading, "The general commanding directs that you close up on Reynolds as fast as possible, and support him."[155] Not only is this cryptic to modern readers but it was confusing to Civil War commanders: To "close up" meant to slide over laterally to take a position in line *beside* Reynolds while to "support" meant to act as a reserve *behind* Reynolds. Furthermore Wood could hardly slide over to Reynolds because Brannon had moved into the way. But once there should Wood take a position in line beside Reynolds or was he to remain in support behind Reynolds?

Under different circumstances Wood might, and probably would, have taken the time to seek clarification either from McCook, his immediate area commander, or more likely from Rosecrans, 600 yards to the rear in whose name the order had been given. However those were not normal circumstances since Rosecrans, who in any event usually operated at a maniacal level, lately had been extremely short tempered with subordinates whom Old Rosey deemed rightly or wrongly to be insubordinate or even acting sluggishly.

Wood had witnessed Rosecrans severely castigating other commanders, including McCook,[156] and indeed earlier in the day Wood—with an ego as large and as sensitive as any general in the army—had been subjected to one of Rosecrans' virulent tongue-lashings in front of Wood's staff when Old Rosey screamed at Wood, "You have disobeyed my specific orders. By your damnable negligence you are endangering the safety of the entire army, and, by God, I will not tolerate it. Move your division at once, as I have instructed, or the consequences will not be pleasant for yourself."[157] Not anxious to be reamed out again, Wood pulled out his three brigades to begin marching to the rear north behind Brannon toward Reynolds' position.[158] Thus not only did this needlessly create a temporary six hundred yard gap, the gap happened to be in an area that was already undermanned, especially since the Union's entire right flank had become weakened by all the other movements of divisions and brigades to bolster the left.[159]

Although the right portion of the Confederate attack had not gone well Longstreet was yet to begin his assault. Although he had been originally ordered to attack much earlier that morning, Longstreet's turn in the oblique order had been delayed by the confusion and disarray in commencing the first attacks in the north. But Longstreet had made good use of the extra time to scout the terrain to his front and equally as important to rearrange his 15,000 soldiers to his best advantage into a formation rarely used in the Civil War. Instead of deploying the customary long line two deep, Longstreet shortened his line by stacking his eleven brigades one behind the other into a battering ram column several miles long.[160] Among other advantages this stacked formation reduced the vulnerability of the attacking column's front while combining attack velocity with concentration.[161] Hood commanded Longstreet's lead division that began its attack at 11:10 a.m. upon Bragg's direct command.[162]

Fortuitously for the Rebels, many who were recent veterans of the Devil's Den and Little Round Top at Gettysburg, by sheer coincidence they struck exactly where the last of Wood's division was departing. Another Union division, under the command of Jefferson C. Davis (no relation to the C.S.A. president), was just beginning to arrive intending to fill the gap[163] but it was too little, too late to have any chance to defend against the onslaught of Hood's hard charging division and the following Rebel attackers.

As though an earthen dam had been breached an unchecked torrent of Confederates suddenly was at the flanks and rear of Union brigades that had little if any chance to do anything other than quickly drop their weapons, equipment, extra pieces of uniform and to flee to safer grounds. Davis' division all but disappeared under the onslaught as did brigades of Wood's and Horatio Van Cleve's divisions. Artillery batteries desperately fired canister before being forced to abandon their positions as well as their guns! Sheridan's division—which was isolated at the Northerners' extreme right flank—gamely tried to make a stand but was soon overwhelmed and forced to join the massive rush to the rear.[164] Worst of all, Confederates began to overrun the lightly defended army headquarters forcing Rosecrans and most of his staff to try to find their way back to Chattanooga. Garfield suggested to Rosecrans that Rosecrans needed to return to Chattanooga to organize those defenses while Garfield would try to find Thomas to assist that portion of the defense.[165] At one point Thomas' provost, Col. John Parkhurst, had rounded up approximately 1,000 retreating Federals; Parkhurst asked Crittenden to organize and to take command but Crittenden just continued to the rear.[166]

Throughout—at least until an hour earlier when he had ordered a total front assault—Bragg's objective correctly had been to turn the Union's left to force a retreat to the south. However, Longstreet's sudden, in all probability unexpected, advances meant there were only remnants of Union forces to Longstreet's left; in effect he and Hood were turning the Union's right, meaning the retreating and routed Union units were trying to escape north toward safe harbor at either Rossville or Chattanooga.

Although it was clear that the Army of the Cumberland was suffering catastrophic losses, it was not yet annihilated. Indeed one of Wood's brigades regrouped to attempt a counterCharge that was unsuccessful except that Hood was seriously wounded in his upper right leg[167]; additionally several brigades from the Union's left flank were beginning to establish new defensive position under George Thomas' resolute leadership.

These Federals managed to establish two compact positions along the crest of the defensive-friendly terrain of Snodgrass Hill, extending along Horseshoe Ridge. The terrain of these positions provided outstanding obstacles against attacks; however the positions were separated by a gap that if exploited would put the attackers around to the rear of the defenders. While Federal defenders had the advantage of excellent terrain, not only were they badly out-numbered, and in danger of being outflanked, their ammunition was becoming desperately low with no prospects for being re-supplied. Although the Confederates had vast numerical superiority—perhaps more than three to one[168]— they missed the battle leadership that Hood might have provided. In Hood's stead Longstreet failed to take tactical advantage since many of the Rebel attacks, while furious, were launched piecemeal.[169]

Although battle-fatigued, Thomas continued to assert his calm, determined leadership as the Yankee defenders held on with grit and fortitude against repeated assaults but the odds, and most importantly the Rebels' numerical superiority, weighed heavily against them. Several division commanders, even those whose brigades had fled, had stayed with Thomas but by early afternoon Negley decided to also retire taking 1,500 men as well as 48 of Thomas's guns with him[170]; Negley would never be forgiven by Wood or Brannon.[171]

But just as all seemed lost, help came from a most unexpected, but welcome source. For most of two days Granger had waited impatiently as he followed Rosecrans' orders to remain in reserve five or six miles to the north. However, on his own initiative—something that was still rare for Union generals—Granger decided he could wait no longer, "orders or no orders." Taking two brigades under the command of BGen. James Steedman, 46, Granger began to march at the double quick southward to the sound of the guns,[172] eventually marching through one of the fields of battle still cluttered with fallen soldiers and detritus of battle.[173]

Not only was Thomas greatly relieved to receive these reinforcements, Granger also brought enough ammunition for approximately ten more rounds per soldier, not an excessive number but certainly more than the two rounds per man that had previously remained in their pouches.[174]

But even with Granger's reinforcements the battles continued as the Confederates repeatedly charged up the 200 foot hills. Garfield, who had ridden to join Thomas at about 4:00 p.m. (a ride that would help propel Garfield all the way to the White House eighteen years later), sent a wire to Rosecrans to recommend that reinforcements with more ammunition be sent to Thomas for a counterattack on the 21st. Instead a half hour later Rosecrans sent a retreat order that Thomas had no alternative except to obey.[175] Still taking a high percentage of casualties, including by regiments that had just arrived with Granger,[176] later that evening Thomas managed to extract most of his soldiers and to relocate via one of the routes that Rosecrans had striven to protect for such purposes, to defensive positions in front of Rossville. Two Union divisions, under Davis and Sheridan respectively, had regrouped to begin the process of returning to Thomas when they met the retreating columns.[177]

## Confederate Failure to Pursue

Although Longstreet had forced a massive retreat of much of Rosecrans' army, neither Longstreet nor Bragg made any immediate attempt to pursue, that is to say to vanquish that part of the 14th Corps that remained with Thomas. It is difficult to ignore a comparison of Longstreet's battlefield management between Chickamauga and 2nd Bull Run. In both instances he allowed units under his command merely to chase the enemy away—admittedly no small task—rather than to plan and to organize a pursuit that would among other things create a blocking position to keep the enemy from escaping. As noted by Holden Reid: "... an effective pursuit demands thought and planning, and this was not forthcoming. Devastating pursuits are rarely improvised, especially with tired, battle-spent troops. They also demand a measure of discipline and operational understanding among commanders that was not to be found in the Army of Tennessee."[178]

But in fairness to Longstreet, since his starting position was on Bragg's left it would have been virtually impossible for Longstreet to have had the leverage to pivot the bulk of Rosecrans's army to the south. Nevertheless, with the advantage of 20/20 hindsight, it seems possible, and probably more feasible, to have assigned a smaller force merely to hold Thomas rather than to continue to relentlessly pound frontally against Thomas' position. Other forces could then be used to bypass Thomas, and to isolate the defenders on Snodgrass Hill and Horseshoe Ridge to compel their capitulation. While this tactic would still not have captured the entire Army of the Cumberland, if successful it might have eliminated the 14th Corps, the largest corps within the Army of the Cumberland.

Nevertheless Longstreet was ecstatic about the success of his attacks that had chased the Federals from the Chickamauga battlefield; at the same time Old Pete could not understand why Bragg—who was "pale and careworn"—seemed less enthused about the battle's outcome.[179] But Bragg was no fool, at least in understanding and weighing strategic objectives. For the past three or four weeks Bragg had planned and been attempting to put the Army of the Cumberland out of business by forcing it south away from its lines of communications and where it could possibly be trapped and forced to capitulate. Despite all his personality flaws Bragg was a strategic realist who knew that a successful pursuit would no longer be feasible, there being no way to block the enemy's path back to Chattanooga. Bragg also realized that once in Chattanooga the Federals—no matter how badly damaged they were—would have a chance to regroup, refit, and resupply to eventually be ready to fight again another day.

In fairness, two days of continuous assaults, and reorganization, had also depleted the strength and crippled the command cohesion of many of Bragg's brigades that simply no longer had the energy to regroup and resume a march to chase the Federals. By the time Bragg and his subordinates had discovered the Federals had abandoned the Chickamauga battlegrounds Thomas had already managed to regroup, organize, and begin to fortify a defense at the critical pass in the Missionary Ridge in front of Rossville, shielding the rest of the army at Chattanooga. More than a quarter of Bragg's army, even as reinforced by Longstreet's divisions, was *hors combat*—killed, wounded, or missing. Furthermore Bragg had thrown all his available forces into the assaults of the 20th failing to keep any brigades as reserves. Even though Longstreet had forced his initial breakthrough, his soldiers suffered horrendous losses—37.7 percent of their numbers—as they launched repeated frontal assaults against Thomas' virtually unassailable defenses. Likewise Breckinridge's and Cleburne's divisions were far below combat strength as a result of their unrelenting charges earlier that morning.

Even though Thomas began his retreat during the late daylight hours of September 20, Bragg and his two new wing commanders, Longstreet and Polk, did not realize the Federals had evacuated Chickamauga until the next morning of September 21, 1863.[180] Bragg refused to believe his army had been victorious, contributing to his failure to initiate an early pursuit.[181] Longstreet immediately made several grandiose proposals, including a movement toward Nashville,[182] swinging into East Tennessee, or moving on the other side of Chattanooga to surround the Federals in that city. But aside from needing sufficient time to allow his mangled army to recuperate, Bragg had other problems that would preclude such endeavors; simply put, he did not have sufficient logistical capabilities for such ambitions.[183]

First, each of these movements meant re-crossing the Tennessee River, which Bragg could not do immediately because he had no pontoon bridge. As it was his army was almost out of rations, a threat that was exacerbated with the arrival of Longstreet's divisions without supply wagons meaning more mouths to feed without any additional capacity to provide food or forage. In other words, even if Bragg could have found the means to have crossed the Tennessee he still had insufficient logistical means to feed his men and animals.

Forrest also complicated Bragg's decision making. At separate times on the 21st Forrest had climbed trees to observe columns of dust that Forrest interpreted and reported as signs of a massive retreat, "evacuating as hard as they can go."[184] Instead these dust clouds were caused by trains of wagons carrying wounded soldiers to the rear before returning with more supplies and replacement equipment needed to replenish the units remaining in Chattanooga. Also on the 21st Forrest sent a report indicating the Chattanooga defenses were ripe for the taking while completely overlooking defensive lines that Thomas established in front of Rossville. Forrest sent a handwritten note to Bragg urging, "I think we ought to press forward as rapidly as possible" which Bragg prudently ignored.[185] Reflecting his penchant for battle, Forrest also encountered enemy cavalry, engaging in a running skirmish during which the neck of Forrest's mount was struck with a bullet. Forrest stemmed the bleeding by sticking his thumb into the horse's wound, an expedient that worked long enough to finish the skirmish at which time the horse collapsed before dying[186]; as dramatic, even gallant, as that incident may have been, more and better intelligence from their cavalry was what Bragg and his wing commanders really needed.

In short, pursuit by Bragg's Southerners after Chickamauga was hardly as feasible as it may have seemed, even in the judgment of many historians, because: (1) Almost as soon as their abandonment of the battlefield was discovered the Federals were constructing fortifications to protect their newly established safe harbor, (2) the Rebels' combat capabilities were reduced as much, if not more, than were the Union's, and (3) in particular the Confederates no longer had the logistical capacity to carry the battle any further.[187]

The cavalries continued to spar and to skirmish for a couple more days. On September 24 Rosecrans ordered the abandonment of Yankee outposts still atop Lookout Mountain[188]; this move enabled the Confederates to establish artillery batteries overlooking supply routes on the river as well as on the best roads and railroads. The next day Bragg rescinded plans to attack Chattanooga and instead ordered Wheeler's cavalry to position itself to attack and to take control of the only remaining overland route between Chattanooga and Bridgeport. In effect the battle of Chickamauga was now over as Bragg began to try to starve the Federals with a siege.

Despite the lack of readily recognizable battles such as Pickett's Charge at Gettysburg or killing fields such as Sunken Road at Antietam, the two-day battle at Chickamauga was a horribly bloody affair with both sides suffering casualties of 28 percent of their effective forces. The Union suffered a total of 16,170 killed, wounded, or missing, including 1,002 officers, while the Confederates suffered 18,454 casualties; the Federal ordinance losses were also high, including at least thirty-six field guns along with almost 10,000 artillery rounds.[189] Measured by casualty rates, the armies at Chickamauga paid a butcher's bill as steep as any in the war. Chickamauga was the Southerners' only major victory in the Western theater but at best it was a shallow feat for the Rebels since they suffered more casualties than did the Yankees who were able—at least for the time being to survive, albeit tenuously—and eventually continue to fight another day.

## Dénouements and Precursors

Neither side was satisfied with the Chickamauga results. The North was of course unhappy that much of the Army of the Cumberland, including its army commander and two corps commanders, had fled from the field; the South was unhappy because the Federals had escaped to Chattanooga meaning that a possible decisive victory had been denied.

John Bell Hood's shattered right leg was amputated four inches below his hip. He recuperated in Atlanta until he went, via a private railroad car, to Richmond in November 1863. Hood was determined to resume command but also knew he would have to show he was physically capable of riding. He was fitted with an artificial leg that would be strapped to a stirrup after he had been hefted onto his saddle.

Dozens of wounded Confederate officers congregated in Richmond where they socialized and were feted as conquering heroes. Hood, shamelessly ambitious, ingratiated himself with Jeff Davis who nominated Hood for promotion to lieutenant general, a rank that the C.S.A. reserved for corps command. With his paralyzed left arm in a sling and using a crutch under his right arm, Hood, at the end of February 1864, reported to the Army of Tennessee, headquartered at Dalton, Georgia, 30 miles southeast of Chattanooga, as it prepared to defend against Sherman's Atlanta campaign.

Braxton Bragg was the target of much Southern criticism, much of it coming from his own subordinates, who of course had been criticizing him for several months. Polk, one serious, long time malcontent, circulated messages critical of Bragg's management of the battlefield. Although Polk had the chutzpah to criticize Bragg for not aggressively pursuing, he—as much as any infantry officer—was to blame for the failure of the Rebels to achieve a decisive victory at Chickamauga. Had the Bishop punctually launched his attack as ordered on the morning of the 20th he would have caught the Union's left flank without adequate fortifications, too weak to make a strong defense. Under these circumstances it is conceivable the Union's left flank would have faltered, forcing the Federals to move south away from their intended retreat routes; however as it was by the time Polk had finished his breakfast to deign it proper to commence his attack Thomas was sufficiently fortified with Negley in place. Polk's dilatory efforts on the 20th—in keeping with his usual habits—contributed significantly, albeit negatively, to one of the most important turning points of the Western campaign.

And Bragg was not about to turn his cheek; instead he demanded that Polk submit a report about the delay in launching the attack on the morning of September 20. Polk's eventual report blamed Hill after which Bragg suspended Polk before dispatching him to Atlanta.[190] Jeff Davis attempted to countermand Bragg's orders but Bragg would not relent; and so Davis appointed Polk to command a widely scattered department headquartered in Meridian, Mississippi.

Longstreet convened a secret meeting of dissident generals—Hill and Buckner being other conspirators—concerning the "mismanagement manifested in the conduct of military operations in this army"; Old Pete then sent a message to C.S.A. Secretary of War James Sedden to contend that Bragg's poor health made him unfit for command.

The disputes and discord were running so deep that they compelled Davis to visit Bragg and his subordinates. Arriving at Bragg's headquarters on October 9, Davis consulted with almost all subordinate commanders, either individually or collectively. Although it was abundantly clear that Bragg had lost the trust and confidence of most his command, Davis had no suitable replacement for Bragg, in large part because Davis had his own acrimonious relationships with the most likely successors such as Joe Johnston or P.G.T. Beauregard.[191] Furthermore since Chickamauga had been declared as a Confederate victory it would be unseemly to relieve the commanding general of such victory. Before departing on October 14 Davis opted to retain Bragg, his old Mexican War comrade, in command while affirming that Bragg would not have to "countenance disobedience of or noncompliance with orders."

Bragg then continued to reorganize his army, relieving Hill of his corps command without giving reasons for such removal. Hill made various appeals even gaining an interview with Jefferson Davis but to no avail. Hill remained without a significant command for the remainder of the war and to add insult to injury the Confederate senate failed to confirm his appointment to lieutenant general. After the war D.H. Hill eventually became president of the University of Arkansas.

But the biggest, or at least the most spectacular, fireworks erupted from Bragg's clash with the volatile, irrepressible Forrest; Bragg's appraisal of Forrest had undergone a complete 180-degree turnabout. Shortly after Forrest joined the Army of Tennessee Bragg commented favorably upon Forrest's "great strength." But now in the aftermath of Chickamauga Bragg commented "[Forrest] is ignorant, and does not know anything of cooperation. He is nothing more than a good raider." Forrest became furious by Bragg's failure to follow Forrest's recommendations to pursue, at one point exclaiming, "What does he fight battles for?"[192] Bragg and Forrest had a couple meetings, accounts of which vary widely, some of which are probably apocryphal,[193] but the upshot was that most of Forrest's command was turned over to Wheeler, after which Forrest with a small retinue was transferred to Western Tennessee and Northern Mississippi where he—operating independently—would gain much of his fame and glory (or infamy).

After Appomattox, Simon Buckner, became a newspaper man, eventually becoming editor of the Louisville *Courier*. He reclaimed property he had sold to a relative before the war and then sold the property for the then princely sum of $50,000. Buckner, a lifelong friend of Sam Grant, was a pallbearer at Grant's funeral. Buckner's son with the same name became a World War II general who was killed while commanding the 10th U.S. Army during the invasion of Okinawa in 1945.

Dana resumed sending wires to Washington to criticize Old Rosey for his continued reliance upon subordinates such as Alex McCook, Thomas Crittenden, David Stanley and James Negley, all of whom Dana generally considered to be useless. Not surprisingly deep schisms developed within the command structure since other generals also had little sympathy toward these commanders. Given the disasters that had befallen upon his corps at Perryville, Stones River, and Chickamauga, Old Gut—the third oldest son in the "tribe of Dan" of the 17 fighting McCooks—had almost no support or sympathy among his fellow generals. And so it was not much of a surprise when toward the end of September 1863, that both McCook and Crittenden were relieved as corps commanders; McCook was also court-martialed for his conduct in leaving the field at Chickamauga but was acquitted. Neither would have another significant position for the balance of the war.[194]

Negley was likewise charged with cowardice and desertion but acquitted. He also received no significant field commands before resigning shortly before the end of the war.

Despite Dana's criticism, David Stanley remained with the Army of the Cumberland, although as an infantry commander, eventually earning a Medal of Honor.

James A. Garfield, Rosecrans' Chief of Staff, had been elected to the U.S. House of Representatives, a position he had yet to assume. In November 1863, claiming that Lincoln told him that he was needed in Congress more than in the Army, Garfield resigned his commission as brigadier general to take his seat in Congress. Garfield was replaced as chief of staff by Joseph J. Reynolds, most recently one of Thomas' division commanders. Although Garfield had several merits, unfortunately there had been some legitimate suspicion that Garfield had not been entirely loyal to Rosecrans, and might have been undercutting his chief as early as the summer of 1863. Certainly Reynolds was an improvement from a military viewpoint.[195]

As a civilian politician Garfield was able to parlay his December 20, 1863, ride to Thomas to additional political fame. He already had a great back story; in addition to his military exploits, somewhat exaggerated in the retelling, Garfield had been born in a log cabin near Cleveland, Ohio, after his father died when Garfield was two years old, he lifted himself from poverty to become a teacher, a lay preacher, and a college president at the age of 26 years before entering the field of Ohio politics.

In 1880 Garfield became the Republican nominee for President, emerging from a field that included U.S. Grant, seeking a third term after being out of office for four years. Garfield narrowly won the general election by beating the Democratic nominee, Winfield Scott Hancock, one of the great heroes of Gettysburg. Garfield won in large part because he had made a wide range of promises, including patronage, in the key electoral state of New York, eventually realizing he had made more promises than he could possibly keep. On July 2, 1881, a deranged office seeker shot Garfield in the back. Garfield, who had never been wounded in the Civil War, lingered for a couple months while doctors tried in vain to find the bullet but Garfield eventually died of massive infections caused by the unsanitary methods of probing for the bullet. Garfield's widow established the nation's first Presidential library.

# 6

# Turnaround at Chattanooga
## October and November 1863

Despite all the problems in Bragg's command, described in the previous chapter, his siege of Chattanooga nevertheless was making matters even worse within the Union fortifications where quartermaster stores, food and forage, and replacement equipment were in dire need. Although the chances of a Confederate attack seemed to lessen each day, rations to the Federals were being drastically reduced while mules were dying in droves from overwork without getting enough forage.[1] Some relief could be gained if Ambrose Burnside were to execute an ordered march with his army of 20,000 soldiers from Knoxville but Burnside simply ignored messages repeatedly sent either from Rosecrans or even from authorities in Washington.[2] Meanwhile the Federals continued to suffer terribly from Bragg's siege.

Rosecrans' own behavior was erratic, buoyant one hour and despondent the next. To his credit he attempted to bolster troop morale by making frequent visits with his regiments[3]; however the grim situation was apparent to almost everyone, including Charles Dana and James Garfield who were sending frequent dispatches to Stanton and/or Halleck.[4] Dana was describing Rosecrans as being broken, unable to focus, and unable to make any decisions about how to break the stranglehold upon vital supply lines; instead, according to Dana, Rosecrans "dawdles with trifles."

Furthermore former commands were merged into a new corps, designated as the 4th Corps.[5] Gordon Granger, who had ridden in the opposite direction as had McCook and Crittenden at Chickamauga, was assigned to command the newly merged corps.[6] Granger, a veteran of the Mexican and Indian Wars, was Regular Army to the hilt, a gruff, strict disciplinarian who was hardly beloved by either his fellow officers or the enlisted men who called him a "red tape soldier." Combining the two former corps also necessitated major reshuffling of subordinate units and their commanders as divisions, brigades, and batteries were also merged; few of these changes set well or were readily received by junior officers or enlisted personnel.[7]

Fortunately Washington authorities were not willing to give up on their Army of the Cumberland and its Chattanooga foothold, tenuous though it may have been. Lincoln wired words of encouragement and "good cheer" to Rosecrans; but Lincoln also recognized that Rosecrans was no longer acting at full capacity, at one point remarking that Rosecrans was acting "confused and stunned like a duck hit in the head." Rosecrans' own reports—pessimistic and fatalistic—gave Lincoln little reason to be sanguine about Rosecrans' capacity to salvage anything from the nearly disastrous predicament. Stanton, Dana's boss at the

War Department, had already decided Rosecrans would have to be replaced as army commander but that was not a unanimous opinion among cabinet members.[8]

BGen. William F. ("Baldy") Smith, 39, arrived to become the army's new chief engineer.[9] Smith was a bright and experienced combat commander whose propensity to express critical opinions caused him to run afoul with the hierarchy, most recently having co-authored a letter to Lincoln to imply his criticism of Burnside's performance at Fredericksburg where Baldy briefly served as 6th Corps commander.[10] At Carlisle, Smith had redeemed himself on July 1, 1863, by rebuffing Jeb Stuart as the latter was nearing the end of his raid around the Army of the Potomac while the fighting at Gettysburg was beginning. (See Chapter 16.) Smith and Rosecrans failed to agree about the necessity of opening the river to relieve the siege; thus Smith went to work upon fortifications.[11]

Even prior to Chickamauga, Halleck ordered Sherman to send a division east from the Mississippi but as soon as Halleck received word of the Chickamauga defeat he ordered Sherman to take three more divisions to Chattanooga. Late in the evening of Wednesday, September 23, 1863—three days after the Federal abandonment of the Chickamauga battlefield—Stanton summoned Lincoln to a hastily called meeting of cabinet and War Department members, including Halleck.[12]

Even with the future addition of Sherman's corps it was painfully apparent that even more reinforcements were necessary but the question remained where would they come from and how would they be transported. One of the most daring proposals was to send the Union's 11th and 12th Corps consisting of 23,000 soldiers along with seven batteries from Meade's Army of the Potomac, a railroad trip of 1,159 miles through six states along railroads of three different gauges,[13] an unprecedented movement that David L. McCullum, head of the Railroad Bureau, quickly calculated would take seven days. Despite Lincoln's trepidation, fearful that many troops could not even get to Washington in less than five days, these two corps, under the unified command of MGen. Joseph ("Fightin' Joe") Hooker, 39, were on their way the next day to Bridgeport.[14] As had been calculated by McCullum, Hooker's army began to arrive seven day later but circumstances forced them to remain in the Bridgeport area for the time being.

This new army bore considerable familiarity from the Army of the Potomac. Hooker had been sitting on the "awaiting orders" shelf since his removal as commander of the Army of the Potomac a few days before Gettysburg. Hooker, yet another veteran of the Mexican War, had resigned from the Regular Army after the Mexican War to try farming in California; not only was this an unsuccessful endeavor but he also managed to acquire a reputation for drinking, womanizing, and dishonoring his debts. Halleck and Sherman, who were acquainted with Hooker during this period, developed a strong dislike for Hooker.[15] Both corps commanders, MGen. Oliver Otis Howard, 33, commanding the 11th Corps, and MGen, Henry Slocum, 36, commanding the 12th Corps, had served under Hooker throughout his tenure as army command in the East but neither enjoyed a cordial relationship with Hooker, who believed neither had performed up his expectations.[16]

Rebel artillery atop Lookout Mountain cut off any resupply attempts via Bridgeport, making Walden Ridge Road, a terrible, narrow trail with uncertain bridges winding its way to and through the Sequatchie Valley across the river from Chattanooga, the only remaining supply route to Chattanooga. Initially the Federals were resupplied via a fifty-five-mile dirt train.[17] However a huge resupply train was scheduled to arrive from Nashville but on

October 2, 1863, Wheeler's cavalry of 5,000 horse riders struck the train seizing or destroying commissary, ammunition, and baggage wagons while capturing 1,800 mules, 800 of which were recaptured in an ensuing cavalry chase that had been dispatched by Rosecrans. Had Burnside been compliant to orders, his army should have been in position to prevent these losses; in frustration Rosecrans sent Burnside a scathing telegram, which Burnside characteristically ignored.

The question arose about the unification of command of the three armies to be assembled at Chattanooga. On October 16, 1863, a secret cabinet meeting decided to create a supreme western commander who would have control over all military units in the Western theater. Sam Grant was designated for this new post, and was given discretionary authority to replace Rosecrans with Thomas.[18] Three days later Grant exercised his authority by relieving Rosecrans from command replacing him with Thomas, although Grant had no particular fondness for either general.[19]

On Monday, October 19, 1863, the same day Rosecrans was being relieved, but prior to the arrival of that order, he and Baldy reconnoitered the downstream banks of the Tennessee River to discover Brown's Ferry, a no-longer used and lightly defended crossing on the river's east bank.[20] Baldy envisioned a plan whereby Brown's Ferry would be the connecting point for two overland routes: One to Kelley's Ferry, further south and out-of-range of Confederate guns, and a second land route west of the Tennessee River but directly to Chattanooga. If implemented this new route should alleviate the resupply difficulties that threatened to starve the Federals out of Chattanooga.

Three days later Grant arrived during the late evening of October 23, 1863, when it was obvious that the most urgent and critical need was to re-establish a resupply line. Since Grant had just arrived in Chattanooga along Walden Ridge Road, muddy and treacherous while still strewn with dead mules and thousands of wrecked and burned-out wagons, and could easily see firsthand the devastation brought by the lack of supplies, he readily agreed that a new line had to be opened.[21] Baldy Smith, whom Grant had not seen since their days at West Point, had already prepared, and Thomas had approved, an audacious plan for a daring complex operation that would have Hooker's army of two corps coming across Raccoon Mountain to converge with a smaller contingent making a middle-of-the-night attack upon Brown's Ferry.[22] After making a personal reconnaissance, Grant gave his approval to proceed on Monday, October 26, 1863. Remarkably the operation succeeded practically without a hitch, and the new supply line, quickly to become known as the Cracker Line, allowed the delivery of back logged tons of desperately needed food, weapons and ammunition, quartermaster items such as replacement uniforms and shoes plus forage for the animals, as well as all the other materials necessary for effective military operations.

On the Confederate side, although Bragg had transferred Simon Buckner and D.H. Hill elsewhere, Longstreet's presence with Bragg's army continued to fester; Bragg could hardly get along with anyone, let alone someone who had been sowing seeds of discord while making almost no effort to acknowledge or respect Bragg's authority. Bragg delegated considerable tactical responsibilities to Old Pete who seemed helpless to divine Union intentions or to grasp the significance of the terrain or the armies' positions.[23] Their relationship soured even more after the Yankees captured Brown's Ferry, which Bragg had previously ordered Longstreet to seize and occupy with sizable force[24]; this was but one of a series of tactical blunders by Longstreet who seemed oblivious to the importance of the routes in and out of Brown's Ferry.

Several factors seemed to converge to provide a solution satisfactory to the Longstreet issue, at least on the surface. First, Lee wanted his top lieutenant back in Virginia so that Lee could resume active operations. Second, Chattanooga was close to becoming a stalemate, although to be sure the Rebels should have recognized the Federals were gaining some advantage with the addition of Hooker's two new corps and having a new resupply line; from the Confederates' perspective it might be possible to dislodge the stalemate by flanking the Federals' left and/or by trying to recapture Knoxville. Third, Longstreet still yearned for an independent command, at least until he would have to rejoin Lee. Finally, almost to cut his nose to spite his face Bragg was willing, even anxious, to release Longstreet even though Longstreet, whom Bragg considered to be overrated, still was Bragg's best and most reliable lieutenant. Ironically with the mutual consent of all parties, on November 7, 1863, Longstreet—with his 20,000 men—began to march away from his position atop Lookout Mountain, thereby reducing Bragg's strength by one-third, and started toward Knoxville. At this point Bragg was left with approximately 42,000 effectives while Grant had mustered about 60,000 troops.

The Federal forces were undergoing additional command changes with MGen. John M. Palmer, 46, replacing Thomas as commander of the 14th Corps and Stanley being put on badly needed sick leave.[25] Palmer was a political general having once been a Democrat before becoming a Republican; he had originally commanded divisions in the Army of the Mississippi before being assigned during the course of the past year to command brigades and divisions in the Army of the Cumberland.

Even though Sherman was normally an aggressive, energetic commander, and even though his soldiers were good marchers, their trek across the width of Tennessee was fraught with difficulties. Sherman was dispirited by the death of his favorite son the day his army was supposed to depart, and he may have not been able to give enough attention to the details of such a large movement. The last of his army—as ordered by Halleck—was underway by September 27, 1863, but its pace was slowed by the necessity to create its own supply line by repairing or rebuilding the railroad along the way to Athens, Alabama. But Washington was asserting pressure upon Grant to get something done in Chattanooga; in response on October 27, 1863, Grant ordered Sherman to cease all work on the railroad and to proceed immediately to Bridgeport. During the evening of November 14, 1863, when Sherman's army had barely reached Bridgeport, Cump was immediately summoned and transported to Chattanooga where he met with Grant, Thomas and Baldy Smith.

The plan, devised by Smith, was relatively simple. Sherman would bring his troops up from Bridgeport, cross the pontoon bridge at Brown's Ferry, march upstream and re-cross the Tennessee River at a point across from the northern foot of Missionary Ridge from whence Sherman would launch his attack against the Rebels. In the meanwhile, Thomas, at the western edge of the center of Missionary Ridge, and Hooker, at the other—or southern—end of Lookout Mountain, would execute feints merely to hold Bragg's units in place at those locations. Grant's rationalized not giving a greater role to Thomas' army that "had been so demoralized by the Battle of Chickamauga that he feared they could not be got out of their trenches to assume the offensive."[26] Sherman was to begin his attack on Friday, November 20, a date Cump agreed was feasible.

However, the proverbial fly in the ointment was that Sherman could not get his troops in position by the scheduled launch date. Several unforeseen factors prevented such a timely launch: first, the pontoon bridge at Brown's Ferry did not have the capacity for large number of troops and vehicles trying to cross at once. Second, the overland path between Brown's Ferry and the upstream crossing point was little more than a narrow, twisting country road deeply rutted from its former use as a resupply route made even worse by continuous downpours. But as significant as anything else the order of march within Sherman's divisions caused the rate of march to creep to a crawl. Each division included its supply and baggage wagons within the marching formation; these wagons not only slowed down that division but also impeding the following division. In order to have facilitated a more rapid rate of march Sherman should have ordered that each soldier carry his rations in his haversack; failing to do so order was costing too much time. And so Sherman's army was not in position to begin to re-cross the Tennessee River until the evening of Monday, November 23. By noon the next day, between the use of a captured Confederate steamer and a hastily constructed 1,250-foot pontoon bridge, Sherman's army was back on Rebel territory on the eastern side of the Tennessee River.

Given only token initial resistance Sherman was easily able to capture two high points along the northern slope of Missionary Ridge.[27] Sherman's next objective was Tunnel Hill. At first glance it appeared relatively easy to capture so instead of proceeding further on the afternoon of November 24, with only an hour of daylight remaining when Tunnel Hill was being defended by only a brigade, Sherman decided not to advance any further but to give his troops a well-deserved rest. To Sherman's surprise, the next morning he discovered a deep ravine, a mile and half long, with steep, rugged sides separated his new position and Tunnel Hill that in turn could be transversed only through a narrow gap. Sherman's failure to reconnoiter put him into a wrong position.[28] Furthermore during the night the single Confederate brigade was reinforced by an entire division commanded by the redoubtable Irish-born Patrick Cleburne, considered by some as the "Stonewall of the West."[29]

There was always an undercurrent of rivalry between Eastern and Western armies within the Federal military. The Western soldier tended to believe his Eastern counterpart was a dandy while the Easterner viewed the Westerner as being an undisciplined slob. Underscoring these differences was the fact that the Army of the Potomac, with R.E. Lee as its nemesis, had suffered several battlefield setbacks while the Western armies, engaged with the likes of Braxton Bragg, had seldom known defeat. Perhaps Joe Hooker was the most prototypical of all Eastern commanders. Always clean shaven, erect of posture whether astride his horse or afoot, and perfectly attired, the egotistical Hooker sensed that Grant, the Western commander, was taking pains to assure that Sherman, Grant's Western cohort, would be getting preferential assignments from Grant. Furthermore Hooker felt slighted by his supporting assignment of merely making a feint while Sherman was assigned the potentially more glorious mission to advance up and to take Missionary Ridge. Besides, Fightin' Joe was anxious to redeem the blight on his reputation that had suffered at Chancellorsville six months earlier.

Chopping at the bit, Hooker requested—Thomas concurring—and was given permission to convert his feint mission to an assault, which if successful, should help squeeze Bragg from both ends. It has been said that terrain is a defending soldier's best friend, and the Confederate defenders at the southern slope of Lookout Mountain could hardly have asked for more favorable terrain. And so as Hooker's soldiers began their difficult climb up the southern slope on the morning of November 24 the rugged terrain provided a more daunting obstacle than did the meager number of Rebel soldiers.[30]

Not only did the foot soldiers have difficulty climbing and/or circumventing sheer cliffs, the artillery vehicles almost demanded to be hand carried in spots. Wheels had to be chocked with rocks to keep the pieces from rolling back down the slopes.[31] But these Eastern soldiers were not about to be denied and proceed until by 2:00 p.m. they had advanced far enough, and were so exhausted, that Hooker order a halt while holding their positions.[32]

That night Bragg, believing he was caught on the horns of a tactical dilemma, but considering that Lookout Mountain was no longer of major importance, ordered the withdrawal of the Lookout Mountain defenders, further ordering they hurry to buttress the defense of Missionary Ridge. Thus the next morning, November 25, 1863, Hooker awoke to find the Lookout Mountain battlefield had been abandoned, setting the stage for the Battle above the Clouds as the Stars and Stripes—one of the most dramatic moments in America's military history—was raised to the cheers of the soldiers of the Army of the Cumberland who were witnesses from below. Subsequently after a four-hour delay by the end of the day Hooker advanced all the way to Rossville![33]

At Tunnel Hill Sherman had a four to one numerical advantage over the Southern defenders. But Cleburne was deftly exerting command of battlefield management at its finest to take full advantage of outstanding terrain, interior lines, and effective artillery fire to repulse Sherman's repeated thrusts.[34] And so despite repeated assaults thrown against the Rebel defenders at Tunnel Hill little was accomplished except to frustrate Sherman and to irritate the impatient Grant. As Sherman's futility continued without abatement into the late afternoon on November 25, Grant reluctantly turned to Thomas for help with his "demoralized" Cumberlanders. Grant ordered Thomas to demonstrate by advancing Granger's newly formed 4th Corps—comprised of corps that had been routed at Chickamauga—to the triple line of entrenched Rebel rifle pits at Orchard Knob in front of the western base of Missionary Ridge.[35]

A line of four divisions consisting of 25,000 soldiers, including cooks and clerks, two and half miles long quickly formed and began advancing almost with parade ground fanfare and precision.[36] Assuming the approaching line was little more than a drill the Confederates watched in disbelief. But as the line came closer and closer Rebel defenders began to fire their rifles and guns, some with devastating effect. But suddenly Federal numbers overwhelmed the defenders in the rifle pits, and those Rebels who were not killed, wounded or captured had no alternative except to try to scramble up the ridge's slope for safety.

Some of the ensuing command details have been muddled in history with the biggest mystery being whether Grant wanted Granger merely to move forward to the rifle pits (the majority view) or did Grant desire Granger's soldiers to continue this assault by scaling the steep slopes in pursuit of the fleeing Confederates. The one certainty was that the newly captured line of rifle pits not a safe place to be since the line was exposed to rifle fire from above. Retreating back across the open fields would likewise be hazardous. And so against the odds the "demoralized" soldiers from the Army of the Cumberland, mostly pursuant to orders from regimental and brigade commanders, began to scamper up the 600-foot slope, weaving and dodging among rock outcroppings, tree stumps, and sometimes shielded from fire atop the ridge by Rebels trying to scurry away from scaling Yankees.

Contrary to usual procedures, lines were no longer centered upon color guards nor did beats of drums provide marching cadences. To be sure there was a mass of Southern artillery but these guns were almost useless because the gunners could not raise the rear of the guns high enough to aim down the slope. In surprisingly quick order the Federal infantry, without artillery pieces or other vehicles, but after fixing bayonets and charging ahead, captured their sector atop Missionary Ridge resulting in one of the most spectacular Federal victories of the war.[37] We will of course never know but it seems fair to conjecture that Longstreet and his 20,000 soldiers would have greatly stiffened the defenses atop the crest of Lookout Mountain and Missionary Ridge.

Given the success of Hooker's and Granger's attacks Bragg had no tenable option except to evacuate his Chattanooga defenses. As darkness neared in the late afternoon of November 25, Sherman discovered there were no longer any defenders at Tunnel Hill, Cleburne's division now acting as Bragg's rear guard. Although the number of their killed and wounded was relatively light, Bragg's army abandoned 6,000 prisoners atop of Missionary Ridge along with 7,000 castaway rifles together with 39 cannons.[38]

Taking the western slope of Missionary Ridge was not without a steep price as the four Union divisions suffered about 20 percent casualties. But there were also some measures of vindication; for instance Thomas Wood's division—the one that created a gap at Chickamauga when it moved to fill another gap that didn't exist—purportedly was the first division to reach the crest.[39] Not to be contained, once he reached the crest Little Phil Sheridan jumped astride and sat on a captured Confederate gun.[40] Then in lieu of any orders led his division down the eastern slope of Missionary Ridge to chase after Bragg and the fleeing Rebels. Although under the circumstances Sheridan's chase was ultimately futile his division did capture nine more artillery pieces as well as several Rebel stragglers, giving Little Phil some sense of vindication for Chickamauga.[41]

Much of the success in overtaking the defenses on Missionary Ridge had been the result of spontaneous, improvised efforts on the part of the soldiers and small units. On the other hand successful pursuits were not improvised maneuvers but instead required an outline of a plan at the division and corps levels. However darkness had set in by the time Union commanders realized the Rebels had abandoned the ridge; plus the terrain did not facilitate organization of units essential for a legitimate pursuit. Although the Chattanooga combat was not—as measured by casualty rates—as brutal or as intense as many other battles, the charge up the slopes of Missionary Ridge had been strenuous and exhausting.

At first Grant was inclined to honor Lincoln's desire to assure that Burnside was reinforced at Knoxville but during the evening of November 24 Grant had somewhat of a change of heart when he advised Sherman that the Union forces should try to "cut off a good portion of [Bragg's] rear troops and trains." Although his generals were not unanimous, Grant did launch a pursuit on Thursday, November 26, 1863—America's first official Thanksgiving Day—but it was short lived.

Once another, better organized pursuit was undertaken the next day under Hooker's control, weather conditions of fog and rain slowed the movements of troops who were, after all, not only still exhausted but badly in need of resupply. Thomas was unable to lend much help since most of his stock of horses had yet to be replenished. Cavalry help—so essential in any successful pursuit—was practically non-existent, most of the horses still being on the other side of the Tennessee River. Furthermore safe harbor for Bragg's Rebels at Ringgold Gap—a steep, narrow passage barely wide enough to accommodate a small stream, the line of the Western & Atlantic R.R., and a wagon road[42]—was a relatively short distance away quickly reached even as soon as the Federals began their movement.

But as much as anything Cleburne continued to be outstanding as commander of the Rebel rear guard, establishing a blocking position at Ringgold Gap.[43] It was barely a half hour after Cleburne's troops took their positions before Hooker's Federals came in pursuit and began an assault.[44] Even with a two-to-one numerical advantage, Hooker was unable to breach Cleburne's defenses thus enabling Cleburne to save the Southerners' trains and artillery vehicles.

As Steven E. Woodworth observes:

> The next two days operations are almost a case study in why Civil War armies were all but indestructible (unless trapped) and why decisively successful pursuits were such a rarity. Grant was a dangerous man to whom to lose a battle. No general in the entire conflict was to show himself more ruthless and skillful in pursuing a beaten foe. Yet in this case even his leadership was insufficient to overcome the enormous odds in favor of the loser's escape.[45]

But as much as anything Hooker's assault against Cleburne's rear guard proved the uselessness of pursuit attempts that did not, or could not, deploy a force against the retreating army's flank, or even better yet its forward units.

Grant ceased any further attempt at pursuit, turning his attention to complying with Washington's orders to save Burnside at Knoxville. Accordingly Grant ordered Granger to go to Knoxville to relieve Burnside but Granger decided he should not be sent to Knoxville and thus shortly returned to Chattanooga. Disgusted with Granger's attitude, Grant then sent Sherman to Knoxville; upon arriving at Knoxville after a six-day hard march Sherman discovered Longstreet had given up on his attempt to siege Knoxville and had moved on, and that Burnside was comfortable with reduced but sufficient supplies.

## *Dénouements and Precursors*

In his after action report Grant failed to mention Hooker's accomplishments. Additionally during the evening of the 25th Sherman and Grant sent each other messages implying that Sherman's attacks at Tunnel Hill were responsible for the success of Thomas' attack. In their respective memoirs, published after Thomas was dead, Sherman and Grant further embellished the truth by suggesting that, against the weight of several contemporaneous accounts, Sherman's attacks were mere feints to support Thomas's assault toward and on the slopes of Missionary Ridge.

Grant was not one normally to gloat or to use braggadocio. Nevertheless he did say that, "Never before was a general so badly defeated as was Bragg." The withdrawal from Chattanooga nullified all the gains and sacrifices of Chickamauga but more significantly gave the Yankees control of the Gateway to the South and a position from which to launch a strategic thrust into the Deep South. The Confederacy's devastating loss of Chattanooga, and coupled with Lee's retreat from Gettysburg as well as the surrender of Vicksburg, both less than five months earlier, greatly shrunk the diminishing chances of military victory or even the fading chances of a favorable settlement of the seceding states' differences with the Federal government. Chattanooga was indeed a turning point in the war in the Western Theater.

At the end of November 1863, Braxton Bragg submitted his after action report wherein he naturally blamed everyone but himself. Shortly after Christmas Joe Johnston arrived to take Bragg's place.[46] Bragg then went to Richmond where he was given a presumably makework position as Davis' chief of staff; surprisingly Bragg's performance exceeded expectations as he brought needed improvements in several areas such as logistical support. Eventually Davis assigned Bragg back to the field to oversee the defenses of Fort Fisher guarding Wilmington, North Carolina, the last remaining Confederate port. Bragg returned to Richmond and was part of the CSA government as it desperately fled to Georgia in April 1865. Bragg suddenly died after collapsing in a street in Galveston, Texas, in 1878. Inexplicably, Fort Bragg in North Carolina, one of the U.S. Army's largest bases, is named in honor of him, one of the least successful, most despised Confederate generals.

Longstreet's reputation took a severe blow as a result of being detached from Lee. Davis was not happy with Longstreet's quarrels with Bragg especially since Bragg seemed to have legitimate grounds to criticize many of Longstreet's decisions. Furthermore Longstreet's failure to accomplish anything at Knoxville revealed further limits of Longstreet's abilities when acting independently. The famed diarist Mary Chestnut wrote, "Detached from Lee, what a horrible failure. What a slow old humbug is Longstreet." Longstreet then moved along to establish winter quarters before rejoining Lee the following May 6, 1864, during the second day of the Battle of the Wilderness where Old Pete was seriously wounded.

After returning to Nashville Sherman was ordered from Vicksburg to Meridian, Mississippi, a major Confederate arsenal and logistical center. Sherman deployed two columns: one comprised of divisions from the 16th Corps and the other comprised from the 17th Corps. After encountering only token resistance from Polk's units, Sherman's two columns arrived at that rail center on February 14, 1864. In towns along the way various buildings had the habit of catching fire but while in Meridian Sherman's troops systemically burned or otherwise destroyed a wide range of public and private buildings and military storehouses as well as miles of railroad tracks and dozens of trestles. As Sherman was withdrawing from Meridian his army was followed by a large number of freed slaves but also by Unionists wanting to escape from the domination of the Confederacy. The immediate strategic effect of the Meridian raid made it more difficult to concentrate Confederate troops in the region. But Meridian was also important because it became a precursor to Sherman's total war strategy later in the war.

Granger's recalcitrance and grousing put him on thin ice with Sherman and Grant, especially in the wake of his aborted mission to Knoxville. Sometime around Christmas of 1863 he was entertaining Grant and Sherman in the home of his mother-in-law in Nashville when she harshly denounced Sherman for his foraging. Granger then beat Sherman to the punch by asking for a leave of absence, which was granted. Thereafter Granger's star quickly fell as he bounced around in various posts, having reached the pinnacle of his career at Chickamauga.

After being relieved of command, Rosecrans "awaited orders" until January 30, 1864, when he was assigned command of the Department of Missouri.

One of the junior officers who led the charge up Missionary Ridge was Arthur MacArthur who was awarded the Medal of Honor for his exploits. Eventually Arthur MacArthur would command troops in the Philippines and became the father of Douglas MacArthur, one of the leading Army generals in the 20th century.

About a month after the battle of Chattanooga Thomas appropriated a 75-acre tract upon which to create a cemetery for fallen soldiers. As the graves were being dug the chaplain supervising the grim task asked Thomas if graves should be separated by state. "No, no," replied Thomas, "Mix them up. I am tired of states' rights."[47] Today the cemetery holds more than 13,000 graves of military dead from all states, casualties of several wars.

# 7

# Sherman's Atlanta Campaign
## 1864

After the Federals had broken the Confederate siege of Chattanooga and had driven the Rebels back to Dalton, Georgia, the respective armies settled into months of restructuring and replenishment. But as important as Chattanooga was as a strategic objective, it was after all a gateway to even more valuable objectives, the first of which would be Atlanta, Georgia. In many respects Chattanooga and Atlanta possessed similar strategic attributes, especially as railroad junctions. Atlanta was a larger and even more important resource to the Confederate logistic effort than had been Chattanooga. Furthermore, while Tennessee's secessionist attitudes were relatively lukewarm with Unionists pockets in some eastern regions, Georgia, one of the original seven states to secede, was still a Confederacy bedrock. Some would argue that while Richmond may have been the capital of the Confederacy, Atlanta was *the* symbol of the South. Ergo both sides realized capture of Atlanta inevitably would be the next strategic conquest.

During the winter of 1863–64 George Thomas' Army of the Cumberland, along with Hooker's *ad hoc* task force of two corps, remained in Chattanooga while Sherman attended to business in Nashville, taking time for his Meridian raid.[1] In the meanwhile Ambrose Burnside returned to 9th Corps, assigned to support, but not be a part of, the Army of the Potomac in Virginia.[2] MGen. John M. Schofield, 33, replaced Burnside as commander of the Army of the Ohio, which for the time being remained in Knoxville.

After graduating from West Point, class of 1853, Schofield remained in the Regular Army until 1860 when he was granted leave of absence to teach physics at Washington University in St Louis, Missouri. Shortly after Fort Sumter Schofield returned to active duty, seeing action August 2–3, 1861, at Dug Spring near Clever, Missouri, and August 10, 1861, at Wilson's Creek for which he was eventually awarded the Medal of Honor. He had honed the fine art of military politics enabling him to maintain good working relationships with a wide variety of commanders. Schofield advanced through the ranks of Union officers, having held brigade, division and department commands throughout the Western theater during which he developed friendships with and gained the trust of Halleck and Grant as well as the influential Blair family.

Schofield was not one of the flashier, egotistical, glory seeking Union generals. Instead his primary characteristics included steady, thoughtful determination, competency, reliability, and attention to detail. He was not known as a fighting general nor was he known as a brilliant strategist prone to take great risks. Instead Schofield tended be an administrator who was methodical and thorough as he approached assignments, the longest of which had been as commander of the Department of Missouri from May 24, 1863, until January 30, 1864.

Essentially Schofield's Army of the Ohio was little more than the 23rd Corps consisting of three infantry divisions[3] plus one cavalry division commanded ironically by MGen. George Stoneman, formerly with the Army of the Potomac and former head of the Cavalry bureau in Washington.[4]

By March 1864, Sam Grant—his reputation and standing enhanced by his success at Chattanooga—was promoted to Lieutenant General and appointed as Federal General in Chief, displacing Halleck, who then became Chief of Staff, a newly created position. Presumably upon Grant's recommendation, Sherman was appointed to replace Grant as commander of the Western armies. Sherman urged Grant to maintain his headquarters in the Western theater but Grant, recognizing the political realities of the Civil War, decided to establish his headquarters with the Army of the Potomac in the East, relatively close to Washington, D.C.

In addition to the Army of the Ohio, Sherman's Military Division of the Mississippi, which he called his Grand Army,[5] incorporated two of the Union's major armies that were veterans of the fighting in the Western theater. Sherman's former command, the Army of the Tennessee, could trace its roots to the earliest days of the conflict with early triumphs in Tennessee at Fort Henry, February 6, 1862, Fort Donelson, February 12–16, 1862, and Shiloh, April 6 and 7, 1862, all under Grant's command.

After Sherman was promoted to command of the Military Division of the Mississippi (Grant's former position before becoming the Union General in Chief) Sherman named MGen. James B. McPherson, 36, as the new commander of the Army of the Tennessee. McPherson graduated first in his class of 1853 at West Point for which he was given choice engineering assignments.[6] For instance among his other assignments, McPherson had been named superintending engineer to complete the defenses at Alcatraz Island. Once the war began, he eventually became Halleck's assistant chief engineer.

McPherson had a long relationship with the Army of the Tennessee, going back as far as January 1862, when Henry Halleck dispatched McPherson to serve as Sam Grant's chief engineer prior to the attacks on Fort Henry and Fort Donelson. Although never officially recognized as such it was widely suspected, even probable, that Halleck had sent McPherson to learn whether Grant was still drinking on duty.

Although it is likely Grant was aware of McPherson's *sub rosa* mission, Grant quickly became impressed with his new staff officer who demonstrated initiative beyond his formal assignments without stepping on any toes. McPherson, who began viewing Grant as his mentor, served with Grant in subsequent battles, including Shiloh. At the same time McPherson was also renewing and continuing his antebellum friendship with Sherman whose temperament was opposite in several ways to McPherson's.

McPherson's conversion from a staff officer to field command began in earnest in October 1862 when Grant assigned McPherson—then a brigadier—to lead an ad hoc unit of four divisions to reinforce the pursuit that Grant had anticipated would ensue after Corinth II. We should recall that McPherson's unit moved quickly from Jackson, Tennessee, to Corinth just as the fighting was ending during the afternoon of October 4. McPherson continued to chase the retreating Rebels for 52 miles before Grant decided to terminate further efforts and ordered McPherson back to Corinth.

Thereafter McPherson was rapidly promoted and given various division commands while Grant commended the Army of the Tennessee. McPherson's star shone brightly during Grant's Vicksburg campaign, including Champion Hill as well as the ensuing siege operations. Grant wrote that McPherson was "…one of our ablest Engineers and most skillful Generals." Even Sherman chimed in that McPherson "is as good an officer as I am and is younger, and has a better temper." Following the surrender of Vicksburg on July 4, 1863, McPherson served as the military administrator of the Vicksburg district.

As McPherson was embarking upon a trip during the spring of 1864 to Baltimore to marry his long time fiancé—the daughter of secessionist sympathizers—he was ordered to report to Cairo, Illinois, where Sherman gave him a new assignment, this being to command the Army of the Tennessee.[7] Although McPherson had consistently excelled in several assignments his lack of command experience beyond the division level would cause some to wonder if his rapid advancement bypassing two levels to army command with its three corps was done in large part due to his friendship with Grant and Sherman.

Of the three armies in Sherman's Grand Army, McPherson's would be the only one without its own cavalry division. In addition to the cavalry division attached to Schofield, there were three cavalry divisions nominally attached to Thomas' army. However, Sherman retained actual control over cavalry, "an arm with which he has had little experience or for which he has less understanding or sympathy."[8]

The Army of the Cumberland was the other major Union army of the Western theater. This army's proud linage went back to the first year of the war.[9] In the spring of 1864, the Army of Cumberland included three infantry corps plus a cavalry division, and was the largest of the three armies in Sherman's Grand Army.

The Confederates' Army of Tennessee was also undergoing command changes in wake of Braxton Bragg's reassignment as Confederate General in Chief, the formal designation as Jefferson Davis' military advisor. After the disastrous Confederate defeat at Chattanooga Davis really had no choice but to reluctantly replace Bragg with Joseph E. Johnston, one of the Confederacy's most senior generals. Davis and Johnston had not been on the best of terms, in large part because Johnston initially complained so persistently and bitterly about not being assigned sufficient seniority among the C.S.A. generals.[10]

But in the winter of 1863–64 their differences had intensified. Davis, along with much of the Richmond political establishment, envisioned an aggressive, and bold, military operation intended to recapture Tennessee and even possibly to wrest Kentucky from Union control.[11] At best such aspirations were naïve and unrealistic given the overwhelming Federal advantages in materiel and manpower. In the simplest of terms, Johnston considered the Davis concept as being high cost and high risk but with minimal chances of success.[12]

Johnston was a military planner who realized, even to the point of obsessing, he would be outmanned, perhaps by as much as two to one. While probably more realistic than were his superiors in Richmond, Johnston still leaned toward the extremely cautious, tending to overestimate the numerical and logistical disparities between the opposing armies.

Another aggravating factor was Johnston's vanity and sensitivity about his reputation and legacy that compelled him continually to pester the authorities for additional resources, especially manpower that Johnston knew, or should have known, were in short supply throughout the entire Confederacy. As a career officer, Johnston had pursued the bureaucratic art of shifting blame toward everyone else for any failure, either past or potential, by either demonstrating that he did not have enough troops, horses, equipment, rations, or alternatively that he was being compelled to follow a strategic policy with which he did not agree nor possibly could execute.

Nevertheless, despite these characteristics Johnston was a sound defensive tactician. First and foremost Johnston was almost always willing to trade territory in order to pursue his objective to preserve and maintain his army's strength and capacities. Johnston was one of the few, if not the only, members of the Confederacy's military hierarchy who realized and appreciated the hopeless folly of engaging in the Union's strategy of using attrition to win the war. In contrast, by 1862 Davis' basic war philosophy was to fight to preserve every parcel of secessionist territory. But Johnston had a long history, going back to his slow, steady retreat in the face of George McClellan's Peninsula Campaign in 1862, of relinquishing territory without necessarily offering much resistance. Johnston's usual rationale was that he was seeking the most advantageous opportunity to strike against an advancing enemy.

Five months after Fair Oaks when he was severely wounded to be replaced by R.E. Lee, Johnston was given command of the Division of the West, which ostensibly included Bragg's army in Tennessee as well as Pemberton's in Mississippi.[13] Although taking Bragg's place as commander of the Army of Tennessee was technically a step down from his department command, the new assignment was a field command, which Johnston cherished.

Another change occurred at the corps level in late February 1864 when John Bell Hood arrived to take command of John Breckinridge's old corps.[14] Hood was one of the most storied warriors in the Confederacy. He was once described as a "Gigantic old Saxon chiefton come to life."[15] Early in the war he had led a famed Texas brigade that won laurels while sustaining heavy casualties during the Seven Days, Second Bull Run, and Antietam.[16] Early in the morning of the Second Day of Gettysburg Hood tried to urge his immediate superior, James Longstreet, to loop around the southern edge of the Federal defenses but Longstreet, apparently miffed because Lee had already rejected a similar proposal from Longstreet simply said, "Lee has already spoken." Shortly after the attack began Hood was shot in his left arm and had to be carried from the field.

Hood was again seriously wounded in his right leg as he began to lead the breakthrough at Chickamauga. As described earlier in Chapter 5, his right leg was amputated four inches below his hip. Nevertheless, Hood recuperated and after being promoted to lieutenant general—backdated to the date of his wounding at Chickamauga—was able to return as one of Johnston's corps commanders.[17]

Shortly after becoming General in Chief of all Federal armies, Grant, with Lincoln's concurrence if not encouragement, formulated an overall strategy intended to bring the maximum amount of pressure upon all the Confederacy's forces. Previously Federal campaigns had been conducted in isolation from other sectors which enabled Rebel commanders to shift and to consolidate their available forces against individual Federal campaigns. If instead several Federal campaigns were launched concurrently the Confederates would not only be outnumbered but also would not be able to shift troops from one sector to another.

The lynchpin of Grant's strategy was to order the Army of the Potomac to attack and eliminate Robert E. Lee's Army of Northern Virginia.[18] Moreover Grant wanted Sherman first to destroy the Confederate Army of Tennessee before moving to the heart of the rebellion where Sherman would then have several options, including the possibility of moving north to join with Meade against Lee, if need be. Toward that end, on April 12, 1864, Grant sent a letter to Sherman instructing that Sherman "move against Johnston's army, to break it up, and get into the interior of the enemy's country as far as you can...."[19]

Grant's plans also ordered a new army, the Army of the James, under the command of MGen. Benjamin ("The Beast") Butler, to proceed up the James River before advancing north toward Richmond. The fourth prong would try to advance up (southward) the Shenandoah Valley to capture the rail lines at Staunton, Virginia, before moving on to the rail hub at Lynchburg, Virginia. MGen. Franz Sigel was appointed to command the Shenandoah Valley campaign. Both Butler and Sigel were political generals appointed at the insistence of Abraham Lincoln as was an earlier appointment of MGen. Nathaniel P. Banks who had been ordered to commence the Red River campaign during the winter and spring of 1864.[20]

In Richmond Braxton Bragg realized Sherman was assembling a large army to attack Johnston; accordingly Bragg ordered Leonidas Polk—whom Bragg once tried to court martial after Chickamauga—to begin moving his forces from Mississippi toward an unspecified juncture with Johnston in Georgia.

By May 4, 1864, Sherman's Grand Army had seven corps comprising three armies including Thomas' Army of the Cumberland, McPherson's Army of the Tennessee, and Schofield's Army of the Ohio. Cump's Grand Army had a combined strength of 110,000 effectives with 354 guns. Thomas's large army would be in charge of repairing/rebuilding the rail tracks that presumably the Rebels would destroy as they retreated.[21] Old Pap also would supply most of the intelligence for the campaign.[22] Sherman wrote, "General Thomas' army ... was provided, and contained the best corps of engineers, railroad managers, and repair parties, as well as the best body of spies and provost-marshals. On him we were therefore compelled in a great measure to rely for these most useful branches for service."[23] A third cavalry division was also added to the Army of the Cumberland with the division of 28-year-old Judson Kilpatrick. Even though Kilpatrick was another reject from the Army of the Potomac, Sherman gladly embraced Kilcavalry's aggressiveness.

Several command changes were made at the corps level. Hooker's two former corps were consolidated into one new corps, the 20th, with Hooker remaining at the head, and made a part of Thomas' Army of the Cumberland.[24] Sometimes rank structure among the major generals in the Union army created awkward situations. In contrast to the C.S.A. army that had four ranks of generals, until the rank of lieutenant general was revived for Grant, the Union army had only two ranks for its general officers: brigadier and major general. Seniority among these ranks was usually determined from date of promotion but several other considerations might be applied. These issues of seniority, particularly Hooker's, contributed to the imbalance of size among the three Union armies. Hooker was senior to all other major generals except Sherman and Thomas and thus was not about to serve under anyone except Thomas.[25]

And so as assembled the abbreviated Union order of battle was as follows[26]:

    Union's Military Division of the Mississippi
    William T. Sherman

  Army of the Cumberland (61,000 effectives)—George H. Thomas
    4th Corps—Oliver O. Howard
    14th Corps—John McA. Palmer

20th Corps—Joseph Hooker
Cavalry—Washington Elliot
Army of the Tennessee (24,000 effectives)—James B. McPherson
15th Corps—John A. Logan
16th Corps—Grenville Dodge
Army of the Ohio (13,500 effectives)—John Schofield

In Dalton, the Confederate order of battle was as follows, Polk not yet arriving:

Confederate Army of Tennessee
Joseph E. Johnston (50,000 effectives)

Hardee's Corps—William J. Hardee
Hood's Corps—John Bell Hood
Cavalry—Joseph Wheeler

Sherman had decided to advance his three armies abreast with Thomas in the middle and either other army on each flank, usually with McPherson on the right and Schofield on the left. For two basic reasons, the march would proceed astride the Western & Atlantic R.R.: first, it was the most direct route to Atlanta, and second, and most important, the railroad facilitated the tremendous resupply requirements of an army of 98,500 men together with perhaps half that number of horses and mules. Supply bases could be established in Nashville and Chattanooga but as a practical matter only the capacity of rail transportation could fulfill the ongoing ravenous needs for food and forage, ammunition and replacement equipment as Sherman's Grand Army advanced further away from these supply bases.

Initially Sherman recognized that frontal assaults would be costly without accomplishing much; therefore Sherman intended usually to employ flanking maneuvers, hopefully to try to get to Johnston's rear without incurring a huge butchers' bill. Conversely Johnston hoped that Sherman would launch frontal attacks against fortified positions[27]; at the same time Johnston fretted that his inferior numbers could not prevent Sherman from extending beyond the defenders' flanks and thus able to envelope Johnston's lines.

## Johnston Is Turned at Dalton[28] (May 11, 1864)

Although he always realized he would be outnumbered, Johnston could have hardly asked for better defensive terrain than existed at Dalton, Georgia, the first major stop southeast of Chattanooga. The Rebel's defenses at Dalton were entrenched at Rocky Face Ridge,[29] part of a thickly wooded chain of heights rising up some seven hundred feet starting seven miles northwest of Dalton and extending southward 25 miles almost to the Oostanaula River.[30] However this chain of craggy ridges had several gaps, passes, or defiles. The northern most defile was found where the railroad from Chattanooga ran first through Tunnel Hill, the northern part of Missionary Ridge, and then curved through Buzzard Roost before entering Dalton. Snake Creek Gap, approximately twelve miles south of Buzzard Roost provided access via a road to Resaca, the next town south of Dalton along the Western & Atlantic R.R.

Even while Grant remained as commander of the Western forces, he had been agitating to do something, even if the odds were slim that anything could be accomplished. As early as February 25, 1864, he ordered Old Pap to conduct a reconnaissance in force against the Rebels in Dalton[31]; not unexpectedly, given how well Johnston's defenders were fortified in the Rocky Face Ridge, this operation produced little except that one of Thomas' cavalry regiments discovered the manmade Dug Gap, where the LaFayette-Dalton road crossed the Rocky Face Ridge five miles south of Buzzard Roost Gap, or Mill Creek Gap, was virtually unguarded.[32]

Because the fortified defenses at the Rocky Face Ridge were too strong to attack frontally, Dalton would be an ideal opportunity to use flanking maneuvers to dislodge Johnston. After finding that Dug Gap was lightly defended in February Old Pap deduced that other defiles or passes could also be lightly defended. Further reconnaissance disclosed that Snake Creek Gap—fifteen miles south of Dalton—was also lightly defended.[33] However, instead of adopting Thomas' earlier proposal wherein his army, including his sizable cavalry, would try to flank Johnston through Snake Creek Gap, Sherman opted to designate his old army—less than half the size of Thomas and without much cavalry but led by Sherman's old friend—as his flanking force.[34] After securing Snake Creek Gap, McPherson would destroy the rail tracks and ambush the Rebel left flank if it attempted to retreat. To occupy the fortified defenders Thomas was ordered to move from Ringgold while Schofield would advance south along the railroad to threaten Johnston's northern flank.

On Saturday May 7, Sherman finally began his Atlanta campaign by sending McPherson toward Snake Creek Gap south of Johnston's left flank. Thomas, via Palmer's 14th Corps, pushed the Rebels toward Buzzard Roost.[35] These frontal attacks against several locations along the Rock Face Ridge continued the next day while McPherson moved to the south.[36] Johnston was aware of the Federal army's movements but could not discern where McPherson was going, even thinking he might be headed for Rome, Georgia, west of the railroad.[37] On May 8 Johnston ordered Cleburne to take two brigades to reinforce the defenses at Dug Gap.

On May 9 the Confederates repulsed five Federal assaults from the crest of Dug Gap, which Sherman called "a terrible door of death."[38] The Confederates also held Buzzard Roost while Wheeler's Rebel cavalry also repulsed Schofield's advance from the north. Further to the south at Snake Creek Gap, McPherson routed a small Rebel force of only 4,000 men.[39] Johnston was criticized for not reacting with more vigor; perhaps this was due to his confusion about McPherson's destination. Johnston may have also been hoping that Polk would encounter McPherson at Rome. Other evidence suggests that Johnston may not have been aware of the significant vulnerability of Snake Creek Gap even though this feature appeared on maps available to his headquarters. Ironically while Thomas had thoroughly scouted the terrain, Johnston had learned very little about the terrain even though he had been in the area for several months and had claimed that he intended to make his fight at Dalton.[40] Wheeler's ineffective scouting—having lost all contact with McPherson on the 8th—also came in for criticism. But in fairness to Wheeler, many of his troopers were engaged with Schofield's lead elements to the north while Johnston had directed other troopers to the east.[41]

Breaching Snake Creek Gap almost brought McPherson's 20,000 men behind Johnston's lines. When Cump heard of the crossing by McPherson's lead column he yelled, "I've got Joe Johnston dead."[42] Although Resaca was within McPherson's reach, without sufficient cavalry to scout,[43] he mistakenly worried there was a sizable enemy before him.[44] Accordingly McPherson over cautiously retired back to the gap and dug in to await his supply train[45] even without destroying the rail line he had been assigned to disrupt.[46]

Upon learning Tuesday, May 10, that Polk was en route, and deciding to follow Thomas' advice to send a large force through Snake Creek Gap, Sherman decided to go ahead and move his entire army toward Resaca via Snake Creek Gap.[47] When he arrived at the gap Sherman was disappointed to learn his friend had not taken Resaca, commenting three days later, "Well, Mac, you have missed the opportunity of a lifetime."[48] Illustrating that confusion permeated both sides, Hood had reported that morning that Resaca was secure and that Johnston should hold onto Dalton.[49]

During the night of May 12, 1864, Johnston retreated from Dalton to Resaca. Being skeptical that Johnston would abandon his fortifications at Rocky Face Ridge, Sherman was failed to move sharply thus allowing Johnston to beat him and dig in.[50] Thus while McPherson's timidity meant Sherman failed to capture Johnston, Sherman's flanking maneuver had at least dislodged Johnston from Dalton, moving the campaign ten miles closer to Atlanta. This was reflected in Sherman's statement that, "The movement was partly, not wholly successful."

Johnston's retreat from Dalton would be the first of several such maneuvers. Both commanders knew, or should have known, that Atlanta was the ultimate objective, and Sherman, who was acquainted with Johnston's propensity for retrograde movements, should have recognized that Johnston's retreat from Dalton would not be his last. Robert E. Lee's ability to anticipate his adversary's intentions helped to make Lee one of the great commanders in America's military history. Sherman had ample resources to plan, prepare, and initiate pursuits to capture or even annihilate Johnston's army before it could reach Atlanta. Would the respective movements of the armies from Dalton to Resaca establish the pattern for the armies as they continued toward Atlanta?

## Resaca (May 13–16, 1864)

Skirmishes frequently occurred as the armies maneuvered into new positions. On the morning of May 13 Howard's 4th Corps began to give chase south along the railroad tracks after discovering the Rebel withdrawal from Dalton. Sherman had hoped the Rebels would continue retreating toward Calhoun on the way to Atlanta[51] but instead the Rebels dug in west of Resaca to establish new defenses that roughly paralleled the Western & Atlantic R.R. before hooking around north of Resaca. Johnston's left, or southernmost, flank was anchored on the Oostanaula River immediately west of Resaca.[52] Again, as he had at Dalton, Johnston hoped Sherman would try to frontally attack the Rebel fortifications.

Polk's corps of 18,000 troops also arrived at Resaca. Polk's arrival—together with a cavalry division led by BGen. William H. ("Red") Jackson, 28—gave Johnston 73,250 effectives.

Late May 14 Hood counterattacked against Hooker's 20th Corps. Although Federal reinforcements stopped the attack, Johnston was encouraged to resume Hood's attack the next day. In the meanwhile Sherman planned for a wheeling movement from the west and around the south: (1) McPherson to press the Rebels' left—this being mildly successful; (2) Schofield and Thomas to attack the Rebel right-center—this being repulsed at the cost of almost 1,400 killed and wounded; and (3) McPherson to secure a crossing and bridgehead on the south bank of the Oostanaula River.[53]

Concerning the third part of Sherman's plan, BGen. Thomas W. Sweeny, 43, the one-armed, feisty, Irish born veteran of the Mexican War, led a division across the Oostanaula at Lay's Ferry, about three miles southwest of the Union right flank.[54] But Sweeny pulled back after fearing—erroneously—he might be cut off.[55] Nevertheless Sweeny's force would still be useful to chase Johnston if he began another retreat. We might recall that Bevin Alexander observes that, "One of the most powerful tools a commander can employ is a rule of cutting off the means of an enemy's withdrawal and supply."[56] Although this objective failed at Dalton, Sherman then had a similar opportunity at Resaca. Sending Sweeny with two brigades to cross at Lay's Ferry was a move in the direction of cutting of Johnston's retreat but realistically a larger force, at least a corps augmented by cavalry, would have been necessary to accomplish interdiction of Johnston's retreat. Moreover, Sherman had been given the resources, specifically hinged pontoons, to allow a large number of troops to cross the river. Had Sherman availed himself of these hinged pontoons he could have had another opportunity to have prevented a Confederate retreat.

On May 15, again Hooker led hard fighting against entrenched positions before taking 1,200 casualties.[57] This effort was without conclusion except that Johnston learned that cavalry with Sweeny had crossed Oostanaula River.[58] Sherman ordered more frontal assaults against the Rebels' entrenched right flank—manned by one of Polk's newly arrived divisions—with predictable results of heavy casualties; on the other hand the Confederate counterattack was severely repulsed after taking almost 1,000 casualties.

Although Sweeny had difficulty advancing a second bridgehead,[59] ironically Johnston became convinced Sherman would reinforce Sweeny. Based upon this assumption Johnston cancelled all further offensive operations before ordering another retreat,[60] he and his subordinate commanders being aware, and concerned, of the Federals' supremacy in numbers. Sherman, not convinced that Johnston would withdraw from his strong position at Resaca, was again slow to react.

Johnston's army retreated from Resaca on Monday, May 16, crossing the Oostanaula on their own pontoons before burning the bridges and pontoons after they crossed. While Johnston's withdrawal in the face of the enemy was once again masterful, even if unnecessary, by the same token Sherman's inert posture practically allowed the Confederates to retreat. And so for the second consecutive time Sherman had used maneuver to coerce Johnston into retreating but also for the second time Sherman was unable to muster an effective pursuit to attempt decisive victory.[61]

As Johnston was retreating on May 17 he had the option of continuing south along the Western & Atlantic R.R. toward Atlanta or instead diverting to the west to protect the war manufacturing faculties at Rome, Georgia, fourteen miles west of Kingston. Rome happened to be the only industrial town of any significance north of the Chattahoochee River; it was where one of only 15 private companies in the entire south that produced cannon. (Rome was probably the target prior to Chickamauga when Rosecrans sent Alexander McCook to Alpine). But Rome's importance paled in comparison with Atlanta's. Accordingly Johnston essentially sacrificed Rome and continued along the Western & Atlantic R.R. toward Calhoun, five miles south of Resaca, hoping to find good defensive positions again. However, as the armies moved south the terrain was changing from heavily forested mountain ranges to the more open rolling hills of the Piedmont Range, meaning there were fewer opportunities for outstanding defensive positions.[62]

## To Cassville (May 19, 1864)

Unable to find suitable defensive terrain at Calhoun and after breaking off firefights the previous evening, the Rebels reached Adairsville, another ten miles to the south.[63] At Adairsville the railroad split in two directions with the western branch bearing toward Kingston while the main branch continued toward Cassville.[64] Sherman decided to split his army along a broad front with Thomas heading toward Kingston while Schofield continued toward Cassville. In the meantime McPherson advanced along the road that was even further west from Old Pap's path. Also recognizing an opportunity to destroy a valuable Confederate asset, Sherman sent a division augmented with cavalry to wreck Rome. Dividing these units in this manner spread the Yanks over more than a ten-mile front.

Without a sufficient number of defenders in Rome the Southerners could do little except to try to keep their factories and the machines from falling into Federal hands. By May 16 the last of the Rebels hauled away machinery and burned many of the buildings before escaping Rome. Nevertheless the subsequent easy capture of Rome exposed the weakness of the Confederate military against Sherman's Grand Army, provoking a sense of panic in northern Georgia.

After stopping on May 19 near Cassville—ten miles south of Adairsville—Johnston believed the Union's extended formation exposed it to attack in detail.[65] He therefore ordered Hood to ambush Hooker's 20th Corps in the Federal center before he could be supported either by Howard's 4th Corps or by one of McPherson's.[66] Instead Hood bungled by turning from his attack to face an imagined Federal threat on his right.[67] In fact Hood had mistaken approaching cavalry—no real threat—for infantry.[68] Given Hood's aborted attack and with Yanks flanking both ends, Johnston canceled Hood's attack; during the early morning hours, the Rebels withdrew to establish another defensive line, this time southeast of Cassville.

However Johnston's new line was an easy target for Union artillery, threatening the Rebel position. Johnston was forced to retreat once again, this time to Allatoona across the Etowah River. At this point the campaign was less than thirty miles from Atlanta. Meanwhile Sherman decided to rest for three days at Kingston. Johnston would later complain that he decided to retreat only under pressure from Polk and Hood to do so.[69] Johnston's profound disappointment in not being able to capitalize upon a rare offensive opportunity against isolated Federal units at Cassville was militated by the news that Lee's army was inflicting heavy casualties upon Meade's army, first in The Wilderness and more recently at Spotsylvania Court House.

## To Dallas (New Hope Church) and Back to the R.R. (May 25 and 27, 1864)

If Sherman were to continue along the Western & Atlantic railroad his army would have to go through Confederate defenses at the Allatoona Pass, a defile in a ridge line that may have been as formidable as had been Rocky Face Ridge. Accordingly, rather than to try to attack this pass from the front, Sherman decided to try to maneuver around Johnston's left by going to Dallas,[70] 13 miles southwest of Allatoona. At this point Sherman had 80,000 effectives at his command. Not only had battlefield related attrition reduced his number of available effectives but the necessity of leaving units behind to guard his supply lines also reduced the number of his available effectives.

Unfortunately for Sherman's grand army, a series of tactical blunders led to nothing except more casualties and to inter-army bickering and a widening breach between Sherman and the Cumberlander's high command. The first miscue occurred in the New Hope - Dallas area where Johnston had also marched his army to parry Sherman's turning movement. Cump failed to heed clear signs of Confederate strength but ordered a series of futile attacks against Hood's entire corps, resulting in Yankee losses four times those of the Rebels. And even though he had grossly misjudged the extent of Hood's defenders, Sherman will later blame the "slowness" of the Army of the Cumberland for the failure of the attack at New Hope Church, inexplicably characterizing this situation as a "splendid opportunity."

By this time Atlanta residents started to become concerned the first time they could hear the muffled sounds of artillery gunfire. Atlanta newspapers began publicly discussing and debating the degree of any threat to their city, and whether citizens should consider leaving.

Two days after New Hope the Yankees again took heavy losses as Sherman deployed Howard's 4th Corps to try in vain to turn the Rebel right after Cump had ordered a heavy morning bombardment.[71] At the last minute Cleburne's division was redeployed to Pickett's Mill, a mile and half northeast of New Hope, to protect the exposed Confederate right.[72] Even without being able to entrench, Cleburne inflicted withering fire upon the Federals' exposed flanks.[73] Reflecting the hopeless futility of the attack, at one point Howard reported back: "I ... am now turning the enemy's right flank, I think."[74] Ambrose Bierce—who was among those in the attack but would later eventually become an insightful writer about the war—will later call the order a "crime."[75] Woods' division alone lost 1,400 men.

During these two days of difficult fighting the Army of the Cumberland suffered 3,000 casualties, leaving three divisions weakened. This series of tactical blunders by Sherman led to inter-army bickering and a widening breach between Sherman and the Cumberlander's high command. Sherman was evasive when reporting these battles to Halleck, incredibly describing them merely as "many sharp encounters, but nothing decisive."[76]

Sherman then realized his large turning movement to circumvent Allatoona Pass had failed. Accordingly he decided to start working his way back to the Western & Atlantic rail line. Reinforcements other than Polk's troops other kept arriving so that by late May 1864 Johnston's army had 70,000–74,000 effectives, making it the largest Confederate army, Lee's included, ever assembled to that point.[77]

## *The Mountain Lines* (June 6–27, 1864)

At this point in the bigger picture Grant's grand strategy was encountering several difficulties. Grant, while "accompanying" Meade, had suffered terrific casualties in his Overland Campaign before eventually withdrawing from North Anna to continue sidling toward

Cold Harbor. South of Richmond Butler was "bottled up" between the James and Appomattox Rivers after being driven back from Richmond. Sigel had failed miserably in the Shenandoah Valley although to be sure BGen. George Crook destroyed rail lines and army supply cashes west of the Alleghenies.

Once Sherman's armies were back on the railroad, the Federals started to draw a closer bead upon Atlanta. Marietta, seventeen straight-line miles from Atlanta, and Smyrna, three miles closer, were the only two towns remaining between the combatants and Atlanta. But there were also two natural barriers, the first being a series of mountains dominated by Kennesaw Mountain, a two-mile ridge with three peaks slanting southwest to the northeast. Smaller mountain ranges two miles in front of the Kennesaw included Lost Mountain and Pine Mountain to the west and Brush Mountain and Blackjack Mountain to the east.[78] (The Chattahoochee River, approximately seven and half miles from Atlanta's outskirts, was the second-to-last natural barrier before Atlanta could be reached.) The rail line ran through a pass in front of Kennesaw Mountain and behind Brush Mountain. Thus as long as Johnston could hold these mountains he would not only enjoy a commanding view of all approaches but he would also control the supply routes to the Chattahoochee River and beyond. It was no wonder the Sherman reported to Washington: "The whole countryside is one vast fort, and Johnston must have fifty miles of connected trenches with abitis and finished batteries.... Our lines are now in close contact and the fighting incessant, with a good deal of artillery. As fast as we gain one position the enemy has another all ready.... Kennesaw ... is the key to the whole country."

By June 6 the usual alignment of Sherman's grand army was inverted with McPherson on the left, Thomas still in the middle, and Schofield on the right where McPherson would normally be aligned. Meanwhile Johnston was positioning his entrenchments to start at Gilgel, nestled along the northern edge of Lost Mountain, and to continue northward across the Western & Atlantic north of the Kennesaw for a total length of approximately six miles.

By June 10 Sherman began to receive reinforcements, most significantly 10,500 soldiers in the 17th Corps commanded by MGen. Francis P. Blair, Jr., 43, another political general, being the brother of Montgomery Blair, Lincoln's Postmaster General.[79]

On Tuesday, June 14, 1864, during a conference of Johnston's staff meeting at the summit of Pine Mountain, a shot fired from a Parrott gun killed Leonidas Polk[80]—Jefferson Davis' friend and the highest ranking general aside from Johnston in the Army of Tennessee. To this day it is not clear whether the shell was randomly or deliberately aimed. One credible account reported that Sherman had ordered a retaliatory shelling after the Confederates had fired shells at Sherman's direction. Regardless, Polk "died a gentleman and high Church dignitary. As a soldier he was more theoretical than practical."

Although Sherman ordered earlier that there be no attacks against entrenched defenses, by Wednesday, June 15 he had again become impatient to do something. Thus, the next day Sherman's three armies resumed their advance and closed in near Marietta. Prior to this campaign Sherman's forte had been rapid movement, especially against light or minimal resistance. He often became impatient or frustrated by Old Pap's deliberate, methodical style of advancing, even when such advances were opposed by fortified positions. In his private letters to Grant, Sherman also took some pains to explain why the pace to Atlanta was not going as rapidly as they had anticipated. Typical of several Civil War commanders Sherman assured his superiors that any shortcomings were the fault of his subordinates, while of course holding himself blameless.[81] Cump's impatience continued, criticizing the Army of the Cumberland: "A fresh furrow in a plowed field will stop the whole column and all will begin to entrench."[82] Sherman falsely blamed Thomas' slowness for the failure to take Dallas at New Hope Church on May 25 and the First Kennesaw Line at Gilgel Church on June 9. But notwithstanding his earlier report to Washington, Sherman seemed to overlook the efficiency and effectiveness of the variety of fortifications constructed by the Confederate engineers. Breastworks (trenches reinforced with logs) were the basic type of fieldworks but the engineers also erected palisades (bulwarks made of wooden stakes driven into the ground), chevaux-de-frise (sharpened poles inserted into holes of larger logs), and abatis (sharpened tops of felled trees).[83] Notwithstanding Sherman's complaints, in order to avoid another envelopment, Johnston ordered his left to pull back from Thomas' front to another mile into Kennesaw Mountain proper.

On Wednesday, June 22, 1864, the Southerners withdrew to their third Kennesaw Line with their right flank at the railroad. From there the line traversed Kennesaw Mountain before bending backwards to form a semi-circular arc. Near Marietta, at the Federals' right flank, Schofield and Hooker reached Widow Kolb's house near the Zion Church, their objective for the day, and began to dig in.[84] Without any reconnaissance, or without informing Johnston, Hood made an unsuccessful attack at Widow Kolb's farm. Hood thought he could strike the Federal's flank but instead it turned into another fruitless frontal assault, the Rebel suffering casualties at a ratio of five to one.[85] One critical commentator saw this attack as "a rehearsal for Atlanta's doom." Hood, who had become very critical of Johnston's passivity, had initiated three unsuccessful and costly flanking attacks: Cassville (May 19); New Hope Church (May 20); and Kolb's Farm (June 22).

After his corps had repulsed Hood at Kolb's Farm the previous day, Hooker's report exaggerated the size of Hood's force; this morning Sherman appeared and severely "dresses down" the former commander of the Army of the Potomac in front of his staff and other subordinates, unfortunately reflecting the intense rancor between Sherman and Hooker.[86] Although Hooker's command was reliable and exceptional in its performance since arriving in the West—indeed his corps was deployed most often as Sherman's lead assaulting unit— Hooker's aggressiveness and arrogance irritated Sherman who distrusted Hooker's motivations and ambitions. On the other hand Hooker was upset by the wide spread and common perception that Sherman unjustifiably favored McPherson and Sherman's former Army of the Tennessee.

After a series of relatively small engagements compelling Johnston to withdraw to other fortified defenses, Sherman was getting tired of his flanking strategy, snapping at one subordinate, "I suppose the enemy, with his smaller force, intends to surround us."[87] Additionally Cump believed, or at least he so stated, that some of his troops wanted a real fight as opposed to continuous marching. (There was also a suggestion that Sherman was envious of the press attention being given to Grant' head-on assaults.[88]) Furthermore Sherman had stretched his own lines from his Big Shanty supply base as he believed to be prudent. Additionally Schofield was so far to the right—eight miles south to the rail line—that his supply lines were exposed to Rebel artillery from the mountain. Probably most important, Sherman—who was always conscientious of logistics—was fearful that trying to circumvent the Kennesaw Mountain would move his army too far from his lifeline, the Western & Atlantic R.R.

And so Sherman ordered a general assault to begin in three days on Tuesday, June 27, 1864. Essentially each corps would charge forward with the Army of the Tennessee to strike the Pigeon Hill summit at the southeastern edge of the Kennesaw Mountain on the left[89] with Schofield on the right while Thomas' Cumberlanders would make the main effort by an assault in the middle.[90] Although Sherman had ordered the strictest secrecy of these plans[91] after receiving these orders Thomas met with Palmer and Howard who encouraged Thomas to communicate their protests with Sherman.[92] Palmer sent a defiant letter to Sherman. One regimental officer said, "…The stupidity of this order is enough to paralyze me." Thomas also made a personal reconnaissance to look for a point of weakness in the Confederates' defense but could not find "…the slightest prospect of success."[93]

Nevertheless on June 27 Sherman ordered three bloody and predictably unsuccessful assaults at Kennesaw Mountain. The attacks had to advance up steep, rocky and thickly forested slopes protected by state of the art earthworks. The formation in McPherson's army was described as "a swarm of desperate men clambering up between boulders and over tree trunks."[94] Nonetheless McPherson briefly captured and held the crest of Little Kennesaw—the middle peak—before a Confederate counterattack recaptured that ground. Following a lengthy cannonade two of Thomas' divisions were launched at the center of the Rebel lines; instead of the usual assault formation of two lines deep Sherman had ordered a concentration of five brigades across a mere thousand-yard front.[95] Unfortunately as they marched across open fields the Cumberlanders were little more than easy targets for Cleburne's well entrenched infantry. The fighting was savage, some shooting was point-blank with hand-to-hand combat using bayonets and rifle butts. Extreme heat, rain, rough terrain, and dense undergrowth doomed the uphill assaults before the Yank attack collapsed 2½ hours after it began,[96] with a casualty ratio in excess of five to one. Logan's corps, which had spearheaded McPherson's attack, lost approximately 11 percent of its numbers, including seven regimental commanders while Thomas lost 2,000 of his numbers.[97]

During these attacks at Kennesaw Mountain the Yankees lost several other senior officers, including BGen. Daniel McCook, 30, brother of Alexander McCook and Sherman's former law partner when they practiced in Leavenworth. Thomas wrote to Sherman, "One or two more such assaults would use up this army."[98] MGen. John Newton, 41, veteran of numerous battles and one of the division commanders in the 4th Corps that suffered greatly, "Well, this is a damned appropriate culmination of one month's blundering."[99] Sherman refused to accept any blame for the disastrous decision, claiming later that he "had to do it" to show Johnston that he could not count on the Federals to sidestep forever.[100] At this stage of the Civil War almost all commanders understood that ratio of at least 3 to 1 was necessary to have any reasonable chance to prevail against fortified defenses but remarkably there were only 16,225 Federals engaged against 17,733 engaged Confederates. Inexplicably but typically for Sherman he blamed "lack of vigor" for the failure of the assaults.[101]

The only Federal success came on Sherman's extreme right where Schofield's "diversion" was able to establish a bridgehead across Olley's Creek. After gaining his bridgehead, Schofield discovered a ridge that dominated Johnston's left flank.[102] To exploit this discovery Cump planned for McPherson to start moving around the Rebel left but McPherson said he needed several days to fill his wagons with supplies.[103] Although Sherman was always anxious for Thomas to quickly attack, Sherman allowed his friend the time he said he needed.

Finally realizing the futility of more frontal assaults, on July 2, 1864, Sherman resumed deploying McPherson to try to flank the Rebel left. But Johnston realized Schofield's diversion had exposed the Rebels' left flank. And so on July 1 Johnston retreated one more time, leaving the Kennesaw to pull back south of Marietta to Smyrna[104]—less than twelve miles from Atlanta.

## *At the Chattahoochee River* (July 9–16, 1864)

On Monday, July 4, 1864, as Sherman was about to once again turn Johnston's left flank at Smyrna, Johnston retreated to his pre-prepared lines along the west bank of the Chattahoochee River northwest of Atlanta. Sherman later called this latest line—complete with redoubts—"one of the strongest pieces of field fortifications I ever saw."[105] But by getting so close, Sherman and his staff were able to see Atlanta—about nine miles to the southeast—from a hill at Vining's Station.[106]

By July 8 Schofield and McPherson had once again exchanged flanking positions. As effective as Johnston's fortifications were in repulsing frontal assaults aimed directly at the breastworks, etc., they could extend only so far. On the other hand with their superior numbers the Yankees could almost always extend their brigades well beyond the length of Johnston's fortifications. And so it was approximately six miles north of Johnston's lines where Schofield was able to start crossing the Chattahoochee and to establish bridgeheads after surprising and overtaking a small cavalry unit.[107]

Once Johnston's defensive line was breached numerous other crossings made it seem almost like the proverbial leak in an earthen dam endangering the entire dam. This time Schofield's bridgehead exposed Johnston's right flank and threatened Johnston's rear, particularly the Western & Atlantic R.R., Johnston's own line of communications with Atlanta. Thus much to the dismay of the Confederate engineer who had prepared these lines that Sherman would admire as "the strongest pieces of fortifications," on July 9 Johnston retreated across the Chattahoochee to the outskirts of Atlanta.[108] Johnston ordered that Atlanta's military hospitals and munitions works be evacuated.[109] In the meanwhile Sherman began accumulating men and supplies for his Atlanta attack.

On Saturday, July 16, while Johnston was working on his fieldworks around Atlanta, Sherman finished crossing the Chattahoochee. McPherson immediately began to circle clockwise around to Decatur, east of Atlanta.[110]

## *Hood Replaces Johnston* (July 16, 1864)

By mid–July Southern leaders, especially Davis, in Richmond had lost almost all patience with Johnston's pattern of retreating without offering any resistance while seeming to not have any plan to defeat Sherman. As early as May 12 Davis had written to Lee to ask Lee's opinion; Lee responded with vague circumspection.[111] Finally on July 17 Davis replaced Johnston with John Bell Hood.[112] Benjamin Franklin Cheatham, 44, A Mexican War veteran but most recently a division commander in Hardee's corps, replaced Hood as corps commander.

Hood had become friendly with Jeff Davis while convalescing in Richmond following his Chickamauga wounds.[113] After returning to the field Hood regularly sent letters to Davis, and although Hood always denied it, it has always been suspected that Hood's letters were critical of Johnston's predilections to readily give ground.[114] The appointment of Hood as army commander was considered a slap in Hardee's face.[115]

Hood liked to proclaim he was a devotee of the Lee and Jackson school of flanking movements as opposed to frontal attacks.[116] It may have been fanciful to say that there was such a school, given Malvern Hill and Gettysburg. At any rate Hood certainly had a well-earned reputation for aggressive, hard hitting fighting, and the officers and men of both sides at Atlanta knew for better or for worse the Army of Tennessee would soon be adopting a new and different character in its defense of Atlanta, with any more retrograde movements highly unlikely. Hood's mission was to defend Atlanta, a mission for which he felt he was well suited by nature and by experience.

## *Peachtree Creek* (July 20, 1864)

By July 16 Sherman's Grand Army crossed the Chattahoochee in preparation for applying a chokehold on Atlanta and Hood's defenders. During the previous year the Confederacy had made extraordinary preparations to fortify Atlanta so that the city was surrounded by extensive earthworks featuring a twelve-mile trench augmented by 20 redoubts and literally thousands of rifle pits.

Realizing the impracticality of direct assaults against the Atlanta earthworks, Sherman intended to destroy all supply routes while besieging the city. To do so, Sherman planned to continue moving clockwise north and then to the east of Atlanta. McPherson—who had already started toward Decatur, a town through which the Georgia Railroad passed six miles east of Atlanta—was selected to lead the encirclement followed by Schofield. Thomas would serve as a fulcrum along the south side of the Peachtree Creek four miles north from the center of Atlanta. These movements would place Federal forces north and east of Atlanta enabling them to be in position to cut off Hood's resupply line to the east.

As Old Pap's army moved southward, Hood's defensive line was one mile north of Peachtree Creek and almost two miles in front of their fortified defensive lines. Thomas was to take high ground, entrench and provide artillery support. As an example of the difficulty to advance in a timely manner Thomas had to use his sabre on the flanks of his artillery horses to prod them through the difficult terrain covered by thick brush.

The next day McPherson moved through Decatur[117] while Thomas continued to push across Peachtree Creek. Schofield was advancing in the middle between McPherson on the left and Thomas on the right. An approximate two-mile gap between Schofield and Thomas presented Hood with an apparent opportunity to attack in detail,[118] indeed the sort of battle that Southern leaders expected Hood to fight.[119] Not wanting to waste an opportunity by waiting, Hood wanted to attack Thomas before he had a chance to "fortify himself."[120]

Attempting to exploit that apparent opportunity on July 20, Hood deployed two-thirds of his army to attack Thomas as his army was moving away from Peachtree Creek through more thick brush. As was often typical with such plans the Peachtree Creek attack started three hours late but even then not all the Rebel units were properly positioned. Furthermore since Sherman anticipated that Hood was likely to attack sooner than later, Sherman had ordered each of his three armies to start advancing toward Atlanta. Accordingly Hood's targets were not where Hood had supposed them to be.[121] In particular, McPherson was advancing (while destroying sections of the Georgia Railroad) through Decatur back toward Atlanta faster than Hood had assumed, meaning among other things he had to order further adjustments to the right. The delays caused by these adjustments allowed Thomas' Cumberlanders to dig in and to construct some rudimentary fieldworks while bringing up some artillery for support.[122] The ensuing battle of Peachtree Creek lasted at least two hours before the Rebels retired after taking severe losses. Uncharacteristically for most army commanders, Thomas was in the thick of the battle, personally positioning some of the battery sites.[123] Although Thomas' performance was comparable to his earlier exploits of Snodgrass Hill, Sherman—who was not even aware of the Rebel attack until later that evening[124]—criticized Old Pap for not advancing fast enough.[125]

Another factor was that like R.E. Lee, Hood tended once battle started to let events unfold under subordinates' command and control. As a result under fluid tactical circumstances coupled with normal "fog of war" Hood's capacity to exert battlefield management could become impaired.[126] The Rebels lost 4,800 men while Thomas lost fewer than 2,000.[127]

Meanwhile the fighting at Peachtree Creek allowed Schofield and McPherson to advance toward Atlanta from Decatur. Once McPherson was within artillery range of Atlanta Sherman ordered the start of an artillery bombardment without giving prior notice, as had been customary when preparing to shell a besieged city where civilian occupants remained.[128]

## *The Battle of Atlanta*[129] (July 24, 1864)

Attempting to apply more pressure upon the Confederates, on Thursday, July 21, 1864, Sherman ordered all three armies to further squeeze Atlanta. For his part Thomas continued to march through Peachtree's dense thickets while McPherson continued to advance cautiously from Decatur. Wheeler's cavalry, McPherson's only opposition, fiercely resisted McPherson's progress but BGen. Mortimer D. Leggett's Union division eventually drove Patrick Cleburne's division off, taking control of Bald Hill,[130] 2½ miles southeast of the center of Atlanta. This provided an excellent site for Union artillery to fire more shells from their 20-pounder Parrott rifles.[131]

Although Hood's attack at Peachtree Creek had failed at a high cost of casualties, and even though the Yankees were tightening their noose, and although Sherman's artillery was able to shell Hood's defenses, Hood was not about to cede any initiative to his enemy. And so on Friday, July 22, 1864, aspiring to emulate Jackson's flanking maneuver at Chancellorsville,[132] Hood planned to attack McPherson's flank east of Atlanta while Wheeler would destroy a Union supply train at Decatur. Hardee—leading the most powerful corps remaining in Hood's army—would try to get behind the Federal position by moving south before swinging to the east to flank McPherson's left that purportedly "was in the air."[133] Other than trying to seize the initiative Hood had several reasons for this attack, but as much as anything else, Hood needed to prevent McPherson's army from swinging back southwesterly to take control of, and destroy, the Confederates' final two rail lines to the east.[134]

However to get into launch position Hardee had to make a night march along 15 miles narrow, dusty roads. Although most of Hardee's men had not slept for two nights, Hood would later characterize them as being "fresh."[135] The march started late and typical for nighttime marches, cavalry and artillery became entangled with infantry, thereby wasting even more critical march time. One of Hardee's division commanders impatiently started his attack before Hardee was ready. As a result, instead of attacking the Federals' rear of hospital tents, supply depots, and wagon trains as intended, the Rebels found themselves attacking Grenville Dodge's well-entrenched, veteran infantry.[136]

As Sherman and McPherson were conferring at Sherman's headquarters they heard sounds of battle. McPherson immediately excused himself to observe the battle first-hand. Later as he saw that the Confederates were about to overrun one of his sectors, McPherson rode to the front to organize and manage a counterattack. Unfortunately McPherson rode into a group of Rebel skirmishers who killed him as he tried to escape,[137] becoming the only army commander killed in the war. Notwithstanding McPherson's brief experience as a combat commander both Grant and Sherman would say that had McPherson not been killed and if the war had lasted longer he would have been recognized as the greatest general of the war.[138] John A. ("Black Jack") Logan, 38—one of the Union's best political generals, a natural leader, and a soldiers' favorite[139]—immediately assumed temporary command of the Army of the Tennessee. Once command devolved to Logan he acted with alacrity, riding along the lines, encouraging the soldiers while moving units to fill holes in the lines

Once the Battle for Atlanta began several charges and countercharges ensued with face-to-face and hand-to-hand desperate struggles, characterized by the soldiers as rudimentary gang fights.[140] But the 27,000 Federal defenders still held Bald Hill even after Hood deployed all 40,000 of his available forces.[141] On the other hand the Confederates still held two rail lines to the south and to the southeast but again the butchers' bill had been costly with Hood losing at least 5,500 men while Sherman lost 3,700 men, his highest single-battle losses of the entire campaign.

Hood's Army of Tennessee, after reaching a manpower peak of 77,000 barely two months earlier in late May, was reduced to no more than 50,000 men—one fifth being cavalry—after the cumulative losses from Peachtree Creek and the Battle of Atlanta.[142] Leadership losses were especially severe with the loss of 60 majors, colonels, and generals in Hardee's corps alone. Eight of the fifteen regimental commanders in Cleburne's division were either killed or wounded.[143] But whether Hood realized it or not the Battle for Atlanta was his last reasonable chance to salvage something other than delay from the entire Atlanta campaign. Hood no longer had, if he ever had, any chance to push the Yankees back to Chattanooga. For all intents and purposes, the loss of Atlanta, with its vital industrial and commercial capacity, had become inevitable!

Hood's involvement in the battle was minimal since he was too ill to come to the field.[144] Nevertheless Hood angrily blamed Hardee for being late in attacking and for failing to extend his position far enough before attacking.[145] Sherman's performance may have even been worse. For instance at first he assumed the Confederates were withdrawing from Atlanta and issued orders for a pursuit.[146] However even when he learned of the pitched battle east of Atlanta Sherman remained in the proximity of his headquarters tent.[147]

On July 26, two days after McPherson's death, Sherman appointed Oliver O. Howard as permanent commander of the Army of the Tennessee,[148] becoming the first outsider to command this army. Howard's appointment bypassed Black Jack Logan notwithstanding his fine performance as interim commander. Although Logan was a political general, he was a first-rate commander and was convinced (with some justification) he was by-passed because he was not a West Pointer. Logan's command performances, beginning as a regimental commander through his brief but inspired stint as McPherson's replacement, had always been dependable and solid, if not stellar.[149] In contrast not only had Howard's corps been routed at Chancellorsville, and later at Gettysburg, his assaults at Resaca and New Hope Church had not been well handled.[150] But while Logan was one of Grant's favorites, Sherman's disdain for non–West Pointers was well known. Sherman's make-weight argument was that Logan was not sufficiently oriented to logistics.[151] Notwithstanding his disappointment Logan reluctantly resumed command of the 15th Corps.

Hooker—who had always blamed Howard for Chancellorsville—was incensed about Howard's promotion. In protest Hooker resigned from Sherman's Grand Army.[152] Not only had Hooker become affronted by the promotion of his former subordinate to army command but bad blood had existed between Sherman and Hooker since pre–Civil War days when Hooker welshed on a debt to Sherman; when even Howard pointed out that Hooker had seniority Sherman snapped, "Hooker has not the moral qualities that I want…." Old Pap tried to help Hooker but to no avail when Sherman himself threatened to resign.[153] MGen. Henry W. Slocum—Sherman's former West Point classmate but also one of Hooker's arch enemies[154]—was transferred from Vicksburg to replace Hooker as commander of the 20th Corps.[155] Slocum had also previously commanded the 12th Corps in the Army of the Potomac, his rise to corps command from regimental command having been one of the quickest rises of command in the Civil War. Slocum had also been senior to Meade when the latter was promoted to command the Army of the Potomac shortly before Gettysburg but Slocum graciously agreed to serve as Meade's subordinate.[156] In another corps of the Army of the Cumberland, Palmer had one too many quarrels with Sherman and asked to be relieved as commander of the 14th Corps,[157] leaving Thomas with three new corps commanders.

Abbreviated Orders of Battle (Revised):

**Union's Grand Army**
William T. Sherman
Army of the Cumberland—George H. Thomas
   4th Corps—Oliver O. Howard → David S. Stanley
   14th Corps—John M. Palmer → Jefferson C. Davis
   20th Corps—Joseph Hooker → Henry W. Slocum
   Cavalry—Washington Elliot
Army of the Tennessee—James B. McPherson → Oliver O. Howard
   15th Corps—John A. ("Black Jack") Logan
   16th Corps—Grenville Dodge
   17th Corps—Frank P. Blair
Army of the Ohio—John Schofield

**Confederate Army of Tennessee**
Joseph E. Johnston → John Bell Hood
Hardee's Corps—William J. Hardee
Hood's Corps—John Bell Hood → Benjamin Franklin Cheatham
Polk's Corps—Leonidas Polk → Alexander Peter Stewart
Cavalry—Joseph Wheeler

## Ezra Church (Tuesday, July 28, 1864)

By late July the Macon & Western R.R., heading southeasterly toward Macon, and the Montgomery Atlanta & Western R.R. (sometimes called the Atlanta & West Point R.R.), heading southwesterly toward Montgomery, were the only rail tracks still open and capable of handling train traffic. Since these two lines merged at East Point, approximately six miles south by southwest from the center of Atlanta, only one former line continued to run all the way into Atlanta. Sherman decided to send Howard's Army of the Tennessee on a wide, counterclockwise movement swinging west of Atlanta, hoping to catch Hood by surprise.[158] Thus on July 27 the Army of the Tennessee, with Howard taking command only that morning, began a counterclockwise leap-frog march hoping to catch Hood's left flank west of Atlanta by surprise.[159] However, Hood was aware of the movement and sent Steward and newly arrived LGen. Stephen D. Lee, 31[160]—replacing Cheatham who reverted to divisional command—to meet the threat.[161] Thus, only six days after the Battle of Atlanta the two Tennessee named armies would engage each other in yet another battle, this time on the other side of the city![162]

Hood planned to use Steward's and Lee's corps to hit the Army of the Tennessee in its right flank from Lickskillet Road while Hardee's corps, with militia help, held the city. Perhaps learning from Hardee's difficulties while trying to move into position on the 22nd, Hood allowed Lee and Stewart ample time to get into position. Not only did plans go awry on July 28 when Howard's corps beat everyone to the Lickskillet Road crossroad where the Rebels had intended to occupy first, but the boys in blue quickly constructed breastworks from materials stripped from the nearby Ezra Church. The newcomer Lee did not wait for Stewart to be in place or for his own troops to be ready before beginning to attack piecemeal as his divisions arrived[163] and letting his badly outnumbered soldiers get caught in enfilading cannon fire. After suffering casualties at a five to one ratio in a badly managed affair, the Rebels withdrew allowing Howard to advance to within two miles of the Macon Railroad at East Point. Hood reported "No decided advantage to either side."[164] Thomas Buell characterizes the outcome as "as waste of Confederate lives."[165]

In just ten days of Hood's command, his Army of Tennessee had been involved in three major battles, or sorties, losing 12,000–15,000 men,[166] almost as many men in those ten days as Johnston had lost in ten weeks.[167] Yet Rebel morale apparently remained high, most Johnnies still believing against all logic and common sense that somehow Hood would drive Sherman out of Georgia.

By August 6 Sherman realized Hood had been reduced to 36,000 effectives, forcing Hood to remain on the defensive. Accordingly Sherman decided to tighten his chokehold even further. To apply more pressure Sherman ordered two 32-pounder Parrott rifles forwarded by rail from Chattanooga. On the other hand, by keeping the rail line to Macon in good repair the Rebels were able to continue to run supplies and other necessities into Atlanta, thus lessening the effect of the siege. And so the siege of Atlanta, which had begun on July 20 when Union artillery began firing from Bald Hill, would continue for the foreseeable future.

## *Jonesboro* (September 1, 1864)

Unhappy with the results of his cavalry's efforts at raiding to disrupt Hood's supply routes, realizing his artillery bombardment was not bringing Atlanta to its knees, and concerned Hood was stalling for time until Bedford Forrest could arrive at the Grand Army's rear, Sherman decided he could no longer rely upon his three-week siege to break the deadlock around Atlanta. Accordingly on Thursday, August 26, 1864, he adopted a plan that had been outlined by Thomas to pull six of his seven corps out of their trenches to start a wide counterclockwise wheeling movement to their right around Atlanta to choke off rail lines to the south, specifically the Macon R.R. at Jonesboro, and the Montgomery Atlanta & Western R.R. to the southwest. Sherman called this his "movement around Atlanta by the south."[168] After Union shelling had ceased and when his pickets found Union positions had been vacated, Hood mistakenly thought the Yanks were retreating.[169] Indeed Hood's mistake compelled him to telegraph Richmond that he, Hood, had achieved a "great victory." However quick examination of extensive debris left in the abandoned Union camps belied any belief that the boys in blue were short of rations and were not being forced by starvation to retreat.[170] Not certain what Cump was trying to do, Hood moved two divisions further to his left. After reinforcing East Point,[171] Rough & Ready, and Jonesboro all along the vital rail line to Macon, Hood's outnumbered army was then stretched 25 miles from Atlanta to Jonesboro.

After leaving Slocum's 20th Corps to guard the Chattahoochee railroad bridges plus the Union supply dumps,[172] by August 27 the Federals had abandoned virtually their entire line west of the city while holding their right-most positions toward East Point as well as their bridgeheads. Since the vital rail line between Atlanta and East Point was well fortified, it made sense to swing the wheel movement south of East Point. Howard's army, minus Slocum, was the whiplash on the right, making a wide western and then southern swing along the outermost arc of the three armies. Schofield, on the left, took the shortest arc headed toward Rough & Ready, a third of the way along the Macon R.R. from East Point to Jonesboro. Thomas was in the center, essentially serving a reserve to the other corps. All six Union corps then on the march were under orders to implement Sherman's compulsion to destroy railroad tracks. Hood, then believing East Point to be the Yanks' objective, began to shift more troops in that direction.

By August 29 Cump continued to press his corps to tear up as much rail line as possible. Although extensive destruction at Fairburn and at Red Oak had already rendered the Montgomery Atlanta & Western inoperational, much time was spent destroying more track for a total of thirteen miles being destroyed between the two operations.[173] Without enough cavalry to act as Hood's eyes and ears, leaving Hood uncertain of Cump's real intent, the Federals were able to move freely almost without detection.

By Tuesday, August 30, 1864, six Union corps, led by Schofield's, left the Montgomery Atlanta & Western line and started along a six-mile front toward the Macon & Western, by then the only rail line still in operation. Two days too late, and without much of his eyes and ears, Hood finally realized the Yanks were not retreating, but instead were headed toward his vital line of communications. Hood had previously deployed Lee's corps at East Point and Hardee's corps at Rough & Ready. But not knowing exactly where the Federals might be attacking along the Macon & Western, on August 30 Hood sent Hardee—still Hood's largest corps with 24,000 men—together with S.D. Lee to defend Jonesboro to the south.¹⁷⁴ This left only Stewart and some militia to guard the city. It was a little more than a seven-mile march for Thomas between Red Oak and the Macon R.R. By this time a couple of Thomas' lead divisions had gone into camp about six miles northwest of Jonesboro. Soon thereafter they spotted Confederate troops (probably Hardee's corps) heading south, presumably toward Jonesboro.¹⁷⁵ South of Thomas, Logan pressed his 15th Corps six miles further to the unfortified Flint River in order to find water for his troops, closer to Jonesboro than Sherman had ordered.

The next day on August 31 a couple of Thomas' division commanders spotted large clouds of dust that told them more Rebels (probably Lee's corps this time) were marching south toward Jonesboro. Thomas pled with Sherman to be able to attack the passing Rebel right flank but Cump refused, possibly because such a move would remove Thomas from a supporting position of lead elements of Sherman's old army, already on the east bank of the Flint River approaching Jonesboro.¹⁷⁶ In any event, the second Rebel corps passed uncontested in front of the constrained Thomas.¹⁷⁷

After reaching Jonesboro without significant challenge, around noon after S.D. Lee prematurely charged Logan's 15th Corps anchoring Howard's front, Cleburne threw his men at Howard's right.¹⁷⁸ The Confederates' bungled, half-hearted attack failed miserably with extraordinarily disproportionate losses. (2,200 Rebel casualties vs. 172 Yankees.¹⁷⁹) The summer's long, arduous campaign was taking its toll, first evidenced at Ezra Church and once again at Jonesboro.¹⁸⁰ After meeting with Cleburne and Lee, Hardee agreed that, "success against such odds could have been only partial and bloody, while defeat would have meant almost inevitable destruction of the army."¹⁸¹ Meanwhile Schofield reported he had cut the last Rebel rail line at Quick Station, about 1½ miles below Rough and Ready—thinly defended because Hood had shifted so many units to Jonesboro—and Stanley's 4th Corps was coming up to secure Schofield's right, or southern, flank.

At this point Sherman had clearly outmaneuvered Hood who had more area to defend than he had available forces. Furthermore Sherman's maneuvers left Hood wondering where Sherman would strike next.¹⁸² Hood, and especially Hardee and Lee, his field commanders who were expected to engage Federal forces somewhere outside of Atlanta, were still handicapped by Wheeler's absence who was still raiding. Although Red Jackson's remaining troopers were providing yeoman service, cavalry deficiency was also a product of insufficient numbers, demonstrating once again the risk, if not the folly, of sending large numbers of cavalry away from an army's main body.

Sherman's enthusiasm for destroying rail track blinded him to an opportunity on September 1 to destroy a major portion of Hood's army. Seeing an opportunity for a decisive victory, Old Pap suggested that two of his Cumberland corps, including Stanley coming south from Rough & Ready, meet with Schofield as his army was destroying track. These three corps would swing southwest and then east toward Lovejoy's Station, thus cutting off any Rebel retreat to Macon. But as he had in response to four previous suggestions by Thomas during the campaign, Sherman rejected this suggestion,¹⁸³ ostensibly on the assumption that Rebels would retreat back to Atlanta, an unlikely possibility since Stanley's and Schofield's extensive destruction of the railroad had already made it impassable. Moreover there were still three other Union corps deployed between Jonesboro and Atlanta. Realistically Thomas's suggestion may have been imperfect given time-and-distance factors but at least if successful it would have fulfilled Grant's directive to destroy Hood's army.

Regardless Stanley and Schofield spent much of the morning continuing to redundantly destroy more track of the Macon & Western. Given that Hood's supply lines were destroyed beyond any reasonable possibility of repair while his army's position inside Atlanta had become precarious, Hood had little choice except to complete the evacuation of the remainder of his army from Atlanta. As their rear guard began to blow up munitions—including 81 railroad cars in the downtown terminal[184]—and other stores, the remaining Rebels started to abandon Atlanta to head southeast along McDonough Road, running roughly parallel approximately six to nine miles east of the Macon R.R. Hood ordered S.D. Lee to march back toward Atlanta[185] until he could meet up with Stewart after which they would countermarch to the south toward Lovejoy's Station. Hopefully they would join Hardee, until then isolated in Jonesboro.

Not until the early afternoon of September 1 did Sherman realize he was facing only Hardee at Jonesboro.[186] In the afternoon Sherman ordered Stanley's 4th Corps forward—while continuing to cut railroad tracks—with Schofield following to close the noose on Hardee's left flank. During the late afternoon of September 1 Sherman also ordered Frank Blair to cut off Hardee's retreat to Lovejoy's Station; also it was late afternoon when Sherman changed Stanley's mission from cutting rail lines to heading down east of the Macon & Western R.R. while Blair's 17th Corps advanced along west of the railroad.

Upon encountering fortified Rebel positions in front of Jonesboro Sherman ordered a double envelopment while Davis' 14th Corps would frontally attack Hardee's middle. Stanley's 4th Corps was ordered to swing around Hardee's right flank northeast of Jonesboro while Blair's 17th Corps was ordered get around Hardee's left flank to gain his rear, thus preventing the anticipated retreat. Davis' frontal attack succeeded in breaching the middle of Hardee's lines, manned by Cleburne's attenuated division, capturing two Confederate brigades, together with two batteries, in the process but also suffering heavy casualties. The frontal assault by the 14th Corps was the only successful frontal attack during the entire Atlanta campaign.[187]

But Stanley did not arrive until dark fall—in Sherman's view Stanley had "dilly-dallied." Furthermore Stanley's path was across difficult ground marked by ravines and marshes, impeding his soldiers from advancing along the Confederate flank, let along getting to the Rebels' rear. Notwithstanding the loss of two brigades, Hardee had shifted an unengaged division to his right to confront Stanley. Hardee had been able to make this shift because of ineffectiveness against his left flank, Blair's 17th Corps getting lost when it attempted to block the road south to Lovejoy's Station. Hardee—whose corps had barely 5,000 men by then capable of fighting—managed to escape after dark through Stanley's sector to await the rest of Hood's army at Lovejoy's Station.[188] Other than Blair's misadventure Howard's Army of the Tennessee had done little, its mission being to maintain its position and make occasional feints to keep the Rebels from concentrating on Thomas' corps.[189] Reflecting the relative degrees of engagement Davis' 14th Corps in Thomas' army incurred 1,272 casualties of the Union's total losses of 1,400.

Notwithstanding the relative inactivity of the Army of the Tennessee and notwithstanding all the hours spent earlier that afternoon by Stanley's 4th Corps in destroying additional track, Sherman blamed Stanley's slowness as the principle reason why Hardee was not bagged.

During the night of September 1–2 Confederate cavalry, serving as its rear guard, continued to blow up ammunition and other munitions, the sounds of which could be heard for many miles, as well setting fires to warehouses.[190] Sherman, continuing to stay with Old Pap, was not certain of the origins of the sounds, believing they might be Rebel artillery. During the evening of September 1 when Sherman could hear the explosions he ordered Slocum to go into Atlanta to reconnoiter the situation. Sherman further ordered that if Hood was abandoning Atlanta, "it is unnecessary for us to go further as this stage." Except of course more railroad tracks were to be destroyed.

As the bulk of Sherman's Grand Army moved south the morning of September 2, continuing to destroy railway track, Slocum's 20th Corps entered Atlanta, whereupon Atlanta's mayor surrendered what was left of the town. The Rebels' destruction of their own railroad cars filled with ammunition, together with other extensive devastation from fires through wide swaths of neighborhoods as the rear guard was leaving, contributed to the Southern mythology falsely blaming most of that carnage upon Sherman. Shortly after that surrender, Sherman learned—while accompanying Thomas who was moving his units into position against Hardee north of the well positioned and strongly barricaded Lovejoy's Station— that the last of Hood's men had evacuated Atlanta during the night. Sherman then wired Washington with the dramatic, electrifying message, "Atlanta is ours, and fairly won."[191] But Sherman's message also included the ominous coda: "I shall not push farther on this raid, but in a day or two will move to Atlanta and give my men some rest. Since May 5 we have been in one constant battle or skirmish."[192] Sherman, becoming curious about the extent of Atlanta's devastation, left to return to Atlanta.[193] Before leaving Sherman cancelled his attack order for Howard's Army of the Tennessee but inexplicably not for Stanley's 4th Corps whose flanking movement proceeded to advance into murderous artillery fire that forced Stanley to retire.

After arriving back in Atlanta, Sherman seemed to lapse into what has been described as a "victor's lethargy," quite uncharacteristic for the normally energetic, high-strung general.

Sherman wrote a self-serving dispatch to Halleck on September 4 trying to explain why Hood had escaped. In essence he blamed many of his subordinates, implying most of the blame fell upon Stanley and Schofield. But in the same dispatch Sherman characterized Thomas as being "slow, but true as steel."[194] Sherman did write that only his former Army of the Tennessee had moved "rapidly" enough to threaten Hood. Stanley, who bitterly resented Sherman's contentions, rightly blamed his late arrival at Jonesboro, and consequently Hardee's escape, on Sherman's delay in changing his orders. Sherman also gave himself credit for the selection of Howard—who had not done anything special— as the new commanding general of the Army of the Tennessee; Sherman could not resist ungraciously and gratuitously remarking that if Hooker were still with the army he would have taken all the credit for capturing Atlanta. In response Grant urged Sherman to not relent saying, "We want to keep the enemy continually pressed to the end of the war."

By Monday, September 5, 1864, Sherman had pretty much disregarded Grant's orders to destroy the Confederate army, instead opting to forego any further pursuit efforts against Hood's army.[195] And so the three armies were ordered by Sherman into garrison in and around Atlanta to rest and to refit, and to allow Sherman to consider his next move.

## *Analysis*

Viewed in isolation Jonesboro was another relatively minor battle, at least by Civil War standards. While it was almost the concluding battle in the entire Atlanta campaign, Jonesboro might not have been even necessary given that all the rail lines, Hood's essential lines of communications, had been extensively destroyed while remaining under the firm control of Federal forces. Without his lines of communications Hood could no longer remain inside his Atlanta fortifications, leaving him with no alternative except to try to escape to his relatively safe haven at Lovejoy's Junction. And while the Jonesboro assaults by Hardee and Lee on September 1 were Confederate failures, the failure of the Union forces to trap and to capture Hardee the next evening was even more significant in terms of achieving a decisive victory.

By being so focused, even obsessive, upon continuing to destroy additional tracks on September 2 when such destruction was militarily meaningless, Sherman became blinded to his opportunity to destroy Hardee.[196] Later that afternoon Sherman decided to try to capture Hardee but only after there was insufficient time to shift Stanley and Schofield from track destruction detail to army destruction missions. It is always dangerous to presume an outcome but certainly the odds in favor of a decisive Union victory at, or immediately following, Jonesboro would have been substantially enhanced had Stanley been able to arrive a couple hours earlier instead of continuing to wreck more railroads. Among other factors, Hardee would not have had time to shift the division to his right; conversely if it had had enough time to arrive before darkness Stanley's corps would have had an easier time navigating the unfriendly terrain that eventually impeded its flanking attempt.

And while it is impossible to impute motives by Sherman based upon circumstantial evidence, it also seems evident that Sherman frequently gave a higher priority to cast fame and glory upon his former army command rather than to seek to destroy the enemy's army. The most obvious example occurred during the morning of September 1 when Thomas sought permission to slam into the exposed right flank of a large Confederate unit, likely S.D. Lee's corps, moving south in front of Thomas. Instead of granting permission to attempt such a decisive action, Sherman directed that Old Pap continue to secure Howard's entrenched right flank, which of course would not have been needed Thomas' protection if the potential attacking force had been emasculated by an attack to its exposed flank. In denying Thomas' proposal, Sherman stated, "You should *follow* the enemy as he retreats."[197] (Emphasis added.) Time and time again during the Civil War it had already been shown, or at least should have been shown, that merely following a retreating army would not result in a decisive victory.

At least five times Sherman rejected suggestions by Thomas to outflank the Confederates.[198] At the same time Sherman had his own favorite ideas, except of course at the Kennesaw Mountains, about using maneuver as opposed to relying solely upon frontal attacks. But Sherman and Thomas differed in their reasons and objectives for using flanking maneuvers. Essentially Sherman liked to deploy smallish, and presumably more mobile, infantry units to flank in order to coerce or threaten his adversary into retreating without any meaningful or effective pursuit.[199] On the other hand Old Pap advocated flanking maneuvers by larger forces, including cavalry, deployed to trap or capture the enemy thereby compelling the enemy to either surrender or attack. Sherman typically was anxious to commence his flanking maneuvers as soon as possible. In contrast Thomas preferred to take the time and effort, for instance some rudimentary reconnoitering, to prepare prior to deploying. At the risk of oversimplification, Sherman's objective was usually to gain ground while Thomas' objective was to conquer the enemy. And even Sherman admitted he "had not accomplished all, for Hood's army, the chief objective, had escaped."

Sherman's decisions after learning that Hood's army had evacuated Atlanta and after learning that Atlanta's mayor had surrendered the city show that Sherman had priorities other than to destroy his enemy. It is true that the capture of Atlanta amounted to a dramatic, important political victory helping to reverse Lincoln's political fortunes while buttressing the will of a war-weary Union population. And it was also true that the capture and destruction of much of Atlanta, including its position as a major rail center, further damaged the Confederacy's war making capacity.[200] And Sherman would always contend that it was imperative to suppress the enemy's will to conduct war. But as Lincoln and Grant had concluded that either capturing or annihilating the enemy's army was the quickest way to end the war.

Albert Castel offers the following observation and commentary:

> ...Sherman's prime purpose was to take Atlanta, not to destroy or force the surrender of the Army of Tennessee. Given the failure to accomplish this at the very onset of the campaign by way of Snake Creek Gap and during several subsequent occasions, this is understandable, perhaps even excusable. One may judge for oneself as to whether Sherman should be left off the hook for letting Hood escape. If raising this question seems unfair, consider the following: George McClellan has come under criticism by historians for celebrating as his greatest victories the occupation of empty cities, yet Sherman is hailed by many authors for accomplishing the same task. Let readers decide for themselves why this is.[201]

And it was not as though Sherman was faced with an either-or choice. In other words, it was not a matter of either capturing Atlanta or eliminating Hood's army, but not both. In fact Atlanta had already been taken and there was no legitimate reason why at least a major portion, if not all, of Hood's army could still not be forcefully pursued to a decisive defeat.[202] One problem was Sherman had no plan beyond capturing Atlanta, a planning deficiency shared with almost all other Union commanders, Grant after Corinth II probably being the most notable exception. Successful pursuits were largely impromptu exercises but conducted in a tactical framework incorporating areas of assigned responsibility. Coordination between infantry and cavalry was absolutely necessary. In this instance there is scant evidence that Sherman was still placing any reliance or responsibility upon his cavalry. In any event merely "following" a retreating army did not constitute a successful plan for a pursuit. While Sherman was certainly a proponent of hard war against a civilian population his military philosophy seemed to still be stuck in the attitude of winning possession of a geographic site, such as Atlanta, but also being content to allow the defeated force to withdraw with relative impunity.

Just how vulnerable was Hood's army to a decisive defeat after Jonesboro? As described by Buell:

> When he received reports that Sherman's army was returning to Atlanta instead of pursuing, Hood could scarcely believe his good fortune. His own army was totally used up, his men battered and embittered. Nearly all his stores and quartermaster supplies had been abandoned in the city, where mobs had ransacked the warehouses even as they burned. Worst of all, his soldiers were down to their last rounds of ammunition, for the twenty-eight railway cars containing Hood's reserve had not been evacuated in time from the city and had to be destroyed in thunderous explosions.[203]

But the military reality was that unless the Federals could, or would, apply a *coup de grâce*, Hood's army, while seriously wounded, remained intact and viable. Once given a chance to rest, to repair, and to resupply the Army of Tennessee could again become a capable fighting force.

## *Dénouements and Precursors*

Although he saw no more Civil War combat duty, Joe Hooker stayed in the Regular Army until 1868 when he suffered his last of a series of severe strokes. But as early as 1864 when he was seen by Theodore Lyman, Meade's volunteer aide, Lyman said Hooker had the appearance of a "used-up man." In 1865 the Joint Committee on the Conduct of the War exonerated Hooker for the Chancellorsville defeat. After Hooker's death in 1879, Grant finally gave Hooker credit for Lookout Mountain, describing it as a "brilliant" achievement while still criticizing Hooker as a dangerous man.

John Palmer, the political general who had risen to corps commander but whose difficulties with Sherman made him more trouble than he was worth, became governor of Illinois before becoming an U.S. Senator from that state. In 1896 he was a minor party's candidate for president.

Ten days after the Battle of Atlanta, Grenville Dodge initiated court martial charges against his subordinate, Thomas Sweeny. The Irishman apparently thinking his one arm was sufficient to out-fight Dodge, struck Dodge in the face after calling Dodge, among other things, "...a God-damned liar, sir" and a cowardly son of a bitch, sir."[204] A few weeks later a Confederate shot pierced Dodge's scalp. Although the wound did not penetrate Dodge's skull, he was incapacitated for field command for the rest of the war. After the war, Dodge resumed his career as a railroad company engineer and became active in politics and veterans' organizations. Fort Dodge, in Kansas, and Dodge City are named for him.

After the war Black Jack Logan remained bitter for the rest of his life about his perception of the West Point clique.[205] He resumed his career in politics, switching his allegiances to the Republican Party. After being elected to the Senate, Logan was able to provoke Sherman's indignation by publicly criticizing West Point and the Regular Army, then commanded by Sherman, and by imposing reductions in military appropriations.

As an example of how Civil War generals were reluctant to let bygones be gone, for several years D.S. Stanley continued to contest Sherman's contention that Stanley's 4th Corps had been slow coming to Jonesboro on September 2. According to Stanley's own memoirs the fault was Sherman's "want of generalship in using a large force to destroy a useless railroad—useless to Hood's army—when that force should have been hastened to hunt up the enemy and to attack him at once."[206] Finally as some measure of concession, in Sherman's 1886 revision of his *Memoirs*, Sherman—by then retired from the army—allowed the inclusion of an appendix with Stanley's and others' version of Jonesboro on September 2.

Commanders of either side persisted in looking for scapegoats. In the case of the Rebels, Hood tried to lay the blame for his failures upon W.D. Hardee, whose corps had borne the bulk of the fighting for Hood. Hardee had been field commander for three of the battles fought under Hood's overall command; Hood's ostensible complaint was that each of those attacks started several hours late giving the Federals extra time to prepare better defenses. Actually Hood's hostility toward Hardee was only a part of the acrimonious relationships among the high command of the Army of Tennessee. As he had eleven months earlier when similar troubles had erupted under Bragg's command, Jeff Davis visited Hood's headquarters in an attempt to mollify the differences among his generals. But as before, Davis' presence only seemed to exacerbate the rancor among the army's high command. Eventually Hardee was relieved of command and sent away to command the Department of South Carolina, Georgia and Florida. Despite its impressive title, this department had an ineffective force that would be powerless when it tried to defend against Sherman's March to the Sea.

At the same time Davis was no longer willing to give free rein to Hood. In order to give some counsel and guidance to Hood, Davis appointed Pierre G.T. Beauregard as commander of the Division of the South. However this new assignment did not give Beauregard any command authority but instead was restricted merely to overseeing Hood. Although Beauregard's latest appointment was to a nominal command, it still represented a remarkable comeback by a general whom Davis once tried to banish. Beauregard's defense of Charleston, South Carolina, was brilliant. As an engineer Beauregard had incorporated several innovations, some of which were precursors of naval warfare. Furthermore he continued to submit several plans and strategic proposals, all of which were either rejected if not ignored altogether by Richmond. In early 1864 Beauregard was transferred to assist Robert E. Lee, specifically in the Richmond sector.

After being relieved of command of the Army of Tennessee, Joe Johnston and his wife retired to the Macon, Georgia, area where they enjoyed the company of family and friends while Johnston began to prepare his memoirs. Johnston also used the opportunity to lash out against his enemies and critics. In particular he was embittered by the mostly unfavorable comparison of his retreat with his friend, Robert E. Lee, who also more than once had been forced to retreat. Finally on February 23, 1865, as Sherman was rapidly advancing on his March to the Sea, Johnston acquiesced to the request of Lee, to assume command of the Department of South Carolina, Georgia, and Florida plus the Department of North Carolina and South Virginia.

Leggett's Hill, formerly known as Bald Hill and the fiercely contested focus of the Battle of Atlanta, eventually was destroyed by the construction of an interstate highway.

# 8

# Thomas After Nashville
## December 1864

### Segue from Atlanta

After Sherman let Hood retreat to a new base at Lovejoy's Station, Sherman seemed to become lethargic, at least concerning what to do about the C.S.A. Army of Tennessee. Sherman did begin to convert Atlanta into an armed garrison, for instance on Thursday, September 8, 1864, while citing military necessity, issuing an order to expel citizens from Atlanta. However two days later, Grant sent a telegram from City Point to Atlanta urging Sherman to drive against Hood as soon as possible. Instead Sherman remained focused upon Atlanta, continuing to expel its residents while converting the city into a logistics base for future campaigns.

While Sherman remained in Atlanta Hood began to revive the remains of his army. Toward that end, on Thursday, September 21, 1864, Hood moved his army about 20 miles west to Palmetto, Georgia, where he planned to rejuvenate and re-equip his army before moving into Alabama to operate against Sherman's supply lines. Although Hood's army had been badly damaged, Hood was not intimidated by Sherman, feeling the Rebel army was free to roam while the Yankee supply lines had become vulnerable to strikes. About a week prior to Hood's move to Palmetto, Bedford Forrest left Verona, Mississippi, to also operate against Sherman's lines while becoming a direct threat to the middle of Tennessee.

On Sunday, September 25, 1864, President Jeff Davis came by train to Palmetto to confer with Hood about several matters, this being Davis' third visit with the Army of Tennessee in three years.[1] Although they had different objectives, Davis and Hood also seemed to agree Atlanta had become Sherman's problem and that Hood was thus free to maneuver while avoiding battle. Ideally, and perhaps unrealistically, they hoped to convert Sherman's capture of Atlanta into an empty victory.

While Sherman had little interest in chasing after Hood and Forrest, he realized he could not afford to ignore them altogether. Accordingly on September 29 Sherman dispatched Thomas back to Nashville to coordinate defenses against cavalry raids against the rail lines.[2] Thomas arrived in Nashville on October 3.

On Saturday, October 1, 1864, Hood moved around Atlanta to assault Union troops at Salt Springs while Forrest continued to hit Sherman's rear. Leaving Slocum behind, on October 3, Sherman marched from Atlanta back toward Marietta only to learn Hood was already moving toward Allatoona, by then a major Union supply depot. After a small garrison held off Hood at Allatoona, Sherman chased Hood all the way back to Resaca.

When Hood arrived at Resaca Wednesday, October 12, 1864, to demand surrender of that badly outnumbered Union garrison, the colonel in command responded to Hood: "...I can hold this post. If you want it come and take it."[3] In the face of such bravado, Hood, being concerned that he could be trapped between Thomas and Sherman, decided to move along toward Dalton.[4] On the other hand, Sherman was becoming annoyed that he seemed to be backtracking along previously captured territory.

Sherman understood that Grant's objective was to destroy armies but Sherman also believed the destruction of infrastructure would hasten the end of the war. After several exchanges with Sherman Grant finally agreed on October 11 to allow his friend to make his trip to the sea coast, leaving sufficient forces with Thomas to handle Hood if Hood should continue to the north.[5] However Sherman also believed, or at least he argued, it was much more likely that Hood would have to follow Sherman south. Although Lincoln had doubts about Sherman's plans, the President, as promised, deferred to Grant's judgment.[6]

On October 15 Sherman received a message from Secretary of War Stanton giving his authorization to Sherman's plan to move to the sea. In anticipation that he would soon have his opportunity to start moving toward the sea, on October 18 Sherman ordered Slocum—still in Atlanta—to prepare massive numbers of rations as well as to prepare the "lightest pontoon bridges and trains ready."

Two days later on October 20, Sherman gave up on any further pursuit of Hood, rationalizing to Thomas, "To pursue Hood is folly for he can twist and turn like a fox and wear out an army in pursuit."[7] Sherman was now fully committed to his March to the Sea.

On Friday, October 21, 1864, Hood received permission to invade Tennessee. Any invasion of Middle Tennessee would of strategic necessity involve Nashville, the state's capital, nestled on the south side of a loop of the Cumberland River. Its 1860 population was 17,000; its diverse economy was not solely based upon manufacturing but instead also served as a wholesale supply warehousing and redistribution center for much of the region west of the Appalachian Mountain range; it connected five railroads and numerous turnpikes and lesser roads.

Upon the Union occupation of Nashville in 1862 its commanders converted the city into a major logistics center where not only supplies and equipment were stored but also where military hospitals were established and where equipment was repaired. Reflecting its strategic importance it became the heaviest fortified city outside of Washington City.

But Thomas probably had only 12,000 "perfectly raw troops" scattered over five states to protect railroads while fighting guerrillas and raiders. Thomas' biggest worry was that Hood's cavalry could capture the Federal outposts, and destroy garrisons, rail facilities, and supply depots, thereby isolating Nashville. Not only did Thomas have to deal with Forrest and Wheeler while preparing to defend against an invasion by Hood, Thomas was also reacting to political turmoil in Tennessee and Kentucky. And while reinforcements were arriving in Nashville each day, Old Pap was also losing equal numbers due either to the end of enlistments or furloughs so that soldiers could go home to vote.

Sherman was transferring convalescents, injured, short-timers—those whose terms of enlistments were about to expire—to Nashville. On the other hand Sherman also retained the best cavalry along with almost the army's entire wagon train, this even though Cump had announced he intended to live off the land. And even though throughout the entire Atlanta campaign Sherman had continuously criticized Thomas' former 14th Corps as being slow and stopping at every plowed furrow, Sherman nevertheless refused to relinquish this elite, veteran corps back to Thomas, now claiming "It is too compact and reliable a corps to leave behind."[8]

Although Grant and the Federal administration were fearful that Hood could reach the Ohio River, Sherman disagreed, saying, "If he'll go to the Ohio River I'll give him rations."[9] But as fears increased that Hood was becoming a threat to invade Middle Tennessee, on October 30 Sherman ordered John Schofield and his 23rd Corps of 10,000 men to report to Thomas.[10] In turn Thomas ordered Schofield to join Stanley, with his 4th Corps of 12,000 men, in Pulaski—75 miles south of Nashville—where they were already watching Hood in Florence, Alabama. Schofield was given overall command in Pulaski with the mission of delaying Hood as long as possible. In addition to these infantry, augmented with artillery, Thomas had 15,000 cavalry scattered among several detachments.

Additionally MGen. Andrew J. Smith, 49, was ordered to bring two of his divisions of 9,200 men from Missouri.[11] Smith was a former dragoon who had seen action in the Mexican war as well as Indian fighting on the frontier before becoming Halleck's chief of cavalry in February 1862. Smith subsequently assumed various levels of infantry command, including posts in the Vicksburg campaign, Sherman's Meridian raid, and the Red River Campaign of 1864. Smith's detachment, now known again as the 16th Corps, was on its way to Nashville when it was ordered back to William Rosecrans' Department of Missouri to help defend St. Louis against Sterling Price's raid. Smith's arrival compelled Price to begin retreating further west. Smith's corps, along with Alfred Pleasonton's cavalry, was part of the pursuit of Price who was decisively defeated October 23, 1864, at Westport, Missouri. Thereafter when Smith was still 200 miles west of the Mississippi River he was once again ordered to join Thomas at Nashville.[12]

As Hood continued to swing westward, it was becoming more and more apparent that Hood was positioning his army for an invasion of Middle Tennessee, to cause Thomas' mission to shift from the defense against railroad raids to the defense of Nashville. On November 1 both Grant and Stanton sent messages to Sherman to question whether it was wise to ignore Hood. Sherman responded with assurances that Thomas would have enough manpower. By November 2, 1864, Hood directed his army northward in three separate columns traipsing through deep mud.[13]

Grant also detached MGen. James ("Harry") Wilson, 27, from the Army of the Potomac to be Sherman' chief of cavalry. Wilson was a self-assured, highly disciplined officer with little tolerance for the foibles and shortcomings of others, either those above or below him in rank. He was a teetotaler in an era of heavy drinking, especially among the officer corps. He was often jealous of other officers whom Wilson perceived as interfering with Wilson's relationship with superior officers, especially Grant. In command positions Wilson was not especially popular with his soldiers who thought he frequently gave higher priority to his ambitions than to their welfare.

In April 1864 Wilson succeeded H. Judson ("Kilcavalry") Kilpatrick as commanding general of the Third Cavalry Division of the Army of the Potomac. When Sam Grant came east to became commander of all Union forces he decided, among other things, to improve the cavalry forces in the Army of the Potomac, and toward that end, he brought Philip ("Little Phil") Sheridan from his post as an infantry division commander in the Western theater to become Cavalry Corps commander for the Army of the Potomac.

Wilson and Sheridan had had a limited acquaintance when both were in the Western theater but as Sheridan's subordinate Wilson quickly came to respect his new commander, especially admiring Sheridan's aggressive and pugnacious attitude. On the other hand, although some fellow commanders, Sherman included, were supporters of Kilpatrick's "audacious" nature, Wilson was also dismayed to discover that his predecessor "had chosen poor locations for his camps and had policed them insufficiently. Some of the troopers appeared to have put on excess weight during the winter, their horses were poorly groomed, and their equipment was in bad order.... He both thoroughly understood and wholly approved of the necessity of ruling with a firm hand."[14] Undaunted, Wilson immediately turned to the task at hand with his usual focused determination, finding better camp sites, initiating frequent and rigorous drills building up manpower, requisitioning more mounts, jettisoning incompetent colonels, and refurbishing equipment. Thereafter as part of Grant's Overland Campaign Wilson led his division in numerous battles, raids and skirmishes, some more successful than others. However, most recently during Sheridan's Shenandoah campaign Wilson seemed docile and cautious.

Although Grant sent Wilson west to organize a cavalry force for Sherman, Sherman made it clear that he was not interested in additional cavalry. Sherman then sent Wilson to Thomas to serve as Old Pap's cavalry chief after stripping Wilson's troopers of their horses and equipment. Undaunted upon his arrival November 6, Wilson desperately tried to remount and re-equip his cavalry from Louisville. Meanwhile Southern cavalries under Forrest and Wheeler were wreaking havoc with Federal outposts and other facilities and could not be ignored as Wilson was attempting to mount and prepare his cavalry.

On Friday, November 11, 1864, Thomas wrote that he was expecting Smith any day. However, Smith was only approaching St. Louis after an exhausting march across Missouri. The next day Sherman left Atlanta with the cream of his army including 62,000 soldiers, Howard's Army of the Tennessee on the right flank and Slocum's Army of Georgia on the left,[15] Kilpatrick's cavalry following its own course. Sherman's engineers also cut the last telegraphic link between Thomas and Sherman.[16]

On November 13 Schofield arrived in Pulaski, Tennessee, where Stanley advised that Hood—Schofield's West Point roommate—could beat them to Columbia, approximately half way to Nashville.[17] Hood was estimated to have 30–35,000 veteran infantry with 10,000 cavalry while Schofield's command had approximately 20,000 infantry with only 3,500 cavalry. Furthermore Hood's numerical advantage in infantry and in cavalry gave him the opportunity to outflank Schofield meaning that Schofield's chief concern was being cut off from Nashville.

On November 15, Hood—with the only Confederate army large enough to impede Sherman but 300 miles to the west—refused to follow, or for that matter to make any move as Sherman abandoned what was left of Atlanta. This was a clear signal that Hood intended to start moving north rather than nipping at Sherman's heels to the east. Indeed four days later Hood advised Davis that he (Hood) would move into Tennessee within two days. That same day Hood sent Forrest's cavalry north across the Duck River ostensibly toward Nashville. While Hood probably hoped to reach the Ohio River, his move into Tennessee, and possibly Kentucky, also abandoned Davis' objective of preserving the Deep South with its capacity to provide produce and other materiel to the upper tier of the Confederacy.

On November 20 Schofield recognized he was on the horns of a dilemma. From

Nashville Thomas notified Schofield that A.J. Smith would not arrive in Nashville until November 25, meaning that Thomas was expecting Schofield to keep Hood from advancing toward Nashville. Concurrently Schofield realized he was not facing a small-scale raiding force in Hood's army, and that it would be difficult if not impossible for Schofield's undersized force to prevent Hood from advancing.

Trying to take advantage of his numerical superiority, after a three week pause, Hood crossed the Tennessee River on November 21 to continue his invasion of Tennessee along three separate columns.[18] Hood's three corps were led by Stephen D. Lee, Alexander P. Stewart, and Benjamin E. Cheatham, 44, replacing Hardee.[19] Hood and Schofield were then in a "race to Columbia," south of the Duck River forty miles further south of Nashville, but the pace of both armies through snow and sleet was slowed by wet, unseasonably cold weather.

Schofield won that race being safely in Columbia's defenses on Thursday, November 24, 1864, two days before Hood finally started to arrive in force on the south bank of the Duck River.[20] At this point neither horses nor equipment had arrived from Louisville meaning that Forrest still outnumbered Wilson at least 2–1. To add to Thomas' quandary, Hood was closer to Nashville than was Smith. Meanwhile Washington and Grant were trying to micromanage Thomas' operation. Grant was reacting largely upon reports in Southern newspapers, some reports being having been fabricated and planted by Beauregard. As an example, over reacting to a totally false newspaper report that Forrest was going after Sherman, Grant instructed Thomas to take an offensive action against Hood.

On November 27 Schofield's civilian cipher clerk abandoned his post and moved to Franklin, meaning that Schofield's means of communicating were limited since messages had to relayed by messenger from Franklin. Nevertheless on the same day Schofield ordered his divisions to cross the Duck River that night.[21] The next day Forrest crossed the Duck at Huey's Mill, 8 miles upstream from Columbia. Although driven back by Forrest, the newly arrived Wilson managed to wire Schofield of the danger but Schofield decided to stay until ordered otherwise by Thomas. Wilson's withdrawal permitted the Confederates to take several crossings near Columbia.

Wilson assumed that Forrest was headed for Nashville and thus quickly led his troopers toward those fortifications. However, instead of continuing his path north, essentially following Wilson, Forrest abruptly changed course to the west to head toward Spring Hill.

Thomas then advised Schofield that Smith would not arrive at Nashville until December 1, at least three weeks later than had originally been expected.

## *Spring Hill* (November 29, 1864)

From the very beginning Spring Hill, Tennessee, and especially the Union army's nighttime escape through or around the Confederate army, has been shrouded in mystery, contradictions, and controversy. Many Civil War students consider the escape to be one of the most bizarre episodes in the Civil War. There are many disputed reports, matters of speculation, and even matters of myths or legend but there are at least some uncontroverted basic facts:

Spring Hill—eight or ten miles north of Columbia—was a village of perhaps a dozen households, including antebellum mansions, astride the macadamized turnpike from Columbia to Franklin and then to Nashville. One of the households belonged to George and Jessie Peters, he being the doctor who in May 1863 had infamously shot Earl Van Dorn.[22] Since other roads also converged at Spring Hill both sides recognized the village as a critical juncture along the road to Nashville.

In the very early morning of Tuesday, November 29, 1864, while S.D. Lee's demonstration was supposed to hold Schofield at Columbia, Hood's infantry began crossing the Duck River to begin its invasion of Middle Tennessee if not beyond. In order to move faster Hood also left behind his supply trains and most of his artillery. As Hood left Columbia, he proclaimed that, "The enemy must give me fight, or I will be in Nashville before tomorrow night." The Rebels did not march along the turnpike but instead marched along a back country road that approached Spring Hill from the southeast. This largely unimproved, narrow road was rough, badly rutted, and in especially poor condition from the rains making it difficult to traverse. Its muddy condition made it so slippery that at one point Hood fell from his horse.[23] Additionally because the road was poorly marked and mapped some of Stewart's divisions became lost and wandered off-course.

Hood's mental condition that day was central to the ensuing controversy. Buell includes the recollection of one of Hood's staff officers as follows:

> General Hood was physically handicapped, if not wholly disqualified from active service in the field. ... He wore a wooden leg, but except when in the saddle, moved only on crutches. ... [L]eaving in the morning his quarters of the night before, he would go on crutches to the side of his horse, pass the crutches over to an orderly, and while another orderly would support his from behind, he would raise his left leg into the stirrup, and then an orderly would pass the right wooden leg over the horse's back, and place the right wooden foot in the stirrup. Thus mounted the General would ride long distances at a slow pace.[24]

Upon hearing Wilson's report that Hood was on the move Schofield sent a division with Stanley forward to Spring Hill to reinforce its small garrison and to block Hood's advance toward Franklin and Nashville.[25] Schofield also had the foresight to send his army's supply train of 800 wagons, together with 40 guns, along the turnpike with Stanley's force. Stanley's van arrived at Spring Hill at approximately half past noon and immediately began to establish two defensive lines. (Stanley called it "the biggest day's work I ever accomplished for the United States."[26]) Soldiers of the existing garrison augmented by one of Stanley's brigades constituted the first of these lines. This line of 4,000 soldiers—north of the village and across the turnpike—almost immediately engaged in a skirmish with Forrest's troopers who had to withdraw around 3:00 p.m. after multiple charges exhausted their ammunition. At first Forrest refused to believe he would be facing much infantry but after being repulsed by the hail of bullets Forrest turned to a subordinate to remark, "They was in there sure enough, wasn't they …?"[27]

Stanley's second line was established east of the turnpike but south of the village to protect the supply train while a hub-to-hub line of eighteen pieces of field artillery was posted northwest of the turnpike.[28] Even as they were digging in the Federal soldiers could spot Confederates approaching from the south and east.

As Hood's army approached Spring Hill Cleburne's lead division encountered the second, and heavier, defensive line south of South Hill. Although Cleburne had been directed to consult with Forrest, Cleburne failed to do so and thus probably did not realize the strength of the Federal defenses to his front. The Confederate effort stalled after Cleburne was turned back by a barrage from the Yankees' 18 guns. Not realizing Stewart's arrival was being delayed, Cheatham ordered Cleburne to pull back. When darkness fell the Confederates set up camps south of the Union line, the closest camp being anywhere from a couple hundred yards to a quarter mile east of the turnpike.[29]

Late in the afternoon, after leaving Cheatham in charge Hood retired to his headquarters at the Absolum Thompson mansion, three miles east of the Columbia Pike.[30] Although obviously tired, even exhausted, whether Hood had taken a tincture of opium, laudanum, to ease his pain is still debated by historians.[31] In any event to celebrate the putative liberation of Tennessee Hood's host served a banquet, complete with libations, to Hood and his staff.

Apparently Hood and Cheatham failed to communicate with each other about the Rebels' objective for that evening. Hood evidentially wanted the turnpike to be blocked while Cheatham understood that the village was to be captured.[32] Hood told Cleburne "to form a line of battle to the left [west] of the road ..., then move forward and take the enemy's breastworks that are just over the brow of the hill."[33] Later Hood apparently changed his orders to Cleburne without telling Cheatham. This confusion among Hood, Cheatham, and the rest of his generals, including probably Forrest, stemmed in large part from the ambiguous objectives of Hood's invasion. Hood had often promised his army that he would avoid battles during the invasion yet there were other indications that Hood was eager to engage Thomas at Nashville. Moreover by leaving Lee's corps together with most of the army's artillery and ammunition that morning on the other side of the Duck River it would appear Hood was not preparing for serious battle at Spring Hill. And it also appeared Hood was not aware that Stanley, with 40 guns, had already arrived at Spring Hill ahead of the Rebel army. And to add to this confusion Hood and Cheatham countermanded each other's orders, thus failing to achieve either objective.

At one point in the early evening three Confederate divisions were aligned in a line of attack against the makeshift Yankee lines. The assault was supposed to be started by the division of MGen. John C. Brown on the right; however despite the urgings of other generals Brown refused to strike, claiming he had no orders. Brown's immediate commander, Cheatham, had gone to Hood's headquarters to seek clarification but Cheatham never returned to Brown's position; thus no attack was launched. Subsequently Brown's soldiers bivouacked in line with arms stacked.

As the evening wore on several Confederate generals visited Hood's headquarters to seek clarifications. Unfortunately for the Rebels these consultations only generated additional confusion as Hood's orders were either vague or contradictory to each other.[34] Belatedly Hood seemed to realize the turnpike was not covered, either north or south of the village. But according to at least one version, Hood eventually accepted it as something that could be corrected the next morning.[35] And by almost all accounts Hood, whether because he was grossly misinformed of the situation or whether he was too exhausted, even possibly impaired from excessive pain and/or laudanum, was optimistic that he had great chances of success, even predicting Schofield's surrender the next day.

On the morning of November 29 Schofield realized Hood might have entrapped any part of his army remaining in Columbia. Although it would be a perilous move, Schofield had no reasonable alternative except to continue retreating north with the remainder of his army. Even if Hood were not successful in capturing Schofield Hood would have a lead in racing toward Thomas at Nashville.

Although Schofield personally arrived around 7:00 p.m. at the Spring Hill area his corps did not begin arriving until sometime around midnight when Union soldiers could see hundreds of the enemy's campfires flickering to the east. Not knowing what to expect, Schofield's officers and soldiers could only fear the worst. One general who had arrived earlier with Stanley said: "It was the most critical time I have ever seen. If the enemy had shown his usual boldness, I think he would have beaten us disastrously."

After determining the road was still clear all the way to Franklin, Schofield then began the task of sending his army, including the 800 wagons and ambulances, through and out of Spring Hill. While Schofield went forward Stanley stayed in Spring Hill to direct the supply wagons that could cross a narrow bridge in Spring Hill only one at a time. As a testament to Stanley's efficiency, the wagon train cleared Spring Hill in about an hour's time. The entire army, including seven or eight miles of wagon and artillery pieces, slipped unchallenged past the camp sites and was gone by daybreak, continuing to march through to Franklin, Tennessee, 15 miles south of Nashville. One Confederate general quaintly summarized the episode: "Schofield ... passed by us while we were dreaming—artillery and wagons, infantry and horse, all gone on to Franklin!"[36] Twice during the night's march the Federal train was attacked by cavalry, which was repulsed each time with only minor losses to the Federals. By 4:30 a.m.—shortly before the Yankee rear guard was leaving Spring Hill—the Federals' lead division reached the outskirts of Franklin.

A veritable plethora of myths, speculation, and loosely based recriminations has emerged against this background of relatively simple, straightforward facts. Perhaps one of the most outrageous myths is that as they were tramping through the Confederate encampments the Union soldiers lit their pipes from the Rebel campfires. In a similar vein there were stories of Federal spies circulating among Confederate commands to spread false orders. Other allegations of excessive drinking and partying among the Confederate high commanders may have been closer to the truth. Spring Hill's mansions were known for their generous hospitality, and one variation of these allegations had Jessie Peters, whose husband was once again out-of-town, entertaining some of the generals to the point of distraction.[37] Cheatham's reputation for hard drinking and womanizing also lent some credence to these reports of excessive partying.

But the military reality was that the performance of the Confederate commanders was simply abysmal. Although Spring Hill did not result from an ordinary retreat and pursuit, the fact of the matter was that Schofield was in a desperate retreat after Hood had stolen a march to be in position to block, entrap and capture Schofield's retreating army. S.D. Lee commented later that Spring Hill was "One of the most disgraceful and lamentable occurrences of the war, one which in my opinion is unpardonable." What inchoate principles of a successful pursuit were lacking or violated that evening in Spring Hill?

Recriminations flew back and forth with none of the commanders escaping criticism. A livid Hood blamed almost everyone except of course himself, conveniently overlooking his own negligence. One observer said Hood was as "Wrathy as a rattlesnake."[38] Cheatham was Hood's primary scapegoat but others, including inexplicably Cleburne, were likewise targeted. In turn the other generals were quick to criticize Hood's command performance, their collective confidence probably having been shaken after they sought clarification and further guidance at the Thompson mansion during the evening of November 29.

While there was ample fault to assign among several of the southern commanders, the top commander was largely responsible for the Spring Hill debacle. As army commander Hood failed to clearly articulate his objectives before retiring to the Thompson mansion thus removing himself from effective management of the combat arena. For a battle hardened veteran commander, Hood was strangely naïve about the mettle and resourcefulness of the Federal generals and their soldiers. Based upon his later comments Hood apparently assumed that good planning—and most historians agree that his original plan was based upon a solid concept—was all that was necessary to achieve the desired result. He also allowed small problems, such as bad maps, difficult roads, lost units, and random appearances of Yankee infantry against his left flank, disrupt and even divert him from the implementation of his plan. But there is also scant evidence that Hood's planning included any specifics, including coordination among subordinate units, of what to do once his army reached Spring Hill. Neither is there any indication that he was able to make any adjustments in his tactical thinking once on the scene where circumstances were no longer as he had once anticipated. Among other things Hood failed to give Forrest, perhaps Hood's most valuable asset at that point, enough direction to allow Forrest, the quintessential self-starter, to know how he was to deploy his troopers later that evening after they were initially repulsed. For whatever reason that evening Hood allowed himself to become complacent, even over confident, about his chance to defeat his former West Point classmate, Schofield.

It was equally inexplicable and inexcusable that Hood and his commanders failed to impose basic military routines such as posting pickets or dousing campfires. In short the most important lesson from Spring Hill about pursuits is that as Lawrence "Yogi" Berra would later observe: "It ain't over 'til it's over!" In other words if one army is in position to either capture or annihilate its retreating enemy nothing should be taken for granted, and regardless of fatigue or other hardships all efforts should be taken to prevent the retreating enemy from reaching its point of equilibrium. This was an ignored lesson that the officers and soldiers Army of Tennessee would soon regret, many at the cost of their lives.

Although it was a non-combat episode, Spring Hill also revealed the widespread turnover of top commanders within the Army of Tennessee was resulting in untested, inexperienced commandeers who lacked much of the élan, decisiveness, and aggressiveness of their predecessors, who in fact may have had their own shortcomings. Unfortunately the Southerners' command performance at Spring Hill did not bode well for the Confederacy's remaining prospects in the Western theater.

## *Franklin* (November 30, 1864)

If Spring Hill was one of the most bizarre events of the Civil War, then Franklin was one of the most tragic. For the Confederacy, Franklin was also little short of being a calamitous harbinger for at least one more battlefield disaster.

Franklin—15 miles south of Nashville—was (and still is) nestled in a loop in the Harpeth River, a northwesterly running tributary of the Cumberland River. When he departed Spring Hill that morning Schofield did not want to fight at Franklin, instead intending to cross the Harpeth to continue to Nashville without delay. But when he arrived at Franklin early in the morning of November 30 Schofield found bridging material but no bridges across the Harpeth River.[39] Thus while his engineers were repairing bridges the Union infantry and artillery began to occupy and improve fortifications that had been previously constructed as part of the Nashville defenses.

More friction began to develop between Thomas and Schofield, both of whom were trying to reconcile competing demands. A.J. Smith's uncertain arrival contributed to command tensions as Schofield kept hoping Smith would be available to reinforce his efforts while Thomas just kept hoping Smith would eventually arrive in Nashville. At one point Schofield claimed Thomas was asking Schofield to hold Hood for three more days while Schofield replied that he didn't know if he could hold Hood for three more hours. Schofield expressed his fear that the slightest mistake on his part or the part of one of his subordinates would prove to be "disastrous."

By noon Schofield's soldiers had erected and began occupying an arc of three lines of earthworks around the south and west of Franklin and anchored on either end on the banks of the Harpeth.[40] Additionally artillery batteries were placed east of the Harpeth thereby providing safe locations from which the batteries could fire enflating rounds. From these new lines of entrenchments Union riflemen and artillerists had a clear view of the broad plain over which the Confederate attackers would have to traverse. There were but only a few isolated farm buildings to obstruct the fields of fire. And so while Schofield had not intended to stop at Franklin where he might have to accept battle he could have hardly asked for better, more formidable defensive positions.[41]

Upon arising the morning of the Federals' escape from Spring Hill Hood was enraged to discover his units were having breakfast instead of forming battle lines. Of course there was no sense in forming battle lines since his soldiers knew Schofield had already vamoosed. Purportedly a private had the courage to tell Hood, "General, the whole dang Yankee army passed by here last night, and we just let 'em go." Hood then concluded his entire army, officers and soldiers, had lost its fighting spirit and accordingly had to be disciplined. Apparently Hood reasoned that thoroughly disciplining his army would renew its sense of pride and esprit compelling it to obey even in the face of certain death. And so Hood, still without his main artillery or Stephen Lee's corps, ordered an immediate march in search of Schofield's army. By 2:00 p.m. Hood arrived at the plain below Franklin and promptly began to deploy available units in battle lines about two miles in front of Schofield's newly occupied works.

By three o'clock in the afternoon of the 30th, and after examining the Union lines through field glasses, Hood abruptly decided to immediately launch a straight-ahead attack. His commanders were incredulous arguing that neither Lee's infantry corps nor the army's artillery had yet to arrive and that it would be fool hardy to attack with less than full strength.[42] Even the normally hard-charging Forrest, having seen the Union fortifications close-up, voiced his objections to a frontal assault, claiming among other things that the Confederacy could ill afford to sacrifice so many soldiers. To his credit Forrest also proposed to take his cavalry across a ford to the east and swing around the Federals' left flank.[43] Insisting that he intended to crush the Federals with a frontal attack, Hood permitted Forrest to take only one of his three cavalry divisions to the Federal rear.[44]

We of course are not in any position to evaluate Hood's mental or emotional state but it certainly seems plausible that Hood was seeking some level of command comfort by reverting to the battlefield tactic that he knew best while punishing his army to instill pride an esprit. Hood may have also taken false hope from isolated signs, such as the debris left by the retreating Federals along the road, that the Blue coats were demoralized and/or panicked.[45] Whatever, and true to reasonable predictions, Hood's decision would result in horrific, irreplaceable loses, including the deaths of six generals.

Earlier as Wilson had been heading back to Nashville he managed to meet up with Schofield's main army in the Franklin area. Schofield had not been very happy with Wilson's performance of the previous day reporting to Thomas: "I do not know where Forrest is. He may have gone east, but, no doubt, will strike our flank and rear again soon. Wilson is entirely unable to cope with him."[46] Always anxious to protect his reputation Wilson became all the more determined to show he was worthy of the trust that Grant had bestowed upon him.

Fortuitously Wilson received two breaks that day: first, when more troopers from remounted camps arrived and, second, when Hood decided to split Forrest's cavalry, sending most of the Gray riders where there would be no significant action. Wilson deployed most of his cavalry east of the Harpeth to help protect Schofield's rear and left flank. Forrest arrived at Franklin at approximately the same time as did the early elements of Hood's infantry. True to form Forrest immediately attacked Wilson in an attempt to cut off Schofield's possible retreat to Nashville. But this time Wilson's strengths matched those of Forrest's, and while the cavalries battled for several hours eventually the Gray riders were forced to withdraw, the first time in the Civil War when Forrest had to withdraw from a battlefield of equal odds!

South of the Harpeth by 4:00 p.m.—about a half hour before sunset—the Rebel bands played various tunes including "Dixie" and "The Bonnie Blue Flag," the guides had unfurled their battle flags (at least 100 of them), and the ranks—perhaps as many as one-fourth without shoes—had formed into orderly formations of perhaps 18,000 men[47] in preparation of Hood's orders to assault the Federals across the open fields to their front. The Confederate lines were almost two miles long, half again larger than the infamous lines for Pickett's Charge at Gettysburg and expected to charge twice as far.[48] As soon as the battle lines started to move forward Hood removed himself from command control when he retired to the rear where an orderly prepared a fire for the general's comfort.

Initially the attack seemed to be succeeding. The Rebels, at least those in the middle of the formation, advanced upon, and indeed breached, the middle of the Union defenses where the turnpike passed. However without orders Union reserves quickly came to the fore counterattacking to close that breach and to repulse any further advances to the Yankee rear.[49]

Winston Groom wrote: "In all its bloody four years, the war had rarely—if ever—seen fighting so ferocious on so large a scale in so confined a space. For nearly an hour, thousands of men within an area no larger than a few acres shot, bayoneted, gouged, and bludgeoned one another to death with rifle butts, axes, picks, guns, knives, and shovels."[50] But the battle continued with indescribable fury as the Confederates made as many 16 charges—described by one Union soldier as "the brown seaweed carried by the white-capped waves"[51]—with any breakthroughs being countered by reserves hustled to the front.

Meanwhile Union artillery, enjoying the relative luxury of not having most of its Confederate counterpart in the arena, was laying down devastating canon fire upon the Confederate infantry exposed in the killing fields. One Confederate division commander, MGen. Edward C. Walthall, 33—who had two horses shot under him during the battle—described the Confederate struggle as follows:

> There was an extensive, open, and almost unbroken plain ... across which we must pass. ... This was done under far the most deadly fire of both small-arms and artillery that I have even seen troops subjected to. [The advance continued] terribly torn at every step by an oblique fire from a battery advantageously posted at the enemy's left, no less than by the destructive fire in front. ... [Still] the line moved on and did not falter till ... it reached the abatis fronting the works. Over this no organized force could go, and here the main body of my command ... was repulsed in confusion; but over this obstacle, impassible in a solid line, many officers and men ... made their way, and some, crossing the ditch in its rear, were captured and others killed or wounded in the effort to mount the embankment.[52]

When the battle was over almost six hours later, Hood's army lost approximately 25 percent of engaged numbers, or 6,300 men. Patrick Cleburne, whose record as a division commander was without equal in the Western theater, after having two horses shot from under him but nevertheless advancing on foot to within fifty yards of the breastworks, was one of the six generals killed or mortally wounded on the battlefield.[53] 59 other division, brigade, or regimental commanders were either killed, wounded, or captured.

Reflecting his lack of comprehension of the severe damage to his army, that night Hood ordered another attack the next day.[54] However arising the next morning his soldiers were stunned to realize, first, Schofield's army had already withdrawn from Franklin, and, second, leaving a battlefield strewn with gruesome gore of bodies, some of them stacked in heaps, of dead, dying, and moaning and groaning wounded Rebel soldiers. Incredibly Hood sent a message to regiments, his message reading in part:

> The commanding general congratulates the army upon the success achieved yesterday over our enemy by their heroic and determined courage. The enemy have been sent in disorder and confusion to Nashville, and while we lament the fall of many gallant officers and brave men, we have shown to our countrymen that we can carry any position occupied by our enemy.[55]

Notwithstanding this lopsided battle, it was not decisive. Hood's army was horribly crippled but not quite mortally. It was still had enough viability to at least try to fight again even though its commanding general failed to recognize its limitations. But despite Hood's illusions the harsh reality was that after its disaster in Franklin the Confederacy would never be able to muster the strength to launch another offensive attack in the Western theater.[56]

## *Nashville* (December 15, 1864)

Nashville's population greatly expanded since the beginning of the Federal occupation in 1862. By December 1864 the influx of refugees, Black and White, together with all the Federal employees and contractors, peddlers, and speculators had grown Nashville's population to as many as 100,000 people.[57] Wartime populations being what they were prostitution proliferated, and Nashville became the first city in America with legalized, regulated brothels.[58]

When Thomas established his headquarters in Nashville the city was well protected with a variety of fortifications, including several forts, and as many as twenty miles of breastworks. Several structures had been razed to provide clear fields of fire in front of the fortifications. Additionally the Cumberland River was essentially a fortified moat patrolled by gunboats.

Schofield's army arrived in Nashville on Thursday, December 1, 1864. Schofield was miffed that Thomas had not sent reinforcements as Schofield was retreating; Schofield also felt Old Pap's greeting was lukewarm,[59] especially considering that his corps was going to be vital to help defend Nashville.

Hot on the heels of Schofield, by December 2 Hood's army invested Nashville—Hood's goal since starting north—with a line 4 ½ miles long covering all southern approaches to the city. Hood's flanks were in the air while the center was stretched dangerously thin. To compensate Hood ordered the construction of a series of redoubts on his left.[60] Although technically Hood had imposed a siege against Nashville, neither the city nor Thomas's army was seriously besieged since they still controlled ample lines of communications in three directions. Furthermore, Hood's army of gaunt, poorly clothed, inadequately armed soldiers was probably outnumbered 2–1. Even Hood knew that assaulting the Nashville fortifications would be worse than assaulting Franklin and that is was impractical, if not impossible, to try going around Nashville. In fact Hood really had no plan except to hope that Thomas would attack in such a manner that Hood could effectively counterattack before seizing Nashville's ample supplies.

While his soldiers were suffering in the harsh weather from lack of clothing, shoes, and blankets, Hood established his headquarters in a private home six miles south of Nashville. One staff member recalled: "We had an abundance of good food: beef, mutton, pork, flour, and potatoes.... At the door of our tent stood a barrel of Robinson County whiskey, for the solace and inspiration of our mess."[61]

Shortly after Schofield's arrival, A.J. Smith also arrived with three divisions (one small division had been added along the way) to give Thomas's command 55,000 soldiers but several were casuals such as convalescent soldiers, quartermasters and supply clerks and hospital orderlies. Thomas' force also included a provisional division, including regiments of unproven black soldiers, commanded by James Steedman who had come to Old Pap's aid at Chickamauga. Thomas' command also included the 4th Corps, now commanded by Wood replacing Stanley who was still suffering from wounds at Franklin. Thomas' cavalry commander, James Wilson, was in Louisville attempting to find more horses to mount his cavalry. The Federals had the advantage of enjoying interior lines while the attenuated Confederate lines were slightly concave or on the exterior.

Grant and the Washington hierarchy started sending telegrams to Thomas on a daily basis. Although Grant initially conceded that "at this distance ... I might err as to the best method of dealing with the enemy,"[62] part of Thomas' problems was that his reports were awkwardly and inadequately worded thus reminding the Eastern authorities of McClellan's and Rosecrans' excuses for delays or even doing "nothing and [letting] the Rebels raid the country."[63] The messages from Stanton and/or Halleck, purportedly speaking for the President, only fueled Grant's "smoldering enmity for Thomas."[64] To be fair to Grant he was also under enormous political pressure to see that something be accomplished as soon as possible. In his *Memoirs,* Grant would claim that everyone was "apprehensive." His own campaign at Petersburg was stalled; Sherman's campaign in Georgia had yet to come to fruition; the price of gold was increasing to reflect the public's impatience with the cost of the war. Furthermore Grant had been forced earlier to apply hands-on pressure to get Sheridan to act against Early in the Shenandoah Valley, and perhaps he could get his subordinates to move only if Grant were personally present. Other historians also suggest that Grant was concerned about the possibility that the Confederates might be able to transfer troops from Southern garrisons to Georgia to oppose Sherman. Nevertheless Grant's posture was quite the contrast to when six months earlier he once admonished a nervous subordinate at The Wilderness that he was, "…heartily tired of hearing about what General Lee is going to do. Some of you always seem to think he is going to turn a double somersault and land in our rear and both of our flanks at the same time." Even Wilson would later say of his patron, "Here, if at any time during the war, Grant lost his head."

On December 5 Hood sent Forrest, together with a couple infantry brigades, to Murfreesboro to operate against a Union garrison of 8–10,000 troops. Not only did Forrest's constitute about 60 percent of Hood's cavalry, but Forrest may have been Hood's most capable commander. As was often the case with Hood's deployments the purpose of sending Forrest toward Murfreesboro was not clear. Perhaps Hood wanted to prevent the Federals at Murfreesboro from being able to reinforce Thomas at Nashville but it has also been suggested that Hood wanted to bait Thomas into sending Nashville troops to rescue the Murfreesboro garrison. But to quote McDonough: "In fact, [Forrest's] expedition in general, whatever the objective, left much to be desired."[65]

Grant continued to hector Thomas by sending a telegram on December 6 directing Thomas to "attack Hood at once and wait no longer for a remount of your cavalry."[66] This message could only prompt Thomas to recall other times—such as Dalton and Chattanooga—when an impatient Grant had improvidently ordered Thomas to attack. But more importantly Thomas wanted to be fully prepared for an offensive action, including cohesive organizations coordinated together sufficient cavalry.

By December 9 Wilson's cavalry was finally mounted with horses impressed from a variety of sources including Vice-President Elect Andrew Johnson's stables, street car companies, and even circuses in the area.[67] With Stanton's blessing Wilson also impressed horses from a variety of sources in Louisville, including horses attached to wagons loaded with produce, milk carts, drays, and butchers' wagons. More importantly Wilson's troopers were also armed with Spencer's repeating rifles.

Old Pap—the only one of the principles with cavalry experience, having been a member of the elite 2nd U.S. Cavalry—wanted more cavalry for two basic reasons: (1) to counteract Forrest, and (2) to deploy cavalry as a massed, mobile strike force against infantry and artillery. Dismounted the troopers would use their rapid-fire carbines to overcome muzzle loaders after which the cavalry would re-mount and pursue relentlessly. In his own methodical, foresighted manner, Thomas was planning not just to stop Hood but rather to use cavalry as part of a quick-hitting, mobile strike force to help destroy Hood's army. The Federal military hierarchy never understood Thomas' concept in part because Sherman thought, and repeatedly stated to Grant, cavalry was useless while Halleck thought want of cavalry was merely an excuse for inaction. Furthermore, even as the Civil War was approaching its fourth anniversary too many of the top commanders were still unable to rely upon any battlefield tactic other than a hurry-up, straight ahead attack.

Typically impatient, especially in issues related to Thomas, Grant issued an order replacing Thomas with Schofield, a choice that did not please Washington since Schofield was perceived, inaccurately, as the general whom Hood had beaten all the way from Columbia to Nashville. In any event Grant rescinded when Thomas reported that he was going to attack on December 10 except for the storm of freezing rains and sleet.

About this time Thomas' chief of staff began to wonder whether someone in Nashville was trying to undercut Thomas' authority as commander. Steedman was assigned to investigate and eventually discovered a telegram from Schofield to Grant wherein Schofield had wired: "Many officers here are of the opinion that General Thomas is certainly too slow."[68] Schofield would deny that this apparently untrue statement was being disloyal but the commanders of the 4th Corps, Stanley and then Wood, warned Thomas that Schofield was a "Judas on his staff."[69]

On December 11 Grant sent more messages telling Thomas to attack regardless of the weather, an order without any plausible logic or reason since neither men nor horses were even able to stay upright on the ice-covered ground. Old Pap conferred with his commanders who concurred with Old Pap's judgment. Thomas wired Halleck to describe how the weather had stymied his army, concluding "Under the circumstances I believe that an attack at this time would only result in a useless sacrifice of life."[70]

Losing almost all self-control, Grant ordered on Sunday, December 13, 1865, John A. Logan to go to Nashville. According to Grant's order, if Old Pap had not attacked by the time when Logan arrived, Logan should replace Thomas. Grant also started to leave for Washington in preparation of going to Nashville himself.[71]

Although on December 14 Thomas advised Washington that he planned to attack on the 15th Grant nevertheless drafted a telegram relieving Thomas. However the officer handling telegrams—realizing Grant "was not favorably disposed toward Thomas"—failed to send the telegram.

As Thomas had planned, on December 15 Union forces attacked with Steedman to feint by "demonstrating" on the Union left with the balance of Thomas' army aligned in a gigantic wheel of several miles maneuver around the right. Although a mere demonstration to draw Hood's army away from the other flank, Steedman's forces—primarily black soldiers—paid dearly with one-third to one-half becoming casualties within the first half hour of their attack.[72]

A gigantic line—at least three times the size of Pickett's Charge—stretched several miles on the right and was comprised of Wilson's 12,000 troopers, 4,000 being dismounted to act as skirmishers, on the outer part of the spoke and three corps of infantry on the inner part. From the beginning Old Pap contemplated the possibilities of a pursuit, hoping to either trap the Confederates before they could escape from the battlefield or at least to be in position to immediately follow Rebel forces as they fled the battlefield. As it was Thomas' army gained five miles after the redoubts were captured one-by-one but Hood's army remained intact, constricting their lines while erecting crude works during the night. Although the number of killed and wounded was relatively light, as many as 10,000 Confederates were captured.

That evening Thomas sent a long telegram to Washington reporting that "the whole action of today was splendidly successful." As soon as Stanton received his copy he delivered it to Lincoln who was already in his night clothing. That evening Grant sent his congratulations but could not help begrudgingly and ungraciously adding, "Push the enemy now, and give him no rest until he is entirely destroyed. … Much is now expected."[73] Lincoln's note of congratulations also admonished that, "A great consummation is within your reach. Do not let it slip."

Thomas was not certain whether the Rebels would retreat or stay at their new lines. Among other losses, the Confederate artillery lost several pieces leaving the already overmatched Rebel long arm with only 80 guns. However, that night, after sending a congratulatory message to his soldiers, Hood gambled against long odds to order his army to stay in their new, hastily-erected lines. And so on December 16 after some initial probing by both sides, the Federals repeated their same basic battle tactic of holding the Rebel right while trying to outflank its left. The Union artillery with its overwhelming superiority in guns and positions was unrelenting. In too many instances the Confederates tried to little avail to match smoothbore with Yankee rifled guns. In short Blue artillery was able to devastate breastworks as well as enemy batteries, including the destruction of their guns as well as the killing of their horses.

Once again soldiers, especially blacks, in Steedman's demonstration against the Southerners' right took severe losses.[74] After some delay most of the Federal units, most notably a division led by recently brevetted MGen. John McArthur, started moving forward on their own initiative. On the other hand Schofield's corps—positioned in the middle of the Union line—failed to advance until virtually shamed into doing so by an unhappy Thomas. Eventually the Northerners' infantry, together with 4,000 dismounted cavalry, captured Shy's Hill,[75] essentially the Confederates' anchor position, a capture that exposed the rest of the Rebels' line. As the day wore on too many of the Rebels' surviving batteries discovered that during the night they had placed their guns on the tops of the hills instead of the military crests thus reducing their effectiveness against charging infantry.[76] The collapse of the Confederate center caused the entire Rebel army to flee as rapidly as possible, many of the soldiers dropping anything not immediately needed. Private Sam Watkins, a Rebel soldier frequently cited in Ken Burns' epic *The Civil War,* described it as "...somewhat like a flock of geese that have lost its leader. I have never seen an army so confused and demoralized." The rout began so suddenly in some areas of the battlefield their numbers of Confederate prisoners exceeded those of their guards.

As the black soldiers began to move from their position on the Union left to join the pursuit along the Franklin Pike, Thomas—the former slaveholder—moved his horse to the side of the road to allow the blacks to pass, remaining "with his head uncovered" until they had all passed.[77]

Thomas' report that evening was full of praise for his commanders to the extent that it failed to clearly describe much of the specifics of the day's actions. His report also failed to mention that he was the commanding general of the only two Union routs in the Civil War against entrenched enemies.

## *The Pursuit Begins* (December 16, 1864)

Wilson's cavalry, many of whom were dismounted either for tactical reasons or for lack of enough mounts, got onto the Granny White Pike behind the Confederate left even as the battle was still underway. Without access to the Granny White Pike most Confederates were forced to skedaddle down a roughly parallel road, the Franklin Pike, their commanders hoping eventually to reestablish some degree of unit cohesion. Union infantry, led mostly by Wood's 4th Corps, immediately chased after their Confederate counterparts down the Franklin Pike.

S. D. Lee's corps—the last to leave the lines—came closest to remaining relatively intact thereby almost by default assuming rear guard responsibilities.[78] Lee also exhorted in a calm and courageous manner to rally some soldiers from all units.[79] One of the members of the general's escort remembered that Lee "…looked like a very god of war."[80] But many other soldiers quickly scattered in wild disarray. Sam Watkins, twice wounded, later recalled, "The woods everywhere were full of running soldiers. Our officers were crying 'Halt! Halt!' and trying to rally and re-form their broken ranks. The Federals would dash their cavalry amongst us, and even their cannon joined in the charge. One piece of Yankee artillery galloped past me … unlimbered their gun, fired a few shots, and galloped ahead again."[81] "Rebel soldiers shook their hats and waved their handkerchiefs from behind every log and tree," noted one Illinois soldier. Another Northern soldier was shocked to see about one-third of the Confederates were without shoes.[82] Running through deep mud caused many already weary soldiers to become too exhausted and debilitated to continue in their flight, surrendering almost in relief. Those Confederates who were not killed or captured scattered as best they could between Franklin and Brentwood.[83]

Because their lines dissolved so quickly Rebel gunners were forced to abandon several artillery pieces. When a crisis struck infantry soldiers could, and often did, simply drop their muskets and any other encumbrances and start running to the rear. However artillery batteries had a more time consuming process since the animals had to be brought forward and hitched before the pieces could be withdrawn. But many animals had been killed while there was not enough time to bring surviving animals forward to be hitched to the pieces.[84] In desperation the soldiers tried to manhandle some of their pieces through the mud but more likely than not half the guns and caissons in Hood's entire arsenal had to be abandoned.[85]

As Federal brigades lurched forward, having tasted the sweet fruits of victory, they soon also disintegrated and intermingled with one another thereby losing their continuity and cohesion. The mud that so thoroughly exhausted the stampeding Rebels likewise consumed their pursuers. Commanders lost management of their soldiers except to join in the chase. Hustling throngs of captured prisoners to the rear quickly became a major task for those commands that had advanced the furthest.[86]

It was getting close to dark before Wilson's dismounted cavalry were able to retrieve their mounts and to initiate a mounted charge down the Granny White Pike.[87] In the meanwhile Hood ordered the Granny White Pike to be held at all hazards.[88] Toward that end two and half miles south of the broken line Rebel cavalry, under the command of BGen. James R. Chalmers, 33, erected crude barricades made of whatever was available, be it fence rails, logs, trees, or even brush.[89] Chalmers' cavalry, mostly Tennesseans, defended these barriers that Wilson's cavalry, including a regiment of Union Tennesseans, attacked in savage saber-to-saber combat.[90] This ferocious, desperate "pandemonium"—called the Battle of the Barricades—continued in the freezing rain even though darkness made it almost impossible to distinguish friend from foe. Wilson thought it had been one of the mast vicious, if brief, encounters of the Civil War.[91] After holding their ground for an extended period the outnumbered Confederates twice fell back to new positions toward Hollow Tree Gap where Granny White Pike met the Franklin Pike. At midnight Wilson ordered his exhausted and fought out troopers into bivouac intending to take up the pursuit early the next day. Wood's infantry bivouacked about a mile from Brentwood, having captured fourteen artillery pieces, almost 1,000 prisoners, and hundreds of small arms.[92] Also that night

Hood dispatched an order to Forrest in Murfreesboro to "rejoin the army with as little delay as possible."[93] In response Forrest immediately began to organize his corps, including attached infantry, for a march to find Hood.[94]

However a significant error occurred that evening when an order dispatching the pontoon train was sent southeast along the wrong road to Murfreesboro instead of Nolensville. It is not clear whether Thomas personally wrote the order but as commander he was responsible, which he eventually, and reluctantly, acknowledged.

## *Hollow Tree Gap and Past Franklin* (December 17, 1864)

Arising early the next morning—the first full day after the rout from Nashville—Wilson's cavalry continued to pursue the fleeing Rebels—still without Forrest. Upon arising the morning of the 17th many Confederates were surprised Thomas had not continued his pursuit through the night and they were not already captured. But since they had not been captured these veteran soldiers went about the soldering process of trying to regroup and prepare for more fighting, stoically hoping to survive yet another day.

Stanley Horn describes what lay in store for the combatants:

> The next ten days were a nightmare of nerve-wracking hardship and struggle to both armies. Alternating marching and fighting and fighting, worn down by battle fatigue and sheer physical exhaustion, they somehow managed to carry on an almost continuous running battle from Nashville to the Tennessee River. The weather was abominable—rain, sleet and snow, with below freezing temperatures. The wagons and guns churned the roads into seemingly bottomless quagmires, which froze into sharp-edged ruts during the cold nights. The heavy rains not only drenched the suffering soldiers but soon flooded the streams and made the passage of each of them a serious problem.[95]

The Battle of the Barricades of the previous evening enabled the retreating Rebels to gain more distance between themselves and their pursuers; by 3:00 a.m. Hood's army reached Franklin and were hustled over the Harpeth River before they could rest for a few hours.[96] Furthermore bad weather confined Wilson's horse riders to the roads, meaning they could not cross fields to try to flank Hood's army marching along the hard surface turnpike.[97] Wilson later recalled, "It was killing work for both sides. The rain was still pouring and the fields on both sides of the road were soaking wet."[98] These conditions meant the best the Blue cavalry could hope to do was to break through the rear guards and create pandemonium among the infantry. While demoralizing the Confederate soldiers—many who were captured or even killed if they resisted capture—it was not a tactic that could capture or annihilate an army.

In the early morning light of Saturday, December 17, 1864, S.D. Lee's corps retreated another few miles to Hollow Tree Gap—about five miles north of Franklin—near Brentwood where the Granny White Pike converged with the Franklin Pike. Lee's corps was joined by major portions of other infantry regiments as well as an artillery battery.

About 9:00 a.m. Wilson's cavalry made another frontal charge at Hollow Tree Gap but was repulsed.[99] Another hour later Lee's rear guard heard reports that Federal cavalry was advancing on both sides of Franklin. Although the rear guard continued to hold a strong, defensible position at Hollow Tree Gap these reports compelled Lee to withdraw or else be threatened with being surrounded. The Union cavalry continued to push south until the

Confederate troopers were shoved "in confusion into the river."[100] Nevertheless Gray infantry, reinforced by artillery, made a determined stand north of the Harpeth until being outflanked and forced to retreat further south.[101]

Multiple rivers and other tributaries flowing to the west to the Tennessee River would be a most troublesome factor in the race between Gray prey and Blue pursuers. Even under normal circumstances streams often made major differences in an army's capacity to move—especially when retreating forces burned bridges—but in December 1864 in southern Tennessee torrential rains converted even the most docile streams into daunting, if not impassable, obstacles. The Harpeth River, twelve miles south of Nashville, was the first such major challenge.

Three weeks earlier the Harpeth had been a major ally for Schofield's army as it nestled in front of Franklin awaiting Hood's late afternoon assault while Schofield's trains scurried northward across the bridge on their way to Nashville. The Harpeth's gentle bends around Franklin provided ample flank and rear protection for the Federals who employed those river banks to help funnel Hood's army into one of the deadliest killing fields of the Civil War. Now that the Rebels had crossed the Harpeth and destroyed the bridge before retreating though Franklin, Wilson had to find some way to get across the roiling waters if the Union pursuit were to continue.

Recognizing the limits of merely attacking his prey's rear guard, Wilson deployed one of his divisions to cross the Harpeth in a wide arc to attempt to reach Franklin ahead of the Rebels. At West Harpeth Branch one of Wilson's divisions broke through an artillery screen to clash with Rebel infantry. But the wet, muddy fields slowed the cavalry so much that the last of the Confederate trains carrying wounded and munitions was crossing the bridge just as Wilson's troopers approached.[102]

Working desperately Confederate engineers and pioneers quickly toppled a wagon bridge and a railroad trestle bridge while disassembling their own pontoon bridge.[103] Hood's army passed through Franklin onto the Columbia Pike barely before Wilson's cavalry arrived on the north bank of the Harpeth, continuing through Franklin so quickly they had little time to take more than a few of their 2,000 wounded comrades left to convalesce after the battle of three weeks hence.[104] Seventeen thousand rations were also left in Franklin.[105]

As Union hunters continued to chase Rebel hunted the Yankees saw tangible evidence of the disintegration of Hood's army as a fighting force. Not only did scores of Southern stragglers willingly continue to surrender but the roadsides together with adjacent fields and woods were littered with a wide range of discarded blankets, small arms, cartridge belts and knapsacks, cooking utensils and canteens together with abandoned artillery pieces and wrecked wagons, some filled with discarded ammunition of various types.[106]

Continuing to follow the Confederates through Franklin, by 1:30 p.m. Wilson aligned his cavalry units in an attempt to get behind the Confederate rear guard newly entrenched approximately two miles south of Franklin.[107] Wilson's cavalry had elements approaching from or along either Rebel flank while Wilson's personal escort detachment—approximately 200 regular army troopers who had seen extensive action going all the way back to the Missouri-Kansas border clashes—was ready to launch frontally along the Columbia Pike. Together with the brigades on either flank Wilson posted a line of almost 10,000 mounted horses a mile and half long.[108]

Initially Wilson's escort detachment fought a fierce, sword versus bayonet struggle before piercing through the Confederate lines. As typical of fights when one side was mounted the wild melee soon scattered but enough Rebel defenders remained in their lines to repulse the Yankee charge. Once again Southern infantry criticized the lack of effort by their mounted comrades, a criticism that might not have been entirely warranted.

But the Yankee troopers on either flank—armed with their Spencer repeating carbine lighting up the night sky—were not to be denied. In fighting that extended well into dark the Blueclads overwhelmed the Rebel rear guard, forcing it to fall back in disorder and disarray.[109] It was by almost all accounts a tremendous victory for Federal cavalry but darkness helped frustrate the fulfillment of Wilson's primary objective, to-wit the capture of Hood's rear guard.[110]

By the evening of the 17th both armies had moved far apart from their supply wagons, forcing Wilson to order already depleted rations be stretched from five days to seven.[111] That night Rebel cavalry bivouacked close to its main army near Spring Hill.[112] Most of Hood's army had marched twenty-one miles that day since its pre-dawn start. One Confederate veteran later remembered, "The weather, still wet, was very cold, the roads desperately muddy, horses and men so hungry and jaded that despondency was now stamped upon the somber [sic] features of the hardiest."[113] In the meanwhile Federal infantry remained stranded north of the Harpeth, out of rations. Thomas, who had been in the saddle almost continuously since the beginning of the rout, requested that gunboats be sent up the Tennessee River to help cut off the retreat.[114]

## *The Slogging Continues* (December 18, 1864)

Sunday, December 18, 1864, would be another fateful day of the pursuit. That early morning Wilson's troopers resumed their advance down the Columbia pike, chasing the last of the Rebel stragglers out of Spring Hill by 11:00 a.m.[115] However, continued bad weather confined Wilson to the roads, meaning his riders were still unable to cross fields to try to capture the rear guard, S.D. Lee observing that, "A more persistent effort was never made to rout the rear guard of a retreating army."[116] Wilson's troopers had nothing to eat since the previous day, no forage was available, and everyone was exhausted after slogging through mud and muck, all to no avail since the enemy was still continuing its retreat.[117] Wood's 4th Corps trudged through ankle-deep slop until stopping to bivouac at 4:45 p.m. about three and half miles from Rutherford Creek. At this point Wood's foot soldiers were leading the Federal pursuit.[118]

Hood, now beginning to recover emotionally from the disastrous rout of his army, stayed that Sunday evening in a private residence in Columbia.[119] Hood's chaplain shared letters from some of Hood's subordinates to try to convince Hood that his army had done well at Nashville except for one division commanded by MGen. William B. Bate, 38, whose soldiers purportedly precipitated the collapse of the entire line by their panic.[120] Following prayers coupled with assurances that God favored the South, the chaplain and Hood's staff tried to convince Hood to retreat no further, citing the expected arrival of Forrest from Murfreesboro as one significant factor for standing firm.[121]

As had been anticipated, Forrest arrived to rejoin what was left of Hood's army later during that evening of the 18th.[122] At this point in the war Forrest, 43, was clearly one of the genuine, toughest warriors of either side in the Civil War. Dabney Maury, another Confederate general, described Forrest as having "…a personal prowess proved in many fierce encounters, he was a king among the bravest of men of his time and country."[123] William Sherman described Forrest as "the very devil" who had to be vanquished before there would be peace in Tennessee.[124] Upon his arrival from a three day horse ride through terrible conditions, upset over Hood's campaign, and still recovering from his third wound, Forrest was hardly in the mood for fanciful ideas, bluntly telling Hood such a stand created too much risk that would completely destroy what was left of Hood's army. Hood acquiesced to Forrest, perhaps recalling the dire consequences of launching a full frontal attack at Franklin instead of following Forrest's recommendations to flank Schofield.[125]

## *Forrest Assumes Rear Guard Command* (December 19, 1864)

Once Hood decided to continue his retreat to Alabama, he made a couple consequential decisions. First, on December 19 the army's wagons and artillery were sent south as quickly as possible. Second, and perhaps most important, Hood put Forrest in charge of the rear guard, reinforcing Forrest's cavalry with a hand-picked infantry division of 1,900 soldiers (as opposed to the 4,000 that Forrest originally requested). Forrest selected MGen. Edward Walthall to lead the newly created division.[126]

The same day, Wilson's cavalry also resumed the chase but the going was not easy. Wilson recounted,

> With five brigades well in hand, [I] lost not an hour night or day that could possibly be avoided , … But with rain and frost to chill and distress both horses and men, and the country getting wilder and more desolate as we pushed into it, we could not get fast enough on the flanks of the enemy's rear guard. … the country … was the worst we had yet seen … entirely stripped of forage and supplies.[127]

Forrest took full, adroit advantage of the terrain—creeks, narrow ravines, and muddy roads—to delay Wilson's riders. A pattern emerged wherein without infantry support Wilson's cavalry could not overcome Forrest's rear guard but by the time Federal infantry had caught up to rejoin its cavalry the Confederate main army was able to continue putting more distance away from its rear guard. An infantry officer serving with Forrest described the usual rear guard tactics as consisting of a portion of the Confederates engaging the enemy while the rest "detached to select and hold a position still further to the rear to which our first line retreated when the increased intensity of the skirmishing seemed to indicate than an assault was about to me made."[128]

Furthermore, without the misdirected pontoons, the pursuers were forced to take two precious days finding materials to build new bridges.[129] Among other aggravations, the Federals sorely missed the expertise an Indiana regiment of trained pioneers and bridge builders that Sherman had taken with him on his Georgia expedition.[130] The rest of Thomas' army followed with determination doing its best to help rebuild bridges and repair rail lines. Nevertheless these vigorous efforts did not stop the Eastern authorities from complaining about what they perceived as unnecessarily sluggish progress.

By Tuesday morning, the 20th, the Federals had completed two bridges enabling Wood's infantry to cross the rain-swollen Rutherford while still believing Forrest's rear guard was in its front.[131] As elements of Thomas's army completed their bridges over the

Rutherford Creek, on December 20 the Confederate army completed its crossing of the Duck River, finished its evacuation of Columbia,[132] and was on its way to Pulaski, Tennessee.[133] Pulaski, another thirty miles to the south, was merely an intermediate stop toward Hood's new objective, Bainbridge, Alabama, a dried-up village and forgotten ferry on the south side of the Tennessee River, about six miles east of Florence.[134]

Once the Federals crossed the Rutherford, and after they determined that Forrest was no longer around, the Federals promptly advanced to the north bank of the Duck where they were again stymied by the want of pontoons.[135] In addition to losing two days to build bridges Wilson lost three more days to cross the Duck before awaiting more rations and forage for his nearly jaded horses.

Despite Grant's reservations, who claimed he wanted to see the "extent of damage done," on December 20 Lincoln promoted Thomas to Major General in the regular army.[136] In contrast, after the earlier Battle of Cedar Creek, Virginia, Grant initiated the promotion of Phil Sheridan—an excellent general but fourteen years junior to Thomas in years of service—to Major General! Even Sheridan admitted Cedar Creek was a victory that should have been credited to one of his subordinate commanders. Furthermore, and as will be discussed later in Chapter 18, while a dramatic counterattack sensationalized by the popular press, Cedar Creek was one of three battlefield victories in the Shenandoah Valley where Sheridan had failed to parlay his battlefield victory with a pursuit.

Henry Halleck, who it must be remembered once pursued at the "glacial" rate of less than two miles per day after Shiloh, on Wednesday, December 21, 1864, sent another patronizing message to Thomas about the "vast importance of a hot pursuit of Hood's army."[137] Halleck's rationale was that a total defeat of Hood's army would benefit Sherman, who after all had taken the cream of Thomas' Army of the Cumberland and had been advancing without any significant opposition ever since leaving Atlanta.[138] His own patience almost exhausted, Thomas replied to Old Brains, "Pursuing an enemy through an exhausted country, over mud roads, completely sogged with heavy rains, is no child's play and cannot be accomplished as quickly as thought of."[139] A mortified Stanton and Grant wrote to assure Thomas that they still had confidence in him although Grant could still not resist also egging Thomas to "push and do all we can."

Back east on December 21 Sherman's force of 60,000 reached Savannah, Georgia. By Sherman's own admission he had been "unopposed except by a few cavalry pickets." Grant nevertheless praised his friend's efforts as "the like of which is not read in past history." But Sherman once again as he had at Jonesboro allowed Hardee's small defensive force of 10,000–15,000 to escape. Accordingly Stanton was not quite so laudatory of Cump's accomplishment, wiring Grant, "It was a sore disappointment that Hardee was able to get off his 15,000 from Sherman's 60,000. It looks like protracting the war while their armies continue to escape."[140]

Stopping in Pulaski gave Hood's three infantry corps brief respite from the rigors of the retreat. While pro-Southern residents gathered shoes for the destitute soldiers, Hood took stock of his army's remaining assets.[141] Although Hood realized Thomas was stuck north of the Duck River, at least for a few more days, Hood was worried about the lack of forage for his animals, a concern mirrored also by Thomas for his animals.[142]

Potentially adding to Hood's concerns, if he were even aware, on December 21 a three brigade cavalry Federal force under the command of BGen. Benjamin H. Grierson, 38, left

Memphis, Tennessee, with the mission to strike and destroy the Mobile & Ohio R.R. and the Confederate supply base at Tupelo.[143] Although not as well known as most other cavalry leaders, this former music teacher had established his *bona fides* during Grant's Vicksburg campaign in 1863 Grierson had conducted one of the most successful Union raids when he led a 600 mile, sixteen day raid throughout northern Mississippi and Louisiana that Grant described as "one of the most brilliant cavalry exploits of the war."

Although the lousy weather continued, after five full days of pursuit both armies resumed their respective marches on Thursday, December 22. Hood's intermediate objective was Sugar Creek, about twenty miles to the south of Pulaski. His three infantry corps would be traipsing along rural roads trains of wagons had churned into mud pits. The conditions of the roads forced the Rebels to leave behind or destroy more wagons and artillery pieces as they bogged through the quagmires.[144] Dead horses and mules, some with eyes still open, lay frozen by the roadside.[145] One of Walthall's staff officers observed, "The sufferings of the troops were terrible. ... Without protection from the severity of the weather, without blankets, and many without shoes, and nearly all indifferently shod, the horrors of the retreat were to be seen as the bare and frost bitten feet of the soldiers, swollen, bruised, and bloody, toiled painfully ... over the frozen pike."[146] Soldiers limped on frostbitten feet so swollen they left blood with every step.[147]

On the other side of Rutherford Creek Thomas was equally determined to catch and capture Hood's army before it reached the Tennessee River. The Union's pontoon train finally arrived at the Rutherford Creek by 1:00 p.m. on December 22, four days later than had been planned. Hoping to cross the Rutherford without further delay, the pontoons were erected while the weather worsened and were completed after dark.[148] Still intending to reach the Duck and hoping to catch the main body of Hood's army, even as troops were crossing the Rutherford, Thomas rushed unused pontoons forward to the Duck, these segments arriving at the north bank of the Duck by 11:00 p.m. However Forrest's cavalrymen firing from across the river at Union engineers and pioneers delayed the start of the bridge's construction.[149]

Once the Duck's south bank was cleared of snipers to allow construction of the bridge, construction was still hampered by 15 degree temperatures and swift currents together with floating ice, not to mention that there were only three pontoniers to direct the work of the inexperienced soldiers.[150] Finally bridges across the Duck River were completed to enable the last of the Federal army to reach the Duck's south bank by early dawn of December 24.[151] After six days delay Thomas' army was once again in full pursuit.[152]

Even though Thomas' army had fought two intense battles within two days at Nashville, followed by an eight-day march through dreadful conditions, including reduced rations, Thomas still wanted to bring Hood's army at bay.[153] Thus, upon completion of the Duck bridge the Union pursuit resumed December 24. The three infantry corps would advance down the roads with Wilson's cavalry riding on either flank across the countryside, having to push their mounts as hard as possible through the continued terribly inclement, wet weather.[154] Another "spirited affair" suddenly erupted at Richland Creek—this time between artillery batteries—with Southern gunners claiming they disabled two Union guns.[155] However the Rebel position became untenable once Wilson started to outflank Forrest who just after sunset ordered another retreat, this one all the way back to Pulaski.[156] Wilson claimed the Rebels retreated so rapidly they were unable to burn the pike bridge over Richland

Creek.[157] But although as before Forrest had been forced to retreat, his stalling tactics allowed the rest of the army to lengthen its lead.[158] Forrest and Walthall spent much of that night in Pulaski destroying wagons of abandoned ammunition as well as a locomotive and five cars.[159]

Despite being exhausted, cold, and hungry, Union cavalry continued pushing forward but the Blue clad infantry was unable to maintain the same pace to provide necessary support. And although they kept struggling to advance, their mounts were suffering an awful toll. Wilson noted, "The horses' legs were covered with mud, and this, in turn, was frozen, so that great numbers of the poor horses were entirely disabled, their hoofs softened and the hair on their legs so rubbed off that it was impossible for them to travel."[160]

On December 25 Forrest's rear guard ambushed Wilson's advance unit at Anthony's Hill (also known as King's Hill), about seven miles south of Pulaski.[161] Here the road climbed into a U-shaped rock formation with thickly treed ridges on either side allowing Forrest to mask his troops and batteries. Forrest sprung his trap with a sudden blast from his guns once the Federal's van approached to within 50 paces.[162] After an initial setback—including the loss of a 12 pounder Napoleon, the Confederates' only prize of the retreat —[163] Wilson's troopers recovered their composure to regain the initiative, capturing another 50 Rebels. Forrest moved back another fourteen miles to Sugar Creek where he bivouacked the night of December 25–26.[164] Meanwhile forty-miles to the south the vanguard of Hood's main army finally reached the Tennessee River at Florence by nightfall on Christmas Day.[165]

Also on Christmas Day, 1864, the Federal cavalry force under Grierson's command struck Verona, Mississippi, a key Confederate supply depot south of Tupelo. Before leaving, the Federals burned or otherwise destroyed two locomotives, thirty-two cars, eight warehouses, and 200 wagons supplies intended for Hood's army. Most importantly, at least for the time being, the Blue cavalry also severed Hood's lone railroad supply line between Corinth and Tupelo.[166]

## Hood Crosses the Tennessee River (December 26–28, 1864)

While Forrest set one more ambush against Wilson's advance on the south side of Sugar Creek on December 26, Hood's army began crossing the Tennessee River,[167] many of the Confederate soldiers being forced to wade through the rigid cold waters.[168] Before arriving at the Tennessee River across from Bainbridge the Confederate engineers realized they did not have enough pontoons to reach across the river. Hood's engineers sent word to Decatur where fifteen additional pontoon boats had been seized by "some blunder" after the Federals had abandoned that garrison in November.[169] Federal gunboats were supposed to have been towed away these abandoned pontoon boats but the Confederates managed to capture these pontoons first.[170] The timely arrival downstream of these addition pontoon boats was critical in saving Hood's army from a wretched situation, with the bridge being completed before sundown.[171]

Meanwhile south of Sugar Creek, during the early morning hours the Federals advanced slowly and carefully while shrouded in dense fog toward Forrest's position. Forrest's rear guard patiently waited until the Federals advanced to within fifty paces before launching an artillery volley "causing the wildest confusion."[172] After chasing the disorganized

Federals back across Sugar Creek in disorder, Forrest waited two hours before retreating, once again having thwarted Wilson's pursuit.[173] Before retreating the Rebels captured enough horses to mount a brigade for their final push to the Tennessee.[174] However Sugar Creek would be the last significant combat of Hood's Army of Tennessee fought on its namesake's soil.[175] Low on ammunition, out of rations, and the infantry far behind—likewise out of rations—Wilson virtually gave up on the main pursuit.[176]

Almost as a last ditch measure Thomas sent Steedman's provisional division by road and rail to Decatur, Alabama, by way of Murfreesboro in hopes of outflanking the Rebels from the east. But this attempt was foiled by bad roads and more inclement weather, and Steedman did not arrive in Decatur—approximately 35 miles east of the Rebel crossing—until December 27. Wilson also requested gunboats to destroy the Confederates' pontoons near Florence, Alabama, but for want of pilots to navigate the shallow shoals, rapids, and sandbars the gunboats could get no closer than a mile downstream from their potential targets.[177]

Also on December 27 to try to prevent Hood's army from crossing the Tennessee River, Wilson dispatched a hand-picked "flying battalion"[178] of 500 hand-picked riders on the freshest horses but this again effort was too late. When the Blue riders reached the Tennessee on the morning of Monday, December 28, 1864, they found the Confederates had completed their crossing at Muscle Shoals before removing or destroying all means of further pursuit.

By the 28th of December Thomas ordered the end of the pursuit that had exhausted and debilitated 5,000 horses. Citing the terrible weather as well as logistical difficulties Thomas also ordered his army into winter quarters. After crossing the Tennessee River the ragtag remnants of the once powerful Army of Tennessee finally arrived in Tupelo January 23, 1865. When Hood inherited command of the Army of Tennessee six months earlier in Atlanta his army had 50,000 soldiers. When he began his Nashville campaign his army had approximately 38,000 men. After losses at Atlanta, Franklin, and Nashville among numerous other minor battles and skirmishes, Hood's army was reduced to barely 18,000 men after re-crossing the Tennessee River. One Confederate surgeon told his wife that nothing was left except "a remnant of a demoralized army."[179] Hood lost 13,189 men taken prisoners in Tennessee alone.[180] In addition to the losses of men, Hood also lost 72 pieces of artillery and 3,034 small arms. Eight generals were taken as prisoners of war.[181]

## Analyses

Although the Federal pursuit did not accomplish its ultimate objective of either capturing or annihilating what was then left of Hood's army it was still as successful as had been any other Civil War pursuit. Edward Longacre—Wilson's biographer—summarizes its success as follows:

> Having come 175 miles since the afternoon of December 16, [Wilson's] command had suffered several hundred casualties and a great number of disabled horses, and had lost one cannon. But in that period they had captured, in a series of skirmishes and engagements, 32 guns, 11 caissons, 12 stands of colors, and no fewer than 3,000 prisoners. Moreover, they had viciously harassed the remnants of a beaten but still dangerous army—not enemy cavalry alone, but foot soldiers and artillerymen as well. It was a record of which Wilson's soldiers could be deeply and justifiably proud.[182]

Also analyzing the impact of the post–Nashville pursuit Einolf—Thomas' biographer—concludes:

> While Thomas did not trap the Confederate army, by pressing the pursuit he inflicted further damage on Hood's force. The rain and icy weather slowed the Union pursuers, but it took a terrible toll on Hood's hungry, poorly clothed soldiers. Many [Rebel] soldiers threw away their muskets along the route, and some units lost all cohesion and degenerated into numerous small bands of stragglers. Hundreds of soldiers deserted or surrendered during the march, and others died of illness, cold, and exhaustion. By the time Hood's men reached Alabama, his army had ceased to function as an effective force. Union control over Tennessee was now certain, and Mississippi, Alabama, and Georgia were almost undefended.[183]

Thomas's own analysis varied from time to time, perhaps depending upon his audience. Once he said he was forced to launch his attack too soon because Wilson still did not have enough cavalry horses but on another occasion he said he had enough cavalry horses. Thomas did cite the bad weather as a reason for not being able to capture Hood's army, certainly a reasonable assertion. But the most interesting, and perhaps the most insightful, came when he said he could have overcome any deficiency in cavalry if he (Thomas) had detached a large force from the main army before the first day and had dispatched the detachment behind Hood's rear. However a Senator in the audience rebuked Thomas, pointing out that such a detachment may have unnecessarily weakened Thomas' army too much. Thomas responded by saying that "a general must be prepared to take some risks."[184]

## *Dénouements*

On January 8, 1865, Sherman announced the victory at Nashville while taking full credit for the victory,[185] strangely claiming that Thomas had "decoyed" Hood to Nashville. Although the pursuit after Nashville was by almost any standard the most successful of any until then in the Civil War, Grant continued his unrelenting personal criticism of Thomas.[186] On January 21, 1865, Grant sent a dispatch to Sherman stating: "[Thomas'] pursuit of Hood indicated a sluggishness that satisfied me that he would never do to conduct one of your campaigns."[187] It is also worth noting Sherman had never seriously pursued and that after Cump arrived in Savannah on December 21, 1864, Grant permitted Sherman to postpone the start of his Carolina campaign for six weeks, waiting among other things on more reinforcements from Thomas.

While black soldiers had proven their mettle in other battles such as Port Hudson and Port Wagner in Charleston Harbor, their courage at Nashville also helped change, at least temporarily, the impression of African Americans as soldiers. Originally the Virginian Thomas was reluctant to deploy the black soldiers on the frontlines, instead intending to use them to man the breastworks. However Steedman was insistent that his mixed detachment be deployed in the front lines. Consequently, as earlier discussed, black soldiers deployed as part of the demonstration fought gallantly and valiantly both days—but while many of the white soldiers in the same demonstration turned and fled—causing Confederate units to remain on their right while Union forces were able to outflank the Confederate left.

At the end of the first day's battle a group of Rebel prisoners were about to be escorted back to Nashville by black soldiers. Some of the Rebels objected to being escorted by former slaves saying they would rather die. Showing little sympathy Thomas simply replied, "Well, you may say your prayers, and get ready to die." Later when Thomas saw the number of dead African American soldiers stacked in front of the Rebel positions Thomas remarked, "Gentlemen, the question is settled; Negroes will fight."[188]

Grant almost immediately countermanded Thomas' orders to go into winter quarters. Schofield continued his pattern of insubordination by advising Grant and Sherman that Thomas had more troops than necessary and requesting that his (Schofield's) corps be transferred back east to fight along Sherman and Grant. (It must be recalled that at one earlier point Schofield had requested that he did not want to accompany Sherman and requested that he be sent instead to Knoxville.) Accordingly in mid–January Grant, without consulting Thomas, ordered the transfer of Schofield's corps to North Carolina to reinforce Sherman's operations.

Grant caused more break up of Thomas' army by ordering, again without Thomas' prior knowledge, that Smith's infantry and a division of Wilson's cavalry be sent to the Mobile campaign. Unit by unit Grant continued to detach Thomas' army without assigning any command responsibilities to Thomas except to support and coordinate cavalry missions. In mid–March, Grant—who had been stalled in front of Lee's army at Petersburg for nine months—blamed his own inaction upon impassable roads.

After Hood's army had encamped at Tupelo the respective cavalries of Forrest and Wilson remained in the Western theater. Forrest was promoted to lieutenant general and given command of all Rebel cavalry in the West. Although Forrest organized his troopers into three division commands, in reality many of his horsemen were scattered throughout Mississippi, Alabama, and eastern Louisiana.

In the meanwhile Wilson was headquartered at Gravelly Springs, in the northwest corner of Alabama. In contrast to the undermanned, poorly equipped Rebels, Wilson had taken great pains to assure that his men were "well-armed, splendidly mounted, perfectly clad and equipped."[189]

One of the Union's remaining goals focused upon Mobile, Alabama. Grant wanted Wilson to conduct a diversionary raid against Selma and Tuscaloosa, Alabama, but Thomas authorized a more ambitious mission of driving deeper into the South to also advance against other important manufacturing and munitions centers at Montgomery, Alabama, and Columbus, Georgia. Thomas also instructed Wilson to defeat Forrest. On Wednesday, March 22, 1865—after heavy rains and swollen streams had delayed his plans for three weeks—Wilson started south from Gravelly Springs, deployed in three columns trying to deceive Forrest.

Despite Wilson's efforts to confuse the Rebels, Forrest correctly determined that Selma—300 miles south of Gravelly Springs—was Wilson's first objective. Accordingly Forrest ordered two of his divisions to join him at Selma where he hoped to attack Wilson from the front as well as from Wilson's rear. However the Rebels failed to arrive in time to reinforce Forrest, meaning that on March 31 Wilson was able to rout Forrest's small force consisting only of his bodyguard and a brigade at Montevello, Alabama, approximately 45 miles north of Selma. The next day Wilson's cavalrymen captured documents that fortuitously revealed Forrest's dispositions and plans for converging with reinforcements. Wilson then proceeded to move directly to Selma, along the way routing another small Confederate force at Ebenezer Church near Plantersville, 20 miles north of Selma, where Forrest's arm was bloodied by saber slashes before he killed personally his 30th victim. As the Rebels fled they abandoned 200 of their wounded comrades as well as three guns.

Although Selma was surrounded with three and half miles of fortifications Forrest had only 2,500 cavalry along with an equal number of militia to occupy and defend the breastworks. Wilson's good fortune continued when the English engineer who had helped build the fortifications decided—after losing faith in the Rebel cause—to provide Wilson with sketches of the works. As Wilson's riders stormed the works on Sunday, April 2, 1865, the Southern militia took flight leaving Forrest no option except to withdraw during the night. Almost immediately fires set by Union soldiers and freed slaves began to engulf the city. Coincidentally as Selma was burning, and of course unknown to Wilson, Richmond was also in conflagrations after Lee had abandoned his works at Petersburg forcing Jefferson Davis and the much of the Confederate government to abruptly flee from the Confederate capital.

Wilson stayed at Selma to complete the destruction of its industrial capacity, rounding up Confederate stragglers, tending to the wounded while resting and refitting his command. Wilson's force was able to destroy the Selma Arsenal, consisting of two dozen buildings, as well as systematically and thoroughly razing other industrial facilities, including the Confederacy's naval foundry, the iron works and machine shops. This destruction was in addition to the capture of 2,700 prisoners, more than 2,000 horses as well as 66,000 rounds of artillery rounds.

Wilson and Forrest met at a pre-arranged conference on April 7 to discuss the exchange of prisoners. The meeting gradually became friendly, Forrest commenting to his guest, "Well general you have beaten my badly—and for the first time I'm compelled to make such an acknowledgement."[190]

By April 9—coincidentally the same day Lee surrendered to Grant at Appomattox—C.H. Wilson began moving on to Montgomery where he arrived Wednesday, April 12, 1865. After hoisting the Stars and Stripes over the original Confederate capital, Wilson then turned east. Wilson next captured Columbus, Georgia, on April 16, capturing 1,200 prisoners plus 52 guns as well as a vast bootie of materiel. As he approached Macon on the 20th Wilson was confronted by C.S.A. General Howell Cobb, then in command of Macon but previously one of the original secessionists, who was angry because Wilson was not honoring the truce that had earlier been arranged between Sherman and Johnston. This was news to Wilson who was advised that Lee had also surrendered.

Until Richard Taylor surrendered May 4 Forrest continued to maneuver what was left of his cavalry, disregarding reports that the war was over and telling his command that they had to remain "firm and unwavering." Afterwards some politicians tried to persuade him to continue some form of resistance, perhaps linking with Kirby Smith in Texas. Forrest responded, "Any man who is in favor of a further prosecution of this war is a fit subject for a lunatic asylum, and ought to be sent there immediately."[191]

Prior to the onset of the war Forrest owned 45 slaves who eventually were freed; it is not clear whether Forrest had voluntarily freed these slaves or whether they had simply been freed as a result of the war. Forrest himself claimed, "I went into the army worth a million and half dollars and came out a beggar." Joe Johnston asserted that Forrest was the war's greatest soldier while historian Shelby Foote would later make a disputed claim that the Civil War produced only two genuises: Lincoln and Forrest. After the war Forrest had murky associations with the Ku Klux Klan, purportedly serving as its Grand Dragon.

Following the Confederacy's surrender, Thomas was assigned to various commands of Southern districts; in these assignments Thomas proved to be an able, even-handed administrator effectively implementing Reconstruction. In this capacity Thomas testified numerous times before Congress and was the first to warn of the emerging dangers of the Ku Klux Klan. In 1868 President Andrew Johnston, once an adversary of Thomas, submitted Thomas' name for promotion to lieutenant general, apparently to obstruct Grant's fledging presidential candidacy. However, Thomas—not wanting to become embroiled in politics—asked as a matter of military loyalty that is name be withdrawn.[192]

Thomas died of a massive stroke March 20, 1870, his weight having increased to 300 pounds, and was buried in his wife's hometown in New York. Thomas' family of Virginians did not attend the funeral, his sisters claiming their brother had died in 1861. A monument honoring Thomas can be found in Washington, D.C.

John Bell Hood was nominated to be the Confederacy's youngest full general (four stars) but the C.S.A.'s Senate never confirmed that appointment.

Upon reaching Tupelo Hood asked Davis to be relieved of command. The day before Hood was relieved, Beauregard visited Tupelo where he found Hood's army with very few provisions with only half the soldiers being still equipped. Hood was temporarily replaced by Richard Taylor before several thousand of the army's men were sent east to try to resist Sherman's Carolina Campaign. Upon the completion of that transfer Joseph E. Johnston once again assumed permanent command of what was still called a greatly diminished Army of Tennessee.

Afterwards Davis sent Hood to Texas to try to raise a new army but by the time Hood arrived Kirby Smith had already surrendered all the Confederate forces in Texas. Hood then surrendered himself to the Federal authorities on May 31, 1865, to be immediately paroled.

In 1866 Hood went to Thomas at the latter's headquarter in Louisville where they met for the first time since their antebellum days in the 2nd Cavalry. Shortly afterwards Hood remarked, "Thomas is a grand man; he should have remained with us, where he would have been appreciated and loved." Hood settled in New Orleans where he married and organized various businesses that eventually fell victim to economic cycles or to the yellow fever.

In 1879 Hood, his wife of eleven years, and the oldest of their eleven children died of yellow fever. P.G.T. Beauregard organized a fund to finance the publication of Hood's posthumous memoirs, the proceeds being used to support Hood's surviving children.

Fort Hood, near Killen, Texas, is the largest active duty armor base in the United States Armed Services, and, in contrast to the modest monument erected for Thomas, is named for John Bell Hood.

# Eastern Theater

## 9

# First Bull Run
## *July 21, 1861*

Irvin McDowell, 43, was one unfortunate example of rapid promotion in rank with commensurate increases of responsibilities beyond his capabilities. Prior to Fort Sumter McDowell, an 1838 graduate of West Point and related by marriage to Ohio's governor, held the rank of major in the Regular Army always serving in various staff positions. At the beginning of the Civil War, McDowell was serving on the staff of General in Chief Winfield Scott in Washington.[1] Within three months, McDowell was brevetted in rank to Major General and given command of all Union troops south of the Potomac with the mission to capture Richmond, 123 miles from the Federal capital.[2]

When he left Alexandria, Virginia, on Wednesday, July 17, 1861, barely more than three months after Fort Sumter, to advance upon Richmond, McDowell had never previously been in charge of more than eight men. Now he was in command of more than 30,000 three-month volunteers along with a couple regiments of Regular Army soldiers, by far the largest army ever assembled on the continent, and approximately two and half the number that Scott led across the Mexican desert fourteen years earlier. Thus McDowell, like the rest of the other Regular Army officers, had no experience managing units near the size of the new Civil War brigades, divisions, and corps. Unlike Scott's Regular Army soldiers and officers, most of McDowell's soldiers and officers were "raw" and "green." Furthermore McDowell had a very small command staff without even the benefit of a chief of staff.[3] This meant that McDowell had little help, something that would prove problematic as the ensuing battle unfolded.

Naturally McDowell's subordinate officers, especially those in command of regiments and companies, also had little if any experience in combat command. One British correspondent riding with McDowell's army characterized most of these officers as "unsoldierly-looking men" and speculated, correctly as it happened, that few of the officers knew how to re-deploy a brigade from a column, the basic marching formation, into lines, the basic combat formation. McDowell was fully aware of his army's shortcomings, observing the army was "not sufficiently drilled and disciplined for an offensive campaign."[4]

It was on open secret that Richmond was the Union's first target.[5] Conversely the Confederate hierarchy recognized Manassas Junction, 29 miles west by south-west of Washington, together with the nearby Bull Run Creek, as strategic points to block any Union advance upon Richmond; not only was Manassas located at an important crossroads, but it set astride a railroad that could be utilized to import reinforcements from the Shenandoah Valley to the west. C.S.A. BGen. P.G.T. Beauregard was assigned to prepare the necessary defensive positions. Beauregard had little more experience, especially in combat command, than did McDowell, his West Point classmate. As a high ranking graduate of West Point, he served as an engineer on Scott's staff in the Mexican war and later was in charge of draining New Orleans before briefly (five days) serving as superintendent of West Point in 1861. Beauregard commanded the Rebel bombardment of Fort Sumter, a prestigious assignment that made him an early Southern hero but one that hardly involved the management of a large number of infantry troops trying to improvise maneuvers on the ground.

Bull Run is a relatively small creek running generally to the southeast before flowing into the Occoquan that in turn is a tributary of the Potomac River. Not only did the Confederates establish a line of defense at Bull Run near Manassas, but the Confederates also had 3,000 troops at Winchester, Virginia, at the mouth of the Shenandoah Valley, under the command of BGen. Joseph E. Johnston.[6] Johnston's lead brigade was commanded by BGen. Thomas J. Jackson, 37, a West Pont graduate who had recently resigned his faculty position at the Virginia Military Institute.[7]

The Federals had 18,000 three-month volunteers at Charleston, Virginia, under the command of MGen. Robert Patterson, 71, a veteran of the War of 1812 and the Mexican War, and who was nominally McDowell's second-in-command. An integral part of the Northern strategy was to prevent the Rebel's much smaller force from leaving the Shenandoah Valley to reinforce Beauregard at Bull Run. But reflecting the lack of aforethought given to Civil War units at that point in the Civil War, Brian Reid has noted Patterson "lacked cavalry, artillery, or even a rudimentary line of supply, and had no telegraph to keep in touch with either Scott or McDowell."[8] And even when they managed to communicate with each other, neither seemed to understand the other.

While of course almost all personnel, enlisted as well as officers, on both sides, were inexperienced, the Confederate forces probably had a distinct edge with better officers in its order of battle, at least down to the brigade level. Among the Federals, Col. William T. Sherman, then a brigade commander, would alone eventually emerge in the top tier of the best warrior generals in the entire war. Col. Ambrose Burnside, was another commander but his was not to be a sterling career. On the other hand, among the Confederates at First Manassas several brigade commanders would eventually prove to, be notable warrior generals, including Jubal P. Early, Richard S. Ewell, J.E.B. ("Jeb") Stuart, E. Kirby Smith, E. Porter Alexander, James ("Pete") Longstreet, Nathan George ("Shanks") Evans, and Wade Hampton. All these officers were West Point graduates except Hampton who was one of the richest men in the South. Evans, a West Point classmate with cavalry officers, William E. ("Grumble") Jones and John Buford, enjoyed a reputation for bravery and fearlessness during the Plains Indian Wars. Once in Kansas Shanks killed two Kiowa warriors in hand-to-hand combat.[9]

Instead of taking action to prevent the Rebels from leaving the Shenandoah Valley, on July 16 Patterson withdrew to begin to establish a base at Harper's Ferry. This relieved any pressure upon Jackson who commenced to march toward the railroad so that his brigade could be transported by rail to Manassas Junction. Instead of engaging Jackson as had been expected, Patterson explained he had not received any orders to attack.

Reflecting the inexperience and lack of training of the green Federal army, coupled with a plethora of bungled logistics,[10] it took two and half days for McDowell's army to march the 20 miles to Centreville, where the Federals paused north of Bull Run. The next morning the two armies were aligned against each other along either side of Bull Run Creek. The battle plan of each side mirrored the other's with each side intending to try to turn the enemy's left flank. In addition to the creek—fordable in only a few locations—some key terrain features included Howard Hill, south of Bull Run at the western edge of the battlefield, Henry House Hill, approximately a mile south of Howard Hill, and the Stone Bridge where the Warrenton Turnpike crossed Bull Run about a mile and half northeast of Henry House Hill. The Federals—who had ordered a number of feints along the entire ten-mile length of the defensive lines—were able to beat the Confederates to the punch in striking early in the morning of July 21; these green soldiers were roused at 4:00 a.m. to start a flank march that, because of a guide's error, took twelve miles. Capt. E. Porter Alexander, acting as a signal officer, wig-wagged to Evans, "Look out for your left. You are being turned."[11] In response, Beauregard cancelled his own plans to attack and began shifting regiments to his left.

Shortly after the battle of Bull Run begun, Beauregard was joined by Johnston who was slightly more senior than Beauregard but deferred overall command to Beauregard because of the latter's familiarity with the terrain of the prospective battlefield. Johnston did have combat command experience having, among other things, led the column storming Chapultepec in the War with Mexico. While Beauregard was responsible for directing the troops on the front lines, Johnston assumed the responsibility for directing newly arrived units to points in the battlefield.

By midmorning McDowell, despite some snafus in bringing his troops across Bull Run, still managed to align approximately 10,000 men, accompanied by sufficient artillery, into a line of battle upon Mathews Hill. This line of battle was opposed by approximately 2,000 Confederates under the command of Barnard Elliot Bee and his life-long friend, Shanks Evans. Their objective was not to defeat the Federal line but instead merely to delay, or buy time, until further reinforcements would arrive. Finally at about 11:30 a.m. with the Louisiana Tigers holding the Confederate left, Bee and Evans prudently withdrew to Henry House Hill where they would have a commanding view of most of the Bull Run battlefield.[12]

Opportunities for pursuits, as well as failures to exploit such opportunities, do not always occur only after one side has fled the battlefield in disarray. Indeed some of the most critical pursuit decisions materialize on the immediate battlefield, often with dramatic consequences. McDowell muffed one such opportunity midway through First Bull Run.

As soon as the Rebels withdrew McDowell ordered a pursuit from Mathews Hill to across the battlefield but halted this advance along the Warrenton Turnpike running in a valley between the two hills. Later that afternoon he posted two artillery batteries of twelve guns together with 2,400 infantry to Henry House Hill.[13] This exposed the Union force to 4,000 Confederate infantrymen with thirteen guns being amassed to contest that key piece of terrain.

Without much doubt McDowell's failure to pursue all the way was a serious tactical mistake. Even with the advantage of hindsight it cannot be said with absolute certainty that taking Henry House Hill alone would have guaranteed a reversal of the outcome of the battle; nevertheless it seems obvious that seizing that critical high ground should have given McDowell's army a significant advantage for the remainder of the battle.

Once the units were realigned the sides faced each other's front, meaning that each side was resorting to frontal assaults and counterattacks, launched in piecemeal, uncoordinated fashion. Hard, ragged fighting ensued back and forth, both sides repulsing attacks by the other. One newspaper reporter compared the battleground to "a boiling crater of dust and smoke."[14]

Indeed at one point while the battle hung in the balance Beauregard and Johnston considered the possibility of withdrawing to another location. But by mid-afternoon confusion crept into the Union lines, part of that confusion being caused by the 33rd Virginia, wearing blue uniforms, when it made an audacious charge that destroyed the Union batteries and their supporting infantry. Furthermore the steady infusion of fresh Rebel regiments, mostly Jackson's brigade that was arriving by rail, began to lead to a panicked collapse of some Union discipline and order. A great deal of Jackson's legend was born that afternoon when Jackson was observed holding his position and someone said "There is Jackson standing like a stonewall."[15]

Although McDowell's initial plan for the battle may have been sound, once fighting started his command decisions probably reflected his inexperience as a combat commander. According to Bevin Alexander in *Lost Victories—The Military Genius of Stonewall Jackson*, McDowell committed three crucial errors: (1) he was reluctant to continue his attack giving the Rebels time to establish a new defensive live on its left; (2) he failed to get four brigades in the final battle; and (3) he did not take advantage of an opportunity to turn the Confederate left flank.[16] Instead he focused on a frontal assault directly against the reinforced Confederate middle line in good defensive positions. To compound these tactical errors the integrity of some Federal regiments started to dissolve under the heat and humidity of the Virginia summer. Soldiers and teamsters from these units streamed toward their rear areas, many throwing away their ten-pound weapons and other equipment while making tracks in disarray toward Washington. McDowell had become "overwhelmed"[17] by the apparent hopelessness of the situation. Some ambulance drivers dumped their wounded passengers or even unhitched their horses to have a means of quick escape.[18] However, it is important to also note that a few Union regiments, particularly those from the Regular Army, managed to maintain good order and discipline, withdrawing from the battlefield with relatively good cohesion.

This might seem to have been one of the most opportune times for a successful pursuit in the entire Civil War. The Federal army was in serious disarray, apparently leaving it vulnerable to total destruction. Furthermore, there were no other defenses in Washington, meaning that if McDowell's army were destroyed, captured or overrun then the Federal capital was there for the taking, possibly ending the war almost as soon as it was beginning.

Indeed when George McClellan arrived in Washington five days after Bull Run he concluded that virtually nothing was in readiness to defend the city, an assertion to which Scott took furious exception.[19] Lincoln's future Secretary of War Edwin Stanton wrote, "The capture of Washington seems now to be inevitable.... The rout, the overthrow, and demoralization of the whole army were complete." However, to be fair, this vulnerability was probably unknown to the Confederate leadership, which would have had every reason to assume Winfield Scott would be overseeing a stout defense of the Federal capital.

The Confederate battlefield became flush with experienced commanders in high places. In addition to the presence of Beauregard and Johnston, Jefferson Davis—another Mexican War veteran and former Secretary of War—had arrived late in the afternoon as the Federals were beginning to flee. But some Confederate regiments had been decimated by the fighting, and even those that remained relatively intact were worn to a frazzle from marching and countermarching, were hungry and thirsty, were emotionally drained, and were low on ammunition. But there were other troops who had not been committed, and presumably were available to make a full-fledged pursuit to capture and/or destroy what was left of McDowell's army, if not to attempt a full *coup de grâce* against the defenseless Federal capital.

Was the Confederates' opportunity for pursuit as golden as may have been seen by many later historians? Perhaps not. In the first place, the Confederate leaders were slow to recognize the extent of their battlefield victory, even being stunned when they eventually realized what had happened. They initially thought the Federals were merely repulsed, regrouping for another counterattack as both sides had done throughout the afternoon. Perhaps being overcautious, there was even concern that McDowell was trying to lure the Confederates into some sort of trap or ambush.

E. Porter Alexander, who became one of the most objective historians of the Civil War, later said First Bull Run was one of the two best chances for the Confederacy to win its independence.[20]

Even after realizing that the Federals were not merely repulsed but instead were retreating, some even in a helter-skelter manner, Confederate commanders had no way of knowing whether, or how many, Union reserves were waiting in Centreville, some five or six miles away. The Confederates were fortunate to have an abundance of officers who would eventually accumulate distinguished military records, but at this point most were still amateurs without experience in commanding large sized units and without experience in the logistics to support units on the move. Marching in a column was yet to be a military skill that could be taken for granted. And while the Confederates won the battle by compelling the equally inexperienced Federals to withdraw from the battlefield, the Southerners had also suffered their share of casualties and thus were far short of enjoying enough numerical superiority to sustain a successful pursuit. Probably as important as anything the Confederate command structure was not clearly defined with Johnston and Beauregard essentially acting as co-commanders but neither possessing the resolve to act aggressively or decisively, especially in the presence of Jeff Davis who seemed as surprised by the outcome of the battle was as almost anyone else.[21]

And for reasons that will be further explored in later chapters, cavalry was an indispensable ingredient of any successful pursuit. Although Stuart's cavalry had arrived in time to make one charge against the Yankees, otherwise it did not play a significant role in the battle, nor was it sufficiently organized to be part of any meaningful pursuit.[22]

David Detzer, in *Donnybrook, The Battle of Bull Run, 1861* (2005), flatly states, "The idea of an all-out Confederate charge at this moment was absurd, the wishful thinking of critics at a later date."[23] Detzer points out that "…the Confederates were as battered as their foes. With the exception of two or three regiments, the brigades that had fought much of the battle … had been pulverized beyond recognition. It would take them a while—a day, a week—to regain the capacity to march long distances and fight. Like the Yankees, the Confederates needed to eat, to quench their burning throats, to rest, to sleep, to regroup."[24]

To his credit, Davis inquired about the possibility of a pursuit, and when advised that none was planned he wrote an order designating a reasonably fresh brigade to lead a pursuit.[25] However, the officers of the brigade objected citing a number of reasons, including roads mired in mud from heavy rains, which also were causing streams to flood. As the rains continued the next morning the orders to pursue were never issued; instead the Rebels embarked upon three probes or reconnaissances in force, none of which produced any meaningful results.

It appears that each side engaged approximately 18,000 soldiers at First Bull Run. The Union suffered about 2,800 casualties while the Confederates suffered almost 2,000 casualties. Of upmost importance to the Rebels they captured badly needed 28 artillery pieces.[26]

## *Dénouements and Precursors*

As noted by Byron Farwell in *Stonewall,* "Failure of the victor to pursue a beaten foe was to be characteristic of almost all Civil War battles, and in this, the Battle of first Manassas (or First Bull Run) was typical."[27] Whether the lack of any meaningful pursuit after First Bull Run was a strategically significant lost opportunity that would have almost immediately altered the history of North America, or whether it is a fanciful "what-if" is a debate muddled by unsettled factual issues. Similar to other Civil War issues it will probably never be settled to anyone's satisfaction. What is clear, however, is that the immediate aftermath of this first significant Civil War battle foretold many of the elements, such as confusion about the status of the enemy, command confusion or indecisiveness, troop exhaustion, ammunition and supply depletion, poor weather conditions, and impending darkness, would continue to be some of the pertinent factors regarding pursuits for the next three years and nine months.

Or perhaps this was but the first example of what von Moltke described as merely "two armed mobs, chasing each other around the country, from which nothing could be learned."[28] Von Moltke's condescending comment was typical of other European observers who felt the American Civil War offered little in terms of military education. Indisputably in July 1861 the Civil War was hardly the first modern war, but unfortunately for the 740,000 lives that would be lost during the remainder of the war, perhaps First Bull Run was merely a harbinger for many other battles to follow.

Beyond the issue of pursuits, recriminations began almost before the last Union soldier drudged back into Washington. Many of the criticisms came from the same major newspapers that had been urgently pressing for the attack in the first place. But within the Union command, Lincoln and Scott did not attempt to scapegoat extensively but rather began to construct a strategy designed to eventually prevail.[29] Robert Patterson, who had failed to prevent Johnston from reinforcing the Rebels at Manassas, was mustered out of the army before the end of the month.

In the tradition of loyalty, Winfield Scott, 75, a hero of the War of 1812 and of the Mexican War, as well as once the Whig's presidential candidate, offered to fall on his sword. The next day after Bull Run, Scott was heard to proclaim, "Sir, I am the greatest coward in America. ... because I did not stand up, when my army was not in condition for fighting, and resist it to the end." Lincoln overheard the remark and inquired of Scott if he was implying that Lincoln had forced the Union troops into battle; Scott, while knowing that indeed that was the case, refused to be rude to his Chief, demurred and simply evaded Lincoln's query.[30] Later Scott submitted his letter of resignation, citing deteriorating health.

Lincoln did not immediately accept Scott's proffered resignation but instead held it in abeyance.

First Bull Run converted one important person in the chain of command from a soft war advocate to a hard war proponent. Prior to Bull Run, Abraham Lincoln had hoped to avoid what he called a "remorseless revolutionary struggle" but almost immediately Lincoln's attitude took a dramatic reversal. Among other things he issued orders to tighten the blockade and to strengthen his forces in Northern Virginia. He also wrote a memo expressing his desire that his four main armies, the ones at headquartered at Cairo, Illinois, at Cincinnati, Ohio, and at Harpers' Ferry, and the one stationed along Arlington and Alexandria, prepare to press forward. Clearly Lincoln had quickly come to realize, long before many of his commanders did, that the war would not be won quickly or easily, but instead the Union would prevail only by hard, difficult fighting. America's War Between the States would not be a soft war to be settled by capturing pieces on a chess board.

After First Bull Run the belligerents took stock and realized the futility of expecting a quick, decisive knockout blow to end the war. Accordingly, they quit relying upon 90-day enlistments with inadequate training and equipment. Instead the armies not only began to massively build up their numbers (Lincoln issued a call for another 400,000 volunteers), but also tried to assure their units were better trained as well as being better armed and equipped to fight over the long haul. At the same time the leaders of both sides began to evolve strategic goals like a fighter who is unable to score an early knockout and who then begins to "work the body," the Union army began to try to weaken the Confederacy with a number of strategic measures such as imposing a naval blockade.

Jubilation was abundant throughout the Confederacy. Because many secessionists also believed one battle alone would decide the entire war, many thought the C.S.A. had already won its independence. At the battlefield itself, hundreds of volunteer militia men believed the war was over and began to return to their homes. This belief that the war was won without more effort may help to explain the lack of any order to pursue further into Washington. Moreover, Jefferson Davis later rued that the victory at Manassas gave the Confederacy "an overweening confidence" that may have led to lax decisions.

The following August Jeff Davis named four full generals, Samuel Cooper, Albert Sydney Johnston, Robert E. Lee, and Joseph E. Johnston, with that order of seniority. Joseph E. Johnston protested that he had been senior to the other three in the U.S. Army and thus should have been designated the senior C.S.A. general. Regardless of its merits Johnston's protest ignited an acrimonious dispute with Davis, one of those disputes that would linger to poison relationships among Confederate authorities throughout the entire war.

During subsequent months McClellan began to campaign aggressively behind the scenes to be appointed to replace Scott as General-in-Chief.[31] Finally on October 18, 1861, Lincoln and his cabinet reluctantly agreed to accept Scott's request to retire, replacing Scott with McClellan, then 34 years old. And so the war began in earnest.

# 10

# Stonewall in the Valley
## Spring 1862

Stonewall Jackson's Shenandoah Valley campaign in the late spring of 1862 may be one of the best case studies to illustrate, examine, and analyze various elements necessary for successful pursuits. Normally, and in a number of different circumstances, Jackson was the pursuer but on at least two occasions he became the prey when Lincoln and Stanton became convinced that Jackson was trapped and ought to be captured.

During the four-year course of the war, the Valley would be subjected to several campaigns initiated by either side, but Jackson's 1862 campaign was a classic example of diversionary strategy. But for our purposes, it was also an exemplary example of extraordinary tactical maneuvering.

The Valley, running more than 150 miles in an approximate north by northeast manner, and being from twenty to forty miles wide, is framed by the Little North Mountain to the west and by the Blue Ridge Mountains to the east. Its topography is complicated by another range, the Massanutten Mountain, which runs up and down the middle of the Valley itself, and which also separates two main tributaries to the Shenandoah River. These branches, or forks, are slightly misnamed with the North Branch located west of and generally parallel to the Massanutten Mountain while the South Branch, being the bigger, and more difficult to ford, of the two branches, runs in a serpentine manner east of and basically parallel to the Massanutten.

Complicating the nomenclature is that the South Branch is formed at Port Republic by the confluence of two rivers: The North River and the South River. These two rivers, and their names, become important when discussing the battle at Port Republic, the final battle of The Valley campaign of 1862. The two tributaries of the Shenandoah River converge north of the Massanutten near Front Royal, Virginia. From this confluence the Shenandoah River continues its flow northward to Harper's Ferry where it joins the Potomac River, some seventy miles upstream of Washington, D.C.

Strasburg, to the west, and Front Royal, to the east, sit at the northern corners of the Massanutten. Harrisburg, at the west, and Conrad's Store (Now Elkton) to the east, are located at the southern edges of the granite range. The area east of the Massanutten is often called the Luray Valley.

Roads also ran on either side of, and roughly parallel to, the Massanutten with the better road being a so-called Turnpike along the west side of the Massanutten. This turnpike was a major route between Winchester and Staunten, Virginia, a Confederate supply base situated at the head, or south end, of the Valley. Much of this turnpike was macadamized, thus providing a hard, normally all-weather, surface. The road on the other, or eastern, side of the Massanutten was not macadamized; it also had four bridges over the South Branch between Front Royal and Port Republic making it vulnerable to heavy rains that could wipe out these bridges.

The Shenandoah Valley, the breadbasket of the Confederacy, was always of strategic importance to Richmond. Furthermore Harper's Ferry, at the lower end of the Valley, was important for two reasons: It was a major armory and armament manufacturing facility but it also was perceived as a gateway to access to the Federal capital some seventy miles downstream. For these strategic reasons, the Valley's major city, Winchester—at the convergence of nine roads, including one connecting to Harper's Ferry—suffered the misfortune of being invaded by one side or the other at least seventy-two times during the hostilities.

## First Retreat Up the Valley

By the spring of 1862 Union forces had managed a string of victories that seemed to portend the beginning of the end of the war. In the autumn of 1861 the Confederacy attempted to annex Arizona and New Mexico by force but badly bungled that attempt. On November 4, 1861, the Union Navy took Port Royal, South Carolina, giving the Union Navy a fueling station that helped to extend the blockade as far south as Florida. Not so incidentally, in January 1862, Edwin Stanton replaced the corrupt and ineffective Simon Cameron as the Federal Secretary of War. In February and March of 1862, BGen. Ambrose Burnside successfully managed the capture of additional coastal areas in North Carolina.

Also in the spring of 1862 the Yankees under David G. Farragut's command captured New Orleans, another sea borne victory. New Orleans, located at the mouth of the Mississippi River, was the South's largest and busiest port, second only to New York City. The capture of this sea port would crimp the C.S.A.'s economy and financial stability for the remainder of the war. And of course Grant's victories at Fort Henry and Fort Donelson created Northern control of the important inland waterways, the Tennessee and Cumberland Rivers. The Union had captured several islands on the upper Mississippi River. The Union victory at Pea Ridge, Arkansas, meant that the Confederates would not threaten Federal control of Missouri. Lastly the Union capture of Corinth, while not a decisive victory, impeded the Confederates' capability to transport troops, equipment, and supplies along the east and west railroads.

Neither Lincoln nor Scott publicly blamed McDowell for the embarrassment of Bull Run. McDowell was allowed to remain in the army, in fact was promoted to major general the next spring and given command of a corps. Nevertheless George McClellan was summoned from what is now West Virginia to take command on July 27, 1861, of the Department of Washington and Northeastern Virginia (Arlington and Alexandria), the genesis of what became known as the Army of the Potomac.

On the surface, at least, McClellan had all the credentials promising he would be a great military leader. After graduating second in his West Point Class of 1846 he served with distinction as an engineer during the Mexican War. Not only had he served as an instructor at West Point, he had been an observer at the Crimean War before resigning in

1857 to become a railroad executive. He was blessed with outstanding physical characteristics—being handsome, broad shouldered, and muscular—that enhanced his charismatic appearance.[1] His report about the Crimea War criticized the allied generals for losing sight of their objective and failing to "press rapidly and unceasingly towards it."[2] Perhaps most important, McClellan won to battles in western Virginia, which perhaps were of marginal significance but no other Union general had yet done better.[3]

As the winter began to fade in 1862, Jackson was headquartered in Winchester, having returned—promotion to major general and a new nickname in hand—after his "Instrumental" role the Confederate victory at First Bull Run. Jackson's original mission had been to defend against a potential Union incursion from western Virginia. Otherwise in early 1862 the Valley had only a secondary strategic importance.

Joe Johnston remained in Manassas with the balance of his army until March 10, 1862, when he withdrew to retreat to Fredericksburg, Virginia, to meet the threat of a Federal invasion of the Peninsula. George McClellan's concept of the war was that the Union should take "their strong places" with overwhelming physical force."[4] McClellan began his Peninsula Campaign, having on April 1, 1862, bringing a massive army to Fort Monroe at the tip of the Peninsula between the York and the James Rivers, and intending to move westward against, and presumably capture, Richmond, some 123 miles south of Washington.[5] Not only was Richmond the capital of the Confederacy it was also part of an important rail hub and the largest, most important industrial city in the South. McClellan had assembled, organized, and trained a tremendously sized army, as only McClellan could do, and planned to overcome the Confederate defenses around Richmond primarily with sheer numerical superiority. Not only did McClellan plan to march his army up the Peninsula, he also wanted McDowell to march south from Fredericksburg to hit the Confederate left flank. Combining McDowell's army with McClellan would give the Union forces a two-to-one numerical advantage over the Confederate defenders. Given other Federal successes around the edges of Confederate territory, capture of Richmond should seriously retard the Rebels' capacity to continue their rebellion.[6]

Although Lincoln had been trying for some time to pressure the Young Napoleon to start moving out of the Washington area—Lincoln still had misgivings about McClellan's specific plans—Lincoln being worried as always about the capital's vulnerability. Nevertheless, upon McClellan's vague assurances that sufficient troops would be left to protect Washington, Lincoln gave his reluctant and conditional approval to McClellan's plans. Thus when Lincoln learned that McClellan had left insufficient numbers of troops, at least in Lincoln's and Stanton's opinion, to protect Washington, Lincoln ordered McDowell, with his army of 40,000, to remain at Fredericksburg, rather than join McClellan as the Little Napoleon had anticipated when launching his invasion of the Peninsula.

Meanwhile, Jackson was chomping at the bits in Winchester to either assemble an army large enough to invade the North or else to join the C.S.A. army defending Richmond. However the Confederacy simply did not have spare troops to reinforce Jackson's ambitions to invade the North. Furthermore from Richmond's standpoint it was imperative to prevent other Union forces, especially McDowell's, from linking up with McClellan. Therefore, Richmond assigned Jackson the mission of diverting McDowell and other Union forces away from McClellan. In practical terms this meant that Stonewall had to draw, and hold, attention to his presence and potential threat in the Shenandoah Valley.

Jackson was in a precarious situation in Winchester. At the most he had only 10,000 troops at his immediate disposal while on the other hand the Federals had several times that number. In addition to McDowell's 40,000 troops to the east in the Fredericksburg area, MGen. Nathaniel P. Banks, 46, with 35,000 troops was in Harper's Ferry to the north, and John Charles ("The Pathfinder") Frémont had 15,000 troops scattered to the west of the Valley.

In this situation the Union was hardly blessed with the best or brightest of military commanders. As previously discussed, prior to First Bull Run Irvin McDowell had been little more than a career pencil pusher. Notwithstanding his lack of command experience, but for a critical tactical mistake at First Bull Run, McDowell could have gained enough fame and glory to have propelled him to the Presidency.[7] Reflecting the dearth of qualified commanders at the beginning of the war, not only was McDowell not relieved of command in the aftermath of First Bull Run, he eventually was named commander of the Army of the Rappahannock headquartered at Fredericksburg.

But despite McDowell's deficiencies he was first rate in comparison to his fellow commanders, Banks and Frémont, both of whom were political generals. Banks, a lawyer, had no prior military experience but instead had been Speaker of the U.S. House of Representatives before becoming Governor of Massachusetts in 1858.[8] Banks succeeded the hapless Robert Patterson after the latter failed to hold Jackson in the Valley during First Bull Run. Granted, as a military general he was considered to be honest and forthright, characteristics not always applicable to other generals. Otherwise Banks consistently proved himself to be an unsuccessful commander, especially when it came to tactical decisions.

Frémont, born in 1813 in Georgia, at least had had some military experience and had gained widespread fame and glory as The Pathfinder as an army explorer, having discovered passes through and around the Rocky Mountains.[9] Nevertheless his combat experience was checkered. During the Mexican War he was convicted by a court-martial proceeding for mutiny and disobedience but President Polk allowed him to resign in order to avoid dismissal. Frémont's political connections were enhanced when he married the daughter of Thomas Hart Benton, an influential U.S. Senator from Missouri. An avowed abolitionist, in 1856 Frémont was the newly formed Republican Party's first candidate for President, losing to James Buchanan. Early in the war Frémont had been put in command of the Western Department, including Missouri, but quickly proved incapable of administering a burgeoning and important command.

The Pathfinder provoked Lincoln when he (Frémont) established martial law in Missouri and freed the slaves in that state. After several military defeats in Missouri, Frémont was relieved of command.[10] Again reflecting the shallow pool of available commanders almost six months later he was sent east to relieve BGen. William S. Rosecrans in the newly created Mountain Department.[11]

Of importance, Lincoln and Stanton failed to appoint an overall commander over these three generals. Instead Lincoln and Stanton—neither of whom had any significant military experience—naively believed they could command and coordinate these three separate armies from Washington.

Few military leaders in American history could have undertaken the task assigned to Jackson against such formidable odds. But the eccentric, pious, quick-tempered, and sometimes abusive Jackson was undaunted by the task at hand. A West Point graduate, finishing seventeenth in a class of 57 in 1846, he immediately had distinguished himself as an artillery officer in the War with Mexico. Five years after his graduation from West Point he resigned his commission to accept an appointment to teach a variety of subjects, including artillery, optics, mechanics, and astronomy at the Virginia Military Institute in Lexington, Virginia. By several accounts he was at best a mediocre professor—his students gave him a variety of unflattering nicknames, including "Tom Fool." Apparently was on the cusp of being fired from VMI when slaveholding Southern states began to secede after Lincoln's election in November 1860.

Notwithstanding his idiosyncrasies and personal shortcomings, as a field commander Stonewall often, but certainly not always, stood head and shoulders above most of the Civil War generals of the first two years of the war. Some Jackson partisans legitimately contend that much of the credit given to Lee for being audacious belonged to his top lieutenant, Thomas J. Jackson. One of Stonewall's maxims was,

> Always mystify, mislead and surprise the enemy, if possible; and when you strike and overcome him, never let up in the pursuit so long as your men have strength to follow; for an enemy routed, if hotly pursued, become panic-stricken and then can be destroyed by half their number.

Another Stonewall maxim was "[T]o move swiftly, to strike vigorously, and secure all fruits of victory,… is the secret of successful war." His new mission in the upcoming campaign of strategic diversion would give him ample opportunities to apply these basic philosophies of combat.

## *Kernstown* (March 23, 1862)

From the onset of armed hostilities, Jackson was often eager to pursue. For instance, as McDowell's Union army was fleeing in disarray after First Bull Run, the newly nicknamed Stonewall allegedly screamed at Jefferson Davis, who was visiting the battlefield, to give him—Jackson—4,000 fresh soldiers and that Jackson would be in the city of Washington that evening. For any number of reasons that story[12] may be more apocryphal than factual since the story did not appear in print until twenty years after the battle. Jackson himself failed to mention anything in his letters to his wife or to a friend about any such encounter with Davis. Neither did he ever bemoan opportunities to have captured Washington. Regardless of whether the story was true it nevertheless reflects Stonewall's reputation as an aggressive warrior eager to achieve decisive victories and being willing to take unconventional risks to do so.

Notwithstanding his strategic ambitions and aggressive tendencies, Jackson was also a realist, both in terms of assessing the immediate situation and in terms of recognizing and adhering to the importance of his assigned responsibilities. Had he attempted to stay and fight in Winchester not only would his overmatched army likely have been defeated but even as important he could no longer serve as a diversion, thereby freeing McDowell to march his 40,000 men to attack the Confederates' left flank at Richmond. Also not to be neglected, Banks and Frémont would have easily been able to capture strategically important positions if Jackson were eliminated as a significant threat.

However, Jackson soon had second thoughts about relinquishing Winchester without first giving battle, and thus circulated among his subordinates a plan to stay and fight.

Essentially Jackson contemplated to quickly turn around and launch an unusual night attack upon an unsuspecting portion of the Union army.[13] His subordinate commanders met in a council of war to decide retreat continued to be the better option. In anticipation of the adoption of this consensus Jackson's supply trains were sent south, much to Jackson's surprise and chagrin when he decided to give battle at Winchester. Becoming furious when he learned that he had been peremptorily countermanded by his own subordinates, Jackson declared in no uncertain terms that he would never convene another council of war.[14] But under the immediate circumstances, Jackson had no choice other than to abandon Winchester to Banks, and sullenly to begin to move south.

Within a week after leaving Winchester Jackson had found an excellent defensive position at Rude's Hill, near Mount Jackson, west of the Massanutten approximately fifty miles south of Winchester. Meanwhile on March 19, BGen. James Shields, commanding a division in Bank's corps, had arrived in Strasburg, eighteen miles south of Winchester, putting him approximately thirty-two miles north of Jackson's position. Shields, born in 1806 in Ireland, was essentially another political general who had most recently been U.S. Senator from Oregon but had some military experience, having fought in the Black Hawk War but also more importantly in the Mexican War where he was wounded.[15] Shortly after Shields reached Strasburg he mistakenly concluded that Jackson had moved east to reinforce Joe Johnston's defenses of Richmond. Accordingly on March 20 Shields began to turn around to return to Winchester as part of a general Union rotation eastward to try to reinforce McClellan. Jackson likewise began to countermarch to head back north as soon as he learned Shields had evacuated Strasburg.

At this point a strange turn of events, based upon faulty intelligence, began to occur. First Jackson's cavalry commander, Col. Turner Ashby, informed him mistakenly that most of the Union regiments have left Winchester.[16] Not one to let apparent opportunity to pass him by—especially one as golden as retaking Winchester—Jackson immediately extended his march to pass Strasburg before heading directly for Winchester.

On Sunday morning, March 23, 1862,[17] Jackson's van arrived at the outskirts of Kernstown, Virginia, three miles south of Winchester. Not being aware that the Federals still had 9,000 troops available, Jackson promptly ordered a flanking attack with his force of less than 4,000 men.[18] Brutal, back-and-forth combat ensued with Jackson issuing a flurry of orders, some of which were contradictory, while others bypassed his subordinate commanders. Eventually a lack of ammunition forced BGen. Richard B. Garnett, the commander of the Stonewall Brigade and Jackson's second-in-command, to order a retreat despite no orders from Jackson to do so,[19] causing Jackson's entire assault to crumble, the only battlefield defeat in Jackson's career. Although he was not on the field during the battle,[20] Shields will claim credit for this victory over Jackson.

Confederate losses were almost a third of those engaged, about the same percentage of Southern losses suffered later at Gettysburg.[21]

But ironically the tactical defeat of Kernstown was turned into a strategic victory when the Federals committed their own intelligence blunder. Although Shields had been provided no information about the strength or composition of C.S.A. forces in the area, the Yanks nevertheless assumed Jackson would not have attacked against such unfavorable numerical odds unless he was part of a much larger force. In fact Shields telegraphed Washington that he had defeated a Rebel force two-and-half times his number of troops! Thus based upon their own faulty estimate of the Rebel forces in the arena the Federals were afraid to launch a pursuit against Jackson's undermanned, out-of-ammunition army.[22] As a result of their faulty intelligence the Federals missed an outstanding opportunity to strike a devastating blow to their enemy,[23] and by April 2 Jackson was once again safely encamped at Rude's Hill.

More importantly, especially at a strategic level, Washington, based upon the same faulty estimation of the size Rebel troops in potential support of Jackson, rescinded McDowell's orders to join McClellan while directing Banks to stay in Winchester. Thus for the time being at least, McClellan was without at least 40,000 reinforcements he thought he desperately needed,[24] ironically all because of Jackson's defeat at Kernstown.

## *Village of McDowell* (May 8, 1862)

At the same time, Jackson's own record as the pursuer during his Valley campaign was a mixed bag, albeit for different reasons. After Kernstown Yankee cavalry came up the Turnpike, and on April 17 pushed across the bridge that had been protecting Jackson's sanctuary on Rude's Hill. In turn this forced Jackson to continue retreating up the Valley to Harrisonburg where on April 19 he turned east. Jackson eventually settled, at least temporarily, at Swift Run Gap, near Conrad's Store, southeast of the Massunutten Mountains.[25]

This new position gave Jackson several options while being relatively safe from Union attacks. One of his obvious options would have been to leave the Valley altogether to reinforce Confederate forces defending Richmond. Indeed on April 29 Secretary of War Stanton thought it was safe to send Banks back down the Valley to Strasburg and again to start Shields east to reinforce McDowell.[26] And joining the Richmond forces was what Jackson apparently was doing when on April 30, 1862, he marched his troops east. However, instead of continuing east toward Richmond, Jackson surprisingly boarded trains west bound toward Staunton, arriving there May 4.[27]

Reinforced by BGen. Edward ("Allegheny") Johnson, 46, in command of 3,000 soldiers, Jackson left Staunton to march northward toward the village of McDowell. Technically the village of McDowell is not in the Valley since it lies west of the Little North Mountain. However the village provided access to two vital points in the Valley: Cross Keys and perhaps more importantly Staunton. Jackson had reason to believe that Frémont was sending elements south from Franklin, now in West Virginia. This advance of Union soldiers would send them through the village of McDowell.

Near the village on May 8, 1862, Jackson's lead units encountered Frémont's advance unit under the field command of BGen. Robert Huston Milroy, 46, who had attended the Norwich Military Academy before fighting in the Mexican War. Milroy, a former judge, was an aggressive Indiana abolitionist described as a general who "will hunt up the enemy and fight him wherever found."[28] Milroy, seldom hesitant about throwing the first punch, launched an improbable two-regiment—the 25th OVI and 75th OVI—uphill assault led by Col. Nathaniel McLean against Jackson's numerically superior forces as they were still preparing their positions.[29] Then during the following night Milroy withdrew from the field and began a retrograde movement through and away from McDowell back toward

Franklin. And although the Yanks were retreating the Rebels were hardly in any position to initiate an immediate retreat. One of Jackson's staff members described the end of the battle as follows, "A great scene of confusion.... It was between 8 and 9 p.m.; our troops were all mingled in the greatest disorder imaginable, like a swarm of bees, calling out for comrades, etc, no one being able to distinguish another in the darkness."

McDowell might be considered a Pyrrhic victory for Jackson since his Rebel defenders, almost twice the number of Yanks, suffered almost twice the casualties than did the Union attackers.[30] The confusion of the battlefield aside, Jackson could not begin his pursuit until the next day because Jackson's supply wagons were delayed—due to Jackson's penchant for secrecy, he had not told even his quartermaster of his plans![31] This delay gave the retreating Union army ample time to prepare several ambushes and set fires to create smoke screens while falling upon its lines of communications.[32] Later Jackson commented admirably of the Yankees' use of smoke screens to cover their retreat, noting that it was "the most adroit expedient to which a retreating army could resort to embarrass pursuit"[33] while falling back upon its lines of communications. Accordingly, after five or six days Jackson abandoned his half-hearted pursuit, turning around at Franklin, to march back to the Valley, deploying cavalry to screen his withdrawal. In any case, Frémont's Federals were content to leave Jackson alone, having no intention to pursue in any event.

Stonewall's march after the battle of McDowell illustrates the difficulty of judging the success or lack of success of a pursuit. Some commentators have decreed this action as one of Jackson's successful pursuits while others have deemed it as a failure, presumably because Jackson did not "bag" the Federals. Not only did the Federals use effective technique to stall the pursuit but any chances of overtaking the Federals' retrograde movement were severely impeded by the day's delay in beginning the pursuit. As would be demonstrated on several occasions during the rest of the war, pursuing units could not afford to allow their prey the luxury of time to maintain, or regain, unit cohesion and to organize effective rear guard tactics, such as ambushes or smoke screens. Establishing and maintaining pressure upon prey was always essential for totally successful pursuits in the Civil War, especially if annihilation of the enemy was the primary objective.

But while it was true that Frémont's Bluecoats were not destroyed or even caught before Jackson decided to return to the Valley, it is necessary to keep in mind that Stonewall's strategic mission had been to keep Frémont confined away from the Shenandoah Valley, a mission that had been entirely accomplished.[34] Furthermore, Jackson also needed to return to the Valley where he had bigger fish to fry. Thus within the strategic context, while destruction or capture of even a portion of Frémont's army would have been a spectacular accomplishment, nevertheless Stonewall's pursuit had accomplished its essential purpose, and accordingly should probably be considered more successful than not. To add icing to the cake, Southern publicists were able to triumph Jackson's success as a counter weight to the recent loss of New Orleans, although of course the situations, and the corresponding consequences, were hardly comparable. Nevertheless McDowell was a badly needed psychological lift for the Confederacy. Even though Jackson had outnumbered the Union forces, McDowell was portrayed as an example of Rebels being able to prevail over great odds.

## Front Royal[35] (May 23, 1862)

After returning to McDowell, Jackson retreated to the Valley, settling his army at Lebanon Springs unbeknownst to the Federals. Members of the Federal hierarchy, perhaps letting their desire to reinforce McClellan cloud the judgment, concluded Stonewall was no longer a threat. And so on May 18 Stanton sent a telegram to McClellan to inform the Young Napoleon that Lincoln had ordered McDowell to resume marching overland from Fredericksburg to reinforce McClellan.

As part of a generally clockwise rotation Banks decided to reposition his army down (northward) the Valley, deploying 7,400 of his men at Strasburg and 1,100 without cavalry at Front Royal, a major Union supply depot ten miles to the east.[36] The remainder of Banks' army was sent to Winchester further down the Valley, essentially forming a triangle of encampments. On May 16, LGen. Robert E. Lee, then still a military a military advisor to Jeff Davis, sent Jackson a message directing Jackson to move "speedily" against Banks.

At Front Royal, Jackson—with the considerable help from a division commanded by MGen. Richard Stoddard ("Dick") Ewell, 44,[37] managed on May 23 to maneuver and concentrate his army against the badly out-manned enemy stuck in an indefensible position.[38] In the anticipation that Jackson would be advancing down the Turnpike Banks established entrenched defenses at Strasburg facing south up the Turnpike but Jackson surprisingly and surreptitiously crossed the Massanhutten at New Market before continuing north via the Blue Ridge's western edge.[39] Although Banks had as many as 1,600 cavalry at Strasburg he poorly deployed his horsemen, thus gaining little useful intelligence about Stonewall's maneuvers. In moving east across the Massanhutten to flank Banks at Strasburg, Stonewall was certainly mystifying, misleading and surprising the enemy but he was also boldly taking a risk that Banks might move suddenly to the south or that Frémont could resume his movement south, possibly trying to capture Jackson's major supply depot at Staunton.[40]

After Ewell's lead brigades, one of which was the exotic Louisiana Tigers, overran the Federal garrison at Front Royal, forcing the Federals to retreat with all possible speed, Jackson adroitly deployed his cavalry units to cut off roads, railroads and telegraph lines.[41] By taking Front Royal Stonewall had severed Banks' link to Washington while foreclosing any possible retreat to the east. Banks had no alternative except to begin a retreat from Strasburg north to Winchester. In reaction to word of the rout of Front Royal, Lincoln cancelled his previous orders to McDowell to reinforce McClellan. By that same time the Young Napoleon had put his army east of Richmond into a vulnerable alignment by deploying two of his corps south across the Chickahominy River. Thus more than ever McClellan felt he needed McDowell to provide reinforcements on the north of the Chickahominy River.

By some measures the Rebel pursuit following the rout of Front Royal was one of the most successful of the entire war. Jackson's horsemen functioned as cavalry had seldom been able to perform during the Civil War, inflicting significant casualties upon fleeing Federal troops and capturing a significant amount of supplies at another supply depot at Buckton Station, about another eight miles north of Front Royal. Acting swiftly and with good coordination, the Rebel cavalry, both those under Jackson's command as well as those in Ewell's division, were able to seize more supplies and equipment than Confederate wagons could possibly carry.[42] Additionally the Rebel horsemen were able to capture hundreds of badly needed replacement horses. On the other hand, amid all the carnage, Banks somehow managed to escape with all but fifty of his 500 supply wagons when the Rebel cavalry focused upon looting rather than capturing more wagons.[43] But while these seizures were an immediate gain for the Rebel cavalrymen, a severe downside would quickly materialize within the next couple days.

## First Winchester (May 25, 1862)

After Fort Royal Jackson quickly continued quickly to sweep northward to storm Winchester, where the Union defenders were once again quickly routed before scurrying across the safety of the Potomac. Some relatively minor aspects of the campaign portended later characteristics of the war. As one example, Union forces complained that citizens fired from downtown buildings as the Yanks retreated through Winchester. This had the effect of blurring the traditional dichotomy between soldiers and citizens, a distinction that continued to fade throughout the remainder of the war. As another example, the Union presence in the Valley had begun to weaken the rigid restraints of slavery. As a result some slaves began to emancipate themselves while seeking the protection of Federal units.

After his smashing victory at Front Royal, Stonewall Jackson began to advance against Union defenders trying to buy time before retreating with their supply trains from Winchester toward the Potomac River. Once again on May 25, 1862, Taylor's Louisiana Tigers led the assault against Union defenders.[44] After Taylor's Louisianans had moved forward in an almost parade ground fashion, Taylor gave the order to his foot soldiers to charge, whereupon the Union defensive line to begin to dissolve. In desperation the Union commander, Col. George H. Gordon, ordered his cavalry to charge against the advancing Louisiana foot soldiers. As the Blue coated horsemen charged forward, Taylor's infantry immediately halted before beginning to methodically fire volley after volley that emptied the saddles of the Union cavalry. Although well-disciplined infantry had begun to learn to protect itself against similar cavalry charges as early as in the Napoleonic wars, the ill-fated charge at First Winchester provided a harbinger of drastic changes in battlefield tactics for cavalry during the Civil War.

As Federal troops were fleeing as fast as possible Banks tried to persuade them to stop halt, yelling "Stop men! Don't you love your country?" To which one of the men replied "Yes, by God, and I'm trying to get back to it as soon as possible."[45]

Although Stonewall saw the opportunity "to reap a richer harvest of the fruits of victory" by unleashing a pursuit, his skilled but sometimes undisciplined cavalry troopers failed to exploit that opportunity.[46] Incredibly most of Ashby's cavalry was nowhere to be found! Instead the cavalry had dissolved into an orgy of looting with many troopers taking unauthorized absences of leave to take their confiscated steeds and other loot home.

Jackson was so frustrated by the lack of available cavalry at such a critical time, he ordered artillery horses to be unharnessed to serve as mounts for his infantry soldiers. Not surprisingly that arrangement did not work since among other problems haul horses were not trained or broken to be ridden. For that matter neither were the infantrymen trained to ride as cavalrymen.

Another problem arose when BGen. George H. ("Maryland Steuart") Steuart, commander of a cavalry unit that was part of Ewell's division, refused to accept a direct order from Jackson's courier, claiming that all applicable orders had to come through Steuart's chain of command.[47] Once Ewell was found to properly issue the needed order it still took another two hours to get Steuart under way.[48] Although Jackson's army captured an impressive number of prisoners and bounty nevertheless an outstanding opportunity to inflict tremendous damage to the fleeing Federal army failed to materialize, a failure that did not go unnoticed by Jackson. In his report Jackson stated, "had the cavalry played its part in this pursuit … but a small part of [the Union] army would have made its escape to the Potomac."[49]

But once again Stonewall's penchant for secrecy also contributed to this failure to pursue.[50] As happened too often Jackson had failed to share his plans with his subordinate commanders, meaning his own cavalry did not realize to stay close at hand. Had Ewell, Jackson's *de facto* second-in-command, been better kept abreast it is also possible Ewell's stiff necked cavalry commander would have been more responsive to the exigencies of the situation.

Another possibility is that unity of command of cavalry would have been productive for the Confederate pursuit. Throughout the war both sides vacillated between making artillery directly responsible to the overall commander, on one hand, or making artillery units part of, and responsible to, subordinate units in the overall command. But, with one exception to be discussed later, until the Union formed a cavalry command in 1863, cavalry tended to be attached to subordinate units instead of answering directly to the top commander. Adherence to a diffused cavalry order of battle hampered many pursuits throughout the Civil War, including the possibility of a decisive follow up after Jackson's triumph in Winchester in 1862.

The exhaustion of Jackson's troops also contributed to his inability to pursue after Winchester.[51] Over the last thirty-five hours Jackson's so-called foot cavalry had been in two battles plus other minor engagements. The battles of course followed extensive miles of marching, for instance one hundred miles in a week prior to Front Royal. Regardless of the legendary status of Jackson's accomplishments, there was a limit to his infantry's stamina.

## *Second Retreat Up the Valley*

Having pursued through Winchester and extending his forward units to Halltown, just three miles south of Harper's Ferry, Jackson was then extremely vulnerable to capture and/or destruction by the very same Federal armies he was supposed to be distracting from the Richmond arena. Although he had chased Nathaniel Banks with his tail between his legs out of Winchester and across the Potomac, Jackson has also moved so quickly that his lines of communications could not keep up, having been extended almost to their breaking point. Accordingly—as can happen if a pursuit gets out of hand—the tables were turned since Jackson and his army were then viewed as targets or potential prey.

The Washington administration became determined than ever to eliminate its nemesis when it realized Jackson's position was so far from his base thereby dangerously stretching his lines of communications. Also by that time the Federals must have realized their post–Kernstown assumptions were erroneous and that Stonewall was indeed isolated without reinforcements or other support in the immediate area. Jackson had proven himself, and his command, to be so disruptive and elusive, but then he was ripe for the taking, or at so it would seem. Accordingly on May 24, after meeting with his cabinet, Lincoln ordered McDowell to send 20,000 men back to the Valley to help capture Jackson.[52] To comply, McDowell returned Shields back west once again.

Also on the same day Lincoln telegraphed Frémont in Franklin to move to Harrisonburg, fifteen miles to the east, a movement that, according to Lincoln "must be made immediately." On paper at least, Jackson seemed to be extremely susceptible to being trapped. Between Frémont, with his army of 15,000, and Shields, back at Front Royal, they had a combined strength greatly exceeding that of Jackson's army, with no more than 15,000 effectives.[53] To further tighten the vise, on May 26 the Federal administration sent BGen. Rufus Saxton, 38, to Harper's Ferry to take command of 3,000 demoralized soldiers stationed at that garrison. Furthermore Banks was regrouped and replenished within striking distance just north of the Potomac.

If these Federal units, which together outnumbered Jackson by at least two to one, could establish a blocking position ahead of Jackson along the Turnpike while bringing a substantial force to Stonewall's rear they would have Jackson trapped without any feasible means of escape. On paper at least, capture of Jackson and his army seemed like, and perhaps should have been, easy pickings.

But Frémont's ineptness promptly began to unravel Lincoln's scheme. As Frémont began to march toward Harrisburg he encountered some relatively minor obstacles, including artillery fire from a few guns that Jackson had ordered down from Staunton.[54] Instead of neutralizing these impediments and continuing on to Harrisburg as directed, Frémont countermarched north one hundred miles first to Petersburg, and then to Moorefield, west of Strasburg. Upon hearing of Frémont's deviation from his direct orders, Lincoln was aghast, telegraphing, "What does this mean?"[55]

However Lincoln was not about to let Frémont's insubordination spoil the opportunity to bag Stonewall. On May 28, while Jackson was still in Winchester, Lincoln ordered Frémont to move from Moorefield to Strasburg and to be there by noon on the 30th. Although Frémont responded by starting his march immediately, he halted at Fabius, only ten miles from the start of his march.

But obviously Jackson, while not panicking, was aware of his jeopardy of lingering too long in Winchester and Halltown. Jackson could still be trapped if Frémont's army and Shields' division from the east converged at Strasburg, some fifty miles to the south of Winchester, ahead of Jackson. A timely convergence of Union forces was feasible because Frémont's advance elements were only 28 miles from Strasburg while Shields had advance elements only 12 miles away from Strasburg. Thus on May 30 Stonewall issued orders to start moving up the Valley again, this being his second retreat.[56] Obviously it was critical to beat the Federals to Strasburg, fifty miles from Stonewall's closest units.

Not only did Jackson have to move his infantry and artillery, but his army had to herd 2,300 captured Federal prisoners. Furthermore, Jackson's train of wagon, filled to the gills with captured food, supplies and equipment seized in the aftermath of Front Royal, was seven miles in length, double filed. Capture of this strung out army, burdened as it was with its enormous baggage, should have been akin to shooting fish in the barrel.

On May 31 Stonewall began to leave Winchester.[57] Soon his army stretched out over twenty miles along the Turnpike. The Stonewall Brigade, Jackson's rear guard, began withdrawing from Halltown to commence skirmishing with the newly posted Saxton. At this point in time Frémont was still only six miles to the west of Strasburg while Shields, claiming he had no orders to move onward, remained immobilized ten miles to the east in Front Royal.[58] Coincidentally, on the same day that Jackson began to leave Winchester, Joe Johnston attempted a preemptory strike against McClellan at Seven Pines and Fair Oaks, seven miles east of Richmond.[59] That attack accomplished little but Johnston was injured and had to be carried from the field. Robert E. Lee was given "temporary" command, a temporary assignment that lasted for the duration of the war.

Incredibly Jackson did escape the Union snare, in part because his army marched 50 miles in two days! Ewell had been sent west to hold off Frémont while Ashby screened to the east allowing the rest of Stonewall's exhausted command to slip through Strasburg. By the time Frémont and Shields eventually converged at Strasburg their prey had slipped the noose and was continuing to drive south. However despite Jackson's extraordinary feat, the failure of the Federals' pursuit rested squarely upon the shoulders of the commanding officers of the pursuing armies that could still have otherwise accomplished their assigned mission of capturing Jackson.

This facet of the Shenandoah Campaign has received a considerable amount of critique, most of which focuses upon the attempt of Lincoln and Stanton to command from Washington. Many Civil War commanders were notorious for their inability or unwillingness to coordinate with one another. In ordering the capture of Jackson, the administration in Washington had issued its orders directly to the three individual commanders, failing to either create a new command in the field or to at least designate one of the three generals as being in overall charge. An example of the criticism of this arrangement can be found in the *Civil War Dictionary*:

> Brilliant as Jackson's operations were, their success was due largely to the blunders into which they led the Federal authorities. [Mathew] Steele says of Stanton, "by his obstinacy and ignorance of the science of war he probably set back the fall of Richmond and the Confederacy just three years." (Steele's *American Campaigns*, 229). The important lesson of the Federals learned from their failure to trap Jackson was "unity of command."[60]

In other words, had there been a field commander it is entirely conceivable that Jackson and his Army of the Valley would have been captured as early as May or June of 1862. Extending this "what if" further, McClellan, reinforced by the newly freed McDowell, would have been able to overcome the Confederate defenses at Richmond.

But the failure to establish unity of command was not the most critical problem. First, it must be noted that no commander of these three separated Federal armies, without effective telegraphic connections, would have been able to coordinate the plans any more effectively than did the authorities in Washington. More to the point, the plan of pursuit and capture was solid. Had Frémont gotten in front of Jackson at Harrisonburg as had been ordered, Jackson would have been surrounded and probably captured. Even after Frémont failed to march directly to Harrisburg, instead of marching to Moorefield, he, along with Shields, were still in position to block Jackson at Strasburg. However their remarkable lethargy allowed Jackson to continue marching southward. This Federal pursuit did not fail because of lack of concept, planning and coordination. It failed because of a lack of execution by inept political generals. James McPherson points out that, "…if Union commanders in the Valley had acted with half the energy displayed by Jackson they might well have trapped and crippled Jackson's army."[61] Lincoln's larger failure may have been in placing so much operational reliance upon political generals such as Frémont, Shields, and Banks.

Surprisingly once Jackson slipped through Strasburg before continuing up the Turnpike, Frémont suddenly became more vigorous in his movement and fairly aggressively began to give chase to Jackson's rear. A small Federal contingent, comprised of cavalry, infantry, and artillery, tried to maintain contact with Jackson's rear guard but as usual had no way of getting around to Jackson's flank.

An ongoing series of cavalry skirmishes ensued, some of which were little more than mounted mayhem fought mainly without decisive results. After one such melee Steuart was roundly criticized whereupon on June 2 Jackson decided to put all cavalry, including those in Ewell's division, under the unified command of Turner Ashby, who was somewhat of a Southern folk hero. However only six days after assuming this new command Ashby was killed near Harrisburg, possibly by friendly fire from Confederate infantry.[62]

Jackson had ordered that all bridges, except one, one either side of the Massanutten be burned or destroyed.[63] However, Frémont, coming up the Turnpike, was operating with a pontoon train that was used to span the North Fork north of Mount Jackson. During the entire retreat and pursuit heavy rains plagued both sides while flooding the streams in the Valley. On June 4, after Union cavalry had crossed the pontoon north of Mount Jackson it became necessary to cut the pontoon's tethers on the south end of the North Branch in order to prevent the entire pontoon from being swept downstream.[64] Cutting the pontoon's mooring stranded the Union cavalry on the enemy side of the North Branch without any support but Jackson failed to exploit that opportunity to cripple Frémont.

## Cross Keys and Port Republic (June 8–9, 1862)

Although the Yanks failed to trap Jackson at Strasburg, they nevertheless continued to chase Stonewall up the Valley. Frémont stayed closely behind on the Turnpike while Banks sent Shields up the quagmired road along the east of the Massanhutten, hoping Shields could still somehow get in front of Jackson's column. Jackson barely won the race, being able on June 7, 1862, to occupy two key locations: Cross Keys, a crossroads near a rural tavern seven miles southeast of Harrisonburg, and Port Republic, a village three miles further southeast of Cross Keys.[65] At Port Republic the North and South Rivers converged to form the South Fork of the Shenandoah River at Port Republic. A single bridge—which Jackson could control—spanned the North River between these two villages. At this juncture Jackson had the option of marching southeast, eventually reaching the Peninsula to reinforce the Confederate defenses in front of Richmond.[66] However Jackson decided to stay to once more engage the pursuing Federal forces that were still isolated on either side of the Massanhutten. Toward that purpose Jackson deployed Ewell to Cross Keys to prevent Frémont from reinforcing Shields at Port Republic.[67]

Sunday, June 8, 1862, also saw one of the great near misses of the Civil War. A Union raiding party of approximately 100 dragoons supported by a couple artillery guns broke though the unburned bridge to roam through Port Republic where Jackson slept the previous night. Jackson, wearing his old blue coat from his VMI days, charged straight toward the Union detachment before it broke off to get out of its precarious position in the village. Jackson narrowly escaped although a couple of his staff members were captured. It was probably Stonewall's closest brush with being either capture or killed.[68]

The next day Ewell engaged and "cowered" Frémont astride the road leading from Cross Keys to Port Republic.[69] Late in the afternoon Frémont—who outnumbered Ewell by two to one—withdrew to new defensive positions but Ewell, in accordance with Stonewall's orders, declined to advance.[70] Instead, during the night Ewell retreated to Port Republic, his rear guard burning the bridge, thus impairing Frémont from being able to help Shields at Port Republic.

On June 9 the Southerners and the Northerners had a vicious, bloody battle north of Port Republic featuring a series of counterattacks by both sides that took a serious toll upon the other. Eventually the Louisiana Tigers outflanked the Federals defenders commanding high ground where the Bluecoats had placed devastating artillery.[71] Once the Rebels seized this key piece of terrain, and the artillery was either silenced or turned against the Federals, the Union had no choice but to withdraw back down the Valley. Jackson's cavalry, followed by infantry, pursued for 13 miles capturing 450 more prisoners together with about 800 rifles and other supplies before relenting from weariness return back to their camps.[72] Essentially both sides decided to not further pursue. The three Union armies withdrew to other locations while Jackson had accomplished his mission of keeping McDowell from joining with McClellan. Union losses at Cross Keys and Port Republic were 181 killed, 836 wounded, and 685 missing while Confederate losses were 139 killed, 951 wounded, and 685 missing.[73] During the 38 days after leaving Swift Run Gap Jackson's men had marched 400 miles while fighting five battles,[74] thus creating the larger-than-life legend of Stonewall Jackson.

But even as spectacular as were Stonewall's accomplishments he failed to achieve any decisive victories since the Federal armies always survived to fight another day. The lack of cavalry discipline, coupled with the fatigue of the soldiers, contributed to these shortcomings. At the same time Jackson's army became extremely vulnerable to its own destruction when its pursuit after Winchester extended too far. On the other hand the ineptness of their commanders meant Federal pursuit efforts were destined to be futile, even when Jackson's audacity bordered upon recklessness. In a nutshell, pursuits had yet to be developed and honed as one of the finer martial arts.

After Lincoln decided to reassign Frémont and Shields to end the Union efforts, Jackson pitched camp just below Port Republic and gave his men a much needed five-day rest. By the following weekend Davis accepted Lee's recommendation that Jackson proceed to Richmond without further delay, thus signaling the end of Stonewall's 1862 extraordinary Shenandoah campaign.

## *Dénouements and Precursor*

Many of the fruits of the Rebels' tremendous haul from Front Royal were short lived. As Jackson proceeded north to Winchester he had left the depot in charge of a Georgia regiment under the command of Col. Z.T. Connor. A week later Federal forces counterattacked to recapture Front Royal including most of the equipment and supplies not burned by the fleeing Georgians. When Jackson asked Connor how many men had been lost in defense of the supplies, Connor proudly answered "None, I am glad to say, General!" whereupon Stonewall promptly placed Connor under arrest.[75]

Otherwise Jackson's Valley campaign was a spectacular triumph against nearly overwhelming odds, and was successful while measured against his objective of diverting Federal strength away from McClellan. On the other hand, Jackson was unable to apply a *coup de grâce* against any of the Federal armies, in part because of some shortcomings of his pursuits, especially when his cavalry did not behave properly. At the same time, when he was the prey Jackson's success in avoiding capture was due in large part to several factors: First and foremost was the lack of military command skills by political generals such as Banks, Shields, and Frémont. But also to give credit where credit where it was due, the horsemanship and courage of Jackson's cavalry in providing screens and rear guard for Jackson's movements contributed a large part toward frustrating the Federals' pursuit. But also not to be overlooked was that Jackson's small army maintained good marching discipline and cohesion allowing it to move extraordinary distances in short time, frequently under adverse conditions.

Jackson's generalship was unquestionably a large part of his success in the Valley. To be sure, although he performed at a high level, Jackson was still not perfect nor absolutely ideal. His penchant for secrecy impaired post-battle after McDowell and after Winchester. While decisiveness was one of his better attributes, his rash, impetuous decision to attack Kernstown cost him dearly in manpower, supplies, and his relationship with subordinates. His decision to no immediately remove his bounty from Front Royal exposed those badly needed supplies and equipment to later retrieval by the Federals. His abrasiveness with subordinates caused considerable disruption among his staff and commanders of his subordinate units.

Nevertheless in many more respects Stonewall's performance epitomized the combination of characteristics for great generalship as described by several commentators, including Brian Reid. During that spring Jackson almost always made choices that reflected his sound grasp of operational imperatives. But just as important Jackson's military leadership was virtually unmatched. Marching the great distance demanded of his troops could be accomplished only by unsurpassed leadership. Although his soldiers often did not comprehend or understand Stonewall's intentions, and although some of his subordinate officers were victims of Jackson's abrasiveness, somehow he gained the soldiers' trust and devotion to be willing to sacrifice themselves way beyond the usual call of duty.

Nathaniel Banks remained in command of his corps until September 12, 1862, when Pope's Army of Virginia was dissolved. As a prominent political general, Banks continued to hold several important commands throughout much of the war, proving himself to be an honest military administrator. However as a military commander Banks encountered several more failures than successes.[76]

Bank's most prominent senior commander, and fellow political general, James Shields, who had been whipsawed in and out of the Valley because of Stonewall's diversions, resigned from the Union army March 23, 1863, after the Senate failed to confirm his promotion to major general.[77] Afterwards he became a U.S. Senator from another state, Missouri, the only person to ever have the distinction of serving in the U.S. Senate from three different states. Shields is one of the Illinois representatives in the Statutory Hall in the United States Capitol.

On April 1, 1862, Jackson relieved Richard Garnett who, without Stonewall's knowledge let alone permission, had ordered the retreat of the Stonewall Brigade from Kernstown. Jackson filed court-martial papers against Garnett, and placed him under arrest. The charges were eventually dropped against Garnett who was reassigned to Pickett's division. While leading his brigade at Gettysburg Garnett was killed on July 3, 1863. Of the six officers who succeeded Jackson as commander of the Stonewall Brigade, three were killed while leading the brigade.[78]

George H. Steuart, the cavalry brigadier who refused to obey an order to pursue from Jackson's courier because the order did not come through the "proper" chain of command, was eventually wounded at Cross Keys. After recovering he commanded infantry at Gettysburg, the Wilderness, and Spotsylvania where he was captured. Later exchanged, he also commanded a brigade at Petersburg.

The Louisiana Tigers, the brigade that led the advance into Front Royal, led the assault at Richmond, and had captured the Union artillery on the commanding ground at Port Republic, begun the war with 5,000 soldiers, the majority of whom were foreign born. This storied brigade continued to fight in several more campaigns, most notably Gaines Mill where their original organizer, Chatham ("Rob") Wheat, was mortally wounded. Once Wheat died it seemed as though much of the battalion's discipline suffered and desertions increased. By the end of the war attrition had left the battalion with only 200 soldiers. Its former commander, Dick Taylor, the only son of former President Zachary Taylor, would be one of the last Confederate commanders to surrender at the end of the war. Taylor may have also been the source of the everlasting impression of Jackson's supposed habit of sucking on lemons. Other than Taylor's recollections there seems to be no other contemporaneous reports of this unusual trait.

## 11

# Lee's Pursuit of Seven Days
## *June 25–July 1, 1862*

In addition to being one of most dramatic events of the Civil War the Seven Day campaign is an outstanding laboratory for military historians and analysts. Within the period of one week there were extraordinary, and surprising, reversals of fortune between two large, but not yet great, combat organizations. Command personalities—some of whom were old comrades—who would remain much longer in the Eastern Theater gathered at that nondescript countryside east of Richmond. During that same span of seven days command reputations were made, some more legitimately than others, some enduring to the present time, while others were diminished and faded into the "dust bins" of history.

But most germane to our perspective, during Seven Days one army executed a magnificent retreat, albeit flawed, costly, and almost certainly unnecessary, while the other army showed us why the mechanisms of a pursuit are so complex and delicate, and thus improbable even in the best and most favorable circumstances.

Of course Stonewall Jackson's earlier brilliant maneuvers in the Valley were strategically relevant because they influenced the relative strengths of the armies in the Peninsula east of Richmond. In March 1862, the Confederates in Northern Virginia, commended by LGen. Joseph E. Johnston, 55, relinquished their base around Centreville, leaving valuable supplies.[1] After being prodded for several months by Lincoln to do something with his army,[2] on April 1 MGen. George B. ("The Young Napoleon") McClellan, 35, finally began his Peninsula Campaign, by bringing a massive army of twelve divisions divided among five corps to Fort Monroe at the eastern tip of the Peninsula—formed by the York River on the north and the James River on the south—and intending to move quickly westward against, and presumably capture, Richmond. However instead of advancing quickly, McClellan maneuvered his force of 100,000 westward on the Peninsula toward Richmond in a cautious, methodical manner—nearly coinciding with Halleck's sluggish march to Corinth—until The Young Napoleon eventually came to almost seven miles of his objective.[3]

After leaving Fort Monroe, McClellan was forced to advance along the York, or northern, side of the Peninsula because the CSS *Virginia*, the highly prized submarine converted from the former USS *Merrimack*, controlled the James; otherwise McClellan could not keep his army resupplied. To meet the resupply needs of his massive army McClellan established a major supply base at White House landing on the Pamunkey River, a tributary feeding the York River.[4]

When McClellan began his Peninsula campaign Johnston withdrew to Confederate defenses around Richmond. In order to disrupt McClellan's advance, on May 31 Johnston launched a preemptive strike of 23 of the army's 27 brigades at Seven Pines and Fair Oaks,[5] a couple hamlets approximately seven miles east of the outskirts of Richmond. The orders for Seven Pines were not clearly provided, or at least not clearly understood.[6] Predictably this was a poorly fought battle—one historian said it "was unquestionably the worst-conducted large-scale conflict in a war that afforded many rivals for that distinction"[7] that decided little except Johnston was twice wounded and had to be "temporarily" replaced by LGen. Robert E. Lee, 55, who was serving again in Richmond as an advisor to C.S.A. President Jefferson Davis.[8]

By war's end, Lee was an icon of American military history, placing him along Abraham Lincoln as a co-hero of the Civil War. To adherents of the Lost Cause, Lee has been, and is, lionized as one of the nation's greatest generals, a commander who was without equal during the Civil War and one who was audacious, cunning but gallant while leading under great handicaps, including having inferior numbers of soldiers and insufficient materiel. In the eyes of many Lee was audacity personified and the most aggressive, combative man in the war.[9]

By almost all accounts he was respected by everyone with whom he dealt, and perhaps more important was beloved by his soldiers, despite their many deprivations and hardships endured under Lee's command. Lee was entirely devoted to the leadership of his command; he was hard working while largely avoiding the internecine backbiting and intrigues that characterized much of the governance of the Confederacy. And there can be no doubt that while astride his horse Lee's command presence was magnificent, no small matter in an age of personal leadership. As a defensive tactician, Lee was probably without any peer.

On the other hand, Lee is not without his critics who contend, among other things, that he possessed a blood lust that resulted in a larger casualty rate than any other commander, including U.S. Grant, supposedly a butcher of his troops. Too often, Lee's critics maintain, he engaged in battles or campaigns of attrition that eventually exhausted the South's lifeblood. Lee's critics further contend that he had a narrow strategic viewpoint that ignored the Confederacy's overall needs outside northern Virginia, these critics assert that much of Lee's battlefield success was due to the extraordinary military skills of his principle lieutenants, specifically Stonewall Jackson, James Longstreet, and J.E.B. Stuart, coupled with engaging Union generalship that ranged from mediocre and weak to pathetically inept, especially during the first two years of the war. The critics also note that Lee often delegated too much discretion to subordinates while failing to pay enough attention to details, especially those related to logistics and operational coordination, Lee would often predicate his plans on conditions as he wished them to be; when conditions were otherwise, as so often happened, Lee would be without contingency plans. Even Lee's admirers admit that he failed to appreciate the improvements of various weapons and munitions, especially that of the Minié ball. As with most controversies, the truth probably can be found somewhere between these two polar positions; the Seven Days campaign provides ammunition to support arguments for either side.

Lee's life story is told in several biographies, including a four-volume work published in 1934 by Douglas Southall Freeman,[10] not without considerable adulation. For our purposes it suffices to say that Lee was born in 1807 in Virginia, the son of an American Revolutionary War hero, Henry ("Light Horse Harry") Lee, who eventually died in financial and social disgrace. After graduating second in his West Point class of 1827, Robert was assigned to the Corps of Engineers. During the Mexican War Lee performed brilliantly as a staff officer for Winfield Scott; in 1852 he began a three-year tour as Superintendent of West Point. By 1859, when he was semi-retired to settle his late father-in-law's estate, Lee was assigned to command a detachment of Marines to quell John Brown's insurrection at Harper's Ferry. As slave holding states began to secede, Lee supposedly spoke to someone, either Scott, still then the Army's General-in-Chief, or Frank Blair, Sr., a veteran Washington figure closely associated with the Lincoln administration, about becoming the Union's principle field commander; if in fact offered, Lee declined the position, instead retiring to his family home in Arlington, Virginia.

On April 20, 1861, six days after the surrender of Fort Sumter and five days after Lincoln's call for 75,000 to suppress the rebellion, Lee tendered his resignation from the U.S. Army. Shortly thereafter he accepted a major general's commission from the Virginia Special Assembly, but soon after that he became a lieutenant general—third in seniority—in the Confederate army, being assigned as a military aide to Davis.

Almost four weeks after assuming command of the Richmond defenses, rather than remaining in passive defenses behind entrenchments, Lee attempted to seize the initiative by striking McClellan to force the Young Napoleon away from Richmond. As McClellan approached Richmond he was confronted with the problem of how to safely cross the Chickahominy River, which runs diagonally northwest to the southeast in front of Richmond. McClellan opted to cross his southern-most corps first until eventually only his right corps, the 5th Corps, commanded by BGen. Fitz-John Porter, 40, remained north, or on the other side, of the Chickahominy.[11] Porter—McClellan's close confidant and political colleague—had a two-fold mission: One, to be in position to link up with Irwin McDowell, hopefully advancing south from Fredericksburg with his 40,000 troops, and then to flank the Confederate left while also protecting access to and from McClellan's supply base at White House landing.

As a result of BGen. J.E.B. Stuart's cavalry "ride around" the rear of McClellan's army, Lee realized that Porter's position on McClellan's right flank was isolated and exposed.[12] Lee also determined that McClellan's supply base at White House Landing was exposed by the Union's failure to have McDowell reinforce Porter.[13] Thus on June 15, 1862, Lee ordered Jackson to bring his army from the Valley to get into position to "sweep down between the Chickahominy and Pamunkey [i.e. Porter's position], cutting up the enemy's communications." With Jackson's army, Lee would have 92,400 men under his command—incidentally the largest number he had ever commanded or would thereafter command[14]—but this number was still smaller than that available to McClellan, even without McDowell's reinforcements.

As McClellan approached closer to Richmond the armies were poised at a tipping point with significant potential for decisive results. Instead of achieving anything of a decisive nature, poor command decisions on either side set the stage for the effusion of blood for almost three more years. Paradoxically the respective army commanders held diametrically opposed assessments of the upcoming campaign. Lee realized that to save Richmond he had to change the contest from a "battle of posts" featuring artillery and engineering for which the Union had superiority to a war of maneuver that would be to the advantage of the South. Conversely, on June 24 McClellan advised one of his corps commanders that his continued advance would "be chiefly an Artillery and Engineering affair."[15]

On June 23 Jackson made a fourteen-hour fast paced, almost non-stop horseback ride of 52 miles from the Valley to confer with Lee and other generals, including Longstreet, MGen. Ambrose Powell ("A.P.") Hill, 37, and MGen. Daniel Harvey ("D.H.") Hill, 41,[16] the latter Hill being Stonewall's brother-in-law. At that point in the Civil War, the Army of Northern Virginia was not tightly organized into a hierarchy of corps but instead was a loose collection of commands, usually the size of divisions. In addition to the aforementioned generals who had division commands, Lee's command structure included MGen. John Bankhead ("Prince John") Magruder, 52, MGen. Benjamin Huger, 57, and MGen. Theophilus Holmes, 58. These divisions varied in size and Lee did not hesitate to give the various commanders varying degrees of responsibilities and authorities.

Lee outlined his plans during this conference but left the room to allow his lieutenants to coordinate their movements and the details of their procedures. Before departing immediately to ride back to his command, Jackson said he would have his troops in position ready to strike at daybreak on June 26. However, when Stonewall left he still knew little about the arena's terrain or for that matter the Federal forces he would be confronting. Indeed Jackson departed too soon to even obtain a copy of Lee's written plan of operations.[17]

At this point in the war, Lee did not have enough competent staff help.[18] Thus Lee was entirely responsible for the concept of his plan, and since he had insufficient staff to prepare and coordinate details of the operation, he had to manage such details himself.[19] Lee's plan was written and distributed as General Order No. 75, a directive written in broad, general strokes leaving several details to his subordinate commanders. More critically, Lee was already developing his habit of formulating offensive plans premised upon what he wished conditions to be rather than as they actually were.

Lee's plan for Thursday, June 26, 1862, was to take advantage of Porter's isolation north of the Chickahominy. Although Lee's entire command—the newly minted Army of Northern Virginia—was smaller than McClellan's, Lee intended to concentrate 52,000 men north of the Chickahominy against Porter's 26,000 men. Lee's concentration was supposed to materialize in two ways: First he counted upon Jackson being in place as he had promised to initiate the attack, hopefully to roll up McClellan's right flank,[20] and second, Lee shifted a large part of his army north across the Chickahominy, gambling that McClellan would not seize the opportunity to strike against the entrenched but grossly outnumbered Rebels remaining south of the Chickahominy. Other than creating a superiority of numbers at the point of attack, timing the launching of the assaults would be the most critical feature of Lee's plan.

## *Day One—June 25* (Oak Grove)

In order to move his heavier guns a mile and half closer to the enemy's fortifications, McClellan desired to seize a crossroads named Old Tavern, almost two miles northwest of Fair Oaks where the armies had battled May 31. Capture of Old Tavern would place McClellan's heavy siege guns to within five miles of the outskirts of Richmond.[21] On June 25, the day before Lee's planned assault, McClellan ordered a probing attack, or reconnaissance in force, in the area north of Oak Grove. This large skirmish gained only 600 yards for the

Federals but the Confederates confused McClellan into assuming he was facing a much larger Southern force.

Even though McClellan had gained some success on June 25 at Oak Grove, that evening he learned Jackson's army left the Valley and was headed for Richmond. Erroneously estimating Confederate strength to be 200,000 men,[22] the Young Napoleon became even more concerned about the safety of his army. Reflecting his anxiety, McClellan said he feared Jackson can "have force enough next morning [the 26th] to force Porter's right." The concern about un-reinforced Porter's right, coupled with the fear that his supply lines on the railroad to White House Landing could be captured, compelled McClellan to begin establishing a new base at Harrison's Landing on the James River, fourteen as-the-crow-flies miles southeast of Seven Pines where the armies had engaged each other on May 31.

Establishing a new Federal base on the James had become possible because on May 1 the Confederates decided to abandon Norfolk and Portsmouth at the mouth of the James River. Federal capture of these sites trapped the CSS *Virginia* upstream in the James. The *Virginia*'s draft was too deep to maneuver in the relatively shallow waters of the James, compelling the Confederates on Friday, May 11, 1862, to scuttle their ironclad with its invaluable firepower. These developments allowed Union gunships to navigate the James with relative impunity, at least as far as Harrison's Landing.

Although not recognized as such at the time, Oak Grove would be McClellan' only offensive action against Richmond and would be the first of what became known as the Seven Days battles, which collectively would engage more men and would spill more blood than any other previous military campaign in American military history. More immediately, McClellan's minor success did nothing to change Lee's plans for the next day.[23]

## Day Two—June 26 (Beaver Creek Dam, a.k.a. Mechanicsburg)

Lee's complex scheme on the 26th began to go awry when Jackson failed to arrive on time,[24] moreover not even contacting Lee's other commanders. A.P. Hill, the youngest of Lee's four major commanders and who had been assigned to strike upon Jackson's signal that his attack had begun, impetuously decided to proceed without Jackson,[25] thus in effect converting a planned turning movement into a frontal assault.[26] When Hill stalled after advancing against Porter, Lee ordered Hill not to advance any further but merely to hold the ground already taken. However, Hill mistakenly believed he had discretion to advance further and ordered a further attack against Porter's troops entrenched behind Beaver Dam Creek.[27] Hill's second assault was gallant in the finest Cavalier tradition but terribly suicidal against withering gun and rifle fire; predictably—at least with the advantage of 20–20 hindsight—Hill's charge resulted in one of the most terrible and unfortunate slaughters in the Civil War.[28]

The lack of accurate maps became a major handicap for Lee's army.[29] After replacing Joe Johnston, Lee—who was not very familiar with eastern Henrico County around Richmond—neglected to order topographical maps. As a result the road network, such as it was sometimes consisting of little more than cow paths, was confusing as were the distances between cultural features such as public buildings and topographical features such as swamps and ridges. Other features, such as thickets, were simply unknown to the Rebels.

This lack of knowledge about the roads, including their locations, surface types, and conditions of the various bridges and/or fords, made it almost impossible to coordinate movements. Ironically the Union made copies of a good map of the area available to subordinate commanders.[30]

Although Lee intended to commit at least 50,000 soldiers against Porter, Lee was able to engage only 14,000 primarily because Jackson still did not deploy as intended. Consequently the Confederates suffered a terrible tactical defeat, incurring almost 1,400 casualties in contrast to Porter's loss of 400 soldiers. More importantly, the Southerners failed their objective of rolling up Porter's right flank. In David Eicher's words, "In theory, [Lee's] plan was masterful if overly complex; in practice it was horribly bungled."[31] Lee went to bed that night not even knowing where Stonewall was.[32]

On the other hand, upon hearing the news of Porter's repulse of Hill, Union soldiers south of the Chickahominy cheered in jubilation. For the first time in weeks, regimental bands were allowed to play music to help celebrate this apparent and most welcome victory.

Just five hours after the fighting ended McClellan felt compelled to retreat,[33] or as he preferred to state it, to protect "the arrangements for the change of base to the James,"[34] now surprisingly and unaccountably McClelland's new objective. And so McClellan ordered Porter, minus his guns and wagons, to remain north of the Chickahominy but to rotate the axis of his battle line from north and south to east and west. Since these lines would no longer face Richmond, their adjustments would enhance Porter's, and by extension McClellan's, ability to protect itself. However, McClellan also relinquished much of the strategic initiative to Lee.[35] Bluntly speaking, McClellan's actions began to resemble those of a general preparing for defeat.

## *Day Three—June 27* (Gaines's Mill, a.k.a. First Cold Harbor)

The next day, Friday the 27th, Lee was still determined to press on to strike Porter. However, Lee also failed to reconnoiter, and consequently did not realize Porter not only had moved his position four miles southeast into strong defensive positions behind Boatswain Swamp, but also had realigned his defensive line to face the north rather than to the west. Among other things this meant that Porter's right flank was no longer exposed making it much more difficult to get to his rear. The ensuing battle would be known forever as Gaines's Mill, but in fact it occurred some distance to the east.

Lee intended to deploy D.H. Hill to strike against Porter's left, Longstreet against the middle, and Jackson on Porter's right. But Jackson was late again[36] after ordering a countermarch that took an extra two hours. Again the lack of decent maps impaired Rebel movements[37]; but even with inaccuracies that among other things failed to show the formidable terrain of Boatswain's Creek or Swamp,[38] Lee could have used, but failed to use, his available cavalry to reconnoiter the area. The available maps did not show among other things there were two Cold Harbors about a mile and half apart. As a result Stonewall was trying to go, and initially did go, to the wrong Cold Harbor. Richard Taylor, commander of the Louisiana Tigers, later commented that "The Confederate commanders knew no more about the topography of the country than they did about central Africa."[39] Had Jackson taken his place in a timely manner, he not only would have been properly placed in the line of battle but also would have been in better position to flank Porter to have gotten into his rear.

Lee amassed 57,000 soldiers, the largest Rebel concentration of the Seven Days, for the battle of Gaines's Mill. Following an artillery barrage from Rebel guns some of the fiercest fighting in the East suddenly erupted through undergrowth, swamps, and broken terrain. Back and forth the sides struggled, much of the fighting hand-to-hand, neither gaining much headway until late in the day when a brigade led by BGen. John Bell Hood, 31, broke through Union defenses in one of most famous charges of the war.[40] Although taking heavy casualties—losing as many men in six hours as the Confederates had lost during two days at Shiloh—Hood's brigade dispersed into loose bands of uncoordinated hunters to force Porter south of the Chickahominy. After this realignment all of McClellan's army was south of the Chickahominy while most of Lee's army was north of the same river with most of the bridges across the river having been burned.[41]

Gaines's Mill was one of the bloodiest days of the Civil War, and certainly *the* bloodiest day of the Seven Days.[42] As a result of Hood's successful charge the Confederates had scored a clear tactical victory on the battlefield but once again suffered more casualties (8,751) than did the Union (6,837). The slaughter of Confederate officers was staggering.[43]

Somewhat ameliorating those losses the Rebels captured 22 cannon.[44] A.P. Hill later mused that while the Rebels were grand, it was "the kind of grandeur which the South could not afford." Notwithstanding the Confederate victory the Union was positioned to have a virtually clear path into Richmond defended by the single Confederate division south of the river. Some of McClellan's subordinate commanders urged an attack but McClellan was convinced the Confederates still outnumbered him.

McClellan was whipped mentally almost to the point of becoming dysfunctional, having failed among other things earlier to send reinforcements to Porter to help stem the Rebel advances. Almost two-thirds of McClellan's soldiers had remained idle while their comrades in Porter's 5th Corps and Henry Slocum's division fought valiantly and desperately. After meeting with his senior commanders that evening, McClellan ordered a total retreat of his army—including the previously ordered abandonment of White House Landing—to Harrison's Landing on the James.[45] Although he had not effectively used the bulk of the manpower available to him, McClellan sent a viciously critical and insubordinate telegram to Secretary of War Stanton blaming Stanton and the rest of the administration for not sending enough troops.[46] The officer in charge of the telegraph office in Washington judiciously deleted McClellan's most scathing sentence before delivering the rest of the message to Stanton.[47]

For all intents and purposes the Young Napoleon was entirely giving up on his much heralded Peninsula campaign and in essence, concluding—while it must be noted in severe intellectual and emotional turmoil—that his paramount mission was now to save his army. McClellan rationalized fairly melodramatically to his lieutenants, "If we were defeated the Army and the country would be lost."[48] A cynic might reply that on the other hand his army would never succeed at anything as long as its commander continuously failed to assume some risks but instead would cut and run when confronted with some obstacles to victory.[49]

McClellan's retreat—he preferred the euphemism of "change of base"—from Gaines's Mill (or more accurately Boatswain's Swamp) to Harrison's Landing involved more than

75,000 men with more than 300 cannon and heavy siege guns.[50] Additionally 3,800 ambulances and wagons together with a herd of cattle attempted to make a 15-mile trek to the James River.[51] To impede any ensuing pursuit Porter's retreating corps burned several bridges across the Chickahominy. Three miles south of the Chickahominy, the White Oak Swamp, seven miles long and as wide as four miles wide in places, was another major impediment to gain access to the James but by the same token was also a major obstacle for Confederate pursuers. Although there were more difficult ways to cross the swamp the most feasible was across the so-call Grapevine Bridge, actually a series of bridges with a long causeway.[52] Once past the White Oak Swamp, the retreating army would go through Savage's Station before being funneled through White Oak Bridge. After that the retreat would pass through Glendale where five roads intersected. From Glendale the Federals would march further south to Malvern Hill before continuing to their final destination at Harrison's Landing.

But evacuation and/or destruction of the massive supply depot at White House Landing also had its challenges. The straight line distance between White House and the James River is 30 miles but the roads were choppy, crude, and most of all unmapped. Few roads in the entire area were laid out in neat, continuous north-south manner while the somewhat better and more numerous roads ran east and west. McClellan retired back to Harrison's Landing without specifying the routes to be taken; he also failed to designate a second-in-command to take charge in his absence.[53] Fortunately for the Army of the Potomac several of McClellan's subordinate commanders assured unit cohesion was maintained, rear guards were deployed, and that McClellan's overall plan was executed.

## *Day Four—June 28* (Garnett's and Golding's Farms, a.k.a. The Pause)

As the armies maneuvered away from their original positions they engaged in a continuation of the battle at Gaines's Mill.[54] Although Lee did not realize it, the ferocity and violence of Days Two and Three whipped McClellan even though his army was still superior in almost all ways to Lee's.[55] Upon learning their army was retreating for the James River, Union rank-and-file reacted angrily with dismay and disbelief,[56] coming to the realization that their efforts and the bloodshed of their comrades were in vain. Many soldiers and junior as well as senior officers could not concede any defeat of their army but rather believed that McClellan had simply let them down.[57]

At White House Landing, Northern troops began to explode ammunition magazines and destroy vast stockpiles of supplies and equipment before their supply wagons started rolling south in long convoys along rugged, inferior roads toward Harrison's Landing. Before fleeing Union soldiers also set fires to the buildings but Stuart's cavalry almost immediately extinguished many of these fires before they became devastating conflagrations. Three corps, the 2nd, commanded by BGen. Edwin V. ("Bull") Sumner, 65, the 3rd, MGen. Samuel Heintzelman, 57, and the 6th, BGen. William Franklin, 39, were positioned to guard the Chickahominy crossings.[58] Keyes' 4th Corps and Porter's 5th Corps were to lead the retreat, but due to a foul-up the division of George McCall was left at the crossroads of Glendale.[59]

Lee failed to order an immediate pursuit simply because he had lost contact with the Yankees, not knowing McClellan's movements.[60] Lee reasonably anticipated McClellan would want to protect his supply base at White House Landing.[61] However two of Longstreet's engineers, while on a reconnaissance, discovered the Federals evacuated key positions south of the York.[62] Although Lee assumed McClellan could be retreating back down the Peninsula eastward toward Fort Monroe, Stuart's cavalry eventually determined McClellan was not heading east.[63]

By the evening of Day Four, Saturday, the 28th, Lee finally understood the Union army was probably making for the James.[64] Upon the "supposition" that the Federals were heading south, Lee belatedly ordered the whole Rebel army to be "put in motion" down five separate routes to pursue the Union army's flight toward the James.[65] Lee's delay of an entire day, while not entirely dispositive, in starting the Rebel pursuit gave the Federals invaluable lead time to move their wagons while preparing defenses to protect the rear and flanks of their columns.

Lee had the option of dispatching a massive column with ample artillery along the River Road, running along the James, to interdict McClellan's retreat before it could reach the river.[66] Instead of Lee's five formations, only Holmes' small division was dispatched to River Road running along the James River.[67] A larger contingent might have permitted the Confederates to intercept the head of the retreating Federals. However, that Southern division, containing only 6,000 men, certainly was not large enough to be of any significant threat against the much larger Yankee army. The other four columns moved behind the Yankees whose rear guard had time to prepare stout defenses at critical junctures.

Inadequate communications was one of the Confederates' chronic problems. Their commanders had difficulty coordinating the directions and timing of their maneuvers while they were separated from one another on the move. Although Lee had ample cavalry to carry messages between himself and among his commanders, he frequently chose to use cavalry for other purposes. Thus it was almost predetermined the Rebels would suffer chronic communications breakdowns during their pursuit.

## Day Five—June 29 (Savage's Station, a.k.a. The Pursuit)

For years military historians have debated, and still debate, whether Lee's initial intentions were to "crush" Porter's corps isolated north of the Chickahominy or instead merely to maneuver to force McClellan's entire army away from Richmond or even perhaps off the entire Peninsula.[68] But once McClellan's army was in retreat, obviously headed for Harrison's Landing, regardless of what his earlier intent may have been, by the 28th Lee clearly seemed intent upon annihilating the entire Army of the Potomac. Thus on the fifth day of the Seven Days, the divisions of Lee's army were aligned in an arc to begin a serious pursuit that by at least one estimation was "bungled."[69]

The Union army retreated in terrible mid-day heat, causing scores of exhausted soldiers to collapse along the roadside. Although organizing a maneuver such as a retreat was McClellan's strong suit, basic logistics were lacking meaning that many soldiers had nothing to eat except hard bread. Some of the participants described this march as a grand skedaddle; notwithstanding widespread chaos, and despite the absence of McClellan, the Union's corps commanders managed to organize a succession of strong defenses to protect McClellan's army.

Earlier while preparing to invest Richmond, the Federals established a forward supply base and hospital that treated thousands of wounded and sick soldiers at Savage's Station along the Richmond & York River Railroad, three and half miles east of Fair Oaks, and fourteen miles southwest of White House Landing. As the Federals rolled back from their positions at Gaines's Mill, fresh troops took up blocking positions west of Savage's Station. McClellan hoped they could hold on long enough for his army to remove or destroy supplies from his White House supply depot while getting those supplies and battered troops across the White Oak Swamp.[70] Upon McClellan's orders, because the railroad across the Chickahominy was being destroyed, Savage's Station would be abandoned and/or destroyed, meaning not only were more supplies and equipment destroyed or burned, the fates of at least 2,500 wounded and sick Yankees were abandoned to the Confederates.[71]

On Sunday, June 29, 1862, Lee hoped to encircle Union forces by striking them in the rear and flanks as they retreated.[72] To do so, Lee devised a complicated plan that among other things had Longstreet and A.P. Hill's divisions looping back toward Richmond's outskirts before turning back to the east to attack the Federal flank at two points along Quaker Road, a thirteen mile march in torrid heat and humidity.[73] Lee's idea also was to sandwich the Federals' rear guard between Magruder, already south of the Chickahominy, and Jackson.[74] Lee ordered Magruder to move down Williamsburg road (roughly paralleling the Richmond & York River R.R.) to be in position to strike the Federal rear or flank.[75] Lee ordered Jackson to repair the bridge across the Chickahominy, a mile north of Savage Station, to cross the Chickahominy, and "to push the pursuit vigorously."[76] Given all these factors, Lee's intended timetable was virtually impossible to meet.[77] Among other things Lee's plan failed to take into account his subordinates' lack of familiarity of the area's thickly wooded terrain as well as their incapacity to communicate with one other. Magruder, who had been suffering from an acute stomach ailment and sleeping little in days, attempted to contact Jackson, who replied he had another "important duty to perform."[78] In his isolation from other commanders, Magruder became convinced Federal forces were preparing to strike him with superior numbers.[79] Accordingly he advanced timorously, awaiting reinforcements.[80]

Rather than assigning the task of rebuilding the bridge to his engineers, Jackson inexplicably assigned the job to Reverend Major Robert L. Dabney, his Chief of Staff, who not surprisingly took much too long to finish. This assignment to a man of the cloth without any engineering experience may have been one of the most incomprehensible decisions of Jackson's career.

There must have also been some confusion about where Lee intended his attacks to occur relative to the White Oak Swamp. Especially with the advantage of 20–20 hindsight, attacking north of that natural barrier would have been more productive than attacking at the south after the Federals had been able to cross. Lee's after action report indicated he directed that attacks be brought both north and south of the swamp. Lee further reported he was disappointed that his divisions were not able to engage as he had anticipated. On the other hand, Jackson—who apparently was supposed to attack vigorously on the south of the swamp—was confused by a directive verbally delivered by a courier from Lee. Without seeking clarification, Jackson opted to remain in a defensive posture north of the swamp thereby contributing little to the execution of Lee's plan. As a result the Union rear guard was not isolated north of the Chickahominy River as Lee must have hoped.

In any event, even though his left had not made contact with Jackson, by late afternoon Magruder's battle line of six brigades began to form west of Savage's Station where the Federal rear guard had formed.[81] The Federal rear guard at that point was supposed to consist of the three corps commanded by Sumner, Heintzelman, and Franklin, respectively. Sumner still thought Heintzelman's 3rd Corps was still on the right and rear of the 2nd Corps but without telling Sumner or Franklin, Heintzelman had continued to march through the White Oak Swamp.[82] Committing only a portion of his division, Magruder was soon met by stout Union resistance, particularly Sumner's 2nd Corps. After a brief but violent clash Magruder withdrew.[83]

For the third time during the campaign, McClellan relinquished hands-on field command by leaving the battlefield.[84] Sumner, an old Indian fighter whose corps had borne much of the rear guard responsibilities, initially refused to obey McClellan's orders to leave Savage's Station. Only after receiving a second message to proceed with the retreat, this message also containing a threat of arrest if not obeyed, did Sumner fall into the retreating columns.[85]

The Southern pursuit's first day was little less than a fiasco, at least when measured against lost opportunities.[86] At the end of the day, ending in severe thunderstorms, Lee simply ordered each of his divisions march down five specified roads, hopefully to converge later at Quaker Road against the retreating Federal column.[87] This has suggested to some of Lee's defenders that Lee's plan had always contemplated a two day pursuit. In any event casualties for the battle at Savage's Station were 1,590 for the Federals (not counting those abandoned in the hospital) and 626 for the Confederates.

## *Day Six—June 30* (Glendale, a.k.a. Frayser's Farm/ White Oak Swamp)

The area's network of east-west roads resembled fingers radiating from Richmond before intersecting with the few north-south roads. Two of those east-west roads, the Darbytown Road and the Long Bridge Road, converged a little more than a mile west of the hamlet of Glendale where the conjoined road crossed the Quaker Road, practically the only north-south road leading from White Oak Swamp by way of Malvern Hill to the James River. Control of the Glendale crossroads was absolutely vital to control Quaker Road. Furthermore, before even reaching Glendale, most Union troops had to cross White Oak Bridge, two miles to the north. Obviously Glendale, and to a lesser extent, the White Oak Bridge, were critical points but they were hardly the most promising points of attack for a pursuit. Arguably controlling Malvern Hill, or for that matter, capturing Harrison's Landing, would be much more lucrative targets with less cost to the Confederates.

Lee's concept envisioned a successful culmination of a short-lived pursuit that would severely cripple if not extirpate the Union's largest, most powerful army. On paper at least, Lee's plan for a massive concentration of force seemed ideal, especially under the right circumstances.[88] Lee hoped at a minimum to sever the Federal column so that remaining pieces could be defeated in detail. If successful, the South would be a long way toward gaining its independence from the North.

The first point of attack, to be led by Stonewall Jackson, would cross the Chickahominy, advance south against the Federal rear guard at White Oak Bridge before advancing down Quaker Road.[89] Lee's second point of attack would have Benjamin Huger move east along Charles City Road (roughly parallel north of the Darbytown Road) toward Quaker Road, while third, Longstreet with Powell Hill in support, to use the Darbytown Road to slice through the Union column hurrying along Quaker Road. Lee ordered Magruder to swing back from Savage's Station and down Darbytown Road to support Longstreet. Lee also sent Holmes' small division to continue back down River Road with instruction to take Malvern Hill.[90]

To protect its column as it moved southward the Union massed seven divisions and a brigade—with approximately 55,000 men—between and the critical White Oak Bridge and Frayser's Farm,[91] immediately south of the village of Glendale. Once again McClellan rode away after conferring with three of his corps commanders. Although Little Mac left the field without designating any second in command, by simple fortuitous circumstance the defenses to Glendale and Frayser's Farm included two of the outstanding divisions in the Army of the Potomac.

Heintzelman, as commander of the 3rd Corps, had a long but not particularly distinguished record. A veteran of the Mexican war, he was personally brave but usually not a commander to take much initiative. Fortunately his command shortcoming were compensated by the fact that two of his divisions were commanded by two fightingest generals in the Army of the Potomac: Joseph Hooker and MGen. Philip Kearny, 45. We have already met Hooker after he was transferred in 1863 from the Eastern Theater to the Chattanooga campaign in the Western Theater. Eventually Hooker's character and personality traits that tended to magnify his subsequent failure at Chancellorsville as well as being abruptly relieved shortly prior to Gettysburg obscured his outstanding success as a division commander. But by June 1862 Hooker's record was that of one of the Union army's best commanders.

Hooker was not commissioned until after First Bull Run but in slightly over a year few soldiers rose faster in rank than did Hooker.[92] After being commissioned he saw virtually every battle fought by the Army of the Potomac. Hooker's early reputation as a hard fighter was clearly established during McClellan's Peninsula Campaign when, as a division commander, Hooker was in the thick of the fighting at Williamsburg where he led a pursuit before being pressed hard by a Confederate counterattack. When McClellan failed to send support as requested, Kearny, on his own initiative, rushed his division to help save Hooker from his peril.[93] When Hooker's soldiers saw Kearny leading his soldiers to the fray they yelled "It's Kearny! It's Kearny!" One of Hooker's officers recalled he "had heard what a fierce fighter he was ... but in all my days I never witnessed anything to equal what I saw him do...."[94]

Later when Kearny received word that McClellan was abandoning his plans to capture Richmond, Kearny and Hooker—who been on the Union left as most of the fighting occurred on the right—stormed into McClellan's headquarters to insist that Richmond could be taken with only a couple divisions. Since Magruder was the chief obstacle between them and Richmond Kearny was convinced Magruder was a theatrical faker meaning that Rebel resistance was too spotty for large forces."[95] In reaction to the Young Napoleon's cool rejection of Kearny's proposal to assault Richmond Kearny flew into such a rage that one observer fully expected Kearny to be placed under arrest. But perhaps even McClellan realized he needed subordinate commanders with Kearny's passion.[96]

Kearny was a member of one of the nation's wealthiest families, his grandfather and father having founded the New York Stock Exchange.[97] As an adolescent he had aspired to pursue a military career but his family pushed him into study of the law. When his late grandfather's will left Kearny with an inheritance of one million dollars, Kearny—now independently wealthy—immediately sought and received a commission as a cavalry officer. Like many other future Civil War officers, Kearny served in the Mexican War where he commanded a cavalry company chosen to accompany Lee on his scouting missions. Very aggressive, Kearny lost his left arm after leading a charge against a Mexican position. Winfield Scott once said of Kearny, "Soldiers will follow such a man to the very gates of hell."[98] Kearny remained in the army until 1851 when he resigned after realizing how slow promotions were in the frontier army.

In 1858 he sailed for Europe where he was attached to the French Army, taking part in numerous cavalry charges, eventually being the first American to receive the Legion of Honor, France's highest honor for military achievements.[99] By 1861 few American men had as much combat experience as did Phil Kearny. Returning from France upon the outbreak of the Civil War, Kearny was given a brigadier's commission to command New Jersey's first brigade of infantry.

Kearny's aggressive nature coupled with his disdain for politically advantaged generals caused him to chafe under McClellan's cautious command. But eventually during McClellan's Peninsula Campaign Kearny was promoted from brigade to division command in Heintzelman's 3rd Corps. On several occasions Kearny had demonstrated he was a genuine warrior; Kearny once told George Custer, "I love war. It brings me indescribable pleasure, like that of having a woman." As much as any other Union general in the Eastern Theater, Kearny—who could be a difficult subordinate—possessed a warrior temperament.

And so fortuitously Kearny's and Hooker's divisions were available to adjoin McCall's division of the Glendale/Frayser's Farm sector after Heintzelman independently withdrew from Savage's Station. Kearny was deployed to the right, or north, of McCall who straddled the Long Bridge Road, while Hooker took a position to McCall's left. Once his brigades were in place Kearny informed his division that it "was the rear guard of all God's creation."[100] There were approximately four and half miles between Kearny's extreme right flank to Hooker's extreme left flank. Following the battle of Savage's Station Franklin withdrew to form a position below the base of the White Oak Swamp north and roughly perpendicular to Kearny; Franklin—with Slocum's division closest to Kearny's, would thus become the Federal rear guard on the 30th. A division commanded by BGen. John Sedgwick, 49, was in reserve behind McCall.[101]

If Lee's planned maneuvers were fulfilled he could concentrate nearly 70,000 soldiers against a smaller, scattered enemy.[102] It has been said that "not one aspect of Lee's plan was executed."[103] What went wrong?

First, while Lee's pursuit should have had many advantages the Federals also had one advantage, invaluable against assaults by larger armies: Specifically, the Federals' divisions were aligned in an arc that was interior to the Rebels' potential points of attack. Not only were the Confederates' columns so widespread they had difficulty supporting one another but the Federal units were deployed so that they could communicate with one another. It was proven throughout the entirety of both theaters that holding interior lines could compensate for other disadvantages, including numerical inferiority.

Moreover, for whatever reason, Jackson—still acting as though he was in a trance—hindered any chance of a Rebel victory by another slow, half-hearted effort against the Federal's rear at White Oak Bridge.[104] Breaching Union lines at White Oak Bridge would have put Jackson in the Federals' rear, thus putting the Union army in severe jeopardy, especially as it was defending against the convergence of Lee's double envelopment. Jackson determined that while his infantry could cross fords through the White Oak Swamp his artillery and wagons could not cross in a similar manner.[105] Rather than aggressively trying to cross with his infantry Jackson was content to allow a desultory artillery duel that accomplished little.[106] One Lee scholar, Clifford Dowdey, opined that Jackson's "failure was complete, disastrous, and unredeemable."[107] Strangely, for reasons remaining a mystery to this day Jackson's failure to exert himself, and by extension his command, during Seven Days consistently demonstrated little of the verve and determination he had displayed during his previous months in the Valley. Some speculate he was tired from the lack of sleep from riding back and forth prior to Seven Days; some speculate Jackson was pouting because he no longer had an independent command. Others wonder whether he was unenthusiastic about defending Richmond because he instead continued to prefer a strategy of invading the North.[108] Since he never had a chance to explain himself in an autobiography or memoir the reasons for his lethargy remain unknown. Nevertheless Jackson's sluggish performance was a significant reason why Lee's army did not accomplish greater success against McClellan, not just at Glendale but also throughout the Seven Days.

Moving counterclockwise along Lee's exterior arc, Huger proved to be astonishingly inept, almost to the point of being comical if not for the tragic consequences. Huger, 54 years old, part of an aristocratic French Huguenot family from South Carolina, was another Mexican War veteran whom Winfield Scott appointed as his chief of ordinance. Huger remained in the Regular Army until the outbreak of the Civil War when he resigned to accept an appointment as a Confederate colonel but D. S. Freeman conjectured that the "slow, peace-time routine of the ordinance service" dulled Huger's fitness for field service. By the evening of the 29th Huger bivouacked his division on the Charles City Road within three miles of Glendale, certainly a feasible distance to meet's Lee's expectations for a noon attack against Quaker Road on the 30th and to initiate the attack by noon by signaling the other divisions by cannon fire.

But instead of advancing as Lee envisioned, Huger became embroiled in what would become known in Civil War lore as the Battle of Axes. Haunted by the specter of possible attacks against his flank or even the rear from Kearny, Huger dispatched a brigade—one fourth of his strength—on a reconnaissance in force, essentially a fool's errand. Advancing with the rest of his division to within two miles of its destination, Huger encountered trees that Federal pioneers had cut across the road.[109] These obstacles, stock-in-trade for retreating armies, completely stymied Huger's infantry as well as his artillery, but more importantly absolutely befuddled Huger.

Huger, and his next in command, BGen. William ("Little Billy") Mahone, 36, a former railroad engineer and executive, then ignored Lee's imperative for speed and timing before deciding to construct a detour. Mahone's soldiers started clearing trees on the alternative route, an effort countered by Federal pioneers felling even more trees along the intended new route. Predictably the Confederates were short of necessary tools, meaning they were out-axed by the better equipped Federals.[110] But eventually late in the day Little Billy's axe-men cut through to a point where an artillery battery was deployed. However this battery was no match for the several awaiting Federal batteries that quickly out-dueled their Southern counterparts.[111] Most importantly and unfortunately for the Southern scheme, Huger failed to advise Lee of the "predicament" caused by the Battle of Axes or of Huger's solution, which was to do nothing. Accordingly not only was Huger flummoxed by the Battle of Axes but the rest of Lee's command, especially Longstreet, was clueless about when to launch the balance of the assault.

Next, the inadequate maps of the area were flawed by confusing nomenclature. For instance two roads were designated as Quaker Road. Naturally Prince John attempted to go to the wrong Quaker Road, got hopelessly lost, and subsequently failed to arrive in position to be of any support to Longstreet.[112]

At the southern portion of Lee's plans, capture of Malvern Hill by Holmes would have given the Rebels' army a huge advantage. However Holmes, being old and deaf, was inadequate for the task.[113] It took no more than shelling from one of the gunships on the James to scatter Holmes' division.[114]

Notwithstanding these difficulties, other portions of Lee's plans began to materialize more or less as anticipated. On the morning of June 30 Longstreet advanced along Darbytown Road; about 2:30 that afternoon —after mistaking the sound of Jackson's artillery exchange for Huger's signal to start the entire assault—Longstreet sent a brigade, led by Col. Micah Jenkins, 27, directly into McCall's position, overrunning two Union batteries.[115] But after deploying two more brigades Longstreet called for help but only A.P. Hill was available.[116] Hill's attack helped to break McCall's center whose men were soon running to the rear allowing McCall to be captured.[117] Once the Federal center was broken Longstreet tried to turn the Federal's right flank by attacking Kearny's position. Kearny's soldiers fought with their customary valor but casualties quickly mounted to the point they either had to retreat or be slaughtered in place.[118] But just as the struggle seemed darkest for Kearny's division, Slocum—who was facing only a nominal threat from Huger—sent Kearny's former New Jersey brigade to help plug the gap. With that help the Federal line held, albeit at the expense of horrendous casualties from a melee, much of which was fought with bayonets and gun butts.[119] While fierce fighting raged as his army desperately struggled survive, McClellan enjoyed dinner aboard the USS *Galena,* a Union gunship on the James.

By 5:00 p.m. when no attack had begun at Frayser's Farm, and as McClellan's army with its herds of cattle and 5,000 wagons continued to pass by, Lee desperately ordered an attack. Even without McClellan's presence, the ferocity of the fighting at Glendale and neighboring villages approached that of Gaines's Mill, three days earlier. Wert says, "In its intensity and bloodletting, it rivaled Gaines' Mill"[120]; Buell called it "...a massive free-for-all, a grand melee of grand proportions in the shadows of the hot setting sun."[121] Porter Alexander would claim Glendale had more hand-to-hand combat than any other battle in the Civil War. Despite the loss of eighteen Union artillery pieces, the Union held firm thus allowing the Bluecoats to pass toward the James River.[122]

Lee blamed the lack of co-operation among his subordinate commands.[123] In his report Lee's rebuke stated, "Could the other commands have co-operated in the action the result would have proved most disastrous to the enemy."[124] But Lee's own performance as commander cannot escape a reasonable, legitimate critique. Although he had been in command of the army for only a month he had had ample time to observe the deficiencies of his command structure, including his individual commanders; previous combat during the Seven Days should have shown the deficiencies of a hands-off command style. At that Civil War period, and with the exception of Antietam, but otherwise continuing until the Wilderness, Lee's command style tended to put his units in place and then to allow, nay expect, his subordinate commanders fully and correctly implement Lee's intentions. Perhaps that style would work when, or if, his subordinate commanders were combat veterans experienced in Lee's methods. But the likes of Magruder, Huger, and Holmes hardly met those standards, and to Lee's later credit would be reassigned elsewhere. But on the 30th one has to wonder why Lee did not try to find out why Huger—not that far away—was not advancing and starting the attack as had been planned. And while Lee apparently consulted with Jackson earlier on the morning of the 30th there was no reason why Lee should not have sent a courier to Jackson to prod Stonewall into some action, even a demonstration, in support of the assaults further down Quaker Road. Although Lee apparently intended to create a concentration of force against the retreating, strung-out Federals, as its unfolded only 20,000 Confederate soldiers were actually engaged while another 50,000 nearby Rebels were unable to help.[125]

Jeffrey Wert is of the opinion that "Glendale had offered Lee his finest chance to inflict a crippling, if not fatal, defeat upon McClellan's army."[126] But converging and attacking at multiple points requires attacks, in order to maximize their effectiveness, be launched at the same time, and once again lack of accurate maps or other means of reconnaissance bedeviled Lee's Army of Northern Virginia as its enveloping units became lost and/or took the wrong roads to their intended destinations. Furthermore Huger was supposed to signal the start of a coordinated attack with cannon fire, always a problematic, erratic means of communication. As a result, only a relatively small portion of Lee's numerically superior army was engaged and the attacks that were launched were uncoordinated and uneven, causing individual attacks to lose potential effectiveness.

Late in the afternoon, and with Jeff Davis at his elbow, Lee ordered more frontal assaults by Longstreet, even though such attacks could not be started in ample time, and even though there was scant chance of success. Longstreet again had help from Hill but a counterattack by Hooker—not concerned by any threat of attack by Holmes—against the Confederates' right, together with the oncoming darkness, thwarted any possible chance of success. Although Longstreet sent his frontal assaults against the Federals at and around Glendale, nowhere—notwithstanding heavy casualties—did the Rebels gain more than temporary advantage. Thomas B. Buell observes,

> It is charitable to call this an attack at all, for the term implies some sense of orderly maneuvering, a plan perhaps, some measure of coordination by a commanding general. Such was not the case on the Evening of Day Six. Let us call it instead a massive free-for-all, a melee of grand proportions in the shadows of the hot setting sun.[127]

But on the other side, McClellan's actions, often called "inexplicable," during this battle were well below the leadership standards expected of commanding generals. As Ethan Rafuse says, "McClellan's failure to return to the scene of the fighting [at Glendale] on the afternoon of June 30, without doubt the critical moment of the retreat to the James, was unforgivable, and Stephen W. Sears is unquestionably correct to describe his actions as 'dereliction of duty.'"[128] Even though McClellan had witnessed none of the fighting, that evening he telegraphed Washington, "My Army has behaved superbly and have done all that men could do. If none of us escape we shall have at least have done honor to the country. *I shall do my best to save the Army.*" (My sarcastic emphasis added.)

C.S.A. BGen. E. Porter Alexander, one of the most objective historians of the Civil War, later said seldom when "we were within reach of military successes so great that we might have hoped to end the war with our independence. ... The first was at Bull Run [in] July 1861.... This [second] chance of June 30th [at Glendale] impresses me as the best of them all."[129] Freeman has said that "...Frayser's Farm was one of the great lost opportunities in Confederate military history. It was the bitterest disappointments Lee had ever sustained, and one that he could not conceal."[130] Although Glendale presented the Confederacy an early, and perhaps its best, chance to deal a near fatal blow to the Yankees, by the end of the day the Bluecoats held firm, almost assuring being able to escape safely to the James.[131] The Union suffered 2,853 casualties but the Confederates lost 3,615. By darkness the Union still held their position but during the night nevertheless withdrew further south another two plus miles back to Malvern Hill.

Although Glendale was indeed an outstanding opportunity to finish the Seven Days pursuit with extraordinary success, and while some might contend a Southern victory would have hastened the end of the war, some perspective remains in order. Time was of the essence as the Blueclads retreated along Quaker Road. Assuming the Confederate attack had begun by noon on the 30th with an immediate victory, clearly a major portion of the Federal army had escaped by the evening of the 29th when a couple of its corps reached the relative safety of Malvern Hill. The parade of Union soldiers, together with their trains of wagons, continued through the night and during the morning of the 30th. The Confederate delay in reaching Quaker Road simply allowed more of the Union army to escape until the Federal interior arc could collapse upon itself continuing their withdrawal to safety in an orderly manner.

Furthermore while the loss of a major portion of McClellan's army would have been devastating, it would not necessarily have been mortal. The Federals still had huge numbers of manpower, including two large, healthy armies in the Western theater plus enough troops to be forming yet another army to protect Washington. Not only did the Union still enjoy a massive naval superiority but its overall effort was led by the steely resolve of Abraham Lincoln and a cabinet likewise dedicated to the preservation of the Union. And so while we can say with some certainty that Glendale was a lost opportunity of significance for the Southern cause we must also measure the magnitude of that loss against other mitigating factors before jumping to any foregone conclusions.

## *Day Seven—July 1* (Malvern Hill)

Malvern Hill slopes to a plateau 150 feet above the surrounding topography.[132] Its clear hillsides created ideal terrain for a static defense, especially if supplemented with 171 pieces of artillery placed almost hub-to-hub. Once Col. Henry J. Hunt, 43, another Mexican War veteran who undoubtedly became one of the greatest artillerist in American military history, carefully placed these guns, the Union army occupied perhaps the best defensive position of the entire war. For the Union army, Malvern Hill—as a "great defensive position afforded by the country"—was Clausewitz's "point where the equilibrium of force is restored." Using Clausewitz's definition of retreat, the Seven Days retreat was concluded but that did not end Lee's quest to give one more battle for good measure. Lee was not in the best of moods this day, impatiently snapping at one subordinate that McClellan was likely to escape again because, "…I cannot have my orders carried out!"[133]

A month earlier Lee had made another unfortunate decision when he reported that he had all the artillery he needed and light mobile batteries could be transferred to "some other branch of the service."[134] As matters would unfold on July 1, 1862, at Malvern Hill, Lee's army could have used all the guns it could muster. The disparity between the respective artillery branches was reinforced by the near incompetence of BGen. William N. Pendleton, 53, a pleasant man who was also Lee's close friend and artillery chief. Other than any training received at West Point, Pendleton's training for artillery came from twenty-four years' experience as an Episcopal priest. Somehow Lee still thought his outnumbered artillery could out duel the Yanks'.[135]

After staying overnight at Malvern Hall, by mid-morning McClellan returned to the river, having given up.[136] On the other hand, Malvern Hill had to be one of Lee's worst command blunders ever, being poorly planned and badly executed.[137] A local citizen had warned D.H. Hill, who passed the message along to Lee and Longstreet, that the Rebels would better leave Malvern Hill alone if the Union army was there in force, a warning that Longstreet, in Lee's presence, scornfully disregarded.[138] Lee's ability to discern or gauge his adversary's attitude and/or intentions from across a battlefield was one of his great strengths. In this instance Lee accurately sensed McClellan's unnerved state but also mistakenly projected that attitude upon the men in the ranks, as well for that matter upon McClellan's senior subordinates.

Jackson was not only late on the scene—again—but once he arrived seemed indifferent to the efforts being exerted by other commands. Lee also had little control over his other lieutenants, his vague, verbal orders having been misconstrued either by his staff or subordinate commanders. Lee accepted Longstreet's proposal to establish two grand batteries but the Rebel gunners could not assemble more than a few batteries at a time, which the Federal batteries destroyed in detail.[139] After receiving erroneous reports that the Federals were withdrawing, by mid-day the Confederates, led by Magruder, began their piece meal frontal assaults. Apparently the Rebels had confused Hunt's adjustments of gun placements with overall movement to the rear; instead, the Union artillery and rifle fire were murderous rendering unabated butchery upon hell-bent assaults. These assaults seemed so senseless that Union defenders surmised that whiskey must have given the Rebel attackers enough courage to continue their heroic charges in the face of such unrelenting, ferocious fire from artillery as well as from infantry muskets. One such charge was led by BGen. Lewis Armistead, 45, who advanced to within 150 yards of the Union defenses before falling back to a safer position.[140] Reflecting Lee's lack of control over his subordinates, Armistead's charge, as were several other such assaults, began after Lee had ordered that the attacks cease and desist.

This carnage lasted a little more than four hours during which the Confederates suffered 5,355 casualties versus 3,214 losses suffered by the Federals. Malvern Hill was one of the few Civil War battles, if not the only, where artillery inflicted more casualties than did infantry. D.H. Hill would later lament about the frontal assaults, "It was not war—It was murder."[141] A Virginian later reflected that. "At no other time did I so realize the horrors of a battle field."[142]

Some of the Union's corps commanders wanted to hold their positions on Malvern Hill, and indeed Porter—McClellan's most loyal subordinate—even urged a counterattack.[143] A flabbergasted Kearny—who was *not* McClellan's most loyal subordinate—raged, "I, Philip Kearny, … protest this order to retreat. We ought, instead of retreating, to follow up the enemy and take Richmond. And in full view of all the responsibility of such a declaration I say to you all, such as order can only be prompted by cowardice or treason."[144] Nevertheless, per McClellan's orders Union forces continued their withdrawal—leaving their wounded on the field—to Harrison's Landing where they could be protected by gun boats, where they could be resupplied via the James, and where they remained a threat to Richmond, only 19 miles to the northwest as the crow flies.

Upon realizing that Harrison's Landing was McClellan's objective, Lee had several options other than chasing the Federals to, and then assaulting the Federals at, Malvern Hill. These options included: (1) Since the James narrows upstream there were ideal locations on the south bank for Rebel batteries to sink Union transports thus impeding McClellan's route of retreat and/or means of resupply; (2) Instead of a frontal assault on Malvern Hill, Lee could have by-passed Malvern Hill and headed with the bulk of his army directly for Harrison's Landing, on McClellan's rear; or (3) As recommended by Longstreet, Lee could have sent artillery to Evelynton Heights which rises about Harrison's Landing and dominates miles of surrounding terrain. Unfortunately for the lads clad in gray or butternut, Lee decided to launch frontal assaults against outstanding defensive positions on the slopes of Malvern Hill.

Had Lee decided to by-pass Malvern Hill with the bulk of his army instead to go straight to seize Harrison's Landing while dispatching his artillery with supporting infantry to Evelynton Heights, not only would he have avoided the debacle and bloodbath of Malvern Hill, he would have placed McClellan's army in the untenable position of either surrendering or else striking the Confederates who would be enjoying excellent defensive position. But the command philosophy at that period of the war was to assault the rear against a retreat rather than to try to block the path of the retreating army. Blocking the path of a retreat would not have been a new concept but had often been used by Napoleon half a century earlier. Given Lee's education and experience, including his stint as Superintendent of West Point, it begs the question why he had not given more consideration to Napoleon's preferred maneuver.

## Analysis

Seven Days resulted in unprecedented carnage with a total of 36,000 men killed, wounded, and missing, a total that exceeded the totals suffered in the entire Western theater during the first half of 1862— including 13,000 more than at Shiloh.[145] Of even more strategic importance it was the first of several turning points in the War Between the States.

Even though Gaines's Mill was the only battlefield victory for the Rebels, on its face Seven Days was a great success for the Confederacy since it appeared Lee had delivered the Confederate capital and its major manufacturing center from certain destruction. At the same time Lee's army suffered terrible casualties—20,000 dead and wounded, one fourth of its original strength and twice the number suffered by the Union—the Army of Northern Virginia also obtained considerable amounts of valuable stores, supplies and equipment plus 52 artillery guns and 35,000 small arms, including Enfield and Springfield rifles captured from or simply dropped by the retreating Federals.

In terms of territory gained, the Confederates gained only seven miles. Lee should at least receive credit for seizing the initiative that in turn quickly persuaded McClellan that his priority was to "save his army." However, once the Young Napoleon began to head toward the James, Lee accomplished little except to debilitate valuable manpower that the Confederacy would have chronic difficulty replacing for the remainder of the war. After Day One at Oak Grove—actually a narrow tactical win for the Union—for any number of reasons, some which were inexplicable, McClellan started moving his support from White House Landing. After Day Three at Gaines's Mill when McClellan ordered a full retreat of his army, Lee's actions were costly in terms of manpower lost, but irrelevant in terms of influencing McClellan's actions not already pre-ordained. The casualty figures for the battles subsequent to Gaines's Mill were 10,037 for the C.S.A. versus 7,025 for the U.S.A., not counting the 2,500 sick and wounded Yankees abandoned a Savage's Station. These attritions were always costlier to the Confederacy than to the Union since the latter had a much easier time replacing its losses.

The dramatic reversal of fortunes of Seven Days helped spawn Lee's iconic status as the hero of the Southern cause.[146] But in terms of Lee's management of the pursuit of the Union retreat, it can be seen Lee's performance fell short of completely competent generalship. On Day Four, the first day of the Union retreat, Lee could not guess the Federals' intentions, even within the relatively confined space of the battlefield. Smoke from the fires at White House Landing—several miles away—was clearly visible during the morning of Saturday, June 28th, and Stuart's cavalry could find no evidence that the Union was retreating to the east toward Fort Monroe. A simple deduction should have told Lee that his adversary was moving south where his most likely destination would be Harrison's Landing. Yet Lee did nothing until later that evening, allowing the fleeing Federals additional time to have separation they would put to good use in subsequent days.

When Lee eventually put his pursuit in motion on Day Five he dispatched his units in five separate columns, thereby making coordinated attacks difficult if not impossible. If his command had had good maps, and if they had effective means of communications, it might have made good sense to disperse his army in such a manner. But it would have made even more sense to try to head off the retreat by sending a bigger, more robust force than the 6,000 soldiers sent by Lee down River Road. In reality Lee's complex albeit naïve pursuit plan was doomed from its very start, especially given Jackson's laggard performance that Lee either ignored or neglected to correct.

Lee's Day Six maneuvers—looping discrete parts of his army to the west toward Richmond and then back toward Glendale—would have been difficult after hours of practice on an open, dry parade field, let alone unrehearsed on unfamiliar terrain, uncharted, muddy roads, under the commands of relatively inexperienced, often timid, indecisive generals. Without any reliable means of communications, it is little wonder the Confederate attacks were piecemeal doing little to thwart the Union retreat. It is one thing to draw up a sophisticated plan that incorporates several tactical components while ignoring difficult terrain features; it is another thing to devise plans that can reasonably be implemented and executed in a coordinated manner by subordinate commanders. Lee's plans depended too much upon conditions and circumstances—including terrain, his own staff capabilities, the skills and attitudes of his subordinate commanders, and the resources or the enemy—as he wished them to be rather than as they really were.

Unfortunately Malvern Hill on Day Seven was an unfortunate omen of the inaccurately labeled Pickett's Charge of just a couple more days than a year later. With our 20-20 hindsight it now seems obvious that launching frontal assaults against heavily and smartly fortified defenses were not going to succeed. But even in 1862 it would be hard to fathom what Lee hoped to accomplish at Malvern Hill, especially when he was advised by subordinates to consider other options.

It is impossible to judge whether alternative measures would have been more successful in capturing or defeating McClellan's army before it reached Harrison's Landing but perhaps, even probably, Lee's main contribution to ridding Richmond from McClellan's threat was little more than simply assuming the initiative and being aggressive.

For any number of reasons, including an overabundance of cautiousness by McClellan, the Federals also lost opportunities to strike devastating blows against the Confederate forces in the Eastern theater. Nevertheless, McClellan was still within striking distance of Richmond.

As a mitigating factor Lee's pursuit might have been hampered by the untimely absence of his cavalry. On Saturday, June 28, 1862, Lee sent Jeb Stuart and his cavalry to cut the rail connections to the White House Landing and to determine the Federal whereabouts and intentions.[147] Sometime in the afternoon Stuart reported seeing immense clouds of smoke coming from White House.[148] Stuart and his troopers saw the fires and smoke as they approached closer to the supply depot before bivouacking for the night.[149]

Upon arising the next morning, the 29th, Stuart spotted a gun boat at the landing, a target Stuart found too tempting to resist. After using his single mortar to drive off the gunboat Stuart's troopers spent the rest of the dousing the fires before helping themselves to the vast stores of supplies, foodstuffs, and equipment that had been abandoned by the retreating Federals. Meanwhile Lee sent a courier to inquire about McClellan's whereabouts and movements. Stuart replied that here were no signs that McClellan was retreating eastward down the Peninsula and that he (Stuart) had no doubt McClellan was moving toward the James.[150] Unfortunately for Lee, without Stuart to reconnoiter close at hand Lee did not know where McClellan was.[151]

Although Stuart had reported with little reservation his intelligence that the Federals were heading south, on June 30 Stuart remained to reconnoiter and guard some bridges across the lower Chickahominy. At this point the only importance of these bridges was that they would have to be re-crossed if the Yanks were indeed retreating to the east—as of course Stuart had determined they were not. If Stuart had determined that the Federals were not heading east, would not the prudent action be to try to find the Federals' exact location?

At 3:30 of the morning of June 31 Stuart was awakened by another courier carrying a message from Lee's Chief of Staff. This dispatch ordered Stuart to re-cross the Chickahominy to cooperate on Jackson's left. However the battle for Malvern Hill was over by the time that Stuart managed to ride 42 miles to reach the left flank of the Confederate army.[152] Thus Stuart contributed no meaningful intelligence or protection to Lee's flank for the entire period of the pursuit. While it is easy to conclude Lee was handicapped without his eyes and ears at least a major portion of the blame rests upon Lee's habit of issuing discretionary orders that in this instance allowed Stuart to linger along the Chickahominy rather than returning immediately to the main army.

## *Dénouements and Precursors*

Although many of Lee's brigades had been severely wounded at Malvern Hill, the next day, Wednesday, July 2, 1862, some of Lee's subordinates, including ironically Stonewall Jackson whose lethargic performance had hampered the Rebels' chances for better success during the Seven Days campaign, advocated further pursuit of McClellan's army, even though these subordinates were not certain of the entire situation. However after consulting with Longstreet and D.H. Hill, both of whom had surveyed the field, Lee determined that further pursuit was not practical.[153]

On Monday, July 7, 1862, Lincoln visited McClellan at Harrison's Landing where his army continued to remain a threat to Richmond, only 19 miles away. The egomaniacal McClellan blamed Lincoln for his failure to send more reinforcements and tried to persuade Lincoln to take a more conservative approach to the war; even as he cowered at Harrison's Landing, the Young Napoleon had the temerity to hand Lincoln a letter that urged that the war "should not be at all a war upon population, but against armed forces and political organizations." Lincoln read the letter in McClellan's presence but placed the letter in his pocket without responding to McClellan. This incident represented a dramatic turning point in the Civil War because it signaled Lincoln's rejection of the possibility of conciliation with the South but instead was committed to take whatever steps were going to be necessary to subjugate Southern interests.

Lincoln suggested McClellan should consider either resuming a movement toward Richmond or else returning to help defend the Washington area. McClellan agreed that he should advance again toward Richmond, provided of course that he received more reinforcements, based upon his preposterous claim that Lee had 200,000 men.[154]

Predictably McClellan and his army remained inert but replenished at Harrison's Landing until on August 3, 1862, newly appointed General in Chief Henry Halleck ordered McClellan to transfer his army back to the Washington area to provide for the defense of Washington and to reinforce Pope's Army of Virginia.[155] Arguably the redeployment of McClellan's army away from Harrison's Landing might have been a strategic mistake. McClellan, regardless of his hesitancy to do anything, was in a position that should have represented a threat to Richmond, especially since McClellan had a reliable supply base and since he was now on the Richmond side of the Chickahominy, which had created such a maneuvering impediment five to six weeks earlier. As long as a viable threat remained against Richmond, Lee's army was, or should have been, obliged to remain in the Richmond area, thus for the time being at least alleviating any threat against Washington.

At this point in the Civil War, gaining individual glory remained the defining motivation for many of the officers on either side of the conflict. Officers' after action reports sill tended to ignore or gloss over mistakes, especially of their own making. But after Seven Days there were two notable exceptions to this philosophy of gaining individual glory. On the Union side, McClellan's chief engineer, BGen. John G. Barnard, 47, a former Superintendent of West Point, scorched both the administration *and* McClellan for bungled opportunities, unwarranted delays, want of initiative, and waffled thinking and reasoning.[156] Barnard's report contradicted McClellan's self-laudatory report in several important respects, but it has rarely been read by historians, other than by Thomas B. Buell, and has never been published intact other than in Vol. 11 of the Official Reports.[157] It should be noted that Barnard retained his position in the Army of the Potomac until promoted to Grant's staff in 1864.

George McCall, the Union division commander who had been captured at Glendale, remained as a prisoner at Libby Prison until exchanged almost two months later when he was placed on sick leave, never able to return to active duty before resigning the next year. One of McCall's brigades was commanded by BGen. George G. Meade who was leading his brigade in the heat of Glendale when struck in his arm and side. Meade winced but did not fall from his horse before riding slowly to the rear. Meade would not return to active duty for seven weeks.

On the Confederate side, Robert Lee quickly realized his command style required subordinate commanders who understood and could act upon Lee's frequently vague directions. Accordingly two of his generals proven to be incapable of such responsibilities, Benjamin Huger and Theophilus Holmes, were re-assigned to the Trans-Mississippi Department. Huger remained there until the end of the war but Holmes asked to be relieved by his assistant, Kirby Smith. Prince John Magruder was sent to command the District of Texas, a command that was enlarged to include Arizona and New Mexico. At the end of the war he went to Mexico where he became a major general in Maximilian's army.

D.H. Hill, one of the few Confederate generals showing consistent initiative during the Seven Days, was the exception to his fellow Confederate officers who submitted reports that tended to be deferential, circumspect, and lacking in any meaningful analysis and recommendations for important, much needed improvements. Among Hill's observations, he alone admitted that the C.S.A.'s loses were greater than those of the U.S.A. He also had the temerity to suggest that Malvern Hill would have had a different result but for "the blundering management of the battle," presumably a criticism of Lee's generalship.[158]

For his efforts, Hill was reassigned (exiled?) to obscurity in North Carolina. In making this reassignment, Lee wrote to Davis, "I feel General Hill is not entirely equal to his present position. An excellent executive officer, he does not appear to have much administrative ability. Left to himself, he seems embarrassed and backward at act."[159] Although recalled later to be part of Lee's army to defend Richmond, Hill never regained his former status within Lee's inner circle, soon being sent West to help Bragg at Chickamauga (see Chapter 5).

Thus, for all the blood that had been spilled at Shiloh, and regardless of the butcher's bill at Seven Days, commanders—apparently even Robert Lee, if Malvern Hill was any indication—continued to stress the capture of locations in the pursuit of honor and glory of giving battle. The idea of using pursuit to gain advantage to capture or annihilate the enemy army was yet to emerge, and certainly was not yet the driving force of combat objectives.

## 12

# Second Bull Run
## August 29–30, 1862

### Pope Commands a New Army

By June 26, after Stonewall Jackson's success in the Valley, and when Lee initiated the battle against McClellan at Beaver Creek Dam seven miles from Richmond, the Federal administration finally decided to unify the command of the three separate armies of MGen. John Charles Frémont, MGen. Nathaniel Banks, and MGen. Irvin McDowell. This new unified command of approximately 40,000 men was ordered to move south toward Richmond (the command also included another 11,000-man division stationed at Fredericksburg). Lincoln appointed the newly promoted MGen. John Pope, 40, recently from Henry Halleck's former command in the Corinth campaign, to serve as overall commander of this new army to be called the Army of Virginia.

Pope, James Longstreet's former West Point roommate, was a relatively junior two-star general who had built a reputation as a tough, give-no-quarter commander, a reputation built largely upon his own exaggerated reports, as well as his braggadocio and some prevarications about his accomplishments.[1] Lee regarded Pope as a "miscreant."[2] In contrast to most West Pointers, Pope was a dedicated Republican, his family having a long relationship with Lincoln. The Radical Republicans were positioning Pope to take McClellan's place. Within the cabinet, Chase and Stanton were big supporters of Pope. Pope quickly expressed a demeaning, denigrating attitude toward Union efforts in the Eastern campaign, a critical attitude that seemed to include McClellan.[3]

Citing his seniority to Pope, Frémont—the second- ranking major general in the Regular Army—refused to serve in the brand new army and resigned from his command.[4] He went to New York where he remained "awaiting orders" for the rest of the war. MGen. Franz Sigel, 38, a graduate of the German Military Academy, replaced Frémont as corps commander. Ever looking for ways to find favor with various demographic groups, Lincoln appointed Sigel largely to impress and attract German immigrants who were thought to make good soldiers.[5]

As reorganized, and with former armies then re-designated as corps, the Federal Army of Virginia, was organized with Sigel commanding the 1st Corps, Banks commanding the 2nd Corps, and Irwin McDowell commanding the 3rd Corps. Artillery battalions and cavalry brigades were attached directly to the infantry corps, meaning Pope would not have direct command of these branches.

While McClellan remained at Harrison's Landing Pope's new army of approximately

47,000 men began to advance southward from the Washington area toward Richmond. By July 12, 1862, it was at Culpeper Court House, Virginia, within striking distance of Gordonsville, a railroad terminus that connected Richmond with the all-important Shenandoah Valley, the Confederacy's breadbasket. For obvious strategic reasons, including the necessity of keeping his army fed, Lee's imperative was to defend that railroad junction!

## Jackson Confronts Pope

In the aftermath of Seven Days Lee streamlined his command structure by reorganizing his seven infantry divisions into two wings,[6] one commanded by Longstreet and the other commanded by Jackson.[7] As measured by brigades, Longstreet's was much the larger with twenty-eight brigades while Jackson's command contained but seven.[8] Lee also consolidated his cavalry into a division to be commanded by Jeb Stuart, newly promoted to major general.[9]

To confront Pope Lee sent Jackson with two divisions and a cavalry brigade under Stuart sixty miles north to Gordonsville, where they arrived July 19.[10] To eliminate Pope's threat, on August 13 Lee ordered Longstreet to take most of the remainder of the Army of Northern Virginia to join Jackson at Gordonsville.[11] At the same time Halleck ordered Pope to not advance any further than the Rapidan.[12] Although the principles did not realize it, the pieces were now in motion toward the Second Battle of Bull Run!

Lee learned from newspaper accounts that Halleck also ordered McClellan to leave Harrison's Landing to start moving by steamboat north to reinforce Pope.[13] Lacking enough steamboats to transport all of his army at the same time, McClellan first sent Fitz-John Porter's 5th Corps to disembark at Aquia Landing, approximately five miles north by northeast of Falmouth. The steamboats would then return to carry other units from the Army of the Potomac to disembark later at Alexandria. From Falmouth Porter began to march along the Rappahannock River intending to meet Pope at Rappahannock Station on the Orange & Alexander R.R. And so the practical effect of Halleck's order to leave Harrison's Landing was to halve the opposition against Lee's forces.[14]

Reasonably confident that McClellan no longer threatened Richmond, and having agreed with President Davis that it was a golden time to initiate some strategic offensive, Lee left Richmond by train to join his army at Gordonsville, arriving August 15.[15] Lee hoped to consolidate his wings before McClellan could join Pope enabling the Confederates to defeat one if not both Federal armies.[16] Shortly after catching up with Jackson and Longstreet, Lee ordered a turning movement on Saturday, August 18, 1862, against Pope's left that was exposed at Cedar Mountain. However this attack was undone in part by Lee's "whimsical" logistical planning, which had failed to take into account all the requirements for feeding an army on the march away from Richmond.[17] Furthermore Lee's plan was undone when Stuart was late in trying to get to Pope's rear.[18] By the time another strike could be launched two days later when Lee had a strength of 54,500 effectives[19] Pope had been able to withdraw to more secure defensive positions behind (i.e., north of) the Rappahannock River.[20] Notwithstanding these setbacks, Stuart captured a cache of papers from Pope's headquarters to learn that within five days more reinforcements would increase Pope's army to nearly 130,000, or more than double Lee's strength.[21]

Lee had reason to consider his position as the two armies probed and maneuvered against each other across the Rappahannock. Although Jackson had done well against Banks a few days earlier, and although Longstreet's arrival had essentially reconstituted Lee's army, Lee also had to take into account the reality that Pope would have an army that would enjoy significant numerical superiority over Lee's army if Pope were reinforced by the arrival of units from McClellan.

Although evidence would later emerge to support speculation that Lee always desired to pursue a strategic offensive into Northern territory, Lee's immediate mission was to defend Richmond together with its supply lines, including the railroads through Gordonsville. However, Lee's defensive mission would be imperiled once sufficient Union forces could be mustered against his smaller Army of Northern Virginia.

## Jackson Flanks Pope

In a move that was a precursor of similar tactics he would employ during the next nine months—tactics cutting across the grain of conventional wisdom of warfare—Lee decided to split his army before reforming to concentrate in force to strike against the still divided Union forces.[22] In other words, within a defensive framework to protect Richmond Lee was taking the offensive, calculating, or gambling as the case may be, that Pope's army would not be reinforced when the divided Army of Northern Virginia would be vulnerable to extinction by vastly superior numbers.

Lee's strategy was to send Jackson ahead to capture Manassas Junction. Not only was Manassas Junction located behind Pope's position but it was also a critical junction on the railroad upon which reinforcements from McClellan would be transported after disembarking at Alexandria. As an additional bonus, Pope's main supply depot at Manassas Junction was ripe for the picking by the perpetually undernourished, poorly equipped Rebels. The Union supply depot at Manassas Junction was much more than a few tents and/or buildings; indeed it occupied a whole square mile of territory! Lee planned for Jackson to leave first, departing Monday, August 25, 1862, with Longstreet remaining to distract and detain Pope's fourteen-mile line along the Rappahannock.[23] Stonewall hoped Pope could be induced to retreat during which Stonewall could win a decisive victory by blocking Pope's retreat![24]

Redeeming his lackluster performance of Seven Days—perhaps because he could operate independently—in two days Jackson proceeded to circle fifty four miles[25] clockwise around and behind Pope's right flank to reach Bristoe Station a short distance from the virtually undefended Union stores at Manassas Junction on Tuesday, August 26.[26] The first leg of Jackson's march had been spotted by the Union army[27] but Pope mistakenly assumed Jackson was retreating west back to the Shenandoah Valley on the other side of the Blue Ridge Mountains.[28] Additionally Pope's over stretched cavalry failed to detect Stonewall's shift at Salem to the east on the 26th. And so Pope remained in the vicinity of the Rappahannock while Longstreet feigned a show of force.

## Pope Withdraws to Manassas

After an orgy of gorging themselves, looting, trashing, and burning the Federal stores at Manassas Junction,[29] Jackson then hid his forces from which he could ambush the Army of Virginia as it would be moving from the southwest to the northeast along the Warrenton Turnpike.[30] When Pope belatedly learned something more than a raid was occurring to his rear, he—without waiting for Porter to arrive from Falmouth—began to withdraw toward Manassas, intending, he bragged, to "bag the whole crowd" Jackson.[31]

On August 26, 1862, the same day when Longstreet was detaining Pope at the Rappahannock while Jackson was sacking the supply depot at Manassas Junction, George McClellan debarked from a boat at Alexandria.[32] Inasmuch as he was accompanied only by his staff he was a commanding general almost without a command. At that time his former 3rd Corps, commanded by Samuel Heintzelman, and the 5th Corps, commanded by Fitz-John Porter, were marching westward overland from Aquia Landing intending to join Pope.[33] The 4th Corps, commanded by Erasmus Keyes, stayed behind at Fort Monroe; William Franklin's 6th Corps preceded the Young Napoleon to Alexandria while Edwin Sumner's 2nd Corps, would arrive two days later.

When Pope arrived at Manassas Junction around noon on Thursday, August 28, 1862, he found his stores destroyed or missing but he could not find Jackson's corps! Jackson had sent one of his divisions along with the supply train to Sudley Spring while the rest of his forces moved to Groveton[34] in a wooded tract behind the railroad cut that ran parallel along the Warrenton Turnpike.[35] On August 28 some of the Rebels came out of the woods when they saw McDowell's 3rd Corps marching along the turnpike from Gainesville to Centreville. During the ensuing battle two of the most storied brigades of the Civil War, the Confederate's Stonewall Brigade and the Union's Black Hats (later "Iron"), were pitted against one another. Fierce, stand-up, ill-directed fighting ensued, two of the casualties being Richard Ewell who suffered the loss of a leg and BGen. Isaac Trimble, 60.[36] When Pope learned of this fight, and still under the mistaken assumption that Jackson was retreating to the Shenandoah Valley, and while ignoring Longstreet's movement to Thoroughfare Gap west of Manassas, Pope directed his troops to Groveton and to Centreville in order to rout what he believed to be Stonewall's remaining Confederates.

Finally late in the day of the 28th Stonewall consolidated his corps of 20,000 troops behind an unfinished railroad embankment at Stoney Ridge, the embankment running parallel with the Warrenton Turnpike. In doing so, Jackson virtually was daring Pope to strike again.

Longstreet, still accompanied by Lee, took the same basic route as had Jackson but took three days instead of Stonewall's two. Upon their arrival at the Manassas area at about noon on Friday, August 29, 1862, Lee and Longstreet were met by J.E.B. Stuart who advised then to turn left onto the turnpike at Gainesville.[37] Longstreet aligned his troops behind woods at a slightly oblique angle to Jackson's right (western) flank. One of Longstreet's divisions was aligned at right angles to and south of the Warrenton Turnpike while his other division continued the line south of the turnpike. Longstreet also posted nineteen pieces of artillery along a low ridge behind the junction of the two Confederate corps. Measured from Longstreet's right flank to Jackson's left, the entire Confederate line was three miles long evenly divided between Jackson and Longstreet.[38]

For some reason Pope acted as though he was not concerned by, or incredibly was not even aware of, Longstreet's impending arrival.[39] Not only was the dust from Longstreet's march clearly visible, John Buford, commander of one of Pope's cavalry brigades, had spotted Longstreet early in the morning, and had sent a written report to Irvin McDowell. Inexplicably McDowell—ostensibly Pope's second in command—simply pocketed that report without sharing that intelligence with anyone.[40]

## Pope Decides to Attack

Late on the Friday afternoon of August 29 Pope gave in to the temptation to make a series of uncoordinated, piecemeal frontal assaults against Jackson's troops sheltered behind the railroad embankment. Lee, still with Longstreet, suggested three times to Longstreet to launch his own counterattack against Pope's exposed left flank as Pope assaulted Jackson's position but each time Longstreet demurred, indicating he did not think the time was ripe for such an attack.[41] Earlier in the afternoon the Confederates had observed a large volume of Federal troops massing approximately two miles to Longstreet's right. Later personal reconnaissance by Lee and Longstreet confirmed that these were Porter's troops, having just arrived from Alexandria by way of Rappahannock Junction. But by 5:00 p.m. Longstreet concluded, and so advised Lee, that Porter was no threat to an assault. Also that evening Jackson withdrew his troops from the railroad embankment.

Pope's original plan for the 29th was to have Porter circle around Jackson's right flank while Pope launched his frontal assaults. This plan had two basic defects: (1) the order was literally impossible to execute since it required Porter to "close in" with Pope's left flank, two miles away, and (2) unknown to Pope Longstreet was covering Jackson's right flank, thus blocking any forward advance by Porter. At about 4:30 p.m. Pope sent orders to Porter to advance with his 10,000 men against the Confederate right then consisting of Longstreet's corps of 25,000 men. However, Pope's order was not received by Porter until approximately 6:30 p.m., or close to sunset.[42] Porter's division commanders protested it was too late in the day without sufficient daylight to launch such an attack. Thus Porter cancelled Pope's order and instead bivouacked for the night.

Also by the 29th the internecine battle in Washington for control between Halleck and McClellan continued to the detriment of the Federals in Manassas. Essentially McClellan was using every excuse to avoid losing all his command if he sent Franklin and Sumner to Pope's aid; meanwhile Halleck was simply trying to assert his authority as General in Chief while also appeasing Stanton who was becoming all the more impatient, if not overtly hostile, with McClellan. McClellan was losing almost all credibility with the Administration, including Lincoln, when he charged that one option was to "leave Pope to get out his scrape & at once use all our means to make the Capital perfectly safe."[43] Finally by the evening of August 29 and after overplaying his hand, and under the threat of being completely relieved of any command—as Stanton was threatening—McClellan was forced to order Franklin to move closer to Manassas.[44]

Very early in the predawn of the 30th, Pope wired Halleck to advise that the enemy was "retreating towards the mountains…."[45] Little did he know!

Early during the same Saturday morning, the 30th, Lee met with Jackson and

Longstreet. They decided Jackson should return to the railroad embankment to await Pope's next attack but if Pope did not attack as anticipated, Jackson was to withdraw from his entrenchments and shift behind Pope's right in order to be able to interdict any attempt by Pope to withdraw back to Washington. The Rebels added eighteen more artillery pieces under the command of Col. Stephen D. Lee, 29, to enfilade the open fields in front of Jackson's position over which the Federals would have to traverse if they should resume their frontal assaults.[46] At the same time Pope apparently but inexplicably concluded Longstreet had moved behind Jackson's lines.[47] Porter tried, with BGen. John Reynolds concurring, to convince Pope that the Confederate's right extended well past the Union's left.[48] So again ignoring Porter's warning about the threat to his left,[49] or even being oblivious to the threat to his left, Pope ordered another frontal assault against the railroad embankment.[50] By now Pope could commit Porter's corps in frontal assaults against Jackson's massed rifles and cannons on Jackson's center and right flank.[51] By shifting the Union attack to Jackson's center and right (also being of course Longstreet's left as well within range of the bulk of the Rebel artillery), Pope and McDowell, in charge of the Union's tactical operations, were directing their attack against the strength of the Confederates' defense!

Furthermore since the attack was directed at the vortex of the Confederate lines there would be limited means of extraction. Bevin Alexander contends the Union's plan for the afternoon of the 30th "ranks as one of the preeminent examples of how *not* to fight a tactical battle."[52] Notwithstanding the tactical ineptitude of some Union commanders these Union assaults resulted in battles of almost unbelievable fury—Porter's corps attacked savagely and with good coordination.[53] At one point the Rebels' ammunition was so depleted they were forced to throw rocks across the crest of their embankments at the oncoming Bluecoats.

## *Longstreet Counterattacks*

Shortly after noon Reynolds dispatched a reconnaissance to discover "the enemy is turning our left."[54] Once again Pope ignored this intelligence. But after scanning the situation McDowell ordered Reynolds to redeploy to Chinn Ridge. Sigel also sent the 55th OVI from a brigade commanded by Col. Nathaniel McLean, 37, to Chinn Ridge with instructions to establish communications with Reynolds.[55] To further bolster the defense of Chinn Ridge, BGen. Robert Schenck, 53,[56] from Sigel's corps, sent the rest of McLean's brigade—consisting of the 25th OVI, the 73rd OVI, and the 75th OVI—along with an artillery battery of four guns that McLean posted on Reynolds' right flank.[57]

Chinn Ridge was an elongated hill with its northern-most tip a half-mile almost directly west of the Henry House. While the Henry House Hill had a commanding view of the Warrenton Turnpike as well as the Stone Bridge, Chinn Ridge likewise overlooked the pike but more significantly was a geographic barrier to the Henry House Hill, especially if approached from Longstreet's launching position. Another prominence, Bald Hill, was east of Chinn Ridge and south of Henry Hill but did not have the same terrain features for defensive positions. Additionally Chinn Ridge was closer to Dogan Ridge, across the Warrenton Turnpike, where Sigal's headquarters and artillery were positioned. Young's Branch, ostensibly the ultimate objective assigned to Hood, was a "Clear and pebbly bottomed branch" that meandered between the Warrenton Turnpike, which the creek crossed twice, and the western slope of Chinn Ridge. Troops and artillery coming either from the pike or from Dogan Hill would have to wade through this tributary before starting to ascend Chinn Ridge.

At the same time McLean was positioning his regiments on Chinn Ridge the attacks ordered by Pope against Jackson were once again repulsed causing the Federals to flee in disarray to the northeast along the Warrenton Turnpike toward Dogan Ridge. As McDowell saw Porter's men retreating toward Dogan Ridge McDowell committed "the most fatal mistake of [his] ill-plagued career" when, in panic, he ordered Reynolds to remove his troops off Chinn Ridge.[58] Reynolds' redeployment left just McLean's three Ohio regiments and their artillery battery to defend the vital Chin Ridge. McLean then did the only thing he could do under the circumstances: He readjusted his three infantry regiments into the positions previously occupied by Reynolds entire division. Scott Patchen observes that "McLean's decision to remain on Chinn Ridge proved pivotal and is all the more commendable given the atmosphere of distrust and intrigue that existed among the various factions of Pope's force."[59]

At some point between 3:00 and 4:00 p.m. as Pope's army was floundering in disarray, Longstreet finally decided the time was ripe to commit his entire command of 25,000 soldiers against Pope's fragmented lines,[60] implementing one of Lee's favorite tactics, the hammer and anvil, with Longstreet providing the hammer this time and Jackson the anvil. Longstreet designated Hood's brigade to lead the attack.

Longstreet directed Hood to head toward Henry House,[61] about a mile and half distant, the same focal point of First Bull Run, "...in order to cut off the [Federal] retreat at the crossing of Young's Branch."[62] Once again Henry House Hill was deemed important because it overlooked the Stone Bridge where the Warrenton Turnpike crossed Bull Run. Capture of the Henry House Hill would give the Rebels' exceptional leverage to impede, if not sever, Pope's retreat. Conversely the Federals had to hold Henry House Hill to maintain possession of the Stone Bridge, once again their most feasible means of escape from the Bull Run battlefield.[63] But instead of approaching the Henry House Hill from the northwest, as the Federals had done a little more than a year ago, now Longstreet's soldiers would approach from the southwest by way of Chinn Ridge.

A small brigade commanded by Col. Gouvernour K. Warren, 32, was the first Unionist command in the way of Hood's onslaught.[64] Warren's brigade included companies of the colorfully uniformed, snazzy drilled National Zouaves. Shortly after Hood advanced The National Zouaves fired a single volley before making "for the rear at first class speed."[65]

Longstreet's counterattack with his 28,000 soldiers soon crushed Porter's corps of 10,000 soldiers, constituting Pope's left flank, before continuing to sweep toward Chinn Ridge. As Longstreet's infantry attacked *en enchelon*, led and guided on the left by Hood's brigade, Longstreet also pushed his artillery in support.[66] But shortly after the attack began Longstreet summoned Hood back to Longstreet's position to caution Hood about moving faster than artillery could maintain its support; however the attack's overall coordination was already disrupted by the time Hood returned to his brigade.[67]

At one point Franz Sigel ordered BGen. Robert Milroy to take his independent brigade of West Virginians to reinforce McLean's four infantry regiments on Chinn Ridge. But before Milroy could deploy Pope countermanded Sigel's order by directing Milroy to move his brigade to Henry Hill; accordingly at least for the time being McLean's Ohio Brigade would defend without reinforcements. Even while witnessing the collapse of Federal resistance below along the Warrenton Turnpike the three Ohio regiments with their single battery were aligned in a battle line facing westward hoping to buy enough time for Pope to shift more units to Henry Hill and save his army from irreparable damage.[68]

One immediate consequence of Hood's failure to maintain command continuity was that two infantry regiments charged up Chinn ridge without any artillery support only to be unmercifully cut down by the score by the 25th and 75th Ohio volunteer regiments.[69] As these battered Rebel regiments fell back along the slope of Chinn ridge a brigade of South Carolinians commanded by Shanks Evans passed through on their way to the front. As a happenstance Evans was returning to the same battlefield where he had achieved his first notable success during the Civil War.[70]

Ironically Evans represented a changing of the guard occurring during the year following First Bull Run when Shanks had been commended for "dauntless courage and imperturbable coolness" along with "skill and unshrinking courage."[71] Subsequently he performed superbly at Ball's Bluff in October 1861 and at Secessionville on June 15, 1862. During both battles Evans' commands inflicted much higher casualties than they suffered.

But for all his tactical brilliance and personal bravery, his penchant for hard drinking, belligerent talk, and being difficult to manage were hampering his chances for advancement, especially within the more genteel culture of Lee's Army of Northern Virginia. Essentially Evans remained at the same command level as at First Manassas while previously more junior officers were now commanding divisions. For his counterattack at Second Manassas Longstreet appointed Evans to command his own brigade plus Hood's division but this appointment was greatly diminished because Longstreet continued to confer exclusively with Hood instead of Evans.[72]

Both sides began to bring artillery to bear against their adversaries, the Northerners positioning substantial metal on Dogan Hill across the way. Federal guns from Dogan Hill and Chinn Ridge hurtled a variety of ordinance upon Evans' Carolinians as they advanced toward their objective, but by cautious maneuvers the Palmettos eventually reached the open ground on McLean's front.[73] About the same time the 55th OVI, which had been detained at the northern end of Chinn Ridge to cover the five hundred yards between the Warrenton Turnpike and Reynolds's position on the ridge, arrived and began to fall in line with McLean's other regiments, adding badly needed reinforcements to McLean's beleaguered rear guard. But although the Buckeyes' muskets wreaked havoc upon the Confederates the numerical superiority of several Rebel brigades began to outflank and overwhelm the Chinn Ridge rear guard.

The 73rd OVI, on the Buckeye left wing, was the first regiment forced to retreat to Henry Hill which in turn caused the 25th likewise to seek the same refuge with the gunners forced to follow suit.[74]

Fortuitously Irvin McDowell began to fully understand the dynamics of the Confederate pursuit, finally realizing the importance of holding Henry House Hill along with its buffer, Chinn Ridge. McDowell personally led reinforcements, led by BGen. Zeolous Bates Tower, 43, who had graduated first in his West Point class before serving on Winfield Scott's staff in the Mexican War, up on Henry Hill before sending Tower and his soldiers further down to Chinn Ridge to relieve what was left of McLean's brigade. After double-quicking to take their new positions on Chinn Ridge these soldiers, mostly from New York and

Pennsylvania, along with the 55th and 75th OVIs, had to hold long enough until Pope secured Henry Hill with other troops.[75] On the other hand it was imperative for the Rebels to drive the Union rear guard off Chinn Ridge and to take Henry Hill if Longstreet were going to achieve his objective.

There never was a formal, explicit order by Pope to commence a retreat. Instead Federal units began to back pedal on their own initiative as brigades in Longstreet's counterattack began to overwhelm and/or outflank the boys in Blue. Even as McDowell was directing Tower's division toward Chinn Ridge Pope, still oblivious to his army's peril, inconceivably queried McDowell whether "he had taken too much from the right," i.e., the retreat route.[76] Once McDowell explained the severity of the situation Pope tacitly "sanctioned" McDowell's actions, thus for the first time Pope started to pay attention to something other than Jackson's corps. Pope remained in nominal command throughout the retreat but McDowell assumed and asserted tactical control.

Although the Confederate attacks were uncoordinated and disorganized, by the same measure they were fierce and relentless. Time and again the outnumbered Federal regiments fired devastating volleys before grudgingly giving ground to new defensive positions. Not to be outdone, the artilleries created mutual havoc with their exchanges of shot, shell, and grape. As regiments were being decimated commanders reformed with the remnants of other regiments, or in some cases, with newly arriving regiments. As he was bringing up reinforcements Schenck was struck three times, the third bullet shattering his right forearm. Schenck—another political general—refused to be carried from the battlefield until someone could retrieve his sword.[77]

Eventually the last of McLean's brigade, the 55th and 75th OVIs, were also forced to retreat from Chinn Ridge. As he was leaving McLean complained to his adjutant "We had been sent up there and sacrificed." But even as they withdrew the Union soldiers halted, turned, and fired at the approaching Confederates whose artillery continue to wreak havoc. Later Confederates approaching within twenty-five yards shot down Tower and his horse as he was trying to position soldiers from New England and New York. As he was being carried from the field Tower shouted to his replacement "Do the best you can to hold the position," but the replacement quickly saw that all was lost.[78] McLean lost nearly one-third of his men while Tower lost almost one-half but between them they gained nearly a precious hour for Pope to finally reinforce his left. Perhaps more important, the Federal resistance on Chinn Ridge punished the Confederate so much that they could not continue until they received further reinforcements.

Both sides proceeded to feed in more reinforcements, mostly by degrees, toward and onto Chinn Ridge. Most of the Southerners were from South Carolina, Texas, Virginia, and Georgia while many of the Northern troops were Germans from Sigal's corps. Tactically the struggle's prize was for little more than to gain or lose fifteen or so more minutes for Pope to secure his avenue of retreat.[79] Even so the fighting was brutal and vicious with Blue and Gray brigades and their regiments suffering hundreds of casualties while losing unit cohesions as commanders were incapacitated or even killed. One Virginian soldier recalled a scene being, "so violent and tempestuous, so mad and brain-reeling that it is to recall it is like fixing the memory of a horrible, blood-curdling dream."[80] Finally after two hours Longstreet captured Chinn Ridge but at the cost of a half-dozen brigades being too crippled for further fighting.

## 12. Second Bull Run

Chinn Ridge fighting continued while Pope began to form another battle line, albeit tenuous, at Henry Hill.[81] Actually the front rank of Pope's battle line was established along Sudley Road, running along the valley between Chinn Ridge and Bald Hill, on one side, and Henry Hill on the other, before intersecting the Warrenton Turnpike at the Stone House, obviously a vital point. The bulk of the line along Sudley Road was under Milroy's charge. John Reynolds' division formed a second rank or line of defense with George Meade's brigade anchoring the rank flank closest to the Warrenton Turnpike. Stragglers from Chinn Ridge crossed Sudley Road to join the newly formed lines around Henry Hill.

South Carolina, Georgia and Texas regiments descended Chinn Ridge and Bald Hill before crossing Sudley Road but some "were forced to secede."[82] Despite these reversals additional Confederate reinforcements arrived to carry on the fight that degenerated into still more brutal, head-on assaults. Federal artillery from top of Henry Hill fired case shot at approaching Rebels while Meade led a headlong charge that helped to secure the intersection, one of Meade's men recalling they had entered "the fire of hell, completely enveloped in smoke and flame."[83]

As various Federal units began their retreat across the Stone Bridge McDowell assigned MGen. Jesse Reno, 39, to go to the Henry House Hill to cover the withdrawal. Southerners still had plenty of troops but no commanders with appropriate rank were available to coordinate further attacks. Although the struggle for control of Henry Hill was fragmented and blundering it was nevertheless intense and horrific. Regimental and brigade commanders rode to and fro attempting to assert some order onto the battles but untold casualties accrued, not only among the rank-and-file but also among the majors and colonels, many who had horses shot from under them.

As dusk began to set in the Confederates were determined to make one last push against Pope's left flank as the southern slope of Henry House Hill. Little Billy Mahone was given the task of leading the last charge. Mahone's brigade was facing Regular Army infantry that skillfully withdrew by retreating thirty yards or so before halting, turning around, and firing a couple volleys before resuming the process.[84] As the regulars were withdrawing in good order McDowell rode up and shouted "God bless you, Regulars! You've saved the army! You shall not be forgotten! God bless you, everyone"[85]

By establishing good defensive positions at critical points, and by hard, brutal fighting, the vastly outnumbered Blue regiments delayed Longstreet's pursuit in heavy rainfall toward Henry House by four hours.[86] As the sun set below the Bull Run Mountains Reno's soldiers rose at least twice to fire lethal volleys into the Johnnies' last gasp charges. At 9:00 p.m. on August 30, 1862, Reno gave orders to relinquish Henry Hill to the Rebels thus quietly ending the Battle of Second Manassas.[87] Although the Army of Virginia suffered a sound defeat, by retaining occupation Henry House Hill Pope narrowly escaped complete disaster as his army fell back upon its lines of communications under cover of darkness, in large part because it won the race to the Stone Bridge, which Sigel's corps destroyed before Longstreet's army could capture that key point. The last of the retreating Federals reached the safety of Franklin's lead elements finally arriving at Centreville from their much delayed march from Washington.[88]

## *Analysis*

Although Second Bull Run is mostly known as one of Lee's most impressive victories, the battle also illustrates several issues related to pursuits at this stage of the Civil War. When reviewing Pope's escape from the battlefield, the most common reasons given were: Given the late start of Longstreet's counterstrike, there was not enough time for the Confederates to fully pursue; Jackson's troops were too exhausted after an extended period of combat; the rainfall hampered Longstreet's advance as darkness approached; and not to overlook the stout defenses of the Union soldiers along Chinn's Ridge and at Henry House Hill.

But there were other reasons: The size of the armies had increased dramatically by the second summer of combat thereby increasing the challenges and difficulties of battlefield management, especially of rapid movement. Although Lee's top command organization had been streamlined to two infantry corps plus Stuart's cavalry, the total number of soldiers in Lee's command was still significantly much larger than had previously fought at First Manassas. At the same time both armies were still seeking combat officers, especially at the division, brigade, and regimental levels, who were capable of managing their commands, especially in fast developing and moving situations such as pursuits.

But the bottom line was that the Confederate hierarchy, meaning specifically in this case Lee and Longstreet, repeated its Malvern Hill mistake of chasing Union forces instead of trying to capture terrain that could interdict the enemy's flight to the rear. Instead of chasing the retreating Bluecoats toward Henry House, the Confederates would have accomplished more toward achieving a decisive victory if they had advanced directly to capture Stone Bridge.

Furthermore, there appears to have been little strategic planning by Lee or his corps commanders about how to coordinate their respective actions in order to accomplish a decisive victory, that is to say a result either capturing the enemy's army or even annihilating it. Jackson had established his defensive positions without consultation with or input from Lee. For almost two afternoons of combat, Lee essentially relinquished to Longstreet the important authority to decide when to initiate Longstreet's counterattack. And once Longstreet sprang into action, apparently he alone decided that Henry House Hill would be the intermediate objective. Once Longstreet started his assault at 4:00 p.m. Lee sent word to Jackson to protect Longstreet's left flank. However Jackson failed to react for two hours, a delay that permitted the Federals to shift brigades to buttress defenses against Longstreet's advance.[89] (However, in fairness to Jackson, it was always difficult for units holding a defensive line for as long as three days to readily convert to an offensive posture.) Thus it can hardly be imagined that there was any significant coordination or battlefield management in concert about how to exploit the battlefield success toward a truly decisive victory.

More importantly, there is little evidence that Lee considered his strategic objectives other perhaps to continue moving toward, and eventually invading, Northern territory. In fairness, given the stout resistance offered by the Union rear guard—surprisingly, in a couple hours of fighting on the 30th the Union rear guard inflicted more casualties upon Longstreet's corps than Pope's assaults inflicted upon Jackson's during three days of battle—(something that is often overlooked by historians who speak of Jackson's troops being mauled behind the railroad embankment) perhaps there was little reason for the Confederate command hierarchy to even anticipate having the opportunity to force the surrender of the Union army.

On the other hand, is it not fair to suggest that the Confederate command hierarchy, especially Lee, simply was so myopic that it lost track, or even overlooked, the most profitable objective, that is to say proceeding directly to the Stone Bridge, where they could establish considerable blockades, instead of chasing the retreating Union forces to the Henry House Hill? Instead of directing Jackson to merely protect Longstreet's left flank (against whom?), suppose Lee had ordered Jackson to advance forward to the relatively short distance to the Warrenton Turnpike whereupon he could turn to his left and proceed directly to the Stone Bridge. And instead of allowing Longstreet to chase the fleeing Federals toward the Henry House, where the Bluecoat regiments were able to make a series of defensive stands that successfully covered the retreat across the Stone Bridge, why not direct Longstreet to advance directly to join Jackson at the Stone Bridge for a concentration of force against the torrent of Union soldiers?

The rationale for advancing directly to the Stone Bridge has been forcefully articulated by Brian Holden Reid:

> Once it was clear that Pope was defeated, organizing the pursuit should have become the top priority because it is a *separate act* of battle. (Emphasis in the original.) As much thought should have been devoted to it as the break-in battle; failure to devote sufficient attention to the pursuit accounts for the comparatively few number of successful examples in military history, not just in the American Civil War. ...The effect of Longstreet's counterstroke was to dissipate his own strength over a large area; advancing toward Henry House Hill, for instance, took him away from the decisive point. The prime objective was the stone bridge that would have cut Pope's line of retreat. By shifting frontally instead of pivoting on his right, Longstreet drove Pope's forces back toward the stone bridge and thus enabled him to rally a defense that prevented an improvised pursuit from gaining momentum. Lee was also culpable in allowing Longstreet to conduct this operation without guidance, and in failing to conserve a pursuit force....[90]

In contrast to Seven Days where the Confederates had little knowledge of the terrain over which they tried to pursue McClellan's retreating army a couple months earlier, the Manassas battlefield was well known was, or should have been, well known to the Confederate leaders. Prior to First Bull Run, Beauregard, with Lee's acquiescence, had selected that site as the most feasible place to contest the anticipated advancement of Federal forces that would be advancing from Alexandria. The Warrenton Turnpike, including the Stone Bridge, provided the best, and most feasible, means of moving an army from the north and vice versa, and thus was an important factor why Manassas was selected as the first battlefield in 1861. Since the Grays won the first battle at Manassas, they were able to continue to occupy the battlefield, at least temporarily, and thus presumably further familiarize themselves with its key terrain features. Although Lee was not in command at First Bull Run, Jackson and Longstreet did play significant roles in that first battle, and were, or again should have been, intimately familiar with the battlefield, especially of the characteristics of the major creek, Bull Run, and its limited crossing points. In terms of a pursuit, capturing Henry House Hill was almost superfluous. All the time and energy of trying to capture that hill was hardly productive but also facilitated the escape of Pope's army as its rear guard stubbornly fought off Longstreet's troops while the rest of Pope's army was frantically trying to get out of harm's way. Thus lack of familiarity with the terrain was not, nor should have been, the excuse that Lee and his army had during their attempted pursuits during Seven Days.

Perhaps the larger point was that army commanders on either side had yet to appreciate that something more than fundamental battlefield tactics were necessary to achieve decisive victories with strategic significance. Because the sides were fairly evenly matched with leaders coming from the same pool of antebellum regular army officers, most of whom were West Point schooled, with essentially the same technology and materiel, it was going to be unlikely that one army could capture or annihilate the other strictly based upon battlefield strengths or maneuvers. Successful pursuits of course could achieve decisiveness but pursuits were not, and would not be, simple matters of hastily chasing a retreating foe, trying to improvise coordinated tactics on the fly. Almost like any other aspect of military operations, pursuits would require at least a modicum of planning and preparation prior to the conclusion of a battle. As of the end of August 1862 that command capability had yet to materialize.

Another factor was that when on the offense Lee often demonstrated a battle lust that could override his command management of the battlefield. In other words, he became so focused upon the immediate issues between the combatants that he could lose sight of overall strategic objectives. One young girl growing up in Virginia once asked her teacher why it was that the Confederates won all the battles but yet lost the war. It is true that the Confederates, especially those under Lee's command, won several great battlefield victories but none were decisive since their Federal adversaries always escaped to fight another day. On a proportionate basis, the Confederate casualties at Second Bull Run, including Ox Hill that immediately followed, were almost as high as those of the Federals yet without a decisive victory the Rebels had little, except for additional ground, to show for their combat accomplishments. If Lee had managed to keep in mind that as an army commander, and indeed the *de facto* commander of the entire Confederacy, his responsibility was to win the war by decisive victories rather than just wining battlefield victories, and thus would have accomplished much more for the Confederacy. And although it was not apparent in early September 1862, additional opportunities for decisive victories by the Confederacy were shortly going to become few and far between.

Of course it is almost entirely conjectural that advancing directly to the Stone Bridge would have been successful in capturing all or even a major part of Pope's army. But the point is that such an approach would have at least had a reasonable chance of strategic success. If Lee always intended to invade, or "raid" Northern territory his chances of doing so would have only been enhanced had he been able to capture a major portion of the Union army at Manassas. Additionally if Pope had been eliminated by capture, while the Union still had more manpower, Pope's army would not have been available for incorporation into McClellan's defense of Washington or for deployment in the upcoming battle of Antietam. Unfortunately for the Confederate's cause, Lee's love of battle may have caused a short-sightedness that meant he lost sight of larger strategic opportunities.

# 13

# Chantilly, a.k.a. Ox Hill[1]
*September 1, 1862*

On Sunday, August 31, 1862—the day of the immediate aftermath of his victory of Second Bull Run, or Second Manassas as Southerners call it—Robert E. Lee would have recognized the following:

- The Eastern theater's arena had been shifted from Richmond to the proximity of Washington[2];
- Despite the magnitude of his victory, Lee had failed to score a decisive victory;
- Although the Union had been driven from the field, John Pope's army had not fled in a rout but instead withdrew in fairly good order to previously constructed fortifications at Centreville, which sits on a crest of a long ridge running north and south.[3] Furthermore Pope was likely being reinforced with and/or replenished by an unknown number of fresh Union troops.[4] Therefore Lee had to assume Pope's army was still capable of defending itself in head-to-head combat;
- Lee's army still had a reasonable chance to score a decisive victory by maneuver if Lee could somehow interdict any retreat by Pope by getting between Centreville and Washington[5];
- Although itself battered by the three days of intense fighting occurring during the period with Groveton on August 28 and August 30, the Army of Northern Virginia had retained its cohesion and capabilities to conduct further operations. Casualties had been high but the army's logistical capacity had been buttressed by the capture and looting of the immense stores at Manassas Junction; and
- Invading Northern territory still remained the primary strategic objective as previously endorsed by President Davis.

However Lee did not realize how severely Pope was personally demoralized and how badly much, if but not all, of Pope's army was mangled beyond reasonable fighting capacity. Also Lee had no way of knowing Pope had put himself into a difficult position vis-à-vis his superiors in Washington. Continuing his long held habit of inaccurate, self-serving reports in order to cast himself into the best possible light, Pope failed to disclose the full extent of his recent losses; instead he reported in such a manner to make Washington believe that he still held a favorable position and intended to resume his offensive against Lee. Based upon these reports, Halleck kept encouraging Pope to resume his attacks as soon as possible. Upon realizing the futility of trying another assault against Lee, and in fact not being fearful that the continued existence of his army was in jeopardy, Pope then changed his tune to suggest to Halleck that the best course of action would be for Halleck to order a retreat back to the fortifications around Washington.

But even without waiting for Halleck's authorization to make such a retreat, Pope initiated orders and made preparations to return his wounded and part of his supply train to Washington by way of Jermantown and then Fairfax C.H. further east along the Warrenton Pike.[6] In the Rebel camp, Lee, without knowing Pope's intentions, but concluding he had much to gain with little to lose, decided his most advantageous move would be to get to Fairfax C.H. or Jermantown, both being located on the Warrenton Pike east of Centreville.[7] If Pope were to try to hit Lee's army while the Rebels remained at Manassas then Lee would be in Pope's rear. Furthermore occupation of Fairfax C.H. or Jermantown would keep further reinforcements from reaching Pope from Washington or Alexandria. On the other hand, if Pope were abandoning the fortifications of Centreville, timely capture by Lee's forces of either of these key locations along the Warrenton Pike would interdict some, if not all, of Pope's retreat. Additionally Confederate occupation of Fairfax C.H.—thirteen miles west of Washington—would create a menacing presence against the Federal capital.

In order to implement this initiative against Pope, Lee planned another turning movement similar to the one that preceded the engagement at Groveton leading to Second Bull Run.[8] Once again Jackson would lead followed by Longstreet who was temporarily detained to bury the dead and to salvage equipment and ordinance left on the battleground.[9]

Their route would go northward a relatively short distance before turning right onto Little River Turnpike (now U.S. Route 50), which ran almost parallel with the Warrenton Pike before intersecting at an acute angel with the latter road at Jermantown. There was a mansion house called Chantilly—now named Greenbrier, but even then a "ghost of its former self, ... being barely habitable"[10]—along the Warrenton Pike east of Centreville. Further east of Centreville, but north of the Little River Turnpike, there was an elevation called Ox Hill. Immediately south of Ox Hill a small, narrow road—little more than a path—called Ox Road ran north and south between Little River Turnpike and Warrenton Turnpike. This short lane, two and half miles west of Jermantown, afforded another possible access for the Rebels to make contact with the retreating Federals.[11] From Jermantown, the Warrenton Pike continues eastward to Fairfax C.H.

Around midday, Sunday, August 31, 1862, Jackson's foot soldiers, many who had not been fed, began their trek by crossing Sudley Ford before turning up Gum Spring Road (currently Rt. 659).[12] A.P. Hill's division was in the lead of 15,000 soldiers in the move. Jackson habitually pressed his subordinate commanders to quicken the pace of the march but in this instance Jackson actually chided Hill for moving too swiftly that, among other things, caused a large number of stranglers.[13]

To ascertain what Pope was doing, and to provide necessary intelligence to Jackson, on Sunday evening, August 31, Lee sent Stuart with some of his cavalry, along with two artillery pieces, around Pope on the Little River Turnpike.[14] Due in large part to the near breakdown of Union cavalry because of fatigue, Stuart met little resistance in the beginning.[15] But sometime before midnight Stuart spotted a massive number of Union wagons moving eastward along the Warrenton Pike toward Jermantown. This of course was the intelligence so eagerly sought by Jackson but Stuart was not able to resist a boyish impulse. Instead of unobtrusively turning away from the unsuspecting Federal trains, Stuart directed his artillery to lob a few shells toward the wagons as "salutations."[16] This pointless gesture of course had no effect except to scare some teamsters while alerting Union officers of a Rebel presence and that it was necessary to intensify the movement while taking further precautionary steps to protect the trains.[17]

Stuart compounded the error of his heedless, incautious judgment by failing to rush to advise Stonewall about the new intelligence. Instead Stuart along with some of his staff visited the home of some old family friends.[18] Stuart did not meet with Jackson until late-morning of September 1, and while Stuart did brief Jackson about the discovery of the Yankees' movement, it is not clear whether he also disclosed the matter of his artillery salutations.[19]

By 7:00 a.m. on September 1 Stonewall's soldiers resumed their march down the Little River Turnpike. The old "Stonewall" division took the lead while Hill's division rotated to the rear.[20] For the era the pike was state-of-the-art, being thirty-foot-wide and covered with wood and stone. For the time being Jackson's main concern was that his right flank could be attacked from the south at Centreville.[21]

Meanwhile Pope's messages to Halleck became more defensive and defeatist. In a message sent at 8:50 a.m. Pope suddenly and surprisingly vented his feeling about the "unsoldierly and dangerous conduct" by unnamed subordinates from McClellan's Army of the Potomac. According to Pope the actions of these unnamed brigade and division commanders were "discouraging, and calculated to break down the spirit of the men and produce disaster." Pope concluded by urging Halleck to "draw back [the] army to the intrenchments in front of Washington,..."[22]

Finally on September 1, 1862, after receiving more candid, realistic reports from Pope, and after viewing the long trains of wounded arriving in Washington, Halleck realized that notwithstanding the infusion of fresh reinforcements from Franklin and Sumner Pope no longer had the strength to try any further assaults against Lee. If Lee were flanking Pope, as indicated by Stuart's salutations, then Washington was vulnerable to capture, especially if Pope's army were decisively defeated. Accordingly, to Pope's immense relief, Halleck sent word to Pope to return his army to the Washington fortifications.

Although Pope had been discombobulated for much of the past seven or eight days, he finally began to regain some of his senses upon realizing the Confederates were moving on his flank to impose a serious threat to his retreat, if not to the balance of his fast-fading career. In response to this double-edged threat, Pope quickly ordered a couple simple counter measures. First he dispatched units to Jermantown to reinforce the defenses at that critical juncture of turnpikes. Pope also sent Joe Hooker to Jermantown to take overall command of that situation, at least until McDowell could arrive with his 2nd Corps.[23]

Second, Pope ordered blocking forces to be established at several locations, including Ox Road. The blocking force directed toward Ox Road consisted of two small divisions from the 9th Corps of BGen. Jesse Reno,[24] these divisions being under the command of MGen. Isaac I. Stevens, Jr., 44. Stevens, who had graduated first in the West Point class, was a distinguished veteran of the Mexican War where he became a close friend with Capt. Robert E. Lee.[25] In 1852 Stevens was probably the only active army officer to support Franklin Pierce's successful candidacy for president against Winfield Scott in 1852.[26] After serving two terms in Congress as a Democrat, Stevens—stridently anti-slavery—eventually accepted a commission to command the 79th New York regiment, a prewar militia unit of Scottish descent called the Highland Guard.[27]

Prior to the time when Stevens had assumed command, the 79th New York had suffered grave loses at First Bull Run, causing the regiment to be demoralized and disgruntled. However under Steven's firm but effective leadership, the 79th had become one of the better Union regiments. By Second Bull Run, Stevens had ascended to division command. As a result of his performance during Second Bull Run—where half his division suffered some sort of casualty—there was speculation that Stevens may have been in line for corps command, speculation that Stevens felt was entirely justified.

Meanwhile Stonewall's march along Little River Turnpike was not advancing at his usual pace.[28] It is not clear whether the rigors of long marches and extended combat had sapped too much energy from Jackson's troops or if Jackson was deliberately holding back until Lee and Longstreet could catch up.[29] Perhaps the mercurial Stonewall simply was not enthused about the maneuver, instead being anxious to get on with an invasion of Maryland, Jackson's long held strategic aspiration. There has even been conjecture that Lee's primary objective was not annihilative defeat of Pope's army. Instead, according to this speculation, Lee was also anxious to launch his intended invasion of Maryland and did not want to be distracted by another encounter with Pope, especially as Pope was being reinforced with an abundance of fresh troops. For whatever reason Jackson's foot cavalry advanced only seven miles before stopping to rest at noon. Stonewall himself found a tree to sit under and took a much needed nap.[30]

Pope's decision to reinforce the defenses at Jermantown could hardly have been more timely. Hooker and his staff arrived at Jermantown at about 3:00 p.m. on the 1st of September. Shortly thereafter Fitzhugh Lee's cavalry met Federal cavalry pickets that Hooker had deployed along the Little River Turnpike. This encounter escalated from cavalry skirmishing as artillery and infantry were thrust into the battle. Eventually Lee had to back off when Stonewall Jackson found he had more important issues and failed to reinforce Lee's cavalry.[31] On the other hand Hooker knew he had no alternative except to deploy whatever reinforcements were necessary to protect Jermantown from Confederate capture. At the same time Jackson also knew he could not afford an attack against his front; accordingly he sent additional infantry brigades to establish defensive positions.[32]

At approximately 3:00 p.m. on September 1 as Stevens and his units along Ox Road to approach the vicinity of Little River Turnpike he observed soldiers in gray and brown uniforms of at least a brigade size deployed as pickets and skirmishers, presumably screening the much larger column headed from Jermantown. Stevens had no orders to attack but he instantly realized his only chance to divert the Rebels from their march upon Jermantown was to strike immediately.[33] Stevens also realized that if he allowed the much larger enemy to assault his position he would have no realistic change to delay the rest of the Rebel column. And so, Stevens quickly made plans to attack. The net effect was that Pope's first objective, that being to protect passage through Jermantown, was being accomplished while the advance elements of Jackson's column were stalled.

Jackson also determined there was a threat to his flank when his pickets and skirmishers were easily overrun by Stevens' lead elements advancing along Ox Road. Therefore Stonewall deployed the balance of his corps in a defensive posture extending along the south of the Little River Turnpike opposite Ox Hill.[34] But even as Stevens was aligning his units—one division to lead with other in reserve—he saw that he was going to be vastly outnumbered by the Confederates. Accordingly he ordered an aide to go to the Warrenton

Pike and try to find a commander who without specific orders to do so would bring reinforcements to support Stevens.[35]

As the Federal assault began to unfold Stevens watched his original command, the 79th NY, unable to make any headway. Despite Stevens' impression from the rear that there was no reason for the 79th to be stymied, its lack of progress was not for want of trying—after all, five color bearers had fallen after being shot; the Confederate position behind a tree line simply was too strong! Finally overcome with anger and frustration Stevens rode to the front and over the objections of the soldiers grabbed the regiment's colors to himself lead another charge. Under the inspiration of the leadership of their commanding general, the 79th NY surged forward, further than even before. But unfortunately Stevens' fate was no different than that of the other brave lads who had carried the colors. At the apex of his marital glory a bullet struck Stevens in the head, killing him instantly.[36]

As word spread that their leader was dead, and there being no second in command to take over, the Union assault floundered and stalled. But ironically even though the Union attack failed to overcome the Confederate defenses, it still had the desired effect of stalling the Rebel column. Jackson could only surmise that Stevens' little strike was but a part of a larger planned attack and so rather than resume his march toward Jermantown leaving his left flank exposed, Stonewall decided to make preparations to defend against such attack.

The aide sent to the Warrenton Pike to find help for Stevens was having little luck convincing commanders of retreating and to engage in another battle. Among other reasons, Union commanders were seldom given the latitude to deviate from orders and/or to take their own initiative. But Philip Kearny was not such a timid commander, and he readily agreed to come to the aid of his fellow division commander, exclaiming "By damn! I'll support Stevens anywhere."[37] By the time of Second Bull Run Kearny was regarded as a first-rate division commander, perhaps the best in the Union army. Accordingly despite his strong anti-abolitionists views but not having aligned himself in any of the political alliances of most other generals, his prospects for advancement in command positions seemed very bright.

Without hesitation Kearny diverted his brigades from the Warrenton Turnpike and aligned them to face the sounds of the firefight.[38] By the time Kearny arrived south of Ox Hill Stevens' troops had floundered without direction; most units were badly disorganized and without any cohesion. One soldier later recalled, "It was evident that each command had lost all connection with the others, and was advancing no one knew where or why."[39] Since Kearny knew Stevens would never tolerate his command to remain in such a condition, Kearny immediately analyzed the tactical situation and fathomed what Stevens had been trying to accomplish.[40] Kearny then set about to organize his own attack against the Rebel defenders: to append the remnants of Steven's divisions and to assist his own division once it arrived.

All of this was happening during a torrential downpour as darkness was approaching. As a result one of the most amusing colloquies of the Civil War happened when A.P. Hill, upon behalf of a subordinate, sent a courier to Jackson to request that Hill's subordinate unit be removed from the line for lack of dry ammunition. Hill's dispatch pled, "My complements to General Jackson and my request to be permitted to take my command out of the line because all my ammunition is wet." Stonewall's response was classic, "My compliments [to General Hill] and tell him the enemy's ammunition is equally wet as his!"[41]

Back on the Federal side of the lines, Phil Kearny had grown impatient about the slow and confused efforts to organize his new line of battle, especially since any opportunity to attack was quickly fading as darkness was fast approaching. Kearny was especially irritated by the apparent inability of one of Steven's regiments to align itself to cover the right flank of the newly aligned line of battle. Frustrated by the regiment's reluctance to resume the assault, Kearny sprinkled his directions with "his sneers, threats, and curses" while threatening to turn his artillery upon them if they continued to hesitate.[42] Kearny then did what he might typically do, and had done, in any similar circumstances: He decided that he would personally lead the ostensibly incompetently led regiment to its assigned position.

As Kearny was riding ahead though a cornfield to find the errant regiment, he suddenly came into a clearing but by now his vision was obscured by the darkness and the mist from the rain. Nevertheless to his front he could see troops in a line of battle. Realizing he may be in some peril, as nonchalantly as possible he called out, "What troops are these?" As soon as the response identifies the troops as being Georgians Kearny turned and spurred his horse to hurry the other way. To reduce himself as a target, Kearny attempted to ride Indian style, with his body lowered and his right arm around the horse's neck. A dozen of shots rang out, one such shot striking Kearny's lifeless body fell onto the muddy ground[43]; his horse, in its riderless confusion, reversed itself to run back through the Confederate lines before being stopped.[44]

As soon as Kearny had fallen, the two opposing lines approached each other in the darkness and rain until they were almost within arm's length of one another. After an exchange of volleys, the enemy lines blindly struggled in a hand-to-hand and bayonet melee; but suddenly and inexplicably they stopped fighting to fall back from one another.[45] The Ox Hill fight lasted for less than three hours but some regiments had higher losses than the three days of combat at Second Bull Run. No field generals had been killed during Second Bull Run but the battle near the Chantilly mansion had cost the Union two of its most promising commanders.[46]

Reinforcements for both sides began to arrive but except for sporadic gunshots it was simply too dark for any further fighting. Jackson and Longstreet, apprehensive that Federals might still eventually launch another attack, continued the halt of their march in order to form a line of battle along the south of the Little River Turnpike.

At first it may have seemed that Pope's army had achieved an equilibrium of force at Centreville; however Centreville was vulnerable because it could be flanked or passed allowing the Confederates to cut off Pope's lines of communications. Therefore the Federals had no intention to do anything except to resume and complete their retreat toward Fairfax C.H. and sanctuary of the Washington, D.C., fortifications. Thus by morning light of September 2 all of Pope's army, even as augmented, was well beyond Jermantown, not only ending the so-called battle of Chantilly but also marking the coda to the battle of Second Bull Run.[47]

Even as Pope had been trying to deceive his superiors in Washington about his precarious situation in Centreville and as the remainder of McClellan's army was arriving from Harrison's Landing it was becoming obvious to Lincoln and Halleck that major decisions about command structure were necessary. Lincoln still had to make a difficult choice to find someone to organize and command the defenses around Washington, but he had few realistic options. Since McClellan had not been circumspect about expressing his unhappiness, there were wide spread suspicions—many of which might have been well founded—that McClellan had deliberately delayed efforts, as ordered, to reinforce Pope. Lincoln was upset with McClellan's callous remark about leaving Pope "to get out of his scrape by himself."[48] Secretary of War Edwin Stanton, once McClellan's strong ally and patron, was among those who believed McClellan had been grossly insubordinate in his failure to render any significant help to Pope.

Pope and McClellan, notwithstanding their political differences, had cordial relationship for a short while immediately after Pope's appointment; but eventually McClellan became apprehensive, even neurotic, about Pope's ascendency in command. That relationship soon turned to mutual scorn and distrust, especially since neither was reticent about expressing his uncharitable, sometimes scathing opinion of the other. Their relationship further soured when Pope made his precipitous retreat from the Rappahannock—where Porter was originally supposed to meet Pope—to Manassas, leaving Porter high and dry after his march from Aquia Landing. Communications among Halleck, Pope, and McClellan were grossly inadequate to prevent serious confusion about locations and arrangements for maneuvers. The inadequacy of communications was exacerbated by Halleck's inability to assert his authority as the most senior general in the army. McClellan was especially anxious and distressed by several issues, for instance who would have overall command should his army be merged with Pope's. More substantively, he was concerned about recklessly rushing troops to Manassas for fear they would meet the same fate as had Taylor's cobbled forces.

Lincoln—who had been furious at McClellan for failing to come to Pope's aid at Second Bull Run[49]—reluctantly decided, despite his repulsion about McClellan's attitude toward Pope's plight and over the vehement objections of cabinet members, especially Stanton,[50] to place McClellan in charge of Washington's entire defense. Unfortunately for Lincoln his alternative choices were limited to Henry Halleck and Ambrose Burnside, neither of whom had sterling credentials as combat commanders.[51] The remnants of Pope's then soon-to-be former army were absorbed into McClellan's newly reconstituted army—still to be called the Army of the Potomac—being organized to defend Washington.

Pope—finally receiving the order to retreat that he had so desperately wanted—continued his rapid retreat toward the safety of Washington, thus narrowly escaping what might have been an opportunity for a decisive victory by the Confederates. However, Pope's career in the Civil War was finished. Lincoln had already decided to merge the Army of Virginia into the Army of the Potomac under the revised command of George B. McClellan. The merger of the two armies along with the change in command was simple and straight forward: As various units—whether or from the Army of Virginia or from the Army of the Potomac—approached the Washington fortifications they were detached from Pope's command and transferred to the Young Napoleon, much to the jubilation of most of the rank-and-file. Lifting his hat to McClellan as a parting salute, Pope, together with his escort, rode quietly away; he and McClellan would never see each other again.[52] Shortly thereafter McClellan reorganized a reconstituted Army of the Potomac at Rockville, Maryland, before starting to move westward to confront Lee's invasion, or "raid," into Maryland that culminated in the Battle of Antietam September 17, 1862.[53]

It is difficult to analyze Chantilly if only because of the uncertain purpose of the Confederate maneuver. Chantilly may have been another instance where the commander of the blocking force was not sufficiently energetic and/or focused upon the pursuit.[54] Jackson's rate of march was not up to his usual standards plus he let potential threats to his flanks distract him from advancing to Jermantown, the presumed strangle point. Although we can never be certain about Jackson's attitude at this point of the campaign, there were strong indicators that Jackson's heart was not in capturing Pope's retreating army; instead Jackson seemed eager to commence his long desired move into Northern territory. In any event Pope's bedraggled army was able to march past Jermantown thereby escaping from its defeat at Second Bull Run before reaching the safety of the Washington fortifications.

But other than pre-empting the possibility of an attack against Lee if he had remained in the vicinity of the Bull Run, Lee's flanking maneuver accomplished little if any military or strategic value. Certainly it was poor effort of pursuit. For instance, BGen. William Dorsey Pender, 28, commander of a North Carolina brigade in A.P. Hill's division, wrote to his wife the next day, "The Yankees had rather the best of it as they maintained their ground and accomplished the object which was to cover the retreat ... none of us seemed anxious or did ourselves much credit."[55] The concept of flanking Pope's army to try to intercept it at some point was sound but any concept or plan is only as good as is the execution of such plan.

In the instance, Stuart's two errors of judgment seriously hurt any reasonable chance of success for a pursuit. His artillery salutations accomplished nothing except to alert the Yankee command that its retreat was in danger while Stonewall—whose march was not evidencing much purpose—was denied the intelligence that could have motivated a more vigorous pace.

But Jackson also assured the failure of any pursuit when he allowed his column to be stalled by the attacks from Stevens, and then Kearny. Getting to the enemy's front was of paramount importance, but Jackson, by stopping his entire column to defend his entire column to defend his right against inferior forces relinquished any reasonable possibility of destroying and capturing any part of Pope's army.

Lee's own words were that the pursuit failed because "the enemy had conducted his retreat so rapidly that the attempt to interrupt him was abandoned." In 1870 Lee explained any further pursuit failed simply because, "[His] men had nothing to eat."[56]

From the perspective of the Union situation, Pope was successfully able to return his army relative equilibrium of force in the fortifications of Washington. Indeed that may have been the highpoint of Pope's brief tenure in command of the short-lived Army of Virginia.

## *Dénouements and Precursors*

Notwithstanding Pope's political connections with Lincoln's family and with the Radical Republicans, and notwithstanding McClellan's duplicity in the defeat at Second Bull Run, Pope's Civil War career was over. On September 6, 1863, Pope was appointed as head of the newly created Department of Northwest to deal with the Sioux and Dakotas in Minnesota, where he performed with much success. Upon submitting his official report Pope gave the Chantilly battle only three sentences, thus contributing to the battle's obscurity.

Prior to Second Bull Run Lee had been given the authority necessary to relieve ineffective commanders at the division, brigade, and regimental levels. Now after Second Bull Run the Federals also recognized the obvious and decided it was necessary to make changes in its chains of command. As part of that reorganization Irvin McDowell—who was not only in charge of tactical operations but was also commander of Pope's largest corps—was again severely criticized for his tactical mistakes but this time McDowell could not use inexperience as an excuse for his shortcomings. After being relieved of command of his corps, McDowell demanded a board of inquiry that eventually exonerated him of blame. McDowell then served on various boards and commission in the Washington area before being assigned to command the Department of Pacific toward the end of the war.

It is easy, and perhaps convenient, to overlook the devastating consequences that battles had upon civilians and their property in the region where the battle occurred. It might be difficult, if not impossible, to rank which region suffered the most but the Centreville and Fairfax C.H. area certainly would be on the short list of areas suffering the most devastation during the course of the Civil War. Stuck upon the pathway between Washington and Richmond the countryside became ravaged, trees and fences gone, livestock slaughtered and water supplies depleted. Following a year of encampment by one army or the other Centreville became a "dilapidated village." The village of Fairfax, which prior to the war had three hundred residents, was converted into a military camp with its former courthouse turned into a Union headquarters, striped of all papers and furniture.[57]

Notwithstanding the despoliation inflicted by the combatants during the Civil War, the region now enjoys a robust economy that, together with years of neglect of historical sites, has rendered the Ox Hill battleground as a "lost." To be sure a small enclosure remains containing monuments honoring Stevens and Kearny, but aside from two or three overgrown and unkempt acres the rest of the battlefield's heritage has been obliterated by commercial and other development. As an example the former cart path is now a multi-lane highway whose present elevations bear little resemblance to those of 1862.

The men of the 79th NY carried Stevens' body from the field as they were retreating from the Ox Road. Eventually Stevens' body was returned by train to Newport, Rhode Island, where it was buried with full military honors at a funeral service attended by governors of Rhode Island and Massachusetts. He was subsequently promoted to Major General pre-dated to July 4, 1862.[58]

After A.P. Hill identified Kearny's body he advised Jackson who exclaimed, "My god, boys, you know who you have killed? You have shot the most gallant officer in the United States Army."[59] When Lee learned of Kearny's demise, he ordered that arrangements be made to return Kearny's remains, together with his personal effects, to the Union army under a flag of truce. Kearny's sword and horse were considered to be confiscated property belonging to the C.S.A. Later, out of respect to Kearny's family Lee had these appraised so that he could pay for them and so that they would be returned to Kearny's widow.[60] Winnfield Scott, for whom Kearny had served, said Kearny was "the bravest man I even knew."

Kearny's death was widely reported in newspapers around the country, and even in England. Kearny was buried in the family plot in New York City but in 1912 his remains reinterred and moved to the National Cemetery in Arlington—Formerly the Lee family home—where he was reburied in a ceremony attended by President Taft, several Congressman and Supreme Court justices.[61]

# 14

# McClellan After Antietam
## September–October 1862

### Lee Invades Western Maryland

Most often in the Civil War the armies would pause for several weeks, even several months after major campaigns. These periods of relatively little combat activity were often necessary to recuperate, to refit, to resupply, and to reassess the relatively new positions. In dramatic contrast, Lee was wasting little time after his victory at Second Bull Run, essentially continuing the string of successes beginning with Seven Days. By Thursday, September 4, 1862, only three days after Jackson's advance stalled at Chantilly, Lee's Army of Northern Virginia crossed the Potomac River into western Maryland with his battle-hardened men, many of whom were ragged and ill-fed. The number of Rebel soldiers who actually crossed the Potomac is unclear since Lee's army was beginning to suffer from extensive straggling and even unauthorized absences of leave.[1] Upon learning the next day of the Confederate invasion, Lincoln directed McClellan to pursue, overtake, and crush Lee's army.[2]

To this date Lee's reasons for invading Maryland at that particular time have never been clearly and convincingly established.[3] Perhaps Lee was trying to influence England and France to give diplomatic recognition to the Confederacy; perhaps Lee was merely conducting a foraging raid to replenish his army[4]; perhaps he intended to march to the Susquehanna River where he could capture the Union's main east to west railroad[5]; perhaps he was attempting a flanking movement that would carry him into Philadelphia and/or Baltimore; perhaps he believed the residents—many of whom were German immigrants—of western Maryland could be persuaded to somehow come to the support and aid of the Southern cause, even bringing Maryland, as a slave state, into the fold of the Confederacy; or perhaps he was simply riding the crest of the momentum of his campaign from Seven Days through Second Bull Run, and was looking to score another victory.[6] In any event by September 7, the Army of Northern Virginia reached Frederick, Maryland, on the National Road about 80 miles northwest of Washington, D.C. On the same day McClellan's army started leaving Washington.[7]

From Frederick, Lee scattered his army in several directions, including a sizable contingent under Jackson's command sent west to capture and hold Harpers Ferry, the site of the huge Federal armory and munitions facility sitting at the juncture of the Shenandoah River with the Potomac. Not only would this provide badly needed bounty of supplies but its capture was also necessary to assure free passage of Lee's supply lines from the Shenandoah Valley. Jackson's contingent was further split into three separate forces in order to completely surround Harper's Ferry. Lee sent a fourth force under Longstreet north toward Hagerstown. Once Harpers Ferry had been captured, Lee planned to reassemble his army to prepare to attack McClellan.[8] These bold divisions of forces incurred the risk that Lee's army, or at least its major portions, could be captured in detail but Lee accepted these risks on the premise—confirmed in part by scouting reports from Stuart—that McClellan would react in his typical sluggish, cautious manner.

Because of the complexity of these maneuvers on Tuesday, September 9, 1862, Lee reduced his plans to writing in a document called Special Order 191.[9] However the fates of war were working against Lee when on September 13 a copy of S.O. 191 was lost (wrapped around three cigars), later to be found outside Frederick by a couple of McClellan's soldiers.[10] Once verified as a true copy the discovery of Lee's plan of action seemed to energize McClellan who could not help making a grandiose public announcement about the discovery of S.O. 191,[11] an announcement heard by a Southern sympathizer and soon carried back to Lee[12]; thus by the evening September 13 Lee was aware that McClellan was not only on the move away from the Washington fortifications but had knowledge of Lee's disposition of troops per S.O. 191.[13]

## McClellan Prepares

Regardless of McClellan's deficiencies as a combat commander he was still without an equal as an organized and administrator. Upon being appointed September 2, 1862,[14] to command the defenses around Washington—a move tantamount to reconstituting the Army of the Potomac—the Young Napoleon's immediate challenge was to reorganize several corps from three sources and to establish a new chain of command to his liking. McClellan's rapid reorganizing at Rockville under these circumstances was little short of miraculous.

In order to assimilate Pope's old Army of Virginia into the newly re-assembled army, McClellan relieved Pope's former corps commanders, McDowell, Sigel, and Banks. McClellan appointed the aggressive and battle seasoned Joseph Hooker to replace McDowell as commander of the 1st Corps.[15] The 1st Corps included some excellent units, including the Iron Brigade and the Pennsylvania Reserves—George Meade commanding.

McClellan re-designated Sigel's and Banks' former commands as the 11th and 12th Corps, respectively, before appointing MGen. Ambrose Burnside, 38, to command Sigel's former corps. Burnside served on occupation duty during the Mexican War after which he served on the frontier before resigning in 1853 to go into the firearms business.[16] While in business Burnside developed an experimental carbine, the fourth type of which, being a breech-loading .54 caliber carbine, was most popular. However Burnside's company went bankrupt after which McClellan gave Burnside a job at the Illinois Central Railroad. Burnside served in Congress before organizing the 1st Rhode Island when the war erupted. Burnside cut an imposing figure but in contrast to many of his collogues did not possess the relentless ambition for promotions. In fact Burnside had refused an offer from Lincoln to replace McClellan as commander of the Army of the Potomac. Prior to returning to Virginia Burnside performed competently as commander of an amphibious expedition that seized control of the North Carolina coast. Most recently Burnside accompanied Halleck when the latter visited McClellan at Harrison's Landing after Seven Days; illustrating the convoluted relationships among higher ranking officers, the President asked Burnside to make inquiries among McClellan's staff and subordinate commanders, which resulted in Burnside learning of their contempt and hostility toward the civilian government, even extending in some case to mention of a possible coup.[17]

McClellan appointed MGen. Joseph Mansfield, 59, to command the 12th Corps, but Mansfield would not arrive from Washington until September 15. Mansfield, an army engineer and career staff officer with almost no experience in combat command, was chosen by McClellan as a desperate measure to replace Banks. The 12th Corps would be Mansfield's largest field command.[18]

Four corps from the old Army of the Potomac retained their original designations as well as their commanders. Edwin V. ("Bull") Sumner, 65, the oldest active corps commander in the Civil War, commanded the 2nd Corps; Samuel Heintzelman, 57, commanded the 3rd Corps, Fitz-John Porter temporarily commanded the 5th Corps, and William Franklin, 39, commanded the 6th Corps. Although Porter's division might have been the logical division to deliver the most devastating blow at Antietam, its two available divisions had recently been badly mauled at the futile and senseless assaults against Jackson's entrenched position at Second Manassas. McClellan regrouped the various cavalry regiments under the unified command of BGen. Alfred Pleasonton, 38, an experienced cavalry officer, including service that began in the Mexican War and continued in the Seminole and Indian Wars through Bloody Kansas and Missouri,[19] was a member of McClellan's inner circle. Notwithstanding his extensive combat experience, Pleasonton was better suited as bureaucrat than as a field commander.[20]

When Lee's order was discovered, the Union army was closer to parts of Lee's army than units of Lee's army were to each other. Accordingly it was entirely plausible that McClellan could score a great strategic victory in detail not only gaining overwhelming military advantage but also propelling him to the powerful political stature which he had been seeking and even plotting. But McClellan still faced some mean challenges before he could completely capitalize upon his windfall discovery.

## South Mountain

South Mountain, a steep, densely wooded geologic northern extension of the Blue Ridge, stretching between McClellan's still dispersed divisions to the east and Lee's scattered units to the west, was the first and foremost challenge. Passage across South Mountain could happen only through three or four passes or gaps, each of which were outstanding defensive positions. The National Road leading westward to Boonsboro had been constructed through Turner's Gap. The old Sharpsburg Road passed through Fox's Gap, set about a mile south of Turner's Gap while Crampton's Gap was found about fifteen miles south of Turner's Gap. The Mount Tabor Church Road passed through a deep gorge about a mile north of Turner's Gap.

The battle of South Mountain would commit thirteen Confederate brigades to defend against seventeen Federal brigades.[21] On September 13 McClellan designated Burnside as commander of a 20,000 strong wing consisting of Hooker's 1st Corps commanded by and the 9th Corps, Jesse Reno taking Burnside's place. Burnside's wing was to push west with a night march and seize Turner's and Fox's Gaps. Together Burnside's wing initially faced D.H. Hill's division of 6,000 Confederates attempting to defend three passes across a three-mile front.[22] McClellan also hoped Franklin could traverse Crampton's Gap—the southernmost gap—to save Harpers Ferry about seven miles to the south where Lee deployed two-thirds of his forces under Jackson's command.

Reno's 9th Corps was advancing along the old Sharpsburg Road with orders to clear the Confederate defenders at Fox's gap. Starting at 9:00 a.m., on September 14, Jacob Cox's lead division from Reno's corps, easily took Fox's Gap.[23] But Cox was concerned about the exhausted condition of his troops following their all night march, and by 11:00 a.m. decided not to follow up on his victory until the rest of the 9th Corps would arrive.[24] Additionally after sundown Reno was shot from his saddle while making an inspection of his troops. As he was being carried to the rear, Reno yelled to a friend, "Hello, Sam, I'm dead." "Yes, Yes, I'm dead. Good-bye." Reno died within an hour of being shot.[25] Although just joining the 9th Corps, by virtue of his seniority in rank Cox assumed interim command of the 9th Corps.

Along the National Road a single brigade—soon to be known as the Iron Brigade—continued to advance toward the summit at Turner's Gap while the rest of Hooker's corps struggled to get to the pass to the north. Once Hooker controlled this pass he would be in position to flank the Confederate defenders before grabbing control of the western slope of the National Road. At Turner's Gap, Gibbon's Iron Brigade[26] attacked Colquitt's brigade as the Rebels, Longstreet having reinforced Hill with eight brigades in the afternoon, put up stiff resistance. Starting at 4:30 p.m. Franklin's 6th Corps forced its way through Crampton's Gap—by then defended by a brigade of only 500 men sent up by McLaws. But Franklin, deciding that getting through the gap was enough work for one day, failed to continue more than three miles beyond Crampton's Gap toward Harper's Ferry as McClellan intended.[27]

By dark Union attacks gained possession of the entire crest of the South Mountain to be able to outflank the defenders on either side.[28] By midnight Lee ordered his Confederate defenders off the mountain,[29] and after abandoning their dead and wounded the Confederates began their retreat down the National Road toward Boonsboro. Each side suffered approximately 1,800 dead and wounded in the struggle for South Mountain.[30]

Also by dark on the 14th, Lee—who received no reports from Harper's Ferry—became so pessimistic that he decided to assemble his forces, except the division of MGen. LaFayette McLaws, 41, at Harpers Ferry, in preparation for a retreat back across the Potomac. However, upon further consideration, Lee became concerned about the possibility that McLaws could be cut off and lost to the Confederacy. And so Lee issued orders to begin consolidating his forces at Sharpsburg, Maryland, a town of about 1,200 residents, where he still would have retreat routes across at least two fords on the Potomac.[31]

Meanwhile at Harpers Ferry, the Federal garrison was completely surrounded without any feasible defense. After its cavalry escaped during the previous night the Union garrison at Harpers Ferry surrendered on Monday, September 15, 1862.[32] The surrender of 12,737 Federal soldiers would be the largest surrender of U.S. troops until the fall of the Philippines during World War II.[33] Additionally, and probably more useful to the Rebels, Harper's Ferry yielded an immense haul of weapons, ordinance, and foodstuffs, all of which could be put to good use by Lee's army.

The next morning at 8:30 a.m. on September 15 McClellan sent a telegram to Halleck to report erroneously that Lee's forces were in full retreat headed for Shepherdstown and that Lee had publicly admitted his army "had been shockingly whipped."[34] Lincoln responded with a telegram, "God bless you, and all with you. Destroy the rebel army, if possible."[35] McClellan then ordered a full pursuit with Hooker to lead and Porter to rush his corps to the front.[36] The so-called pursuit consisted of forming long columns that marched down the western slopes until they would reach Boonsboro where presumably they would turn to the south to chase after Longstreet and D.H. Hill.

The Union pursuit captured more than a thousand prisoners before reaching Boonsboro.[37] But by the afternoon of the 15th at Boonsboro McClellan began to realize Lee's army had not been "shockingly whipped." Indeed Lee was not even in full retreat toward Shepherdstown but instead was establishing a battle line north near Sharpsburg on high ground west of Antietam Creek. In response the Federal columns turned west on the road to Sharpsburg.[38] The Union column then stopped at Keedysville, mid-way between the villages, to await the rest of McClellan's army.

## *The Armies Converge*

Although Jackson was yet to arrive from Harpers Ferry, McClellan's estimate—based in large part upon his own observations through a telescope—gave Lee credit for twice the number of Rebel troops already at Antietam. Moreover much of McClellan's army would not be available and in place at Antietam on the 15th. Thus McClellan decided to wait to attack Lee thereby effectively ending what passed for a pursuit from South Mountain. In reality it was unlikely that any pursuit on the 15th would have succeeded regardless of whether the Rebels were headed south to cross the Potomac as McClellan had supposed or else headed for Sharpsburg as Lee had actually ordered. As stated by Richard Slotkin: "An attack in sufficient strength could not have been launched until late in the day, by troops tired from long marches and [for Hooker's and Burnside's corps] a day of hard fighting. The Army of the Potomac had no doctrine for pursuit, and neither cavalry nor infantry was prepared for it."[39] Moreover the Confederates had been able to break away undetected in good order during the night from the battlefield and had put sufficient distance between themselves and the Federals before establishing their battle lines along the ridge between Sharpsburg and Antietam Creek.

Upon receiving a message about the surrender of Harpers Ferry Lee ordered Jackson to join the rest of the army at Sharpsburg, leaving A.P. Hill at Harpers Ferry to finish various chores, including paroling the thousands of Union prisoners captured from that garrison.

McClellan's advance divisions continued to arrive east of Antietam Creek on September 15. Part of McClellan's caution was based upon his propensity to grossly overestimate the size of Lee's army. Instead of deploying his ample cavalry to scout and reconnoiter,[40] the Young Napoleon continued to rely upon Pinkerton's detectives who had been notoriously inaccurate going back to McClellan's Peninsula campaign. Furthermore the Young Napoleon continued to see himself and his army as the only means of saving the nation.[41] Given this view he had little to gain by achieving a decisive victory that would only play into the hands of Lincoln, Stanton, and the Radical Republicans who were advocates of hard war, the antithesis of McClellan's soft war philosophy. To accomplish McClellan's soft war objectives it was only necessary for McClellan to prevent Lee from staying in Northern territory. Since McClellan calculated he had little to gain by taking unnecessary risks but much to lose if Lee should get the upper hand, McClellan felt he had every reason to remain risk adverse. But among other things McClellan's delay of two days allowed more of Lee's army to arrive at Sharpsburg to take and prepare their positions west of Antietam Creek.

Although Lee was able to establish interior lines along a four-mile arc, he might have made a mistake in establishing a defensive line between Sharpsburg and Antietam Creek.[42] At that point the meandering Potomac forms a cul-de-sac that unfortunately for Lee would restrict his opportunities to maneuver around either flank. And since the Potomac was at Lee's back he had only one feasible route of retreat across the Potomac.[43] Furthermore, the countryside around Sharpsburg was open, gently rolling farmland, providing outstanding fields of fire for artillery, almost always an advantage for the Federals.

Early on the morning of September 16 McClellan informed Halleck that he intended to "attack as soon as the situation of the enemy is developed" but that he was having difficulty ascertaining the Confederates' strength and location.[44] The respective artillery forces engaged in sporadic duels. However, it is unlikely that McClellan actually had any plan of attack for the 16th.[45] In preparation for a push on the 17th McClellan did order Hooker to cross the Antietam and to make a reconnaissance in force against Lee's left, a maneuver that accomplished little except to tell Lee that McClellan's attack would likely come from that direction.[46]

## The Bloodiest Day

On paper McClellan's general plan of attack on Wednesday, September 17, 1862, appears to be solid but not particularly imaginative or well defined.[47] Essentially he planned three major frontal assaults, the first to start at the north end of his exterior lines guided toward the Dunker Church while a second attack at the southern end of the battle line would begin shortly thereafter. A third attack would be launched in the middle. McClellan intended to force Lee to shift his defenders to meet the first attack thus weakening Lee's line of defenders against the subsequent thrusts.

As seemed typical for battle plans in the Civil War, McClellan's plans, relatively simple as they might appear, were poorly managed and executed, starting to go awry almost immediately.[48] The first attack, initially led by Joe Hooker, who was severely wounded early in the attack, started on time but quickly turned into massive bloodshed. Hooker was replaced by the senior division commander, George G. Meade. But since all orders, from McClellan on down the chain of command, had been given verbally Meade was not cognizant of Hooker's plan of attack, thus was unable to do anything except to hold his ground.

One constant fault of Civil War offensive actions was that attacks were launched in a piecemeal fashion, meaning the attacking forces were not able to achieve concentration of forces at the point of attack. As one of the many examples of such poor battlefield management, particularly on the Federal side, Mansfield's 12th Corps was supposed to join with Hooker's attack toward the Dunker Church. But not only did Mansfield have to take a longer route to the battle—not arriving until Hooker's attack was exhausted[49]—but he foolishly opted to ride at the head of his column. Unfortunately Mansfield, who had taken command only two days earlier, was mortally wounded as his corps met the same devastating fate that had befallen Hooker's corps. Thomas Buell notes that "When Hooker was wounded and Joseph Mansfield killed, the division commanders on the right wing were on their own in a free-for-all."[50]

For a third piecemeal attack McClellan belatedly ordered Sumner's 2nd Corps to cross the Antietam and to advance in support of Hooker's and Mansfield's late attacks.[51] Sumner was also riding with John Sedgwick's lead division that was ambushed from the rear precipitating another bloody debacle.[52]

Instead of following in the path of Sedgwick's division, Sumner's two following divisions veered off course to the south where they encountered the center of Lee's defenses, commanded by D.H. Hill, entrenched in a sunken road.[53] Again this attack was piecemeal, but eventually Sumner's second division arrived enabling the Federals to gain an enfilading position. The same approximate confusion among Rebel commanders created an unintended retreat soon to be known as Bloody Lane, the site of one of the most horrific carnages in the Civil War.[54] As the center of the Rebel defenses crumbled, Franklin—being uncharacteristically aggressive—pleaded with McClellan to unleash his fresh corps to exploit the opportunity to sweep the field but the ever cautious McClellan refused.[55] McClellan's decision might have been influenced by Sumner's report that his corps, along with those of Mansfield—who was replaced by BGen. Alpheus Williams, 52—and Hooker were "all cut up and demoralized."[56] Jeffrey Wert observes, "[McClellan] would never know, nor would history, if one more assault would have brought a crowning victory. He would never know because he could not bring himself to ask of his men what Lee and his subordinates had required of their men all day."[57]

Ambrose Burnside was in charge of the left or southern-most attack that was supposed to occur shortly after Hooker's attack to the north.[58] As his 9th Corps attempted to cross the stone arch bridge across the Antietam his soldiers encountered effective resistance from a small group of Georgian sharpshooters firing from the hillside on the west side of the bridge. Once across, Burnside, rather than promptly charging up the slopes against but a small number of Rebel defenders, stopped to replenish his troops' ammunition.[59]

Burnside eventually moved up the slope toward Sharpsburg. But the delay of a couple hours in crossing the bridge—ironically a ford was available a short distance downstream—coupled with the delay of resuming the advance once the bridge was crossed meant that Burnside's attack became the third attack in sequence instead of being the second such attack. But just as Burnside did succeed in organizing his attack to begin advancing against Sharpsburg in the nick of time A.P. Hill's Light Division arrived after a sixteen mile forced march from Harpers Ferry to stem any further Union advance, possibly preventing the annihilation of Lee's army.[60]

At the end of the day the Union forces—despite several command mishaps—managed to gain ground, taking positions across, or west of, Antietam Creek. But the Southern defenders, while also badly bloodied, remained on the battleground in decent defensive positions.

In contrast to Lee's personal hands-on management of his forces, except for one occasion McClellan remained at his headquarters east of the Antietam a mile and half from the battle observing the battles through his telescope. He directed his subordinates via messages carried by couriers or staff members. McClellan's leadership during the battle has often been characterized as that of an interested spectator. Lee's principle subordinates, Longstreet and Jackson, along with Stuart and A.P. Hill, were superb while several of McClellan's subordinate commanders suffered from either wounds or death; otherwise a couple of the Young Napoleon's lieutenants were inebriated or, as in the case of Burnside, inept almost to the point of being incompetent.

Despite the fierce infantry and artillery fighting that produced the bloodiest single day of fighting by American forces, McClellan made little use of his cavalry. For the most part his mounted soldiers were kept either near or behind headquarters, presumably to be launched for a possible breakthrough.[61] Thirty three years later Wesley Merritt, former cavalry commander, wrote, "The cavalry under him [McClellan] was decimated instead of being concentrated, and each corps, division, and even brigade commander, was supplied with a force of this expensive arm, which necessarily reduced the available force of the cavalry proper."[62] McClellan also deployed a cavalry unit in a skirmish line behind the battlefield in order to stop stragglers. McClellan made such little use of cavalry to scout or reconnoiter that his extensive reliance upon Pinkerton's spy reports almost always produced an exaggerated estimate of Lee's strength and capabilities.

But McClellan's deployment of his infantry was hardly any better. Because he kept deploying his infantry in a piecemeal manner, he never managed to get more than 20,000 of his men into action at the same time while another 20,000 soldiers never were committed.[63] Within a 12-hour period on Wednesday, September 17, Lee lost 10,000, or approximately one third, of his 35,000 men.

On Thursday, September 18, 1862, the sides left each other alone without much action except for some tentative scouting. Otherwise the respective commanders could not agree to terms for a truce meaning the 19,000 battleground wounded suffered grievously. Both armies suffered grievous loses in the chains of command that would be difficult to repair quickly but McClellan was being reinforced with 13,000 fresh troops, these being in addition to 26,300 veterans from Porter's 5th Corps and Franklin's 6th Corps that had not been engaged in the battle.[64] Also Pleasonton's cavalry was fresh and eager to engage. The new reinforcements together with the 20,000 troops kept in reserve during the battle on the 17th totaled more fresh troops than the total of Lee's remaining effectives![65]

After considering whether a further artillery attack might be feasible, Lee contracted and compacted his lines. McClellan ordered further attacks but cancelled those orders upon learning of his own severe shortages of artillery ammunition.[66] Several of McClellan's corps commanders warned of the risks of repulse and possible counterattacks that if successful would have exposed Washington. Buell writes that, "...on the eighteenth, the generals began beating their chests and contriving excuses to explain away their inertia for the benefit of history."[67]

## Lee Begins to Retreat

The lack of any significant action on the 18th allowed Lee's staff to plan and to organize an orderly retreat should it become necessary or advisable. Early during the morning of the 18th Jackson reported to Lee that any further attack would be futile.[68] At approximately

2:00 p.m. Longstreet sent a note to Lee recommending a retreat. During the evening of the 18th Lee apparently concluded his position was untenable because his losses had been too high while his ammunition and supplies were running too low. And so under cover of darkness Lee began a retreat back across the Potomac River, first sending the wagon train, then the artillery, and finally the ambulances carrying the wounded prior to allowing the infantry to abandon its lines prior to marching to the crossings.[69] Before departing Longstreet left a battery of rifled guns "in the main street of Sharpsburg for Stuart's cavalry."[70] A.P. Hill's Light Division of Jackson's corps was last to abandon its position leaving nothing between it and McClellan's army except a squadron of cavalry and a single piece of artillery.[71] Before leaving Harper's Ferry the Rebels destroyed the pontoon bridge during the afternoon of September 18. They also tried to burn the railroad bridge but despite five attempts to blow up the piers the piers remained intact.[72] Altogether it took a little more than twelve hours to cross Boteler's Ford (sometimes called Shepherdtown's Ford) a mile and half downstream from Shepherdstown, West Virginia.[73]

## *McClellan Makes a Move*

Crossing the Potomac River in the face of Lee's rear guard, reinforced with artillery, would be difficult but Lee's army was not going to be able to defend every possible crossing. When McClellan—suffering from an outbreak of chronic dysentery—received reports of Confederate activity upstream at Williamsport, he promptly dispatched a force of 18,000 men toward Williamsport to protect his right flank.[74] After Stuart withdrew back across the Potomac Lee reported to Davis that his proposed offense could not be sustained, explaining that, "It was my intention to re-cross the Potomac at Williamsport, and move upon Hagerstown, but the condition of the army prevented [it]."[75]

The Union victory could hardly have been deemed overwhelming or decisive, and despite the Rebels' massive losses certainly they were not retreating with any degree of disarray. However McClellan's dispatches made it sound as though he had decisively won a great struggle.[76] Many fully expected McClellan to follow up to complete the task of finishing Lee and his army, or at least to punish them further. Pleasonton, McClellan's cavalry commander, was one who assumed that a pursuit would be forthcoming; accordingly he set out immediately Friday morning, September 19, almost as soon as McClellan learned of Lee's withdrawal.[77] Pleasonton, eager to enhance his reputation, later commented, probably with considerable self-serving embellishment, "I was convinced a rapid and energetic pursuit would have routed them, if it could cause Lee himself to surrender."

McClellan's first message to Halleck about the Confederate retreat was posted 10:30 a.m. on Saturday, September 19, 1862, when he reported (somewhat misleadingly), "Pleasanton [sic] is driving the enemy across the river. Our victory was complete. The enemy is driven back into Virginia, Maryland and Pennsylvania are now safe."[78] In short, this was another example of a soft war commander being content to drive the enemy from the field instead of attempting to eradicate the threat of future action by the enemy.

In short order, the Union horsemen moved toward the rear of the retreating army. At Boteler's Ford, the Blue cavalry attacked the Confederate's rear, being able to capture some stragglers. In the anticipation of moving forward, McClellan ordered his army to form a line between the two loops of the Potomac River.[79] Porter followed up to send a brigade across Boteler's Ford to seize four artillery pieces that had been left behind.[80] But upon learning BGen. William Nelson Pendleton, 53, Lee's Chief of Artillery, had positioned an arc of 44 guns creating a cross fire at Boteler's Ford, McClellan decided that any pursuit across Boteler's Ford would be futile. Thus he ordered any activity to cease at that point.[81]

Immediately after Lee retreated McClellan, while still not committed to a full-scaled pursuit—he was reluctant to take further action without "absolute assurance of success"— nevertheless ordered another attack across the Potomac on September 20, this time with two of Porter's divisions; Lee countered by reinforcing his rear guard that was able to strike back against Porter's divisions with overwhelming success. Tragically new recruits in a Pennsylvania regiment, known as the Corn Exchange Regiment, were issued defective rifles at Shepherdstown before being left isolated. A.P. Hill's Southerners struck the unfortunate recruits with appalling fire, driving the Pennsylvanians "pell-mell" into the river.[82] Within only a few minutes these young Pennsylvanians lost one third of their ranks.[83] Accordingly nothing further happened and thus, on that unfortunate note, the Federal pursuit, such as it was, was over with Lee being restored to what Clausewitz defined as the "equilibrium of force," at least against an adversary with McClellan's conservative, soft war mentality.[84]

## *Dénouements I*

No further action was taken in serious pursuit for approximately seven weeks while the opposing armies stayed on either side of the Potomac to rest, recuperate, and resupply. During this period Lee sent mixed messages about his intentions for future actions. For example on September 24 Lee wrote that he hoped to draw McClellan into the Shenandoah Valley; the next day Lee added he hoped to retain McClellan's army on the Potomac but on the same day Lee advised Davis that "the best move ... would be to advance upon Hagerstown and endeavor to defeat the army at that point."[85] Apparently Lee's army was well supplied for meat and flour for the soldiers but Lee worried about the condition of his horses.[86]

Although he was not inclined to engage his army in any further significant military action, McClellan deemed his political position was sufficiently strengthened to the point that he could demand further powers. Such sentiments were completely disconnected from reality because on September 22 Lincoln further diminished the Young Napoleon's political influence and military powers by announcing the Emancipation Proclamation to go into effect January 1, 1863.[87]

A week after the battle McClellan began to relocate his base of operations to Harpers Ferry,[88] a move not to Halleck's liking, still concerned with the protection of Washington.[89] There was also ample evidence that during this period McClellan continued to spend much time and effort promoting the idea that he should be replacing Stanton and/or Halleck, if not even the President.[90]

While McClellan's main army was not particularly active post–Antietam, Pleasonton's troopers were not to be allowed to remain idle.[91] For starters on Sunday, September 21, and again on the 23rd, cavalry regiments launched small-scale reconnaissance on the south side of the Potomac in and around the Shepherdstown area. Later Pleasonton found and paroled 600 wounded Rebels who had been left to recuperate in private homes. But to rub more salt, on October 9—the day when McClellan was making intensive preparations for his proposed move up the Shenandoah Valley toward Winchester—Jeb Stuart began another "ride around McClellan" that reached its apex at Chambersburg, Pennsylvania, where it arrived after dark on the 10th[92]; Stuart's raid of three or four days covered 180 miles and captured over 1,200 horses,[93] destroying extensive machine shops, railroad depots, burning several trains of railroad cars, as well as 5,000 muskets, pistols, and sabers.[94] Although Stuart's ride was not especially significant from a strategic basis (most damaged or stolen items were quickly repaired or replaced), the Union's widely scattered cavalry was compelled to give chase—covering 70 miles in the last twenty-four hours—no matter how futile given Stuart's head start. Furthermore McClellan ordered Burnside to deploy his infantry along the Potomac to prevent any such future raids.[95]

Additionally the Union cavalry's sluggish, feeble attempts to capture, or at least to confront, Rebel intruders greatly embarrassed the entire Union army, especially McClellan's command. The chase had a debilitating effect upon the cavalry's troopers and horses, as a consequence "no more than one-half of our cavalry are fit for service."[96] These embarrassments, coupled with the failure of infantry to lend much support, precipitated the usual finger pointing among the army's elements. More importantly as far as McClellan's standing was concerned, Stuart's raid simply added weight, perhaps redundantly, to convince Lincoln and Stanton that McClellan would have to go. Lincoln's less than sympathetic comment was "…if the enemy had more occupation south of the river, his cavalry would not be so likely to make raids north of it."[97]

## *Lincoln Pressures McClellan*

On Thursday, October 2, Abraham Lincoln visited Antietam to tour the battlefield, to confer with McClellan, and to inspect the troops. During his three-day visit the Federal Commander in Chief attempted to encourage a quick resumption of an offensive against the Army of Northern Virginia, but to no avail. There is reason to believe that as he left to return to Washington the President had come to the conclusion he had no choice except to find another commander for the Army of the Potomac.

On October 13 Lincoln sent McClellan a lengthy and carefully honed letter, in the voice of a displeased parent, outlining the campaign Lincoln expected from the Young Napoleon.[98] Lincoln's letter was a mix of encouragement and proffered support, military maxims, Euclidean geometry, as well as a challenge of McClellan's manhood.[99] Citing Jomini's principles,[100] Lincoln also observed that by moving east of the Blue Ridge, instead of along the other side as McClellan proposed, McClellan could be closer to Richmond than would be Lee, still west of the Blue Ridge. Lincoln no longer expected a pursuit that could necessarily result in the elimination of Lee's army; instead Lincoln was merely trying to goad McClellan into initiating some sort of offensive maneuvers on the "inside track" that perhaps would force Lee to give battle, if only to protect Richmond.[101]

Nevertheless McClellan and Halleck, the latter with Lincoln's solid support, continued to squabble with each other about a plan of attack against Lee. McClellan continued to espouse the establishment of a base at Harpers Ferry in order to launch his advance up the Shenandoah Valley, i.e., west of the Blue Ridge, which was exactly what Lee hoped McClellan would do.[102] Their exchanges continued through October 20.

As Lincoln pressed McClellan to advance against Lee, the state of the horses in the Army of the Potomac became a contentious issue between McClellan and the Administration. McClellan of course had a litany of excuses about why he could not begin a vigorous advance, complaining for instance about the lack of shoes and clothing for his soldiers, but he complained most consistency about the poor condition of his cavalry horses, arguing with logic that without adequate cavalry he would be at a decided disadvantage against Lee and Jeb Stuart's cavalry. When not chasing Stuart the Blue riders were required to conduct non-ending, 24 hours per day picket duty for as many as twenty miles away from the army's main encampments. The requirement to stay in the saddle for extended periods exhausted both man and beast. Finally 4,000 horses were put out of service in late October by the onslaught of an epidemic of hoof-and-mouth disease, an acute, highly contagious degenerative viral disease, characterized by fever and the eruption of vesicles around the animal's mouth and hoofs. According to a reliable count McClellan's army had fewer than a thousand horses fit for various duties such as guarding possible crossings on the Potomac but Stuart had as many as 6,400 mounts.[103]

Eventually in late October 1862, the Young Napoleon sent a telegram reporting that most of his horses were "positively and absolutely unable to leave the camp, from ... sore-tongue, grease, and consequent lameness, and sore backs. ... [H]orses, which are still sound, are absolutely broken down from fatigue and want of flesh." On October 26 Lincoln famously responded, not without a small degree of sarcasm, "Will you pardon me for asking what the horses of your army have done since the battle of Antietam that fatigues anything?"[104]

McClellan calmly but belatedly responded that his cavalry had been in constant deployment, not only since Antietam, but indeed ever since leaving Washington on September 7. (Had he chosen to have done so Mac could have also legitimately argued some horses and riders had been working continuously much longer than that, perhaps extending to Second Manassas, perhaps even to the Seven Days battles.) Among other things McClellan reported his cavalry had been continuously "engaged in picketing and scouting one hundred and fifty miles of river front ... and has made repeated reconnaissances ... engaging the enemy on every occasion."[105] Unfortunately for McClellan, even though his arguments might have been factually valid, by that time he had lost too much credibility for his reports to carry much weight with the Washington administration.

Finally on October 22, 1862, McClellan reluctantly agreed to moving "upon the line indicated by the Presdt in his letter of the 13th"[106] In short McClellan would move his army in the valley between the east slope of the Blue Ridge and the Bull Run-Catoctin Mountains. A critical part of this plan was to block Lee from moving through one of the passes in the Blue Ridge, a task made all the more difficult by the diminished capacity of Pleasonton's cavalry. And of course it was essential to move faster than Lee could react. Otherwise Lee could once again gain the "inside track."

Finally on Sunday, October 26, 1862, McClellan began another attempt to confront Lee in Virginia,[107] taking six days to complete the crossing of the Potomac at Berlin (present

Brunswick), Maryland.[108] Afterwards it took McClellan's army another seven days to march fifty miles to the vicinity of Warrenton, Virginia, which Reynolds seized November 6.[109] From there McClellan had hoped to advance further south to Culpeper on the other side of the Rappahonnock before moving to Fredericksburg where he could try to threaten Richmond either by way of the James River or the Peninsula.[110]

On October 27 McClellan warned Lincoln that many of the Young Napoleon's regiments were greatly reduced and that it was necessary "to fill up those skeletons before taking them again into action."[111] Lincoln, who apparently had lost all patience with McClellan's excuses, pointedly asked McClellan "Is it your purpose not to go into action again until the men now being drafted in the States are incorporated into the old regiments?" Even McClellan could sense his Chief's irritability and hastily explained that without Mac's authorization an aide had added the phrase about not taking the regiments into action again.[112]

Throughout much of October Lee continued to reposition his army, on October 28 ordering Longstreet to Culpeper to block McClellan while leaving Jackson at Winchester to guard against and to decoy McClellan's rear units.[113] Lee—aside from Longstreet—was moving southward west of the Blue Ridge Mountains. On November 3 Longstreet began to occupy Culpeper, establishing positions on the Orange & Alexandria R.R. that had been intended to be McClellan's main supply route.

At the time McClellan—who suspected Lincoln was considering a change of command—did not realize this but Longstreet's capture of Culpeper, together the results of the national elections the next day, sealed McClellan's fate. Eventually Stuart's counter-reconnaissances enabled Lee's main body to get to its objective, the familiar, and easily defended, terrain of the Rappahannock River basin, thus thwarting any threat against Richmond or Fredericksburg.[114] On November 6 McClellan had 114,000 troops concentrated in front of Longstreet. However, instead of moving in with vigor and speed to destroy Longstreet, McClellan stopped to consider what mischief Jackson could do.[115] Soon all of Lee's army safely arrived at Culpeper, Virginia, without McClellan having been able to contest, let alone interdict or even contact, that movement.

And so ended the extended campaign of 1862.

## *More Dénouements and Precursors*

Strategically Lee's Maryland campaign was a calamity seriously impeding the Confederacy's war aims.[116] Despite the costs and losses of the Rebels, none of Lee's objectives were attained.[117] To the contrary Northern territory, including the cities of Washington, Baltimore, and Philadelphia, remained secure at least for the time being. Instead of joining the rebellion, the citizens of western Maryland turned their backs to the Confederacy. Great Britain and France were persuaded to remain neutral, and perhaps most important Lincoln gained strategic cover to announce his Emancipation Proclamation. The eminent Civil War historian, James McPherson has opined that "No other campaign and battle in the war had such momentous, multiple consequences as Antietam."[118]

McClellan would claim that Antietam was his finest accomplishment[119]; he boasted in a letter to his wife that, "I feel my military reputation is safe … this last short campaign is a sufficient legacy ... so far as honor is concerned."[120] In the view of his biographer, Ethan S. Rafuse, although McClellan "clearly missed what was the greatest opportunity to destroy the Army of Northern Virginia that would come to a Union general before 1865" Rafuse argues that

> ... the decisions that prevented McClellan from taking full advantage of the opportunity to destroy Lee's army, which his conduct of operations created, were also a consequence of the fact that such an outcome, although desirable, was not critical to McClellan's strategic vision in September 1862. Victory north of the Potomac was not in McClellan's mind an end in itself but merely one step in a logical, clearly reasoned program for returning the Union war effort to the path of enlightened statesmanship from which he believed it had foolishly departed in the summer of 1862. ... Once the Army of the Potomac was once again a well-ordered, adequately supplied, and properly trained and disciplined force, he would undertake a new and truly decisive campaign against the rebels.[121]

That McClellan-friendly assessment is not shared by many historians or scholars. Brian Reid, contends:

> ... [McClellan] had failed to seize the greatest single opportunity handed to a federal general to destroy a Confederate army. Such opportunities were far from uncommon in the Civil War; what was more rare was the single-mindedness, forethought, and courage to seize such changes.[122]

And Jeffrey Wert comments:

> McClellan and his generals could have inflicted a decisive, if not devastating, tactical defeat upon Lee's army. To do so would have required aggressiveness, even daring, at critical junctures. But within the Union army's senior leadership those attributes were rare.[123]

On October 1, 1862, John-Fitz Porter, almost certainly with McClellan's prior consent, if not substantial input, wrote a letter to the editor of the *New York World* to outline why McClellan did not renew the battle at Antietam. Among other things Porter cited the army's limited remaining supplies of ammunition, its loss or officers, a large number of new troops, and Sumner's resistance to renewing the battle after Sedgwick's defeat. Porter further complained that the government was grumbling about delays in renewing offensive operations but not providing what was needed in a timely manner, specifically accusing Halleck and Stanton of mismanagement.[124] While the complaints about lack of supplies and personnel losses had some validity, Lee's army was suffering under the same, if not worse, handicaps. Even more revealing, Porter objected to a strategy based upon a war pursued with an intention to oppress the South and to extinguish slavery, objections that were becoming contradictory to the Administration's objectives.

And while McClellan can, and should, be severely criticized for settling so easily after the repulse at Botener's Ford, it is unrealistic to suppose a more aggressive attack at that point, while certainly helpful, would have necessarily caused total destruction of Lee's army. Although McClellan's army gained possession of the Antietam battleground, that gain did not result from an overpowering, dominating victory. Instead Lee withdrew because, as so often happened after other Civil War battles, his ammunition and other supplies were close to being exhausted and he could not foresee any opportunities to take offensive or counteroffensive moves. While suffering a high rate of casualties, Lee's army was hardly "whipped" to the point of being vulnerable to a *coup de grâce*.

In order to accomplish an annihilative pursuit the Northern army would have needed to somehow block any further retreat by Lee. Otherwise his army could simply continue to fall back upon its lines of communications up the Shenandoah Valley—Stonewall Jackson's briar patch—all the while jabbing with crippling rear guard actions against McClellan's army burdened with its own supply and manpower problems. In the absence of any natural terrain obstacles to stop Lee as he withdrew, McClellan would have to deploy a flanking detachment, presumably a mix of cavalry and infantry. Again establishing an effective flanking attack would have been easier said than done since the Blue Ridge and the Bull Run Mountains provided substantial protections to any army retreating up the Valley. Additionally Stuart was available to block, or at least deflect, almost any flanking force McClellan could have mustered. And to be redundant, it is worth repeating Richard Slotkin's earlier comment that "the Army of the Potomac had no doctrine for pursuit," a doctrine that as a practical matter would not materialize for another two years. Otherwise it becomes one armed mob chasing another armed mob.

Therefore, while a major push against a retreating Southern army would have gained more valuable buffer space for Federal territory north of the Potomac, as well as continuing to apply pressure upon Lee thus preventing him from seizing the initiative, it is improbable that Lee, even with a wounded, diminished fighting force, would have jeopardized his army's survival by getting trapped or cornered to the extent that it could not defend itself.

In a rare instance of venting his frustration toward the soft war advocates who had command or other important staff positions, Lincoln angrily, and on the spot, cashiered a War Department staff officer who was also the brother of McClellan's chief of staff[125] who had been sent to prod Burnside at the bridge. The offending officer, Major John Key, had stated in private conversation that Lee's army had not been "bagged" after retreating from Antietam because that was "not in the game." When confronted directly by Lincoln, Key admitted that he'd said "The object is that neither army shall get much advantage of the other; that both shall be kept in the field till they are exhausted, when we will make a compromise and save slavery."

After Key made an appeal to Lincoln to reconsider, Lincoln, in his letter rejecting such appeal, advised Key:

> ... I had been brought to fear that there was a class of officers in the army ..., who were playing a game to not beat the enemy when they could, on some peculiar notion as to the proper way of saving the Union; and when you were proved to me, in your own presence, to have avowed yourself in favor of that 'game,' and did not attempt to controvert the proof, *I dismissed you as an example and a warning*... [emphasis added].

McClellan's failure to strenuously capitalize upon his narrow victory at Antietam contributed to the end of his military career. But the differences between Lincoln and McClellan went deeper. Lincoln's Emancipation Proclamation clearly and strongly signaled he intended and expected to pursue the war in contrast to the outline contained in McClellan's letter handed to the President at Harrison's Landing. And although Lincoln never made and major policy speeches, nor did he ever write any papers concerning theories of warfare, by the autumn of 1862 he had become a full-fledged convert to the philosophy of hard war, as clearly evidenced by this rumination made in early November 1862:

> General McClellan thinks he is going to whip the rebels by strategy; and the army has got the same notion. They have no idea that the war is going to be carried on and put through by hard, tough fighting, that will hurt somebody; and no headway is going to be made while this delusion lasts. ... General McClellan is responsible for the delusion that is intoning the whole army—that the South is going to be conquered by strategy.

After the general election of 1862 when Lincoln no longer needed any more political influence than may have been provided by McClellan, Lincoln—who always had reservations about letting McClellan resume command at least after Second Bull Run, and perhaps as early as their meeting at Harrison's Landing—relieved McClellan ending his sixteen month reign as commander of the Army of the Potomac, commenting that he was tired of trying to "bore with an auger too dull to take hold."[126] The Young Napoleon was replaced by Ambrose Burnside who did not want the position but took it only because of the threat that Joe Hooker would be appointed if Burnside refused the appointment. Politics aside, the differences about how the war should be pursued undoubtedly meant the split between Lincoln and McClellan, these highly intelligent, strongly motivated, but self-assured leaders, was not only inevitable but moreover was necessary in order to attain unity of command in pursuit of national as well as strategic objectives.[127]

Burnside had a good start, feinting toward Gordonsville and managing to place himself between the two wings of Lee's army, a position that could have allowed Burnside to attack the Army of Northern Virginia in detail. However, Burnside changed his mind and decided to attack Fredericksburg, using a plan that depended upon the timely arrival of a large pontoon train to bridge the 400-foot Rappahannock River.

On Saturday, December 13, 1862, Burnside's forces suffered a disastrous defeat—one of the most one-sided battles of the war—at Fredericksburg, Virginia, suffering 18,000 casualties. A Federal soldier commented: "It was a great slaughter pen ... they might as well have tried to take Hell." While observing the slaughter Lee simply said. "It is well that war is so terrible—we should grow too fond of it."[128] Had Burnside's attack been launched in a timely manner it might have succeeded but the attack was delayed because someone, probably Halleck, failed to send the necessary pontoon bridges in time. Lee commented, "I wish these people would go away and leave us alone." The survival of Lee's army after its defeat at Antietam meant that even without Longstreet, who had been dispatched to North Carolina, the Army of Northern Virginia recuperated sufficiently to have more than enough strength to defend itself at Fredericksburg three months later.

The next day Burnside withdrew back across the Rappahannock, and shortly thereafter began to make preparations again to cross the Rappahannock upstream for another attack upon Fredericksburg. However, the weather changed from snow to rain causing severe transportation difficulties for Burnside's army, resulting in the infamous Mud March as the Rebel soldiers laughed and shouted derisively from across the Rappahannock. Faced with mud everywhere after 30 hours of rain, Burnside, on January 22, 1863, decided to withdraw from his position, thereby abandoning any further possibility of attacking Fredericksburg.

Three days later, on Friday, January 25, 1863, Lincoln removed Burnside as commander of the Army of the Potomac, appointing Hooker as the next commander of the Army of the Potomac.

Burnside remained in the Federal army in lesser positions, for instance commanding the Army of the Ohio throughout most of the remainder of 1863. His successes in that command included the capture of C.S.A. raider BGen. John Hunt Morgan and the siege of Knoxville. On the other hand, McClellan had no other commands but did become the Democratic candidate for president in 1864 running on a platform featuring a call for a negotiated end of the war.

After Union defeats, scapegoating was almost as common as were burial details. In

Pope's dispatch of September 1, 1862, to suggest that he should be ordered to return his army to the defenses of Washington, Pope also complained to Lincoln that, "I think it my duty to call to your attention to the unsoldierly and dangerous conduct" of "many" unnamed officers of the Army of the Potomac. Upon returning to Washington on Wednesday, September 3, 1862, and after his command had been pulled from him, Pope submitted a report to Halleck charging McClellan with a lack of support at Second Bill Run. Pope noted his urgent need for reinforcements from McClellan when attacking Jackson and alleged McClellan's men, especially those under Porter, were tardy.[129]

After Pope's allegations, Porter was allowed to remain in command of his corps through Antietam. Lincoln's order relieving McClellan also relieved Fitz-John Porter from further corps command thereby clearing the way for formal charges to proceed against him. (Although Porter's restoration to command was tenuous at best after Pope filed his charges, Porter's chances of remaining in command were probably wrecked after his previously described letter of October 1 to the *New York World* included a vicious attack upon the issuance of the Emancipation as well as an argument that the war should be prosecuted conservatively in classic soft war terms.) That November Porter was charged with willful disobedience of an order—specifically the order he received at 6:30 p.m. on August 29—convicted by court-martial, and cashiered from the army. Notwithstanding the severity of the penalty, Radical Republican Zachariah Chandler thought Porter should have been shot.[130] Porter continued to appeal his conviction, finally winning reversal in 1887[131] and restored in rank as a colonel in the Regular Army thanks in large part to the testimony of Longstreet and other Confederate generals to the effect that Longstreet's unassailable position of the 29th made it impossible for Porter to have carried out Pope's order. To some degree Porter—who enjoyed a very successful post-war civilian career—was the victim of Republican vindictiveness, especially since he was McClellan's principle subordinate and most trusted confidant. However, Porter—who made some of his comments in writing—was not exactly circumspect about Pope, who some called McClellan's "pet," had expressed his displeasure about being attached to Pope's Army of the Potomac and at one point called Pope an Ass, perhaps an accurate and widely held assessment. However Porter was hardly endeared to those in power who were antagonistic to the Democratic West Pointers who seemed to be unable to win battles.

Field artillery played a major tactical role. Indeed, because of the destruction wrought by the armies' long arms, Stephen D. Lee called Antietam "Artillery Hell," a nickname that has stuck through the ages.

Less than a year after the conclusion of his Valley campaign Jackson died of pneumonia contracted after being shot in the arm by friendly fire at Chancellorsville; he had been shot upon returning after-dark reconnaissance behind enemy lines purportedly looking for a way to cut off a potential retreat by the Union army the next day. As had become his habit, Jackson had not disseminated word about his reconnoitering. Thus his longtime penchant for secrecy played at least an indirect part of his death. In the view of some historians, the untimely death of Stonewall deprived the Confederacy of its most legitimate chance for victory. Richard Garnett, who had protested Jackson's action in relieving Garnett of command and in bringing charges, nonetheless proudly served as one of Stonewall's pallbearers.

George McClellan, who never received another Union command, ran for President against Lincoln in 1864 but was defeated in the aftermath of Sherman's capture of Atlanta. After serving as governor of New Jersey from 1878 until 1881, McClellan died October 29, 1885, at the age of 58.

Tradition holds that visitors to the Antietam battlefield do not see elaborate statues and other memorials to generals because of their many costly blunders.

# 15

# Eastern Horse Soldiers

## Union Cavalry Evolves

Although Union cavalry began the war lagging behind its Confederate counterpart, their relative positions were beginning to equalize by the early part of 1863. Not only had Confederate cavalry begun with inherent advantages, but throughout the first part of the conflict Union infantry commanders almost always failed to make best use of their horse soldiers. As an example, George McClellan had cavalry background, having observed firsthand how the French used their cavalry; McClellan had also written a manual of cavalry tactics and had designed a saddle widely used by cavalrymen. Yet as commander of the Army of the Potomac he seldom made maximum use of his cavalry to reconnoiter or to cover and/or screen the flanks of his army. Instead during battles he tended to use cavalry as headquarters security. It is telling that on September 17, 1862, at Antietam, the bloodiest single day of the war, Union security suffered only 28 casualties as Little Mac kept most of his cavalry close at hand at his headquarters a mile and half east of the Antietam Creek.

Notwithstanding McClellan's poor use of his cavalry, his appointment of BGen. John Buford, 37, not only the Union's third most senior cavalry officer but also one of its best horse soldiers, as Chief of Cavalry was an important step in reorganizing cavalry structure and command, even if Buford's position carried no field command responsibility.[1]

But further organizational changes were forthcoming. In early December 1862—after Ambrose Burnside replaced McClellan but before the Fredericksburg debacle—BGen. Alfred Pleasonton submitted a detailed memorandum suggesting a number of changes, including most significantly the creation of a cavalry corps within the Army of the Potomac.[2] Pleasonton also suggested the army's commanding general should issue orders directly to the cavalry division commanders bypassing and thus undercutting the authority of the cavalry corps commander.

Although a skillful and confident officer, Pleasonton—the Union's second most senior cavalry officer—resembled several cavalry officers on either side of the conflict: A self-promoter who could shamelessly embellish his accomplishments. For example Allen Guelzo describes Pleasonton as "a kid-glove-wearing dandy, a ladies's man, a vivid talker with ... a sharp eye for the main chance, and an open door for reporters who might obligingly puff his name in the papers."[3]

After the great losses at Fredericksburg in December 1862, and after the subsequent embarrassment of the Mud March in January 1863, Burnside was dismissed as commander of the Army of the Potomac with his implied acquiescence. To replace Burnside, Lincoln appointed MGen. Joe Hooker, in most ways Burnside's polar opposite. Hooker was a capable corps commander whose combat performances were hardly matched by any other Union general.[4] But Hooker was also brash, ambitious, and not above backbiting in order to advance his career goals.

In many ways Hooker knew as well as McClellan how to organize and motivate his command. He was a popular choice with the rank-and-file who appreciated his efforts to improve their lots with, among other things, more and better food, cleaner camps, and clearing out corrupt quartermasters. Hooker also implemented several changes for his cavalry, changes closely reflecting Pleasonton's earlier recommendations.[5] As a result of Hooker's changes, cavalry in the Army of the Potomac was consolidated into one single corps consisting of three cavalry divisions plus a reserve brigade of Regular Army cavalry commanded by Buford.

Jeb Stuart, the highest ranking cavalry officer in the Army of Northern Virginia, commanded a division consisting of five cavalry brigades and one horse artillery brigade. Cavalry brigades in the Army of the Potomac were combined into three divisions which in turn were grouped into the newly organized cavalry corps. The Union's horse artillery was divided and assigned to various brigades rather than being consolidated into one brigade.

## Stoneman Commands the Cavalry Corps

Hooker appointed MGen. George Stoneman, 44, a former dragoon and McClellan's friend and West Point classmate,[6] to command the entire cavalry corps of the Army of the Potomac. Stoneman was the army's most senior cavalry officer with vast experience extending to the Mexican War. From the beginning of the Civil War Stoneman advanced through various cavalry commands but following McClellan's Peninsula campaign Stoneman took command of an infantry division and eventually commanded the 3rd Corps at Fredericksburg.[7] His appointment was generally approved throughout the corps but the corps was also rife with jealousies and personal frictions among many of its senior officers. Unfortunately Stoneman also suffered from a medical malady most uncomfortable for saddle riding; specifically he suffered from a severe case of hemorrhoids![8] Additionally his status as a Union general was weakened by the fact that shortly before the war he had married a Southern belle half his age.

The three cavalry divisions were commanded by brigadier generals Pleasonton, William Woods Averill, and David McM. Gregg, each of whom was widely experienced in cavalry operations. The Reserve Brigade, consisting of four Regular regiments, was commanded by John Buford whose rank justified command of a division but who preferred command of the Regular reserves.[9] Averill had served with numerous cavalry posts and had been seriously wounded in the Indian wars. In many ways Averill's traits resembled those of George McClellan stressing the need for extensive training and drill but being a cautious, conservative battlefield commander. Like McClellan, Averill was a Democrat who did not trust politicians, especially Lincoln. Consistent with the views of many other Regular Army officers, Averill had little use for amateur soldiers, and believed that only professional officers should command large units. Although lacking McClellan's charisma Averill was well liked and respected by his troopers who felt Averill had prepared them to become an elite cavalry division.

Hooker and Stoneman were not content merely to rearrange organizations on paper. Rather they made several other improvements intended to create an *esprit de corps* to replace the former cavalry attitude to either surrender, die, or run when encountering Rebel cavalry. To help develop an effective fighting force, they imposed a wide range of long overdue improvements, ranging from mounting a better quality of horses while directing that such horses be given better care by the cavalrymen.[10] Other elements were also improved including better weapons, better equipment, more rigorous drills, even assuring that better food and forage for the horses was available. Not insignificantly, processes were incorporated also to improve the quality of cavalry leadership, even to the extent of eliminating ineffective officers.[11]

Soon after Stoneman was appointed cavalry corps commander, he reported that he had 8,943 cavalrymen as well as a brigade of 459 horse artillery present and fit for duty. Within a relatively short time the cavalry corps strength had increased to more than 11,000.

Given Hooker's personality together with the intensified training and other improvements, it would not be long before his newly revamped cavalry would be tested in the field.

## *Hartwood Church*

The first of these tests occurred on Friday, February 27, 1863, when a relatively small band of 400 Rebel cavalry under BGen. Fitzhugh ("Fitz") Lee crossed the Rappahannock River—more or less the line of demarcation between the two armies—at Kelly's Ford upstream from Fredericksburg. Lee's mission was to raid the Union right flank at Hartwood Church, less than 12 miles from Falmouth, Virginia, where Hooker's headquarters were located.[12]

Fitz Lee was Robert E. Lee's nephew and attended West Point while his uncle was the academy's superintendent. Fitz and Averill became close friends while attending West Point,[13] and as reflected by his class standing, Fitz's behavior at the academy had been problematic and perhaps he was allowed to graduate only because of his uncle's position. Nepotism aside he was "born in the saddle," having served as an Indian fighter on the frontier prior to the Civil War, by 1863 Fitz was an experienced, battle tested cavalry officer. Among other things, Fitz was well known for his puckish sense of humor, still being fond of making mischief if the right opportunity arose.

Like most other raids, Fitz Lee's raid was not intended to capture and occupy territory; instead Lee's mission was to learn Hooker's intentions[14] but perhaps given Fitz's mischievous character he once again wanted to demonstrate an upper hand against his old West Point friend. Hooker became incensed that Lee's force had penetrated the Union picket lines before rampaging through Averill's encampment. Hooker then ordered Stoneman to organize an immediate pursuit. Union cavalry not already on picket duty was rousted in the middle of the night to begin a disjointed chase in the midst of a heavy rain storm. After accomplishing his mission of confirming that Northern infantry still occupied the area in force,[15] Lee was able to escape back across the rapidly rising Rappahannock; by the time Averill's lead brigade reached the river, the Rappahannock had risen too high to allow a further crossing compelling the cession of any further pursuit.

## Kelly's Ford

While rummaging through Averill's area, Lee left a note to Averill daring his classmate to make a return "visit"; Lee further taunted Averill to "send me over a bag of coffee."[16] Hooker admonished Stoneman, "You have got to stop these disgraceful cavalry 'surprises.' I'll have no more of them."[17] When he learned of the note, Hooker enthusiastically approved such a return visit.[18]

Accordingly three weeks later on Tuesday, March 17, 1863, Averill made his return visit but it would not be made with a force similarly sized to Lee's raid. Instead the Union retaliatory raid would be made with 4,000 troopers, or a force ten times larger than Lee's. The Blue horsemen were able to cross the Rappahannock, again at Kelly's Ford, "a very easy ford, and shallow."[19] A Rebel outpost contested the incursion for an hour or two before Fitz Lee's main body at Culpeper C.H., approximately six miles away, could respond.

A fierce five-hour battle of swirling charges and countercharges ensued once the two opposing cavalries engaged.[20] The Union riders were becoming adept at the use of swords or sabers while the Confederates continued to rely upon their pistols at such close quarters. Not only were the Confederates surprised by the Yankee incursion across the Rappahannock, the Rebels were also surprised by their adversaries' increased fighting skills and battlefield confidence. And although Union cavalry apparently was getting the best of the battle, the cautious Averill eventually seemed to lose heart and ordered a withdrawal[21] after failing to press his advantage.[22]

As noted by Eric Wittenberg, "Averill crossed the Rappahannock with a force nearly four times the size of Fritz Lee's."[23] Although Averill's orders were to find the enemy and to destroy it, Averill allowed Lee to reclaim the initiative, forcing Averill to take the defensive. Had Averill pushed ahead to make a charge at the end of the battle he very well may have won a decisive battle.[24] Being satisfied that his efforts to improve his horsemen by reorganization and intensive drilling, upgrading the quality of the horseflesh, weapons, equipment, and provide better care of his troopers were beginning to bear fruit Hooker was pleased that his cavalry had acquitted itself so well. Nevertheless Hooker strongly condemned Averill for failing to accomplish his assigned mission.[25]

## Cavalry Raids During Chancellorsville

Hooker's Chancellorsville campaign would provide the next major test of his cavalry's new capabilities. It would also demonstrate deficiencies in command relationships between infantry and cavalry, especially as those relationships pertained to the tactical deployment of cavalry during battles. Hooker's well-conceived plan was to flank Lee's position strung along the Rappahannock before getting to the rear of the Southern army.[26] Central to Hooker's strategic plan was that Stoneman's entire cavalry corps—minus one brigade retained with the infantry—be detached from the main body of the army[27]; after crossing even further upstream the cavalry would then sweep behind Fredericksburg. From there six brigades of Union cavalry plus four brigades of horse artillery would sever Lee's railroad connections to Richmond and be prepared to block, or at least harass, any Rebel retreat from their Rappahannock lines.

After crossing the Rappahannock Stoneman divided his force into two columns.[28]

Averill commanded one column comprised of his reinforced division while Stoneman retained control of the remaining column.

Averill's mission was to head southwestward along the Orange & Alexandria R.R. that ran toward Gordonsville. Somewhere in Culpeper County he was expected to meet and defeat a Rebel cavalry brigade. After that task would be accomplished Averill should rejoin Stoneman, presumably near Richmond, to seize and block the Richmond, Fredericksburg and Potomac R.R.[29]

On Thursday, April 30, 1863, the day after his troopers had crossed the Rappahannock, Averill's troopers entered Culpeper where they captured, and then burned, a large cache of foodstuffs and other supplies meant for Lee's army.[30] Continuing further down along the Orange & Alexandria, Averill passed Cedar Mountain before late afternoon when he approached the Rapidan River, a tributary of the Rappahannock River. That evening Stoneman, Averill's immediate superior, sent a message ordering Averill to move on to Rapidan Station, located across the river, and to drive the Rebels further ahead of him.

Gazing across the Rapidan, Averill's Federals saw that the Rebel defenses seemed strong and skillfully built. However Averill did not realize he still vastly outnumbered the Confederates.[31]

Meanwhile, after the Federal infantry broke its winter camp on April 27 and crossed the Rappahannock River at Kelly's Ford and then the Rapidan at Germanna Ford,[32] the battle at Chancellorsville between R.E. Lee and Hooker began in earnest. Once reaching the mansion house that constituted Chancellorsville on April 30, all Hooker had to do was to keep marching east toward Fredericksburg to encircle Lee's undersized army.[33] After successfully attacking Jackson's diminutive corps on May 1, Hooker inexplicably—and against the advice of his subordinate commanders—pulled back to take a defensive position awaiting an attack from Lee. In contrast to all his previous bravado, Hooker was conceding initiative to Lee, never a smart concession![34]

As he was assuming his defensive alignment, Hooker also had somewhat of an epiphany upon realizing he had no available cavalry to cover his exposed right flank. Accordingly when Hooker learned Averill had not rejoined Stoneman, nor was Averill not—in Hooker's view—engaged in battle, Hooker ordered Averill to return and to report to Hooker, presumably to cover the main army's right flank.[35] Averill responded that he had been fighting Rebel cavalry as well as destroying Lee's lines of communications, implying that he either could not, should not, or even would not return as directed.

The next day instead of reporting back to Hooker, Averill decided to cross the Rapidan in an effort to rejoin Buford. But late that afternoon Hooker sent a second order for Averill to report back to the main army. Responding to Hooker's second order, Averill's command started back toward Ely's Ford, essentially Hooker's westernmost crossing if it were to become necessary to retreat from Chancellorsville; however Averill did not rush back, instead stopping for several hours to allow his animals to graze.[36]

As Averill's troopers approached Ely's Ford they heard sounds of heavy fighting, undoubtedly coming from Stonewall's assault as the Rebels rolled upon Hooker's right flank consisting of Oliver O. Howard's 11th Corps. Instead of sending Stuart to chase after Stoneman, Lee had prudently kept most of Stuart's cavalry close at hand to scout and to protect Lee's flanks. While scouting Stuart had discovered that Hooker's left flank was hanging in the air, in other words it was not anchored against a natural barrier or reinforced by artillery.

Stuart also discovered, and diligently reported, the absence of Union cavalry that would otherwise be able to detect any threat against these exposed positions. Lee promptly acted upon Stuart's intelligence by sending Stonewall's corps on a looping 16 mile flanking movement that put Jackson's foot cavalry in position to attack the Union's unsuspecting 11th Corps. Late in the afternoon of Saturday, May 2, Stonewall was able to catch Howard's infantry almost by complete surprise before rolling up the unprepared Federals for a couple miles before the Rebels were too exhausted and too disorganized to continue.[37] Averill's command was able to encamp in the area at about 10:30 p.m.; early the next morning, May 3, Averill dispatched a reconnoiter party to try to scout Lee's right flank. Averill then rode to report to Hooker whereupon Averill first learned the Northern army had taken tremendous losses from the Confederate attacks.[38]

At that point, Averill's career with the Army of the Potomac was forced into limbo. Averill reported to Hooker that the tangle of second growth of shrubs and brush was unsuited for cavalry. In response Hooker promptly relieved Averill from command, claiming that Averill had disobeyed Hooker's orders for Stoneman's expedition and further charging that Averill was guilty of lack of zeal in not finding an enemy to engage. Hooker claimed it had been Averill's "duty to do *something*. ... If the enemy did not come to him, he should have gone to the enemy."[39] Hooker, looking for a scapegoat, was contending that Averill had accomplished little in his disobedience, and that when Hooker discovered Averill was no more than a day's march away Hooker recalled him to be in position to protect Hooker's right flank, too late as it turned out. Reporting the obvious that The Wilderness around Chancellorsville was not suitable for cavalry became the proverbial straw that broke the camel's back, in other words Averill's command.

More than anything Averill was victimized by at least a couple factors, the first being so attentive to the care and condition of his troopers and their horses. While horses may be big and strong they are also fragile and in need of care and subsidence, including forage and water. Although Averill's reinforced division had advanced only fifty miles beyond Hooker's main body, it had also been living off very impoverished land for five days during which it was actively and continuously engaged in skirmishes.

Another factor probably leading to Averill's downfall was the old bugaboo of the Army of the Potomac, specifically its politics. Fightin' Joe was a longtime critic of George McClellan's battlefield timidity, loosely associating that timidity with McClellan's Democratic politics. Since Averill's Democratic affiliations were well known, and since Hooker was anxious to curry favor with the Republicans in Congress, Averill, and his cautiousness—whether real or merely perceived—made an inviting target to scapegoat. Averill was replaced by Col. John B. McIntosh, 33, very unhappy about the relief of his mentor.[40]

But Averill, as were and would be other cavalry commanders of both sides, was victimized an even more important factor, that being the failure of infantry commanders to make most effective use of cavalry, especially during battles. In polar contrast to McClellan who kept cavalry close to his headquarters well behind the battle lines, Hooker sent the bulk of his cavalry well in front of the projected lines of battle. The rationale for such deployment was to disrupt the enemy's lines of communications, to block any potential retreat, and to otherwise create disruptions and/or distractions to the enemy's main body. But the downside of such deployment was that the main army could flounder without having the eyes and ears that cavalry could provide if kept closer at hand.

Undoubtedly Hooker needed to find scapegoats because by Monday, May 4, he ordered a withdrawal back across the Rappahannock after coming to the realization that his grand plans to flank Lee's left were not coming to fruition.[41] Although Hooker's army had withdrawn from the field, both sides had taken heavy casualties, the Federals suffering a total of 17,287 dead, wounded, and missing while the Confederates suffered 12,764 dead, wounded, and missing. On a percentage basis the Confederate losses were twice as high as the Union's, an attrition rate the Confederacy could ill afford.[42] Lee's assessment was ironically downcast: "Our people were wild with delight—I, on the contrary, was more depressed than after Fredericksburg; our loss was severe, and again we had gained not an inch of ground and the enemy could not be pursued."[43] Stonewall Jackson's loss of his left arm was the most significant of the Confederate casualties; he had to be taken from the field to recuperate. Unfortunately for the Confederacy's command structure, as well as for its cause, Jackson contracted pneumonia that caused his death while recuperating eight days after being wounded.

During the Chancellorsville excursion Stoneman remained with his larger column; after reaching Louisa Court House on May 2 this column severed five miles of Lee's main supply line, the railroad to Richmond.[44] Stoneman then further divided his command into one and two regimental sized groups—he called it his bursting shell[45]—to scatter in various directions. But Stoneman eventually discovered that "to take the enemy by surprise and penetrate his country was easy enough, but to withdraw ... was a more difficult matter." On May 8, the exhausted and bedraggled bulk of Stoneman's command re-crossed the Rappahannock and finally rejoined the Army of the Potomac on May 16.

Stoneman's raid lasted ten days, during which his troops created some panic among Virginians; additionally they destroyed twenty-two bridges, seven rail junctures, five canal boats, and four supply trains.[46] However, this Union cavalry success was made at the cost of at least 1,000 horses (Pleasonton later claimed the loss of 6,000 horses) that had to be either shot or abandoned from the wear and tear of the raid. On the other hand Lee's Army of Northern Virginia was not forced to retreat from their positions along the Rappahannock, and so there was no occasion to use Union cavalry as a blocking force.

The measure of any success of Stoneman's Raid *per se* was controverted at the time and remains difficult to assess to the present time. Since Blue clad horse soldiers could not remain on site of their destruction, any damage to the Confederate infrastructure was readily repaired.[47] But although Stoneman's raid had little impact upon Lee's capabilities or tactical decisions, the Union troopers were enthused, even ecstatic, because they had never before remained so long in the enemy's rear.

Not surprisingly, Hooker and Stoneman had different opinions about the cavalry's impact, Stoneman claiming that he had followed Hooker's directions to the letter and that his "primary objective ... was fully complied with and carried out."[48] In contrast, Hooker reported that, "...the raid does not appear to have amounted to much" and further accused Stoneman of "entirely disregarding" Hooker's instructions.[49] Hooker also accused Stoneman of going "so far around that they never accomplished anything."[50]

On the other hand Hooker's decision to send almost all his cavalry away from the main army was criticized from the beginning with that criticism continuing to the present. Such deployment nullified two of cavalry's most important capabilities, those being (1) the ability to scout and reconnoiter, thus providing eyes and ears to the commander of the main body, and (2) the capacity to screen and cover the main body's most vulnerable parts, its flanks and rear. Even Stonewall Jackson, after being wounded but before dying eight days later, observed that "[Hooker] should not have sent away his cavalry; that was his greatest blunder. ...had he kept his cavalry with him, his plan would have been a very good one." As more recently stated so forcefully by Brian Holden Reid:

> The deployment of Stoneman ... aimed to strike at Lee's lines of communication and cause alarm and despondency to Richmond, but any damage it caused was more than canceled out by the loss of reconnaissance and intelligence gathering. Hooker had 130,000 men but they stumbled about like partygoers pushed from a brightly lit anteroom into a deep, pitch-black cellar. Even when the cavalry returned to the main body they were of little use. General Fitzhugh Lee, recalling his experience with Stuart, wrote that, "Cavalry raids are dazzling, but do not generally accomplish enough to compensate for the number of broken-down horses and men." [Hooker's] misuse of the mounted arm was perhaps Hooker's single-most significant error in an otherwise well-planned maneuver.[51]

In retrospect, several aspects of the raid seem ironic. First, it should be recalled that Pleasonton's original memorandum of December 1862 argued that cavalry should be unified to constitute a massive fighting force; however in their first major engagement Hooker and Stoneman split the cavalry corps into three groups, including the brigade that remained the main army. Furthermore, the larger detached group that remained with Stoneman split itself further into regimental size units that may have harassed isolated outposts and/or local citizens but offered little assistance to the main army's efforts. By splitting his cavalry into smaller units, Stoneman diminished the fighting effectiveness of his corps.

Second, while encamped at Falmouth Hooker had extensively used his cavalry for picket duty, ostensibly so that his encamped army would not be taken by surprise by any unforeseen maneuvers by Lee; yet as his Chancellorsville operation unfolded Hooker had inadequate cavalry to screen or guard his flanks, a deficiency that was devastating since it permitted Stonewall Jackson to make his flanking movement without being detected in a timely manner. It is almost as though Hooker had learned nothing of Lee and Jackson's propensity to try bold, unconventional tactics, including wide flanking movements when least expected to do so. Perhaps Hooker had fooled himself by his bold predictions that Lee would be forced to either fight on Hooker's terms or else flee.

## Pleasonton Resumes Command

On May 20 Stoneman decided to take medical leave to seek treatment for his hemorrhoids. Hooker having no objection to Stoneman taking medical leave, appointed Alfred Pleasonton to take Stoneman's place while Stoneman recovered. Characteristically Pleasonton had exaggerated his accomplishments during the Chancellorsville campaign,[52] one reason why Pleasonton may have been appointed instead of John Buford, who would have been a more popular and more meritorious choice. In any event Buford was appointed as commander of the 1st Cavalry Division, replacing Averill. Because Pleasonton tended to claim all the glory to the exclusion of others he was not highly admired nor trusted by other officers who among other things were dubious about his courage. Nevertheless Pleasonton gained a public image of being a great warrior because he ardently cultivated cozy relationships with journalists who were willing to write favorable stories about his exploits.

Because of the increased size of cavalry units throughout the entire Union army, the

War Department created a Cavalry Bureau in Washington. After leaving to try to attend (unsuccessfully) to his medical problems, Stoneman on July 18, 1863, became the first Chief of the Cavalry Bureau to support this growth in its cavalry. One major difference between Union cavalry and its Confederate counterparts was the manner in which horses were supplied. The Federal government, or in some cases the respective state governments, provided horses to their cavalrymen; on the other hand, Confederate cavalrymen had to supply their own horses.

One immediate result of this difference was the Rebel riders had every incentive to take better care and to provide better maintenance for their mounts than did Union riders. A Confederate cavalryman had to find his own replacement mount if that horse became lame or sick. (If a Gray rider's horse was killed as a result of combat the Confederate government would pay for the cost of a replacement horse.[53]) Should a Union horse soldier lose his horse, regardless of the reason, a replacement would be provided without cost or too much effort to the trooper.

Attrition took a heavy toll upon the horses of both cavalries; while Rebel cavalrymen may have taken better care of their mounts, Union cavalrymen were more easily able to get replacement horses that had been killed, seriously wounded, became lame or struck wan equine illness such as hoof and mouth disease. As it did in almost all logistical efforts, the Federal government developed a massive system via the Cavalry Bureau for procuring and then providing horseflesh for its cavalry in all sectors of the war.

Eventually the Union War Department established five horse depots around the country.[54] These depots were intended for "the reception, organization, and discipline of cavalry recruits and new regiments, and for the collection, care, and training of cavalry horses." The largest such depot could hold 12,000 horses and had facilities to treat and rehabilitate horses that had become jaded from overuse. However the system continued to be terribly corrupt with contractors not providing horses of a specified type or quality. (This pattern of graft would not be abated until BGen. James H. Wilson, 27—another of the Union's "Boy Wonders"—served a three-month stint as Cavalry Bureau Chief in early 1864.) Eventually about a half-dozen corrupt contractors had to be imprisoned as a deterrent against some of the misfeasance. Notwithstanding its inefficiency the massive size of the Federal system provided a significant advantage to blue coated cavalry, especially as the war advanced into its third and fourth years.

The Cavalry Bureau also developed another advantage for its riders by supplying Spencer repeating carbines. Carbines had a much shorter effective firing range than did rifled muskets but as a practical matter carbines were easier to carry, to reload, and to aim for mounted riders than were rifles. During the war seven shot carbines were developed—and personally tested and promoted by none other than Abraham Lincoln—but logistic officers resisted their initial use because the new carbines would naturally require more ammunition.

## Brandy Station

After his appointment as temporary commander of the cavalry corps, Pleasonton probably wanted additional time to rest, remount and replenish his command from the wear and tear of the Chancellorsville campaign. But circumstances would not permit an extended period of recuperation. Instead Union cavalry was kept busy trying to suppress guerrilla and other small unit raids in various sectors, including areas between the main army's rear and Washington. More importantly, Union cavalry would soon become engaged at Brandy Station, one of the most famous, and certainly largest, cavalry-against-cavalry battles ever fought on American soil.

Union scouts had discovered that elements of Lee's Army of Northern Virginia were shifting their bases from the Fredericksburg area westward to Culpeper County,[55] a movement that begun Wednesday, June 3, 1863.[56] Such a movement might have several implications, including most ominously an effort by Robert Lee to establish a new launching point for another invasion of the North. In order to learn the possible Confederates' disposition and to try to "bust up" any concentration of Rebel cavalry, Hooker ordered Pleasonton's cavalry corps to cross the Rappahannock River to conduct a reconnaissance in force "to disperse and destroy the rebel force assembled in the vicinity of Culpeper."

Hooker had valid reason to suspect that something was astir. Lee—wanting to avoid remaining on the defensive and sensing that a prolonged war of attrition was weighing against the Confederacy's chances—persuaded the Richmond authorities, actually meaning Jefferson Davis, of potential advantages to be gained by another invasion of Northern territory. Realizing Hooker's position at Falmouth blocked a direct path to the north, Lee planned to launch a wide westward flanking movement into the Shenandoah Valley from whence the Rebels would be able to invade central Pennsylvania.

As part of those preparations Stuart had brought his five brigades into the area of Brandy Station, Virginia—a hamlet of a few, ordinary buildings—sitting along the Orange & Alexandria R.R., approximately five miles southwest of the Rappahannock River.[57] Stuart's division had recently been expanded by the addition of a brigade commanded by BGen. William E. ("Grumble") Jones' brigade from the Shenandoah Valley in exchange for the smaller brigade of BGen. Albert G. Jenkins.[58] Additionally Lee and Stuart were able to have two regiments under the command of Beverly Robertson transferred from North Carolina. To inspect the readiness of his subordinate brigades and to show off his division—some 10,000 strong, his largest ever assembled—Stuart staged a series of reviews, one occurring on Friday, June 5, 1863, replete with pomp and circumstance[59] followed that evening by a moonlight ball attended by dignitaries, apparently oblivious to the Northerners just across the river.

Three days later on June 8 Stuart conducted another review, this one primarily for Lee's benefit.[60] In deference to Lee's wishes to conserve energy and assets, this review was more restrained; horses did not gallop nor was artillery permitted to fire ammunition.[61] Later that evening Stuart sent his five brigades back to their separate camps within a few miles of Brandy Station while Stuart himself and his staff remained at Fleetwood Hill near Brandy Station. The brigade of William Henry Fitzhugh ("Rooney") Lee—Robert E. Lee's second oldest son—camped two miles north of Brandy Station while Wade Hampton's brigade of horse riders camped two miles south. Stuart intended to lead his cavalry across the Rappahannock the next morning to screen the further movement of Robert Lee's army.

In the meanwhile, Union cavalry was making final preparations to launch its raid. Pleasonton—less than three weeks into his new assignment as temporary cavalry corps commander—divided his corps into two major wings or columns, one under Buford's immediate command consisting of his own division of 3,000 riders plus 1,500 infantrymen and 34 guns. David McM. Gregg, 30, commanded the other wing, consisting of Gregg's division plus the division of the French-born Col. Alfred Napoleon Duffié, 28.[62] Gregg's wing had a little more than 4,000 cavalry plus 1,500 attached infantry and 18 guns. Each cavalry wing was reinforced by infantry because the Federals correctly believed Lee's army was also in the area. Both Buford and Gregg were talented, experienced cavalry officers who enjoyed their troopers' trust and confidence. Gregg's troopers had nicknamed him "Old Reliable" but Pleasonton—himself not particularly popular—disliked the third division's foreign born commander, Duffié.[63]

At 5:00 a.m. on Tuesday, June 9, 1863, Buford's column, accompanied by Pleasonton, crossed the Rappahannock at Beverly Ford.[64] After crossing, Buford was supposed to advance southwesterly straight toward Brandy Station. Gregg's column, Duffié in the lead, was supposed to cross Kelly's Ford, approximately eight miles downstream (towards Fredericksburg). After crossing, Gregg was supposed to swing northward to his right, hoping to catch Stuart's flank while Duffié would continue to Stevensburg,[65] a crossroads town a little more than four miles south of Brandy Station.

Apparently the Beau Sabreur was so pleased with the successes of his extravaganzas that he had not seen any necessity of posting pickets or vedettes north of the Rappahannock.[66] Thus the Union cavalry was able to cross without particular incident. However as soon as the van of Buford's column crossed Beverly Station it was detected by Rebel pickets who quickly dispatched alarms back to Stuart's headquarters at Fleetwood Hill. Notwithstanding his total surprise, Stuart promptly sent couriers to various brigade commanders to go to the sound of the guns and to deploy toward other possible approaches. Stuart then headed toward the river to organize a defense. Before leaving, Stuart left his adjutant general, Maj. Henry McClellan, in charge of coordination and communications at Fleetwood Hill.

Stuart's other tactical error of June 8 occurred when he bivouacked 16 guns plus 600 horses of his artillery in an open area a mile and half from Beverly Ford. While this was an expedient location for moving out the next morning, it left the batteries exposed if, as happened, the Yankees should cross the Rappahannock first. But once the Rebel gunners realized their peril they immediately harnessed their teams in preparation for a retreat while at the same time turning a couple guns to fire canister to discourage the approaching Federals. Additionally Grumble Jones quickly deployed his cavalry brigade to reinforce the horse artillery. Together this only impeded the enemy's advance, it allowed the retreating pieces of artillery to find better, more secure firing positions.

By 7:00 a.m. Buford had gotten all his cavalry with its artillery across the Beverly Ford and had pushed forward approximately two miles. However by then Stuart had organized three brigades into a line of defense along St James Church Road running roughly parallel with the Rappahannock and about a mile in front of Fleetwood Hill—which actually was a ridge two miles in length. Over the course of the next three hours the sides charged and countercharged while the respective artilleries traded barrages. The Yankees fought with uncommon valor, determination, and tenacity but being vastly outnumbered were unable to make any headway. By mid-morning Buford realized he did not have sufficient numbers to force a breach of the Gray defenders. Buford then divided his wing into two groups with one group assigned to defend whatever little ground that been taken. Buford took his other group in an attempt to get around the Rebel left flank, hoping to get to Brandy Station where he assumed he would meet Gregg. However, Buford did not have the strength to hold his advance, and was driven back to his original position. By 11:00 a.m. Buford's troopers backed off from the St. James Church Road position creating a lull in the fighting.

However the Gray defenders would not enjoy any meaningful respite. At approximately 11:00 a.m. Stuart learned to his dismay and initial disbelief that more Union cavalry was approaching Brandy Station from the south.[67] While Buford's crossing had initially gone without any significant hitches, the same could hardly be said of Gregg's crossing at Kelly's Ford. Since Duffié would proceed on to Stevensburg, he was scheduled to cross Kelly's Ford first. However, Duffié inexplicably became lost arriving late at the Union staging area. Rather than have his other units, including infantry and artillery, cross while awaiting Duffié, Gregg waited for Duffié before any other units were directed to cross. And so it was close to 9:30 a.m. when the Kelly's Ford crossing was completed; by that time gunfire could be heard in the distance, a clear indication that Buford's part of the fighting had already begun.

Stuart immediately ordered two brigades to leave St. James Church Road to block Gregg's new threat from the south. But in the meanwhile Fleetwood Hill was virtually undefended. Fortunately for the Rebels, Henry McClellan, who had remained on Fleetwood Hill, also spotted the approaching Yankee column; in desperation McClellan—George's cousin—created a ruse by having his only cannon fire defective rounds at the column from the top of the hill. Although its only available ammunition was defective this single cannon remarkably convinced the Yankees that the fire was coming from at least a full battery. This simple deception slowed the advance of Gregg's column sufficiently to give a brigade of Confederate cavalry enough time to assume a defensive line as the Union riders approached to within only 50 yards.

This precipitated another intense, swirling struggle at close quarters lasting several hours.[68] This time the Federals were able to make some progress but just as they reached the top of Fleetwood Hill Rebel more reinforcements arrived. More furious and ferocious fighting ensued with riders for either side fighting with sabers and/or pistols, no quarter asked nor given. Ultimately Rebels' sheer numbers forced the Yankees off the crest down the slope and past Brandy Station.[69]

Meanwhile as Duffié was approaching Stevensburg he received word from Gregg to turn around and move his division to Brandy Station where Gregg badly needed reinforcements.[70] Duffié did as requested but took a roundabout route that included more temporary resistance. When Duffié reached Gregg, Pleasonton had terminated all Federal attacks against Brandy Station and ordered all units to cross back over the Rappahannock.

The losses at Brandy Station on June 9 totaled 525 men for the Confederates and 485 for the Federals.[71]

Although the overall attack, especially its staging, was planned in considerable detail, it had several major flaws that doomed any chances of decisive success. First, the inception of the plan was to have the two columns converge at a specific place, to-wit, Brandy Station, at an undetermined time. As discussed elsewhere, plans based upon convergence seldom, if ever, succeeded in the Civil War. Of course if Buford and Gregg had been able to converge at the same time at Brandy Station they very well may have enjoyed an incredible victory over Stuart; on the other hand, "ifs" and "buts" seldom were synonymous with successes on the battlefield.

Second, by having Buford advance from the northeast while Gregg would be advancing from the south, Stuart had an enormous advantage of holding interior lines allowing him to shift brigades relatively easy from point to point along his defensive lines. Conversely, the Union forces, operating on the exterior, were never able to link their divisions in a coordinated manner, especially since they arrived on the scene at different times.

Third, the penchant of cavalry commanders to split their commands caused a devastating dilution of force. In the beginning Hooker had directed that merely a regiment be diverted to Stevensburg; instead Gregg apparently decided that if a regiment was good then an entire division would be even better. Unfortunately for the Northerners, this diversion of an almost entire division nullified any chance that Gregg may have had in his attack when he was atop Fleetwood Hill, especially when the Rebels enforced their effort with another brigade.

Furthermore, the Union's ambitious venture was undertaken without sufficient intelligence. Scouts had of course detected the general movement of Marse Robert's army but apparently the location and size of Stuart's cavalry was not known. Additionally the nature of the terrain and condition of the roads between Kelly's Ford and Brandy Station had not been ascertained; better intelligence would have warned about the difficulties to be encountered on the roads south of Brandy Station, Gregg's intended route. Likewise better intelligence would have negated any thought of sending an entire division to Stevensburg.

Thus it was no wonder that Pleasonton's cavalry corps failed in its primary mission to determine the whereabouts and intentions of Lee's army; for that matter Pleasonton hardly came close to his mission to "disperse and destroy" either Lee's army or Stuart's division. Although it took six days for Stuart's cavalry to refit, Lee did not wait to resume the movement of the rest of his army.[72] Instead on Wednesday, June 10, 1863, the day following Brandy Station, Lee resumed his westward movement that within a couple weeks would lead to his invasion of Western Maryland and then Central Pennsylvania.[73]

## *Dénouements and Precursors*

Although the Federals had to withdraw from the field without being able to accomplish their primary missions, within the larger scheme of things all was not lost for the Blue riders. As never before Union troopers and their officers more than held their own in close quarter battles. The riders of both sides recognized the horse soldiers of one side were now as good as those of the other side. Pleasonton ordered the withdrawal because of fatigue of horses and riders, not because his troopers were beaten and forced to retire; furthermore the withdrawal was made in a relatively leisurely manner without any pursuit by the Confederates. At last the Yankees were able to match their Southern counterparts in horsemanship, in unit cohesion, and in the use of their weapons; the mystic of Rebel superiority in cavalry was quickly fading, something being noticed even by Stuart's cavalrymen.

And while Stuart was once almost deified for his audacious, romantic ride a year earlier around George McClellan as the latter approached Richmond, Stuart was now subjected to severe criticism, even ridicule, for being caught off guard at Brandy Station. It mattered not that the Union horsemen had not been able to halt, let alone detect, Lee's movements; nor did it matter Stuart's horsemen retained their positions in and around Brandy Station, having fought long and hard to preserve such positions. Newspapers, particularly Southern press, were scathing and acerbic in their comments about Stuart not acting efficiently as Lee's eyes and ears, criticism that cut the publicity conscious Stuart to the quick.

The cavalry of the Army of the Potomac also enjoyed an advantage of better arms and equipment. Union cavalry was among the first to possess breach loading weapons; not only were breach loaders faster and easier to reload, they could be reloaded from a prone position while muzzle loaders had to be reloaded from a standing, more exposed position. And though the manufacturing of repeating Spencers did not begin until the summer of 1863, even by June 1863 some of the troopers in two Michigan cavalry regiments already had such repeaters. The Union's other arms, such as pistols and artillery, also benefitted from better quality control than those possessed by their Rebel counterparts. Even equipment such as Confederate saddles was inferior to those used by the Bluecoats. Although the Union's emerging advantages of more and better horses, more rigorous training, better artillery support, and better training were incremental, they still helped the Federal cavalry, especially the Army of the Potomac's, overcome the distinct superiority once enjoyed by Confederate cavalry.

At this point the Confederate cavalry still enjoyed, among other things, a decisive edge with its leadership; certainly Alfred Pleasonton was no Jeb Stuart, even after Jeb's reputation was diminished by Brandy Station. Furthermore the quality of Rebel brigade commanders such as the Lee cousins, Wade Hampton, and Grumble Jones was still hard to find in the Union table of organization; however bold, aggressive, and younger cavalry leaders such as Judson Kilpatrick, George Custer, Wesley Merritt, Ulric Dahlgrem, and James Wilson were beginning to emerge, perhaps to fill some of the leadership voids that remained and needed to be filled if Union cavalry would surpass the overall effectiveness of Confederate cavalry. As we shall shortly see, even though Union horse soldiers had become skilled fighters, and were closing the gaps between themselves and their Southern counterparts, several holes still remained in their skill set before they would be the entire equal of their Southern counterparts, and thus be an effective component of decisive pursuits.

A pistol ball seriously wounded Rooney Lee in his leg causing him to be taken to a private home north of Richmond for his recovery. After newspapers reported his location he was captured June 26 during a Northern raid and held until March 1864. In the meantime his wife Charlotte died. Rooney resumed cavalry command after returning to active duty.

# 16

# Gathering at Gettysburg
## June–July 1863

## *Lee Reorganizes*

After the battle of Chancellorsville—widely acclaimed as Lee's greatest triumph but at the cost of the death of Jackson[1]—Lee once again reorganized his army and its command structure. Instead of having two corps of about 30,000 men each, Lee reshuffled his infantry divisions and brigades into three corps of three divisions each with Longstreet retaining command of his slimmed down 1st Corps. Although Stuart had performed admirably on an interim basis as Stonewall's replacement at Chancellorsville, and apparently would have liked to continue as an infantry corps commander, Lee instead appointed Richard S. ("Dick") Ewell and Ambrose Powell ("A.P.") Hill as commanders of the two other newly constituted corps.[2]

Ewell was another well-connected Virginian, having grown up near Manassas. A former cavalry officer who had once fought against the Indians, once he linked up with Jackson prior to Front Royal, he served as Stonewall's trusted right hand subordinate—a role that he fulfilled with distinction under Stonewall's detailed and specific instructions.[3] After Ewell lost the lower part of his leg while leading one of his brigades at Groveton, he went on convalescent leave to allow the stump of his leg to heal. While recovering Ewell, previously a lifelong confirmed bachelor, romanced and married a wealthy, widowed cousin. Whether or not by coincidence Ewell seemed to have lost some of his fighting spirit that had characterized his services with Jackson. For example, once Ewell liked to lead from the front; but after returning from his convalescence, while still able to ride his horse, albeit with difficulty, he found it more comfortable to ride in a buggy. Capable of extraordinary profanity, he was perhaps Lee's most eccentric general, and for that, coupled by his gentle, compassionate nature, was loved by his rank-and-file. Essentially Ewell assumed command of Jackson's downsized corps.

The relatively young A.P. Hill was the son of a Culpeper, Virginia, merchant, and had married the sister of the Kentucky raider, John Hunt Morgan. Hill had lost a previous courtship when his intended instead married George B. McClellan, then president of the Illinois Central R.R. Hill suffered from fragile health due in part to an advanced case of gonorrhea, contracted while a cadet at West Point. A.P.—who was not closely related to the other General Hill, Daniel Harvey—had served fifteen years in the Regular Army before resigning to join the Confederacy. His character was contradictory in many ways: Gentle and gracious on one hand but impetuous and prickly on the other. He had had personal clashes with Longstreet as well as with Jackson. His Civil War record was marked with inconsistencies: He had served with distinction during Seven Days, at Cedar Mountain, at Antietam (where he had arrived in the nick of time after a grueling 17-mile march from Harpers Ferry), and at Chambersburg where he had served briefly as Jackson's first replacement before himself being wounded. However he had also suffered serious lapses at Second Manassas and at Fredericksburg. Some believed he may have gained his corps command mostly by virtue of being a Virginian.[4]

While the Union cavalry raid at Brandy Station may have been a jolt to Stuart's pride and prestige, still the Federal cavalry failed in its primary mission to determine the whereabouts and intentions of Lee's army. Although it would take six days for Stuart's cavalry to refit, Lee did not wait to resume the movement of the rest of his army, sending Ewell out of Culpeper on a northwestern course on Wednesday, June 10, 1863, the day following Brandy Station.[5]

Lee seemed to have a multitude of reasons for invading Northern territory again.[6] Among other reasons he wanted to negate pressures to send troops west to help relieve the siege upon Vicksburg by demonstrating he was making good use of his own units in the East. There were also excellent prospects for obtaining supplies, livestock, grains, and other foodstuffs in Maryland and Pennsylvania while at the same time relieving the burdens upon the farmers in Northern Virginia.[7] Lee was also looking for an opportunity for a victory on Northern Soil that might compel the Washington administration to open negotiations,[8] especially since Lee and other Southern leaders felt time was running against them, especially given the prospects of losing Vicksburg to U.S. Grant.

As the rank-and-file joined in the respective deployments to the North few had reason to anticipate, or even to care, that one of the epic military battles on American soil would soon ensue. For that matter even the senior officers had little reason to anticipate a great battle. For the Southern officers, Lee had tried to make it known he wanted to avoid a major conflict. Northern officers, under the command of Fightin' Joe Hooker, knew even less about their mission or about the possibilities of even encountering the Confederate army. The common soldiers had concerns of the ordinary, mundane variety of keeping their weapons clean, and of feeding their hunger and quenching their thirst.

Hoping his army would be well into Northern territory before Hooker realized what was happening, the Gray Fox's plans for moving his army into central Pennsylvania were based upon basic elements of speed and deception.[9] In order to deceive Hooker, A.P. Hill lingered in the Frederick area while Lee deployed Ewell west of the Blue Ridge and then north toward Pennsylvania via Winchester, Virginia. Longstreet moved to take a blocking position east of the Blue Ridge while Stuart had the primary mission of screening Longstreet's position.[10]

## Hooker's Lieutenants

But Lee's command structure was a model of solid stability in comparison with its counterpart in the Army of the Potomac. In the Spring of 1863 the Army of the Potomac consisted of seven infantry corps plus a cavalry corps. At this point Hooker's artillery was dispersed among the various infantry commands.

Remember that between 2nd Bull Run and Antietam McClellan relieved Irvin McDowell as commander of the 1st Corps, replacing him with Fightin' Joe Hooker. When Hooker needed time to recuperate from his Antietam wounds, McClellan appointed MGen. John F. ("Josh") Reynolds, 43, to command the 1st Corps, in effect bypassing MGen. George Gordon Meade, 48, one the 1st Corps' senior division commanders. Reynolds was another Mexican War veteran who had good relations with other senior generals, including Meade, perhaps because he kept his opinions about politics and personalities to himself. After being captured at Gaines Mill he was exchanged in time to be available at 2nd Bull Run where he won kudos from other corps commanders.[11] Reynolds had been one of McClellan's closest personal friends, almost coming to tears during a private farewell for McClellan after Lincoln relieved Mac.[12]

After suffering horrendous losses at Antietam, the 2nd Corps underwent two command changes prior to marching toward Pennsylvania nine months later. Edwin V. Sumner—who had been in command during the Peninsula campaign through Fredericksburg—took a "temporary" leave of absence to recover from the stresses of those campaigns. Unfortunately the beloved Sumner died March 21, 1863, while on the way to a new command in Missouri.

Sumner was replaced by MGen. Darius Couch, 41, with a distinguished military background as well as connections to the top of the Army of the Potomac, including McClellan his West Point roommate.[13] But Couch was not popular with his subordinates. Moreover, Couch became profoundly discontented with Hooker's command, holding Hooker, and not Howard, Sedgwick, or Stoneman, responsible for the Union defeat at Chancellorsville. After recommending that Meade, Couch's junior in rank, replace Hooker, Couch resigned from the 2nd Corps to take command of the Department of the Susquehanna.[14]

Hooker then appointed MGen. Winfield Scott Hancock, 39, to lead the 2nd Corps, an appointment that would shape the 2nd Corps for the rest of the war. A West Point graduate and another Mexican War veteran, Hancock (nicknamed "the Superb") was an aggressive and fiery leader, both courageous and unflappable.[15] In camp Hancock was after the hearts of his men by taking care to appear immaculately dressed at all times.[16] Once William Franklin wrote of Hancock, "I never met a man, who as a general officer, ... combined so well as he did the prudence which cherished the lives of his command, with the dash which was his distinguishing characteristic."[17] Although Hancock had a long period of service under McClellan's tutelage, when Hancock heard talk of a march upon Washington to force McClellan's reinstatement, Hancock responded, "We are serving our country, and not any man."[18]

The background and characteristics of the 3rd Corps commander, MGen. Daniel Sickles, 38, deviated the most from the other corps commanders. Sickles was not a West Point graduate nor did he have any military experience prior to raising a New York brigade while being commissioned as a colonel.[19] A lawyer (who had studied under Ben Butler) and a former Congressman, he was mostly known in legal circles for being the first murder defendant to be acquitted on the grounds of temporary insanity.[20]

Not only did Sickles not attend West Point, he despised the Point's graduates as being "cliquish, cautious, calculating."[21] "Ambitious, determined, unscrupulous, and charismatic," he naturally became Hooker's kindred spirit.[22] After Hooker transferred Stoneman from the 3rd Corps to cavalry command prior to Chancellorsville, Hooker appointed the colorful but controversial Sickles to command the 3rd Corps. Although Sickles' bravery under fire was acknowledged by the professionals, he was also one of the two corps commanders at Chancellorsville who urged withdrawal, his reasoning being that any chances of success were "doubtful" versus the danger to Washington in case of a defeat.[23]

Fitz-John Porter remained in command of the 5th Corps pending his court-martial until relieved by Lincoln November 5, 1862, in the same order that dismissed McClellan.[24] Upon Porter's removal, Burnside appointed BGen. Daniel Butterfield, 32, "an energetic, ambitious, and charming man" to command the 5th Corps.[25] Again Meade was not happy since he easily outranked Butterfield; when Meade complained to Burnside, Burnside apologized using the lame excuse he did not realize Meade's seniority. After Fredericksburg—where Meade's division advanced further than any other division after which Meade discovered his hat had two new bullet holes—Burnside appointed Meade, one more West Point graduate and another veteran of the Mexican War, to command the 5th Corps.

Meade was born in Spain of well-to-do American parents; he entered West Point at the age of sixteen but resigned one year after graduation to become a civil engineer. Failing to prosper in civilian life Meade rejoined the army in 1842.[26] Meade's appointment effectively reverted Butterfield back to division command. On the surface Butterfield accepted his demotion gracefully but Butterfield—"first and foremost a political animal"[27]—contacted powerful Senators while cementing an alliance with Hooker. Meade's corps was not heavily engaged at Chancellorsville but Meade strongly advocated against withdrawal, arguing that the "army had already too long been made subservient to the safety of Washington."[28]

The 6th Corps—the army's largest—also underwent rapid command changes. Starting during the Peninsula campaign, MGen. William B. Franklin, 40, commanded this corps until Burnside elevated him to Wing commander prior to Fredericksburg. Upon Franklin's ascension to Wing, the 6th Corps command fell upon Baldy Smith, Franklin's close friend. Although Baldy was very capable, McClellan once described him as "quick tempered, ... very selfish, and had a most bitter tongue which very often ran away with him and got him into trouble."[29] After Fredericksburg, Burnside and the Joint Committee for the Conduct of the War blamed Franklin for that debacle but in turn Baldy and Franklin also wrote to Lincoln to criticize Burnside's performance.[30]

Baldy Smith, Hooker's mirror image as a chronic complainer and intriguer, was the only corps commander Hooker wanted to remove when Hooker became commanding general of the Army of the Potomac. Accordingly, Hooker arranged to transfer Smith to command the 9th Corps that was being ordered to Fortress Monroe prior to being transferred to the Department of Ohio.

Having rid himself of Smith, Hooker promoted MGen. John ("Uncle John") Sedgwick, 50, a professional soldier to the core who had seen almost every military conflict—including extensive service in Mexico and on the frontier—since his graduation from West Point in 1837. He was often ill or injured as he advanced in rank and command levels but in February 1863 he was given command of the 6th Corps. As was typical for many of the regular officers with his West Point education and professional background, Sedgwick—a devotee of McClellan's conservative philosophy—was cautious and risk adverse, prone to overestimating the adversary's strength. Twice wounded—Glendale and Antietam—Sedgwick was a "humble, phlegmatic, unobtrusive, and unglamorous bachelor," who avoided the politicking and backbiting that characterized much of the army's officer corps.[31] Difficulties arose between Hooker and Sedgwick at Chancellorsville when Sedgwick was deployed below Fredericksburg. According to Hooker's orders, Sedgwick was to pursue the Confederates still at Fredericksburg but he should "attack and carry their works at all hazards" if those Rebels moved toward the main body of Yanks remaining at Chancellorsville. Unluckily Uncle John became overwrought with the dangers in front of him, failing to go to the sounds of battle at Chancellorsville. Jeffry Wert observes that this "...required of Sedgwick alertness, initiative, and flexibility amid fluid circumstances. Unfortunately, caution and deliberateness characterized his generalship."[32]

Again citing Wert, Sedgwick became "'perfectly satisfied' with minimal performance [and had] searched only for obstacles that prevented him from performing his primary mission."[33] Once Sedgwick retreated back to Fredericksburg, Lee had greater freedom to maneuver against the rest of Hooker's army and unfortunately Sedgwick's retreat back to Fredericksburg was another factor contributing to Hooker's defeat. After the battle Sedgwick, along with Stoneman[34] and Howard became Hooker's scapegoats. Specifically Hooker accused Uncle John as being "slow and afraid to fight; also of disobeying orders directly." Nevertheless, Hooker took no further action against either Sedgwick or Howard.[35]

The 11th Corps had the army's worst reputation by this period in the Civil War. Not constituted as such until September 12, 1862, it derived from Pope's Army of Virginia that was in turn composed of separate commands that chased in vain against Stonewall Jackson during his 1862 Valley campaign.[36] The corps contained a high percentage of German immigrants in divisions led by commanders with Teutonic names. Franz Sigel, its original commander, was relieved at his request February 22, 1863, to be replaced by Carl Schurz.

Although at least three German immigrants had sought the appointment, Hooker decided to assign the 11th Corps to MGen. Oliver Otis Howard, 33, another West Point graduate. Heading a brigade at Fair Oaks, Howard was seriously wounded, necessitating the loss of his right arm. Unlike most West Point graduates or other Regular Army officers, Howard as "an abolitionist and devout Christian without ... martinet mannerisms."[37] But Howard's appointment was not a good fit with the German "freethinkers" who began calling Howard "Old Prayer Book" and began resenting his attempts to "make a Sunday School class of a military organization."[38] Unluckily the 11th Corps, and by extension Howard's reputation, suffered a rout when Jackson struck the corps exposed on the Federals' right flank at Chancellorsville. Contrary to Hooker's instructions, most of the regiments, the 75th and 82nd OVIs, the 58th NY, and the 26th Wisc excepted, failed to stay in any state of readiness, having stacked arms prior to Jackson's late afternoon attack. Even though he had been warned by Hooker to be alert, Howard falsely assured Hooker, "I am taking measures to resist an attack from the west."[39] As a result of their stampede to the rear the German element became known as the Flying Dutchmen, despised by other native born regiments in Howard's command. Later Howard admitted, "I wanted to die. ... That night I did all in power to remedy the mistake, and I sought death everywhere I could find an excuse to go on the field."[40]

The 12th Corps was the third of three units that began as independent divisions in the 1862 Valley campaign before being incorporated as corps into Pope's Army of Virginia. In this instance Nathaniel Banks was the original commander before McClellan decided to replace him with the elderly J.F.K. Mansfield, who was mortally wounded at Antietam after only two days in actual command. Mansfield was temporarily replaced by BGen.

Alpheus Williams, who did a good job under very difficult circumstances. But as a brigadier Williams had insufficient rank, especially with so many Major generals available and wanting the assignment, so on October 15, 1862, McClellan appointed MGen. Henry ("Harry") Slocum, 36, as permanent commander of the 12th Corps.

Slocum, a former school teacher, was in the minority at West Point with his strong anti-slavery stance. After three years' active service he resigned his commission to practice law in upstate New York. Rejoining the army after Fort Sumter, the "small, spare man with considerable poise" whipped the 12th Corps into shape while earning the friendship and trust of his fellow officers, including Williams.[41] But even though Slocum was a competent manager of military assets, as noted by Noah Andre Trudeau, "he lacked the spirit of a warrior."[42]

By early June 1863 it had become clear, or should have become clear, that Lincoln's means of prosecuting the war were contrary, if not antithetical, to McClellan's soft or limited war, and while some commanders might not have been happy with Lincoln's policies, they were resigned to the reality that McClellan was unlikely to ever regain his former command. And while not in the direct chain of command, the specter of the Joint Committee on the Conduct of the War, dominated by the Radical Republicans, lurked in the background. Furthermore most senior military commanders were quite capable of changing with the political winds. Butterfield was an outstanding example of fluctuating attitudes. When McClellan was dismissed in November 1862 Butterfield rashly made noise about marching upon Washington in order to compel Mac's reinstatement. But by the spring of 1863 Butterfield, after being bumped aside from command of the 5th Corps to make room for Meade's appointment, alighted to become a fiercely loyal chief of staff for Hooker, McClellan's antagonist, meaning Butterfield no longer had any interest in promoting McClellan's reinstatement.

Unknown to Hooker, but adding to the command turmoil, Washington was looking to replace Hooker, apparently offering the command to four of Hooker's subordinates, including Couch, Reynolds, Sedgwick, and Hancock.[43] Reynolds declined the appointment purportedly because he failed to receive assurances that he would be given a free hand.[44] The other three also declined the appointment, apparently because they did not want correct the problems created by Hooker; on the other hand these three also recommended that Meade replace Hooker.

To briefly summarize, none of the seven infantry corps commanders had held their respective slots at Antietam. Only two had been appointed by McClellan, the other five by Hooker. Not so incidentally sixteen of the army's nineteen division commanders had been appointed subsequently to Antietam. Edwin Coddington considered that: "On the whole Hooker had a very competent set of corps commanders, although some of the generals commanding his divisions and brigades did not measure up to their standard."[45]

## The Cavalries Maneuver

Union cavalry under its recently appointed temporary commander, Alfred Pleasonton, was forced to quickly resume operations after Chancellorsville. The Cavalry Bureau supplied hundreds of fresh horses while the Quartermaster Department also provided ample quantities of supplies such as ammunition, saddles, and weapons.[46] This resupply and replenishment was largely responsible for enabling the Federal cavalry to embark upon its surprise attack at Brandy Station on June 9.

Notwithstanding his general satisfaction with his cavalry's performance at Brandy Station, on Thursday, June 11, 1863, Hooker further reorganized his cavalry command. Buford and Gregg retained division commands but the French émigré A. N. Duffié—who had not fared well at Brandy Station—[47] was reduced to regimental command while the rest of his division was dissolved.[48] Thus for the time being Hooker's cavalry corps consisted of just two divisions. However another division being transferred from Washington would soon become the cavalry corps' third division, eventually under the command of the newly promoted BGen. Judson Kilpatrick, 27, another of the Union's "Boy Wonders," so nicknamed for graduating from West Point in 1861 before rising rapidly in rank.

Lee's infantry movements triggered considerable maneuvering by the cavalries of either side. Hooker was desperate to learn Lee's location and intentions, knowing that some of Lee's army had already shifted west beyond the Bull Run Mountain range. In his new corps command Ewell was anxious to emulate the rapid, decisive movements of his successor, Stonewall Jackson.[49] Indeed, on June 14, 1863, Ewell's advance unit had come down from the Shenandoah Valley to "gobble up"[50] Winchester, capturing supplies, wagons, artillery pieces, and nearly 4,000 prisoners from three brigades that would never be reconstituted.[51] The next day the van of Lee's army waded across the Potomac at a ford at Williamsport.[52]

Finally realizing Lee was moving, but not knowing exactly where, on June 14 Hooker began moving his army away from the Rappahannock. The seven infantry corps were divided among three groups: the first group being Reynolds' 1st Corps, Sickles' 3rd Corps, and Howard's 11th Corps; the middle group really only Meade's 5th Corps, and the rear group being Hancock's 2nd Corps, Sedgwick's 6th Corps, and Slocum's 12th Corps.[53]

The movements of these armies only served to agitate the Washington authorities who were pressuring Hooker to assess Lee's intentions. Hooker made an indirect slap at Pleasanton with a complaint to Lincoln that, "We can never discover the whereabouts of the enemy, or divine his intentions, so long as he fills the country with the dust of his cavalry."[54] Pleasonton, trying to placate Hooker by finding the rest of Lee's army, deployed his cavalry toward Little River Turnpike (now U.S. Rt. 50), running east and west between the Bull Run Mountain and the Blue Ridge. Three villages were located along the turnpike west of the Bull Run Mountain, Aldie being nestled in Aldie's Gap of Bull Run Mountain while Middleburg and Upperville were found further west toward the Blue Ridge.

On Wednesday, June 17, 1863, as Longstreet was moving from Culpeper westward to the Blue Ridge, Fitz Lee's brigade (under Col. Thomas Munford while Fitz was recovering from wounds) went to Aldie to cover Longstreet's movement. At the same time David Gregg's division was sent from Manassas Junction to search for Rebel formations west of Aldie with Kilpatrick's brigade of Gregg's division reaching Aldie at 4:30 p.m. The Rebels, supported by artillery, built up a defensive position while the Federals launched a series of mounted and dismounted attacks until dark when Munford was ordered to withdraw. Stuart claimed these were some of the bloodiest fights of the Civil War.[55]

Pleasanton felt he could report to Hooker that "from the information I can gather, there was no force of consequence of the enemy's this size of the enemy." Pleasanton reported this even though Longstreet's corps of approximately 20,000 men was at the foot of the

Blue Ridge, only ten miles away! Clearly Union cavalry's ability to reconnoiter was still inferior to its emerging capacity to fight. Hooker was not sympathetic to Pleasanton's situation, telling him in effect that Pleasanton's job was to find where the enemy was, not where he wasn't.[56]

On June 19 Pleasanton's cavalry continued a series of charges to sustain pressure upon Stuart, who fought defensively in order to protect Lee's movements rather than becoming involved in a general engagement. Eventually Stuart withdrew about a half mile to defensive positions that the Federals decided not to attack.

Two days later on June 21 Pleasanton made another concerted effort to go after Stuart's cavalry and "to cripple it up." After leaving a couple brigades of horse soldiers to guard communications at Middleburg, Pleasanton unleashed a two-pronged assault against the Rebel cavalry, driving Stuart's five brigades back through Upperville toward Longstreet's main body at Ashby's Gap in the Blue Ridge. Upon reaching Ashby's Gap Pleasanton broke off contact to return to Aldie, now being satisfied his efforts had accomplished everything he was supposed to do, even though Pleasanton still had not discovered Longstreet's presence or ascertained Lee's intentions.

On the whole this series of on-again-off-again cavalry engagements over five days along the Little River Turnpike were bloody but indecisive as both cavalries survived to fight another day; certainly any impact upon Lee's movement was short lived. However, once again Union cavalry had demonstrated increased prowess in its fighting ability,[57] and once again some Southern newspapers wrote scathing but partly erroneous criticisms of Stuart's inability to fully screen and protect Lee.[58] Unfortunately for Hooker he still had insufficient intelligence to allow him to fathom Lee's intentions except that by Wednesday, June 24, 1863, it was obvious that Lee was headed north somewhere between Washington and Pittsburgh.[59] On June 25 Lee, accompanying his "Old War Horse" Longstreet, crossed the Potomac.[60] That same day Hooker started his army in motion toward Frederick, Maryland.[61]

## Stuart Begins Another Ride

On the Confederate side Stuart was anxious to redeem a reputation that he perceived had been damaged, especially at Brandy Station and later at Upperville. Lee desired Stuart to do two things: (1) to screen the corps of Hill and Longstreet as they followed Ewell to the north, and (2) to serve as the army's right flank guard while keeping Lee informed of the Federals' movements and actions.[62] Thus Stuart was given ostensible opportunity for some redemption on June 22 when Lee wrote the first of two orders to Stuart: "If you find that [Hooker] is moving northward, and that two brigades can guard the Blue Ridge, and take care of your rear, you can move with the other three into Maryland and take a position on General Ewell's right, place yourself in communication with him, guard his flank and keep him informed of the army's movement."[63] Guarding Ewell's right was especially important because Old Baldy's mission was to forage all the way to the Susquehanna River.

Historians have debated whether Lee's June 22 order allowed Stuart too much discretion but by June 23 Lee knew Hooker's army began to cross the Potomac River via a pontoon bridge at Edward's Station.[64] Lee's second order was much more specific than had been his first order stating among other things that: "...I think you had better withdraw this side of the mountain to-morrow night, cross at Shepherdstown the next day, and move over to [Frederick, Maryland]. ... I think the sooner you cross into Maryland, the better."[65] During the early morning of June 25 Stuart, with 5,600 cavalrymen from three of his brigades[66]—under his most trusted commanders, Wade Hampton, Fitz Lee, and John R. Chambers, substituting for the still recuperating Rooney Lee—together with six artillery pieces, took advantage of Lee's authorization left Salem (now Marshall), Virginia, to begin another ride around the Army of the Potomac. Before leaving Stuart, per Lee's order, left the brigades of William ("Grumble") Jones and Beverly Robertson—Stuart's two least favorite generals—to guard gaps in the Blue Ridge.[67] Stuart would have been in complete compliance with Lee's discretionary directive by crossing the Potomac upstream of Hooker to head straight north between Ewell and Hooker. Instead Stuart chose a more circuitous route, riding downstream to Hooker's right, going east toward Washington before turning to begin a counterclockwise, hopefully another triumphant, ride to redeem his reputation.

Given Stuart's character, including his sense of boldness together with his craving for publicity, it was almost preordained that he would once again try the same basic maneuver that twice before had given him fame and glory.[68] But almost as soon as Stuart got underway he encountered an unexpected delay near Haymarket, Virginia, where his route crisscrossed Hancock's 2nd Corps.[69] Although Stuart could not resist lobbing a few rounds at Hancock's passing corps (shades of Jermantown following Second Manassas), Stuart had no alternative except to allow Hancock to continue to pass. Stuart did send a dispatch to Lee about this discovery but the single courier carrying this valuable intelligence was never heard from again,[70] and Lee was thus not immediately aware of the extent of Hooker's movements. In any event, Stuart immediately fell a day behind his projected schedule.

To avoid other Union movements, Stuart could have reversed his course and still have taken the more westward route closer to Ewell's column. However doing so would have cost Stuart two more days and would have relinquished the prospect of more glory since Hooker would be between Stuart and Washington. Predictably Stuart continued along his originally chosen route.

Stuart's next two days after Haymarket were better for him, and by the end of the second such day, Saturday, June 27—the same day Hill and Longstreet were arriving in the Chambersburg, Pennsylvania, area—Stuart had reached the Potomac at Rowser's Ford; but Stuart had marched for 50 hours while covering only 34 miles.[71] Moreover, Stuart found the Potomac was two feet higher than normal causing considerable difficulty in crossing, particularly for his artillery.[72] Nevertheless by 3:00 a.m. Stuart's crossing was complete.[73]

Lack of forage for the horses was another unexpected impediment encountered by Stuart. As a result Stuart was forced to halt from time to time to allow his otherwise starving horses to graze.[74]

After a few hours sleep, Stuart captured some Federal soldiers and Blacks from whom he learned that the Army of the Potomac was moving toward Frederick, Maryland. This news should have underscored the importance of linking up with Ewell as soon as possible. But as Stuart was crossing the National Pike near Rockville, Maryland, approximately 25 air miles southeast of Frederick, Stuart's troopers discovered a Union train of 150 supply wagons—eight miles in length—headed for Hooker's army.[75] These wagons—each pulled by four mules—were filled with a variety of valuable supplies, including grains, meat and even whisky.[76]

Teamsters of twenty-five wagons managed to either escape or at least wreck their wagons. Under normal circumstances, the Confederates were always eager and thankful to capture all possible booty but, unknown of course to Stuart, Ewell and the independent cavalry divisions were also gathering even more plunder. Whatever, Stuart had to take several hours to burn the overturned and wrecked wagons while awaiting the return of Fitz Lee's brigade that had given chase and attempted to round up Union teamsters trying to escape.

## *Meade Replaces Hooker* (June 28, 1863)

On the same day when Stuart was adding (and burdening himself with) 125 supply wagons—almost seven miles in length altogether—to his entourage, dramatic changes were occurring in the Army of the Potomac. The first of these changes happened when newly promoted Kilpatrick assumed command of the 3rd Cavalry Division recently arrived from Washington. Fiercely ambitious and relentlessly aggressive, sometimes to the point of recklessness, Kilpatrick was still a West Point cadet when the war began; he was scorned and ridiculed as well as admired. He was shot in the buttock at Big Bethel, thereby purporting to be the first Union officer to be wounded during the Civil War. Although married and a father, he was well known as a frequent patron of prostitutes; he had also served a couple weeks in jail for allegedly selling confiscated livestock. One of his distracters referred to "Kil-cavalry" as a "frothy braggart, without brains."[77] Nevertheless his propensity for fighting and fearlessness earned him a quick succession of command assignments and promotions.

But an even larger command change occurred on June 28. Almost as soon as Lee started to move Ewell's corps westward, leaving A.P. Hill in the Fredericksburg area, friction began to build and accrue between Hooker and Washington authorities. Hooker—who had previously intimated his political ambitions, including the possibility of establishing a dictatorship—was not amenable to taking advice from anyone, even from someone as senior, as learned, and as experienced as General in Chief Henry Halleck. More substantively the parties had differing strategic viewpoints for dealing with Lee.

Upon realizing that A.P. Hill had been left alone in Fredericksburg, Hooker wanted to attack Hill and move on to capture a lightly defended Richmond. On the other hand, Lincoln's position—as described to Hooker when he was first given command in January—was that "...*Lee's* army, and not *Richmond,* is your true objective point."[78] Additionally any move by Hooker toward Richmond would make eastern cities, including Washington, vulnerable to capture by Lee. Indeed, to validate Lincoln's apprehensions, Lee probably would have been happy if Hooker were no longer between Washington and the remainder of Lee's forces in order to attack Hill who probably would have simply retreated away from any such attack.[79]

Later as Lee's long column continued to lumber to the west and then north, Hooker's inclination was to try to find and attack the column's tail. Not only was Hooker having a difficult time finding that tail, but as seen in other venues, attacks against a rear guard seldom accomplished much except to frustrate the pursuer. Lincoln in his own wry, but astute, manner was urging consideration of another point of attack: "If the head of Lee's army [Ewell's vanguard] is at Martinsburg and the tail of it [Hill's rear] on the Plank road between Fredericksburg and Chancellorsville, the animal must be very slim somewhere. Could you not break him?" But again Hooker seemed hesitant to engage Lee's main body, even strung out as it was. We do not have the benefit of a psychoanalysis of Hooker, but it seems apparent that Chancellorsville had given him a new found respect for Lee, and that Hooker was hardly demonstrating the same aggressiveness, or bluster, that he seemed to demonstrate prior to Chancellorsville.

The final straw was related to the defense of the Federal arsenal at Harper's Ferry. The Federal garrison at Harpers Ferry had been relocated from the town itself—which sits in a practically indefensible valley—to the heights overlooking the town. Hooker wanted to remove that garrison of 10,000 soldiers from Harpers Ferry, in effect to forfeit the arsenal to Lee, and to attach those troops to the Army of the Potomac.[80] Hooker believed the Harper's Ferry garrison, when added to Slocum's corps of 15,000 soldiers, could attack the rear of Lee's column while the main body of Hooker's army could move westward to strike at Lee's "slim" mid-section. Lincoln was fearful that Lee would repeat his maneuver of 1862 prior to the battle of Antietam; accordingly Lincoln insisted that the garrison remain intact. In other words the Harpers Ferry garrison would not become attached to Hooker's army.

Since Hooker seemed to not understand or appreciate Halleck's, and by extension Lincoln's, grand strategy of going after Lee, Lincoln and Halleck—while appreciating that Hooker had some desirable characteristics—were fast losing confidence as Hooker as an army commander. Some in the Federal administration, including Secretary of War Stanton, thought they were beginning to see signs of another McClellan on its hands. Hooker contended that as the commander in the field he was entitled to more authority and latitude with less interference from Washington but seemed at odds with the administration about how such authority and latitude should be deployed against Lee. Either because of sincere frustration or as a bluff to gain more command leverage, on Sunday, June 28, 1863—while Stuart was processing his newly captured bounty—Hooker requested that he at once be relieved,[81] which to his apparent surprise, was promptly accepted.[82] And so Hooker's five-month term as commander of the Army of the Potomac came to an abrupt end.

Upon acceptance of Hooker's resignation, the army command was thrust upon Meade, commander of the 5th Corps. Meade had been a solid if not spectacular division and corps commander. He was known as being honest and straightforward while being thorough and painstaking in attention to details.[83] Unfortunately he was short of command charisma, giving the appearance of being a thoughtful, but cranky professor. He was also junior in rank to three of his seven corps commanders who still tended to have residual inclinations between pro- and anti- McClellan backgrounds.[84]

Beyond his basic professional competence, Meade's most prominent attribute for being selected—other than the fact that nobody else wanted the assignment —was that he was from Pennsylvania and thus was assumed to want to fight harder to defend his home state. When Meade's name was being considered for promotion to army command, purportedly Lincoln said Meade would fight well "on his own dunghill."[85] Being born while his parents were in Cadiz, Spain, he was ineligible to become President.[86] It was thought that this ineligibility meant he, unlike his predecessors, had no political aspirations or agenda. Furthermore, unlike many of his colleagues Meade had not sought promotion to army command,

and, after protesting that the army, including himself, expected Reynolds to succeed to command,[87] accepted the position only because he was told he had no choice.[88]

Perhaps more than anything else, other than being a hard, determined fighter, Meade was defined by what he wasn't: He wasn't likely to lose a battle out of Hooker-like loss of confidence and wasn't going to persist in a Burnside-like attempt to do the impossible even after it was clear that it was not possible.[89] While respected by most of his fellow officers, the appointment of this career soldier with "extraordinary moral courage" as met by vast indifference by the common soldiers who were mostly aware of his quick, nasty temper.[90] If the soldiers had any reactions to the change of commanders many would have been to reinstate McClellan.[91] Lastly, Meade had no experience with or intuition for public relations, meaning the press was unlikely to try to glorify his accomplishments.

Although Lincoln had selected Meade to replace Hooker, Halleck wrote the appointment order that included the phrase, "You will … maneuver and fight in such a manner as to cover the capital, and also Baltimore, as far as circumstances will admit."[92]

Upon his appointment, Meade knew he did not have the luxury of taking his time to adjust to his new command structure. He immediately reached out to Reynolds, "a lieutenant important to me in his services … a friend and a brother."[93] After Reynolds came to Meade's tent, the latter hurried outside to meet his friend before taking Reynolds inside the tent where an unobserved aide heard Meade assure Reynolds that he [Meade] counted on Reynolds for the support he would have given his friend had the latter been placed in the same situation.[94]

Once Meade became army commander, somebody had to take his place as 5th Corps commander. This time Meade deferred to seniority to elevate MGen. George Sykes, 41, an old army, tireless, methodical soldier who "enforced discipline like a machine."[95] Sykes was a West Point graduate who had scouted and fought on the frontier and in the Mexican War. At several levels Sykes commanded Regulars, demonstrating ample steadiness and courage but never displaying much initiative or dash.[96] Stephen Taaffee opines that Sykes "was not … the man to fill Meade's shoes as a corps commander."[97]

Beyond this immediate appointment, Meade discovered that other than going after Lee's tail end, Hooker had made no plans.[98] In fact Meade did not even know the locations of the other Federal corps.[99] Also on the same day of his new appointment Meade received an intelligence report generated by a citizen in Hagerstown that Lee had at most 80,000 troops supported by 275 cannons.[100]

Meade quickly, and reluctantly, decided to retain Daniel Butterfield, Hooker's chief of staff and close friend, as his own chief of staff.[101] Meade had little experience in or with cavalry, forcing him to rely initially upon Pleasonton for most cavalry matters. Based upon Pleasonton's recommendation Meade did promote three cavalry captains, Elon J. Farnsworth, 26, Wesley Merritt, 29, and George Armstrong Custer, 24, to brigadier general.[102] Furthermore, Meade's limited view of cavalry was that its primary duty was to obtain reliable information while Pleasonton's view was that cavalry should fight battles.[103] Otherwise, no matter how exhausted the boys in blue were from days of hard marching, the search for Lee's army began immediately as the Army of the Potomac began moving north.[104] According to Edwin Coddingham, "Without missing a beat in tempo, in a little over two days after assuming command Meade had made a general advance of thirty miles and put his army in good position to meet a challenge from the enemy."[105]

## Stuart's Ride Continues

After processing his prisoners captured at Rockville, Stuart rode another thirty miles before arriving at Cooksville the next day, still 27 or 28 miles south of the Pennsylvania border. After quickly dispatching guards at Westminster, Maryland, the Federals' forward supply base, Stuart's troopers enjoyed their first good meal and some decent rest since June 24. Additionally forage was found for the horses but naturally distribution and feeding of the forage cost more time and sleep for the troopers.[106] Seventeen or 18 miles along the way after Cooksville, Stuart's cavalry captured another 400 prisoners.

With the extra burden of more prisoners, Stuart's pace was slowed even further, a pace that caused his advance unit on June 30 to run into Kilpatrick's rear guard at Hanover, Pennsylvania,[107] a town where six roads intersect six or seven miles north of the Pennsylvania line and just 14 miles east of Gettysburg. To avoid further engagements with Kilpatrick who was blocking the road to Carlisle,[108] Stuart had to take a five-mile detour before hiding until dark. Stuart then led a forced 20-mile march in the dark to the northeast—some riders sleeping in their saddles, others even falling from their mounts from sheer exhaustion. The next morning, Sunday, July 1, Day One of the Gettysburg battle, Stuart's exhausted riders finally reached Dover, Pennsylvania. Not only were the horses and riders exhausted, but the captured mules were badly fatigued, hungry, and thirsty, frequently becoming unmanageable, sometimes stubbornly refusing to move to cause more inconvenient delay for the rest of Stuart's column.[109]

Also, whereas Hanover was only 36 miles on a direct road from Lee's headquarters near Chambersburg, Dover was an additional eight air miles distant and no longer on a direct path to Chambersburg. But while his men rested at Dover, Stuart at last sent a small detachment to try to find Ewell,[110] who at that point was moving south to converge with Lee.

Stuart was beginning to realize Stoneman's lesson of the Chancellorsville raid that "to take the enemy by surprise and penetrate his country was easy enough, but to withdraw ... was a more difficult matter." Lee was also being reminded of the peril to a main army commander if he should allow cavalry, his eyes and ears, to remove itself from the main army while either on the move or in battle. Any gains from such raids or detached rides were seldom worth the costs of not knowing enemy deployments, not to mention the toll upon men and horses. Porter Alexander made essentially the same point as follows:

> ... in my humble opinion, it was bad play to let our cavalry to get out of touch & reach of our infantry. The first axiom of war is the mass one's strength. Then & only then can its fullest power be brought into play. As before stated, in the account of Chancellorsville, I think Hooker's defeat was due to the absence of his cavalry on just such a useless raid as this. I cannot say exactly what would have happened, but our force in hand at [the] opening of the [Gettysburg] fight would have been greater—& that might easily have changed the whole result. We took unnecessary risk, which was bad war, & the only bade war, too, I think in all our tactics. Everything else in the advance was excellently planned & executed....[111]

But while Lee complained about not having his eyes and ears due to Stuart's absence, Lee had after all directed that two brigades of cavalry remain to guard passes in the Blue Ridge where there would be very little action. Those two brigades had been ordered to report to Lee once the Federal cavalry crossed the Potomac but stayed back at the Blue Ridge. Furthermore two smaller, irregular cavalry units, one of which was essentially mounted infantry, were attached with Ewell. Together these two irregular cavalry units totaled approximately 5,800 riders.[112]

Nevertheless, Lee still managed to gather important intelligence from a civilian scout to alert Lee that Federal units were swiftly moving along a path roughly parallel with his army strung-out between Chambersburg and York.[113] Lee also learned from the same source that Meade had replaced Hooker. Lee promptly sent orders, the first being dated June 28, to his subordinate units to converge at Cashtown Gap near Shippensburg, Pennsylvania, north of the pike between Chambersburg and Gettysburg.[114]

Meanwhile on Stuart's ride, Fitz Lee also learned that Jubal Early, commanding Ewell's northern-most division, was returning from his advanced position near the Susquehanna River. Stuart also learned Lee's army was converging near Shippensburg; but rather than heading directly towards Shippensburg, Stuart started riding toward Carlisle, Pennsylvania, 22 miles to the northwest, where he hoped to find desperately needed provisions as well as Ewell's corps. But upon arriving at Carlisle, instead of finding other Confederate forces, Stuart found local militia, reinforced by artillery and a detachment of cavalry, altogether under the command of Baldy Smith.[115]

As previously noted, Smith was a capable veteran officer seldom reticent about criticizing the tactics or policies of his superiors. And so in the summer of 1863, being in disfavor with the Union military hierarchy because of his outspoken criticism of the Union tactics at Fredericksburg, and after a six week stint in command of the 9th Corps, Baldy found himself assigned to the relatively minor outpost of Carlisle.[116] Stuart, somewhat surprised by finding a Union garrison instead of Ewell's corps, made a demand for surrender that Smith promptly rejected, saying that he was willing "to meet J.E.B. Stuart in hell before he gave up the place."[117] In response to Smith's ungracious rejection, Stuart started shelling the town but soon received word of Lee's location. After burning the cavalry barracks as well as destroying parts of civilian buildings, Stuart at last headed for the main army, thirty miles to the south at Gettysburg, leaving at 1:30 a.m.

## Fighting Erupts at Gettysburg

In addition to ordering Ewell to finish foraging and instead to return toward the Cashtown area, Lee began to move his other two corps, first Powell Hill starting June 29 from their bivouac near Chambersburg to be followed by Longstreet, along the Chambersburg Pike toward Gettysburg.[118] Lee also assigned one of Longstreet's divisions, commanded by George E. Pickett, 38, to remain in Chambersburg to guard the immense bounty until the arrival of John D. Imboden's independent cavalry, expected to arrive in two days with its own impressive haul of captured bounty.[119] Lee also ordered that the two cavalry brigades guarding the passes in the Blue Ridge rejoin the main army[120] to move into the Cumberland Valley to protect the main army's line of communication as well as Lee's rear.[121]

As the successor to Stonewall Jackson's command of the 2nd Corps, Ewell began the Pennsylvania invasion in high fashion. Following his smashing success in overcoming the Federal garrison at Winchester, Old Baldy diligently complied with Lee's instructions to march to the Susquehanna River, south of Harrisburg.[122] As he progressed north through the Pennsylvania countryside Ewell's main task was to gather supplies, particularly foodstuffs, and toward this objective Ewell had performed as well as, if not better than, could have been expected. Between June 10 and June 29 Ewell's corps captured 28 guns, almost 4,000 prisoners, 5,000 barrels of flour, 3,000 head of cattle, trainloads of ordinance and medical stores at Chambersburg, in addition to food, horses, and quartermaster supplies that were seized and issued to his own men.[123] Despite his cavalry's laggard performance Ewell had moved briskly and efficiently to the point that on June 29 Early's division had Harrisburg in its sights when Ewell received Lee's orders of June 28 to rejoin the rest of Lee's army.[124]

Lee was always aware of the numerical odds against him, and usually tried to concentrate his forces so that he would have the numerical advantage at that particular point. A couple days while in Chambersburg, Pennsylvania, in late June 1863, Lee purportedly said, "I shall throw an overwhelming force on their advance, crush it, follow up the success, drive one corps back on another, and by successive repulses and surprises before they can concentrate create a panic and virtually destroy the army."[125] This sounded much like his success a couple months earlier at Chancellorsville, reflecting Lee's desire to be able to find and defeat individual corps isolated from the rest of the Northern army.

Meanwhile, Union cavalry was staying busy. In order to scout across the widest territory, the Blue riders were ordered to "fan out." Toward that end BGen. John Buford's 1st Cavalry division was thoroughly reconnoitering the area around Gettysburg, a village of 2,400 situated 26 miles east of Chambersburg. Sometimes it may seem as though the great battle of Gettysburg was the result of an accidental or random encounter but its geography almost made the encounter inevitable. At that point of Lee's invasion, control of eastern and southern Pennsylvania was a strategic imperative for both sides. Although the village itself was of little military significance, Buford knew the network of a dozen roads, including three which had all weather surfaces, intersecting at Gettysburg meant it was highly probable the two armies would meet there with the Confederates converging from the north and from the west[126]; by the same token, Union corps would be arriving via roads from the east and from the south. Once the respective armies arrived where these roads intersected the area's terrain, particularly the parallel ridges that offered linchpin positions for either side, created an ideal venue for a classic battle.

Buford entered the village from the south shortly before noon on June 30 just as the Gray brigade of BGen. James Pettigrew, 35—of Henry Heth's division in Hill's corps—was withdrawing to his main body in Cashtown to the west. Anxious residents in Gettysburg told Buford about Rebel activity in and around the village; from this information he adduced that the amount of activity was more than cavalry scouting. Accordingly Buford sent vedettes well beyond his defensive lines to gather additional information about the Rebel disposition. Buford then concluded that units of Lee's army would soon be approaching from the west along the road from Chambersburg. Accordingly he posted one of his brigades, William Gamble's, along the ridge to the south of the Chambersburg Pike while posting another, Thomas Devin's, astride and along the north of the road. A third brigade, to be used as Buford's reserve, was escorting the supply wagons and had not arrived by the evening of June 30.[127]

Pettigrew had withdrawn because he had been on a foraging mission under general orders from Lee to avoid any general engagement until Lee's army could be consolidated. When Pettigrew reported back to his superiors—A.P. Hill and Heth[128]—that cavalry had been spotted entering Gettysburg they—not realizing the extent of Union movement—

surmised that such cavalry must have merely been local militia. Responding to the rumors that badly needed shoes might be found in the village, Heth asked Hill if there would be any objection to looking for some such shoes.[129] Hill responded with a shrug, "None in the world."[130]

The lack of Gray cavalry—or more precisely Stuart—positioned close at hand for Lee meant he was operating with grossly inadequate information about the Federal units in the area. Had Stuart been scouting from Lee's headquarters, Stuart undoubtedly would have not confused Buford's division with local militia. While Lee probably would have still advanced toward Gettysburg (after all his army once consolidated should have easily overwhelmed an isolated cavalry division), most certainly he would have proceeded under drastically different alignment, including sending Stuart to scout ahead and to protect his flanks on the march.[131]

The van of Heth's division began to approach along the Chambersburg Pike at about 8:00 a.m. Wednesday, July 1, 1863. In classic dragoon fashion, Buford's dismounted troopers fired their breach loading carbines as rapidly as possible before retreating to their next defensive position. Buford was able to impede Heth's advance, but Heth also enjoyed the advantage of superior numbers; exploiting this advantage by 9:00 a.m. Heth began to spread out to envelope Buford's lines. Adding to Buford's concerns, he was also receiving reports that another Confederate formation was approaching from the north.

About that time Buford's friend, John Reynolds, rode up to Buford's headquarters. When Reynolds asked for a quick assessment Buford replied succinctly, "The devil's to pay!"[132] Reynolds then asked if Buford could hold on for one more hour until infantry reinforcements should arrive. Buford simply replied, "I reckon I can."[133]

Reynolds quickly decided that it was crucial to gain time so that defenses could be established along the ridges south and east of the village. He also sent couriers to hurry the 11th and 3rd Corps to Gettysburg and to send a message to Meade that a battle was developing.[134] Deftly using his horse artillery of six three inch rifles to supplement his carbines, Buford was able to hold McPherson's and Seminary Ridges west of Gettysburg until two infantry brigades arrived. Tragically Reynolds was shot dead from his saddle almost as soon as he sent these two brigades to the front,[135] and the Army of the Potomac abruptly a leader lost who many believed may have been its best general.

But Buford's work was not finished by the arrival of some infantry, welcome though it may have been. As the Union foot soldiers took their positions, Federal troopers deployed to protect either flank while feeding battlefield intelligence to the infantry commanders. Devin's brigade was aligned with Howard's 11th Corps. Devin's brigade gave ground as reluctantly as possible against Ewell's attack from the north but the 11th Corps met a fate similar to when Stonewall Jackson had launched his surprise flanking attack at Chancellorsville a mere two months earlier.

Within the larger frame of the three days of combat at Gettysburg, Buford's actions or Stuart's early absence might not have been, either individually or collectively, irreversible turning points, and no argument is made here that they alone were the principle reasons for the Gettysburg results.[136] What they do help to illustrate is that the proper use of cavalry could create a significant edge to the main army's efforts, especially when the main armies were on the move—with one army essentially in pursuit of the other—, and/or while preparing for battle. Union cavalry was at last becoming a positive factor while Confederate cavalry could no longer be deemed as always a major advantage for the Confederate infantry, especially if improperly deployed away from the main body. Only time would tell whether these lessons were learned, retained, and applied during the remainder of the war.

## *The Confederates Fail to Pursue*

By 1:00 p.m. when Meade received word of the death of Reynolds Meade instructed Winfield Scott Hancock to turn command of his 2nd Corps over to John Gibbon before proceeding immediately to take charge of the Federal forces at Gettysburg.[137] Hancock reminded Meade that Howard was senior to Hancock but Meade responded that he knew Hancock better than he knew Howard.[138] Hancock arrived at Cemetery Hill sometime between 4:00 and 4:30 p.m., and immediately met with Howard, who although senior in rank to Hancock,[139] would act as his subordinate on the battlefield.[140]

Although Hill's two lead divisions were having an uneven day, Ewell continued his superb afternoon. Notwithstanding his disappointment in not being able to capture the prize of Harrisburg, and not being aware of any great emergency, in two days Old Baldy had brought his first two divisions, including Early's, to within striking distance of Gettysburg; Ewell diverted his third division, commanded by Edward ("Allegheny") Johnson, to Chambersburg to protect and deliver the immense train of quartermaster and subsistence stores purchased, impressed, and simply confiscated during Ewell's foraging campaign of two weeks.[141] By the middle of the afternoon his two lead divisions linked with two of Hill's divisions to form a wide arc north and west of Gettysburg.[142] As Ewell's first two divisions approached Gettysburg the timing of his commanders had been perfect on several occasions.[143] Moving south and while beginning to form a battle line with Hill's two divisions to his right, he watched them rout the Federals at Oak Ridge and across the valley north of Gettysburg.[144]

Notwithstanding their initial overall success, by the end of Day One the Confederates nevertheless committed a failure of pursuit, specifically the failure to capture either Cemetery Hill or Culp's Hill, eerily reminiscent of Irvin McDowell's failure to pursue across the field during First Bull Run. Allen Guelzo characterizes this failure "as the most sensational Confederate misjudgment of the war,…"[145] Scott Bowden and Bill Ward go even further to determine that "Ewell's failure to pursue the foe he and his troops had vanquished was one of the most costly errors in American military history."[146]

Approaching the battlefield along with Hill, Lee became visibly disturbed by the possibility that matters had gotten out of hand.[147] But upon his arrival, Lee was pleased that Ewell and Hill, who had been "unwell all day,"[148] had severely damaged the Federal 11th Corps to the north of Gettysburg and the 1st Corps to the west of the village. Lee could also observe streams of survivors escaping through the village, making their way to the high ground east and to the south of the village.[149] Lee also knew the battle would continue as other Federal troops would arrive and that in all probability these new troops would assume positions along the ridge line extending to the south of the village, a ridge line we now know as Cemetery Ridge.

Although Powell Hill believed he and Ewell had accomplished a "complete" rout of the enemy,[150] Lee's trained eye immediately told him of the importance of seizing Cemetery

Hill to the north of the ridge since that prominence could dominate the ridge line where the Federals were likely to establish their defenses.[151] More immediately, since the Baltimore Pike ran across Cemetery Hill, Lee hoped to use occupation of the hills with their control of access to the pike to implement his plan to pick off more Union corps as they fed into the Gettysburg battlefield. Furthermore Cemetery Hill would dominate a possible escape route if the Federals were defeated and forced to leave the battlefield. By courier Lee, who believed Hill's units were in no shape to continue fighting, told Ewell that "…he [Lee] could see the enemy retreating over the hill…, that it was only necessary to press 'those people' in order to secure possession of the heights, and, if practicable, he wished General Ewell to do this."[152] Lee's courier caught up with Ewell in Gettysburg sometime after 5:45 p.m.[153] Ewell then conferred with his two available division commanders, Early and Robert Rodes, to ascertain the feasibility of taking the hill; collectively they became convinced it would not be a simple matter of walking up the hillside to take it.[154] Shortly after scouts reported that Culp's Hill was apparently unoccupied Ewell decided to concentrate instead upon that elevation,[155] located across the Baltimore Pike east of Cemetery Hill. However, when Ewell checked with Jubal Early, commander of the division closer to Culp's Hill, Early responded that "*his* command had been doing all the hard marching and fighting and was not in condition to make the move." (My emphasis added.)[156] Early also asserted that it was essential for somebody's soldiers to take Culp's Hill, a remark that Johnson took as an insult.

Leaning upon Lee's phrase "if practicable," coupled with Rodes' added protest that "the men were tired & footsore & he did not think would do any thing 'one way or the other,'"[157] Ewell determined that the lateness of the day coupled with the fatigue of the soldiers in both available divisions meant it was not practicable to take Culp's Hill either. Other factors that might have influenced Ewell's decision where he felt he could not position his artillery effectively to support an infantry attack upon the hills, he had to contend with approximately 4,000 prisoners, and he still lacked Allegheny Johnson's division.[158] Furthermore earlier in the day the one-legged Ewell had been knocked to the ground when a shell fragment killed his horse beneath him. Finally a message from Lee made clear to Ewell there would be no support to Ewell's right from Powell Hill.[159] Nor can we discount Stuart's absence, and the resultant lack of intelligence about how the hills were lightly defended at time, as another factor in Ewell's decision making process.[160]

Many of Ewell's subordinates, still being accustomed to the late Stonewall Jackson's aggressive style of command, were stunned by Ewell's reluctance to pursue. A Confederate private grumbled, "Why we failed to push on and occupy the heights around and beyond Gettysburg is one of the unsettled questions."[161] In an oversimplified exaggeration one officer claimed, "There was not one officer, not even a man, that did not expect that the war would be closed upon the hill that evening, for there were still two hours of daylight when the final charge was made, yet for reasons that have never been explained nor ever will be … someone made a blunder that lost the battle of Gettysburg, and humanly speaking, the Confederate cause."[162]

Later that evening Lee met personally with Ewell and his two division commanders who were still with him, Johnson being absent while trying to align his units in front of Culp's Hill.[163] It was Lee's first personal meeting with Ewell since June 9 when Ewell had set forth on his foraging mission. In essence Ewell and his division commanders still agreed that taking either Cemetery Hill or Culp's Hill was important but neither division commander felt his division was then up to the task. According to Jubal Early, Lee's disappointment was evident but was serious about attacking "the enemy as early as possible the next day"[164] thereby implicitly agreeing that the attack would not be made that night.

The next day, July 2, Johnson's division took all of Culp's Hill except for the very crest held by one Union brigade, the rest of their Federal comrades being redeployed to reinforce the Bluecoated left.[165] Arguably this was the real high water mark of the Confederacy but in any event the next day most the Union's 12th Corps, under acting commander Alpheus Williams, retook, repulsed, and reoccupied Culp's Hill for the remainder of the battle.

Given the importance of this issue it is not surprising there are differing, if not diametrically opposed, opinions about what portion, if any, of the responsibility for this failure rests upon the shoulders of Robert E. Lee. Most notably upon Lee's behalf Douglas S. Freeman, and other critics, argue that Lee, as a Southern gentleman, was merely being polite in the use of the term, "if practicable," and that Lee fully intended Ewell to take Cemetery Hill despite these other factors. In particular Freeman claimed Ewell simply was not accustomed to Lee's looser style of command that was in contrast to Ewell's former commander, Stonewall Jackson, whose orders were more explicit, more forceful, and more detailed.[166] Stackpole went even further in stating that, "[Ewell] lacked the self-assurance and initiative, possibly even the character necessary to exercise corps command in a decisive way."[167]

On the other hand Coddingham concluded that "Responsibility for the failure to make an all-out assault on Cemetery Hill on July 1 must rest with Lee."[168] While acknowledging Ewell was no Stonewall who might have successfully regrouped his units for another assault, Coddingham points out the narrow streets of the village proved to be a difficult obstacle, meaning "the Southern assault lost its momentum after the Federal lines were crushed."[169] According to Coddingham the chances for a successful pursuit were rapidly decreasing within an hour after the Federals retreated through Gettysburg, that retreat starting about 4:00 p.m. By 5:25 p.m. Hancock proclaimed the Union position was one that "cannot be well taken."[170] Instead of relying solely upon Ewell's corps that had recently marched twenty-five miles, Lee should have acted sooner to have also deployed other, relatively unscathed units from Hill Corps.[171] Guelzo notes the decision not to continue the pursuit was "neither Hill's nor Ewell's—if Robert E. Lee had thirsted to drive the Yankees off Cemetery Hill or Culp's Hill, he certainly knew how to give the orders for it."[172] After all there would be time tomorrow to finish the job, or so they thought.

The foregoing opinions tend to reflect near unanimous conclusions that for several reasons Ewell did not measure up to the standards usually set by his predecessor, Stonewall Jackson. (These standards normally excuse Jackson's less than stellar performance during Seven Days or even Ox Hill.) But Lee, notwithstanding Ewell's shortcomings, bears the ultimate responsibility for the irreparable failure at Cemetery Hill at the end of Day One. While not in direct, face-to-face contact with Ewell until after it was too late to occupy either hill that evening Lee was on the battlefield, able to observe the situation, and able to communicate with Ewell at least by courier. Much is made by the ambiguity of the word "practicable," a word used by Lee and for which he alone bears the responsibility for the difficulty it may have created or caused. And even if Lee did desire that the hill be taken that evening, and indeed he was visibly disappointed when it became evident that it would not be taken that evening—as Early contended—a commander's desire is often not enough to accomplish the intended result. The commander must use the tools at his disposal, including the quality of his orders, to bring intended results to fruition! And even further if Lee was merely being polite, as Freeman contended, style matters for little on battleground management. By giving Ewell some degree of latitude Lee cannot escape the ultimate responsibility for the manner in which that discretion might have been exercised.

Lee was also guilty of, and bears the responsibility for, underestimating his enemy's capacity to mount a proper battlefield defense, including the primary target of Cemetery Hill. Apparently Lee—not realizing how quickly more Federal corps could arrive at Gettysburg—concluded his conference with Ewell and Old Baldy's subordinates with the thought that there would be time tomorrow to finish the job. Indeed to do just that, i.e., finish the job, Lee planned that Ewell would continue to attack the hill from the north the next morning while Longstreet, arriving with two of his divisions, would march up or northward along Emittsburg Pike to attack the hill from the south. This reflected Lee's tendency to predicate his plans on conditions as he wished them to be rather than reality; instead of finding Cemetery Hill to be lightly defended the next morning the Confederates discovered not only Howard entrenched on Cemetery Hill but Slocum finished his march to occupy Culp's Hill, becoming the barb of the Union's fishhook defensive line. Additionally Hancock had moved his 2nd Corps along the ridge south of Cemetery Hill and, more discombobulating, Dan Sickles had moved his 3rd Corps almost directly in front of Longstreet's intended line of march.

Although Ewell and Hill had probably inflicted about as much damage to Federal personnel as was possible for Day One, the failure to pursue to capture Cemetery Hill had momentous consequences during the remainder of the Gettysburg battle. The Federals' new defensive posture on the morning of Day Two forced Lee and Longstreet to change their plan of attack and while, as will be described in the next chapter, the Confederates still achieved significant battlefield gains during Day Two the Southerners were never able to gain occupation of either eminence for the remainder of the battle. Accordingly by not pursuing to take Cemetery Hill—the more valuable piece of real estate—the Confederates forfeited an opportunity to dominate the Federal defenses being established along Cemetery Ridge and to be able to lend devastating artillery support to subsequent Southern infantry attacks on Days Two and Three. Several years after the war, Meade, in answer to Ewell's question, "stated flatly that if Ewell had pushed his advantage and attacked Cemetery Hill during the afternoon of the first day (as Lee had directed him to do, "if practicable") he would unquestionably have driven the disorganized off the hill, which in turn would have uncovered the rest of Cemetery Ridge and changed the entire complexion of the Federal buildup."[173]

## Dénouements and Precursors

Federal command of the battlefield remained in flux throughout the remainder of July 1. After Henry Slocum eventually arrived at the battlefield with his 12th Corps and assumed overall command, Hancock returned to Meade's headquarters at Taneytown. Meade then rode to the battlefield, arriving shortly after midnight, to assume overall charge meaning that seven Union generals had been in successive control of the battlefield during the first day's start of the battle.[174]

Upon his arrival at Gettysburg, Meade—no stickler to seniority—also bypassed Doubleday to appoint the Virginian MGen. John Newton, 40, to take Reynolds' place as commander of the 1st Corps. Another West Point graduate, Newton's record had much in common with Meade's, having been engaged prior to the war in the construction of fortifications, lighthouses, rivers and harbors. But once the war began Newton was involved in several battles in the Eastern theater. Most recently Newton had been a division in the 6th Corps; shortly after Fredericksburg, Newton and a brigadier took a leave of absence to meet with Lincoln to express their opposition to Burnside's plan for another offense against Fredericksburg, an act they probably realized was insubordinate.[175] Purportedly Newton was a "pet" of Meade's who had an "animosity" toward Doubleday based on "past political differences."[176] Newton was an affable, fidgety, good-natured man with ability to scrutinize the terrain. Regretfully he squandered his talents with his laziness, self-indulgence, and heavy drinking.[177] Taaffe says Meade would have done better to give the corps to someone else.[178]

The value of occupation of Cemetery Hill was vividly proven on Day Three when Federal artillery upon Cemetery pummeled Rebel infantry without mercy as the Johnnies in the so-called Pickett's Charge attempted to get into position to assault the Federal defenses along Cemetery Ridge. And again this is conjectural, but Lee and Ewell should have had better intelligence about the lack of strength of defenses on Cemetery Hill had Stuart's cavalry been available for scouting that key piece of terrain on Day One. All of this underscores the importance of pursuit on the battlefield, as well as afterwards, and why the availability and proper deployment of cavalry was an integral, essential element of successful pursuit.

# 17

# Lee and Meade After Gettysburg
## July 4-14, 1863

## Ending the Battle

Jeb Stuart finally arrived at Robert Lee's headquarters sometime during the afternoon of Day Two. According to legend Lee's terse comment was, "Well, General Stuart, you are here at last."[1] When Stuart tried to mitigate the matter by saying he had captured 125 wagons, Lee brusquely replied, "They are an impediment to me now."[2]

Much of the genesis of the Myth of the Lost Cause is rooted in Day Two when James Longstreet urged Lee to take another tack before he—Longstreet—belatedly started to implement Lee's initial plan.[3] Stuart's continued absence on the morning of Day Two meant Lee's plan of attack was devised upon faulty intelligence about the disposition of the Federal defenders.[4] In the absence of cavalry to do his reconnoitering, Lee sent small group of staff officers[5] who apparently were mistaken about the location of the Federal units. Additionally cavalry would have been available to discover the Sickles Salient that at the very least caused last minute confusion, and more delay, by Longstreet's command.

By the time the Confederates' attack finally was launched additional Federal corps had arrived to be placed in critical positions in the Union defenses along Cemetery Ridge. Noah Andre Trudeau notes that Day Two was one of the Civil War's most intense battles.[6] Day Two also generated several Civil War iconic landmarks, known for instance as the Fishhook, the Devil's Den, Plum Run, the Wheat Field, the Peach Orchard, Sickles Salient, Cemetery Hill, and perhaps most famously Little Round Top. Aside from Daniel Sickles' 3rd Corps, which was mauled before being forced to retreat hastily from its salient, most of the Union defensive lines held their positions but undoubtedly the Confederates had been able to make significant advances beyond their original positions on or near Seminary Ridge.[7] By most accounts, and notwithstanding several intelligence and command difficulties—for instance purportedly Lee was not feeling his best—Day Two at Gettysburg was a narrow victory for the Confederates even though they were unable to drive the Federals from the field.[8]

Accordingly by nightfall of Thursday, July 2, 1863—Day Two of Gettysburg—Robert E. Lee believed he was at the cusp of achieving a hugely important, decisive victory.[9] Various historians may disagree about Lee's strategic objective for coming north into central Pennsylvania, some contending that Lee was making a wide flanking movement before turning east to attack one of the Northern cities; there is also some indication that Lee believed he could find, catch and destroy several of the isolated Union corps; others believe Lee intended little more than a sizable raid to replenish badly needed and scarce supplies, hopefully without having to engage the enemy.[10] But for whatever reason or reasons Lee may have had for crossing the Potomac River less than a week earlier, he was now quickly making plans and preparations to annihilate the Union's largest and most prominent army, a victory that would gain tremendous strategic importance for the Confederacy.[11]

In his book, *Gettysburg: A Testing of Courage*, Trudeau claims Lee's reasons for renewing "his offensive on July 3 were largely illusory."[12] Illusory or not, from Lee's perspective during the evening of July 2 and morning of July 3 he still had several reasons to believe his army was in position and capable of gaining a great decisive victory for the Confederacy. For instance at the northern corner of the Union's lines, Dick Ewell's corps seemed to be in position to take Culp's Hill—the barb of the Union's Fishhook—which if taken would give the Confederates a commanding position of much of the northern sector of the battlefield, including Federal defensive positions.

In order to parlay the gains of Day Two into an annihilative victory, Lee planned to complete the capture of Culp's Hill while launching a massive frontal assault that would concentrate against the center of the Union lines, identified then and forever as the Copse of Trees. Lee's aim was that such a massive concentration following a lengthy cannonade would force a breach of the Union line, a rupture that would precipitate a collapse of the entire defenses along Cemetery Ridge. Lee also anticipated such a collapse would result in a mad, uncontrolled scramble to the rear; to prevent the Federal forces from escaping, Lee dispatched Stuart to go around the northern end of the Union positions—in other words around the Fishhook—and then to get to the Union rear where Stuart would be able to capture or kill Yankees fleeing in disarray.[13]

However, Lee's best laid plans started to go astray from the very beginning. First, during the evening of Day Two George Meade anticipated that Lee would attack the center of the Union lines and advised his generals to be prepared for such an attack.[14] Winfield Scott Hancock's 2nd Corps, probably the strongest corps in the Army of the Potomac, and led by the army's most capable commander, manned this portion of the Union lines while Meade took pains to assure reinforcements would be available during the ensuing attack. Second, pre-dawn on Day Three the Federals made a preemptive strike to recapture Culp's Hill thereby denying those potential artillery positions to the Confederates.[15] Next the artillery cannonade—so loud that it could be heard almost a hundred miles away—was largely ineffective in terms of softening Union defenses.[16]

Finally, the frontal assault—infamously the so-called Pickett's Charge—apparently was not given Lee's intended full support. Lee never said so in so many words but, according to Porter Alexander, Lee envisioned three assault lines of fourteen infantry brigades—initially extending more than two miles in length—would be formed for the charge but for reasons still not clearly understood only two of those lines of nine brigades participated in the charge.[17] Later in the night Lee purportedly told John Imboden that "…if [Pickett's Division] had been supported as they were meant to have been—but for some reason, not yet fully explained to me, were not—we would have held the position, & the day would have been ours."[18] Alexander's conjecture was that Lee's undersized staff simply failed to prepare or distribute the orders necessary to direct the five additional brigades to form a third line.[19]

But Federal efforts should not be overlooked or ignored. When asked several years later what went wrong, George Pickett[20] replied he "always thought the Yankees had something to do with it."[21] As mentioned, Meade did correctly anticipate the focus of the Confederate attack and positioned his defenders accordingly. The Union enjoyed enflating positions, not only by the 8th OVI from the north but also by the 13th and 16th Rhode Island from the south; although the Rebels pre-assault cannonade was largely ineffective, afterwards Federal artillery poured devastating fire into the Rebel ranks as they approached the largely entrenched Yankee defenders.[22] The combination of artillery and musket fire decimated the Rebel lines as they kept closing ranks to advance toward the Copse of Trees. But despite all these advantages in favor of the Union, some of the lead elements of the Confederate assault still managed to force a small breach of the Union line some fifty yards north of the Copse of Trees, only to be quickly repulsed by Federal reinforcements. Meade—with extraordinary individual help from Hancock—was able to amass a larger number of soldiers at the breach, thereby compelling the attackers to relent before trudging back to their original positions where by a distraught Lee met them. The temporary breach by Pickett's Charge of the Union lines has been remembered forever, and perhaps inaccurately, as the High Tide of the Confederacy.

## Cavalry Encounters on Day Three

The other thrust of Lee's plan, i.e., Jeb Stuart's movement to the rear of the Federal lines also met with failure. Stuart led his three available brigades, along with fourteen pieces of artillery—altogether about 8,000 riders—three miles to the east of Gettysburg. Stuart's objectives, in addition to capturing Federal soldiers who would supposedly be in retreat, were to get into and disrupt the Union rear while cutting off its lines of communications along the Baltimore Pike. If Pickett's Charge were to succeed Stuart would be in position to apply the *coup de grâce*.[23]

The Union cavalry division of BGen. David McM. Gregg, 30, was patrolling that sector with approximately 5,000 men supported by 10 artillery pieces. Gregg had been assigned to scout and protect the right or northern flank of the Union lines while H. Judson Kilpatrick was at the southern portion of the Yankee defenses near the Round Tops. Given all the wear and tear of the men and horses of John Buford's division, on Day Two Meade had sent that division back to Westminster, Maryland, the Union supply base twenty-five miles east of Gettysburg, for rest, refitting, and re-shoeing.

Gregg also had three brigades at his disposal; one of these brigades—commanded by George A. Custer, now a brigadier general after holding a captain's rank less than a month earlier at Brandy Station[24]—was detached from Kilpatrick's division. Paradoxically the Confederate assault on the other side of Cemetery Ridge and the Union's cavalry defense behind Cemetery Ridge would feature generals—Custer and Pickett—with one thing in common: both had finished last in their respective graduating classes at West Point![25]

After Stuart had looped around the top of the Union's Fishhook and was turning south toward his intended destination, at about 1:00 p.m. two of his brigades were met by Gregg's troopers blocking the way to the Baltimore Pike.[26] Stuart fired his artillery, most of which was aimed at Custer who responded in kind. Just then Alfred Pleasonton, the Union's cavalry corps commander, sent a message ordering Custer to return to his parent division under Kilpatrick to the south.²⁷ However, when John B. McIntosh, commanding the brigade at the right of Gregg's line, became engaged in an artillery duel with Stuart, McIntosh sent word asking Gregg to countermand Pleasanton's order and keep Custer in the fight against Stuart. Not requiring much prompting, Custer was glad to join McIntosh's tussle with Stuart. The brigades led by McIntosh and Custer fought mounted and dismounted, attacking and counterattacking.

The sides furiously see-sawed throughout the afternoon until Wade Hampton led his brigade in a last ditch effort to break the blue jackets' defenses. Custer led his brigade to meet Hampton head on, the two enemy columns clashing as they rushed toward one another. In particular Custer—with his long blond hair—led a spectacular charge that propelled him to fame as a flamboyant but effective man at arms until Little Big Horn a few years later.²⁸ "So sudden and violent was the collision that many of the horses were tuned end over end, and crushed their riders beneath them. The clashing of sabers, the firing or pistols, … now filled the air."

Finally a lull occurred at 4:00 p.m.²⁹ when another Confederate brigade, led by Wade Hampton, appeared. But McIntosh had been gathering loose, unattached groups of troopers to form an attack against Hampton's flank. The Rebels were repulsed when Hampton was badly wounded during McIntosh's flanking attack, Hampton being almost blinded by blood flowing from a re-opened wound on his skull.³⁰ Under attack from his front as well as from his flank, Hampton had little choice except to withdraw back to his starting point. Once Hampton's brigade withdrew the sides had fought to a standstill but the Confederates had no more fresh troops while the Federals still had another fresh brigade in reserve. But more importantly the Confederates failed to reach their objective of disrupting the Federal rear.

Although this cavalry battle ended in a tactical stalemate, Gregg summarized the engagement's results as "[Stuart's] was to do, ours to prevent." In the immediate sense, Stuart's offensive was immaterial since there was no significant rupture of the Union lines along Cemetery Ridge; this cavalry battle—one of the larger such engagements of the Civil War—once again showed that when properly led Union cavalry was as capable at fighting as were its Rebel counterparts.

Another cavalry engagement on Day Three demonstrated the polar extremes of effective Union cavalry. To the Federal left at about 5:00 p.m.—after Pickett's Charge was dissipating—Kilpatrick ordered one of his regiments to make a cavalry assault across terrain that was unfavorable to horsemen against dug-in Confederate infantry.³¹ Indeed the Union regiment, led by the newly promoted Elon Farnsworth, had already made two predictably unsuccessful charges against infantry lodged along the western base of Big Round Top. After Farnsworth said there was not "the slightest chance for a successful charge," Kil-Calvary—showing convincingly his nickname was well deserved—taunted Farnsworth by insinuating that Farnsworth was afraid to lead the third charge.³² Farnsworth then proceeded to lead his troops in a brave, gallant charge, prescient of the Charge of the Light Guard made famous several years later by Alfred Tennyson. As should as have been foreseen by any sensible commander, Farnsworth's charge was disastrous with almost a quarter of the 300 Union troopers being killed or wounded. Farnsworth himself was retrieved from the battlefield with five mortal wounds just a few weeks short of his 26th birthday.

Had Stuart with his three brigades stayed closer to Lee, and if Lee had a better assessment of what lay ahead, perhaps the general engagement that Lee wanted to avoid would

## 17. Lee and Meade After Gettysburg

never have happened, at least not at Gettysburg.[33] Or perhaps Lee would have deployed Hill's corps in a more effective manner. Or once the combatants were engaged, perhaps Lee and Ewell would have been in a better position to have tried to take either Cemetery Hill or Culp's Hill on Day One.

If the Confederates' pursuit could have captured either hill in a timely manner and could have established artillery on either prominence the balance of firepower should have shifted in the Confederates' favor in support of their assaults on Days Two and Three.

Regardless of these might-have-beens, Lee certainly realized the abrupt turning of his army's fortunes; within twenty-four hours he had gone from seeming to be at the cusp of a great victory to urgently needing to salvage his army's future. Lee lost 28,000 men or a remarkable 33 percent of his army; in comparison Meade lost "only" 23,000 men but more significantly only 20 percent of his army.[34] Despite the profound disappointment of suffering this turn of events, Lee did not dither but instead immediately began to make plans for the withdrawal of his army from Gettysburg and the subsequent retreat back to Virginia. As was typical for Lee he never articulated a list of reasons for his decision to retreat; but he had seen first-hand that he had delivered his best shot without defeating or even dislodging the Army of the Potomac. Furthermore, and most ominously, the Rebels' ammunition chests were running low with perhaps only enough for one day's fighting.[35] Another major consideration was that Ewell's raid of central Pennsylvania, extending almost to Harrisburg, had—together with Imboden's efforts—been extraordinarily successful and profitable, yielding badly needed plunder, including more than 100,000 head of livestock. Delivering these captured supplies and livestock back to Virginia would salvage some degree of success for Lee's foray into Northern territory, but more importantly would go a long ways in sustaining the Army of Northern Virginia so that it would have the capacity to fight another day.

## Lee Starts His Retreat

Retreating from Gettysburg was not going to be a simple matter of just reforming his army into a column before departing in a leisurely manner. To the contrary Lee had a multitude of challenges if he and his army were to reach Virginia without being rendered *hors de combat*. There was of course the matter of wrangling the herd of 50,000 head of cattle, 50,000 sheep, plus a huge number of hogs and other animals. Controlling and moving 4,000 captured prisoners also added to the difficulties of staying ahead of Meade's army. Lee proposed to Meade that they exchange each other's prisoners but Meade knew that he could and would simply send his prisoners to the rear where they would not be a burden to his efforts.[36] Thus Meade sensibly declined Lee's offer to exchange prisoners, probably no surprise to Lee.[37]

And then Lee had to manage the transportation of his wounded. During the three days of the battle of Gettysburg the Confederates suffered 14,497 wounded; Lee left 6,8902 of these wounded in houses, barns, churches, schools, other public buildings in the Gettysburg area as well as on the battlefield, mostly to be entrusted to the care of an treatment by Union medical personnel[38] together with a handful of Confederate surgeons selected to also remain in Gettysburg.[39] Lee's concern for those wounded soldiers not abandoned in and around Gettysburg extended past humanitarian reasons; the Confederate pool of personnel was limited much more so than was the Federal manpower pool. Accordingly it was imperative that the Confederacy recover, treat, and hopefully rehabilitate as many wounded soldiers as soon as possible for return to active duty, especially if the war were to become a contest of attrition, something that seemed more likely since Lee's gamble for a knockout victory had failed. Altogether the non-ambulatory among the 7,695 wounded taken back to the medical evacuation network in the Shenandoah Valley required a train of wagons and ambulances seventeen miles in length. Once in Staunton, 200 miles away, the wounded would be forwarded by train to Richmond.[40]

Lee's tactical challenge was to extract his three corps, stretching five miles from end-to-end, and to reform these three corps along with his wounded and the captured bounty before setting forth to the Potomac River, some 35 straight-line miles distant at Williamsport—a thriving river port town—via Hagerstown. To reach Hagerstown, Lee's army had to cross the South Mountain range, which could be traversed only through six narrow, steep passes gaps or passes, the strategically important passes being the Cashtown Pass and Monterey Pass, ten miles further south. Although the approaches to the passes were steep and narrow making them difficult to climb they would also provide excellent terrain for obstructing any pursuit. One other gap, the Fairfield Gap, was between the eastern foot of South Mountain and the northwestern slope of Jack's Mountain; this gap provided passage to Monterey.

By most accounts, Lee—given his undersized staff—himself planned and orchestrated his army's retreat. Kent Masterson Brown is confident Lee, as a student of the military arts, would have been aware of the axioms for retreating by Jomini and Clusewitz, including the necessity of make a slow fighting retreat.[41] Lee decided to divide his command into two separate retreat components with one of those to consist mainly of the wounded not left at Gettysburg. The other much larger component would consist of Lee's three infantry corps that of course would also have their own supply trains together with the remainder of Stuart's cavalry brigades.

By 11:00 p.m. at the end of Day Three BGen. John D. Imboden was already summoned to report to Lee's headquarters. Imboden, a forty-year-old lawyer, former legislator, and businessman, commanded an independent, undisciplined cavalry unit that was largely viewed as a group of foragers rather than as a conventional fighting cavalry.[42] Two hours later, after Lee had returned from A.P. Hill's headquarters where orders had been issued for the rest of the Army of Northern Virginia, Lee instructed Imboden to accompany and protect the so-called train of wounded to Williamsport.[43] Imboden would be augmented with five batteries of artillery selected from Lee's three corps. Additionally the cavalry brigades of Fitz Lee and Hampton would protect Imboden's rear and flanks.[44] Imboden should leave as soon as possible[45] to take his train of wounded toward Chambersburg through the Cashtown Gap before turning south toward Williamsport.[46] Imboden's wagon train—described by one observer as "a motley procession of wagons, ambulances, wounded men on foot, straggling soldiers and band boys,…"[47]—was completely assembled in the afternoon of the 4th and by 4:00 p.m. immediately began to leave Gettysburg before climbing into the Cashtown Gap. Imboden left Cashtown at 8:00 p.m. to ride toward the head of the column, taking four hours to do so.[48]

Lee's other column consisted of his three infantry corps, plus Ewell's reserve or supply train then 40 miles long[49]—largely consisting of the livestock herd and other booty captured or seized by Ewell prior to returning to Gettysburg, but also including the 4,000 Union prisoners. Lee directed this column—led by Ewell's massive supply train followed by Hill's corps—to follow the Fairfield road through the village of Fairfield—at the eastern base of Jack's Mountain, part of the South Mountain—the shortest way to Hagerstown.[50]

The Fairfield road forks at Fairfield with neither fork offering easy passage, especially considering how the rains of the past few days were turning surfaces into knee-deep quagmires. The right fork, called the Maria Furnace road, circled around the north of Jack's Mountain before continuing through the Fairfield Gap to eventually connect with the Emmitsburg-Waynesboro Turnpike atop Monterey Pass.[51] After clearing the Monterey Pass Ewell's reserve train would proceed down the mountain's western slope. Once in the Cumberland Valley the column would turn south proceeding approximately eleven miles to Hagerstown. The Fairfield route meant Lee's main body would be taking a shorter arc inside Imboden's train of the wounded.

Late during the night of July 3—Day Three—Dick Ewell instructed his quartermaster, Maj. John A. Harmon,[52] who had served so admirably in the same capacity for Stonewall Jackson, "to get [Ewell's] train safely across the Potomac or he wanted to see his face no more."[53] Lee's Army of Northern Virginia, by then reduced to 47,000 effectives, began to constrict its lines closer to its retreat routes while preparing for a possible counterattack.[54] After consolidating into interior lines along Seminary Ridge, Lee's army slowly and methodically began to head back toward Virginia. By 3:00 a.m. of July 4, Ewell's reserve train under Harmon's command, with all the confiscated and/or "impressed" bounty, formed along the Fairfield Road, and began to leave the Fairfield area, heading for the Fairfield Gap. Lee expected Ewell's trains to take fifteen hours to clear Fairfield.[55]

Obviously the village of Fairfield—approximately eight miles southwest of Gettysburg—was a key juncture. Ironically during the Day Three battle a single Union cavalry regiment rode unsupported to Fairfield after a small column of wagons was reported to be in the area. The Yankees blundered into Grumble Jones' cavalry brigade on picket duty that had been recalled from the Blue Ridge. After a brief but brutal fight, the Blue riders fled in a wild rout.[56] Since this encounter was along the route where the Confederates would be retreating, it might seem the Union had inadvertently squandered a great opportunity[57]; however holding that juncture for long by a single cavalry regiment might have been problematic against the weight of Lee's entire army.

A torrential rain began shortly after noon on July 4. Hill's corps, in the center of the line along Seminary Ridge, withdrew first to follow and to protect the trains; as they were leaving Hill's soldiers lit pine tar fires to create thick, black smoke along their fortifications in order to further screen their movements. By 9:00 on the evening of July 4 Harmon was leading the head of Ewell's wagon train into Hagerstown,[58] forty miles by road from Gettysburg,[59] while the rear of the train was still passing through Monterey Pass followed by quartermaster, subsistence, ordinance, and ambulances from the various divisions in Lee's main army.[60]

As the sun set on July 4 the Rebel's main army began its "retirement," led by the remnants of Pickett's division, reduced to that of a good sized regiment.[61] Pickett's down-sized division was guarding 4,000 Federal prisoners, most of whom had not eaten for three days and for whom there would be few if any rations from their captors.[62] Hill's corps—still in the center of the constricted line—was next in line followed by Longstreet then Ewell bringing up the rear to serve as a screening force. As commander of the last corps Ewell tried to assure the column covered as much distance as possible over the rough, winding roads.[63] This order of march would be rotated each day, in part to assure that the rear guard remained fresh.[64]

## *Meade's Initial Reaction*

As early as July 4 when a couple Union patrols tried to find the location of the Confederate lines, fragmentary reports—including some from village residents and others from Rebel deserters—began to indicate the Confederates were withdrawing from their Seminary Ridge lines. Slocum personally led a brigade-sized expedition shortly after 10:30 a.m. to discover the Confederates had withdrawn to undetermined positions at least a mile behind their previous positions. Additionally signal station sent reports late that same afternoon suggesting a Rebel withdrawal[65] but the question about their new location remained.

As commanding general George Meade was responsible for organizing and managing the Army of the Potomac's counter stroke. History's conventional assessment of the events immediately after Gettysburg is that Meade lacked the will power or aggressiveness to effectively pursue Lee's retreat and thus forfeited a golden opportunity to bag Lee before he and his army could reach the safety of Virginia across the Potomac. Unfortunately for Meade and his legacy much of that assessment is colored by Lincoln's reaction using King James rhetoric expressing his disappointment after Lee returned across the Potomac back into Virginia.[66] Additionally a good portion of Lincoln's reaction was based upon reports from generals who were either misinformed themselves or else had little to no reason to put Meade in the best possible light.

This is not an apologia for Meade nor is it an attempt to promote him to the pantheon of leading Union generals—that pantheon usually thought to consist of U.S. Grant, W.T. Sherman, Phil Sherman, and George Thomas. However when analyzing Meade's command decisions and actions during the nine day period starting July 4, it is useful, if not essential, to put Meade in the context of his circumstances at the time. In looking at the proper context—and without hoping one way or the other whether Lee's army should have been somehow eliminated—we can, or ought to, realize that an analysis of combat decisions often incorporate more factors than mere statistics or lines drawn on a map.

The first and most obvious consideration of course was that Meade was not appointed as commander of the Army of the Potomac until only three days prior to the opening salvos of Gettysburg. Meade had not sought the appointment and accepted it only because he was told he had no choice. His appointment occurred during a very fluid period when the seven infantry corps of the Army of the Potomac were separated by several miles on the move to an undefined objective, hardly an ideal situation for establishing command relationships or procedures. And of course the next three days of battle hardly gave Meade or his subordinates much opportunity to plan or to prepare for any post-battle action, especially since the outcome of the battle would remain in substantial doubt until Pickett's charge was repulsed.

It is difficult to find another instance when a major army commander was appointed on such short notice before a major battle, let alone a battle as momentous as Gettysburg.

Lincoln's appointment of George McClellan shortly before Antietam might come to mind but McClellan's "new" command included his temporarily downsized Army of the Potomac. McClellan's staff remained intact while he and most of the corps commanders were familiar and comfortable with each other. Furthermore, while McClellan's rapid reorganization of the bedraggled, demoralized units in and around Washington was extraordinary by any measure, it must also be noted that 16 days lapsed between McClellan's appointment of his enlarged command and the onset of the battle along Antietam Creek.

Henry Halleck's original orders to Meade were to stay between Lee, on one hand, and Washington and Baltimore on the other.[67] Accordingly Meade saw his mission not to destroy or capture Lee's army but rather to protect these east coast cities from Lee. Sometimes one difference between good or merely competent commanders on one hand and great commanders on the other hand is that the former tends to be hidebound to specific or literal orders while the great commanders are able to envision larger objectives and/or possibilities and to take initiative accordingly. It simply was not Meade's character to deviate from strategic orders.

It is only conjectural whether Meade would have reacted differently—in other words more audaciously or decisively—if he had been in command for a significantly longer period before determining the proper course of action upon the repulse of Pickett's charge on Friday afternoon, July 3, 1863. But having been elevated to army command only a week earlier he evidently did not feel confident to expand significantly upon Halleck's orders. When appointed to command the entire army, Meade was junior in seniority to three of his corps commanders and by the end of battle Meade had lost the services of two of his best commanders, John Reynolds, who was killed, and Winfield Scott Hancock, who was badly wounded on the final day of Gettysburg. Additionally Meade had to replace a third corps commander, Daniel Sickles, but whether that was a gain or loss may be an open question.[68]

Another factor not sufficiently appreciated by those not on the field was that by the end of July 3 the Union soldiers were fatigued and under-nourished after days of extraordinarily arduous and long marches followed immediately by three days of battle.[69] Many, perhaps as many as half in some corps,[70] Yank soldiers were unshod form the hard marching bringing them to Gettysburg. The Federal army needed to replace 2,000 cavalry horses plus another 1,500 artillery horses.[71] The surviving horses in Meade's army—so vital in any pursuit—had not been fed or shod for several days.[72] Furthermore the Union's highly heralded supply system had not been able to stay with the army and it would be another day before the army's quartermaster would finally be able to get urgently needed supply trains rolling along the Baltimore Pike to Gettysburg.

Meade was also handicapped when he inherited Hooker's Chief of Staff, MGen. Daniel Butterfield, a good and gallant soldier but without a good relationship with Meade. Essentially Butterfield's loyalties remained with Hooker, Butterfield being reluctant to share vital information with Meade. Butterfield received a painful wound on Day Three, forcing him to go home on July 5 to convalesce.

Additionally, prior to his Gettysburg defense, much of Meade's combat experience had been to lead offenses against Rebel defenses, including as a brigade commander during the Peninsula campaign, and as a division commander at Antietam and at Fredericksburg where his division advanced as far, if not further, than any other Union division. Although

Meade had little experience as a troop commander prior to the Civil War, as an engineer and given his experience in these unsuccessful ventures, he readily appreciated the difficulties of taking the offensive against entrenched Confederates. Adding to Meade's innate apprehensions, BGen. Francis Barlow, 29, who had been behind enemy lines recovering from a wound since Day One, sent Meade a message on July 4 that Lee's apparent evacuation was a feint designed to entrap Meade.[73] Meade probably was not surprised to learn the Southerners were pulling out of their Gettysburg lines; the question was whether Lee was leading his army in retreat back to Virginia or was Lee merely repositioning his defenses to be entrenched somewhere in the South Mountains. During that evening Meade said in a letter to his wife that he had notion of giving the Rebels the chance to "play their old game of shooting us from behind their breastworks."[74]

Meade's relative inexperience with cavalry in his command was another factor working to his disadvantage compounded by having to rely upon his ineffectual cavalry corps chief, Alfred Pleasonton. Despite his seniority in cavalry, Pleasonton basically remained a desk general unprepared to lead his command in the most concerted, productive manner. For instance, Pleasonton was still in Frederick on Day One when Buford was performing extraordinary service against the approaching Rebels. Later Buford's division was sent to Westminster to refit, re-shoe his horses and to draw more ammunition; accounts differ about the actual necessity of sending Buford to the rear but regardless Pleasonton seemed to have forgotten to replace Buford at Gettysburg.

Furthermore, for unknown reasons, Pleasanton split much of David Gregg's division among infantry and other cavalry commands. Not only did this fragmentation reduce the combat effectiveness of Gregg's troopers but it left Gregg—an experienced cavalry commander—with practically nothing to do.[75]

As soon became evident, on Saturday, July 4, 1863, Meade did not have a comprehensive plan of action, in large part because he was unsure of Lee's movements. Rather than devising a deployment of cavalry that might be complementary to Meade's main army, Pleasonton sent his cavalry to strike at the enemy's rear and lines of communication to "harass and annoy him as much as possible in his retreat."[76] Since Meade was in the dark about his enemy he could have made more productive use of his cavalry if its primary mission had been to scout and discover Lee's movements. Not only would this deployment hamper Meade's capacity to gather badly needed intelligence, but trying to harass and annoy Lee's army, including Stuart's now fully reconstituted cavalry, would inflict needless wear and tear upon the Union's troops and their mounts. It had been shown repeatedly during the first two plus years of the Civil War that cavalry was ineffective against large groups of infantry but that lesson seemed to have escaped Pleasonton.

Meade also lost two factors that contributed in his success during the Gettysburg defense. Specifically during the last two days of Gettysburg Meade was able to anticipate Lee's intended points of attack and thus was able to move units accordingly. Now Meade was uncertain about Lee's whereabouts and/or direction, and instead of moving regiments or brigades among his divisions or corps, Meade had to keeps those units intact in order to create and maintain his most effective pursuit. Furthermore, Meade had had Hancock's able assistance to implement and coordinate those shifts of units. Although he had been a corps commander for only a few months prior to Gettysburg, Hancock was not only a natural leader of troops but he was also an excellent tactician who paid attention to detail.

Hancock was the rare Union commander not afraid to exceed his authority as the situation required, one fellow general commenting that "Hancock was our genius, for he at once had brought order out of confusion and made such admirable dispositions that he secured [Cemetery] ridge and held it." Unfortunately for Meade—and indeed for the entire Army of the Potomac—Hancock suffered a serious wound in his upper thigh shortly before the repulse of Pickett's Charge and would be *hors de combat* for several months.

July 4 was a busy, eventful day for Meade and for the Army of the Potomac that was now reduced to about 67,000 effectives. As noted by Freeman Cleaves, one of Meade's biographers:

> The immediate and most pressing task was to supply and refit a battered army that obviously needed rest after several days of marching and fighting. The field was roughly strewn with dead and wounded, the bodies of horses [at least 5,000], arms of all description, blasted chunks of metal, wagon wheels, pieces of clothing, shoes, cartridge belts, mess gear, and other items to be salvaged or scrapped. ... Barefoot soldiers, some weak from hunger, scouted the field for shoes and rations.[77]

Among his other activities Meade issued a congratulatory, but unfortunate, message to his troops; Meade—whose message may have been largely pro forma—congratulated his soldiers for removing Lee from Pennsylvania.[78] This message distressed Lincoln who was expecting more, specifically the destruction of Lee's army.[79] In terms of being able to successfully comply with Lincoln's strategic objectives, Meade had been handicapped by not having the opportunity to consult personally and directly with Lincoln, Halleck, and other Administration officials during his short period of army command prior to July 4, Meade's only contact coming via Halleck's telegrams directing Meade to protect Washington. In contrast, Lincoln and/or Halleck had met with each of Meade's predecessors on multiple occasions giving those commanders opportunities to learn of the Administration's wartime objectives and what was expected of the army commanders. The generals, McClellan and Hooker especially, frequently resisted any acceptance of Washington's views about how the war should be prosecuted but at least they were, or should have been, acquainted with how Washington felt the war should be conducted. To be fair, Meade—as a corps commander—probably knew some of Washington's views; in fact he had been present during part of at least one prior conference between Halleck and Hooker, but generally this knowledge would have been filtered through the eyes and prejudices of Meade's superiors in his chain of command.

The fact that Halleck and Lincoln did not always hold, or articulate, the same strategic views at this stage of the war was another chronic disservice to commanders in the field, especially since Halleck's wires often contained a caveat that the field commanders should use their own best judgment regardless of whatever else was said—particularly Lincoln's position—in the order. In any event, Meade's congratulatory message to his soldiers and Lincoln's reaction to Meade's message demonstrated that on July 4 they did not share the same strategic goals.

Many of Meade's men spent the day burying the dead, tending to the wounded and gathering up tons of weapons and ammunition left on the battlefield[80]; many Union soldiers helped themselves to Springfield rifles left by the Confederates to replace their own Enfields, which they considered to be inferior.[81] At last a Union supply train had arrived from Winchester to start replenishing Meade's fatigued and starving troops. To reorganize his command, Meade ordered his corps commanders to regroup their units and to prepare for further operations.[82] Given the number of casualties—23,049 killed or wounded—that reduced some regiments to company size, regrouping was not a perfunctory task. In addition to the battlefield casualties, the army suffered from large numbers of soldiers who simply left their units during or in anticipation of the battles.

Not only did Meade have to reorganize much of his command to replace the wounded or killed commanders throughout his army, including replacements for four corps commanders; seven brigade commanders had been killed with several others wounded. Meade was also preoccupied by having to deal with MGen. Abner Doubleday's grievance about being bypassed to take command of the late John Reynolds' 1st Corps.[83] Beyond these administrative matters Meade ordered MGen. William H. French, 48, commanding the Federal Garrison at Harper's Ferry, which had moved to Frederick, to return part of his command to Harper's Ferry and to block the passes through South Mountain with the rest of his command.[84] Later in the day Meade changed his mind and countermanded his order.[85]

Finally late in the evening of July 4 Meade held another council of war that was still reluctant to leave Gettysburg.[86] The council's majority position would have cavalry alone pursue the retreating Confederates with the implication being that the infantry corps would take a route parallel to that of the Rebels.[87] Meade, knowing that he could not remain in Gettysburg much longer—after all he still had to stay between Washington and Lee as he was apparently moving to the south[88]—announced his intention to send a probing force at dawn under the direction of his Chief of Engineers, BGen. Gouvernour K. Warren, 33,[89] toward Lee's last known position at Gettysburg. Meade authorized Warren—one of the Day Two heroes—to take whatever sized he deemed necessary for the probe.[90]

Meade initially intended to move his headquarters to Creagerstown, ten miles north of Frederick. But before Meade had a chance to ascertain clearly where Lee was heading he was visited after midnight on July 5 by Herman Haupt,[91] who was badly misinformed about the situation, partly because a distracted Meade seemed to be unclear about his intentions. Because Haupt—fresh from Washington—did not fully appreciate the depleted condition of Meade's soldiers, he also became annoyed when Meade said his men needed a rest.[92] Haupt suggested that part of the Union army be sent across the Potomac to trap Lee's Rebels but Meade recalled the difficulty encountered by McClellan when he split his army across the Chickahominy.[93] Haupt then made an unfavorable but misleading report to Halleck in Washington.[94]

## First Encounters

Mid-afternoon on the 4th Kilpatrick's division departed Gettysburg south for Emmitsburg where he heard reports of Confederate trains heading for, even passing through, the passes east of South Mountain. Kilpatrick then immediately turned west along the Emmitsburg-Waynesboro Turnpike toward Monterey Pass where five roads intersect, including the Emmitsburg-Waynesboro Turnpike and the Maria Furnace Road. Monterey Pass was defended by a twenty-two man detachment of dismounted cavalry armed by a single Napoleon with less than a dozen rounds of ammunition[95]; this small detachment was commanded by Capt. George M. Emack, 21.[96] By 9:00 on the evening of July 4 as Ewell's wagon train was arriving at Hagerstown,[97] the quartermaster, subsistence, ordinance, and ambulances from the various divisions in Lee's main army were still passing through Monterey Pass.[98] Emack heard reports of cavalry coming up the Emmitsburg-Waynesboro Turnpike; accordingly in order to avoid exposing the Confederate column to attacks from this cavalry, Emack ordered a halt to the column still climbing up the Maria Furnace road.

Kilpatrick's troopers continued west during the night and after climbing the steep, narrow, winding road, they approached the eastern edge of Monterey Pass where they were surprised and startled when Emack's Napoleon fired one of its rounds from about fifty feet away.[99] The narrow profile of these mountain passes constricted the ability of Kilpatrick's cavalry to maneuver, especially to try to outflank the defenders. The small band of Rebels was using the same tactics Buford used on Day One west of Gettysburg by fighting, retiring, fighting, and then redeploying, except that in this case attackers could not spread out to outflank out-numbered defenders. Additionally pitch-black darkness prevented the attackers from seeing almost anything, including the defenders.

Grumble Jones and Beverly Robertson were ordered to guard these passes. Since Grumble had had an encounter with Federal cavalry the previous day and appreciated their significance of the area he asked to protect Monterey Pass. He then rode ahead accompanied only by couriers and his personal staff.[100] Along the way on Maria Furnace road to Monterey Pass Grumble noticed all Rebel traffic had stopped and pulled off the road per Emack's orders, which Jones countermanded causing the column to resume its trek toward Monterey Pass and beyond. And so as he withdrew toward the intersection Emack was surprised to discover herds of cattle and sheep being driven together with wagons and ambulances lumbering behind his back through the intersection.

Eventually Kilpatrick sent Custer ahead to clear the way; on the other side of the line Jones commandeered cavalry from the trains to come back to the summit to reinforce Emack's detachment.[101] After five hours and three separate hand-to-hand battles, Custer's dismounted troopers scattered the Rebel defenders from the mountain's summit.[102] Custer's break-through allowed Kilpatrick to descend a half-mile down the west side of the mountain to force the rear of the then moving Confederate wagons and ambulances off the road tumbling down the ravines.[103] Kilpatrick also captured 250 wagons and 1,300 officers, enlisted, slaves, and free blacks together with cavalrymen from three Confederate regiments.[104] Before moving further down the mountain to Smithsburg for a short rest, Kilpatrick also seized or recovered some slaves, more plunder and booty plus the quartermaster's payroll.[105] Furthermore pre-dawn on July 5 another Kilpatrick detachment corralled and captured another segment of Ewell's trains resulting in the capture of another hundred prisoners and a "drove of cattle."[106] Although Kilpatrick probably exaggerated the extent of his accomplishments, measured by statistics alone Monterey Pass was still one of the most lopsided Union victories of the war.[107]

But frankly Kilpatrick's "victory" was of insignificant, if not negative, value in pursuit operations. Any bounty re-captured from Ewell's reserve trains was hardly essential for Meade's purposes once Federal supply wagons started rolling on July 4 from the Union supply depot at Winchester.[108] And while such captures certainly irritated Ewell and Stuart, Lee was not about to allow such proportionately minor losses from trains more than 40 miles in length to deter him from his paramount objective of getting his main army safely back to Virginia.

Furthermore, as had happened a few weeks earlier to Stuart, the captured booty quickly became a burden to Kilpatrick's cavalry, hampering its mobility and agility while at the same time consuming valuable manpower necessary to handle the wagons and to wrangle recaptured livestock.[109] To lighten his load Kilpatrick ordered many of the quartermaster wagons and their contents to be burned.[110] Later while Kilpatrick had come to rest at Smithsburg, Stuart attacked Kilpatrick, who despite holding favorable terrain and positions, soon disengaged and decamped for Boonsboro,[111] 20 miles to the south, ostensibly wanting to hand off his captured wagons, materials and prisoners to French but possibly intending to try to capture more bounty from Lee's line of retreat elsewhere. But in so disengaging from Smithsburg, Kilpatrick cost the Army of the Potomac valuable initiative it could never fully regain.[112] Furthermore by operating west of the mountain Kilpatrick failed to act as Meade's eyes and ears, a major factor in Meade's vacillation in deciding how to pursue Lee's retreat. Later at Boonsboro Kilpatrick met with Buford to plan further attempts to cut off Lee's retreat but without any coordination with the main army.

Lee's retreat began and continued during a hard, torrential rain that agonized all the men and their animals. The roads quickly became virtually impassable quagmires, at least 12 inches deep in places. As so vividly described by Kent Masterson Brown, "All of the fences had been torn down along the roadway. Because the road was so deep in mud and so cut up, ambulances and wagons, together with their cavalry and artillery escorts, were making their way across the fields, crushing the wheat, corn, and grasslands of the neighboring farms. All along the route, this great [retreat] column had left the debris of broken-down ambulances, wagons, caissons, horses, and mules."[113] And of course the foraging continued during the retreat, forcing farmers to do everything possible to save their livestock from the retreating Rebels.

Earlier as Rebel rear guard commanded by BGen. John Gordon of Ewell's corps was finally leaving Gettysburg, Harmon led Ewell's reserve wagon train, including more than 5,000 head of cattle, into Williamsport.[114] Shortly after dawn on July 5 after riding all night the ubiquitous Grumble Jones was next to arrive at Williamsport where he found only chaos in control,[115] Harmon apparently finally being over his head.[116] Grumble immediately began to impose some order and within a couple hours was able to resume the ferry operation.[117]

Next, the front of Imboden's train started to arrive at Williamsport during the afternoon of July 5 about the same time when Meade was still trying to ascertain Lee's intentions! Upon Imboden's arrival he immediately began to deploy pickets to guard the roads while placing 23 pieces of artillery on the high ground to cover the road network.[118] When Lee came north in late June he crossed the Potomac by using a pontoon bridge erected at Falling Waters, a few miles downstream from Williamsport, as well as a ford at Williamsport. However, detached Union cavalry from Harper's Ferry captured and destroyed the Rebel pontoon bridge along with four pontoon transport wagons, various bridge parts and equipment, and the stores of the engineer department[119]; additionally the rains that continued almost without interruption since July 4 had raised the level of the Potomac to the point that it could no longer be forded. Accordingly Lee and most of his army was stuck on the north side of the Potomac at least until the river's level would subside and/or a new pontoon bridge could be built.

Upon finding the pontoon gone, Imboden found a flat ferryboat that could carry approximately 30 men each trip. To have additional ferries the Confederates also began using boats from the canal running parallel with the river. Helping to alleviate the Rebel's shortage of ammunition and other supplies, the 54th North Carolina arrived across the river with a resupply train. Without delay the Confederates began shuttling their most seriously wounded back across the Potomac while bringing supplies back on return trips.

Also by the morning of July 5, with Meade's concurrence Warren decided to take Sedgwick's entire 6th Corps for his "probe." Beloved by his soldiers, nevertheless some of Uncle John's professional peers were more critical. The army's Provost General, Marsena Patrick, opined, "Sedgwick, I fear, is not good enough a general for [corps command]. He is a good honest fellow and that is all." Even from the Confederate perspective, Porter Alexander—referring to Chancellorsville—chimed in with the opinion that, "I have always felt surprise that the enemy retained Sedgwick as a corps commander after [Salem Church], for he seems to me to have wasted great opportunities, & come about as near to doing nothing with 30,000 men as it was easily possible to do. …With a little help from McLaws, Wilcox was able to drive the enemy back & recover the position. After this Sedgwick seemed to make no further effort to advance, but went into camp to wait for another day."[120]

On Gettysburg's Day One his corps was still at Manchester, Maryland 34 miles distant from Gettysburg. After one of the hardest marches of the war, Sedgwick's corps reached the Gettysburg battlefield during the afternoon of Day Two enabling Hancock's 5th Corps to defend and repulse Longstreet's attack on the Union left.

On Day Three Sedgwick's corps was used as reserves with its individual brigades being detached to plug holes in the lines of the other corps. Reflecting its lack of heavy action, Sedgwick's corps suffered fewer casualties than did several regiments. Because Sedgwick's corps remained less wounded than any other corps, it seemed natural to take it for Warren's probe while other corps rested and resupplied.

Meade's intended to wait upon the result of the Warren/Sedgwick probe. Depending upon such results, Meade could then send his army either westward directly toward Lee's rear or alternatively to try to flank Lee by going south along the eastern side of the South Mountain before turning west. However Meade's options were spoiled by the uncontrollable Butterfield, who—on his last day before leaving for convalescent leave—issued provisional orders sending everyone south toward Middletown, Maryland.[121] Is it any wonder when Marsena Patrick said of Butterfield's departure that it was fortunate "for him & to the joy of all."[122] During the few days before Butterfield could be replaced his staff duties were split between Warren and Pleasonton.[123]

Furthermore Meade's order for the probe created some confusion—at least in Sedgwick's cautious mind—about whether Sedgwick was supposed merely to reconnoiter to uncover Lee's intentions or should he engage Lee in battle. Sedgwick left Gettysburg with his entire corps during the early afternoon of July 5, employing a formation with a line of heavy skirmishers hardly conducive to a rapid advance.[124] Despite Meade's urging to move aggressively, Sedgwick moved very carefully as he approached Fairfield at the end of July 5.[125]

The Fairfield Gap, a little more than two and half miles southwest of the village of Fairfield, and being less than 100 yards wide, gave the retreating Rebels a potential chokepoint.[126] Accordingly, on the morning of July 5 Lee wanted to induce the Yanks into a fight, telling Ewell "If 'those people' will only come out of their entrenchments and give us an open field fight, we will smash them."[127] Being quite unhappy over his losses at Monterey Pass the previous night, Ewell was also itching for a measure of revenge.[128]

That night Lee had Ewell's and Longstreet's troops construct breastworks and build campfires in the vicinity of Fairfield along the eastern edge of the South Mountain range as though they were preparing to stay and to fight.[129] All the campfires fooled Warren and Sedgwick, whose line was a mile and half away, into thinking Lee was not moving beyond Fairfield.[130] Later that evening when Warren returned to Meade he reported Sedgwick believed Lee had concentrated his main force around Fairfield.[131]

Even before hearing from Warren, during the afternoon of the 6th Meade finally heard from other sources that Lee was not at Fairfield but was in full retreat. Meade also learned of Kilpatrick's encounter at Monterey Pass; this report included Kilpatrick's typically exaggerated estimate of how much damage had been done to Ewell's reserve train. Given these reports, Meade concluded his best option was to chase directly after Lee; accordingly he tried to reverse Butterfield's the previous order sending the entire army—minus Sedgwick—to Middletown.[132] Trying to turn his army around to head back to join Sedgwick at Fairfield caused Meade to spin his wheels for the next 30 hours; however Meade was fearful, among other things, of precipitously exposing his supply base at Westminster if Lee could advance from Fairfield back to Gettysburg and then southeast down the Baltimore Pike.

Damage to image and reputation aside, the substantive effect of the badly handled "probe" was to cost a delay of thirty hours in the race between two armies to reach the approaches to the river crossings. Not only was the Army of the Potomac now taking the longer route to the Potomac, it was further handicapped by starting another thirty hours later than Lee's army.[133] (Lee had already gained an initial 24-hour head start by his surreptitious departure late on July 4.) Thus it was almost preordained that Lee would win the race making Meade the big loser, not only in terms of getting to the river approaches after Lee did, but also, and perhaps more important, looking bad in the eyes of his Commander in Chief.

Almost every day during this period of retreat and pursuit saw conflict and engagements between the elements of the respective armies. But some days were more significant than others. For instance on Monday, July 6—the same day that Sedgwick was cautiously approaching Ewell's rear guard at Fairfield on the east side of the South Mountain while Lee's lead element was emerging from the west side of the mountain—the Union cavalry, or at least its two divisions still intact, would engage in separate battles that created a profound effect upon the pursuit operations.

Jeb Stuart, realizing the importance of Hagerstown where Lee's army would pass before continuing toward Williamsport, started sending brigades in that direction to assure Lee's safe passage.[134] In contrast, Alfred Pleasonton continued to relinquish tactical control to two of his division commanders, John Buford and Judson Kilpatrick, allowing them to create and assign their own missions. On July 5 John Buford's 1st Cavalry Division, after mounting up in Westminster, headed through more rain and mud for Frederick, Maryland, about 25 miles away, hoping to take out Imboden before he could transfer his and Ewell's trains across the Potomac.

Buford's column got to within five miles of Frederick before stopping to make a soggy camp in the rain. Buford and Kilcalvary then met pre-dawn July 6 to decide upon a two-prong attack with each division advancing along separate prongs but to cooperate as the two operations unfolded.[135] Buford and Kilpatrick decided Buford would continue to try to attack Williamsport while Kilpatrick—apparently intending to add to his tally of Monterey Pass booty—would go directly after the trains going through Hagerstown.[136] Kilpatrick, entered Hagerstown largely unopposed before encountering barricades and rifle fire from church steeples.[137] A terrifying horse artillery duel at short-range ensued with charges and countercharges—mounted as well as dismounted—in the streets before the Rebels stiffened at Church Street[138]; Iverson's Rebel infantry arrived shortly thereafter to flank Kilpatrick's right forcing the Union horse riders to withdraw, the glory-seeking Eric Dahlgren arriving with a commandeered squadron too late to help. Dahlgren's squadron found itself engaged in a savage battle but after six hours of brutal combat both Kilpatrick and Dahlgren were forced out of and from the town.[139]

Meanwhile at Williamsport, instead of finding undefended positions, Buford encountered infantry that—albeit composed largely of convalescent soldiers—was fortified and supported by ample artillery. Upon learning that 7,000 Union cavalry were heading his way at Williamsport (actually by that time Buford was reduced to no more than 4,000 effectives), Imboden mustered about 700 newly armed wounded on the high ground around the town.[140] Additionally Imboden deployed about two hundred teamsters and wagoners into two companies under the command of wounded but ambulatory officers. Eventually Imboden mustered about 3,000 men committed to the defense of his base at Williamsport; not insignificantly Imboden—a former artillery officer—also had 23 pieces of artillery at his disposal. With Imboden's line so close to its quartermaster and subsistence trains there was no way they could be protected from capture and/or destruction if Buford's cavalry could break through any part of the line![141]

Buford's cavalry continued to push westward along Boonsboro Road, still mistakenly believing Williamsport to be lightly defended.[142] The Union attack started at 1:30 p.m. with an artillery barrage; the Rebels returned fire almost running out of ammunition before more ammunition could be ferried across the Potomac.[143] As Buford applied pressure at various points throughout the battle and edged closer to the Confederate wagons Imboden remained active along his defenses, moving units from place to place and summoning more help as needed.[144] Toward the end of the day Buford was able to push to within a half mile of the Rebels' parked wagon trains but Fitz Lee, bringing up the rear of Imboden's train of wounded, sent word to Imboden to hold on for another thirty minutes until Fitz could arrive with his brigade of 3,000 cavalry.[145]

When Buford heard the gunfire from Hagerstown he sent a distress call to Kilpatrick to send help to Williamsport.[146] But as Custer started directly toward Williamsport to reinforce Buford, and thus protecting Kilpatrick's left flank as he attempted to retreat, Stuart pushed Custer away forcing Custer to fight his way back to the rear.[147] Fitz Lee's timely arrival forced Kilpatrick's fractured commands to withdraw causing Buford to be overmatched and also being forced to withdraw in a rout late in the day.[148] As a result of these separate actions, the day ended as a fiasco with the Federals being unable to seize either Hagerstown or Williamsport. Brown notes that both actions demonstrated how ineffective cavalry could be when it operated far from its quartermaster trains for more than four or five days.[149] Both instances also verified among other things once more that cavalry against entrenched infantry supported by ample artillery was seldom a favorable proposition for cavalry.[150]

These battles also demonstrated once again the folly of dividing cavalry before engaging in combat. For scouting purposes it usually made sense to divide and spread cavalry across wide expanses of territory; this maximized cavalry's mobility and ability to act as the eyes and ears of the main army commander. However as earlier propounded by Pleasonton, for fighting purposes it was almost always better to concentrate the forces in place, hopefully to gain a numerical advantage at the point of contact with the enemy.[151]

But the larger, more pertinent point is that during pursuits it was imperative to coordinate cavalry operations with the main army. And as part of that coordinated effort, cavalry's mission had to be more definitive than merely to "harass and annoy" the retreating enemy. To illustrate, suppose that Union cavalry, either by Kilpatrick alone or by Kilpatrick together with Buford, had on July 6 captured Hagerstown. But on that same date Sedgwick with his single corps of infantry was still struggling to overcome Ewell's rear guard at Fairfield while the remainder of Meade's army was a day from even beginning its pursuit. This begs the question of how long could Union cavalry have blocked Lee's army, which was still a capable fighting force of 47,000 effectives that included Stuart's intact cavalry. We will never know of course but it would seem reasonable that Union cavalry without infantry or artillery support, or in the absence of terrain favorable for defensive purposes, could hardly have blocked Lee's army for more than a couple hours. A couple hours' delay might have sufficed if the main army were close at hand but not so when the main army was still a couple days hard marching away.

In short, while the cavalry of the Army of the Potomac had made great strides in fighting enemy cavalry of a similar size, its overall effectiveness, including acting as the eyes and ears for the main army commander, was impaired by poor combat management that among other things failed to deploy the horse divisions in a coordinated manner to maximize the cavalry's ability to perform useful missions.

During the morning of July 7 Meade ordered Sedgwick to push forward but Sedgwick demurred saying such a movement was too dangerous.[152] In fact Lee continued to try to draw Sedgwick in and then smash Sedgwick's corps with Ewell's entire corps but to his credit Sedgwick was not willing to take the bait.

## *Meade's Pursuit Begins in Earnest*

After almost 30 hours lost investigating—or dithering about—which route to take, by noon of the 7th, Meade finally decided to forego any thought of pushing his entire army through the South Mountain passes, instead reissuing Butterfield's original orders to proceed to Middletown.[153] By the late afternoon almost the entire Army of the Potomac, other than a light division from Sedgwick's corps, was plodding through deep mud and muck along three routes leading to Middletown, sitting astride the National Road immediately east of Turner's Pass. Not only did the infantry and artillery units have to change directions but Meade's new plan also required a massive realignment of all his army's quartermaster and subsistence trains of 6,000 wagons.[154] Sedgwick's light division cautiously advanced to eventually get through the Fairfield Gap but of course by then even Lee's rear guard was gone.

At last, on Tuesday, July 7, Meade's army began its full pursuit by heading at last toward Middletown. By the end of the day, as torrential rains continued to fall, the three wings in Meade's army made marches of between 15 and 34 miles through mud and mire.[155] Meade and his staff rode ahead of his army, arriving at Frederick, the largest town on the National Road between Wheeling, West Virginia, and Baltimore; after establishing his headquarters Meade had his first change of fresh clothes and enjoyed his first good night's sleep in ten days. Although Meade and his army had made remarkable progress on his first day's march, he still needed at least one more day to get through the more-southern passes over the South Mountain into the Cumberland Valley where Hagerstown and Williamsport are located.[156]

Lincoln, worried that Lee would escape, continued—via Halleck—to urge Meade to attack without delay.[157] Meade continued to plan to have his army rendezvous at Middletown thereby keeping his army between Lee and Washington, D.C. However this decision meant Meade's army was taking a longer route toward Hagerstown making it even less likely that he could block Lee's escape.

After a brief rest in Leisterburg, Lee's army, including its rear guard, reached the outskirts of Hagerstown on the same day that Meade was finally getting his army underway. Had Union cavalry captured and held Hagerstown on the 6th, it might have been in position to block or at least impede Lee's retreat.

Although it is doubtful whether even the entire Union cavalry could have blocked Lee's advance for an indefinite period, it is possible concerted, massed effort by the three cavalry divisions could have impeded Lee's progress to help Meade's main army. Once it was determined that Lee was retreating via Fairfield, the remainder of his route down the Cumberland Valley should have been obvious. If Pleasonton had seized the reins of his command—and we realize this would have been in the realm of hypothetical—he could have established a series of blocking positions between Cavetown and Hagerstown. A tactic of delaying Lee by the use of cavalry from point to point might have slowed Lee enough to have allowed Mead's army to catch up before Lee could cross the river or, as it would turn out, could establish defensive fortifications, to cover his final preparations prior to crossing. However, the hypothetical also presumes Meade's main army would be following closely to apply direct pressure to Lee's rear as opposed to twice reversing itself before taking a more circuitous route to Lee's destination. Unfortunately, by this time not only was the Union cavalry fragmented, but the Union horses were tired and jaded from being ridden endlessly from point to point thereby becoming of little use until rested. Up to the point of July 8 in the Gettysburg campaign, nearly 15,000 horses and mules had been abandoned by Meade's army or had broken down and became unserviceable.[158]

Even as his army began a mass movement in pursuit Meade continued to reorganize his army, appointing William French to replace Dan Sickles as commander of the 3rd Corps and MGen. Andrew A. Humphreys as his new Chief-of-Staff. Humphreys was a 32-year veteran who had languished under poor to incompetent commanders for much of his career[159]; he was generally regarded as being iron-willed, confident, methodical and precise whose services were highly valued by Meade. French, 47, was known as "Old Blinky" because he blinked excessively when he spoke[160]; French also had a foul disposition with a fondness for whisky.[161]

A common perception had been created that the Army of the Potomac was timid and lethargic as it approached toward Lee's position. Lincoln was certainly impatient, unable to understand or appreciate why Meade had not already attacked and perhaps destroyed Lee's army before it could cross the Potomac. Halleck—the paragon of do-as-I say, don't-do-as-I-did—kept prodding Meade to move faster, suggesting that Meade should employ forced marches, a suggestion that caused Meade to react immediately with considerable irritation.[162] Even Porter Alexander has piled on with his opinion that, "…the enemy had pursued us as a mule goes on the chase of a grizzly bear—as if catching up with us was the last thing he wanted to do."[163] But the fact was that once underway Meade's army moved about as fast and certainly as hard as could be reasonably expected under the circumstances. Reflecting the rigor by which the army moved, after spending all of the 8th and until noon on the 9th pulling artillery pieces out of the mud across wretched roads to get over South Mountain, the horses were totally spent compelling the 1st and 6th Corps to advance without their artillery.

Lee arrived at Hagerstown on July 7 (the same day Meade's army began its retreat in earnest) and almost immediately began inspecting the roads connecting Hagerstown, Williamsport, Falling Waters, and Downsville as well as the approaches to the Potomac River.[164] The horses and mules, together with the thousands of cattle, sheep, and hogs in and around Williamsport had created an almost unbearable stench.[165] Since Lee was being forced to stay on the northern side of the river at least for awhile, it became necessary to construct defenses for his troops and materiel in the Hagerstown and Williamsport areas while covering the approaches to the river crossings. Lee and his staff identified and began to establish a nine-mile defensive line—mostly with open fields in front with excellent artillery positions—starting at Downsville,[166] near Falling Waters on the Potomac on the right, and extending northward to Hagerstown.[167] Under Lee's personal supervision this line was constructed along a ridge in front of a road network, including the Downsville Road, which would allow easy transfer of units from position to position.[168] Lee and his engineers made extensive use of stone fences as fortifications; furthermore the so-called Downsville line was effectively covered by artillery batteries placed in the heights behind the lines.[169] The swollen Marsh Run (or Creek) also ran in front of Lee's line creating another obstacle—indeed a killing field—against any attacking forces. Furthermore the canal path provided a connecter between Williamsport and Falling Waters, allowing for additional mobility for Lee's forces.

Between July 7 and July 9 the Union army advanced in fits and starts with encounters at Beaver Creek and Boonsboro together with sniping along the lines. Meade also continued to re-supply, rest and refit his soldiers in preparation for what promised to be difficult fight ahead. Also during this period Imboden's engineers had been able to build and launch a second ferry to help alleviate the log jam of ambulances and other wagons waiting along the roads between Williamsport and Hagerstown.

On July 10, 1863, Meade's army started to move with more determination through the muck and mire toward Lee's forces, gathered in and around Williamsport. Several skirmishes erupted in nearby towns, including a serious encounter at Falling Waters, downstream from Williamsport. Meanwhile Lee's engineers and pioneers began gathering materials for the construction of a bridge across the Potomac at Falling Waters.[170]

To give Lee's engineers and pioneers additional time to complete the Downsville line, Stuart engaged in a battle along the National Road east of Funkstown to contest Buford who was in support of Sedgwick.[171] To assist Stuart, Longstreet sent some infantry forward but the Rebels were pushed back to Antietam Creek before beginning to stand their ground.[172] Eventually both sides brought in additional cavalry, infantry and artillery, with heavy fighting ensued on some of the richest farmland in Maryland.[173] Eventually the weight of Federal forces prevailed and Stuart withdrew clearing the way for Meade's army to advance all the way to the Potomac[174]; however by the end of the day both sides were still in the same approximate positions they had occupied that morning. Since the Confederates were trying to buy time, and conversely since the Federals were being pressed to launch an attack, this standoff represented a tactical victory for the Confederates. That night Stuart's troopers unsaddled their horses for the first time in ten days.[175]

## Standoff and Escape

By Saturday, July 11, 1863, Meade was moving all seven corps to within seven miles of the Downsville entrenchments and fortifications.[176] Meanwhile Lee's engineers almost completed construction of the Downsville line to defend the roads from Hagerstown to Williamsport and on to Falling Waters.[177] These stout breastworks of fence rails, straw and dirt rivaled the strongest built by Confederate engineers during the war including those at Fredericksburg.[178] Some of the parapets were six feet high while guns were placed for perfectly converging fire.[179] And as they approached the completion of their Downsville line fortifications Lee's engineers began construction in earnest of a new 26-pontoon 800-foot bridge at Falling Waters.[180] In order to have materials for the pontoons, Major J.A. Harmon, now Lee's "handyman," stripped every warehouse in Williamstown of siding.[181] They also stripped roofs from local buildings in order to melt tar that could be use as sealant.

While Lee's forces waited for the Potomac to subside, Meade's army continued to reposition in preparing for an attack. These preparations included contact between Federal skirmishers and Rebel infantry extended well in front of Hagerstown and Antietam Creek. Sedgwick's 6th Corps took possession of Funkstown after it had been abandoned by the Rebels in the process of consolidating their lines.[182] In the anticipation of heavy casualties for the upcoming assault an additional 50 surgeons and many volunteer nurses arrived at the army's headquarters.[183]

On Sunday, July 12, 1863, as the Confederates were completing their Downsville line fortifications, Meade brought his main army into position to begin some light and generally ineffective reconnaissance. Having completed their pontoon bridge at Falling Waters, the Confederates continued to abandon Hagerstown.[184] As the Rebels withdrew their skirmishers around Hagerstown Kilpatrick ordered Custer to charge into the town after which the entire 11th Corps followed to anchor Meade's right flank between Hagerstown and Funkstown.[185]

By the 12th of July the Potomac fell to a five-foot depth at Williamsport. The Federals were receiving reports about the Confederates sending supplies Williamsport but for reasons still not clear the Federals failed to make an effective effort to interdict that re-supply effort.[186] While Lee was beginning to move across the somewhat subsided Potomac on boats and the newly constructed pontoon bridge at Falling Waters Meade continued to act cautiously, apparently still haunted by the disastrous assaults at Fredericksburg.[187] Eventually Meade contemplated a full-fledged assault for that day but a chaplain complained about attacking on the Sabbath. While not acquiescing directly to the chaplain, Meade decided attacking the next day was the better option. After telegraphing Halleck that he [Meade] intended to attack the next day, Meade contemplated a reconnaissance in force that could be converted to an attack; however that evening his council of war—only two infantry corps commanders voting to attack as proposed by Meade—dissuaded him from even considering such an attack, claiming they still had insufficient intelligence about Lee's positions.[188]

To placate his resistant corps commanders, Meade and Humphreys personally reconnoitered the lines on Monday, July 13, while many troops waited in frustration; based upon that reconnaissance Humphreys issued an order to attack at 7:00 a.m. the next day.[189] Although Lee had hoped Meade would attack the Rebel entrenchments, he also knew he could not afford to linger any longer and ordered a withdrawal.

Heth's division was deployed as the rear guard at Falling Waters. Fitz Lee's cavalry was to provide a screen in front of Heth, except that once, or if, the pontoon bridge was cleared, Fitz's cavalry was "otherwise to cross at the ford at Williamsport."[190] However, instead of remaining between Heth and the Federals, Fitz Lee mistook the rear of Longstreet's column for Heth's rear guard, thereby assuming the pontoon bridge was clear, his cue for moving upstream to cross at Williamsport. Since Heth was not aware that Lee moved upstream, Heth did not realize his front was left without a cavalry screen.[191]

During the night Ewell's corps completed its evacuation by fording across the Potomac at and above Williamsport[192]; the water was still about five feet deep in the middle of the river but the tallest men stood at mid-stream to pass the shortest men along the line.[193] Meanwhile Longstreet, along with the wagons and artillery pieces—some being swept away into the river—crossed the newly completed pontoon bridge at Falling Waters. Poor visibility from fog and smoke prevented Meade's signalmen from spotting the evacuation; however late in the evening Howard thought he spotted a Rebel column leaving the area.[194] Although this information was passed along to Meade, it was too late in the day to react.

Before dawn on Tuesday, July 14, Union cavalry detected Lee's retreat across the Potomac. (Query: Why was this information not promptly sent to Meade's headquarters?) Kilpatrick rushed from Hagerstown to Williamsport, where he found only empty entrenchments and stragglers. Without delay Kilpatrick began to gallop toward Falling Waters, capturing more stragglers and horses along with discarded arms and equipment,[195] while Buford came west from Downsville.

En route Buford informed Kilpatrick to hold the attention of the Rebel rear guard at long distance while Buford would drive to the bridge to cut off much of the Confederate rear guard.[196] Arriving prior to Buford, Kilpatrick became impatient and after countermanding Custer's to make a dismounted attack, Kilpatrick ordered two companies to make a mounted charge. Still unaware they were without cavalry screening, Heth's soldiers initially thought the approaching horse riders belonged to Fitz Lee but they recovered in time to slaughter all but a few of the Blue troopers.

Still undeterred by his tragic folly of directing mounted charges, Kil-Cavalry ordered another charge but this time acquiesced to Custer's deployment of dismounted troopers. Kilpatrick's impatience pushed the Rebel rear guard to the bridge before Buford could arrive when the Confederates cut their pontoon bridge loose from its Maryland-side moorings, thus foiling any further pursuit.[197] Notwithstanding the lack of coordination between Kilpatrick and Buford, some of Heth's rear guard were captured. R.E. Lee vociferously denied there was even such a battle at Falling Waters, perhaps a convenient way of not having to explain his nephew's mistake in leaving Heth without a cavalry screen, while Kilpatrick reported as much as an entire brigade of 1,500 Rebels was captured. Perhaps the most accurate account came from *Harpers Weekly,* which reported almost six weeks later the prison at Point Lookout had nine hundred prisoners who had been captured at Falling Waters.[198]

Also at 6:35 a.m., after reporting the Confederates had abandoned their works to his front, Howard immediately began to move forward.[199] By 7:00 a.m. it seemed obvious the Rebels were no longer trapped. At 8:30 a.m. the Union army began its approach toward the Confederate defenses. But pressing forward to attack, the Federals' infantry discovered the Rebels had abandoned their positions and the Yank soldiers settled into the vacated Rebel lines to enjoy their first real meal in days.[200] Meade promptly ordered a pursuit but aside from Buford's and Kilpatrick's attack against Lee's rear guard, the pursuit was too late!

Henry Heth's division, the first Confederate division to enter Gettysburg thirteen days earlier, was the last to cross the Potomac. John Buford, whose cavalry division spotted and then skillfully thwarted Heth's approach on Day One, had been in position to attack Heth as he crossed.[201] James Pettigrew, who had approached Gettysburg on June 30 before returning to Cashtown after observing Union cavalry, and who had commanded one major thrust during the ill-fated charge of July 3, lay mortally wounded at Falling Waters. Once the pontoon bridge was on the West Virginia side, the Confederate engineers and pioneers disassembled the bridge taking components with them for the remainder of the retreat.

Upon inspecting the abandoned fortifications, some of Meade's more capable officers concluded they had averted a disaster by putting off the attack.[202] Col. Wainwright, the Chief of Artillery for Union's 1st Corps, reported the line the strongest he had yet seen, "built as it they [were] meant to stand a month's siege."[203] Meade's new chief-of-staff, Andrew Humphreys, a thirty year topographical engineer, later testified "A careful survey of the intrenched position ... showed that an assault upon it would have resulted disastrously to us."[204]

Although still short of shoes and some supplies, Lee's army continued to move southward along the Shenandoah Valley to good defensive positions west of the Blue Ridge. Perhaps equally as important, Lee's army had captured and retained a tremendous amount of booty of animals (approximately 30,000 head of cattle and an equal number of sheep survived the entire retreat), equipment and other supplies critically needed to sustain the army. But the bottom line was that even after losing the bloodiest battle on American soil, the Army of Northern Virginia, while badly wounded, had survived to fight another day. Lincoln's reaction was one of unhappy despair exclaiming, "We had them within our grasp. We had only to stretch forth our hands & they were ours. And nothing I could say or do could make the Army move."[205]

Despite the tremendous toil and horrific bloodletting by the men and their officers of either side Lee's escape across the Potomac ended the Gettysburg campaign with neither side able to claim any sort of triumph. And despite his battlefield defeat at Gettysburg Lee's successful retreat also restored the immediate balance of power between the combatants.

## *Analysis*

In brutally stark terms, completion of the Downsville line signaled the end of Meade's pursuit, at least in military measures as opposed to political terms. The Downsville line definitively meant Lee had restored an unparalleled equilibrium of force; accordingly from that point the armies' maneuverings were discretely converted from retreat and pursuit to Lee preparing to receive a conventional battleground assault while Meade cautiously and carefully prepared that assault, which of course never materialized. While Lee still had to prepare and manage the additional step of withdrawing from his Downsville line before crossing the Potomac, certainly a difficult step with some vulnerability, completion of the Downsville line permitted Lee to have a commanding battlefield position while assigning Meade to the inevitable task of assaulting a fortified position, which statistically and realistically was going to be a losing proposition.

In a sense, the Union pursuit was doomed from the moment Ewell's rear guard left Gettysburg virtually undetected thus giving the Southerners a lead they never had to relinquish. But there were several other critical tipping points—such as the Rebel's stalwart, determined defense at Monterey Pass, or the failure of Buford and Kilpatrick to capture or destroy trains at Williamsport or Hagerstown, or Sedgwick's falling for Lee's ruse at the Fairfield Gap, or Meade's delay to launch his full-fledged pursuit, or the inability of the Union cavalry to be able to delay Lee's main army—that foretold, or at least should have foretold, the failure of any pursuit. Any of these events meant that the balance of power inexorably was being restored in Lee's favor.

Conducting a successful pursuit meant connecting several elements into a chain. Like any other chain, a pursuit operation was only going to be as strong as its weakest link, but unfortunately for the Union in July 1863 its chain had several weak links, some of which were external beyond Meade's control, such as Lee's brilliant plan and management of his retreat. At the very top of the chain of command, Halleck failed to communicate Lincoln's desire that Lee's army be "bagged." But some of these weak links were inherent within the Army of the Potomac, starting with Meade's appointment shortly before the Gettysburg battle with "marching orders" from Halleck to remain between Lee and Washington. Unfortunately Halleck's guidelines were not entirely consistent with Lincoln's strategic aspirations for an annihilative victory, something that was not conveyed to Meade in a timely manner. And while Meade's management of the field was extraordinary during Days One and Two, the timing of his appointment meant Meade had virtually no opportunity to plan and/or prepare for a pursuit, apparently not even being certain when the fighting had ended at the end of Day Three.[206] Furthermore at that point in Meade' career his persona—still typical of almost all Regular Army officers—was that of a good defensive commander rather than being an aggressive pursuer. While he had proven his personal courage beyond any doubt in several battles, Meade lacked another form of courage, that being the confidence to risk going above and beyond the basics of his level of command to envision a national objective.[207]

Some of these shortcomings might be understandable from a humanistic standpoint: A lack of confidence from his short duration of his new command and his lack of seniority over a couple corps commanders. But Meade also allowed too many administrative and logistic issues distract him on July 4 when he should have been focusing upon the most important issue: What to do about Lee?

But perhaps even worse the next lower level of command, that of corps commanders, including the cavalry corps, was largely lacking in the basic command skills and attitudes necessary to seek an annihilative result against Lee's army. For whatever reason, probably because of his desire to defer and to accommodate input from former seniors and equals in rank, Meade compounded his management deficiencies by convening a series of councils of war.[208] Meade's apprehensive and divided council of war could not even determine whether the enemy was in fact retreating. While the deployment of an entire infantry corps to try to determine Lee's whereabouts and intentions was a serious management mistake, the specific assignment of John Sedgwick was little short of a tactic blunder. Whenever the issue was put to a vote the majority of corps commanders overwhelmingly voted against moving directly against Lee's army. But even when Meade eventually asserted his authority he was met with doubt and resistance from his subordinates who found excuse after excuse not to aggressively attack Lee. The losses of Reynolds and Hancock, the best corps commanders, only exacerbated these command deficiencies.

Additionally, and most critically, the Union Army failed to make the most effective use of its cavalry. The cavalry's nascent capability to scout could have been put to good use initially when Lee's location and intentions were unknown. Instead cavalry was instructed to harass and annoy, a silly, myopic mission that accomplished little either in scouting or in combat effectiveness. Beyond a possible mission to scout and reconnoiter, rather than amassing its horsemen in order to try to delay Lee's main army, the two still intact division commanders were allowed to ad lib, which as a result one division commander, Kilpatrick, used that latitude to try to garner as much glory as possible by needless plundering.[209]

Pleasonton contributed virtually nothing in cavalry management when effective command would have been most productive; the fact that he was available to be temporary co-chief of staff during that critical time period reflects his minimal value as cavalry commander. Eric Wittenberg and his co-authors conclude Pleasonton deserves much of the blame for the failure of the Army of the Potomac to destroy Lee's army north of the Potomac.[210] In contrast Stuart realized his mission was to protect Lee's main army during its retreat and thus deployed his subordinate commands with that overriding purpose in mind. As a result Stuart was able to successfully delay Meade's army at critical junctures as it approached along the National Road toward Lee's positions.

And while the bulk of historians emphasize Meade's pursuit shortcomings it is seriously mistaken to overlook Lee's brilliance in planning, preparing and implementing the retreat of his army. Lee's plan was eloquent in its simplicity replete with attention to detail. While Lee might be legitimately criticized for delegating too much during the battle, and for making some of his orders too vague and ambiguous, and for not closely supervising some, even many, aspects of his plans, Lee was extremely and exhaustively hands-on during all phases of his retreat, including the soldiers' actual crossing of the Potomac. In short Lee's retreat was a military masterpiece that arguably would have thwarted any pursuit, no matter how well planned and prepared.

Finally, and perhaps most importantly, the pursuit failed because a series of Federal command miscalculations and faulty assumptions. As previously noted, Meade did not fully understand, at least initially, what Lincoln expected of him during the entirety of the Gettysburg campaign. He and his corps commanders miscalculated the importance of keeping constant pressure upon Lee's retreating army, which as a result could prepare a stout, practically impenetrable defensive position. Meade and his subordinates miscalculated how to make the most effective use of cavalry that when properly commanded had become the equal of the Rebel cavalry. And most significantly, Meade and his councils of war miscalculated the results of taking a circuitous route in pursuit that naturally took longer than the more direct route of the retreat. These miscalculations directly permitted Lee to construct and to occupy an equilibrium of force that brought an end to this crucial phase of his retreat as well as ending the corresponding pursuit.

## *Dénouements and Precursors*

On July 13 five days of bloody rioting and chaos broke out in New York City as a result of the beginning of the first draft lottery. The War Department declared martial law and ordered Meade to send troops to New York City to help quell the riots, for which Kilpatrick volunteered.[211] Within weeks Meade was forced to send thousands of his battle hardened troops to help with the New York crisis.

Continuing to "pursue," on Saturday, July 18, 1863, four days after Lee had escaped across the Potomac, the Union army also moved across the Potomac at Harper's Ferry and at Berlin (now Brunswick), Maryland. For several weeks Lee's army remained west of the Blue Ridge while Meade's army stayed east of the same range, being careful to remain between Lee and Washington while both armies rested, refitted and replenished.

As early as July 21, 1863, Lee's army was observed making a further retreat up the Shenandoah Valley.[212] On July 23 Meade ordered French,[213] still commanding the Union's 3rd Corps, to cut passage through Manassas Gap to cut Lee's column into two parts at Front Royal, perhaps the Union's best chance to defeat the Confederates in detail. However at the little known Battle of Manassas Gap, a.k.a. Wapping Heights, French proceeded at such a leisurely pace that he could not inflict any significant damage even after successfully forcing passage of the gap.[214] The Federals occupied Front Royal the next day but the Confederates had withdrawn up the Luray Valley, well beyond any chances of pursuit. Humphreys would later testify that Meade realized Reynolds or Hancock probably would have better managed the attack and was more disappointed than he had been at Williamsport.[215]

After Lee was forced to make what was until then his longest retreat of the Civil War, Meade recommended that his army move to destroy crops growing in the Shenandoah Valley. However Lincoln and his cabinet rejected Meade's recommendation on the rationale that Lee and his army were the objective. No further response was forthcoming when Meade inquired what kind of campaign was expected of him.[216]

In August 1863 Jeb Stuart attempted to settle his score with Grumble Jones by relieving Jones from command, blaming Jones for the loss of wagons at Monterey Pass. Jones responded with a letter that typical for him probably was not respectful whereupon Stuart placed Jones under arrest and filed court martial charges. A court martial found Jones guilty of one of the charges but Lee simply had Jones transferred to another department. On June 5, 1864, while defending Staunton at Piedmont Jones was killed leading a cavalry charge.

At one point in early September 1863, Meade confirmed that Longstreet and his corps had been sent west to reinforce Bragg at Chickamauga; trying to take advantage, Meade was in the process of launching a turning movement against Lee east of Clark's Mountain when word was received of the desperate situation of the Federal army in Chattanooga following the Yank's rout from Chickamauga.[217] To relieve the besieged Federal army, the Lincoln administration decided on September 21, 1863, to detach two corps, the 11th and the 12th, from Meade and to send these two corps—under Joe Hooker—to Chattanooga.[218] Although this left him with 76,000 men present for duty,[219] Meade was compelled to scrap his turning movement then underway against Lee.

Butterfield went west with Hooker, serving as Hooker's chief-of-staff. After the war Butterfield became a successful business man who would be asked to organize events such as Sherman's funeral, the Washington Centennial, and the parade celebrating Dewey's return after the Spanish-American War. However Butterfield might be best known as the composer of "Taps."

In October 1863 Beverly Robertson was transferred to South Carolina under Beauregard's overall command but a month later went with Longstreet to Knoxville where he was relieved of command for making mutinous remarks.

John Buford continued to command his cavalry division but in late October 1863 he received orders to command the cavalry of the Army of the Cumberland, apparently in hopes that he could contend with Nathan Bedford Forrest in the West. However Buford's long years in the saddle were accumulating a toll on his body. Before he could go west to assume his new command, Buford stayed with the Army of the Potomac as it pushed against Lee's army, attempting to regain the ground between the Rappahannock and the Rapidan. The apex of that push occurred November 7 and 8 at Rappahannock Station where the Union forces were able to capture 1, 600 prisoners as well as 2,000 stands of arms before Lee could escape back across (south) the Rappahannock.[220] Although this highly successful effort enabled the Yanks to reoccupy a forty-mile line along the Rapidan's north bank, Buford was exhausted from non-stop riding during these two days of action forcing him to go on sick leave from fatigue and with dysentery. While trying to recover Buford contracted typhoid fever with his condition quickly deteriorating. When it became apparent Buford would not survive, Lincoln asked Secretary of War Stanton to facilitate Buford's promotion to major general. Slipping in and out of his delirious condition, Buford's last words before dying December 16, 1863, were, "Put guards on all roads, and don't let the men run back to the rear."

Buford's death was another damaging loss not just for the Union cavalry for the entire Union command structure. Jeffry Wert summarizes the loss of Buford as follows:

> No one in the Cavalry Corps measured up to this excellent horse soldier. Whether dismounted or mounted, [Buford's] men fought with a gritiness reflective of him. Although he appeared rough on the edges, he was a quiet and unassuming man, who, unlike Alfred Pleasonton, had little time for newspapers and self-aggrandizement. Upon learning of his death, an officer stated, "He was decidedly the best cavalry general we had."[221]

Shortly after returning from his 30-day leave, Meade found himself in the middle of another controversy hardly of his own making. Again Kilpatrick was the principle culprit since he had gone over Pleasonton's head to obtain Lincoln's and Stanton's approval for cavalry raid to free Union prisoners held in Libby Prison and on Belle Isle.[222] Wert characterizes the plan—based upon faulty intelligence that these prisons were lightly defended—as "myopic at best, harebrained at the worst."[223]

Demonstrating that Murphy's law that whatever-can-go-wrong-will-go-wrong is frequently applicable to military operations, especially those that are poorly planned, Kilpatrick's raid never came close to accomplishing its objectives, losing 300 men as well as 500 horses. Ulric Dahlgram, another immature, ambitious Union cavalry officer, was among the dead; he had been carrying papers that purported to show how Richmond should be burned and how Jefferson Davis would be assassinated.

The Confederacy reacted with outrage; Lee sent Meade a letter asking if the plans "were authorized, sanctioned, or approved." The Administration, Meade, and Kilpatrick all denied any prior knowledge but Kilpatrick's denial certainly was implausible. This "ugly business" caused one officer to describe Kilcavalry as a "frothy braggart without brains…." At the very least the Kilpartick-Dalgram raid, and its consequences, did not make Meade's command any easier.

Politically Meade was forced to go the defensive against an array of ambitious critics, some of who were Hooker allies wanting to see Fightin' Joe restored to command of the Army of the Potomac.[224] Abner Doubleday—who incidentally despite his claims did *not* invent baseball—still felt scorned because Meade did not promote him to corps command, also did his best to stir criticism of Meade. And of course, the ubiquitous Daniel Sickles—who still sought to be restored to his command despite losing a leg—could not resist chiming in with his criticism of Meade, especially since Sickles himself had endured a good deal of criticism because of his Day Two antics. For some reason, perhaps because they both enjoyed good stories, Sickles became one of Lincoln's confidants, returning to the White House as early as July 5 with his unsubstantiated version of how his insubordination had saved the Union on Day Two.

On March 5, 1864, Meade was also forced to endure an "investigation" by the Joint Committee on the Conduct of the War whose radical members whose prejudice had been reinforced by behind-the-back criticisms of Meade from Hooker—a favorite of the committee that inexplicably still wanted to see Hooker restored to command[225]—and Hooker's allies, including Doubleday, and of course from Sickles. The committee, chaired by Ohio's Ben Wade—with "his talent for profanity and invective plus his utter intransigence and an unmistakable aura of self-righteousness that won him so many enemies"[226]—conducted an inquisition wherein Meade was not even informed of the nature of allegations against him.[227]

Pleasonton and Meade had some differences but Meade still attempted to protect Pleasonton—regarded by one cavalry officer as "the greatest humbug of the war" who owed his position to "systemic lying"—from his many critics. However Pleasonton's perfidy before the Committee on the Conduct of the War betrayed Meade who was justifiably enraged. Grant then arranged to have Pleasonton transferred to Missouri where he would serve under Rosecrans, another exile from the Eastern Theater. Together they participated in the repulse of Price's Raid, the final major campaign west of the Mississippi.[228] As alluded to in Chapter 13, Pleasonton led a cavalry force against Price's rear that was repulsed October 23, 1864, at Westport, Missouri, perhaps the largest Civil War battle west of the Mississippi River. Phil Sheridan replaced Pleasonton as Meade's cavalry commander.

Wade's committee had questionable authority and as usual Lincoln simply ignored the committee's findings.[229] Nevertheless, although Lincoln was not going to relinquish his Constitutional authority as Commander-in-Chief to a Congressional committee, Lincoln had come to the realization that while Meade was an honest, competent general, someone else was needed to achieve a decisive victory over Lee and his Army of Northern Virginia. Instead Lincoln would eventually delegate that decision to his new Commanding General, U.S. Grant, who would decide to leave Meade in command of the army.[230] While Meade remained in command of the army throughout the course of the war, Grant's appointment of all Union forces, together with Grant's decision to establish his headquarters in the field with the Army of the Potomac, eventually superseded and constricted Meade's authority, almost consigning him to a historical footnote.

The McIntosh-Custer stand of Day Three was aided by the first extensive use of repeating carbines. Some units had yet to learn fire discipline and thus ran out of ammunition; nevertheless the enhanced firepower by a couple Michigan cavalry regiments gave them a decided advantage. One captured Rebel horse rider commented to his capturer, "You'ns load in the morning, and fire all day." The use of carbines increased later during the Mine Run campaign the following December. Although supply officers continued to resist widespread distribution of the repeaters, the enthusiastic feedback from the field overcame the reluctance of those in charge of logistics. Confederates horse soldiers tried to obtain repeaters in almost any way possible, including scavenging from battlefields, but as the war continued the Union's widespread use of increased firepower began to give it an important edge over the Rebel cavalry.

John Sedgwick remained as a corps commander, even after the number of corps in the army was reduced from five to three; in fact he became temporary commander of the entire army when Meade was on leave of absence for a month in early 1864. Sedgwick's numerous wounds had always been serious and painful requiring extensive periods of recuperation. After his last wound Uncle John said, "If I am ever hit again, I hope it will settle me at once. I want no more wounds." Unfortunately Sedgwick's wish came to fruition during the Overland Campaign when on May 9, 1864, while overseeing the placement of his troops at Spotsylvania, Virginia, and after chiding one of his soldiers for flinching from Rebel sharpshooters, a bullet struck under his right eye slaying him instantly.

Sherman called Kilpatrick a "damned fool" but nevertheless requested that Kil-Cavalry be transferred to Sherman's army where he served for the remainder of the hostilities.

# 18

# Little Phil Comes East
## *1864*

In the early spring of 1864 Union's new General-in-Chief, U.S. Grant, with Lincoln's concurrence if not encouragement, formulated an overall strategy intended to bring the maximum amount of concurrent pressure upon the Confederacy's military. Grant's strategic lynchpin featured the Army of the Potomac attacking and trying to eliminate Robert E. Lee's Army of Northern Virginia. Grant's orders to George Meade were simple and straightforward: "Lee's army will be your objective point. Wherever Lee goes, there you will go also." Grant also wanted Sherman to destroy the Confederate Army of Tennessee in the Western theater before moving to the heart of the rebellion at Atlanta. Grant also ordered a new army, the Army of the James, under the command of Benjamin Butler, to proceed up the James River before advancing north toward Richmond. Grant's fourth prong had the Department of West Virginia advance up (southward) the Shenandoah Valley to capture the rail lines at Staunton, Virginia, before moving on to the rail hub at Lynchburg, Virginia.[1] Initially MGen. Franz Sigel, 40, another political general without any notable command success, was appointed to command the Union's Shenandoah Valley campaign with an army of 8,900 men.

## *Cavalry Corps Command*

Even before Gettysburg, Secretary of War Edwin Stanton was not satisfied with Alfred Pleasanton's command of the army's Cavalry Corps, believing—with considerable justification—that Pleasanton lacked sufficient aggressiveness. To replace Pleasanton, in late March 1864, Grant had transferred the 33-year-old Irish-American MGen. Philip H. ("Little Phil") Sheridan from infantry division command in the Army of the Cumberland. Grant's second move was to transfer one of his ambitious protégés, BGen. James H. ("Harry") Wilson, 27, from the Cavalry Bureau in Washington to command of the 3rd Cavalry Division, replacing Hugh Judson Kilpatrick who was sent west after his failed raid on Richmond.[2] Although he was referred to as one of the army's "Boy Wonders," Wilson had accrued a wide range of experience since graduating from the Point in 1860. Originally a topographic engineer, he had served on the staffs of Sherman, Hunter, and McClellan, among others, seeing action during a variety of campaigns including Antietam and Vicksburg and having been a part of the advance party for Grant at Chattanooga prior to the breakout upon Missionary Ridge. The other cavalry divisions were commanded by holdovers BGen. David

McM. Gregg, 31, and BGen. Alfred T.A. Torbert, 31, another former Indian fighter who most recently had several commands of New Jersey infantry.

Part of Sherman's meteoric rise through the officers' ranks has already been described in Chapter 7. Despite these rapid promotions he was hardly a prototype commander, Lincoln once describing Little Phil as a "brown, chunky little chap, with a long body, short legs, not enough neck to hang him, and such short arms that if his ankles itch he can scratch them without stooping." He and Grant had had a sporadic acquaintance in the Western theater. For instance, in a rare billet for him as a cavalry commander, Sheridan led a pursuit after Corinth II before Halleck cancelled that operation. Sheridan often claimed he was the first to reach the crest of Missionary Ridge, a claim also made by others, but nevertheless it was a climb that would have come to Grant's disbelieving attention.[3]

Despite his physical shortcomings Sheridan had other attributes that often made him an outstanding combat leader. He was energetic, aggressive, normally eager to engage an enemy. Furthermore Sheridan exhibited an abundance of combat charisma, as an infantry commander almost always leading from the front. He could also be controversial, for instance he was opinionated and some of his actions could be construed as insubordination.[4] Paradoxically as a commander he could overreact, sometimes mistakenly, to actions by subordinates that he perceived as insubordination.

Sheridan assumed his new command Wednesday, April 6, 1864, at Brandy Station, Virginia, where he found horses to be in horrible shape from excessive picketing. The ensuing relationship between Meade and his new cavalry commander was never cordial or even compatible. Meade had a conventional, perhaps even unimaginative concept of the use of cavalry, that is to say Meade expected his horse riders to be subordinate to the needs of the infantry. Meade expected cavalry to stay close to the infantry to screen its movement, to clear the roads and intersections along which the infantry would be marching, and to protect the army's trains and lines of communications. To give Meade credit, the experience of several Civil War campaigns, including in the East, had shown this concept to be the most efficacious use thus far of cavalry, providing among other things the critical element of eyes and ears to the main army.

On the other hand, Sheridan's immense ambitions were not satisfied with serving in a closely supervised, constricted support role. Instead Little Phil envisioned, perhaps even lusted after, the prospects of the glory of cavalry-to-cavalry combat independent of the needs of the main army. Again pragmatically such deployments had been shown—most recently Stoneman's raid during Chancellorsville and Pleasanton's deployment of his cavalry divisions during the retreat from Gettysburg—to be counterproductive toward gaining an overall advantage against an enemy.

The respective personalities of the commanders impaired any chances for a compatible relationship. Although Grant initially said he did not intend to interfere with Meade's command decisions it was increasingly more evident that Grant and his staff were asserting more direct operational control of Meade's Army of the Potomac. With specific reference to cavalry operations, Meade could not help but resent having to deal with an upstart from the Western Theater who openly chafed at serving the needs of the infantry. Unfortunately both commanders had harsh tempers with two of the shortest fuses of all Union generals.

The Army of the Potomac began its Overland Campaign toward Richmond on Tuesday, May 3, 1864. When beginning his push toward Richmond,[5] Grant hoped for a relatively quick passage through The Wilderness. However, a number of circumstances, most notably logistical difficulties—specifically getting 5,000 wagons in the Union supply train through The Wilderness—coupled with Lee's hammering attacks along the path of the intended advance, intervened to result in one of the most horrid battles of the Civil War. Unfortunately the terrain, most notably its thick secondary growth, prevented cavalry from contributing much help during the struggles of that battle. Furthermore, after Sheridan urged that his cavalry be allowed to fight Confederate cavalry, early in the morning of May 5, 1864, Wilson's cavalry division suffered a serious defeat when it was driven from the field at The Wilderness.[6] As an immediate result Lee's entire army was approaching undetected and Wilson was prevented from warning Meade that Lee blocked Meade's path.

Although the Federals took almost unimaginable losses, instead of ordering the army's customary retreat, Grant ordered a rapid movement down Brock's Road to Spotsylvania to commence the late afternoon of Saturday, May 7, 1864.[7] The quick deployment might have caught almost all other adversaries off guard, but Lee uncannily anticipated Grant's move to likewise order his own army to start driving south.[8] Essentially the two opposing armies were racing along two roughly parallel roads trying to reach Spotsylvania first.[9] Although Spotsylvania, located about ten miles southwest of Fredericksburg, was but a small town, it had strategic value as an intersection of several roads in open ground with terrain that should have been to the advantage of the Union's superior numbers in manpower and artillery. However, Fitz Lee had already moved his division of Gray cavalry to Todd's Tavern, a critical intersection on Brock Road.

To facilitate the Union army's progress toward Spotsylvania, Meade ordered Sheridan to clear Brock Road as far south as possible. After believing they would be fighting infantry, two of Sheridan's divisions fought almost all day against Fitz Lee's riders only to be ordered to retire at the end of the day to bivouac back at Todd's Tavern.[10] Not only did this retirement relinquish at least a mile of Brock Road but the next morning, May 8, the Federals' own cavalry blocked the infantry's progress at Todd's Tavern. Meade became furious when he found the two cavalry divisions still at Todd's Tavern and that Brock Road still was not clear. In order to get his infantry on its way to Spotsylvania, and in Sheridan's unexplained absence, Meade then issued direct orders to one of the cavalry divisions to clear the rest of Brock Road. When Sheridan appeared at Todd's Tavern he was angered that Meade had given a direct order to one of Little Phil's divisions. An open, loud, ugly argument erupted with Sheridan finally accusing Meade of, "mixing up infantry with cavalry." Sheridan further bellowed that, "If he [Sheridan] could have matters his own way he would concentrate all the cavalry, move out in force against Stuart's command, and whip it."

Later that day when Meade complained to Grant about Sheridan's rank insubordination, instead of supporting his army commander Grant surprisingly responded, "Well, he generally knows what he is talking about. Let him start right out and do it."[11] Accordingly during the evening of May 8 Meade's headquarters issued orders for Sheridan to "to detach any portion of your command for offensive operations."[12] Not only did this episode undercut Meade's authority over his cavalry but it also marked the point at which Grant began to assume more direct control over the Army of the Potomac. Moreover, and more significantly, the Federals lost the race to Spotsylvania where the armies would engage in another prolonged series of bloody, indecisive battles.

## Yellow Tavern

After leaving one regiment with the army, the next day Little Phil departed with 10,000 troopers in four columns, each thirteen miles long, headed south searching for Stuart's cavalry. On Wednesday, May 11, 1865, after two days of hard riding Sheridan's cavalry destroyed Confederate supplies and liberated captured prisoners headed for Southern prisons.[13] The Yankee riders also met and engaged Stuart, with his force of 3,000 troopers, at Yellow Tavern at the north edge of Richmond. During an afternoon of intense mounted and dismounted fighting, Stuart led a counterattack against George Custer's troopers but was mortally wounded by a dismounted Union rider.[14] Although the road to Richmond was then open, Sheridan did not try to seize the Confederate capital, still heavily defended. Instead Little Phil opted to turn northeast to try to link up with Butler's Army of the James still deployed on the eastern end of the Peninsula. But the Rebels were not about to allow Union horse riders to roam the territory entirely as they pleased. Instead the Confederates set a trap at Meadow Bridge, a critical crossing over the Chickahominy River.

The day after their victory at Yellow Tavern, the Federal troopers were almost out of food, forage, and ammunition, but even more importantly found themselves surrounded by a combined Rebel force of cavalry, infantry, and clerks from Richmond. But George Custer's division saved the day when it forged a breakthrough while his pioneers repaired a railroad bridge that allowed the rest of Sheridan's troops to escape. Once across the Chickahominy Sheridan led his troopers to Butler's camp, arriving there on May 14, where Sheridan rested his men and horses until returning to rejoin the main army on Wednesday, May 25, 1864, six days after the battle at Spotsylvania was over and two days after the beginning of the battle at North Anna River.

But while Sheridan was exhilarated about causing the death of the vaunted Stuart, as a result of his cavalry's failure to properly clear Brock Road, including the intersection at Todd's Tavern, Lee had won the race to Spotsylvania, another combat venue where both sides incurred nearly unprecedented butchers' bills, including the fighting at the infamous Bloody Angle on May 12 that Ed Bearrs describes as "arguably the most severe of the war."[15] Furthermore during his two weeks absence from the main army, and notwithstanding the high cost of horses lost because of the heat and fatigue, Sheridan had failed the other objectives of defeating the Rebel cavalry and of entering Richmond.

Historian Gordon C. Rhea, in *To the North Anna River: Grant and Lee, May 13–25, 1864*, considers Sheridan's Yellow Tavern raid as being ill-advised, writing,

> Severe criticism can be leveled against the broader features of Sheridan's campaign. By taking his cavalry from Spotsylvania Court House, Sheridan severely handicapped Grant in his battles against Lee. The Union army was deprived of its eyes and ears during a critical juncture of the campaign. And Sheridan's decision to advance boldly to the Richmond defenses smacked of unnecessary showboating that jeopardized his command.[16]

## Old Cold Harbor

As the armies sidled southward they skirmished at various locations, encounters that gave Grant great confidence that, "Lees army is really whipped. ... I may be mistaken but I feel that our success over Lees army is already insured."[17] In order to buttress the Army of the Potomac, Grant ordered the transfer of Baldy Smith's 18th Corps from the Army of the James. On May 30 Meade ordered all commanders to leave at dawn the next day to sortie. Instead of leaving at dawn on the 31st, Sheridan left at 4:00 p.m. shortly before engaging Fitz Lee at Old Cold Harbor, a crucial intersection of five roads two miles east of Gaines Mill, one of the battlegrounds of Seven Days. Aided by the advantage of repeating carbines, Sheridan's troopers gained occupation of the crossroads, which Meade ordered to hold "at all hazards" until infantry could arrive. Baldy Smith was supposed to reinforce Sheridan but Grant's headquarters issued erroneous directions causing Smith to be delayed behind Horatio Wright's 6th Corps.[18] As soon as Wright arrived at ten o'clock the next morning Sheridan's cavalry retired almost four miles, leaving Wright without any cavalry support. Later that afternoon, in an attempt to drive the Confederates back to Richmond, Wright's corps attacked but unsupported by cavalry was unable to avoid a stalemate.

After two days fighting, the last and bloodiest day of fighting occurred on Friday, June 3, 1864, at New Cold Harbor, a mile and half west of Old Cold Harbor, where the armies had shifted before heavily entrenching. Although Lee was greatly outnumbered, his interior line stretched without reserves between the Totopotomoy and Chickahominy rivers, making it impossible to be flanked. In frustration about not being able to flank Lee's entrenchments, Grant and Meade ordered a frontal attack. Unfortunately for the Federals, the ill-advised attack was not properly coordinated, quickly resulting in horrendous number of casualties.[19] Later Grant admitted he had, "…always regretted that the last frontal attack at Cold Harbor was ever made."

At this point in Grant's Overland Campaign—including the major battles of The Wilderness, Spotsylvania, North Anna River, and Cold Harbor—had accumulated a previously untold mass of casualties, 55,000 or 37 percent of those engaged for the Union versus 32,000 or 32 percent for the Confederates. Because cavalry commanders, including most recently Sheridan, possessed a penchant to embark upon raids rather than providing direct support, such as screening, scouting, clearing of roads, impeding or even blocking enemy movements, and protection of trains, for the main army, the Army of the Potomac—never known in the first place for rapid mobility—was never able to outpace Lee's Confederates as the enemy armies moved from battlefield to battlefield, and thus was never able to gain any strategic advantage against its outnumbered, out-gunned foe.

## *Trevilian Station*

After the bloody debacle at Cold Harbor Grant decided to change his strategy. Instead of trying to draw Lee out of his fortifications into a hopefully decisive battle in the open, Grant determined the better strategy would be to outmaneuver Lee by crossing the James River and attempting to capture Petersburg, the railroad junction on the Appomattox River south of Richmond. If successful, this would sever an immense share of the Confederates' lines of communications while isolating Richmond from most of the rest of the Confederacy.

On May 15 MGen. John Breckinridge, together with Imboden's cavalry and augmented by cadets from the Virginia Military Institute, routed Sigel at New Market, half way between Winchester and Staunton.[20] Later Sigel delayed the Confederates at Harper's Ferry but

Grant still relieved Sigel for "lack of aggression," replacing the German ex-patriot on May 21, 1864, with MGen. David ("Black Dave") Hunter, 62.[21]

Hunter's new command had a total force of 11,000 infantry and 5,000 cavalry divided between two columns. The Rebel resistance was led by Grumble Jones—whom we had last seen helping to organize the assembly at Williamsport—with 5,000 cavalry augmented with 3,500 infantry. Hunter began to advance up the Shenandoah Valley on May 26 but on June 5 at Piedmont, Virginia, Jones tried to keep Hunter's two columns from uniting. After a see-saw battle, a rout of the Rebel force ensued with Jones being killed. Moreover, Hunter moved unopposed to Staunton the next day where was joined with his other column on June 8.

In order to create a diversion away from his planned move toward Petersburg, and to provide more strength to Hunter operating in the Shenandoah Valley, Grant ordered Sheridan upon another raid with several objectives, including linking with Hunter at Charlottesville before the combined force would return to the main army that hopefully would be at or at least around Petersburg.[22] The primary objective of this ambitious plan was to destroy beyond repair the rail lines and facilities between Charlottesville, Lynchburg, and Gordonsville. If accomplished this would breach access to the Confederacy's breadbasket in the Shenandoah Valley.

Leaving Wilson's division behind with the main army, on Tuesday, June 7, 1864, Little Phil departed with two divisions of 9,000 men, many who were dismounted for lack of healthy horses. As planned, Sheridan moved west for Louisa C.H. aiming to make his first attack at an obscure place called Trevilian Station, six miles southeast of Gordonsville. Sheridan intended to tear up track starting at Trevilian Station before converging with Hunter. Although the plan required Sheridan's cavalry to ride more than one hundred miles, his troopers were allowed to carry only three days' rations for themselves and two days forage for their horses.

While the maneuver might have looked good on paper, it was impossible to hide 9,000 troopers as they fanned out over enemy territory. By that evening Confederate cavalry—under the command of Wade Hampton leading five sevenths of Lee's cavalry strength—learned of the raid to quickly give chase,[23] intercepting the Blue riders at Trevilian Station on June 11. Two days of the largest cavalry-to-cavalry fighting in the Civil War ensued. Eric Wittenburg tells us the battle "...featured mounted charges with sabres glinting in the bright sunlight, desperate hand to hand fighting, valiant service by the horse artillery, and protracted, brutal dismounted conflict."[24] On the first day Union cavalry gained the tactical edge under Torbert's direction but by the end of the final battle on the second day the outnumbered Rebel riders routed the Federal cavalry from the field. In a departure from his days as an infantry commander, Little Phil was largely disengaged during both days, even failing to commit Gregg's division during the second day.

Sheridan had yet to accomplish any of his original objectives, including linkage with Hunter, but he had no realistic alternative except to begin a retreat back to the safety of his main army. But he also knew that after two days of intense fighting at Trevilian Station—and his horses having not been fed for two days—such a retreat would of necessity be at a slow pace. Accordingly, after leaving about 100 wounded and four attending surgeons behind,[25] his cavalry began its retrograde movement during the very early morning of June 13. Not only did Sheridan's withdrawing force include the usual components of his wounded plus the enemy's captured, many of whom were also wounded, but there were also approximately 2,000 contrabands to slow the pace.[26] Hampton wanted to pursue but first he had to take time to bury his dead and also take rehabilitative efforts for his command, including *his* horses, which were also in serious condition from the hard riding, intensive fighting, and a similar lack of food and forage. And so Hampton could not begin his pursuit until Sheridan had gained a day's head start.

## Lost Opportunity

While retreating eastward from Trevilian Station, Little Phil received orders to head for White House Landing on the York River. There Sheridan was to oversee the dismantling of the Northern supply base before escorting the White House Landing garrison and its equipment to a new supply base being re-established at Harrison's Landing on the James River. The relocation of the Union supply base from White House Landing to Harrison's landing might reasonably seem reminiscent of a similar relocation ordered two years earlier by George McClellan as part of his retreat during Six Days Battles. However this time Grant had a more audacious ploy in mind; he was not retreating but instead was trying to steal the march toward Petersburg, starting to lay the groundwork for such move as early as June 6 when he sent two aides to obtain topographical information about the James![27]

On May 15, 1864, while Lee and Grant were still skirmishing near Spotsylvania Court House, Beauregard defeated Ben Butler at the Battle of Drewery's Bluff, also known as Ware Bottom Church. In doing so Beauregard nullified that prong of Grant's Grand Strategy against the Confederacy.

After nightfall on the evening of June 12 the Army of the Potomac resumed shifting to the south. Before starting to move the entire army, Grant cleverly disguised his principle objective. Specifically he sent Warren's corps, accompanied by Wilson's cavalry division, toward Richmond; concurrently Baldy Smith's 18th Corps retraced its steps back to White House Landing to board riverboats before circling around the end of the Peninsula to start back up the James River to land at Bermuda Hundred.[28]

After Lee—who could ill afford to allow Federal access to Richmond—fell for Warren's feint, and once Smith's corps cleared the roads, the rest of the Union army, including three infantry corps and the army's baggage trains, carefully withdrew from its Cold Harbor trenches to begin a 55-mile march to Charles City C.H. near the James. During the night of June 14–15 they started traversing a 2,100-foot bridge laid across 110 pontoons. After supervising the crossing, Grant established his headquarters at City Point where the Appomattox River flows into the south bank of the James. Although Sheridan's Trevilian Station raid failed to achieve its primary objectives, Grant's march to and across the James was successful in part because Sheridan had drawn two Rebel cavalry divisions away from Lee's main army while Warren's ruse, accompanied by Wilson's cavalry that blocked reconnaissance and made demonstrations,[29] had held Lee in place at Cold Harbor.

At this point the Union had a rare, golden chance to strike a nearly mortal blow against the Confederates. Jeffry Wert tells us that because of its rail linkage between Richmond and the rest of the South, "Petersburg was a prize of inestimable worth."[30] While Lee was still responding to Grant's Richmond ruse, the Petersburg defenses were stretched dangerously thin with little help close at hand. After Seven Days the Confederacy had constructed a series of concentric fortifications around Petersburg but the works were grossly undermanned. P.G.T. Beauregard was in overall charge of the Petersburg defenses but he had already detached his largest division to Cold Harbor to reinforce Lee. The ten-mile length of fortifications in front of Petersburg was manned by only 3,200 soldiers including 2,400 men under Virginia' ex-governor (1856–60), the acerbic BGen. Henry Wise, 58.[31] Another 4,000 had been assigned to the Bermuda Hundred area to continue corking Benjamin Butler's 10th Corps in that bottle. Accordingly Beauregard was forced once again to use all his considerable wiles to disguise the undermanned status of his Petersburg fortifications.

For just a short period Grant had tens of thousands of soldiers available to attack the paltry defenses in front of Petersburg. On Wednesday, June 15, 1864, Baldy Smith had two of his own divisions, plus a black division augmented by BGen. August V. Kautz's small cavalry division from Ben Butler's Army of the James, in place to attack these attenuated Petersburg defenses. But Kautz allowed a Rebel attack to delay him, which in turn discouraged Smith from advancing until mid-afternoon. But even with that delay Smith still had 15,000 soldiers at his immediate disposal with Hancock's in the area with another 20,000 men. Despite these overwhelmingly favorable odds, Smith continued to move cautiously, perhaps as a result of his harrowing experience in charging Confederate fortifications at Cold Harbor.[32] Indeed throughout the entire Overland Campaign Union officers and soldiers saw trenches and other fortifications that Grant had time-and-time again ordered to be assaulted to the cost of tens of thousands of lives. As a result of these repeated attacks the assaults were becoming half-hearted as best.[33] Even so, by late evening Smith's Black division managed to breach about a mile of the Confederate's outer lines at Petersburg, including capture of a half-dozen batteries.[34] But then Smith could hear a locomotive approaching that Smith correctly surmised meant Rebel reinforcements were beginning to arrive. But even still with an overwhelming numerical advantage Smith was too timid to press his advantage, instead halting at the outer works.

By next morning, June 16, Confederate numbers increased from 3,200 soldiers, plus the home guard, to 10,000 men. Both sides were bringing reinforcements to the Petersburg arena so that by the evening of June 16 Beauregard's numbers increased to 14,000 soldiers while the Federals had 55,000 men in the area.[35] Grant had intended that Hancock's corps would join Smith's but that order failed to reach Hancock until the morning of June 17. In fact when the order arrived Hancock's corps was still 15 miles from Petersburg awaiting three days rations that never arrived. The 2nd Corps' march to the front was impeded by faulty maps and by the lingering effects of Hancock's Gettysburg wounds that would soon require him to seek a temporary leave of absence. Hancock's corps relieved Smith's by midmorning of the 17th but the 2nd Corps was also too slow in resuming the attack to capitalize upon its continuing superiority in numbers. Essentially Hancock's corps made a charge that was met with severe fire before Hancock's corps quit upon him despite his futile efforts. Reflecting the toil extracted from the Overland Campaign, veteran soldiers who once fearlessly charged entrenched positions at Fredericksburg, Antietam, and Spotsylvania had become reluctant to charge, if they would charge at all.[36]

Although Baldy Smith deservedly received much, if not most, of the blame for the failure to exploit the Confederacy's vulnerability, in fact the failure of the 2nd Corps on June 17 was also largely responsible for wasting the Petersburg opportunities. And it is a matter of reasonable speculation whether scouting by additional Union cavalry would have been able to ascertain how vulnerable the Confederate lines were, especially during the first two days of the Petersburg battle.

Burnside's 9th Corps then joined the fray, capturing some works before being repulsed by counterattacks by the ever growing number of Rebels. From Petersburg Beauregard had been desperately seeking more reinforcements. After Warren's corps had pulled back from its feint to join the trek down to and across the James, finally by June 19 Lee brought the remainder of his army to undertake the defenses of Petersburg. Accordingly when the Union army once again assaulted the fortifications on the 19th they were met with murderous artillery and musket fire, described by the veteran soldiers—verified by casualty statistics—as the worst day they had ever encountered. One regimental commander claimed the Rebels "cut our men down like hail cuts the grain and grass."[37] Many soldiers throughout the army described the Petersburg attacks as horrid massacres with men being sent forward merely to "get shot."[38]

During these four days of attacks, the Federals suffered almost 10,000 casualties, a higher casualty rate than that suffered at Cold Harbor. As terrible as were the casualty rates for the Union's 2nd Corps, Burnside's corps suffered even worse. Jeffry Wert summarizes those four days thusly, "For a few critical days, Petersburg was a vulnerable prize, weakly defended against a powerful foe. But misunderstandings, timid generalship, and the exhaustion of the troops denied it to the Federals."[39] Grant realized that the Army of the Potomac was worn to a frazzle, essentially ceasing to exist as a cohesive, viable fighting force. Grant decided against any more assaults saying, "Now we will rest the men and use the spade for their protection until a new vein has been cut."[40] As a result of Beauregard's stand, Grant was forced to resort to investing in a siege against Petersburg, again stymieing Federal progress in the war. Grant was converting the strategy from Lee's superb infantry to Union engineering, artillery, and superior numbers.[41]

Meanwhile Hampton's cavalry was still chasing Sheridan as he continued his slow retreat from Trevilian toward White House Landing. Hampton caught up with Little Phil at White House Landing on June 21 when several spirited skirmishes erupted but without any consequential results. Both opposing cavalries took their first day off in two weeks to rest and to care for their horses. The next day, Thursday, June 23, 1864, Sheridan began moving the column of 900 wagons extending for more than ten miles. Despite repeated Rebel attacks against this tempting target, Sheridan adroitly managed to get the train to and across the James by that evening. However, one cavalry officer from Massachusetts succinctly observed "I don't think these giant raids amount to much."[42]

The record of Union cavalry was decidedly mixed during Grant's Overland Campaign that concluded with the failure to exploit the Rebel weakness at Petersburg. There were isolated successes such as the mortal wounding of Jeb Stuart but overall the raids contributed little to attaining the objectives of the Overland Campaign. On the other hand much of the blame for the failures rested with Grant who either allowed or initiated orders that sent Sheridan's cavalry upon raids meant to divert Lee's attention from Grant's maneuvers. But regardless of who was responsible for the raids, the absence of much of the Union cavalry for large portions of the Overland Campaign meant the main army was deprived of its principle source of intelligence to help determine the enemy's strength, locations, and movements. At this point it is merely conjectural but there were several instances when the Army of the Potomac should have had greater success if it had not been operating blindly without more and closer cavalry support. One cannot help but wonder if better, and frankly more conservative, deployment of Blue cavalry might have meant success for the Overland Campaign in terms of the defeat of Lee's Army of Northern Virginia by June 1864 or at least the early capture of Petersburg, which in turn would have resulted in a quicker strangulation of the Confederacy.

## Sheridan's Army Command

Sheridan's ascension to command of an army began as a counterstroke to Lee's deployment of his 2nd Corps into the Shenandoah Valley. The 2nd Corps commander, Richard Ewell, was undergoing long term health issues, some related to the amputation of his leg from Second Bull Run but further aggravated by Ewell exerting himself ceaselessly.[43] Although Ewell was so ill that he became prostrate in his tent, he was also reluctant to take any sick leave but Lee insisted that he do so and on May 29, 1864, named Jubal ("Old Jube") Early as Ewell's permanent replacement.[44]

Early, whom Lee called his "bad old man," was a rarity among Civil War generals on either side. A lifelong bachelor who fathered four illegitimate children, he had none of the usual Confederate ideological beliefs, indeed having opposed secession. He was a gruff, blunt atheist who was completely indifferent about gaining any popularity. Early was one of the most respected combat officers in Lee's army yet his irascibility, arrogance, derisive, and abrasive nature meant his was also despised by almost everyone. Early was a non-stop talker with an endless litany of opinions on a wide variety of subjects.[45] He had a general appearance of carelessness and disarray who carried an "inevitable canteen," supposedly filled with Kentucky "Old Crow."[46]

Early's Civil War service began when he commanded a regiment at First Bull Run, and with few exceptions, compiled an excellent record as a subordinate commander. Fiercely independent, even insubordinate at times, he possessed considerable tactical skills, especially on the defensive side. Early had served mostly under Richard Ewell in the Confederate's 2nd Corps but he had also served short stints as substitute commander of the 2nd Corps as well as substitute commander of the 3rd Corps whenever A.P. Hill was too ill to perform. Early's 2nd Corps was once part of Stonewall Jackson's command and was considered as probably the Confederacy's finest corps.

Black Dave Hunter was creating havoc with his rapid advance up the Shenandoah Valley, including torching the Virginia Military Institute at Lexington, Virginia, on June 11, the same day the opposing cavalries began their fight at Trevilian Station. In response to Hunter's rampaging, on Sunday, June 12, 1864—as Lee and Grant were maneuvering away from Cold Harbor—Lee detached Jubal Early and his 2nd Corps—including three infantry divisions plus two artillery battalions—north to drive Hunter from the Confederates' breadbasket in the Shenandoah Valley. Lee detached a fourth of his strength at Petersburg in the strategic hopes it could match its accomplishments of two years earlier.[47] Lee also hoped Early could threaten Washington and/or Baltimore to the extent that Grant would be forced to divert a sizable number of troops away from Lee's defenses.

The Shenandoah Valley mission would be Early's first independent command. To underscore Early's mission, as Old Jube was preparing to leave Lee told his subordinate among other things, "We must destroy this army of Grant's before he gets to the James River. If he gets there it will become a siege, and then it will be a mere question of time."[48]

In essence, Early's 2nd Corps became a reconstituted (and undersized) Army of the Valley. Even though this army still carried battle flags from Stonewall's original force of more than two years ago, it had suffered savage wear and tear since that glory period. For instance it had suffered extensively May 12, 1864, during the Bloody Angle at Spotsylvania when most of the Stonewall Brigade was cut off and captured without even being able to fire more than a few shots.[49] It was comprised primarily of three infantry divisions, led respectively by MGen. Robert Rodes, 35, MGen. John B. Gordon, 32, and MGen. Stephen D. Ramseur, 27. Although these commanders were younger than had been their predecessors at comparable command levels, by 1864 they were battle tested, combat hardened commanders who among other things helped save the day at Bloody Angle. Rodes had been blamed by some for a lack of initiative on Day One at Gettysburg, he had nevertheless become widely respected as a pillar of the Confederate war effort.[50] Gordon, once a Georgia lawyer, was a rising star in the Confederacy whom Early seemed to resent.[51] Ramseur took his first command position prior to Seven Days but had been wounded three times, the last being at the Bloody Angle. BGen. Armistead Long, 39, Lee's former military secretary, commanded the artillery battalion consisting of two batteries. Initially Early's army had no cavalry but Lee intended to add more units as Early advanced into and down the Valley. For instance, the division belonging to MGen. John C. Breckinridge, 43, was expected to soon join Early's army even though Early did not even know where Breckinridge was located.

After Early marched west to Charlottesville he boarded trains to Lynchburg, the vital railroad junction linking the Shenandoah Valley with eastern Virginia. On June 17 his advance units joined forces with Breckinridge to coerce Hunter to abandon plans to enter and occupy Lynchburg. Hunter then retreated west into West Virginia eliminating any possibility to join Sheridan either at Lynchburg or any other point, including Charlottesville, to the east while giving Old Jube an unimpeded path down the Shenandoah Valley..[52] Lee had gambled by reducing his immediate Petersburg defenses to two corps when he sent Early to the Shenandoah Valley but he also prevented Hunter's small army from becoming a further threat. More importantly, Lee still retained control of the Confederacy's vital breadbasket.

Early moved down the Shenandoah Valley to destroy portions of the Baltimore & Ohio Railroad before crossing the Potomac River at Harper's Ferry. After crossing the Potomac, Early advanced into Maryland and even into Pennsylvania, where in June 1864 a Rebel cavalry brigade burned Chambersburg to the ground before beginning to threaten Baltimore and/or Washington.[53]

On Friday, July 8, 1864, MGen. Lew Wallace with a cobbled force of 5,800 men at Monocacy south-east of Frederick, Maryland, attempted to block Early's 14,000 men advancing toward Washington.[54] Although Wallace was blamed for a tactical defeat at Monocacy he also achieved a strategic gain by buying time while sufficient reinforcements were being rushed to the capital's defenses.

But after Lew Wallace managed to stall Early's advance at Monocacy, Old Jube was easily able to approach the outskirts of Washington still ringed with numerous fortifications.

However, unlike earlier years the fortifications were no longer fully manned, almost all able bodied soldiers having been transferred elsewhere, mostly as replacement troops for the Army of the Potomac.

By the next day Early's army approached some of the fifty-three forts, including Fort Stevens, surrounding Washington. The War Department was desperately finding and bringing in other units, most notably the battle hardened 6th Corps, commanded by MGen. Horatio G. Wright, 44,[55] whose appearance apparently persuaded Early to withdraw during the night of July 12–13, 1864, before resuming his destruction of more sections of the B&O R.R. As a side note, prior to Early's withdrawal Abraham Lincoln visited Fort Stevens while it was being subjected to sniper fire from Rebel sharpshooters. As Lincoln exposed himself by peering over the parapet a young officer yelled out, "Get down you damned fool!" The officer probably was Oliver Wendell Holmes, Jr., who would eventually become a long-standing, influential Justice on the U.S. Supreme Court.[56]

Having determined that his raid into Maryland had maximized its gain, Early began his retreat from Fort Stevens the morning of July 12, with his rear guard leaving the area in the late afternoon.[57] Finally, by mid-afternoon of the 13th Horatio Wright, with 14,000 infantry, left Fort Stevens in the most meaningful pursuit of Early's retreat. After marching fifteen miles over a five-hour span, Wright rested until early the next morning when his chase resumed. That same day, July 14, Early's Army of the Valley completed its crossing of the Potomac.[58] Old Jube decided to rest his soldiers on the 15th because he felt Wright was not pursuing aggressively.

Horatio Wright, a career soldier who had graduated second in his West Point class, served mostly as an engineer prior to the Civil War. Taking on infantry command after the war began, Wright was steadily competent, particularly within a larger command, but without exhibiting any brilliance or aggressiveness. Even worse Assistant Secretary of War Charles Dana once observed that Wright possessed "no predilection for fighting."[59] Although Wright had struggled at Spotsylvania and at Petersburg, there might have been no alternative to retaining Wright as corps commander.[60]

Wright likewise rested his soldiers on the 15th, not crossing the Potomac until July 16 while Early was already crossing the Blue Ridge at Snicker's Gap.[61] Lincoln's reaction to Wright's careful pace was scathing: "He [Wright] thinks the enemy are all across the Potomac but that he has halted and sent out an infantry reconnaissance, for fear he might come across the rebels and catch some of them."[62]

In fairness, Wright's pursuit was hampered by two factors, one being beyond his control. First, Grant's orders were unclear and even contradictory. Publically Grant wanted Wright to destroy Early's Army of the Valley but Grant also wanted Wright to pursue only so long as there was a chance of "punishing" Early. After that Grant wanted Wright to return to Petersburg where Grant already had a two-to-one advantage over the besieged R.E. Lee. Realistically Grant, in his headquarters in City Point, was too far removed from the Shenandoah Valley to provide effective guidance to Wright, especially through the intermediary of Henry Halleck. But given any ambiguity about Grant's posture, Wright was likely to seek the least risky course of action.

Wright's relationship with David Hunter was also problematic. After being chased away from Lynchburg into West Virginia, Hunter was slowly returning eastward, having arrived at Cumberland, Maryland, on July 8.[63] On July 15 Hunter received a telegram from

Halleck directing Hunter to turn over portions of his command either to Wright or BGen. George Crook, 35, one of Hunter's division commanders who had been interrupting Southern rail communications between Lynchburg and Eastern Tennessee. Feeling insulted, Hunter asked to be relieved of command while ordering 7,000 of his infantry under BGen. Jeremiah C. Sullivan, 34, plus 2,000 cavalry under BGen. Alfred Duffié, to march toward Aldie at the eastern foot of the Blue Ridge.[64]

From Aldie the Sullivan-Duffié group was in position to interrupt Early's march toward the Snicker's Gap. Instead they encamped out of harm's way until Crook arrived to take charge. Crook ordered his new command of cavalry to find Early's army, which they did, capturing 37 wagons and burning 40 other wagons of Early's train.[65] Although Crook assumed command of an additional portion of Hunter's overall command (Hunter was not completely relieved until August 8), the new relationship between Wright and Crook was hardly an improvement over Wright's relationship with Hunter. For an unfortunate instance, as Early continued to move through Snicker's Gap and on across the Shenandoah River, Wright followed to the point that the armies faced each other across the difficult-to-ford Shenandoah. By July 17 one of Crook's brigades marched north to cross at Island Ford.[66] The Rebels attack forced this small force to take cover behind a stone wall. When no other Federals crossed the river to lend reinforcements, Crook sought permission from Wright to withdraw but Wright refused.[67] Wright ordered one of his divisions to cross over to the beachhead but that division commander refused after witnessing the Confederate attack. According to Steven Bernstein, Crook never forgave Wright and claimed Wright had allowed a "useless sacrifice" of Crook's soldiers stranded on the Cool Spring farm west of the Shenandoah.[68] Although the enemies continued to skirmish against each other, for all intents and purposes it was obvious Wright was avoiding a full-scale confrontation with Early, and that the Federal pursuit of Early was over.

Without a unified command any Federal effort of four separate military departments against Early seemed futile.[69] Given our perspective of 150 or so years of hindsight it may often seem as though little military knowledge had been gained during the course of the Civil War. However the Federals at least came to understand and appreciate the importance of unity of command, in large part because of its frustrations against Stonewall Jackson in the same Shenandoah Valley a little more than two years earlier. Accordingly the Federals decided to create another command unified to protect Washington and to drive Early back up the Shenandoah Valley. Several possible commanders, including Meade, were considered. Halleck was considered a logical possibility, at least on the surface, but Old Brains had already shown his ineptitude as a field commander. Furthermore his tenure in Washington had exposed his inability to make command decisions under virtually any circumstances. Ironically given Halleck's previous suspicions, and professed disapproval, about Grant's drinking there were reports that Halleck's mind was "regularly muddled after dinner every day" from his own heavy drinking.[70]

To unify command of the Union corps already in the Washington area, on August 1, 1864, Grant appointed Sheridan as commander of the new army, called the Army of the Shenandoah, with orders to rid the Shenandoah Valley of Early, to destroy the Confederacy's breadbasket, and to destroy the Virginia Central Railroad.

As with numerous other Civil War command issues there is a substantial difference of opinion about Sheridan's bona fides to be elevated to army command, especially given

## 18. Little Phil Comes East

his age and lack of infantry corps command experience. Albert Castel and Brooks Simpson contend Sheridan's elevation was due to his performance during the recent Overland Campaign during which, according to Castel and Simpson, Little Phil had

> ... transformed the Army of the Potomac's cavalry from what hitherto been mainly picket service and escorting trains into a highly mobile, hard-hitting combat force capable of holding its own and increasingly more than that when engaging Lee's cavaliers, thanks to repeating carbines and fighting as much, if not more, on foot rather than astride a saddle.[71]

These esteemed historians seem to have overlooked that more than a year earlier the Union cavalry had broken away from the tethers of strictly picket and escort service. At a minimum there was Stoneman's raid during Chancellorsville, Brandy Station, Buford's stalwart stands during the first day of Gettysburg, the operations of Kilpatrick and Buford during the pursuit of the Rebels after Gettysburg, and the Kilpatrick-Dahlgren Raid. While not all these operations were entirely successful they at least showed that Union cavalry had been coming of age and had been undertaking more ambitious missions long before Sheridan's arrival.

On the other hand, Eric Wittenberg, probably the preeminent historian of Federal cavalry in the Eastern Theater, disputes the conventional historical conclusions about Sheridan's performance as a cavalry corps commander. Wittenberg's evaluation of Sheridan's cavalry command performance is that,

> Aside from his dubious record of success, Sheridan employed unimaginative tactics. His cavalry often fought as infantry, and he rarely demonstrated a true understanding of the nature of mounted combat. Further, his troopers had a significant advantage in both manpower and firepower as a result of their repeating weapons. They should have bested their Southern adversaries on almost every battlefield, but poor tactics often negated these advantages, as at Trevilian Station on June 12.[72]

It is also worth noting that by the end of the Overland Campaign both cavalries were exhausted and depleted. However the Federal cavalry still enjoyed better recuperative power because of their remount stations as well as a more efficient, more robust system to resupply weapons and other essential equipment. In the final analysis Grant's eventual appointment of Sheridan may have been influenced by Grant's personal fondness for commanders who appeared to be bold, aggressive, and decisive, characteristics that certainly fit Sheridan.

On August 6, 1864, Sheridan met with Grant at Monocacy Junction where Sheridan took command of the newly created Army of the Shenandoah, the infantry consisting of the 6th Corps, commanded by Wright, two divisions of the 19th corps, commanded by BGen. William H. Emory, 53, and the Army of West Virginia, by then commanded by George Crook, Sheridan's West Point classmate, replacing Hunter. Crook's Army of West Virginia was augmented by the transfer of two divisions from the 8th Corps.

Emory, a former topographical engineer, a former artillery officer, and a former cavalry commander, was yet another Mexican War veteran who had fought in almost all sectors of the Civil War. Most recently Emory led a division in the 19th Corps in Louisiana where Emory acquitted himself well in an otherwise disastrous campaign. Emory was expected to provide old army reliable performance but without much initiative or aggressiveness.[73]

Although George Crook was Little Phil's oldest and closest friend the two had radically different personalities. Whereas Sheridan was normally eager and frequently impulsive, Crook was "a notably keen and clear headed man, whose equanimity was rarely, if ever, disturbed, even under the most trying of circumstances."[74] Crook's limited educational opportunities prior to West Point contributed to his modest academic ranking but nevertheless he quickly exhibited an aptitude for battlefield tactics. Prior to the Civil War Crook experienced combat fighting Indians in the Pacific Northwest before being commissioned as a colonel in the 36th Ohio at the start of the war. He was an affable, unaffected officer who, unlike most of his comrades, did not smoke or drink, even coffee.[75]

The cavalry in this new army also had disparate sources but three years of contending with Stuart's Rebel horsemen had created cavalry units that were tough and battle tempered. William Averell's cavalry accompanied Crook from West Virginia; in effect, Averell was returning from the exile imposed by Joe Hooker during Chancellorsville.[76] Alfred Torbert and his 1st Cavalry Division together with James Wilson with his 3rd Cavalry Division were sent north from Petersburg leaving David Gregg's cavalry division at Petersburg. These infantry and cavalry units, including artillery among the infantry, gave Sheridan a combined force of nearly 45,000 men to operate against Early's 20,000 mostly veteran soldiers, only 4,000 of whom were cavalrymen.[77] Of the 29 cavalry regiments, fifteen were completely armed with Spencer repeaters, giving these mounted soldiers firepower that not even some Southern infantry could match.[78]

Sheridan designated Torbert, upon whom Sheridan relied so heavily during the previous four months, as chief of his three divisions of cavalry, jumping him over the more senior and cautious Averell, a McClellan Democrat.[79] Wesley Merritt, an 1860 West Point graduate with a reputation for coolness in battle, was bumped up to take command of Torbert's former division. After two years as a cavalry staff officer, shortly before Gettysburg Merritt assumed command of a cavalry brigade that distinguished itself at Gettysburg, Todd's Tavern, and Yellow Tavern.[80] One of Torbert's staff officers described Merritt as having, "…a constitution of iron, and underneath a rather passive demeanor concealed a fiery ambition."[81] Exact numbers are not available but the Union cavalry of 8,000 riders was estimated to comprise 18–19 percent of the army, or about twice the usual percentage of cavalry in Civil War armies.

Later in August Early was reinforced by the arrival of another infantry division (4,500 men) commanded by Joseph B. Kershaw and by Fitz Lee's cavalry (2,000 riders).

Preliminaries out of the way, the stage was then set for a series of significant battles that constituted the major, and decisive, portion of the Shenandoah Valley Campaign of 1864. One side would emerge entirely triumphant with its commander becoming a national a hero. The vanquished would not only lose the campaign but would be forced to relinquish a valuable, strategic resource for its side. Furthermore the commander of the losing army would be sent home in disgrace, never again to being part of the remaining struggle.

## *Third Winchester*[82]

The sides had scattered, having only accidental contact with each other during the early days of September 1864. The Rebels withdrew to behind (the west side) of the Opequon Creek, running north to south along the east side of Winchester. Grant had cautioned Sheridan to be careful, an admonition that Little Phil apparently took to heart. Sheridan's relative inactivity was causing apprehension by Northern politicians as well as consternation by the C.E.O. of the B&O R.R. Additionally, on September 17 Early was emboldened to divide his force, sending a couple divisions twenty-two miles northward to strike the B&O at Martinsburg, close to the Potomac River, and another division down the Pike to Bunker Hill.[83] Unfortunately for Early, his strength was diminished when Kershaw's division was withdrawn, something that Sheridan learned on September 16 from a local Quaker and schoolteacher, a Union sympathizer who ran a boardinghouse frequented by Confederate soldiers.[84]

The same day Grant visited Sheridan who shared his attack plans with Grant who was happy to approve. But when Early learned Grant was conferring with Sheridan Early presciently assumed Sheridan would soon be launching an attack[85]; accordingly Old Jube withdrew his divisions to the northern and eastern edges of Winchester. At that point Early had 13,000 to 15,000 men at hand while Sheridan commanded a combined force of 39,000.

The next day, Monday, September 19, 1864, Sheridan started operations that became the Third Battle of Winchester (also being the seventh engagement inside the town).[86] Predicated upon coordinated speed, Sheridan planned to have his infantry pressing along an arc from east and north of Winchester, hopefully to smash the Rebels into bits and pieces. Averell's and Merritt's cavalries, under Torbert, would advance from the north on the right flank. Wilson, with his cavalry division of 3,300, followed by 20,000 soldiers in Wright's and Emory's two infantry corps, was supposed to open the attack by crossing the Opequon, clear a confined canyon two miles in length, seize the open ground on the other side of the canyon, and strike on the left (or southern) flank before changing direction, to cut off any Confederate retreat.[87] Crook, with 10,000 soldiers in his small Army of West Virginia, would be held in reserve east of the Opequon, two miles to the rear.

As often happened in Civil War operations, several circumstances, most critically terrain, hindered the implementation of Sheridan's tactics. Moreover, Early anticipated Sheridan's maneuvers and Confederate cavalry exploited the narrow confines of the ravine to delay Wilson's advance.[88] More importantly Wright's advance following Wilson was impeded even more by the limited road, "crowded with artillery, ammunition wagons, and ambulances," together with roadsides through which the columns "stumbled over rocky, guttered ground, and straggled through the underbrush."[89] Furthermore Wright made the mistake of bring his ammunition train, which added to the congestion along the narrow canyon.[90] Trying to make things happen as quickly as possible, Sheridan rode along the front lines, "treating the infantrymen to a taste of the sweetest swearing they had ever heard."[91] But much of the delay was of Sheridan's own making since he sent this sizable force along only one road when two other roads were also available.[92] True to his character, Sheridan never accepted responsibility for the delay, blaming Wright for the delays and contending for years later that, "...I have always thought that by adhering to the original plan we might have captured the bulk of Early's army."[93]

During the first couple of hours the Rebel defenders fought valiantly, inflicting twice as many casualties as they suffered. As Rebel generals John Gordon and Robert Rodes were preparing to send their divisions through a gap in the Union lines, an artillery shell exploded to crush Rodes' skull, killing him before he fell to the ground. The Confederate counterattack—featuring hand-to-hand combat—eventually failed in its main objective of breaching Sheridan's lines. However the counterattack against the gap forced Sheridan to urgently summon his reserve, Crook's corps with its 10,000 soldiers still east of the Opequon, to strengthen the Union right. But until Crook's corps could take its new position, the situation was best described as being "…extremely critical and the Union army was on the verge of a serious defeat, if not an absolute disaster, … considerable time must necessarily elapse before [Crook's Corps] could possible reach the field."[94]

That looming disaster was thwarted by a Union brigade, under BGen. Emory Upton, 25,[95] that stemmed the Confederate counterattack while plugging the gap long enough for Crook's army to arrive.[96] Crook's arrival was delayed when his army took the same debris-strewn path taken by Wright's and Emory's corps earlier in the morning. Prior to Crook's arrival fewer than 13,000 Confederates fought approximately 30,000 Federals to a standstill. On the other hand, Crook's redeployment allowed a flanking attack led by Col. Rutherford B. Hayes, 42, through a swamp around Early's left side. By 5:00 p.m. the left side of the Rebel army began withdrawing toward Winchester.

Also five brigades of Union cavalry on Sheridan's right side, with its overwhelming numerical advantage continued to advance southward along either side of the Valley Turnpike[97] to overcome the Southern resistance, Fitz Lee taking a bullet in his thigh; one infantry soldier recalled the charge was "the most gallant and exciting cavalry charge I ever saw."[98] Merritt's cavalry continued to press the fight, launching repeated charges against the Rebels' rear guard. In one of the rare instances when cavalry prevailed over infantry, Merritt's division alone captured 775 prisoners, including 70 officers, and two pieces of artillery.[99]

On Early's right side, Wilson working with Wright and Emory slowly pushed the overwhelmed Rebels's line backwards until it collapsed altogether.[100] By the end of the day, the demoralized survivors in Early's army were stampeding pell-mell through Winchester and toward Strasburg, ten miles to the south, leaving burning caissons and ambulances in its wake. But Little Phil's hopes to interdict any pursuit failed to materialize when Wilson was bluffed into unwarranted passivity by fewer than 1,400 shoddily armed and mounted Rebel troopers[101] Despite having a sizable numerical advantage, and despite having troopers armed with Spencer repeating rifles supported by a six-gun battery, Wilson timidly failed to charge through Early's outmanned flank while the Rebel main army hurriedly headed south. Scott Patchan opines that—perhaps stating the obvious—if Wilson had broken through the attenuated lines ahead of him he might have also had Merritt's success.[102] One Confederate colonel mused, "Why this great body of horse was not hurled upon General Early's army is a mystery to me."[103] But the fact of the matter was that without infantry support, Wilson's 3,300 cavalry would not have seriously impeded the whole of Early's army, no matter how disorganized.[104]

Early suffered 4,000 casualties or nearly 30 percent of his effectives.[105] On the other side, Sheridan's army suffered 5,000 casualties (including the death of one of a respected division commander, David Russell) with his infantry being too tired and too bloodied from ten hours of marching and fighting to join in any pursuit. Crook's redeployment also meant he was not available to help Wilson, Wright, and Emory with the planned pursuit south of Winchester. Nevertheless Wilson later commented that "Winchester was the first large scale action of the war in which foot soldiers and cavalrymen were employed in proper conjunction."[106] Rutherford Hayes was also impressed, exclaiming, "Sheridan's cavalry is splendid. It is the most right thing I have seen during the war."[107] And Early later lamented "The enemy's very great superiority in cavalry and the comparative inefficiency of ours turned the scale against us."[108]

Third Winchester was the harbinger of the destruction of what was left of Stonewall

Jackson's former army, Early's Army of the Valley. The loquacious John Gordon neatly summarized the Confederate plight, "There was no limit to lofty courage, to loyal devotion, and the spirit of self-sacrifice; but where were the men to come from to take the place of the maimed and the dead? Where were the arsenals from which to replace the diminishing materials of war?"[109] Finally, after the frustrating setbacks at The Wilderness, Spotsylvania, North Anna, and Cold Harbor, and despite some tactical errors by Sheridan, the Federals had their first undeniable victory in Grant's Eastern campaign of 1864.[110]

## Fisher's Hill

After stopping to rest the evening of the 19th, Sheridan pressed his cavalry and infantry to resume pressure as Old Jube was forced further south along the Valley Turnpike up the Shenandoah Valley where Stonewall Jackson had launched his army to resounding success in 1862. As described in Chapter 10, the landscape is dominated by the northern end of Massanutten Mountain approximately 20 miles south of Winchester. The Shenandoah Valley continues west of the mountain while the area east of the Massanutten is often called the Luray Valley. Strasburg, a "dingy, dilapidated village" to the west, and Front Royal, to the east, sit at the northern corners of the Massanutten.

Sheridan's cavalry van skirmished with Early's rear guard at several locations, including near Middletown, Strasburg, and Cedarville. About two miles southeast of Strasburg, Early created a new defensive line at Fisher's Hill, the eastern, or left, end of the line almost at the North Fork of the Shenandoah River. This battlefield's name is misleading since the line was not on a single hillside but instead was along two roughly parallel low knobs running between the Valley's steep slopes. While this nearly four-mile line was well conceived—perhaps the best available defensive position in the Shenandoah Valley—Early's losses at Winchester as well as by the redeployment of Breckinridge's division back to southwestern Virginia thinned his already diminished army.[111] At this point Sheridan enjoyed, and intended to take advantage of, a 4–1 numerical advantage over Early.

Sheridan aimed to strike Early's army from the north while the Blue cavalry would cross one of the Massanutten's few gaps to establish blocking positions to the south. In preparation for Sheridan's overall pursuit, on September 20 he sent Wilson to attack the Rebels' rear guard at Front Royal.[112] After a fierce fight the next day in dense fog, Wilson's troopers sent the Confederates scurrying south.

By the afternoon of Thursday, September 22, 1864, Crook crossed Cedar Creek between Strasburg and Middletown, before marching mostly unseen under cover of ravines and heavy woods adjacent to Fisher's Hill, eventually taking position against Early's far left. In order to create a diversion from Crook's flanking attack, Averell's cavalry was positioned to the right of the infantry line—across from dismounted Rebel cavalry that was undermanned, hungry, and poorly armed.[113] Apparently, or at least they would later claim, some Confederate defenders observed Crook getting into position but Early would later claim he was never aware of the threat on his left. In any event no effort was taken to buttress the left of Old Jube's defensive line before Crook and Averell began their flanking attack shortly before sunset.[114] Unfortunately for Early his dismounted cavalry on his left were outnumbered, perhaps by as much as 5–1, and despite pockets of gallant resistance, were soundly whipped and scattered. Gordon succinctly summarized what happened: "To all experienced soldiers the whole story is told in one word—'Flanked.'"[115] As Crook was collapsing Early's left, Sheridan personally led a fierce frontal attack that once again scattered Early's dwindling army. In his report to Grant that evening Sheridan claimed that "only darkness has saved the whole of Early's army from total destruction."[116]

But Sheridan's claim about darkness might have not been totally forthcoming. Despite the darkness Sheridan's infantry divisions continued their chase up the Valley, albeit with disorganized, broken ranks. The Confederate stampede continued for miles, as described by Jedediah Hotchkiss, the famous Confederate mapmaker, "The rout of wagons, caissons, limbers, artillery, and flying men was fearful as the stream swept down the pike toward Woodstock, as many thought the enemy's cavalry was aiming to get there by the Middle Road and cut us off."[117] That is exactly what Sheridan intended and anticipated!

To help implement his plan of capturing the fleeing Rebels, Sheridan sent Torbert with Merritt's division to meet Wilson's division before heading up the Luray Valley east of the Massanutten. Sheridan wanted Torbert to cross the Massanutten at the New Market Gap to be in position at New Market—thirty miles south of Fisher's Hill—to block Early's anticipated retreat.[118] Early in the morning of the 22nd, Wilson pushed some Gray horse riders back six miles up the Luray Valley east of the Massanutten before encountering a couple brigades of fortified Rebel cavalry. Rather than to press his overwhelming numerical advantage, and not realizing Sheridan was routing Early from Fisher's Hill, after a couple hours exchanging artillery fire, Torbert broke off before countermarching to return down the Luray Road to Front Royal.[119] Since Torbert's two cavalry divisions were not in a blocking position, Early's army escaped up the Valley 25 miles to Woodstock, something Sheridan never understood or forgave later commenting, "To this day I have been unable to account satisfactorily for Torbert's failure.... Torbert ought to have made a fight ... it does not appear he made any serious effort at all to dislodge the Confederate cavalry."[120]

Federal losses were light, altogether 162 killed, wounded or missing. Confederate losses were much heavier, approximately 1,000 prisoners alone being taken. Additionally the Rebels were forced to abandon at least twelve invaluable artillery pieces.

Although Sheridan's army had won overwhelming victories in the space of three days, Federal cavalry was altered by ongoing command changes. First, as early as September 1 Grant had authorized Sheridan to relieve Averell for a perceived lack of aggressiveness. After helping Crook roll up the Confederate left at Fisher's Hill, Averell broke off his pursuit after seven miles to encamp for the night.[121] The next day, at Woodstock Averell and Sheridan had a loud, testy argument, the surface issue being why Averell had not aggressively pursued Early's army as it skedaddled from Fisher's Hill during the night. Averell complained he had received no orders or other direction from Sheridan or his headquarters; Sheridan retorted that he had not been able to find Averell. In turn Averell—who it should be recalled had previously been removed by Hooker during Chancellorsville—complained that he had "...unfortunately incurred the displeasure of a few small politicians, and they have left no stone unturned to inure me publically and privately."[122] Despite his foul mood Sheridan decided to give Averell another chance admonishing the division commander, "I do not advise rashness, but I do desire resolution and actual fighting with necessary casualties, before you retire."[123] On September 23 Averell encountered an enemy infantry division supported by five pieces of artillery.[124] Averell's failure to attack before encamping became the basis when, two days later, Sheridan relieved Averell, ostensibly for lack of aggressiveness in pursuing Early, replacing him with George Custer.

Next, on September 30 Grant ordered Wilson to report to Sherman in the West, advising Sherman that "Wilson will add 50 percent to the effectiveness of your cavalry." George Custer was shortly re-assigned to replace Wilson, a move that was unpopular with some troopers of the 3rd Cavalry Division. However, most others in Wilson's former command welcomed the change in command, one subordinate commander writing, "The Div feel very much pleased at the change. Think you will hear better accounts of us now that we have a gallant leader."[125] Separating Wilson from Custer may have worked for the best in terms of cooperation between division commanders since Wilson and Custer hated each other.[126] Both were ambitious and glory-seeking, and neither was reluctant to voice his disdain for the other. Col. (later BGen.) William H. Powell, 42, an Ohio manufacturer in civilian life, but most recently from the 2nd WV Cavalry, was appointed to command Averell's former 2nd Cavalry Division.[127]

Even after these cavalry command changes, Sheridan continued to advance up the Valley, by October 1 reaching Waynesboro, 20 miles west of Charlottesville.[128] Early's army was encamped near Brown's Gap, a few miles east of Staunton and west of Waynesboro. After two devastating defeats followed by a long, punishing retreat, Early's army was hungry and dirty, with huge numbers of wounded scattered in throughout hospitals, churches, and private homes all the way to Harrisonburg.[129] Sheridan reported to Grant, "From the most reliable accounts Early's army was completely broken up and is dispirited."[130]

As soon as Grant learned of Sheridan's success at Fisher's Hill, Grant began urging Sheridan to turn east toward Charlottesville to help squeeze Lee at Petersburg. By capturing Charlottesville the Federals would be positioned to destroy the Virginia Central railroad track as well as the James River canal, thus severing the supply lines between the Southern breadbasket in the Shenandoah Valley and Lee's army in the Petersburg and Richmond area. More importantly, Sheridan could also pressure Lee from the west, conceiving ending the war, at least in the East, by that fall. Sheridan was reluctant to comply, mostly because of insufficient stores and partly because he believed further excursion would substantially weaken his command (Crook would have to be left behind to protect the B & O) while making his rear vulnerable to hit-and-run attacks by enemy rangers. Moreover Sheridan contended the best strategy, "will be to let the burning of the Valley be the end of the campaign, and let some of this army go somewhere else."[131] Little Phil suggested, successfully, that he be allowed to fall back to Winchester where he would be closer to his supply base before moving on by boat and train to reinforce Grant at Petersburg. Sheridan was able to convince Grant; however, he has not convinced the Civil War historian Jeffry D. Wert, who has observed,

> In a day or day and a half of good hard marching, the Union infantry and artillery could have been at Charlottesville. Early, if he contested the advance, would have had to do it at Waynesborough, with his outnumbered army with its back against the [Blue Ridge Mountain] and its escape route through one narrow gap. Sheridan had the chance to strike a mortal blow to the Confederacy, most likely shortening the war in the East by months.[132]

Fisher's Hill was another terrible defeat for the Confederacy's once proud, formerly invincible 2nd Corps. Its strength was being sapped and its members were beginning to have doubts about itself and its commander in particular. Moreover its retreat to Mount

Jackson exposed miles of the Valley to the marauding Blue cavalry. At the same time, without having to contend with an all-encompassing pursuit, Early was able to withdraw in good order to his safe haven where his corps could rest and refit as a viable, albeit weakened fighting force.

But even as the Federal forces were withdrawing to Winchester, destruction of the Valley's infrastructure remained their primary objective. Sheridan's army drove off livestock, destroyed all supplies and burned mills filled with grain, an operation known as "The Burning." But as the Federals continued their destructive withdrawal, Rebel cavalry—incensed by the destruction of the Valley's beautiful bounty—continued its harassing attacks.

On October 5, 1864, Early received reinforcements, including Kershaw's return. Nevertheless on October 7 Sheridan was able to report from Woodstock, ten miles south of Strasburg, that upon his completion of "the destruction of wheat, forage, etc, down to Fisher's Hill, … the Valley, from Winchester to Staunton, ninety two miles, will have little in it for man or beast."[133]

## Tom's Brook

On October 5 Early's bedraggled cavalry was reinforced by the addition of 600 mounted troopers led by MGen. Thomas Lafayette Rosser, 28.[134] While riding at the head of his column on the evening of October 7 as his army was heading back to Winchester, Sheridan learned Rosser's cavalry was striking effectively at Little Phil's rear guard. Sheridan—"mad clear through"[135]—angrily and emphatically ordered Torbert to retaliate immediately, telling Torbert to, "Whip the rebel cavalry or get whipped himself."[136]

At Tom's Brook—approximately three miles southwest of Strasburg—two of Torbert's cavalry divisions made a mass attack on Sunday, October 9, 1864, against the Southern cavalry that had irritating Sheridan. After two hours of pitched combat, Custer led his brigade on a flanking movement that Rosser ignored. Caught in a vice, the Southerners broke to begin scurrying up the Valley Turnpike leaving wagons and artillery behind.[137] The Blue riders gave chase for twenty miles before the Gray riders reached the safety of their infantry lines at Rude's Hill.[138] Collectively the two Union cavalry divisions captured eleven field guns, 68 horses, and a wagon filled with Enfields but more significantly the capture of 300 Gray riders meant that Rebel cavalry should no longer be able to bother Sheridan's Valley operations.[139] After the chase—known as the Woodstock Races—Early reported to Lee, "…the fact is that the enemy cavalry is so much superior to ours, both in numbers and equipment, and the country is so favorable to the operations of cavalry, that it is impossible for ours to compete with his."[140]

Of all the branches of Early's army, cavalry was subject to the most criticism. But as observed by Joseph Glatthaar:

> Yet in fairness the [Confederate] cavalry, it had suffered badly. Strength had been worn by attrition, horses were emaciated, and the equipment so deteriorated that disaster was almost inevitable. In one brigade alone, almost one in every six horsemen carried an unserviceable weapon into combat. If they fought on foot, they could adapt, but on mounts, they entered combat at an extreme disadvantage, especially against Federals on excellent animals and armed with repeating weapons.[141]

## Cedar Creek

Blissfully thinking Early's army was no longer capable of any significant threat, Sheridan continued his retrograde movement back toward Winchester, on October 10 ordering his army into bivouac astride the Valley Turnpike a little more than a mile south of Middletown along the northern side of Cedar Creek. Meanwhile Lee—who grossly underestimated Sheridan's strength—continued to urge Early to mount an offensive. Accordingly Early began to move north in preparation of re-occupying his old lines on Fisher's Hill, a short distance south of the Union encampment. Still believing the Southerners posed no further threat. Sheridan began to prepare to send Wright's 6th Corps back to rejoining Grant at Petersburg.[142]

Grant and the Washington authorities wanted Sheridan to swing south to Charlottesville to be able to destroy two of Lee's vital supply lines. However, Sheridan disagreed, contending that Early was no longer a threat and that other than leaving a cavalry detachment his (Sheridan's) army should be deployed elsewhere.[143] To resolve the matter, on Thursday, October 13, 1864, Stanton and Halleck summoned Sheridan to confer with them in Washington. After leaving Wright in charge in his absence, and satisfied the Rebels at Fisher's Hill were no threat, on October 15 Sheridan decided to travel to the capital to meet with Stanton and Halleck. After a conference that Sheridan deemed to be pointless even though he prevailed, on October 18 he returned to Winchester where he stayed overnight. But during that same evening Early set a complicated plan in motion to spring a surprise attack upon Sheridan's encampment at Cedar Creek. The key to the Confederate plan, devised and to be led by Gordon, was to launch the attack from the presumably impassable north face of the Massanutten Mountain against the lightly defended Union's left flank east of the Pike.[144] For some inexplicable reason Old Jube also dispatched half his cavalry to Front Royal, twelve miles to the southeast, where his horse riders were supposed to turn to get into the Federal rear.

On the early morning of October 19 Sheridan awoke in Winchester to the distant sound of artillery.[145] At Cedar Creek, Wright ordered a reconnaissance in force to try to ascertain the Confederates' dispositions. But Early's massive attack caught the Federals completely by surprise, some of the Northern lads being still asleep in their tents. Union troops retreated in mass confusion from their fog shrouded camps leaving 18 guns and much of their camps behind while 1,300 Yankees were captured by 7:00 a.m.[146] In the words of one Union officer, it "was a blind, confused, feeble scuffle."[147] But by 9:30 a.m., west of the Pike Wright's 6th Corps begun to collect itself and to resist the Rebel onslaught. Wright also made perhaps the most important decision of the day when he posted Torbert's entire cavalry east of the Pike where they threatened the Confederate's right flank.[148]

Following the Southerners' initial, overpowering success, they paused before reforming while Early met with Gordon sometime between 7:30 a.m. and 10:30 a.m. What transpired next to the Rebel offensive is confused and controverted.[149] During this hiatus many of the Rebel soldiers and some of their officers began to plunder the kettles of cooking coffee, food, clothing, blankets, and equipment left in the Union camp. One version is that pillaging caused Rebel discipline to disintegrate to the point that further military action was not feasible. But the prevailing, but not necessarily exclusive or persuasive, version is that Gordon insisted the Federals could be destroyed in an hour but Early decided there had been "enough glory for one day" and that—to Gordon's mortification—further pursuit was unnecessary, Early having assumed the Federals would continue to withdraw without being pressured. Gordon would later claim he had a "vision of the fatal halt of the first day at Gettysburg."[150] In any event, within the next hour and half or two the Confederate attack began losing its momentum as units lost their cohesion and soldiers were exhausting after advancing for several hours. Also, to add to the uncertainty about Cedar Creek, by some reports during this time Early either had a change of heart or a change of mind about his army's posture, Old Jube becoming hesitant and apprehensive. According to Douglas Freeman who argued, "…as the forenoon passed, the thought of the wreck of his Divisions by absentees began to say Early's soldierly vigor. His state of mind changed subtly and progressively from one of confidence to one of concern."[151]

As Wright was attempting to reorganize his new line, Sheridan galloped back to where his soldiers were preparing for a further retreat. At about 10:30 a.m. Sheridan reached the bulk of his army, including some of his cavalry, "the appalling spectacle of a panic-stricken army—hundreds of slightly wounded men, throngs of others unhurt but utterly demoralized, and baggage wagons by the score, all pressing to the rear in hopeless confusion, telling … plainly that a disaster had occurred at the front."[152] Some of Sheridan's tactical decisions can legitimately be criticized but without doubt his battlefield charisma was hardly equaled as his officers and soldiers responded immediately and with energy to his presence and exhortations. "Retreat hell!" Sheridan assured everyone there would be no further retreat and that they would be back in their camps by that evening.

By early afternoon the Confederates approached the southern outskirts of Middletown where they remained to rest and reorganize their lines depleted by casualties and straggling from the morning's looting. The Confederates did little except to try a reconnaissance in force that accomplished nothing before being easily repulsed, Sheridan having anticipated the Rebel effort. Glatthaar believes the strength of Federal cavalry was another reason Early was dissuaded from continuing his forward movement.[153] But for whatever reason or its cause, this period of Confederate inactivity has become known as "the fatal halt" in Civil War lore.[154]

While the Rebel soldiers were celebrating their apparent victory in part by continuing to loot the Union camps, Sheridan was enthusiastically going about the business of reorganizing his lines in preparation for a counterattack. Once the Union infantry began its counterattack by 4:00 p.m., shortly thereafter Custer's cavalry (which Little Phil had shifted to the Union's right flank as he reorganized his lines) came in at a thundering gallop to sweep behind Gordon's attenuated left flank causing the entire Confederate line to crumble like falling dominos before taking flight. One Confederate later wrote they were "…running as fast as a herd of wild, stampeded cattle. We just had to get out or be captured, and as we saw it, our officers were losing all controls over us."[155] As Early watched helplessly, being able to only yell, "Run, run, God damn you, they will get you," the Rebels rushed back across Cedar Creek to Fisher's Hill, leaving 2,000 dead and wounded on the battlefield with another 1,000 comrades captured. One significant casualty was Stephen Ramseur, one of Early's division commanders, who was mortally wounded after having three horses shot from under him.[156]

Sheridan's rally of his army converted a rout into a spectacular albeit incomplete Union victory. Two cavalry regiments from Custer's division as well as another two regiments from Merritt's division sliced through the retreating chaos between Cedar Creek and Strasburg.[157] The Union horsemen cut down horses, and captured scores of wagons and ambulances, dozens of cannon, and hundreds of prisoners, some of whom were able to escape in the darkness. Otherwise Sheridan, apparently not realizing or anticipating the completeness of his victory, failed to plan and organize a pursuit, meaning the residue of the badly beaten Confederate army remained intact. Rosser, one of the Rebel cavalry leaders commented, "If [Sheridan] had pursued vigorously on the morning of the 20th, he could have galloped over every obstruction we could have thrown in his path and could have captured Early and his army."[158] Even Old Jube's report groused. "Nothing saved us but the inability of the enemy to follow us with his infantry and his expectation that we would make a stand there."[159] In the absence of a pursuit, the next day the Confederates withdrew further up the Valley Turnpike to New Market where the seeds of the Shenandoah Valley Campaign of 1864 had been sowed a little more than five months earlier.

Early's explanation to Lee was, "The enemy subsequently made a stand on the pike and in turn attacked my line and my left gave way and the rest of the troops took a panic and could not be rallied, retreating in confusion. But for their bad conduct I should have defeated Sheridan's whole force."[160] Early also publicly lambasted his army, criticizing it for yielding "to a disgraceful propensity for plunder."[161] Early added fuel to the mutual discord with Gordon by implying Gordon had participated in the plundering, remarks that helped to perpetuate the controversy for many years.

After Cedar Creek the cavalries sporadically engaged each other before Sheridan removed his army back to Kernstown, south of Winchester. On Wednesday, November 16, 1864, Early's infantry began pulling out of its lines before moving back to Lee at Petersburg, neutralizing Early as an individual force in the war. "The Burning" continued relentlessly and systematically as Sheridan moved his main force to Harrisonburg to conduct his scorched-earth campaign designed to deprive the Confederacy of its Shenandoah Valley "breadbasket."

## Analysis

Among the campaign's three major battles, plus Tom's Brook, there were five possible opportunities for pursuits. Prior to Third Winchester Sheridan had anticipated his overwhelming numerical superiority would cause Early's army to withdraw. Accordingly he positioned Crook's 6th Corps in alignment with Wilson's cavalry for such pursuit. However battle factors—some stemming from poor tactical decisions by Sheridan—necessitated a realignment of Crook to the opposite end of the Federal lines. This redeployment, together with the stiff resistance to Wilson's early advance, compounded by Wilson's later cautiousness, impeded any realistic chance for a pursuit when the Gray coats eventually fled through and from Winchester.

Prior to Fisher's Hill Sheridan again wisely planned for a pursuit. However his cavalry commander, Torbert, who had been entrusted to lead two cavalry divisions to a blocking position, misjudged the strength of enemy cavalry that was confronting him. Rather than try to force his way to his assigned position, Torbert decided to countermarch thus forgoing any chance to implement Sheridan's pursuit strategy.

In the cavalry versus cavalry action at Tom's Brook, the smaller Rebel cavalry eventually broke loose before starting to high tail south with Blue riders in hot chase. However after a 24-mile race the Rebel cavalry was able to return to the safety of its infantry lines; while the so-called Woodstock Races took a severe toll upon Rebel riders, and especially their horses, Federal riders were unable to either annihilate or capture the entire cadre of the Rebel horsemen.

At Cedar Creek Early's now reduced army brilliantly executed a surprise attack, overrunning the Yankee encampment before driving the Union units back at least three miles. However, rather than attempting to pursue further, Early's army—for whatever reason—halted for several hours. During that lull the Federals—with considerable efforts from their just returning commander, Little Phil—regrouped, reorganized, and reformed for a counterattack that not only drove the Confederates from the battlefield but forced them back up the Valley. But unlike Third Winchester or Fisher's Hill, no preparations were made for a pursuit allowing Early's army to make a relatively leisurely retreat to safety up the Valley.

Finally, rather than continuing to pursue Early's beaten army up the Valley, thus allowing the Rebels to take refuge at Brown's Gap where it remained until the next spring, Sheridan was focused upon the destruction or capture of the crops, livestock, agriculture infrastructure in the Valley. The timely elimination of Early's army would have allowed Sheridan to bring pressure against an undermanned Lee during the autumn of 1864 instead of waiting until the spring of 1865.The lack of successful pursuits helps to explain in part why Sheridan's streak of battlefield victories did not result in a decisive campaign for the Union that could, if materialized, have significantly shortened the war.

Jeffry Wert observes that Sheridan as:

> The Union commander forged an army from an amalgam of commands, gave the North and Abraham Lincoln's reelection campaign three timely, major victories, seriously crippled the best fighting corps in the Army of Northern Virginia for the duration of the war, laid waste the granary of the Confederacy and began the descent of the Confederacy in Virginia to Appomattox. For these accomplishments, Sheridan received from a grateful government the commission of major general in the Regular Army, and from a grateful people, a place alongside Ulysses Grant and William Sherman in that triumvirate of victors.[162]

But Wert also notes Sheridan's strategic shortcomings, quoting L.W.V. Kennon's conclusion that, "'it is remarkable that a campaign so completely victorious in the field should be so barren of decisive results, and this can be accounted for only on the supposition of very faulty strategy.'"[163] Steven Bernstein also takes note of Sheridan's failures:

> Most any competent Federal commander, enjoying great advantages in manpower, supply, and firepower, would have defeated Early; yet it took Sheridan nearly seven months to destroy the Army of the Valley. ... Had he not assumed the Valley Army was finished after Fisher's Hill and pursued through Brown's Gap, and had he extended his supply lines, destroyed the James River Canal, and pressured Lee's army from the west, the war might have ended that fall. Instead, Sheridan chose to burn the valley, ensuring several more months of fighting and a long residue of bitterness afterwards.[164]

Perhaps the most remarkable feature of the Shenandoah Valley Campaign of 1864 was that Union cavalry had become demonstrably and indisputably superior to the Confederate cavalry, at least in the Eastern Theater. Beginning with John Buford's efforts more than two years earlier, and continuing with the development of the remount depots and the acquisition of repeating carbines, Union cavalry had improved in almost every aspect, most importantly the quality and numbers of its horseflesh, its firepower, and the aggressiveness of its leaders. On the other hand, Southern cavalry was roundly criticized by several sources, including its own infantry. For example, on infantryman from Georgia complained, "All of our misfortunes were caused by depending on our cavalry to protect our flanks. In neither of the late fights was our infantry whipped but forced to fall back because the Cavalry let the Yankees flank our position and get behind us."[165] Time after time Federal cavalry overcame Gray troopers, whether mounted or dismounted, causing Rebel flanks to collapse, which in turn made Rebel infantry lines become untenable. There was no longer any doubt that the Blue cavalry had attained the capacity to turn any battle into the Northern advantage. And to his credit, Sheridan was not adverse or hesitant to use that superiority relentlessly to his best advantage.

## *Dénouements and Precursors*

Sheridan's spectacular victory at Cedar Creek, together with Sherman's earlier capture of Atlanta and Foote's victory at Mobile, assured an easy, landside Electoral College victory for Lincoln against McClellan.

Within a month starting at Third Winchester and ending at Cedar Creek, Early's reputation suffered a complete reversal from being a Rebel hero, perhaps second in standing only to Lee, to becoming a total command disaster. Although Early's courage could never be questioned, his irascible and caustic nature prevented him from developing any meaningful rapport with his associates and subordinates. Letters from Rebel soldiers are replete with harsh criticisms, even condemnations, of their commanding general. Furthermore his loses in the Confederacy's breadbasket, upon which so much depended, brought unrelenting public scorn, much of which might have been exaggerated and even unwarranted. And while Early could be energetic and resourceful, he also had tactical blind spots, especially in the deployment and utilization of his numerically overmatched cavalry, that were often exploited by Sheridan and his subordinate generals.

By December 1864 much of what was left of Early's 2nd Corps was transferred back to Lee's Petersburg defenses. However Early himself remained in the Shenandoah Valley with a small force of 1,600 that on March 2, 1865, was almost annihilated at Waynesboro, Virginia. Thereafter—realizing that Old Jube no longer enjoyed the confidence of soldiers, other commanders, or public opinion—Lee relieved Early from further command responsibilities. When Lee surrendered to Grant, Early fled to Texas hoping to join Kirby Smith who had already surrendered by the time Early arrived. Although the Myth of the Lost Cause has many origins, Early's vitriolic writings, many of which were critical of Longstreet who had had the audacity to criticize Lee at Gettysburg, were prominent contributions to the cult belief that the Confederacy had good, noble purposes, but that notwithstanding the superiority of Southern soldiers and generals its war aims were overwhelmed by the North's greater population and material resources. Early died in 1894.

After being detached from Early's army, John Breckinridge, Buchanan's Vice-President and one of Lincoln's opponents in the 1860 election, served briefly as commander of the Department of Southwest Virginia before being appointed February 4, 1865, as Secretary of the Confederate Secretary of War, succeeding James Seddan, who had resigned for health reasons.[166]

After the 1864 Presidential elections Grant, with Lincoln's concurrence, decided it was finally time to relieve Ben Butler as commander of the two-corps Army of the James. Although Grant apparently once considered Baldy Smith as Meade's replacement, he also blamed Smith for failing to take Petersburg against what were attenuated defenses.[167] Nevertheless—and reflecting the frequently irrational bases for command promotions—Grant determined Smith was his choice to replace Butler. But although Butler was an inept battlefield commander he was nevertheless an adroit politician who successfully maneuvered to retain his position. Smith reacted with displeasure when he learned he would not be promoted to army command but instead would remain as corps commander. Grant simply responded, "You talk too much" referring to Smith's constant criticism of Meade and his handling of the Army of the Potomac, particularly at Cold Harbor. In fact, Baldy long had the reputation as a difficult troublemaker. Tired of Smith's rants, Grant relieved Smith of corps command, whereupon Smith moved back to his home in Vermont where he transferred his criticisms targets to Grant, accusing his former friend of drunkenness, poor generalship, and "utter disregard of truth."[168]

After relinquishing the opportunity to take the unified command the defense of Washington, Black Dave Hunter—who had a Confederate bounty on his head because he had sanctioned the 1st S.C., the first Negro regiment—served on various courts martial until the end of the war. He had accompanied Lincoln from Springfield, Illinois, in 1861 after Lincoln was elected and after Lincoln was assassinated in 1865 Hunter escorted Lincoln's body back to Springfield. Hunter returned from Springfield to preside over the military commission that tried those charged with the assassination conspiracy.

George Crook was captured February 21, 1865, in Cumberland, Maryland, by 70 Rebel cavalrymen wearing Union uniforms. Crook was imprisoned in Libby Prison before being exchanged after which on March 26, 1865, Crook became commander of the cavalry corps of the Army of the Potomac, replacing Alfred Torbert who had been transferred to take command of the downsized Army of the Shenandoah. After the Civil War Crook became one of the nation's leading Indian fighters. In 1883 Crook tracked Geronimo down in Mexico before persuading the Indian warrior to surrender. Two years later after Geronimo escaped from his reservation, Crook asked to be relieved when Sheridan ordered Crook to cease a pursuit in order to take defensive postures to prevent further raids. Written after Sheridan's death, Crook's autobiography bitterly criticized his former friend claiming among other things that all the praise heaped upon Little Phil had "caused him to bloat his little carcass with debauchery and dissipation."

As a corps commander, Horatio Wright seemed to be transformed under Sheridan. After succeeding the late John Sedgwick, Wright continued to conform to the typical command style of the Army of the Potomac, that is showing little initiative, adhering to cautious advances, and exhibiting little personal leadership in combat. These characteristics continued through Third Winchester but there Wright observed Little Phil's more forceful, hell-be-damned leadership style. Whether consciously, Wright began to emulate some of Sheridan's decisiveness and flair, characteristics that became quite apparent in Sheridan's absence at Cedar Creek.

Lew Wallace had a mixed record as a general throughout the Civil War. In 1878 he was appointed governor of New Mexico during which time he wrote the novel for which he is best remembered, *Ben Hur: A Tale of the Christ* (1880).

## 18. Little Phil Comes East

Shortly after the stunning victory at Cedar Creek, Sheridan was accorded the highest praise for converting a bad defeat into a rout. A widely published poem, exaggerating the length of Sheridan's ride prior to arriving back at the battlefield, made Sheridan a popular hero approaching cult status. *Harper's Weekly* featured an article accompanied by a drawing of Sheridan galloping upon the scene. And while Little Phil deserves credit for galvanizing his command and personally leading a dramatic counterattack that afternoon, the fact remains that Horatio Wright had already stabilized the Union situation prior to Sheridan's arrival while the Confederates' fatal pause in failing to pursue immediately was a gross tactical error that set the stage for Sheridan's counterattack. Once again immediately after the battle Sheridan conceded much of the credit for the day's work belonged to Wright, a concession that Sheridan was not willing to continue as time passed.

Sheridan's refusal to give due credit to his subordinates seems to be in keeping with a major character flaw. As described by Eric Wittenberg, admittedly a harsh critic, "…Philip Sheridan's ambitious drive for self-aggrandizement knew no bounds. Lying was just a part of his aggressive plan for advancing his own self-interests. He regularly lied to cover his mistakes at all costs. He seems to have been a congenital liar, and his perfidy often exposed him to public ridicule and criticism. Sheridan did not care. He lied anyway."[169]

Regardless, Sheridan's accomplishments as an aggressive, decisive commander utilizing cavalry as previously seldom seen would mean he would soon be assigned further, and greater, command responsibilities.

# 19

# Grant's Ultimate Pursuit
*April 1865*

## Brief Review

By 1864 the Federal command structure had undergone enough personnel changes to better reflect Lincoln's desire for decisive victories from his commanders in the field.[1] Grant's ascension General in Chief—effectively extinguishing any remaining embers of George McClellan's soft war philosophy—portended much of that change of attitude. Grant tried to make it clear that his aim was not just to win battles but instead he wanted to win the war and intended to do so by defeating Confederate armies. As previously described elsewhere Grant's overall strategy was to initiate four separate but simultaneous campaigns designed to destroy enemy armies. However none of the campaigns developed as intended, and in particular Grant was forced to modify his Overland Campaign by flanking Lee to lay a siege against Petersburg instead of continuing to direct attacking Lee as had been previously ordered.

Grant's siege began immediately on June 1864 after Baldy Smith's lost opportunity to capture Petersburg. Instead of continuing to rely upon rapid movement or tactical maneuver, Grant employed classic siege tactics by patiently pressing forward, yard-by-yard, while at the same time trying methodically to extend his southern flank to threaten Lee' supply lines while stretching the Southern threadbare lines even further. The Union's infantry efforts were augmented by continuous artillery shelling together with sniper fire from sharpshooters.

As the Shenandoah Valley campaign wound down after Early's defeat at Cedar Creek, both Lee and Grant brought infantries back to their respective Petersburg lines until the Shenandoah Valley essentially became cavalry engagements. As examples of these infantry realignments, Horatio Wright's 6th Corps rejoined the Army of the Potomac while John Gordon replaced Jubal Early of the greatly diminished 2nd Confederate corps before it also returned to Lee's army at Petersburg. At Petersburg Gordon became one of Lee's chief lieutenants, complementing Longstreet who was still recovering from his Wilderness wounds.

By the first of January 1865, the noose was tightening around the last of the Confederate resistance. Atlanta had been captured after which Sherman cleaved Confederate territory as he marched to the Atlantic seashore. Hood failed to capture Nashville after which Thomas chased the remnants of Hood's army to Tupelo. The final pieces of the original Anaconda strategy fell into place with the captures of the ports of Mobile and Wilmington, the latter being the last of the blockade running ports. Although other Southern armies remained,

Lee's Army of Northern Virginia aligned in the trenches stretching between Richmond and Petersburg remained as a viable fighting force, albeit being slowly emaciated, and as such was the final lynchpin of any hopes for Southern independence.

And although from afar the Petersburg lines seemed static with relatively little maneuvering, the Union lines did manage to inch forward while lurching counterclockwise to Lee's right flank. As a practical matter, Lee's soldiers in the trenches were getting the worse of the situation. The Federal logistics were in high gear with tons of supplies being delivered daily to City Point—then the busiest port in the world—from which supplies were redistributed via a twenty-one-mile rail line extending from City Point along the Federal positions.

In contrast to the Union's plentiful situation, the Confederacy was suffering terribly from the ravages of the war, including the loss of its Shenandoah Valley breadbasket. The Wilmington port had provided some degree of support to Lee's army but that resource was no longer available. The losses of the various supply sources had tangible consequences in the trenches where men and animals were seriously undernourished. Replacement clothing and shoes were difficult to find with many Confederate soldiers trying to cope as best they could without complete uniforms or footwear. Elizabeth Varon, a Professor of History at the University of Virginia, has noted, "The last year of the war had been a prolonged nightmare for the Army of Northern Virginia."[2]

Sherman's march northward through the Carolinas was causing Confederate soldiers to fear for their families' safety and welfare. These concerns, coupled with the nearly insufferable deprivations from living in the trenches, was causing many Rebels to desert, perhaps at a rate of forty desertions per each forty-eight-hour period. As the lines kept extending counterclockwise to the southwest, and as the Confederate numbers kept shrinking because of desertion and other forms of attrition, fewer Confederate soldiers were available to defend more territory.

Lincoln was becoming anxious that the war would soon be over. He was personally fatigued from carrying his multitude of duties as Commander in Chief but even more telling was his profound concern about the horrendous lists of casualties suffered by both sides. And to be fair Lincoln was also impatient to be able to begin the process of healing and reconciliation that although already begun in isolated sections could not begin in earnest until the South had surrendered.

After active combat in the Shenandoah Valley was over, and as infantry units returned to the Petersburg lines, Sheridan, along with his 1st and 3rd cavalry divisions, encamped for the winter near Winchester, Virginia. Grant did not want Sheridan to come to the Petersburg lines, and toward that end on February 20 Grant ordered Sheridan to ride to Lynchburg to destroy rail road lines at that junction before moving south to join Sherman in North Carolina. However Sheridan, by his own admission, wanted to ride to Petersburg where he sensed the end was near and where he could gain the most glory.[3] Toward the end of February 1865, Sheridan moved his force up the Valley to Staunton where he learned that Early remained with the remnants of his force near Waynesboro. Moving through terrible weather on Thursday, March 2, 1865, as described in Chapter 18, Sheridan's cavalry stuck at Early's flanks and front to obliterate Old Jube's little force at Waynesboro. In addition to capturing several battle flags, Sheridan captured 1,600 prisoners, 11 guns, and 200 loaded wagons.[4]

By March 14 Grant, realizing that he was virtually powerless to force Sheridan to ride south to join Sherman, bowed to the inevitable, ordering Little Phil to move to the Petersburg lines with "no halt."[5] Not only was Sheridan elated to receive orders to join Grant in Petersburg, Sheridan further realized from Grant's orders he would be operating as an independent command not subject to Meade's control.

It is not clear why Grant had been reluctant to bring Sheridan and his cavalry to Petersburg. It is possible that Grant's principle objective had contemplated a convergence with Sherman who would help to defeat Lee's army, and that Grant anticipated that Sheridan could help make that convergence happen. If so then Grant seemed to not fully appreciate the advantage that a numerically superior, well-armed, aggressively led cavalry would add to his efforts to force Lee to succumb.

Although Sheridan's earlier performance as a cavalry commander can be, and has been, criticized,[6] his subsequent performance in the Shenandoah Valley showed he had developed skills beyond his pugnacious nature that were virtually unmatched in the Eastern Theater. In assessing Sheridan's use of cavalry during the Shenandoah Valley campaign Jeffry Wert concludes that:

> ... Sheridan's use of the mounted arm exceeded that of any army commander, North and South, during the war. He not only enjoyed a decisive superiority with this arm, he exploited it. The cavalry, under his direction, became the equal of the infantry and artillery, the spearhead of the offensive at Winchester and Cedar Creek. He extended the field use of the arm.... The contribution of the Union cavalry to the outcome of the campaign was decisive and attributable to Sheridan.[7]

Moreover Sheridan's experience in the Shenandoah Valley had cemented his tactical conviction that cavalry, infantry, and artillery deployed together could form a mobile force more lethal than the sum of the individual parts, especially when aggressively, fearlessly, and relentlessly commanded. As events would eventually transpire Grant was fortunate that Sheridan more or less forced his services, as well as those of his cavalry, upon Grant's remaining struggle against Lee.

## *The Beginning of the End*

By late March 1865 the trenches zig-zagged for an estimated forty miles starting just south of Richmond and continuing southward toward Petersburg where the fortified ditches curved westward to the Petersburg & Weldon R.R. Lee's defenders consisted of Longstreet's 1st Corps, Gordon's 2nd Corps, A.P. Hill's 3rd Corps, Richard Anderson's 4th Corps, and Fitz Lee's cavalry. Altogether the Confederate strength aggregated to approximately 56,000 soldiers, exact numbers are difficult to determine because the Confederates were always imprecise about personnel strengths. Additionally some other units such as militia and home guards, even some naval units, had joined in the defenses of Petersburg and especially in Richmond under Richard Ewell's command.

Aligned in their trenches against the Rebels, Grant had two and half as many soldiers organized among six corps each commanded by veteran military commanders. In turn these six infantry corps were organized between two armies, the Army of the Potomac still commanded—at least nominally—by George Meade, and the Army of the James, commanded by Edward O.C. Ord, who had replaced Ben Butler in January 1865 following Butler's folly at first Fort Fisher. Butler had tried a hair-brained idea of floating a barge filled with explosives toward the fort. The barge exploded but without any effect. Lincoln did not object or intercede when Grant sent Butler home, by then Butler no longer serving any political purpose.

Subsequent to being wounded at the Hatchie Bridge, as described in Chapter 4, Ord commanded various corps including one at Vicksburg under Grant. Although Ord, a Maryland Democrat opposed to abolitionism, could be temperamental, his loyal service in the Army of the Tennessee gained him entry into Grant's inner circle, and at Grant's request Ord was transferred east along with Sheridan.[8]

The corps commanders of Meade's Army of the Potomac were A.A. Humphreys, Meade's former (and excellent) chief of staff, commanding the 2nd Corps, in place of the physically infirmed Winfield Scott Hancock[9]; Gouverneur Warren, commanding the 5th Corps; Horatio Wright, still commanding the 6th Corps; and John G. Parke, commanding the 9th Corps in place of Ambrose Burnside who had been retired after the Crater debacle. Henry Hunt, who had brilliantly commanded the Army of Potomac's artillery since Antietam, was still in charge of Grant's artillery.

The corps commanders in Ord's Army of the James were MGen. John Gibbon, 38, commanding the newly created 25th Corps, and MGen. Godfrey Weitzel, 30, commanding the 25th Corps, consisting of two divisions of United States Colored Troops. Gibbon, a former Indian fighter, was an outspoken and independent career officer with several command billets throughout the Army of the Potomac, including the Iron Brigade. Prior to taking command of the 25th Corps Weitzel had served primarily in engineering capacities. Ord's army was positioned along the northern sector of lines across or near Richmond.

## *Fort Stedman* (March 25, 1865)

Not only had the siege taken its toll but the Southerners felt threatened by the prospect that Sherman's march north would at the very least destroy their remaining supply lines. As winter turned to spring the Rebels were desperate to break Grant's siege. John G. Gordon planed an elaborate scheme designed to force the Federals to abandon some of their southern fortifications thus permitting the Southerners to have a shorter line to defend.[10] Accordingly on Saturday, March 25, 1865, Rebel forces—led by Gordon and his 2nd Corps— attempted a pre-dawn breakout by attacking Fort Stedman located on the left of the Union lines.[11] The plan's objective was predicated upon a faulty intelligence that three more Federal outposts were located behind Fort Stedman; Gordon believed that once these outposts were captured Confederate cavalry could occupy the territory and destroy Grant's communications.[12] Although their stratagem breached Union lines to capture the fort, as described by Joseph Glatthaar the Federals "were too numerous, too well equipped, and too responsive for the [Rebel] plan to work."[13] Furthermore the Rebel guides could not find the three outposts, which in fact were non-existent.[14] Upon daybreak the adjoining Union batteries went to work while Union infantry quickly and effectively counterattacked to drive the Gordon's corps back to its original positions. Hundreds of Confederates surrendered to the Federals rather than to try to run the gauntlet of murderous fire across the fields to the original Rebel lines.[15] Additionally Meade correctly surmised that the Southerners must have weakened other sectors in order to have had enough troops for their attack upon Fort Stedman. Accordingly Meade ordered a series of sorties that seized sections of the Confederate picket lines. Confederates lost 4,000 casualties, or approximately 7 percent of Lee's army. Union casualties were half of those of the Confederates.[16]

Realizing that Sheridan would soon be arriving to augment Grant's lines, Lee fully appreciated the consequences of losing the Fort Stedman gamble when he advised Jeff Davis the next day, "I fear now it will be impossible to prevent a juncture between Grant and Sherman nor do I deem it prudent that this army should maintain its position until [Sherman] shall approach too near."[17] Although the soldiers probably did not realize it at the time, the Rebel attack upon Fort Stedman would be the last offense ever launched by Lee's Army of Northern Virginia.

## *Five Forks* (March 30, April 1, 1865)

But even before the Rebel strike at Fort Stedman, Grant—as anticipated by Lee—had initiated an offensive designed further to strangle Lee's army. On Friday, March 24, 1865, Grant ordered Meade to prepare for an offensive aimed at the Southside R.R., Lee's remaining supply line as well as his best route for a possible escape to reach Johnston in the south.[18] Grant's plan was to deploy Warren's 5th Corps and Humphreys' 2rd Corps toward the Boydton Plank Road that fed into the Confederate lines from the south. Upon Sheridan's arrival with his cavalry, Little Phil would head for Dinwiddie Court House, eight miles south of the Southside R.R. In the meantime most of Ord's Army of the James would shift southward to take supporting positions behind the Union left flank.

On March 26, 1865, Sheridan with his two divisions of cavalry crossed the James River before going into camp the next day near the Union's military railroad. The same day the 2nd Cavalry Division, now under the command of recently exchanged George Crook, joined Sheridan's two other divisions under the respective commands of Thomas Devin and George Custer, giving Sheridan an effective force of 9,000.[19] Wesley Merritt was bumped down to become Sheridan's second-in-command. Shortly thereafter Grant further enhanced Sheridan's independent authority by designating Little Phil as a wing commander.[20]

Douglas Southall Freeman observed that, "The week beginning March 27, 1865, was one on which the survivors of the Army of Northern Virginia were loath to dwell, because it was to them, in memory, the first stage of a gruesome nightmare;..."[21] By March 29 Sheridan had taken occupation of Dinwiddie C.H. The next objective was Five Forks, the critical junction of the road from Dinwiddie C.H. to the Southside R.R. and the Boydton Plank Road from Danville. Because the Boydton Plank Road led easterly to Lee's right flank, Lee could ill afford to allow the Federals to occupy this intersection.[22] Torrential rains caused a couple days' delay while driving Sheridan almost to distraction. Riding to Grant's headquarters on March 30 Sheridan told aides "I can drive in the whole cavalry force of the enemy with ease and if an infantry force is added to my command, I can strike out for Lee's right, and either crush it or [make] him so weak in his entrenched lines that our troops in front of them can break through and march to Petersburg."[23]

Realizing the Federals were preparing to attack his right flank, thereby threatening the collapse of his entire line as well as cutting off his remaining supply lines, Lee tried to reinforce his defenses by sending George Pickett's division to the area of the Five Forks, ordering Pickett to hold Five Forks "at all hazards."[24] Unfortunately for Pickett his division was isolated at least four miles from the rest of the Rebel lines. During the late afternoon on April 1, 1865, Pickett and Fitz Lee, the cavalry commander, assuming it was too late in the afternoon for an attack, went to the rear to partake in a shad bake. To the complete surprise of these Confederate commanders, Sheridan's cavalry and Warren's infantry—which had marched all night to join Sheridan—attacked and collapsed Pickett's detached division, resulting in most one-sided Union victory since the Overland Campaign began at The Wilderness the previous June. Not only did the Union attack demolish a Confederate infantry division but by the end of the day Sheridan's group was within an easy march of taking the Southside R.R. Moreover, capture of the Five Forks intersection meant the Federals could use the Boydton Plank Road to roll up the remainder of the Confederate's defense lines. Freeman observed that, "…Five Forks was only one scene removed from the dread dénouement."[25]

The Federals captured another 5,000–6,000 prisoners[26] all of whom were offered their release and passes to return to their homes if they would merely swear allegiance to the United States government. However, fewer than 100 of the Rebels opted to take the necessary oath, the rest of the prisoners staying loyal to the Confederacy (or perhaps not anxious to undertake a long difficult trek back to their homes).

Although the Federal victory was about as overwhelming as could be expected, in his battle rage Sheridan was unhappy with Warren's performance as corps commander.[27] Using authority delegated by Grant, Sheridan summarily canned Warren, replacing one of the storied heroes of Gettysburg with BGen. Charles Griffin, 40,[28] a veteran of multiple campaigns in the Mexican, Indian, and Civil wars.[29]

On Sunday, April 2, 1865, the day after his army's stunning victory at Five Forks—coincidentally the same day when Harry Wilson was crushing Nathan Forrest's cavalry at Selma, Alabama—Grant ordered an assault all along Confederate lines crippled by the loss of one-fifth of its strength during the Fort Stedman and Five Forks attacks. A.P. Hill was killed when he rode forward to check his lines and ran into a couple of Yankee soldiers.[30] Within the larger picture, Confederate resources were stretched too thin to defend all possible points of attack, especially since its anchor from the right flank had been destroyed. By the end of the day not only had the Federals driven the Confederates from their trenches but perhaps more importantly the Federals had secured control of the Southside R.R., which until then had been Lee's remaining lifeline for supplies.

As the Confederates defenses began to collapse, Lee had no alternative except to order at 3:00 p.m. the evacuations of Petersburg as well as of Richmond.[31] Mad melees ensued as governmental officials as well as other civilians tried to find ways to flee the cities. Fires set to tobacco warehouses turned into uncontrolled conflagrations sweeping through much of Richmond.[32] Repeated explosions of ammunition ships in the harbor were adding to the distress of those civilians remaining in the city.

Lee's army withdrew in six columns, five of which were expected to converge at Amelia Court House, 23 miles west of Petersburg.[33] The largest of the Rebel columns consisted of parts of the 1st, 2nd, and 3rd Corps that were tramping westward north of the Appomattox River. Richard Ewell, incapacitated at Bloody Angle at Spotsylvania before assuming command of the defenses at Richmond, was leading a small patchwork force of 3,000 from

Richmond. In addition to the columns of infantry, the Confederates' largest wagon train, including 1,400 wagons and extending for 30 miles,[34] set out under Custis Lee from Richmond along a route north of the infantry routes.[35] The plan was to turn the army southwest at Jetersville sitting astride the Richmond and Danville R.R. before heading toward Danville, in southwest Virginia, hopefully to meet Johnston's army, which recently had been engaged with elements of Sherman's army at Snow Hill, North Carolina.

Richmond, the Confederacy's capital, had been the focal point of Union objectives almost as soon as Virginia seceded shortly after Fort Sumter. As Confederate soldiers were abandoning Richmond the way was open for Federal soldiers to take occupation of their enemy's capital, almost without opposition. But unlike Sherman who had been distracted about the prospect of capturing Atlanta, Grant's attention turned immediately to the tasks of organizing and preparing for the pursuit of Lee. Unlike Sherman, who had rushed to Atlanta to be part of its capture, Grant did not even bother to go to Richmond. Instead he moved his headquarters forward to Petersburg where he went about the business, in a matter-of-fact manner without any particular emotion, of issuing necessary orders for the next phase of his campaign, that being the pursuit and defeat of Lee.[36]

Although Union commanders were aware that the Rebels were withdrawing from their positions during the night of April 2–3 the Federals did not start their full-scale pursuits immediately, thus giving Lee's army at least a half-day's head start.[37] Nevertheless, a brigade of Custer's cavalry under Colonel William Wells attacked Fitzhugh Lee's cavalry near Namozine Church, seventeen miles due west of Petersburg, the first of many such harassing rearguard actions that would continuously plague Lee's retreat. Furthermore on Monday, April 3, 1865, Grant had made arrangements to use the Confederates' former supply line, the Southside R.R., to help keep his armies resupplied during the retreat. But since the Southside line had a five-foot gauge the Federal pioneers had to lay a third rail to accommodate the narrower gauge of the Northerner's locomotives and trains.

It may be instructive to compare the Petersburg retreat and pursuit with similar maneuvers after Gettysburg. Both retreats were of course organized and managed by Robert E. Lee. Although it had failed to overcome the Federals at Gettysburg, as Lee's army was retreating in July 1863 it was in good health and spirits, even believing with some plausible justification that it had not been driven from the field but instead merely was returning to Virginia where it could resupply with more ammunition and refit itself for future offenses. Ewell had captured thousands of animals from the Pennsylvania farms meaning the army was well fed. Although Lee was handicapped from the earlier death of Stonewall Jackson he was still left with a group of experienced subordinate commanders in their primes. The main army's retreat routes were through mountain passes that provided excellent tactical opportunities for rear guard actions to stall a pursuit. Southern cavalry, under Jeb Stuart's adroit and focused command, performed brilliantly as it screened and protected the main army's flanks and rear.

In contrast Lee's army left Petersburg in desperation hoping to escape and to survive. Southern soldiers were in terrible physical condition from several factors including their debilitating existence in the trenches. For months Lee's soldiers had been on a diet with half the protein necessary to sustain bodily mass. Their diet was also woefully lacking in many vitamins causing the soldiers' to suffer skin ailments, night blindness, anemia, scurvy, and diarrhea.[38] Signs of demoralization became evident as soon as the Federals began their chase. For example the roads were cluttered with broken and abandoned wagons and artillery pieces as well as other debris such as bed rolls, knapsacks, and cooking gear discarded by soldiers trying to lighten their loads.[39] Rebel stragglers were beginning to surrender, either individually or in clusters, rather than continuing to flee while at the same time the woods were full of Confederate deserters who were either unable or unwilling to continue marching with their units along the roads. Even many of the soldiers who remained with their units disarmed themselves by sticking the bayonet end of their muskets into the ground. Too exhausted or too famished to continue, hundreds of horses and mules dropped by the wayside to await their deaths.

The war had also taken a terrible toll upon Lee's subordinate commanders. Jeb Stuart, upon whom Lee had so heavily depended, had been killed at Yellow Tavern. Lee had to send an incapacitated Ewell home from North Anna and although Ewell had returned to take charge of a small force at Richmond he was no longer the feisty, energetic commander of pre–Gettysburg. Out of mercy Lee also had to send Early home from the Shenandoah Valley, Old Jube's reputation in ruins. Equally as important scores of brigade and regimental commanders had become casualties of dozens of battles and could not be adequately replaced by the Confederacy's shallow pool of qualified officers.

In contrast to the plight of the Confederate army, the Union forces grew stronger, especially after the Petersburg siege began. For starters the Union's robust system of logistics kept its men and animals in fit fighting form. Grant brought an entirely different command attitude to the fore. He was not merely content surviving battles but instead was determined to win the war almost it sometimes seemed at any cost. As he reconfigured his command structure Grant appointed subordinate generals and colonels whom he knew, who were to his liking, and who shared Grant's attitude about the prosecution of the war. There was no longer any need for political generals, or for soft war advocates, or for those without basic battlefield management skills. Gone were the likes of David Butterfield, Meade's disloyal chief of staff, the alcohol loving William Henry French, who had replaced Dan Sickles immediately after Gettysburg, and the popular but super cautious, indecisive John Sedgwick. Although Hancock's Gettysburg's wound diminished his leadership capacity to the point that he had to be replaced and sent to a less demanding position, on the whole the six infantry corps then at Grant's disposal were commanded by capable, experienced professional military men upon whom Grant could depend to carry out his orders.

Finally, to give Grant an unprecedented edge his cavalry corps commander, Sheridan, brought unmatched determination, zeal and combativeness to a numerically superior, well-armed and equipped cavalry that Little Phil had learned, and was not hesitant, to deploy as a lethal strike force. Sheridan's chief of staff would later recall that Little Phil's tactics were not complicated:

> ... the method to be pursued by the cavalry corps was immediate and simple. It was to pursue and attack the left flank of the retreating army at any possible point with the cavalry division that first reached it, and, if possible, to compel it to turn and defend its wagon trains and artillery. ... Then to send another division beyond and attack the Confederate army again at any possible point, and to follow up this method of attack until at some point the whole army would be obliged to turn and deliver battle.[40]

And finally, the terrain west of Petersburg was without mountain passes or gaps that could be used to deter pursuits. On the other hand there were multiple routes that were more or less parallel to each other thus providing the pursuers ample access to the retreating army's flanks and front. The Southside R.R. and the Appomattox River were the two most topographical features running west of the Richmond and Petersburg area. At first they diverge before converging near Farmville before again going in separate directions before meeting again near the village of Appomattox. In short Lee had lost many of the important advantages his army enjoyed after Gettysburg while the Federals gained significant advantages not available to them in July 1863.

## *Amelia Court House* (April 4–5, 1865)

Lee began his retreat by moving his main column parallel to the north bank of the Appomattox.[41] His first planned stop was the redbrick town of Amelia Court House where sustenance supposedly was waiting in boxcars on the railroad. But unfortunately for Lee his original plan immediately was unraveling. Just as a logistical mistake—sending the pontoon wagon train in the wrong direction—impaired Thomas' pursuit of Hood, another logistics mistake was about to dearly cost Lee. Lee had previously ordered food, forage, and ammunition to be pre-staged at Amelia Court House. But without food or forage since leaving Petersburg Lee's men and animals were in bad need for something to eat. Unfortunately the train commander had taken the food to Richmond where the food was destroyed as part of the evacuation.[42] When the Confederates arrived at Amelia C.H. on Tuesday, April 4, 1865, they found only ordinance,[43] something the Rebels not only did not need but weight their starving animals could hardly haul.

This logistics mix-up forced Lee to order his men to scour the countryside for food.[44] Not only were the foragers unable to find nearly enough to satisfy the starving army, but the process of scavenging for food and forage cost the Confederates much of their head start in their efforts to stay ahead of the pursuing Federals. Lee later acknowledged that "The delay was fatal and could not be retrieved."[45]

Upon leaving Petersburg, Grant together with Ord's Army of the James marched along the tracks of the Southside R.R. while Sheridan, including his cavalry and Meade's Army of the Potomac, took the straightest course due west, between Lee's line and Grant's.[46] When Sheridan realized Lee was stalled at Amelia C.H., Little Phil organized a rapid march to Jetersville, further west where the Southside R.R. intersected with the Richmond & Danville R.R. where Sheridan hoped to interdict if not capture Lee's army. By that evening the Union blockade—consisting of one cavalry division plus portions of Humphreys' 2nd Corps, Griffin's 5th Corps, and Wright's 6th Corps—faced the northeast, the first time a line of battle for the Army of the Potomac ever faced that direction.[47]

Even without any food for breakfast for his hungry troops, Lee was forced to put his soldiers on the road again early the morning of Wednesday, April 5, 1865. But Sheridan's forces blocked Lee's intended route toward Jetersville, where Lee had planned to turn south heading for a convergence with Johnston at Danville. Because Lee—after making his own personal reconnaissance—decided he could not attack with his weary, famished troops,[48] he was compelled to take a northerly detour looping toward Farmville, another 18 miles due west. Lee again hoped among other things to then find 80,000 desperately needed rations that had been part of another shipment from Lynchburg.[49] Thus although Lee managed to circumvent Sheridan's blocking force, by taking a northern loop Lee did so at the cost of bypassing the point where he had wanted to start moving south to meet Johnston. Furthermore Lee's troops were still without badly needed rations that were supposed to have been waiting for them at Jetersville. Gary Gallagher says "Jetersville marked the defining moment of the campaign."[50] In any event Meade immediately ordered the chase of Lee's rear guard to continue.

Also on April 5 one of the Federal cavalry divisions, led by BGen. Henry Davies, 29, was scouting to see whether Lee may have been circling to the north. Instead at Paineville,[51] five miles north of Jetersburg, the Yankee horsemen found and attacked the Confederate supply train that had turned south hoping to join the main column. The train's small contingent of Confederate cavalry was virtually helpless against the much larger number of Blue riders who scattered or destroyed large parts of the column, including wagons carrying papers from Robert E. Lee's headquarters. In addition to destroying at least 300 wagons of badly needed supplies, Davies' cavalry captured at least 600 Southerners (half of whom were black teamsters) plus six pieces of artillery that had been part of the train. While armies never wanted to lose guns, more immediately the loss of loaded supply wagons greatly exacerbated Lee's supply problems.[52]

Again the odds were shifting further against the Confederates. Soldiers on both sides were being asked to march as many as 35 miles per day, sometimes through muddy roads or even through swamps. While the boys in blue were at least receiving daily rations provided by way of the re-configured Southside R.R. the boys in ragtag gray or butternut forced to continue marching under near-starvation conditions. Furthermore Lee's slim hope of reaching a restoration of equilibrium by joining Johnston was becoming more distant, less likely.

## *Sailor's Creek*[53] (April 6, 1865)

Sheridan sent a message to Grant—riding with Ord's headquarters—that he should ride forward to join Little Phil who was concerned that the pursuit might consist entirely of Meade's chase against the rear guard. Late during the evening of April 5 Grant determined, based largely upon Sheridan's recommendations, to alter the pursuit tactics to include getting ahead of Lee's retreat again rather than merely following and attacking from the rear or the flanks. As a result of this conference Grant ordered Meade with two Union corps to continue toward Amelia C.H.—already vacated by Lee—while Sheridan's cavalry together with two other infantry corps headed west, trying to get ahead of Lee's van.[54] This alignment still allowed two additional infantry corps from Ord's Army of the James to be held in reserve thus giving Grant the additional advantage of tactical flexibility. Although Meade's authority as the field commander had been in steady decline ever since Spotsylvania, at Jetersburg Grant finally delegated all tactical control of the pursuit to Sheridan.

While detouring northward around Jetersville Longstreet's corps led Lee's column followed by Anderson's corps. Ewell's scratch force from Richmond was followed by those wagons that had escaped from Paineville with Gordon's corps being the army's rear guard.[55] Altogether the column stretched for more than ten miles as it trudged westward toward Rice's Station located along the Southside R.R. Not only did Lee want to regroup the column at Rice's Station but also once there his army could double back to Burkeville, eight miles south by southeast, where hopefully Lee's army could there resume its southward journey.

The Union's superiority in numbers of horse soldiers allowed Sheridan to deploy his brigades in a variety of manners. Because of the circumstances, specifically the Rebels' weakened condition negating a reasonable possibility of a counterattack, Sheridan did not have to concern himself with protecting the main army's flanks or rear. However Sheridan did understand the advantages of scouting and reconnoitering, and used smaller units for those purposes. Sheridan also believed in massing his cavalry as dismounted infantry, sometimes even entrenched. At the same time he would send detached brigades to harry and raid against the Confederate column, especially its trains. Douglas Freeman had observed that, "There could hardly have been a stretch of Virginia countryside better suited for an attack by cavalry on an encumbered column of infantry."[56] Although these attacks were usually on a piecemeal basis they were nevertheless still taking a toll as the Blue horse soldiers cut the harnesses or disabled the wheels by axing the spokes or even burning or upsetting the wagons beyond possible repair.

At Holt's Corner—a crossroads six miles northeast of Rice's Corner on the road between Amelia C.H. and Farmville—Anderson halted the march of his corps to defend against an attack by the main body of Union cavalry. Not being aware of these attacks to his rear, Longstreet continued toward Rice's Station. But Anderson's halt created a gap between his lead division and Longstreet's rear unit.[57] When Anderson was able to resume his march toward Rice's Station Ewell's troops followed Anderson before crossing Little Sailors' Creek, a small tributary flowing northward toward the Appomattox. However, before the army's wagon trains and artillery trains crossed the creek Ewell directed them to turn to the north. Ewell also wanted Gordon to follow Ewell's trains to provide a stronger rear guard. However Ewell did not tell Gordon of the trains' diversion causing Gordon to follow the trains to the north instead of continuing toward Rice's Station with the rest of the column. Gordon's mistaken turn meant Ewell became the main column's rear guard but without the benefit of any artillery support.

These miscues split the Confederates into three groups: (1) Longstreet accompanied by Lee waiting unaware at Rice's Station five miles to the west of Anderson; (2) Anderson followed by Ewell; and (3) an isolated Gordon following the trains that had taken a wrong turn to head north toward the Appomattox.[58]

The column's separations resulted in disastrous havoc as the Federals struck two of the separated segments from all directions. The battle of Sailor's Creek—essentially three individual battles—turned into an unmitigated disaster for the Rebels almost as soon as the Union cavalry discovered the vulnerabilities of the detached segments. Sheridan's entrenched cavalry, with its repeating carbines, blocked Anderson's lead brigades from advancing while Wright's 6th Corps, complete with artillery as well as infantry, crossed Little Sailor's Creek to batter the rear of Ewell's small unsupported force. Miraculously Ewell's ragamuffin force from Richmond pushed the 6th Corps back across the creek before a brigade of Confederate marines and Georgia artillerymen, dressed in scarlet-trimmed parade ground uniforms,[59] foolishly countercharging across the creek where their valiant efforts were blasted with canister. Ewell frantically tried to coordinate his defense with Anderson's but his group was soon outflanked before also crumbling. The survivors of this "bloody slaughter" had no recourse except to surrender.[60]

Further ahead Anderson attempted a frontal assault trying to catch up with Longstreet's rear but his soldiers exerted only half-hearted efforts against a numerically superior entrenched force, many of Anderson's soldiers quickly dropping their arms before surrendering. In addition to attacking supply wagons, at one point on April 6,[61] Custer, leading, leading his 3rd Cavalry Division, captured about 800 horses and mules, 300 wagons plus 15 artillery pieces, including the battalion's commander.[62] Observing helplessly from a distant hilltop as Anderson's corps melted away, the normally stoic Lee could only bemoan "My God! Has the army been dissolved?"[63]

Two miles to the north where Little Sailor's Creek joins Big Sailor's Creek, the Yankees' 2nd Corps by Andrew Humphreys—whom Thomas Buell characterized as a wolfhound[64]—pummeled the wagon train while forcing Gordon's corps into utter disarray. Gordon later wrote of the experience that the Federals "struck my command while we were endeavoring to push the ponderous wagon trains through the bog, out of which the starved teams were unable to drag them."[65] Humphreys later wrote the Rebels' route of retreat was "literally lined with their tents, baggage, and cooking utensils," cast away in the Johnnies' desperate efforts to stay ahead of the pursuit.[66] The Northern 2nd Corps captured 20 percent of the wagon trains, 1,700 Rebel soldiers, 70 ambulances plus 11 battle flags.[67] By the end of the day Gordon was driven in massive disorder across the Appomattox before regrouping along the Lynchburg railroad at the High Bridge.

The devastating outcomes of these battles, resulting in another 8,000 Rebel casualties, including eight generals taken prisoner, would greatly influence Lee's eventual decision to surrender. Richard Ewell, once Stonewall Jackson's top subordinate, Joseph Kershaw who had served with Early in the Shenandoah Valley, and who was considered one of Lee's hardest fighting generals,[68] and Custis Lee, Robert E. Lee oldest son who was leading field troops for the first time, were among the eight captured Confederate generals. Additionally Lee soon relieved Anderson and two other generals, Pickett and Bushrod Johnson, from the army thereby reducing Lee's inner circle of infantry generals to Longstreet, Gordon, and Mahone.[69]

Professor Glatthaar observes:

> The Saylor's Creek disaster marked the beginning of the very end for Lee's army. Not only did it lose 8,000 men and large numbers of guns and wagons, but the battle was emblematic of the collapse of the army's fighting prowess. Exhausted physically and emotionally, the men of the Army of Northern Virginia could no longer resist the vicious strikes of the Union army. Sheridan and his command sensed the Confederates' enervated condition and closed in for the kill.[70]

But surprisingly all was not lost for the Confederates! Rebel cavalry was still able to repulse Union forces trying to capture the important High Bridge and the adjacent wagon bridge that gave access to Farmville from the north. Nevertheless what had been the greatest of the Confederacy's armies—reduced to no more than two effective corps, one still led by Longstreet and another cobbled together under Gordon—was horribly wounded, "limping pathetically in its efforts to get away" from Grant.[71] In order that his army would have something to eat, and after ordering his army's third night march, Lee ordered more supplies to be sent from Lynchburg to a Southside R.R. depot at Appomattox Station, 32 miles due west of Sailor's Creek.

## Farmville (April 7, 1865)

In contrast to Hood's post–Nashville retreat that went along a relatively straight road crossing several streams whose high banks made it difficult to cross once the rear guard burned the bridges, Lee's retreat was along meandering roads. Although the Appomattox River flowed through several roads there were also an ample number of bridges traversing the river. Furthermore as the Appomattox continued westward it became more shallow, and easier to ford, as it approached its headwaters. This meant there were few terrain features that could be incorporated as obstacles by rear guards, especially since the trailing Federals were pressing too close to allow the Rebels enough time to construct barricades, cut trees, or dig ditches.

The Southern remnants left Sailor's Creek in two main columns with Longstreet's group, including Lee and his headquarter section, staying south of the Appomattox River to continue to Farmville, a town of 1,500 near the south bank of the Appomattox River, where they arrived on Thursday, April 6, 1865. Lee's other column, headed by Gordon, took a longer, more circuitous route to Farmville moving northwest toward the High Bridge, one of the four area bridges spanning the Appomattox River. The Southerners received rations at Farmville, the first for many since leaving the Petersburg lines five days earlier. However Lee's command enjoyed little respite when Lee soon learned the wagon bridge beneath the High Bridge was controlled by the Federals.

Estimates of Lee's remaining strength were always inexact since circumstances did not permit daily musters to count available soldiers. Casualties were high but uncounted as the Southern army could not pause even to count its losses. Furthermore the Rebel forces were dissipating in droves. Porter Alexander reported that thousands were leaving their commands and wandering about the devastated country in quest of food, and they had no muskets.[72] In all likelihood even Lee would have had difficulty calculating the remaining effective strength of his army. Post-war estimates have been made even more difficult to compute because so many headquarters records were lost or destroyed as wagons were burned or overturned during the retreat. Given these uncertainties Bevin Alexander estimates that Lee's army had only 30,000 men remaining but with only 12,000 still carrying their rifles.[73]

To continue westward from Farmville Lee had a choice of taking roads either north of the meandering Appomattox or south of that stream. Lee determined his better advantage was to march both of his remaining corps across to the north side of the Appomattox River before continuing to the west. Thus by crossing the Appomattox at Farmville Lee had decided to take a longer, indirect route to the Appomattox community, a decision that is not self-apparent nor has been satisfactorily explained. Lee began a 25-mile march winding through many hamlets and villages toward Appomattox. An integral part of Lee's plan was to try to separate his army from the Federals by stranding the Northerners south of the Appomattox River. To do so Lee ordered Billy Mahone—former president of the Southside R.R. Co.—to destroy 24 bridges, including the High Bridge as well as the adjacent wagon bridge across the Appomattox. However, Mahone's rearguard division was able to burn only four of those 24 bridges. Unfortunately for the Confederates the wagon bridge beneath the High Bridge was one of the bridges not destroyed. Nevertheless Little Billy was able to repulse the Federal attack, allowing the Confederates' retreat to continue.

Lee also ordered Alexander to burn the railroad and highway bridges that crossed at

Farmville.[74] Although Alexander tried burning the bridges, Federal cavalry and infantry began arriving in force at Farmville and were still able to cross the Appomattox by dousing the flames and by finding a nearby ford. By midmorning the Federals were resuming their chase with Humphreys' 2nd Corps continuously pressing the Confederates' rear guard.

Furthermore not only were the Federals able to cross the Appomattox to resume harrying Lee's rear guard but the Federals also realized that staying south of the Appomattox provided a route shorter than the route that Lee was taking. Meanwhile a Union scout sent word that several railroad cars of supplies were waiting for Lee at Appomattox Station, 25 miles away. Based upon this information Sheridan with his cavalry followed by Griffin's 5th Corps and much of Ord's army marched relentlessly and without rest to take the more direct, shorter route to Appomattox that Lee had eschewed.

Grant, wearing his mud splattered clothes and being exhausted from an ongoing severe migraine, arrived in Farmville in the afternoon of Friday, April 7 a few hours after Lee's departure. On this day Lincoln telegraphed Grant, "Gen. Sheridan says 'If the thing is pressed I think Lee will surrender.' Let the *thing* be pressed." After establishing his headquarters in the same hotel occupied by Lee the previous evening Grant sent a short message to Lee, "The results of the last week must convince you of the hopelessness of further resistance on the part of the Army of Northern Va. in this struggle. I feel that it is so and regard it as my duty to shift from myself the responsibility of any effusion of blood by asking of you the surrender of that portion of the S.C. army known as the Army of Northern Va."

Lee received Grant's message at 9:30 p.m. on the 7th before showing the note to Longstreet who simply said "Not yet."[75] Without consulting further with Longstreet Lee then responded to Grant by disputing Grant's premise that further resistance was hopeless but still asking Grant what "…the terms you will offer on the terms of [the army's] surrender."[76]

Grant's second note to Lee—sent the early Saturday morning of April 8, 1865— answered Lee in part, "…there is but one condition I insist upon, namely: that the men and officers surrendered shall be disqualified for taking up arms again, against the government of the United States, until properly exchanged." In response to Grant's second note Lee inquired about the possibility of surrendering all Confederate forces, not just his Army of Northern Virginia.[77] However, Grant knew Lincoln had not delegated such wide authority and his authority to negotiate was limited to terms of surrender of individual armies.

## *Appomattox* (April 8–9, 1865)

After hard, overnight marching Sheridan's cavalry arrived in Appomattox Court House Saturday morning, April 8, ahead of Lee's vanguard. In the afternoon Little Phil sent Custer's cavalry division down the road into Appomattox Station. Taking a 4,000-man Confederate detail completely by surprise Custer also captured four trains bulging with supplies loaded at Lynchburg for Lee's starving army.[78] Sheridan sent the trains a couple miles back to the west assuring these supplies remained beyond the reach of the intended recipients. Custer also managed to capture 25 guns as well another thousand prisoners.[79] Furthermore, the Confederate lines of communications, including badly needed supplies, were totally severed beyond reach. Sheridan sent an urgent message to Gibbon to push his 24th Corps ahead so that "they may have handsome results in the morning."[80]

That Saturday evening Lee convened a rare (for him) council of war that decided to try one last ditch effort to break through the Federal cordon.[81] The plan was for Gordon, with help from Fitz Lee's cavalry, to force a breach in the Union lines to the west after which Longstreet, together with Lee and his headquarters group, would follow before turning south toward Johnston. It was also agreed that Lee would have no alternative except to meet with Grant to discuss surrender if Gordon were unable to punch through the Union lines.

Three miles northeast of Appomattox Station at Appomattox Court House, as planned on Palm Sunday, April 9, 1865, Gordon's infantry and Fitzhugh Lee's cavalry formed a line of battle in a last ditch, desperate effort to break out along the Lynchburg Road. This force, led by one of the most determined, valiant Confederate generals but being a shell of its former 2nd Corps self, enjoyed initial success against the Union's cavalry pickets. However this early success was not only short-lived, but was illusionary as Gibbon's 24th Corps, reinforced by two infantry brigades of the U.S.C.T., together with Griffin's 5th Corps, arrived just in time to emerge from the woods to attack Gordon from three sides. At this point the Army of Northern Virginia was surrounded by Union cavalry reinforced by infantry to the front, to the rear by Meade's 2nd and 6th Corps, and to the south. Three regiments of black regiments after rapidly marching twenty miles to take their positions along a stage coach road blocked the Confederates intended escape route.[82] Within an hour Gordon reluctantly reported back to Lee "Tell General Lee I have fought my corps to a frazzle, and I fear I can do nothing unless I am heavily supported by Longstreet."[83] Upon learning of the failure of Gordon's attack, and after eschewing Porter Alexander's advice to disperse his army to become guerrillas in the woods and mountains rather than surrendering, Lee decided he had no choice but to meet Grant to discuss terms of surrender. And so Lee sent word to Grant asking to meet at a convenient location.[84]

By mutual agreement the respective representatives arranged that their commanding generals would meet at McLean's House in Appomattox C.H. McLean had formerly lived in the Manassas, Virginia, area but moved westward hoping to avoid additional collateral dangers of warfare. In McLean's house, and before discussing terms of surrender, Lee told Grant that the South then was as opposed to human bondage as was the North, thus removing the only fundamental issue dividing the two sections. Thereafter in an obscure village with no particular strategic significance the son of an Ohio tanner dictated terms of surrender to the scion of a First Family of Virginia. Much to Lee's surprise he was not taken prisoner. At Lee's request, his men were allowed to keep their own horses and side arms[85]; furthermore, after Lee mentioned his army had not been fed for several days, Grant also ordered that three days' rations be distributed to the former Rebels.[86]

Looking back it is hard to imagine how Lee's army could have escaped the Grant-Sheridan juggernaut. In order to escape, Lee's his entire command would have to execute the retreat to perfection. But in contrast, Lee's retreat encountered several problems beginning with the logistics blunder at Amelia C.H., which meant the already malnourished Confederate soldiers had to continue their long, desperate trek without food. But perhaps more importantly the delay at Amelia also meant Lee's army lost the half day's lead it had gained from its head start. Moreover Lee's retreat was plagued by a series of other mishaps including the dismembering of the supply train at Paineville, the debacle at Sailor's Creek, the failure to burn bridges across the Appomattox, and Lee's decision to take the longer route from Farmville to Appomattox. Any of these miscues might have been enough to doom Lee's chances to escape but collectively they were absolutely fatal!

Perhaps against earlier iterations of the Army of the Potomac Lee still would have managed to lead his army to a safe harbor. But by 1865 Lee was finally matched against a superbly well oiled war machine whose tenacious tactical commander was committed, and knew how, to finish the rebellion. Not only did Sheridan's cavalry spearhead an unmatched strike force but Union infantry had commanders such as Wright, Humphreys, and Gibbon who led marches at unprecedented rates to provide reinforcements to cavalry blocking positions at Jetersburg, at Sailor's Creek and finally with conclusiveness at Appomattox Station. Together they assured the entire noose prevented any reasonable chance for their prey to escape. The most successful, indeed the only entirely successful, pursuit of the Civil War struck the blow that was mortal to four years of the rebellion!

## *Dénouements*

Before departing for Washington Grant ordered there be no firing of salutes. Grant also insisted that there be a formal ceremony of surrender before Confederate soldiers could be allowed to return to their homes. Although neither Grant nor Lee participated, the formal surrender occurred at Appomattox C.H. April 12, 1865, four years to the day after the beginning of the cannonade upon Fort Sumter.

Lee dictated General Orders No. 9, a farewell message to his troops.[87] But even in surrender Lee maintained a strain of defiant intractability saying his soldiers were being "compelled to yield to overwhelming numbers and resources."[88] Lee signed his parole and with a small retinue rode from Appomattox on April 12, arriving in Richmond mid-afternoon April 16. There a small crowd warmly greeted Lee, 58, who responded courteously before entering his house without making any remarks.[89] Lee's war was over.

Technically the war was not yet entirely over but the Appomattox surrender shattered the Confederacy's backbone with Lee's departure crushing the Rebellion's heart and soul. Furthermore the C.S.A. government was no longer functioning as Jeff Davis and much of his administration continued on the run attempting to avoid capture by Federal pursuers.

On the day before the formal surrender ceremonies Lincoln made some brief remarks to a crowd gathered on the White House lawn. John Wilkes Booth, a 26-year-old actor with strong Southern sympathies, was in the crowd and became infuriated when he heard Lincoln say he would like to give voting rights to certain Blacks. Three days later Booth slipped into the back of the President's Box at the Ford Theater in Washington where he mortally wounded Lincoln with a shot to the back of the President's head. The nation was overcome by grief by this assassination while one immediate effect being to harden Secretary of War Stanton's attitude toward future terms of surrender.

Porter Alexander had urged Lee not to surrender because Alexander realized what the effect would be upon other Confederate armies. On April 9, 1865, Alexander said, "If there is any hope for the Confederacy it is delay. For if the Army of Northern Va. surrenders every other army will surrender as fast as the news reaches it. For it is the morale of this army that has supported the whole Confederacy." Alexander's prediction materialized when Joe Johnston requested an armistice to negotiate terms of surrender of his army in North Carolina. Initially Sherman—believing he was negotiating pursuant to Lincoln's guidelines—agreed to extend the same terms as Grant had given Lee. However an embittered Stanton refused to agree to allow Johnston to surrender on those same terms. But Johnston knew that further combat was futile while Sherman was anxious to disengage so that he and his army could be part of the national ceremonies in Washington. Accordingly Sherman and Johnston agreed to new terms of surrender on April 26.

Smaller units steadily surrendered. For instance on April 21 the famous raider, John Mosby, disbanded his band of rangers, most of whom surrendered. On April 24 in Charlotte, North Carolina, Jeff Davis, while continuing to flee from the Federals, held his last cabinet meeting. On April 26 Federal troops cornered John Wilkes Booth in a barn south of the Rappahannock River in Virginia. Before he could be captured alive he was shot and killed. It has never been clearly established whether the shot was self-inflicted or from a Union soldier.

The last of Southern resistance—at least east of the Mississippi River—was ended on May 4 when Richard Taylor, who once led the Louisiana Tigers as part of Stonewall's Jackson's Valley campaign of 1862, surrendered. As previously noted on May 9, 1865, Forrest sent his troopers home. On Wednesday, May 10, 1865, a detachment of Union cavalry, under the command of Harry Wilson, captured Jefferson Davis, his wife, and several staff members in the woods near Irwinville, Georgia. West of the Mississippi Simon Bolivar Buckner surrendered the last large group of Confederate soldiers on May 26, 1865, a capitulation not approved until June 2, 1865, by Kirby Smith.

On December 18, 1865, after approval by twenty-seven states the Thirteenth Amendment abolishing slavery became the law of the land. For several years Blacks retained justifiable pride in the numerous contributions of the U.S.T.C., especially in helping to capture the Army of Northern Virginia at Appomattox. They realized that without infantry reinforcements following long and exhausting marches, it is unlikely Sheridan's cavalry would have been unable to block Gordon's breakout along the stage coach road.

Edwin Stanton remained as Secretary of War but the former pro-slavery Democrat's radical views about Reconstruction brought him into constant conflict with President Johnson. Although Congress had enacted the Tenure in Office Act intended to require Congress' approval before a cabinet member could be fired, Johnson sent Stanton an order of removal, which Stanton ignored by locking himself in his office for weeks. Eventually Johnson was impeached, in part because of his attempt to remove Stanton without Congressional approval. By one vote Johnson avoided conviction whereupon Stanton submitted his resignation from the cabinet.

President Grant nominated Stanton to the United States Supreme Court, the only office Stanton ever truly wanted. But shortly after being nominated in December 1869 Stanton suffered a severe asthma attack causing his death at the age of 55.

Ulysses S. Grant succeeded Andrew Johnston to become the 18th President of the United States serving two terms (1869–1877). For years after his departure from office Grant's performance as President was rated as one of the worst, mostly because of the corrupt activities of his trusted aides, but more recent evaluations give Grant higher rankings as President. After leaving office Grant was forced into bankruptcy after he had lent his name to a brokerage firm that defrauded both Grant and the firm's clients. As Grant was suffering from painful throat cancer he began to write his memoirs so that his family would have some income after his death. Grant died at the age of 63 years on July 23, 1885, shortly after his highly successful, but sometimes factually dubious, memoirs were published.

William T. Sherman wanted nothing to do with Reconstruction. As a war hero he was able to choose to administer the pacification of the West, specifically supervising the removal of hostile Indians from areas desired by Whites. His harsh, vindictive methods—which tried to destroy all Indian resources, including food sources, villages, while targeting women, children, and the elderly without discrimination—drew criticism from several Eastern quarters, but typically Sherman hardly cared.

Sherman was determined to avoid involvement with partisan politics, even rejecting Andrew Johnson's attempt to appoint Cump as Secretary of War to replace Edwin Stanton, whom Sherman detested. (Sherman had refused to shake Stanton's hand at the parade celebrating the Union victory.) However Sherman was delighted when President Grant appointed him as General-in-Chief but Sherman eventually became embroiled in a power struggle with Grant's secretary of war. That struggle ended in Sherman's favor when the war secretary was forced to resign upon being implicated in one of the many scandals of Grant's administration. During his 14-year term as General-in-Chief he laid the foundation for advanced education in the officer corps.[90]

Sherman took the time to write several commentaries that were widely published. His central theme was that war is terrible and ought to be avoided at all costs. Sherman lived the last four years of his life in New York City where he died of pneumonia in February 14, 1891.

Philip Sheridan continued in the Regular Army after the war. His Reconstruction administration in Louisiana and Texas was so harsh Andrew Johnson was forced to transfer Sheridan to Missouri. For several years Sheridan served on the Western frontier where his ruthless methods against Indians raised the hackles of several religious and humanitarian organizations. Whether he actually said it Sheridan will forever be stigmatized for a statement attributed to him that "The only good Indian is a dead Indian." In 1884 Sheridan succeeded Sherman as General-in-Chief, being promoted to full general shortly before his death in 1888 at the age of 57 years. The head of his casket was adorned by the battle flag he had carried at Cedar Creek.

After the war George Meade remained in the Army undertaking several major commands, including the Reconstruction District headquartered in Atlanta. However Meade became bitterly disappointed when Sheridan was promoted ahead of him to lieutenant general after Sherman became General-in-Chief. At the age of 57 years, Meade died November 6, 1872, of pneumonia without ever fully recovering from his wounds suffered at White Oaks Swamp in 1862.

George Custer continued in the cavalry, taking command of the 7th Cavalry in 1867 and fighting Indians almost continuously until 1876 when he encountered Sitting Bull at Little Big Horn in Montana where Custer and 276 of his troopers were killed. The relief column, arriving too late except to bury the victims, was led by John Gibbon who had remained in the army after the Civil War to resume Indian fighting.

Gouverneur Warren's career was destroyed by Sheridan's abrupt dismissal and so in protest of his treatment Warren resigned his volunteer commission May 1865. However he continued to seek redemption by asking for a board of inquiry, which Grant refused to allow. Finally when Grant was no longer president his successor, Rutherford B. Hayes, ordered that a board of inquiry be convened. After hearing testimony from dozens of witnesses, including Grant and Sheridan, the board completely exonerated Warren. Although the board did not find any fault with Sheridan he was nevertheless sufficiently indignant to send a letter of protest to the Secretary of War. Although Warren's name was cleared he had already died in August 1882 before the inquiry was completed.

After the war Harry Wilson transferred back to the engineers where he remained until his resignation in 1870. Wilson then had several well paid positions until 1897 when he re-entered the army as a major general to fight in the Spanish-American War. In the 1900s Wilson published several biographies of other Civil War generals as well as his own autobiography, *Under the Old Flag*. Before dying at the age of 88 years in 1925, Wilson was the last surviving member of the West Point class of 1860.

Jeff Davis was imprisoned for two years after the capture. Although charged with treason he was never tried. Instead Davis was released on a $100,000 bail. After his release from prison Davis travelled to Europe. Upon returning to his home in Mississippi Davis maintained a low profile but sometimes spoke out against the centralization of power in Washington. Davis died in New Orleans at the age of 89 years in 1889 and was posthumously restored to full citizenship by a joint resolution of Congress.

After returning to his home in Richmond, Robert E. Lee became president of Washington College (later Washington & Lee University) in Lexington, Virginia. Lee died at the age of 63 years on October 12, 1870, apparently from pneumonia related to heart ailments similar to the ones that plagued him intermittently during the Civil War. Although Lee wrote some letters he was one of the few Civil War generals not to write memoirs. Although other generals might receive higher marks as strategists or tacticians no other Civil War general is accorded Lee's iconic status, especially by Southerners.

In the early 1870s Sherman resumed contact with his old adversary, Joseph E. Johnston. Over the ensuing years Sherman and Johnston became close friends, exchanging correspondence and visiting with each other as circumstances permitted. In 1888 Sherman interceded upon Johnston's behalf to help the latter retain his position as a railroad commissioner.

Johnston served as an honorary pallbearer at Sherman's funeral and burial. In respect to his friend Johnston refused to cover his head in the chilling rain. Unfortunately Johnston caught a severe cold that weakened his frail heart and a month later Johnston was dead at the age of 84 years.

After trying several businesses in New Orleans, James Longstreet started to depend upon political appointments after the war, even becoming a Republican to curry favor with Grant and other Republican presidents of the era. After Lee died Longstreet published a critique of Lee's leadership which precipitated a running and bitter war of words with Jubal Early, who blamed Longstreet for among other things the Confederate defeat at Gettysburg. Fearing for his safety as a result of the Lost Cause controversies, Longstreet moved to Gainesville, Georgia, where paradoxically his house burned, destroying a trove of Civil War materials. Longstreet died January 2, 1904, of pneumonia related to the complications of cancer.

P.G.T. Beauregard received offers to command Romanian as well as Egyptian armies but instead he became wealthy as a railroad company engineer and executive. In 1888 Beauregard was elected commissioner of public works, holding that position until he died February 20, 1893.

In contrast to the other Confederate officers who were allowed to go home soon after the Appomattox surrender, after his capture at Sailor's Creek Richard Ewell remained a prisoner until August 1865. Upon his release from prison Old Baldy returned to his wife's farm near Spring Hill, Tennessee, where he died January 25, 1872, at the age of 55 years.

In many ways John Gordon was the last surviving Confederate. He served as governor of Georgia as well as three terms in the U.S. Senate where he strove vigorously to restore Georgia to its former status. As a member of the Ku Klux Klan he attempted to subjugate Blacks while espousing—often using selective memory—the myths of the Lost Cause and of the virtues of the antebellum South.

As a businessman Gordon was constantly on the cusp of financial ruin while still managing to stay just ahead of bankruptcy. After finishing his *Reminiscences of the Civil War* Gordon died January 10, 1904, at the age of 72 years.

# 20

# Conclusions

And so the mighty scourge ended, a little more than four years after it began with sacrifices and costs that still stagger the imagination. There had been 76 battles with 6,000 skirmishes and engagements. With a population of one-tenth of today's population there were an estimated 750,000 deaths, two thirds caused by disease. Those costs in lost lives and debilitating injuries remained for decades with families that lost loved ones and communities that were left without leaders and other prominent citizen-soldiers. In many other instances, communities near the battlefields or close to the encampments were almost completely destroyed and had to be rebuilt with their economies to be resuscitated and/or resurrected, incurring tangible and intangible costs practically impossible to measure.

Given that the North had several important advantages including superior numbers of manpower, industrial and commercial resources, and naval capabilities, and given several internal problems within the Confederacy, three questions emerge: (1) What took so long for the North to prevail, (2) Could use of effective, successful pursuits have enabled one side to more quickly vanquish the other, thus mitigating the immediate and long-term suffering as well as other societal losses, (3) What factors prevented more successful pursuits leading to decisive victories,?

## *What Took So Long?*

In answer to the first question there were a myriad of reasons why the war took so long. No one could dispute the dedication, courage, valor and gallantry consistently, but not always, displayed by the soldiers of both sides during four years of combat on American soil. But all too often these sacrifices meant little in terms of settling the differences between the belligerents or of their respective governments. Strategic points, usually territory, were seized or lost but the respective armies—no matter how badly mauled or mangled—managed to survive to, and did, fight another day.

Since almost all Civil War battles concluded with one side withdrawing and being able (even being allowed in some instances) to retreat to a safe haven, the armies continued to fight again and again, albeit with considerable attrition but certainly not with enough attrition to render either side *hors de combat*. Despite regular bloodbaths the Civil War is typically regarded by military historians for its lack of decisive battles.

After citing a litany of reasons for the lack of decisive battles in the Civil War, Paddy Griffith, the esteemed British military historian, opines in general that:

## 20. Conclusions 349

> At the end of the day ... the indecisive outcome of so many Civil War battles must be put down to the individual personalities of the generals. Many of them seem to have been cautious men, rather too ready to call off their battle when victory was in sight, or to refuse combat if the odds were not to their liking. Despite the Lees and the Jacksons, the Hoods and the Burnsides, the predominant military culture was not deeply rooted in rapid manoeuvre and crushing assault. A more tentative and sedate style of war seems to have been more generally preferred.[1]

To an extent Griffith has a point. Certainly in the early stages of the Civil War for a variety of reasons commanding generals seldom had whole hearted commitment to either capturing or annihilating their defeated enemies. However this lack of commitment was not merely because of their "cautious" natures as claimed by Griffith. In some cases, especially on the Federal side, commanding generals—McClellan and his many adherents being prime examples—simply did not share the national objectives of their respective commanders in chief. Instead many generals—especially engineers with West Point educations—still adhered to the ideals of soft war whereby the objective was to prevail on individual battlefields with only secondary thoughts, if any, given to eliminating enemy armies. Ironically Lincoln—the self-taught strategist—realized long before most of his military leaders that hard war was the key to defeating the Rebellion. Frankly some of the commanding generals seemed to remain more intent upon gaining personal glory or satisfaction than upon putting the enemy completely out of commission.

On the other hand, as the war continued, and as many of the more conservative or passive generals were shelved, and as the butchers' bill accrued to theretofore unimagined tolls, the "tentative and sedate style of war" became an outdated memory. Thereafter cautiousness was not as much of a problem as was the myopic strategic vision of commanders such as Buell and Meade who had difficulty envisioning anything beyond the immediate tactical or logistic challenges before them.

Although some military historians oriented toward Napoleon doctrines have contended, and perhaps still do, that the war would have ended sooner with more concentrated artillery barrages, infantry blitzes and/or large forces of saber-armed cavalry, those doctrines became passé by 1861. Two changes occurred to make decisive battlefield victories difficult if not almost impossible. The Minié ball used in conjunction with the rifled musket provided defenders greater killing power while the advent and extensive use of a wide variety of fortifications gave defenders extra capacity to remain on the battlefield, even in the face of numerical odds against them. Frequently heavily wooded, hilly terrain impeded maneuvering, especially by cavalry, that might have resulted in decisive battlefield victories. Although the North enjoyed better numbers in terms of manpower and material resources, both sides were similarly equipped and armed.

We can also see with the benefit of 20/20 hindsight that several strategic mistakes prolonged the war. At the very onset of hostilities Federal military leadership assumed the war would be fairly short and it was therefore unnecessary, even imprudent, to take the time and effort, and to spend the money, to develop a strong, robust cavalry. Lacking cavalry's mobility, the options available to offensive commanders were almost limited to frontal assaults, only one of which—Missionary Ridge at Chattanooga—was unquestionably successful. Lincoln also committed serious military error when he decided the politics of the day required the prominent use of political generals, almost all who were incompetent combat commanders. Errors were also made in the appointment of traditionally oriented

West Point generals—many with their knighthood rules of conduct and soft war philosophies—as commanders of large armies. The early obsession upon Richmond as the primary strategic target became another error of judgment because the South was not going to capitulate so soon even if its capital were lost.

Attrition was a major factor allowing the Union to eventually gain an upper hand. Certainly by 1865 the South had suffered a multitude of grievous, irreparable losses caused in large part by suffering higher rates of casualties in almost all major battles, Fredericksburg being the most notable exception. Rebel armies were emaciated while the Southern manpower pool was reduced to conscripting young boys and old men as replacement troops. Its territory shrunk in almost all directions. Its ports became closed. Its war making capacity had been substantially reduced while its domestic economy was in tatters especially since a large portion of its bonded manpower had either escaped or been set free. In short, defeat almost became a matter of when, not if. Nevertheless the Rebels had shown remarkable resilience throughout much of the Rebellion, but attrition was a slowly moving factor as were other factors such as the Anaconda strategy.

But to Griffith's point, initially the commanders on both sides had similar military backgrounds but arguably the Federals better learned by trial-and-error to select more competent commanders and subordinates while the level of Confederate commanders remained stagnant if not diminished. The North also enjoyed a superior political administration and a better War Department organization. Ironically strict adherence to states' rights sometimes hurt the Confederacy when recalcitrant governors refused to cooperate with Davis. But neither side seldom had the resources, tactical advantages, or will power to compel the other side to totally succumb, thus achieving decisive victories. The failure to compel the vanquished to quit the war as a result of battlefield combat meant pursuit of armies in retreat were necessary to finish the job by either annihilating or capturing the enemy's retreat.

## Could *Pursuits Have Ended the War Sooner?*

In response to the second question, history cannot change what has already happened. The question then becomes whether successful pursuits would have lent decisive results to end or at least shorten the war. Although as a practical matter the war was probably going to be won or lost in the East where the capitals were located, as more importantly were most of the major population centers, manufacturing hubs, financial centers, as well as harbors or ports for imports of essential military supplies, the Western theater also had significant ancillary value. From the very beginning both sides invested in large armies in the struggle for the control of the river and rail systems that sustained the economies of both regions. Furthermore populations were moving westward making cities such as Cincinnati, Louisville, Vicksburg, and Nashville attractive targets. Accordingly capture of one of the other side's Western armies would deal a crippling, but not necessarily fatal, blow to that side.

In the West the Confederates had at best only limited opportunities for decisive victories, including those by successful pursuits. From the start Jefferson Davis committed his Western armies to the defense of an immense amount of territory but his armies in that region were undersized for that herculean task. And so except for the Kentucky excursion in 1862 and except also for Hood's Tennessee invasion in late 1864, these Confederate armies had, or chose, to fight on the defensive, often resorting to strategic retreats.

Although the Confederates won close or even tactical victories at Perryville and Stones River, their only clear cut victory was at Chickamauga. But notwithstanding an impressive battleground victory, command mistakes, coupled with the exhaustion of the soldiers, precluded an opportunity for a decisive victory; the huge Army of the Cumberland escaped capture in some part because Longstreet failed to close off the escape route, instead hammering away with frontal assaults at Thomas' heavily fortified position at Snodgrass Hill continuing along Horseshoe Ridge instead of closing off retreat routes. In all likelihood Bragg's army was not in position to prevent the escape of Rosecrans's entire army as it retreated from Chickamauga but had Longstreet sought to block Thomas' escape route he might have destroyed or captured much of the Union's largest army in the West.

We can only speculate about the consequences of the loss of a large Federal army, but it is only fair and reasonable to contemplate first whether the Washington administration would have bothered to muster and commit the extra forces to save Chattanooga and second whether the breakout out of Missionary Ridge could have occurred in the absence of Thomas's Army of the Cumberland. Regardless it is difficult to envision even the loss of the Army of the Cumberland being enough to overcome the overwhelming numerical advantage enjoyed by the Northern forces in the Western theater.

On the other side of the equation, the Federals won several victories in the West, most of which were against the Army of Tennessee. But starting at Shiloh, continuing at Corinth II, Perryville, Stones River, Chattanooga, and several times during the Atlanta campaign, these Federal victories were incomplete, the defeated Southerners always being able to survive to fight another day. Shiloh, Perryville, and Stones River were not especially good opportunities for pursuit, if only because the respective Federal armies were beaten up by almost as much, if not more, than were the Southern forces.

Anticipating that Rosecrans would repulse Van Dorn's small Southern army at Corinth II, Grant sent extra troops to reinforce Rosecrans, both in the chase as well as to establish a blocking force. Although the blocking force muffed allowing Van Dorn to continue his retreat, Rosecrans likewise continued his pursuit. In retreating Van Dorn's army showed all characteristics of a beaten army, strewing debris hither and yon along the way. However for reasons not clear Grant ordered an end to the pursuit thus allowing Van Dorn to reach his safe haven. While elimination of Van Dorn's army would have been a crippling blow to the Confederacy, its loss would not have tipped the scales significantly in the Federals' favor.

At first glance it might appear the Union conquest at Missionary Ridge was a good opportunity for pursuing Bragg's Rebels as they fled the ridge to go scampering down the valley. However Grant had not anticipated that turn of events and thus made insufficient preparation for such a pursuit. Furthermore, because of the earlier toll taken by the siege against Thomas's army at Chattanooga his animals were too malnourished to be of any help.

In the East the Confederates also had chances for decisive victories, especially during the first two years of the war, but as brilliant as Stonewall Jackson performed during his Shenandoah Valley campaign of 1862 he nevertheless failed to achieve any successful pursuits. In the first instance, after Winchester I Stonewall's chances to thoroughly destroy a stampeding Federal force were thwarted by the absence of his cavalry, which had taken French leave with their newly acquired mounts.

Despite Jackson's slowness in leaving his entrenched positions at Second Bull Run the bulk of the blame for that failed pursuit rests upon Longstreet who became so focused upon driving the Yanks toward Henry Hill that he also ignored the tremendous advantage of establishing a blocking position at the only point where the Federals could escape the battlefield. Although Lee's army would score further victories at Fredericksburg and Chancellorsville, Second Manassas and Chantilly were wasted chances by the Confederacy to capture or destroy major Union armies.

In order to start a successful pursuit it was necessary to score a battlefield victory. Unfortunately for the Federal cause such victories were rare in the Eastern theater. To be sure the Confederates left the field at Antietam thus giving the Yankees a narrow tactical victory. While McClellan could have, and probably should have, pushed Lee further away from the Potomac River, as a practical matter a decisive pursuit probably was not going to happen. In the first place, the margin of McClellan's victory was so narrow with both sides suffering sizable losses that the Northerners had insufficient superiority to try to capture or annihilate the Southerners.

Furthermore, Lee had a significant advantage in that he had crossed the Potomac to take excellent positions to impede, if not entirely block, any meaningful crossing by McClellan. Eventually Lee would have to withdraw from his Potomac positions but when he did so it was under his terms and conditions, not under the pressure of a pursuit. (Obviously the analysis would be different if McClellan could have acted quickly enough to have kept Lee from reaching and crossing the Potomac, but that simply did not happen, being one significant consequence from Burnside's delay in crossing the bridge at Antietam Creek.)

On its surface, Gettysburg was the next and perhaps the most famous, or at least most debated, opportunity to gain a decisive victory against Lee's army. Unfortunately Lincoln's metaphor of letting Lee slip through the Federals' fingers has helped to distort the historical analysis. First, Lee had a masterful plan of retreat that was almost perfectly executed by his subordinates. Looking back we can see that Meade could have but didn't anticipated Lee's retreat, and could have, but didn't immediately send a mixed force of cavalry and infantry to Hagerstown and/or Williamsport to block Lee's re-crossing of the Potomac.

But prior to retreating from Gettysburg, Lee's army had squandered its own chances for seizing a significant battlefield advantage. Again we can only speculate about what might have been the consequences, but as it turned out the Confederacy's last best chance to inflict major damage to the Federals occurred when they failed to pursue completely to capture Culp's Hill at the end of Day One. Historians still debate who, and what, was responsible for that failure to take this critical terrain, but it is hard to deny that the odds shifted dramatically away from the Confederates' favor on Day Three when Federal artillery had decided superiority to decimate the ranks in the so-called Pickett's Charge. It is conceivable that instead of being forced to retreat, Lee's army could have continued to advance to Washington or Baltimore, thus giving the C.S.A. a strategic leverage is was never able to command for the remainder of the war.

## What Prevented More Successful Pursuits?

For the Union, well before his leading generals came to the same conclusion, Lincoln realized that destroying the enemy army was more important than capturing territory, even capitals. As early as 1862 Lincoln was determined to defeat Stonewall Jackson in the Shenandoah Valley but Lincoln's efforts were undone by several factors including a non-unified command coupled with inept generals such as John Frémont. But in the East—where realistically the war was going to be won or lost—prior to 1865 the Federals had gained only two other opportunities to pursue because of battlefield victories, these being after Antietam in September 1862 and after Gettysburg in July 1863. However a significant amount of revisionist history ignoring or rewriting several factors, including the make-up of the commanders and of their command structures, is necessary to formulate any reasonable, logical conclusions about these possibilities. So why didn't either side use pursuits to gain a *coup de grâce* to end the war earlier than 1865?

Essentially there were four roughly hewn, often overlapping reasons why pursuits were either not used, or if used, did not succeed. These reasons can be categorized as follows: (1) After most battles both sides were too exhausted to continue any further fighting; (2) The commanders did not have sufficient attitudes or capabilities to deploy or manage pursuits; (3) Subordinate commanders did not have what to would take to fulfill their assigned missions; and (4) Ineffective use of cavalry.

Regarding the first reason, Douglas Southall Freeman offered his perspective when he commented upon Lee's lack of capacity to pursue McClellan's Federals as they retreated to Harrison's Landing:

> The Army of Northern Virginia, at the close of the action at Malvern Hill, was in the condition in which both it and the Army of the Potomac were to find themselves after nearly every major engagement of the next two years. The adversary put up so good a battle, winning or losing, that the opposing army was exhausted and incapable of pursuit. The margin of superiority was so narrow, on either side, that a victory could rarely be developed into a triumph.[2]

Although Freeman was referring to the armies' exhaustion after the Severn Days Battles, this factor arose in several other bloody instances, most notably after Shiloh, after Stones River, after Chickamauga, probably after Perryville, and maybe after Antietam.

Regarding the second reason, Brian Holder Reid, had pointed out that: "Success in battle—which includes the pursuit—can be measured by a general's skill in organizing and judiciously expending the forces under his command"[3] Reid makes this observation specifically in reference to Braxton Bragg's failure to pursue after Chickamauga but the same can be said about a host of other generals throughout the Civil War—the most notable exceptions being Thomas, Sheridan, Lee, and to a lesser extent, Grant.

Shifting from the notion of gaining territory to the objective of capturing and/or destroying enemy armies required much more than simply Lincoln saying to do so. The change of objectives required several transitions, including the appointment and promotion of generals who were no longer hidebound to outmoded notions of gaining individual glory and/or of soft war, or who were primarily seeking personal fame or glory. Instead the transition required generals who had successfully commanded at smaller levels such as regiments, brigades, and divisions, and who understood the dynamics of the battlefield were no longer the same as had been taught at West Point and who were committed to the execution of the commanding general's plan of operations. Recognizing the need for these changes was slow in coming, e.g., Ben Butler still held an important command until after the 1864 election, while finding the best commanders who could be weaned from Jomini's defensive theories was a perpetual work in progress.

It is difficult to imagine that McClellan—even if directly ordered to do so by Lincoln—would have been inclined to organize a successful pursuit by venturing to send his cavalry across the Potomac to try to block Lee's retreat. It is almost asking whether frogs could fly if they have wings. For example McClellan hardly tapped his cavalry's potential when he kept his troopers close to his headquarters to serve as his security or as a courier service. Furthermore there was little in his management of the Antietam battlefield to suggest McClellan would have judiciously expended his infantry for a vigorous chase.

While Meade, with a lot of help from Hancock and some, but not all, of his other subordinates, masterfully prepared and coordinated the Union defenses at Gettysburg there is scant evidence, then or later, that he and his array of staff and remaining subordinate commanders were ever going to capture and/or annihilate Lee's army. Union cavalry after Gettysburg fought long and hard but the individual brigades of horse riders operated without significant coordination with infantry or for that matter even with the other cavalry units. Meade was not able to capture Lee before the Army of Northern Virginia re-crossed the Potomac back into Virginia, and once Lee was back in Virginia his army enjoyed too much freedom of movement to permit Meade to develop any meaningful trap. For more than a year after Gettysburg until Grant had superseded Meade's role as army commander no evidence emerged that the Army of the Potomac had the overall command skills to capture Lee's army, admittedly a most difficult challenge.

But beyond the conservative, risk adverse nature of many commanders, other commanders, cautious or otherwise, failed to properly plan and prepare for pursuits. As previously noted pursuits were largely improvised operations but to be successful they still required a simple, fundamental framework with essential roles that could be discharged without close supervision from commanding generals. As a consequence, some pursuits failed because the commanders did not provide necessary planning and preparations. Sometimes subordinate commanders were unable to finish their assigned tasks.

As examples of subordinate commanders not having what to would take to fulfill their assigned missions, Stonewall's unexplained lethargy during Seven Days repeatedly undercut Lee's attempt to capture a major portion of McClellan's retreating and vulnerable army. And within another few months Jackson could have helped establish a blocking force at the Stoney Bridge to keep Pope's army contained at Second Manassas. And finally, a few days after Second Manassas a better, or at least a more focused, effort during Chantilly could again have helped capture Pope's army but Jackson became distracted by a relatively minor attack against his flank. Jackson's failures as the Federal armies were retreating during Seven Days, Second Manassas, and Chantilly cost the Confederacy dearly.

In the West, Sherman eventually adopted Thomas' plan to cut off Joe Johnston's retreat from Dalton at the beginning of the Atlanta campaign but McPherson, assigned to establish a blocking position at Snake Creek Gap, badly misjudged the size of Rebel forces in the area before allowing Johnston's unimpeded retreat thereby costing McPherson his "opportunity of a lifetime." But later at Atlanta and Jonesboro Sherman himself bungled another

## 20. Conclusions

excellent opportunity to capture a large portion, if not all, of the Confederate Army of Tennessee—by then commanded by John Bell Hood—when he became distracted to lose sight of his strategic objective as Grant had directed. Eliminating the Confederate's principle Western army would have given the Union several attractive options, not the least of which would have immediately been to increase the pressure upon Lee in his Petersburg trenches.

At the onset of the Overland Campaign in 1864 Grant probably envisioned the immediate destruction of Lee's army but again too much revision of history is necessary to speculate whether a Union victory would have been possible prior to investing in the Petersburg siege. In short, during the Overland Campaign the Federals failed to win any battle that could have set the stage from which to launch a pursuit. However once Lee bit on Grant's feint toward Richmond the Union had a golden opportunity to seize a tremendous advantage before Baldy Smith failed to capture the Petersburg fortifications in June 1864. Perhaps that would have compelled Lee to retreat westward away from Richmond that much earlier but Baldy had been too cautious in large part because of the lack of sufficient cavalry to ascertain the Rebel numbers entrenched in the fortifications. Thus even if Lee would have retreated as a result of the loss of Petersburg, Sheridan's absence would have meant Grant would still have had insufficient horse riders to pursue effectively.

Much of this book's narrative tells the story of how the Federal cavalry emerged, coinciding with the gradual decline of Confederate cavalry, to become spearheads of tactical mobile strike forces that became the lynchpins of successful pursuits. In the beginning of the Civil War Federal authorities treated cavalry as an expensive, time consuming afterthought but gradually began to facilitate the improvement of horseflesh, the riders and their commanders, weapons and other equipment.

The change of strategic objectives required new allocations of resources among the three major arms. Specifically cavalry, with its unmatched mobility and firepower (especially once armed with repeating carbines) had to be buttressed in numbers, quality of its horseflesh, and armament. But equally as important, it took time for commanders to learn and appreciate that cavalry had the most impact when used in conjunction with infantry as an attack or strike force rather than as a diversion by raiding or merely as the infantry's eyes and ears. This new concept had its American genesis when John Wilder mounted his infantry on horses (or mules), armed them with repeating carbines, and used that mobility to deploy his brigade throughout the theater in Tennessee where it would have the most impact. Finally, commanders such as Phil Sheridan, and his former subordinate, Harry Wilson, begin to realize the great advantage of using cavalry, together with hard marching infantry, to create blocking positions that would at the very least impede retreating armies long enough so that the main army in pursuit could apply the decisive blow.

Even through 1864 Grant failed to grasp the tactical advantage of closely coordinating cavalry's striking power with rest of the main army. When Meade complained about Sheridan's rank insubordination at Todd's Tavern, instead of ordering Little Phil to clear the road ahead as Meade wanted, Grant allowed Sheridan to go after Stuart. And while there was some advantage to the Union when Stuart was killed that advantage was at the larger cost of losing the race to Spotsylvania and even to North Anna. Instead of subsequently using Sheridan in concert with the rest of Meade's army Grant sent Sheridan on a long diversionary mission to Trevilian Station at a time when a full force of cavalry would have been invaluable as Grant kept sidling southward toward the James River.

It was not until Third Winchester in late 1864 that Federal cavalry and infantry fought in concert with one another. Soon after Third Winchester at Fisher's Hill Sheridan tried again to coordinate an infantry attack, which he was confident would succeed, with cavalry moving forward, not to raid, but instead to establish a blocking position force against the potentially retreating enemy. However the commander of the cavalry sent to establish the blocking position did not do so and the pursuit failed. But Sheridan's concept was correct even if his subordinate commander's execution let him down.

To further illustrate the difficulty of winning decisive victories, that is to say annihilating or capturing the enemy's army, it is not necessary to look any further than the ten days immediately after Nashville. Frank Varney opines Thomas' victory at Nashville was the most complete Civil War field victory "of them all."[4] Yet Thomas was one commanding general who, at least at this point in the war, looked beyond the immediate battlefield to deploy his cavalry in position to attempt such pursuit. Thomas used the cavalry of Harry Wilson, who had previously participated in Third Winchester, as part of a long spoke in a wheeling maneuver to flank Hood's Confederate defenders. Almost as soon as the Rebels started to retreat Wilson's troopers rode aggressively under difficult conditions in their attempt to get ahead of the fleeing Rebels, who were shielded by Forrest's extraordinary command of the rear guard, but the Tennessee terrain, coupled with torrential rains that swelled the streams, prevented Wilson's troopers from getting in front of the Rebels to establish a blocking position. The pursuit was also temporarily hampered when Thomas' pontoon train was sent in the wrong direction. And so while the Union pursuit battered Hood's army to the point that it was reduced to a mere shell of its former self, and while Hood was forced to retire from further command, circumstances as much as anything prevented Thomas from applying his much desired *coup de grâce*.

In analyzing Thomas' pursuit after Nashville, Christopher Einolf, who—contrary to Varney—deems that pursuit as a failure, concludes that:

> ... Thomas's pursuit failed in part due to his own errors, in part due to the poor weather and roads, and in part due to the same difficulty that all Civil War armies had in exploiting battlefield victories. Pursuing and retreating armies moved at the same pace, a walk, and retreating armies could slow their pursuers by destroying bridges and fighting delaying actions with cavalry. Furthermore, a retreating army fell back on its own supply line, while a pursuing force tended to outrun its own supplies. ... There were very few examples of successful pursuits after victory in any theater of the Civil War.[5]

(It should also be remembered that although Einolf classifies Thomas' pursuit as a failure, i.e., Thomas was unable to either capture or annihilate the Army of Tennessee, Einolf also recognizes, as previously noted in Chapter 8, that by pressing the pursuit, Thomas was able to inflict substantial damage to Hood's retreating army. Varner describes Hood's army as being a "hallow shell" after the pursuit ended.)

And parenthetically it should not be overlooked that Grant was almost completely oblivious of the importance of cavalry to Thomas at Nashville. In short for all his outstanding command attributes at various levels, including as General-in-Chief, Grant simply did not appreciate the value of cavalry as a vital weapon for gaining decisive victory. And as late as the spring of 1865 Grant wanted to send Sheridan with his two divisions to Sherman instead of preparing a final thrust against Lee at Petersburg. Grant was lucky that Sheridan had other ideas to virtually force himself, and his cavalry, upon Grant.

Both sides had intermittently attempted pursuit throughout most of the Civil War but for one reason or another no pursuit ever fully succeeded. So why did the pursuit to Appomattox succeed when similar operations had failed? Many of those circumstances have been addressed in the preceding chapter but in a nutshell Grant—a perpetual opportunist—took full advantage of a virtually unprecedented opportunity to pursue and capture the enemy's main army; on the other hand Lee was unable to reach a safe harbor to attain at equilibrium in force as he had done after Gettysburg and to a lesser extent after Antietam. At the onset once Sheridan arrived in Petersburg with his two divisions of cavalry, soon being joined by a third, Grant finally had all the necessary elements at hand to vigorously use pursuit to resume his original objective of destroying Lee's army. Sheridan and his cavalry would become Grant's ace card to trump anything that Lee might try as his army retreated.

As the respective armies moved west from the Richmond/Petersburg area the Union forces enjoyed substantial numerical superiority, perhaps by as much as two and half to one. They also enjoyed other important advantages including being better fit, better equipped and supplied, and frankly better commanded. Neither terrain nor weather would be an impediment but more than any other factor the Yankees, seeking a chance to end the war and to go home, were better motivated.

Joseph Wheelan, one of Sheridan's biographers, describes the Union victory at Sailor's Creek as a "tour de force by Sheridan, who brilliantly coordinated the operations of large cavalry and infantry forces in a running fight over unfamiliar terrain to trap and destroy two Confederate corps.... No other Union general could have accomplished what Sheridan had done."[6]

And so the most that can safely be said is that the Union was fortunate in the spring of 1865 to have a commanding general with Grant's strategic vision that was consistent with and supported by his Commander in Chief, and had combat managing skills and perseverance to command a group of subordinates with the zeal, determination, and capacities of the likes of Sheridan and Humphreys to apply the *coup de grâce* against a badly wounded, albeit still dangerous, enemy. The Federals' pursuit to Appomattox was executed so well and so convincingly that in hindsight its success can almost be taken for granted. However against a commander as determined and as wily as Lee, even in the direst of circumstances Lee's immediate surrender was not pre-ordained. Certainly the Confederacy seemed to be on its last legs in 1865 but there were other times during the war when it appeared the Federals were about to win the war, once for instance closing recruitment stations. In contrast to those other times when victory seemed so close, it took the one most decidedly successful pursuit to assure the Confederacy would not somehow survive to fight another day. And so Grant and the commanders in his two armies must be given much credit for using pursuit in a precise, ruthless manner finally to bring the war to the cusp of closure.

In sum, although common sense tells us the war probably took too long to conclude, we can only speculate if it could have ended sooner. However we have identified a number of times when either side had reasonable opportunities to use pursuits as a means of gaining decisive victories that could have shortened, if not ended, the conflict. When launched, and aggressively deployed, pursuits had devastating effects, even if they failed to "bag" the vanquished, for instance after Nashville. When fully successful, such as after Petersburg, the pursuit directly brought the terrible conflict to a close. Again we can only speculate what might have happened had Lee escaped to Danville, or wherever, but certainly if not for Grant's successful pursuit the war could, and doubtlessly would, have extended for an indeterminate additional period with even more death and destruction. Thus, although speculative, we can still be reasonably certain that if the North had launched earlier pursuits it would have ended the war that much sooner.

# Chapter Notes

## Chapter 1

1. Alexander, Bevin, *How Great Generals Win*, Paperback Edition (2002) New York: W.W. Norton & Company, 123.
2. Hagerman, Edward, *The American Civil War and The Origins of Modern Warfare: Ideas, Organizations and Field Command* (1992) Bloomington: Indiana University Press, Introduction.
3. Reid, Brian Holden, *America's Civil War: The Operational Battlefield 1861–1863* (2008) New York: Prometheus Books, 36–37.
4. Reardon, Carol. *With a Sword in One Hand & Jomini in the Other: The Problem of Military Thought in the Civil War North* (2012) Chapel Hill: University of North Carolina Press, 22.
5. Jones, Archer. *Civil War Command & Strategy: The Process of Victory and Defeat* (1992) New York: The Free Press, 8–9.
6. Jones, 21.
7. Hagerman, 7.
8. Goss, Thomas J. *The War Within the Union High Command: Politics and Generalship During the Civil War* (2003) Lawrence: University Press of Kansas, 200–01.
9. *Ibid.*, 112, 120.
10. Reid, Brian Holden. *The American Civil War* (1999) London: Cassell & Co.,39–40. Dragoons were trained to fight from the saddle and on foot. Dragoons were commonly deployed in Indian warfare.
11. Reid, *The American Civil War*, 75.
12. See Dugard, Martin. *The Training Ground: Grant, Lee, Sherman, and Davis in the Mexican War, 1836–1848* (2008) New York: Little, Brown and Company. In addition to introducing us to many future Civil War generals, this book is an excellent introduction to one of our forgotten wars.
13. Born in 1780, the son of a Prussian military officer, von Clausewitz entered the army at the age of 12 years, eventually becoming chief of staff to Field Marshal Gneisenau during the Polish insurrection of 1830. Previously he wrote his seminal book on the theory of war while director of the War Academy in Berlin. Clausewitz died in 1831.
14. Clausewitz, Carl von. The Essential Clausewitz: Selections from *On War*; edited by Joseph I. Greene (2003) Mineola, NY: Dover, 83.
15. *Ibid.*, 83.
16. Born in 1779, Jomini's first exposure to war occurred when he was a staff officer in Napoleon's armies. Jomini's writings were most prominent until Germany victories in 1870 pushed Clausewitz' writings to the forefront.
17. Jomini, Antoine-Henri. *The Art of War* Translated by Capt. G.H. Mendall and Lt. W. P. Craighill (2007) Mineola, NY: Dover Publications, 211.
18. Logs that were camouflaged to look like artillery guns.
19. Jones, 36.
20. Sometimes commanders were reluctant to leave the battlefield prematurely because the "winner" was perceived as being the side that captured, and stayed on, the battlefield.
21. Berimber et al., 116. Unfortunately much of the Civil War was fought on rough or forested terrain not well suited for effective chases.
22. Griffith, 67–8.
23. Brian Holden Reid maintains that failure to devote sufficient attention to the pursuit accounts for the comparatively few number of successful examples in military history, not just in the American Civil War. *America's Civil War: The Operational Battlefield 1861–1863* (2008) New York: Prometheus Books, 182.
24. Jones, 2.
25. Articulation refers to the process of organizing large military units into smaller commands, for instance in the case of ground forces, into divisions, brigades, regiments, battalions, and companies.
26. Reid asserts that thought should be given to the pursuit before the battle begins. *America's Civil War*, (44).
27. Alexander, Edward Porter. *Fighting for the Confederacy: The Personal Recollections of Edward Porter Alexander / Edited by Gary C. Gallagher* (1989) Raleigh: The University of North Carolina Press, 236.
28. The side that remained on the battlefield assumed the responsibility for cleaning the battlefield, including burying dead soldiers from both sides and disposing of dead animals, frequently by burning the carcasses. The extent to which this should delay the start of a pursuit would depend upon the commander's aggressiveness.
29. Nofi, Albert A. *A Civil War Treasury: Being a Miscellany of Arms & Artillery, Facts & Figures, Legends & Lore, Muses & Minstrels, Personalities & People* (1992) Edison, NJ: Castle Books, 172; Guelzo, Allen C. *Gettysburg: The Last Invasion* (2013) New York: Alfred A. Knopf, 40.
30. Guelzo, 40–41.
31. Katcher, Philip. *Union Cavalry 1861–65* (1995) Osprey, 3.
32. *Ibid.*, 4.
33. *Ibid.*, 11–12.
34. *Ibid.*, 23.

## Chapter 2

1. Also known as Pittsburg Landing, especially by Southerners.

2. These were major elements of the so-called, sometimes derisively, Anaconda Plan.

3. It is easy to overlook the fact that the Confederacy covered as much territory as did France, Spain, Germany, Italy, and Great Britain combined.

4. Also known as Logan Cross Roads. George Thomas led a relatively small Federal force to crush a Confederate force that broke and ran before making a nighttime escape across the Cumberland River. It did not occur to Thomas to pursue but he did capture 12 guns and their caisson plus several wagons, horses and mules. The fleeing Rebels were so demoralized that many deserted.

5. While Carlos Don Buell remained commander of the region east of the Cumberland River.

6. Dugard, Martin. *The Training Ground: Grant, Lee, Sherman, and Davis in the Mexican War, 1836–1848* (2008) New York: Little, Brown and Company, 171–77, 223–24.

7. In his memoirs, Grant claimed he resigned because he could not support his family on a captain's pay.

8. Chadwick, Bruce. *1858: Abraham Lincoln, Jefferson Davis, Robert E. Lee, Ulysses S. Grant and the War They Failed to See* (2008) Naperville: Sourcebooks, 220–21.

9. Shortly after Fort Sumter Grant traveled to Cincinnati where he had hoped to gain an interview with McClellan to seek an appointment. However, McClellan ignored Grant who was later able to gain a commission through the intervention of his Congressman, Elihu Washburne, from Illinois. Peter Cozzens notes that Regular Army officers who had known Grant before he had resigned might have resented his rapid rise in rank upon his return to active duty. *The Darkest Days of the War: The Battles of Iuka & Corinth* (1997) Chapel Hill: The University of North Carolina Press, 13.

10. Steve Earle's album *Train a Comin'* on Winter Harvest (1995) includes a very unromantic rendition of soldiering under Ben McCulloch.

11. Pea Ridge was the only major Civil War battle in which American Indians—about 1,000 Cherokees for the South—participated.

12. The designation of this army is confusing. Steven E. Woolworth in his extensive history of the Army of the Tennessee refers to Grant's five divisions as the Army of the Tennessee, which will become the eventual permanent designation of this organization. See *Nothing but Victory: The Army of the Tennessee, 1861–1865* (2005) New York: Alfred A. Knopf, 141. To add to the confusion there were other Armies of the Mississippi, one commanded by McClernand and the other commanded by John Pope and by Rosecrans.

13. Halleck had tried to replace Grant as his field commander but Grant's Washington patron, Congressman Washburne, intervened with Lincoln upon Grant's behalf.

14. Woodworth, Steven E. *Nothing but Victory: The Army of the Tennessee, 1861–1865* (2005) New York: Alfred A. Knopf, 144.

15. Arnold, James R. *Jeff Davis's Own: Cavalry, Comanches, and the Battle for the Texas Frontier* (2007) Edison: Castle Books, 23–24, 36–53.

16. Axelrod, Alan. *Generals South, Generals North: The Commanders of the Civil War Reconsidered* (2011) Guilford, CT: Lyons Press, 54–8.

17. As the Confederacy's officers' corps was being organized much of its seniority was determined by Jefferson Davis's personal preferences. After Beauregard's victory at First Bull Run he was promoted to full general but was not given a command fitting for such rank. Seldom willing to suffer such slights in silence, Beauregard complained much to the displeasure of Davis who assigned Beauregard to serve under Albert Sidney Johnston's command. First Bull Run is described in further detail in Chapter 14. Archer Jones describes Beauregard as having "In person ... a compelling magnetism and demonstrate[ing] a clear grasp of any strategic situation. His confidence and optimism communication themselves to those around him. Yet, in action, he was competent, circumspect, and orthodox, completely belying the air of unreality of his writings. But his eccentricity in the presentation militated against his selection for more responsible command; ..." *Civil War Command & Strategy: The Process of Victory and Defeat* (1992) New York: The Free Press, 173–74.

18. Eicher, David J. *The Longest Night: A Military History of the Civil War* (2001) New York: Simon & Schuster, 224.

19. Buell's Report (O.R., X, pt 1, 291–92). Although Buell's observations were corroborated by the reports of his subordinate officers Grant always disputed the extent to which the Union soldiers "cowered" beneath the banks.

20. Woodworth, *Nothing but,* 198–99; Bruce Catton observes that Sherman may have recovered too well from his previous loss of nerve, and flatly refused to believe Johnston was about to attack when his patrols warned him that "something .ominous was building up," *Terrible Swift Sword* Paperback Edition (1963) London: Phoenix Press, 229. See also Varney, Frank P. *General Grant and the Rewriting of History: How the Destruction of William S. Rosecrans Influenced Our Understanding of the Civil War* (2013) El Dorado Hills: Savas Beatie, 12–17.

21. Entrenching and other forms of fortifications were known and used as defensive measures in other parts of the world. But at this point in our Civil War many commanders did not allow entrenching because the commanders felt such measures caused the soldiers to lose confidence in their positions. Soon thereafter soldiers began to entrench on their own initiative almost to the point that they would start digging or building other fortifications almost as soon as their unit halted.

One of Sheridan's regimental commanders, Thomas Worthington, Jr., son of a wealthy and powerful Ohio family and a West Point graduate, was among those who charged Sherman with a "lack of preparedness." While others moved on, Worthington was so obsessed with finding vindication he demanded a court-martial that not only found against him but ordered that he be cashiered from active duty. While Worthington's charges had some plausibility as well as corroboration from other witnesses, both military and civilian, one suspects the army command had no interest in dwelling upon the distraction created by Worthington's charges. For a full account of the matter see Brewer, James D. *Tom Worthington's Civil War: Shiloh, Sherman, and the Search for Vindication* (2001) Jefferson, NC: McFarland.

22. Catton, *Terrible Swift,* 233.

23. Hess, Earl J. *The Civil War in the West: Victory and Defeat from the Appalachians to the Mississippi* (2012)

Chapel Hill: The University of North Carolina Press, 46. McClernand was a political general from Illinois who fought well during Shiloh, especially during the first day. However his ambitious nature eventually caused him to fall out of favor with Grant and Sherman. See Work, David. *Lincoln's Political Generals* (2009) Urbana & Chicago: University of Illinois Press.

24. *Ibid.*, 46.

25. Reid, Brian Holden. *America's Civil War: The Operational Battlefield 1861-1863* (2008) New York: Prometheus Books, 140.

26. *Ibid.*, 141. Although most historians credit Prentiss with a heroic stand that gave the Federals much needed time to reform, in his *Memoirs* Grant inexplicably blames Prentiss for causing a break in the line. Varney, 17–19.

27. Eicher, *Longest Night*, 226.

28. Cunningham, O. Edward. *Shiloh and the Western Campaign of 1862* Edited by Gary D. Joiner and Timothy B. Smith (2007) New York and California: Savas Beatie, 343.

29. Woodworth, *Nothing but*, 188.

30. *Ibid.*, 192; Wallace's division—which had to march six miles to reach the battlefield—arrived much later than expected. Controversy continues to this day about the reason for the delay in arriving but it seems clear that for some reason Wallace did not take the most direct route to the battlefield. See Varney, 19–23.

31. Catton, *Terrible Swift*, 237.

32. After being captured and meeting Beauregard that evening, Prentiss bragged to a disbelieving Beauregard that Buell would be arriving that evening. See Cunningham, 332.

33. Eicher, *Longest Night*, 230.

34. Woodworth, *Nothing but*, 195.

35. *Ibid.*, 196–97.

36. Cunningham, 364.

37. Eicher, *Longest Night*, 230.

38. Catton, *Terrible Swift*, 238.

39. Sometimes spelled "Breckenridge."

40. Stevenson, William G. "Behind Enemy Lines" part of Cannon, John. *War in the West: Shiloh to Vicksburg* (1990) New York: Gallery Books, 80.

41. Woodworth, *Nothing but*, 204.

42. Shelby Foote described it as "…a lesson hunters sometimes learned from closing in too quickly on a wounded animal." Foote, Shelby. *The Civil War, a Narrative: Fort Sumter to Perryville* (1958) New York: Vintage, 349.

43. Perhaps apocryphal. But even if it was not something Forrest ever said it still describes his typical actions.

44. Cunningham, 373–75.

45. Woodworth, *Nothing but*, 205.

46. Cunningham, 368.

47. Catton describes the relationship between Grant and Buell as "delicate." *Terrible Swift*, 238.

48. Cunningham, 368.

49. Varney, 25–27.

50. Castel, Albert with Brooks D. Simpson. *Victors in Blue: How Union Generals Fought the Confederates, Battled Each Other, and Won the Civil War* (2011) Lawrence: University Press of Kansas, 81.

51. Eicher, *Longest Night*, 230.

52. There were more casualties at Shiloh than in all previous wars in American history.

53. Castel with Simpson, 81.

54. Even many of Grant's soldiers were critical that Grant may have been surprised and/or that their positions were not fortified. Cunningham, 381.

55. Woodworth, *Nothing but*, 205.

56. *Ibid.*, 207.

57. *Ibid.*, 207.

58. Essentially this meant Thomas—who did not arrive at Shiloh until two days after the battle—was replacing Grant's field command. Is it possible this was the root cause of the animus that existed between these two generals for the remainder of the war?

59. Cunningham, 387.

60. Cozzens, *Darkest Days*, 29.

61. Earlier while in command of Fortress Monroe, Butler—an astute criminal lawyer and active politician—had devised the legal theory for retaining runaway slaves, contending they were captured property that the Federals could keep. This was the root of the term "contraband" used to describe such slaves who thus became virtually free even prior to the Emancipation Proclamation.

62. Castel with Simpson, 89.

63. Grimsley and Woodworth have noted that most historians have tended to characterize Halleck's pace as being "glacial," an adjective they say fits. Grimsley, Mark & Woodworth, Steven E. *Shiloh: A Battlefield Guide* (2006) Lincoln: University of Nebraska Press, 141.

64. Woodworth, *Nothing but*, 206.

65. Halleck's sluggish march to Corinth nearly coincided with George McClellan's maneuvering of his force of 100,000 on the Peninsula toward Richmond in his cautious, methodical manner. Further described in Chapter 16.

66. Morris, Roy, Jr. *Sheridan: The Life & Wars of General Phil Sheridan* (Paperback Edition) (1992) New York: Vintage, 58.

67. *Ibid.*, 39.

68. See Chapter 18 for further descriptions of Sheridan.

69. Morris, 60.

70. The size of Halleck's army increased when it was joined along the way by Pope's army.

71. Morris, 62.

72. *Ibid.*, 63.

73. *Ibid.*, 65.

74. Daniel, Larry J. *Days of Glory: The Army of the Cumberland, 1861-1865* (2004) Baton Rouge: Louisiana State University Press, p. 86 footnote.

75. Reid, *America's Civil War*, 144.

76. *Ibid.*, 144.

77. Beauregard did return to Charleston, South Carolina, the site of his first great triumph, the bombardment of Fort Sumter, where he was treated as a returning hero. While at Charleston Beauregard commanded the repulse of several assaults upon the numerous fortifications, many which had been engineered by R.E. Lee, that surrounded Charleston as part of the Confederacy's coastal defenses. See Kelly, Joseph. *America's Longest Siege: Charleston, Slavery, and the Slow March Toward Civil War* (2013) New York: Overlook Press, 205–309.

78. Morris, 74–75.

## Chapter 3

1. Daniel, Larry J. *Days of Glory: The Army of the Cumberland, 1861-1865* (2004) Baton Rouge: Louisiana State University Press, 5.

2. The late Bruce Catton (1899–1978) observed that "Halleck, although diligent, shared with General McClellan a singular genius for making war in low gear. ... He could crowd a weaker opponent into a corner, but instead of exterminating him there he would give him a chance to get out: ..." *Terrible Swift Sword* Paperback Edition (1963) London: Phoenix Press, 371.

3. One of several nicknames given to George Thomas. His troops most often called him Old Pap.

4. Earl J. Hess compares Buell with McClellan thusly: "They were conservative generals, both militarily as well as politically, believing the war should be made only on the armies and that the object of strategy was to outmanuever the enemy rather than to kill him. Neither general had a sense for the jugular, an overriding desire to close with the Rebels, or a willingness to embrace the messy uncertainties of a life-or-death struggle." *Banners to the Breeze: The Kentucky Campaign, Corinth & Stones River* (2000) Lincoln: The University of Nebraska Press, 13.

5. Twiggs' action might have been the only treacherous action taken by Regular Army officers who resigned their commissions prior to joining the Confederacy.

6. Symonds, Craig L. *Stonewall of the West: Patrick Cleburne & The Civil War* (1997) Lawrence, Kansas: University Press of Kansas, 85.

7. *Ibid.*, 85.

8. Hess, *Banners*, 19.

9. Buckner should not have been surprised by the perfidy of Pillow and especially Floyd. While governor of Virginia, Floyd's term was characterized by a banking scandal and other financial irregularities. Later when he served as Buchanan's Secretary of War, Floyd distributed a disproportionate share of arms to Southern state militias while transferring rifles and muskets to Federal arsenals in the South where they could easily be seized by Rebels. Floyd also appointed a number Southern sympathizers to key military posts, including David Twiggs to command the large Department of Texas.

10. Hsieh, Wayne Wei-Siang. *West Pointers and the Civil War: The Old Army in War and Peace* (2009) Chapel Hill: The University of North Carolina Press, 78–79.

11. Hess, *Banners*, 23.

12. Woodworth, Steven E. *Nothing but Victory: The Army of the Tennessee, 1861–1865* (2005) New York: Alfred A. Knopf, 217; Castel, Albert with Brooks D. Simpson. *Victors in Blue: How Union Generals Fought the Confederates, Battled Each Other, and Won the Civil War* (2011) Lawrence: University Press of Kansas, 123.

13. Castel and Simpson, 123–24.

14. Dougherty, Kevin J. *Great Commanders of the Civil War: The Battles of the Civil War* (2008) San Diego: Thunder Bay Press, 104.

15. Symonds, 91–92.

16. Daniel, 111.

17. Castel and Simpson, 124–24.

18. Daniel, 114–15.

19. Foote, Shelby. *The Civil War, a Narrative: Fort Sumter to Perryville* (1958) New York: Vintage, 657.

20. Dougherty, 110.

21. *Ibid.*, 110.

22. Daniel, 124–25.

23. *Ibid.*, 127.

24. *Ibid.*, 130–31.

25. Daniel, 134–135.

26. There has never been a definitive answer about why Thomas rejected this appointment but one of his biographers, Christopher J. Einolf, has remarked, "Thomas's refusal to take command from Buell lay not in his apprehension of changing commanders on the eve of battle, but from Thomas's abhorrence of politics and his extreme concern for his own honor. ... Thomas did not want command of an army unless he could be assured that the political authorities would not dispute and overrule his decisions." *George Thomas: Virginian for the Union* (2007) Norman: University of Oklahoma Press, 133.

27. Foote, 715.

28. Daniel, 137.

29. An obvious reference to Gilbert.

30. One of the fighting McCooks of Ohio, a family divided into two branches or "tribes" that altogether contributed 15 army and naval officers to the Union efforts.

31. Daniel, 142.

32. Foote, 712.

33. Hess, *Banners*, 83.

34. Symonds, 94.

35. Foote, 729.

36. Daniel, 142.

37. *Ibid.*, 146.

38. Hess, *Banners*, 87. At this point the 31-year-old Sheridan had received his brigadier's star only two weeks earlier and had been division commander for only nine days.

39. Daniel, 148.

40. Foote, 730.

41. Daniel, 151.

42. *Ibid.*, 152.

43. Symonds, 96–97.

44. Daniel, 152.

45. *Ibid.*, 153.

46. Hess, *Banners*, 100.

47. McPherson, James M. *The Battle Cry of Freedom: The Civil War Era* (1988) Oxford University Press, 519.

48. Foote, 735.

49. Daniel, 148.

50. Foote, 738.

51. Hess, *Banners*, 107.

52. Castel and Simpson, 151.

53. Daniel, 168.

54. Foote, 739.

55. *Ibid.*, 739.

56. Hess, *Banners*, 111.

57. Daniel, 168.

58. *Ibid.*, 169.

59. Symonds, 97.

60. Foote, 740.

61. Hess, *Banners*, 111.

62. Daniel, 169.

63. Foote, 740.

64. Symonds, 97–98.

65. Hess, *Banners*, 112.

66. Daniel, 171.

67. Hess, *Banners*, 113.

68. Castel and Simpson, 152.

69. Daniel, 172.

70. Foote, 742.

71. Catton, *Terrible Swift*, 471–72.

## Chapter 4

1. Hess, Earl J. *Banners to the Breeze: The Kentucky Campaign, Corinth & Stones River* (2000) Lincoln: The University of Nebraska Press, 123.

2. Castel, Albert with Brooks D. Simpson. *Victors in Blue: How Union Generals Fought the Confederates, Battled Each Other, and Won the Civil War* (2011) Lawrence: University Press of Kansas, 121.

3. Cozzens, Peter. *The Darkest Days of the War: The Battles of Iuka & Corinth* (1997) Chapel Hill: The University of North Carolina Press, 34.

4. Smith's command will not be part of this chapter but will be a central part of the following chapter.

5. Price's brevet as a Brigadier General was the second highest of Mexican War veterans who became Confederate officers.

6. Woodworth, Steven E. *Nothing but Victory: The Army of the Tennessee, 1861-1865* (2005) New York: Alfred A. Knopf, 217.

7. *Ibid.*, 217.

8. Although born in Charleston, South Carolina, Hurlbut was a political general from Illinois. Work, David. *Lincoln's Political Generals* (2009) Urbana & Chicago: University of Illinois Press, 13.

9. Upon further review of many of my sources I have substantially revised and revamped my original draft of this chapter, particularly evaluations of the actions of Grant and Rosecrans. My original sources had extensively sourced Grant's *Memoirs* that other scholars have convincingly shown to be inaccurate when discussing certain other generals, especially Rosecrans. The gist of more recent scholarship about Grant's *Memoirs* is that Grant tended to rely upon his memory when he wrote his *Memoirs* some 24 to 26 years after the fact, and that his memory must have been distorted by personal feelings, including animosity, toward some of his fellow generals. Castel and Simpson, 334 fn 16, contend that "Grant's account of the Iuka operation in his *Memoirs* contains so many falsehoods as to make it worse than worthless." Those historians who relied upon Grant's memory without checking other sources, including the Official Records, or even some of Grant's earlier writings, have done so at their own peril.

10. Hess, *Banners*,128.

11. Woodworth, *Nothing but*, 218.

12. Castel and Simpson, 127.

13. Varney, Frank P. *General Grant and the Rewriting of History: How the Destruction of William S. Rosecrans Influenced Our Understanding of the Civil War* (2013) El Dorado Hills: Savas Beatie, 39.

14. Woodworth, *Nothing but*, 219.

15. Hess, *Banners*,131.

16. *Ibid.*, 132.

17. Cozzens, *Darkest Days*, 127-28.

18. Woodworth, *Nothing but*, 220.

19. Varney, 41.

20. Castel and Simpson, 130.

21. Eicher, David J. *The Longest Night: A Military History of the Civil War* (2001) New York: Simon & Schuster, 372.

22. Hess, *Banners*,136.

23. Also known as an acoustic anomaly.

24. Cozzens, *Darkest Days*, 130.

25. Varney, 49-53.

26. Hess, *Banners*,137.

27. Cozzens, *Darkest Days*, 124.

28. One Union soldier described the "scene, and with it that of our dead heroes and those of the enemy lying thickly over the ground and the look of destruction and desolation that abounded in the vicinity, was the grandest and most awful spectacle of war that I viewed during a service of four and a half years." *Ibid.*, 124.

29. *Ibid.*, 119-21.

30. *Ibid.*, 124-25.

31. *Ibid.*, 130-31.

32. Varney, 56.

33. Cozzens, *Darkest Days*, 132.

34. *Ibid.*, 132.

35. *Ibid.*, 132.

36. Foote, Shelby. *The Civil War, a Narrative: Fort Sumter to Perryville* Paperback (1958) New York: Vintage, 720.

37. *Ibid.*, 720.

38. Redoubts were hastily built small field fortifications enclosed on all sides.

39. Hess, *Banners*,142.

40. Varney, 91.

41. *Ibid.*, 143.

42. Foote, 722.

43. Woodworth, *Nothing but*, 227-28.

44. Hess, *Banners*,147-53.

45. Hess, *Banners*,154; Woodworth, *Nothing but*, 230.

46. *Ibid.*, 234.

47. Cozzens, *Darkest Days*, 272-73.

48. After graduating from the University of Virginia and studying law, Maury—a small, spare man—entered West Point. Maury was another veteran of the Mexican War where a musket ball paralyzed his left arm. Maury later taught at West Point for five years and also served as superintendent of the cavalry school at the Carlisle Barracks, Pennsylvania. In 1859 he published a textbook *Skirmish Drill for Mounted Troops* that was still being used at the turn of the century. At the beginning of the Civil War Maury was dismissed for "treasonable designs."

49. Hess, *Banners*,66.

50. Woodworth, *Nothing but*, 229. Woodworth's writings seem to be heavily influenced by Grant's *Memoirs*.

51. Varney, 115.

52. Woodworth, *Nothing but*, 235; Varney, 15.

53. Hess, *Banners*,166; Varney, 94.

54. Varney, 95.

55. *Ibid.*, 93.

56. *Ibid.*, 93.

57. Cozzens, *Darkest Days*, 276.

58. *Ibid.*, 276.

59. In his *Memoirs*, Grant claimed he was confident the Confederates would be defeated at Corinth II after which they would be in retreat. Thus even before any initial contact between skirmishers occurred he started thinking—or so he recalled 24 years after the event—how to cut off the anticipated retreat and to capture Van Dorn's and Price's entire army. However no contemporary documents have been found to substantiate Grant's version of the events.

60. Woodworth, *Nothing but*, 237.

61. Cozzens, *Darkest Days*, 289.

62. *Ibid.*, 289.

63. Woodworth, *Nothing but*, 238.

64. Cozzens, *Darkest Days*, 276-77.

65. *Ibid.*, 293.

66. *Ibid.*, 293.

67. Varney, 95-96.

68. Cozzens, *Darkest Days*, 295.

69. Cozzens, *Darkest Days*, 295.

70. Hess, *Banners*,170.

71. Varney, 96.

72. Cozzens, *Darkest Days,* 299.
73. Ibid., 290.
74. Castel and Simpson, 135.
75. Cozzens, *Darkest Days,* 300.
76. Varney, 97.
77. Hess, *Banners,*172.
78. Castel and Simpson, 135.
79. Ibid., 137.
80. Ibid., 136.
81. Varney, 90–91.
82. Foote, 725; Woodworth, *Nothing but,* 240; Cozzens, *Darkest Days,* 301–03.
83. Varney, 97.
84. Foote, 762.
85. Castel and Simpson, 137.
86. Ibid., 132.
87. Regardless of whether Rosecrans had leaked reports of Grant's drinking to the press, there were circumstantial as well as personal reports of such drinking. Grant's chief of staff, John Rawlins, whose main duty was to keep Grant away from the bottle, was absent during Iuka. Additionally several officers as well as enlisted personnel wrote that Grant was drunk in his Huntsville headquarters. However it is not established if these personal reports were based upon direct observations or upon camp hearsay. See Cozzens, *Darkest Days,* 130.
88. Cozzens, *Darkest Days,* 311.
89. Woodworth, *Nothing but,* 224.
90. For instance see Woodworth, *Nothing but,* 239.
91. Castel and Simpson, 154.
92. As further described in Chapter 5.
93. Powell, David A. *Failure in the Saddle: Nathan Bedford Forrest, Joseph Wheeler, and the Confederate Cavalry in the Chickamauga Campaign* (2010) New York and California: Savas Beatie, 17.

## Chapter 5

1. As discussed in the preceding chapter, these hard feeling apparently developed during the Iuka campaign and festered during Corinth II.
2. Daniel, Larry J. *Days of Glory: The Army of the Cumberland, 1861–1865,* 181. The situation became awkward because Washington failed to notify Buell that he was being relieved although to be sure he had to have known that the axe was about to fall on his command.
3. Lincoln once commented that selecting a general was "like putting one's hand in a sack to get one eel from a dozen snakes."
4. Rosecrans graduated from West Point in 1842, a class that produced 17 Civil War generals, including John Pope, D.H. Hill, Earl Van Dorn, and James Longstreet.
5. Woodworth, Stephen E., *Six Armies in Tennessee: The Chickamauga and Chattanooga Campaigns,* 2.
6. Daniel, 181.
7. The historian Peter Cozzens says that Rosecrans was "perhaps … the only true genius to command a Union army in the field." Bruce Catton observed that "Washington seems to have forgotten that [Thomas] was the one western general who had really wanted to carry out Mr. Lincoln's plan for an invasion of eastern Tennessee. Finding a good fighting man [meaning Rosecrans], the government had failed to notice a better one. *Terrible Swift Sword* Paperback Edition (1963) London: Phoenix Press, 474.

8. Einolf, Christopher J. *George Thomas: Virginian for the Union* (2007) Norman: University of Oklahoma Press, 141.
9. Ibid., 143.
10. Ibid., 143.
11. Daniel, 183.
12. Ibid., 192–93.
13. Symonds, Craig L. *Stonewall of the West: Patrick Cleburne & The Civil War* (1997) Lawrence: University Press of Kansas, 101–02.
14. Also known as Battle of Murfreesboro.
15. December 1862 was terrible month for the Union that suffered defeats or setbacks at Fredericksburg, western Tennessee where Forrest captured 2,500 men, Holly Springs where Van Dorn captured 1,500 men, as well as Grant's failures to make any progress in his Vicksburg campaign. Additionally Morgan's Raiders were causing havoc and damage in Kentucky. See Woodworth, *Six Armies,* 5.
16. Castel, Albert with Brooks D. Simpson. *Victors in Blue: How Union Generals Fought the Confederates, Battled Each Other, and Won the Civil War* (2011) Lawrence: University Press of Kansas, 155.
17. Einolf, 143.
18. Hess, Earl J., *The Civil War in the West: Victory and Defeat from the Appalachians to the Mississippi* (2012) Chapel Hill: The University of North Carolina Press, 127.
19. Einolf, 145. Wheeler was an aggressive commander who led from the front but who had difficulty controlling his troopers unless he was physically present. He also had the habit of exaggerating his claims.
20. Daniel, 202.
21. Morris, Roy, Jr. *Sheridan: The Life & Wars of General Phil Sheridan* (Paperback Edition) (1992) New York: Vintage, 103.
22. Ibid., 104.
23. Hess, *War in the West,* 129; Symonds, 107.
24. Hess, *War in the West,* 129.
25. Purportedly the North and the South each had regiments recruited from the same county in Kentucky. These regiments, the Union's 23rd Kentucky, and the Confederate's 3rd Kentucky, confronted and fought against each other on the Federal right.
26. Catton, Bruce, *Never Call Retreat* Paperback Edition (1965) London: Phoenix Press, 41.
27. Daniel, 210; an entire brigade had to be assigned to assist the regular provost guard in rounding up all the soldiers from McCook's corps who had skedaddled during the rout. Within an hour the Union provost guard had collected one thousand cavalrymen, nearly two regiments of infantry, and seven artillery pieces.
28. Symonds, 111.
29. Daniel, 217.
30. Another version has Thomas saying, "General, I know of no better place to die than right here." See Daniel, 218. See also Einolf, 150.
31. Hess, *War in the West,* 130.
32. Castel and Simpson, 169.
33. Daniel, 222.
34. Castel and Simpson, 169.
35. Daniel, 223.
36. Stephen Woodworth notes that Bragg came "within a whisker" of prevailing. *Six Armies,* 3.
37. Roy Morris notes that Rosecrans took to his bed, probably suffering from a nervous collapse. Morris, 113.
38. As thoroughly analyzed by Frank Varney, at this

point in the war Grant and Rosecrans did not agree upon much. *General Grant and the Rewriting of History: How the Destruction of William S. Rosecrans Influenced Our Understanding of the Civil War* (2013) El Dorado Hills: Savas Beatie, 123–29. Accordingly it seems possible that Grant wanted to make it appear that Rosecrans had not exercised sufficient command influence to accomplish anything at Stones River but for Sheridan's efforts. It may also be noteworthy that Grant's statement also failed to acknowledge Thomas' superb efforts in the center of the Federal defenses.

39. Daniel, 224.
40. *Ibid.*, 225–26.
41. Daniel, 257. The Federal administration was pressing Rosecrans to take some action that would relief pressure on Grant's Vicksburg campaign. Garfield wrote one letter, probably intended for public consumption, that undercut Rosecrans' position of being thoroughly prepared before taking further action against Bragg. Peter Cozzens. *This Terrible Sound: The Battle of Chickamauga* (1996) Urbana and Chicago: University of Illinois Press, 16–17.
42. Einolf, 155.
43. *Ibid.*, 155.
44. Daniel, 232.
45. *Ibid.* The intrepid Wilder took financial matters in his own hands by agreeing to be a cosigner of notes to permit every man in his brigade to buy his own repeating carbine at the cost of $35 per weapon.
46. Daniel, 237.
47. Castel and Simpson, 206.
48. In reality Garfield was more than a liaison but was probably another spy for the War Department.
49. "Tullahoma" is Greek for *more mud.*
50. Woodworth, *Six Armies,* 13–14.
51. Daniel, 267.
52. Buell, Thomas B. *The Warrior Generals: Combat Leadership in the Civil War* (1997) New York: Three Rivers Press, 254.
53. Coincidentally the Tullahoma campaign started during the same period when Lee's Army of Northern Virginia was beginning its maneuvers to cross the Potomac River into Maryland prior to Battle of Gettysburg.
54. Powell, David A. *Failure in the Saddle: Nathan Bedford Forrest, Joseph Wheeler, and the Confederate Cavalry in the Chickamauga Campaign* (2010) New York: Savas Beatie, 2.
55. Woodworth, *Six Armies,* 22–25.
56. Daniel, 269. Cozzens attributes this statement of gratitude to Rosecrans, *Terrible Sound,*18.
57. Daniel, 271.
58. Woodworth, *Six Armies,* 36.
59. *Ibid.*, 36.
60. Daniel, 272; Powell, 4. Minty's Sabre Brigade was the other mounted infantry.
61. This date coincided with the first day of battle at Gettysburg.
62. Woodworth, *Six Armies,* 40.
63. Daniel, 274.
64. The Confederates' command structure became so dysfunctional that Steven Woodworth, *Six Armies,* 41, speculates Hardee was contemplating mutiny and replacing Bragg with Simon Buckner.
65. Morris, 120.
66. Woodworth, *Six Armies,* 42.
67. *Ibid.*, 42.
68. The same day when Lee withdrew from Gettysburg and Vicksburg surrendered to Grant.
69. Woodworth, *Six Armies,* 43 ; see also Daniel, 275 and Buell, 255.
70. Hess, *War in the West,* 186.
71. Powell, 5.
72. Einolf, 158; Woodworth, *Six Armies,* 45.
73. Hess, *War in the West,* 186; Daniel, 276.
74. Woodworth, *Six Armies,* 43.
75. Daniel, 275, summarizes a critique by Keith Poulter that the Tullahoma was a failure in conception as well as execution because it allowed Bragg to escape.
76. Woodworth, *Six Armies,* 2.
77. Daniel, 287; Powell, 33.
78. Daniel, 288.
79. *Ibid.*, 47.
80. *Ibid.*, 53.
81. Hess, *War in the West,* 190.
82. Minty, born in Ireland, was the son of a British officer and served as an ensign in the Royal Army, seeing action in the West Indies, Central America, and Africa.
83. Woodworth, *Six Armies,* 54.
84. Jefferson Davis had proclaimed August 21 as a day of fasting and prayer. As Wilder's batteries began their fire, Confederate generals and Chattanooga's citizens were gathered in a local Presbyterian church to hear a visiting preacher equate God's will with Confederate aspirations. Buell, 257.
85. Daniel, 290.
86. Woodworth, *Six Armies,* 54.
87. Powell, 38. Hardee and D.H. Hill were two talented Confederate generals whose truculent temperaments caused them to be shifted from command to command. After being replaced by Hill, Hardee briefly commanded the Department of Mississippi and East Louisiana under Joe Johnston before returning to Bragg's army.
88. *Ibid.*, 57.
89. Einolf, 158.
90. Morris, 123.
91. Woodworth, *Six Armies,* 65.
92. *Ibid.*, 59.
93. Buell, 258.
94. Woodworth, *Six Armies,* 59.
95. *Ibid.*, 60.
96. Daniel, 298.
97. Woodworth, *Six Armies,* 62.
98. Buell, 259; Buell claims Thomas was "appalled."
99. Einolf, 159.
100. Also spelled "Lafayette."
101. Castel and Simpson, 220.
102. Daniel, 300; Woodworth, *Six Armies,* 62–63.
103. Apparently Bragg was aware of Rosecrans' intentions that had been reported in a Northern newspaper.
104. Powell, 53.
105. Apparently a spy employed by Sheridan had tried to tell Rosecrans that the Rebels were preparing for a major fight.
106. Powell, 57.
107. Woodworth, *Six Armies,* 66.
108. Cleburne was the son of a prominent Protestant physician. In 1849 he migrated to the United States and lived in several states before settling in Helena, Arkansas where he became a successful attorney. Although he enlisted as a private he was soon elected as a captain and continued to rise in rank, as a colonel commanding a brigade at Shiloh.

109. Reid, Brian Holden. *America's Civil War: The Operational Battlefield 1861–1863* (2008) New York: Prometheus Books, 352.
110. Woodworth, *Six Armies*, 68.
111. Steven Woodworth, *Six Armies*, 69, describes Hindman as "colorful a man as one could hope to find…" who could be "rude, insulting, and imperious." Holden Reid, *America's Civil War*, 352, describes Hindman as "a strutting *poseur*, but one who did not lack ability."
112. Woodworth, *Six Armies*, 73; Symonds, 141.
113. Castel and Simpson, 221.
114. Einolf, 160.
115. *Ibid.*, 304.
116. Castel and Simpson, 222. Since McCook had almost all the cavalry it was going to be difficult to get the word to concentrate to McCook.
117. Daniel, 313.
118. Woodworth, *Six Armies*, 74.
119. Einolf, 161.
120. Powell, 72.
121. Hess, *War in the West*, 190.
122. Hess, *War in the West*, 190; Bowers, 49.
123. Woodworth, *Six Armies*, 80.
124. Daniel, 311; Woodworth, *Six Armies*, 82.
125. Phil Sheridan's former West Point classmate.
126. Powell, 94.
127. Reid, *America's Civil War*, 353.
128. Most records describe Chickamauga as a two day battle occurring on the 19th & 20th while other records add the 18th, making it a three day battle.
129. Daniel, 315–14; Powell, 131.
130. Einolf, 161.
131. Woodworth, *Six Armies*, 85.
132. Daniel, 312.
133. Einolf, 162.
134. Daniel, 316–17; Bowers, 71–72.
135. Powell, 134–38.
136. Einolf, 163; Woodworth, *Six Armies*, 86–87; Buell, 263.
137. In a rare flash of humor occurring during the heat of battle, after encountering more than he had expected Croxton sent a message back to Thomas to ask which of the four or five brigades he was supposed to capture. September 19 also marked the first time that Forrest commanded a couple infantry brigades along with a couple cavalry brigades.
138. Woodworth, *Six Armies*, 87.
139. Woodworth, *Six Armies*, 89; Bowers, 77–78.
140. Woodworth, *Six Armies*, 102.
141. Reid, *America's Civil War*, 354–55.
142. Woodworth, *Six Armies*, 103.
143. Buell, 264.
144. Einolf, 167; Bowers, 95–97.
145. Einolf, 168; Buell, 263.
146. Hess, *War in the West*, 191.
147. Daniel, 325.
148. Negley arrived later than planned because his promised relief, Wood's division, failed to arrive in a timely basis. This potential blunder could have been avoided if Rosecrans had simply ordered Wood, rather than Negley, to report directly to Thomas. Hardin Helm, Abraham Lincoln's brother-in-law leading a Confederate brigade, was mortally wounded during this repulse. See Bowers, 104–05.
149. Woodworth, *Six Armies*, 111.
150. *Ibid.*, 113.
151. Daniel, 325.
152. Wood was Sam Grant's first roommate at West Point.
153. Woodworth, *Six Armies*, 114.
154. Buell, 265.
155. Woodworth, *Six Armies*, 114; Buell, 265.
156. Daniel, 324; Rosecrans' stinging rebuke of McCook included a pointed reminder of McCook's failure at Stone's River.
157. Daniel, 324. In the opinion of Larry Daniel, Rosecrans "…appeared to be losing control."
158. Woodworth, *Six Armies*, 115; Thomas Buell infers that Wood hated Rosecrans so much that he "wanted revenge" and thus betrayed Rosecrans "in an act of insane vindictiveness." Buell, 265.
159. Daniel, 328–29.
160. Bowers, 118–19.
161. On the other hand the disadvantage of this formation was vulnerable from artillery aimed at the flanks of the formation that could also lose its cohesion in heavy woods.
162. Daniel, 329.
163. Woodworth, *Six Armies*, 117.
164. Daniel, 330. One of Sheridan's biographers, Roy Morris, Jr has noted that Sheridan *might* have had time and opportunity to join Thomas that afternoon. Morris, 133–34. Indeed while Sheridan was riding back with LCol. Gates P. Thurston, McCook's assistant adjutant general Thurston proposed that Sheridan try to link up with Thomas. After Sheridan declined Thurston departed and was able to find Thomas at Snodgrass Hill. Morris, 134–35. Eric Wittenberg, a harsh critic of Sheridan's veracity, gives Sheridan a pass, pointing out that Rosecrans had left without orders to his subordinates leaving them to fend for themselves. *Little Phil: A Reassessment of the Civil War Leadership of Philip H. Sheridan* (2002) Dulles: Brassey's.
165. Castel and Simpson, 225–26.
166. Daniel, 331; Buell, 266–65.
167. Hood had to be carried from the field after he was toppled from his horse. At the field hospital his leg was amputated just below the hip.
168. Buell, 269.
169. Woodworth, *Six Armies*, 122.
170. Buell, 267.
171. Daniel, 332.
172. Woodworth, *Six Armies*, 124.
173. Larry Daniel, 333, describes Granger as being "short-tempered, crude, and at times a sadist" and Steedman as being "an addict to drink, women, cursing, and cards."
174. Woodworth, *Six Armies*, 125.
175. Daniel, 334; as is typical for such actions, the exact time is inexact but Cozzens, *Terrible Sound*, 476–77, estimates it to have been received at 4:30 pm.
176. Steedman's brigades suffered almost 50% casualty rates that afternoon.
177. Daniel, 334. Cozzens, *Terrible Sound*, 511, describes how Thomas shared some brandy with Sheridan after they met and rested a few minutes that night.
178. Reid, *America's Civil War*, 361. Castel and Simpson, 227, also opine that the Confederates failed to pursue Thomas from Snodgrass Hill because they did not expect him to withdraw.
179. Woodworth, *Six Armies*, 126.
180. Woodworth, *Six Armies*, 132; Buell, 272.

181. Symonds, 152.
182. Hess, *War in the West,* 192.
183. Hess, *War in the West,* 192; Woodworth, *Six Armies,* 132–33.
184. Powell, 178.
185. Woodworth, *Six Armies,* 134.
186. Powell, 176; Cozzens, *Terrible Sound,* 519.
187. Buell, 273.
188. Woodworth, *Six Armies,* 135.
189. Daniel, 336.
190. As will be noted in Chapter 7 Polk will return to the Army of Tennessee after Bragg leaves.
191. One of the Confederacy's internal weaknesses at this point in the war was that beyond Lee, Davis had little choice except to keep rotating Bragg, Johnston, and Beauregard among the top command positions while at the same time when other generals, such as Hood, Buckner, D.H. Hill, and Polk, were found wanting even for consideration for army level command.
192. Woodworth, *Six Armies,* 134.
193. David Powell calls these stories "fanciful." Powell, 182.
194. Castel and Simpson contend that Wood should have also been court-martialed, striped of rank and removed from the army, 233. However Wood continued to serve, eventually becoming a corps commander.
195. After the Civil War Reynolds continued to serve in the Regular Army and during the winter of 1875–76 he captured the winter hideout of Crazy Horse. However Reynolds did not capture or destroy the dismounted warriors who contributed the following spring to the massacre at Little Big Horn.

## Chapter 6

1. Woodworth, Stephen. *Six Armies in Tennessee: The Chickamauga and Chattanooga Campaigns,* 142. Mules were reduced to eating the bark off trees.
2. Cozzens, Peter. *This Terrible Sound: The Battle of Chickamauga* (1996) Urbana and Chicago: University of Illinois Press, 523. Woodworth, *Six Armies,* 136.
3. Daniel, Larry J. *Days of Glory: The Army of the Cumberland, 1861–1865* (2004) Baton Rouge: Louisiana State University Press, 340.
4. And to be sure, neither Dana nor Garfield was particularly loyal to Rosecrans. Dana was a well known spy for the War Department while Garfield had his own political agenda.
5. Granger's 4th Corps was formed from McCook's 20th Corps and Crittenden's 21st Corps.
6. Woolworth, 146; Cozzens, *Terrible Sound,* 524. Granger also happened to be a friend of Dana's.
7. Daniel, 349.
8. Cozzens, *Terrible Sound,* 524.
9. Daniel, 342.
10. See Chapter 16.
11. Daniel, 342.
12. Castel, Albert with Brooks D. Simpson. *Victors in Blue: How Union Generals Fought the Confederates, Battled Each Other, and Won the Civil War* (2011) Lawrence: University Press of Kansas, 230.
13. Cleaves, Freeman. *Meade of Gettysburg* (1960) Norman: University of Oklahoma Press, 195.
14. Cozzens, *Terrible Sound,* 522.
15. Cleaves, *Meade of Gettysburg,* 174.
16. See Chapter 11 for more details about Hooker's early war record.
17. Castel and Simpson, 235.
18. Hess, Earl J., *The Civil War in the West: Victory and Defeat from the Appalachians to the Mississippi* (2012) Chapel Hill: The University of North Carolina Press, 194.
19. Daniel, 353, says that "While Grant distrusted Thomas, he detested Rosecrans." Grant was fond of dismissing Thomas as a strictly defensive general but as Bruce Catton observed about Thomas' performance at Mill Springs, "…Thomas, who looked so ponderous, could strike swiftly and powerfully once battle had been joined. His whole campaign, as a matter of fact, had been well handled, despite the wastage of the hard march down from Lebanon." *Terrible Swift Sword* Paperback Edition (1963) London: Phoenix Press, 140.
20. Castel and Simpson, 236. See also Cozzens, *Terrible Sound,* 527–28.
21. Castel and Simpson, 237. The path was so treacherous that Grant's own horse slipped and fell upon Grant, who fortunately was not seriously injured this time.
22. Bowers, John. *Chickamauga and Chattanooga: The Battles that Doomed the Confederacy* (1994) New York: Post Road Press, 188.
23. Woolworth, 157.
24. Hess, *War in the West,* 195.
25. Castel and Simpson, 240.
26. Bowers, 199–200.
27. *Ibid.,* 203.
28. Castel and Simpson, 244.
29. Symonds, Craig L. *Stonewall of the West: Patrick Cleburne & The Civil War* (1997) Lawrence, Kansas: University Press of Kansas, 164.
30. Bowers, 206.
31. *Ibid.,* 208.
32. Castel and Simpson, 244.
33. Bowers, 220. Rossville was of course where Thomas established his initial defenses after withdrawing from Chickamauga.
34. Symonds, 169; see also Woolworth, 191–93.
35. Woolworth, 180–81.
36. This line contained almost twice the number of soldiers than in Pickett's Charge.
37. Hess, *War in the West,* 197.
38. Castel and Simpson, 246.
39. An honor that would forever be contested by Sheridan who had also ascended to the crest.
40. Perhaps apocryphal, but the tube of the canon was still hot thus burning Little Phil's thighs and rump.
41. Bowers, 233–34.
42. Symonds, 172.
43. *Ibid.,* 170.
44. Symonds, 173; Woolworth, 205.
45. Woolworth, 203–04.
46. Woolworth, 185; Castel and Simpson, 244; Symonds, 169.
47. Bowers, 239.

## Chapter 7

1. Cleaves, Freeman. *Rock of Chickamauga: The Life of General George H. Thomas* (1948) Norman: University of Oklahoma Press, 205.
2. Because Meade was junior in rank to Burnside, the latter's command was independent of the Army of the Potomac.

3. Castel, Albert. *Decision in the West: The Atlanta Campaign of 1864* (1992) Lawrence: University Press of Kansas, 88.

4. Castel calls Stoneman a "conceited incompetent." *Ibid.*, 116. On the other hand, Benson Bobrick rates Stoneman as "one of the great cavalry officers of the war." *Master of War: The Life of General George H. Thomas* (2009) New York: Simon & Schuster, 236.

5. Sherman's overall command was properly called the Military Division of Mississippi.

6. Castel, 80.

7. *Ibid.*, 81, 83.

8. *Ibid.*, 116.

9. This was the original Army of the Cumberland before being merged to form the original Army of the Ohio. In October 1862 it once again became the Army of the Cumberland, then under Don Carlos Buell whose most important battle occurred October 8, 1862, at Perryville, Kentucky. Buell's replacement was William S. Rosecrans who led the Cumberlanders in battles at Stones River near Murfreesboro, December 31, 1862 and January 2, 1863, the Tullahoma campaign, June 23–30, 1863, and Chickamauga, September 18–29, 1863. After Chickamauga—the worst Union defeat in the Western theater—Rosecrans was replaced by George Thomas who was in command at Missionary Ridge near Chattanooga, November 23–25, 1863.

10. Davis, Stephen. *Atlanta Will Fall: Sherman, Joe Johnston and the Yankee Heavy Battalions* (2001) Wilmington: Scholarly Resources, 9. As the senior Regular Army officer to defect to the C.S.A., Joe Johnston always contended he should be the senior officer in the C.S.A. The acrimony between Davis and Johnston extended back to 1857 when Davis, then a U.S. Senator, opposed Johnston's appointment as Quartermaster.

11. Longacre, Edward G. *Worthy Opponents: William T. Sherman & Joseph E. Johnston—Antagonists in War, Friends in Peace* (2006) Nashville: Rutland Hill Press, 236.

12. Buell, Thomas B. *The Warrior Generals: Combat Leadership in the Civil War* (1997) New York: Three Rivers Press, 350. Buell characterizes the Confederates' strategies as "not predicated on such practical considerations as military capabilities, relative combat power, logistical support, transportation, and the like, but rather by self-delusion."

13. *Ibid.*, 16.

14. Symonds, Craig L. *Stonewall of the West: Patrick Cleburne & The Civil War* (1997) Lawrence: University Press of Kansas, 199.

15. *Ibid.*, 199.

16. Davis, *Atlanta Will Fall*, 127–28.

17. Buell, 349.

18. Cleaves, *Rock of Chickamauga*, 208.

19. Eicher, David J. *The Longest Night: A Military History of the Civil War* (2001) New York: Simon & Schuster, 697; Davis, *Atlanta Will Fall*, 19–20; Castel, 90.

20. Longacre, *Worthy Opponents*, 246–47.

21. Additionally as Sherman's Grand Army was being formed in the spring of 1864 Thomas was responsible to feed and to supply all three armies from his depot in Nashville. Buell, 353.

22. Buell, 359–60.

23. Bobrick, 229.

24. Cleaves, *Rock of Chickamauga*, 211.

25. Personal hatreds arising at Chancellorsville remained among some of these Union generals. For instance Hooker and Howard despised each other as a result of Howard's Corps being overrun by Jackson's surprise attack while Slocum was vivid about Hooker's failure to counterattack Lee at Chancellorsville. Furthermore, Sherman and Hooker had issues with antebellum roots. For instance, see Daniel, 385.

26. Eicher, *Longest Night*, 696–97.

27. Longacre, *Worthy Opponents*, 248.

28. Also known as Rocky Face Ridge.

29. Longacre, *Worthy Opponents*, 248.

30. Davis, *Atlanta Will Fall*, 34–5.

31. Buell, 355.

32. Davis, *Atlanta Will Fall*, 35.

33. Buell, 357.

34. Davis, *Atlanta Will Fall*, 36; Buell, 358; Daniel, Larry J. *Days of Glory: The Army of the Cumberland, 1861–1865* (2004) Baton Rouge: Louisiana State University Press, 394. Cleaves, *Rock of Chickamauga*, 210.

35. Catton, *Never Call*, 387.

36. Daniel, 397.

37. *Ibid.*, 38. See also Castel, 130.

38. Catton, Bruce. *Never Call Retreat* (1965) Paperback Edition London: Phoenix Press, 320.

39. Woodworth, Steven E. *Nothing but Victory: The Army of the Tennessee, 1861–1865* (2005) New York: Alfred A. Knopf, 495.

40. Buell, 361.

41. Longacre, *Worthy Opponents*, 250.

42. Davis, *Atlanta Will Fall*, 44. Longacre, *Worthy Opponents*, 250. Cleaves, *Rock of Chickamauga*, 213, has a slightly different version: "McPherson is through the Gap. Johnston's army is mine."

43. Davis, *Atlanta Will Fall*, 40.

44. Eicher, *Longest Night*, 699.

45. Woodworth, *Nothing but*, 495.

46. Benson Bobrick—certainly no fan of Sherman—points out that Sherman provided three versions of McPherson's mission: (1) To feint at Snake Creek Gap; (2) to seize and control the railroad; and (3) to cut the railroad before withdrawing to the gap. Bobrick also asserts Sherman suppressed evidence that might have militated in McPherson's favor. 231–33.

47. Woodworth, *Nothing but*, 497.

48. Ecelbarger, Gary. *The Day Atlanta Died: The Battle of Atlanta* (2010) New York: St. Martin's Press, 17. Historians of the Atlanta campaign have argued over who was at fault for allowing the Snake Creek Gap to be virtually undefended. Johnston's defenders tend to blame Wheeler's cavalry but the fact of the matter is that Wheeler was deployed to the north observing Schofield's advance from the Knoxville area. See Davis, *Atlanta Will Fall*, 42–44.

49. Symonds, 205.

50. Buell, 363.

51. Davis, *Atlanta Will Fall*, 46.

52. Daniel, 399, describes Johnston's position as roughly resembling "a large shepherd's crook, with the end of the crook resting on the Connasauga River. The three-mile-long 'staff'" ran south east toward Resaca, eventually connecting with the Oostanaula River."

53. Davis, *Atlanta Will Fall*, 46–47. Thomas had suggested the use of the wheeling movement but with a much larger force. Daniel, 399, fn 15.

54. Davis, *Atlanta Will Fall*, 47; Woodworth, *Nothing but*, 503–04.

55. Longacre, *Worthy Opponents*, 251.

56. Alexander, Bevin. *How Wars are Won: The 13 Rules of War from Ancient Greece to the War on Terror* (2002) New York: Three Rivers Press.
57. Davis, *Atlanta Will Fall,* 49. One Confederate attack was repulsed by an Indiana regiment led by Benjamin Harrison, future president of the United States.
58. Longacre, *Worthy Opponents,* 253.
59. Woodworth, *Nothing but,* 503–04.
60. Buell, 363.
61. Davis, *Atlanta Will Fall,* 50–51; Stephen Woodworth, *Nothing but,* 505, comments that: "Whether McPherson could and should have taken and held Resaca anyway is one of the unknowable might-have-beens that will always be part of welfare as long as generals are human and have to proceed on the basis of imperfect knowledge."
62. Davis, *Atlanta Will Fall,* 51.
63. *Ibid.,* 52.
64. Woodworth, *Nothing but,* 506.
65. Longacre, *Worthy Opponents,* 256.
66. Catton, *Never Call,* 324.
67. Daniel, 400.
68. Davis, *Atlanta Will Fall,* 55.
69. Davis, *Atlanta Will Fall,* 57; Longacre, *Worthy Opponents,* 257.
70. Eicher, *Longest Night,* 700.
71. Cleaves, *Rock of Chickamauga,* 216.
72. Symonds, 212–14.
73. Longacre, *Worthy Opponents,* 262.
74. Davis, *Atlanta Will Fall,* 64; Daniel, 403.
75. Bobrick, 234.
76. *Ibid.,* 65.
77. *Ibid.,* 58.
78. *Ibid.,* 517.
79. Work, David. *Lincoln's Political Generals* (2009) Urbana: University of Illinois Press, 15.
80. Eicher, *Longest Night,* 702.
81. Buell, 364.
82. Davis, *Atlanta Will Fall,* 79; Buell, 364; Daniel, 406; Cleaves, *Rock of Chickamauga,* 220. Cleaves notes that this letter, dated June 18, was sent was a private letter but with the anticipation that Grant would publish it for the world to see, which Grant did. The complete text of this letter is found at Bobrick, 235–37.
83. Symonds, 217.
84. Davis, *Atlanta Will Fall,* 82; Longacre, *Worthy Opponents,* 268.
85. Davis, *Atlanta Will Fall,* 82.
86. Daniel, 408.
87. Davis, *Atlanta Will Fall,* 86; Daniel, 408.
88. This suggestion came from Black Jack Logan who happened to be visiting in Sherman's headquarters when observing Sherman reading newspaper accounts of Grant's assaults. Cleaves, *Rock of Chickamauga,* 216. See also Bobrick, 243–44. Edward Longacre, *Worthy Opponents,* 268, opines that Sherman acted act out "sheer frustration" from being beaten by a "wily and agile opponent exploiting to the fullest the advantage of interior lines of movement."
89. Woodworth, *Nothing but,* 520.
90. Longacre, *Worthy Opponents,* 268.
91. Woodworth, *Nothing but,* 520.
92. Daniel, 408. Apparently Thomas responded that he has "protested so often against such things that if I protest again Sherman will think I don't want to fight." Cleaves, *Rock of Chickamauga,* 221. Nevertheless Thomas made two visits to Sherman's headquarters the night before the assaults.
93. Daniel, 409.
94. Woodworth, *Nothing but,* 523.
95. Symonds, 217.
96. Davis, *Atlanta Will Fall,* 87.
97. Woodworth, *Nothing but,* 525.
98. Davis, *Atlanta Will Fall,* 87; Cleaves, *Rock of Chickamauga,* 225.
99. Davis, *Atlanta Will Fall,* 87; Daniel, 410.
100. Longacre, *Worthy Opponents,* 269–70; Bobrick, 246–47.
101. Longacre, *Worthy Opponents,* 269.
102. Woodworth, *Nothing but,* 526.
103. *Ibid.,* 526.
104. *Ibid.,* 526.
105. *Ibid.,* 526.
106. Cleaves, *Rock of Chickamauga,* 226.
107. Woodworth, *Nothing but,* 527.
108. Cleaves, *Rock of Chickamauga,* 227.
109. Davis, *Atlanta Will Fall,* 97.
110. Woodworth, *Nothing but,* 529.
111. Davis, *Atlanta Will Fall,* 109; Buell, 365.
112. Eicher, *Longest Night,* 707.
113. Ecelbarger, 24.
114. Buell, 366; see also Symonds, 219, 223.
115. Symonds, 219.
116. Davis, *Atlanta Will Fall,* 83; but compare Buell's assessment that Hood's tactics were "entirely frontal" citing Hood's fighting instructions. Buell, 352.
117. Ecelbarger, 19. One Union soldier described Decatur as "…a very old dilapidated, wooden town, of perhaps 400 inhabitants."
118. Longacre, *Worthy Opponents,* 274.
119. Davis, *Atlanta Will Fall,*131.
120. *Ibid.,* 133.
121. Davis, *Atlanta Will Fall,* 134.
122. *Ibid.,* 135.
123. Buell, 370–71.
124. Daniel, 414.
125. Sherman had not anticipated that Hood would attack Thomas' position, instead believing Hood would attack to the east leaving Thomas "to walk into Atlanta, capturing guns and everything." Buell, 370. See also Cleaves, *Rock of Chickamauga,* 229.
126. Davis, *Atlanta Will Fall,*136.
127. Longacre, *Worthy Opponents,* 275.
128. Davis, *Atlanta Will Fall,* 136–37.
129. Also known as Hood's Second Sortie.
130. Woodworth, *Nothing but,* 534–36.
131. The Irish born Cleburne—Sherman's nemesis from Tunnel Hill—was Hood's most experienced and reliable field commanders but had been passed over for corps command several times, perhaps he had had the audacity to suggest that slaves be armed to fight in the Confederate army. See Buell, 351.
132. Davis, *Atlanta Will Fall,*138. Ecelbarger, 48, says Hood's plan was "unlike any seen in the Western theater of the Civil War to date."
133. Ecelbarger, 53; Buell, 372.
134. Ecelbarger, 49. Sherman also casually eschewed a suggestion from Thomas that Thomas attempt to enter Atlanta from the north during the battle. Daniel, 415.
135. Symonds, 219.
136. Davis, *Atlanta Will Fall,*198.

137. Ecelbarger, 114–18; Woodworth, *Nothing but,* 550–52.

138. Arguably this assessment by Sherman and Grant might be inconsistent with McPherson's relatively brief and mixed record as a combat commander. Even after his failure to advance upon Receca McPherson remained cautious throughout the Atlanta campaign, and even though Sherman constantly gave McPherson's army choice assignments, McPherson never achieved any notable success during the campaign.

139. Work, 19–20.

140. Ecelbarger, 143.

141. Woodworth, *Nothing but,* 568. Although that day's battle is commonly called the Battle for Atlanta, in some quarters it is also called the Battle for Bald Hill.

142. *Ibid.,* 214.

143. Symonds, 230.

144. Davis, *Atlanta Will Fall,* 46–47.

145. Eicher, *Longest Night,* 708.

146. Ecelbarger, 63; Woodworth, *Nothing but,* 540.

147. Davis, *Atlanta Will Fall,*148.

148. Longacre, *Worthy Opponents,* 279.

149. Ecelbarger, 73–76.

150. Steven Woodworth, *Nothing but,* 540, notes that despite Howard's battlefield setbacks, the War Department recognized "him as an officer of merit." Woodworth also characterizes Howard as "brave, conscientious, aggressive, and solidly competent."

151. Ecelbarger, 217–18.

152. Eicher, *Longest Night,* 710. Frank Blair remained in his headquarters giving rise to widespread speculation that he was drunk during the battle; Ecelbarger, 141.

153. Thomas apparently also had a preference that Logan not be given the army command. Cleaves, *Rock of Chickamauga,* 234.

154. Cleaves, *Rock of Chickamauga,* 235.

155. Castel, Albert with Brooks D. Simpson. *Victors in Blue: How Union Generals Fought the Confederates, Battled Each Other, and Won the Civil War* (2011) Lawrence: University Press of Kansas, 272.

156. Slocum had also tutored Hood when the latter was studying for his entrance exams at West Point.

157. Eicher, *Longest Night,* 711.

158. Davis, *Atlanta Will Fall,*150.

159. Woodworth, *Nothing but,* 571.

160. Lee, no relation to the other Lees, was the youngest lieutenant general in the Confederate army.

161. Davis, *Atlanta Will Fall,*150.

162. Ecelbarger, 219.

163. Davis, *Atlanta Will Fall,*153.

164. Symonds, 232.

165. Buell, 374.

166. Symonds, 232.

167. Ecelbarger, 220.

168. *Ibid.,* 175.

169. Longacre, *Worthy Opponents,* 283.

170. Davis, *Atlanta Will Fall,* 175.

171. Hood wrote to Davis, "To hold Atlanta, I have to hold East Point."

172. Woodworth, *Nothing but,* 578.

173. Daniel, 421. Castel and Simpson, 274, note that Sherman's destruction of these tracks that were useless to the Confederates made the "Improbable impossible."

174. Longacre, *Worthy Opponents,* 284.

175. Daniel, 422.

176. Cleaves, *Rock of Chickamauga,* 238.

177. Daniel, 422.

178. Woodworth, *Nothing but,* 580–81; see also Symonds, 239.

179. Davis, *Atlanta Will Fall,*185 .

180. Woodworth, *Nothing but,* 581.

181. Symonds, 239.

182. Davis, *Atlanta Will Fall,*188.

183. Daniel, 423; Cleaves, *Rock of Chickamauga,* 238.

184. Buell, 376.

185. Longacre, *Worthy Opponents,* 284.

186. Castel and Simpson, 276.

187. *Ibid.,* 277.

188. Longacre, *Worthy Opponents,* 285.

189. Woodworth, *Nothing but,* 582.

190. *Ibid.,* 582.

191. Eicher, *Longest Night,* 714; Ecelbarger, 223.

192. Buell, 376.

193. Cleaves, *Rock of Chickamauga,* 240.

194. Buell, 377.

195. Woodworth, *Nothing but,* 582.

196. Castel and Simpson, 277, bluntly state that Sherman "botched" an opportunity to demolish Hardee's corps and so wreck Hood's army.

197. Buell, 375.

198. Larry Daniel, 426–27, identifies these five occasions as follows: "(1) to use the Army of the Cumberland as the flank army at Snake Creek Gap; (2) to use [Hooker's 20th] Corps to reinforce the Army of the Tennessee in crossing the Oostanaula; (3) to outflank the Confederate position at Kennesaw Mountain on their right; (4) to attack the Confederate in flank at Rough and Ready, though this is not verified in contemporary evidence; and (5) to send the Army of the Cumberland on a flank march to Lovejoy's Station to block the Confederate escape route." Albert Castel, in his extensive, in-depth study of Sherman's Atlanta campaign, counts six times when Sherman had opportunities to destroy or to mangle, or at the very least, to drive Hood's army to the eastern edge of Georgia. See Castel, 539.

199. Thomas Buell claims that Sherman—"a raider accustomed to swift action, to movement"— neither understood, nor had he mastered, the complex warfare characterized by the stop-and-go pursuit of Johnston.

200. Of course many other historians consider the capture of Atlanta alone as a great and significant accomplishment. For instance Steven Woodworth, *Nothing but,* 583, considers "The capture of Atlanta [as] one of the great epochs of the war, on a level with the seizure of Vicksburg."

201. Castel and Simpson, 277.

202. Bruce Catton, *Never Call,* 387, the esteemed Civil War historian, put it this way: "As a matter of fact Sherman had done less than he had set out to do. Hood's army had escaped,.... He had been told to destroy the Confederate army and he had not done it, and the capture of Atlanta had been no more than incidental to his plans."

203. Buell, 378.

204. Ecelbarger, 216–17.

205. Woodworth, *Nothing but,* 570.

206. Cleaves, *Rock of Chickamauga,* 239.

## *Chapter 8*

1. Hess, Earl J. *The Civil War in the West: Victory and Defeat from the Appalachians to the Mississippi* (2012) Chapel Hill: The University of North Carolina Press, 248.

2. Hess, *War in the West*, 249.

3. Bailey, Anne J. *The Chessboard of War: Sherman and Hood in the Autumn Campaigns of 1864* (2000) Lincoln: University of Nebraska Press, 34.

4. The encounter at Dalton became ugly. The 44th USCT comprised approximately 60 of the garrison's 800 men. Perhaps it was the first time Hood's Army of Tennessee had confronted Black troops but after the overwhelmed Federal garrison surrendered it is possible, at least according to a report in the *Charleston Mercury*, that most of the Black prisoners were either returned to bondage or were hanged. See James Lee McDonough. *Nashville: The Confederacy's Final Gamble* (2004) Knoxville: The University of Tennessee Press, 36–38. See also Bailey, 35–38.

5. Bailey, 30.

6. Bobrick, Benson. *Master of War: The Life of General George H. Thomas* (2009) New York: Simon & Schuster, 261.

7. Bailey, 44.

8. Daniel, Larry J. *Days of Glory: The Army of the Cumberland, 1861–1865* (2004) Baton Rouge: Louisiana State University Press, 430.

9. Bobrick, 263; Cleaves, Freeman. *Rock of Chickamauga: The Life of General George H. Thomas* (1948) Norman: University of Oklahoma Press, 247.

10. Hess, *War in the West*, 251.

11. Castel, Albert with Brooks D. Simpson. *Victors in Blue: How Union Generals Fought the Confederates, Battled Each Other, and Won the Civil War* (2011) Lawrence: University Press of Kansas, 292.

12. Grant—who continued to harbor his grudge against Rosecrans—was so angered that Rosecrans had borrowed Smith's corps that Grant almost had Rosecrans arrested.

13. Symonds, Craig L. *Stonewall of the West: Patrick Cleburne & The Civil War* (1997) Lawrence: University Press of Kansas, 248.

14. Longacre, Edward G. *Grant's Cavalryman: The Life and Wars of James H. Wilson* (1972) Mechanicsburg, PA: Stackpole Books, 108.

15. Slocum's army included two corps, the 14th and the 20th, formerly in the Army of the Cumberland. Sometimes this army would thus also be called "Slocum's Army of the Cumberland" but for all intents and purposes the original Army of the Cumberland was disbanded when Thomas was transferred to Nashville.

16. Bobrick, 265.

17. In 1860 Columbia was the second largest city in Middle Tennessee.

18. Part of Hood's delay was because of poor planning; part because of bad luck. See Bailey, 71.

19. Cheatham was born near Nashville. Although he had fought in the Mexican War he had little military experience prior to the Civil War. However once the war started he saw combat in several battles in the Western theater.

20. Symonds, 249.

21. See Bailey, 80.

22. *Ibid.*, 82. The legend was that upon George's death Jessie attended the burial and was heard to mutter, "I never loved George but I guess I owe him this much."

23. McDonough, 63.

24. Buell, Thomas B. *The Warrior Generals: Combat Leadership in the Civil War* (1997) New York: Three Rivers Press, 388.

25. Bailey, 83.

26. McDonough, 61.

27. *Ibid.*, 61.

28. Symonds, 250–53.

29. According to various maps the exact locations of the Confederate encampments remain somewhat of a mystery.

30. Bailey, 83.

31. For instance see Bobrick, 270.

32. McDonough, 65.

33. Symonds, 250.

34. McDonough, 68.

35. Bailey, 87.

36. McDonough, 70.

37. *Ibid.*, 75.

38. Symonds, 254.

39. Bailey, 94.

40. *Ibid.*, 94.

41. McDonough, 84.

42. *Ibid.*, 94–5.

43. Bailey, 97.

44. Castel and Simpson, 293.

45. McDonough, 93.

46. Longacre, *Grant's Cavalryman*, 172, 174; McDonough, 58.

47. Compared to the estimated 13,000 men in Pickett's Charge at Gettysburg.

48. Symonds, 258; Bailey, 99.

49. Castel and Simpson, 294.

50. Groom, Winston. *Shrouds of Glory: From Atlanta to Nashville: The Last Great Campaign of the Civil War* (1995) New York: Pocket Books, 182.

51. *Ibid.*, 200.

52. McDonough, 108.

53. Symonds, 258.

54. McDonough, 110.

55. *Ibid.*, 111.

56. McDonough, 110–11, argues with considerable persuasion that Franklin is the most underappreciated battle of the Civil War, even among many Civil War readers.

57. McDonough, 129.

58. Bailey, 136. See also McDonough, 130–31.

59. McDonough, 140.

60. Small elevated forts containing four artillery pieces with interlocking fields of fire.

61. Buell, 397.

62. McDonough, 149.

63. Bobrick, 279.

64. Buell, 398.

65. McDonough, 143.

66. Bobrick, 280. Bobrick calls this part of the "most remarkable exchange of telegrams in the annals of war."

67. *Ibid.*, 279.

68. After the war no such message could be found.

69. Bobrick, 289.

70. *Ibid.*, 285.

71. *Ibid.*, 286.

72. Steedman's forces also included a brigade led by Charles Grovesnor of Athens, Ohio, this author's hometown. Grovesnor, an attorney, was eventually elected to Congress where he promoted the establishment of national parks of former battlefields. His former home in Athens currently is the headquarters for Ohio University's Alumni Association.

73. McDonough, 215.

74. This author's great-great grandfather, part of the

18th OVVI assigned to Steedman's "demonstration," was killed this day.

75. So named for C.S.A. Col. W.M. Shy, of the 20th Tennessee, who was killed in defense of this hill.
76. Placing guns on top of the hill instead of on the military crest, slightly downhill from the top, was the same mistake made earlier at Missionary Ridge.
77. Bobrick, 297.
78. Smith, Derek. *In the Lion's Mouth: Hood's Tragic Retreat from Nashville, 1864* (2011) Mechanicsburg, PA: Stackpole Books, 81.
79. Smith, *Lion's Mouth,* 83.
80. McDonough, 258.
81. Smith, *Lion's Mouth,* 81. An out-of-shape Ed ("Alleghany") Johnson, whom we would have met at Culp's Hill during the Gettysburg campaign if these chapters were presented in chronological order (see Chapter 16), was one of the generals captured as Rebel units scattered.
82. Sword, Wiley. *The Confederates' Last Hurrah: Spring Hill, Franklin, & Nashville* Paperback Edition, first published as *Embrace an Angry Wind* (1992) Lawrence: University of Kansas Press, 384.
83. *Ibid.,* 391.
84. Smith, *Lion's Mouth,* 82.
85. *Ibid.,* 82.
86. *Ibid.,* 87.
87. Sword, 386. In his *Memoirs* Grant claimed this was a major reason why, in his opinion, the pursuit did not have more success.
88. Smith, *Lion's Mouth,* 89.
89. McDonough, 262.
90. Paradoxically Wilson's Northern cavalry also included a regiment of Tennesseans.
91. Sword, 389; McDonough, 262.
92. Smith, *Lion's Mouth,* 97–98.
93. *Ibid.,* 98.
94. *Ibid.,* 98–99.
95. Horn, Stanley F. *The Decisive Battle of Nashville* Paperback Edition (1991) Baton Rouge: Louisiana State University Press, 154.
96. Smith, *Lion's Mouth,* 107.
97. On numerous occasions this author has heard Ed Bearrs say that the sight of a flanking enemy was the retreating army's worst nightmare.
98. Smith, *Lion's Mouth,* 105.
99. Sword, 395.
100. Smith, *Lion's Mouth,* 117.
101. *Ibid.,* 117.
102. Sword, 395; Longacre, *Grant's Cavalryman,* 189.
103. *Ibid.,* 396.
104. Smith, *Lion's Mouth,* 108.
105. *Ibid.,* 116.
106. *Ibid.,* 118; Sword, 394.
107. Wright, 486.
108. Smith, *Lion's Mouth,* 119; Sword, 397.
109. Sword, 399; Smith, *Lion's Mouth,* 123.
110. Sword, 400.
111. Longacre, *Grant's Cavalryman,* 190.
112. Smith, *Lion's Mouth,* 127.
113. *Ibid.,* 128.
114. *Ibid.,* 132. Those Federals who paused at Franklin were dismayed and sobered by what they found. Many dead soldiers had been buried in shallow graves that the torrential rains had washed away the covering dirt to expose jumbled, decaying bodies, many which had been stripped naked. In some instances hundreds of corpses had simply been dumped in pits serving as mass graves.
115. Sword, 401.
116. Horn, 160.
117. Smith, *Lion's Mouth,* 137.
118. *Ibid.,* 138–39.
119. Sword, 404.
120. Smith, *Lion's Mouth,* 138.
121. Sword, 405; Smith, *Lion's Mouth,* 141.
122. Wills, Brian Steel. *The Confederacy's Greatest Cavalryman: Nathan Bedford Forrest* (1992) Lawrence: University of Kansas Press, 289.
123. Smith, *Lion's Mouth,* 142.
124. *Ibid.,* 143.
125. Sword, 406.
126. *Ibid.,* 407.
127. Cleaves, *Rock of Chickamauga,* 271.
128. Wills, 291.
129. After being originally dispatched the pontoon train advanced about fifteen miles before the error was discovered. After trying unsuccessfully to cross overland to Franklin the train returned to Nashville, reaching its original starting point on December 18. The train then resumed its trek south on December 19.
130. Cleaves, *Rock of Chickamauga,* 272.
131. Smith, *Lion's Mouth,* 157–58.
132. After the Confederates passed through Columbia a resident wrote, "They were the worst looking, and most broken down set I ever laid eyes on."
133. Sword, 408.
134. Smith, *Lion's Mouth,* 154.
135. *Ibid.,* 160.
136. Sword, 413; Bobrick, 302.
137. Smith, *Lion's Mouth,* 169; Cleaves, *Rock of Chickamauga,* 271.
138. In his biography of Halleck John Marszaek, while admitting that Halleck was basically a paper pusher, contends this shows how much Halleck's attitude had changed over the course of the war. Marszalek, *Commander of all Lincoln's Armies,* 218. Suffice to say that others may respectfully disagree, contending instead that Halleck was merely echoing Grant's complaints.
139. Cleaves, *Rock of Chickamauga,* 271.
140. Smith, *Lion's Mouth,* 171; Bobrick, 304.
141. Smith, *Lion's Mouth,* 166.
142. *Ibid.,* 166–67.
143. *Ibid.,* 174.
144. *Ibid.,* 175.
145. Sword, 414.
146. Smith, *Lion's Mouth,* 178.
147. Sword, 414.
148. Smith, *Lion's Mouth,* 169.
149. Smith, *Lion's Mouth,* 176; Sword, 413.
150. Sword, 413; Smith, *Lion's Mouth,* 177.
151. Smith, *Lion's Mouth,* 178.
152. Sword, 413.
153. Smith, *Lion's Mouth,* 178.
154. Longacre, *Grant's Cavalryman,* 190.
155. No Federal accounts corroborate this claim.
156. Wills, 292.
157. Sword, 416–17.
158. Smith, *Lion's Mouth,* 191.
159. Sword, 417.
160. Smith, *Lion's Mouth,* 194.
161. Sword, 417.
162. Smith, *Lion's Mouth,* 201–03.

163. Longacre, *Grant's Cavalryman*, 191; the piece was later recovered in fighting at Selma, Alabama.
164. Wills, 292; Sword, 419.
165. Cleaves, *Rock of Chickamauga*, 272; Smith, *Lion's Mouth*, 194.
166. Smith, *Lion's Mouth*, 214.
167. Sword, 419.
168. Smith, *Lion's Mouth*, 195.
169. *Ibid.*, 206.
170. *Ibid.*, 201.
171. *Ibid.*, 215.
172. Wills, 292.
173. Sword, 419.
174. Smith, *Lion's Mouth*, 218.
175. *Ibid.*, 218–219.
176. Sword, 419.
177. Wilson's version blamed "the independence of the navy and the natural timidity of a deep-water sailor in a shoal-water river."
178. Longacre, *Grant's Cavalryman*, 191.
179. Bailey, 167.
180. *Ibid.*, 168.
181. Sword, 425.
182. Longacre, *Grant's Cavalryman*, 192.
183. Einolf, Christopher J., *George Thomas: Virginian for the Union* (2007) Norman: University of Oklahoma Press, 287.
184. *Ibid.*, 285–86.
185. Bailey, 168.
186. Cleaves, *Rock of Chickamauga*, 273, added, perhaps with a note of sarcasm, that "Grant could see only sunny skies and a wide-open road for Thomas."
187. Grant's criticism continued unabated almost until his own death. Chapter 21 of his *Memoirs* citing distorted facts, criticizes several aspects of the pursuit. Although this portion of the pursuit was led by Grant's protégé, James Wilson who was still living when Grant's memoirs were published in 1885, Grant does not mention Wilson by name.
188. Einolf, 288.
189. Walsh, 402.
190. Longacre, *Grant's Cavalryman*, 210.
191. Wills, 316.
192. Despite Sherman's complaints that Thomas was slow and/or sluggish, Sherman's memoirs still ranked Thomas as the second best general in the Civil War, behind Grant but ahead of Lee. Einolf, 297.

## Chapter 9

1. Winfield Scott, born 1786 in Virginia, was one of the most distinguished soldiers in American history. Scott had become a national hero during the War of 1812, had forced South Carolina to capitulate during the Nullification crisis, and scored a tremendous success at little cost in leading the invasion of Mexico. Known as "Old Fuss and Feathers" he had become grossly overweight and infirm at the outbreak of the Civil War. But his military acumen was still unmatched.
2. David Detzer suggests that McDowell might not have been Scott's preferred choice to lead this new army, and that Scott was not enthusiastic about the march to Richmond, preferring instead to build up the defenses around Harper's Ferry. See Detzer, David. *Donnybrook: The Battle of Bull Run, 1862* (2004) Orlando: Harcourt Books, 82–83.
3. Reid, Brian Holden. *America's Civil War: The Operational Battlefield 1861–1863* (2008) New York: Prometheus Books, 56; Detzer, 85.
4. Detzer, 85.
5. The first real big battle had occurred at Big Bethel, Virginia, at the time considered to be a major victory for the Confederacy.
6. Aside from two years as a civil engineer in Florida Johnston had served in various positions during an entire career in the Regular Army. Although early on appointed to full general in the Confederate army he was still junior in rank to three other generals who had been his juniors in the Regular Army, a situation than annoyed Johnston and caused continuous strife between him and Davis.
7. Jackson was born in what is now West Virginia. After graduating from West Point he served with distinction in an artillery battery during the Mexican War, earning two brevets. In 1859 he commanded a company of V.M.I. cadets at John Brown's hanging.
8. Reid, *America's Civil War*, 60.
9. Patchan, Patrick C. *Second Manassas: Longstreet's Attack and the Struggle for Chinn Ridge* (2011) Washington, D.C.: Potomac Books, 40.
10. Detzer, 167–68.
11. *Ibid.*, 175–76.
12. The Louisiana Tigers, also known as the Wheat Tigers after their founder, Chatham ("Rob") Wheat, were recruited from a variety of sources, including prisons and newly arrived immigrants in New Orleans. Purportedly three women were in their ranks although none of the ladies made it to Manassas. The outfit was dressed as Zouaves and liked to march with fancy dance-like steps. At First Bull Run Wheat was shot through both lungs but declared he "don't feel like dying yet" to recover to fight in several more battles.
13. Reid, *America's Civil War*, 64.
14. Berimger, Robert E., Hattaway, Herman, Jones, Archer; & Still, William N, Jr. *Why the South Lost the Civil War* (1986) Athens: University of Georgia Press, 114.
15. Farwell, Byron. *Stonewall: A Biography of General Thomas J. Jackson* (1993) New York: W.W. Norton & Company, 180. Another, less popular, version has another commander saying, "Yonder stands Jackson like a stonewall, let's go to his assistance."
16. Alexander, Bevin. *Lost Victories: The Military Genius of Stonewall Jackson* (2004) New York: Hippocrene Books, 26.
17. Reid, *America's Civil War*, 64.
18. Farwell, 184.
19. Perret, Geoffrey. *Lincoln's War: The Untold Story of America's Greatest President as Commander in Chief* (2004) New York: Random House, 77–8.
20. Alexander, Edward Porter. *Fighting for the Confederacy: The Personal Recollections of Edward Porter Alexander*, Edited by Gary C. Gallagher (1989) Chapel Hill: The University of North Carolina Press, 110.
21. Part of the legend of Stonewall Jackson is that he had a chance encounter with Davis wherein Jackson supposedly yelled at Davis, "We have whipped them! They ran like sheep! Give me 5,000 fresh men [or 10,000 men, depending upon the version] and I will be in Washington city tomorrow morning." However this statement was not reported until 20 years later and Jackson made no mention of such as statement in his letter that evening to his wife. See Farwell, 194.
22. Jones, Archer. *Civil War Command & Strategy: The*

*Process of Victory and Defeat* (1992) New York: The Free Press, 36–7.

23. Detzer, 466.

24. *Ibid.*, 465. Detzer, 483, also says it was unlikely that Jackson told Davis that he, Jackson, could be in Washington the next day if given 10,000 fresh soldiers.

25. Farwell, 193.

26. *Ibid.*, 196.

27. *Ibid.*, 193.

28. Jones, 2.

29. The reaction the defeat at First Bull Run, along with the defeats at Wilson's Creek and Ball's Bluff, were part of the considerations that led to the formation of the Joint Committee on the Conduct of the War.

30. Foote, Shelby. *The Civil War, a Narrative: Fort Sumter to Perryville* (1958) New York: Vintage, 85.

31. Perret, 97–8.

## Chapter 10

1. Taaffe, Stephen R. *Commanding the Army of the Potomac* (2006) Lawrence: University Press of Kansas, 23.

2. Reardon, Carol. *With a Sword in One Hand & Jomini in the Other: The Problem of Military Thought in the Civil War North* (2012) Chapel Hill: University of North Carolina Press, 25.

3. Taaffe, 6.

4. Reardon, 26.

5. McClellan also planned that after seizing Richmond his army would turn to the South, taking Charleston, Savannah, etc., and New Orleans to "crush out this rebellion at its very heart."

6. Bevin Alexander argues that attacking Petersburg, to the south of Richmond, would have been a more effective move. *Lost Victories: The Military Genius of Stonewall Jackson* (2004) New York: Hippocrene Books, 41.

7. And yes, we know that if the frog had wings he could fly.

8. Work, David. *Lincoln's Political Generals* (2009) Urbana: University of Illinois Press, 10–11.

9. Because of his exploits Frémont probably was the best known American soldier at the beginning of the Civil War. After resigning from the army in 1848 Frémont acquired vast amounts of real estate and grew rich as a result of the gold rush.

10. Work, 42.

11. T. Harry Williams describes Frémont as being "weak and unstable." *Lincoln and His Generals* (1952) New York: Dorset Press, 35.

12. Another version has Jackson demanding 10,000 troops.

13. Farwell, Byron. *Stonewall: A Biography of General Thomas J. Jackson* (1993) New York: W.W. Norton & Company, 225.

14. *Ibid.*, 226.

15. Work, 22–23. Shields once challenged Lincoln to a duel but the two patched up their differences and eventually became good friends.

16. Farwell, 229; Alexander, *Lost Victories*, 45.

17. The pious Jackson ostensibly tried to avoid launching attacks on Sundays. However he often had to explain to his even more pious wife why his efforts at restraint were not successful.

18. Jackson had marched his men so hard that many of his soldiers had fallen by the wayside from fatigue and exhaustion. Alexander, *Lost Victories*, 45.

19. Farwell, 234; Alexander, *Lost Victories*, 46.

20. Shields had to be carried from the field after being struck by multiple shell fragments as he approached the battlefield.

21. Farwell, 238.

22. Alexander, *Lost Victories*, 46.

23. Farwell, 239.

24. Alexander, *Lost Victories*, 47.

25. *Ibid.*, 51.

26. *Ibid.*, 54.

27. Farwell, 257. Alexander, *Lost Victories*, 53. While at Staunton Jackson donned a new Confederate uniform replacing his old VMI uniform.

28. Patchan, Patrick C. *Second Manassas: Longstreet's Attack and the Struggle for Chinn Ridge* (2011) Washington, D.C.: Potomac Books, 80.

29. Farwell, 262; Patchan, *Second Manassas*, 13. McLean, an Ohio lawyer, was the son of John McLean the long serving U.S. Supreme Court Justice who wrote a blistering dissent in the *Drew Scot vs Sanford* case in 1857. As a result Justice McLean was adopted by Northern abolitionists as their champion. Nathaniel McLean had recruited and organized the 75th OVI.

30. Farwell, 264.

31. *Ibid.*, 265.

32. Eicher, David J. *The Longest Night: A Military History of the Civil War* (2001) New York: Simon & Schuster, 259–60.

33. Farwell, 265.

34. Alexander, *Lost Victories*, 57.

35. Also sometimes called the Battle of Brothers, both sides having infantry brigades from Maryland.

36. Bevin Alexander, *Lost Victories*, 61, also notes that Jackson's actions against Frémont at the village of McDowell had the effect of isolating Banks against a potentially much larger army under Jackson.

37. Aside from his stint in Mexico, Ewell had spent his entire twenty-one army career fighting Indians. As soon as the war began Ewell resigned as a captain to become a colonel in command of a Confederate cavalry training camp. Within a month Ewell was promoted to brigadier to command a brigade at First Bull Run.

38. Prior to this time Ewell's chain of command was not clear. Originally Ewell had been placed under Jackson's command by Lee, then still only an advisor to Davis while Joe Johnston was the actual commander of the region in which Ewell was operating and had yet to give explicit orders for Ewell to continue operating under Jackson. Indeed after Lee had advised Jackson to attack Banks Johnston sent orders to Jackson and to Ewell prohibiting them to attack Banks. The record is not clear how Jackson resolved these contradictory orders. See also Alexander, *Lost Victories*, 62.

39. Farwell, 277; Alexander, *Lost Victories*, 63.

40. Farwell, 279.

41. Alexander, *Lost Victories*, 64, 66–7.

42. Farwell, 283.

43. Reid, Brian Holden. *America's Civil War: The Operational Battlefield 1861–1863* (2008) New York: Prometheus Books, 111.

44. Farwell, 291.

45. Eicher, *Longest Night*, 262.

46. Alexander, *Lost Victories*, 71.

47. Farwell, 295.
48. Alexander, *Lost Victories*, 72.
49. Farwell, 295.
50. Alexander, *Lost Victories*, 72.
51. Reid, *America's Civil War*, 113.
52. Farwell, 298; Eicher, *Longest Night*, 262.
53. Alexander, *Lost Victories*, 74.
54. *Ibid.*, 74.
55. Farwell, 304.
56. *Ibid.*, 307.
57. Alexander, *Lost Victories*, 80.
58. Farwell, 308.
59. Alexander, *Lost Victories*, 81.
60. Boatner, Mark M. III, *The Civil War Dictionary*, New York: Vintage Books, 742.
61. McPherson, James M. *The Battle Cry of Freedom: The Civil War Era* (1988) Oxford University Press, 460.
62. Farwell, 317; although Ashby had been nominated for promotion to brigadier general, his commission had never been confirmed by the Confederate senate.
63. *Ibid.*, 310.
64. *Ibid.*, 313.
65. Alexander, *Lost Victories*, 84. While retreating up the Valley Jackson had hoped Richmond would send him reinforcements so that he would be able to initiate an invasion of Maryland, a dream Jackson had held almost since the beginning of the war. However shortly before reaching Port Republic Jackson received word that Richmond would not be providing the requested reinforcements.
66. Eicher, *Longest Night*, 265.
67. Farwell, 318.
68. *Ibid.*, 320–22.
69. Alexander, *Lost Victories*, 86.
70. Eicher, *Longest Night*, 266.
71. Farwell, 328; Alexander, *Lost Victories*, 87.
72. Farwell, 330–31, provides a harsh critique of Jackson's generalship at Port Republic quoting among others Douglas Southall Freeman's evaluation that "this was, on Jackson's part, a poorly managed battle."
73. Eicher, *Longest Night*, 266.
74. *Ibid.*, 266.
75. Farwell, 301.
76. Work, 228–33.
77. Stanton succinctly endorsed Shields' letter of resignation as follows: "Accepted."
78. Citing Jackson's six-month period during which he either brought court-martial charges against four senior officers or provoked others to the point that they threatened to resign, Harwell, 332, states, "No other general, North or South, had shown himself so abrasive and so clumsy in [Jackson's] personal relations with subordinates, and he never improved."

## Chapter 11

1. Alexander, Ted. *The Battle of Antietam: The Bloodiest Day* (2011) Charleston, SC: The History Press, 17.
2. Hoping that a lighter load of responsibilities would enable McClellan to focus upon his duties as commanding general of the Army of the Potomac, on March 11, 1862, Lincoln relieved McClellan as General in Chief of all Federal forces.
3. McClellan's advance was slowed considerably when he opted to lay a month-long siege against badly outnumbered Rebel forces at Yorktown.
4. Col. W.H. F. ("Rooney") Lee, R.E. Lee's second oldest son owned the plantation at White House where the senior Lee's wife and daughter were also in residence. Upon McClellan's arrival he extended every possible courtesy, providing these ladies an escort to accompany them to the other side of the Confederate lines.
5. Wert, Jeffry D. *The Sword of Lincoln: The Army of the Potomac* (2005) New York: Simon & Schuster, 84–85.
6. Stempel, Jim. *The Battle of Glendale: The Day the South Nearly Won the War* (2011) Jefferson, NC: McFarland, 19.
7. Foote, Shelby. *The Civil War, a Narrative: Fort Sumter to Perryville* (1958) New York: Vintage, 445.
8. Before appointing Lee to replace Johnson, Davis appointed Gustavus Smith as Johnston's temporary replacement. However Smith suffered an attack of paralysis, perhaps from nerves, and was quickly relieved and replaced by Lee. Smith eventually served as interim Secretary of War before resigning when six other officers were promoted to Lieutenant General ahead of him.
9. Guelzo, Allen C. *Gettysburg: The Last Invasion* (2013) New York: Alfred A. Knopf, 18.
10. Freeman, Douglas Southall, *R.E. Lee, A Biography Vol. I* (1934) New York: Scribner, is the first of the four volume series.
11. Wert, *The Sword*, 91.
12. *Ibid.*, 95.
13. Alexander, Bevin. *Lost Victories: The Military Genius of Stonewall Jackson* (2004) New York: Hippocrene Books, 96.
14. Buell, Thomas B. *The Warrior Generals: Combat Leadership in the Civil War* (1997) New York: Three Rivers Press, 71.
15. Rafuse, Ethan S. *McClellan's War* (2005) Bloomington: Indiana University Press, 221.
16. Glatthaar, Joseph T. *General Lee's Army: From Victory to Collapse* (2008) New York: Free Press, 136.
17. *Ibid.*, 136.
18. Freeman, Douglas Southall, *R.E. Lee, A Biography Vol. II* (1934, 1936) New York: Scribner, 233–35.
19. Buell, 75. Buell also reports that Lee had never before written such an order.
20. Wert, *The Sword*, 101; Buell, 72.
21. *Ibid.*, 98.
22. *Ibid.*, 99.
23. Eicher, David J. *The Longest Night: A Military History of the Civil War* (2001) New York: Simon & Schuster, 283.
24. Freeman, *Lee Biography Vol. II*, 122.
25. Glatthaar, 136–37; Freeman, *Lee Biography Vol. II*, 130.
26. Alexander, B., *Lost Victories*, 102.
27. Eicher, *Longest Night*, 284.
28. Wert, *The Sword*, 102, says "The Southerners never had a chance." See also Alexander, B., *Lost Victories*, 103.
29. Buell, 70.
30. *Ibid.*, 70–1.
31. Eicher, *Longest Night*, 283.
32. Buell, 76.
33. Stempel, 24.
34. Rafuse, 221.
35. Wert, *The Sword*, 102.
36. Glatthaar, 137.
37. Freeman, *Lee Biography Vol. II*, 138.
38. Buell, 79.

39. Alexander, B., *Lost Victories*, 103.
40. Glatthaar, 137.
41. Buell, 80.
42. Wert, *The Sword*, 106.
43. Alexander,B., *Lost Victories*, 109.
44. Wert, *The Sword*, 106.
45. *Ibid.*, 106–07.
46. Rafuse, 223. Initially McClellan had considered Stanton to be one of his closest allies in McClellan's hopes to take control of the government. However that relationship quickly soured when Stanton started working closely with Lincoln and the rest of the administration.
47. Wert, *The Sword*, 107; Eicher, *Longest Night*, 288.
48. Wert, *The Sword*, 107.
49. McClellan's biographer, Ethan S. Rafuse, relying heavily upon risk analysis, and stating that "From the time he reached the Peninsula McClellan had seen his best-laid plans upset by factors outside his control"; tries to make the case that McClellan really had no other feasible option except to move his base to the James River. See Rafuse, 223–25.
50. Wert, *The Sword*, 108.
51. *Ibid.*, 108.
52. Eckenrode, H.J. & Conrad, Bryan. *James Longstreet: Lee's War Horse* (1936, 1986) Chapel Hill: The University of North Carolina Press, 72.
53. Eicher, *Longest Night*, 289.
54. *Ibid.*, 289.
55. Buell, 81.
56. Wert, *The Sword*, 108.
57. Eicher, *Longest Night*, 284, characterizes this decision as "…a new and heightened level of illogical thinking for George McClellan." Noting that "The situation in fact still favored McClellan greatly."
58. That night Phil Kearny issued red patches to be sewed to the caps of the soldiers in his division. These red patches became the forerunners of unit patches eventually used throughout all military units.
59. Wert, *The Sword*, 108, 109–10.
60. Freeman, *Lee Biography Vol. II*,159.
61. Bevin Alexander, *Lost Victories*, 114, observes that Lee should have quickly realized that McClellan was prepared to abandon the supply depot at White House Landing when Lee's couriers advised him that morning that Federal forces had moved south of the Chickahominy before burning all the bridges behind them.
62. Wert, Jeffrey D. *General James Longstreet: The Confederacy's Most Controversial Soldier* (1993) New York: Touchstone, 140.
63. Wert, *The Sword*, 109; Stempel, 32.
64. Eckenrode & Conrad, 71.
65. Eicher, *Longest Night*, 289.
66. Alexander, B., *Lost Victories*, 116.
67. *Ibid*, 116.
68. General Order No. 75, dated June 24, 1862; Freeman, *Lee Biography Vol. II*,166, stated, "The aim of the campaign had been to force McClellan to retire or to come out from behind his entrenchments so that he could be attacked to advantage."
69. Buell, 82.
70. Glatthaar, 137.
71. Wert, *The Sword*, 110.
72. Freeman, *Lee Biography Vol. II*,167–70.
73. Wert, *Longstreet*, 140; Eckenrode & Conrad, 77.
74. Glatthaar, 139.
75. Stempel, 37.
76. Wert, *The Sword*, 109.
77. Glatthaar, 139.
78. Wert, *Longstreet*, 141.
79. Stempel, 37–38.
80. Glatthaar, 139.
81. Wert, *The Sword*, 111.
82. *Ibid.*, 111.
83. Freeman, *Lee Biography Vol. II*,174; Stempel, 39.
84. Wert, *The Sword*, 112.
85. *Ibid.*, 112.
86. Freeman, *Lee Biography Vol. II*,76.
87. *Ibid.*, 176.
88. Eckenrode & Conrad, 74.
89. Bevin Alexander, *Lost Victories*, 121, states that "Lee's decision [to mass troops against the Union's rear guard instead of trying to take Harrison's Landing] demonstrates, perhaps more clearly than at any other point in the war, his lust for a trial by battle and his inability to see a strategic alternative that would have had a better chance of success and caused fewer casualties."
90. Stempel, 41.
91. Wert, *The Sword*, 113.
92. Stempel, 43.
93. *Ibid.*, 44.
94. *Ibid.*, 45–46.
95. Wert, *The Sword*, 48.
96. *Ibid.*, 48.
97. *Ibid.*, 43.
98. Stempel, 47.
99. Wert, *The Sword*, 47.
100. Welker, David A. *Tempest at Ox Hill: The Battle of Chantilly* (2002) Cambridge: Da Capo Press, 56.
101. Eckenrode & Conrad, 78.
102. Wert, *The Sword*, 114.
103. Buell, 82.
104. Freeman, *Lee Biography Vol. II*,194–98.
105. Eckenrode & Conrad, 75.
106. Wert, *Longstreet*, 145.
107. Dowdey, Clifford, in *The Seven Days: The Emergence of Robert E. Lee* (1964) New York: Skyhorse Publishing, 308
108. See also Eicher, *Longest Night*, 284; see also Alexander, B., *Lost Victories*, 132, fn 20. See also Freeman, Douglas Southall. *Lee's Lieutenants: A Study in Command—Manassas to Malvern Hill Volume I* Chap XLII (1942) New York: Scribner.
109. Stempel, 69.
110. *Ibid.*, 103.
111. *Ibid.*, 104.
112. Eckenrode & Conrad, 76.
113. *Ibid.*, 76.
114. Buell, 83. These gunships, as well as artillery batteries atop of Malvern Hill, were directed by spotters at the crest of Malvern Hill using semaphore flags to signal adjustments, probably the first instance of indirect naval gunfire controlled by spotters ashore.
115. Wert, *Longstreet*, 142.
116. Eckenrode & Conrad, 79; Wert, *Longstreet*, 143.
117. Welker, 56; Wert, *Longstreet*, 143. As McCall was being led to the rear he encountered Longstreet, McCall's subordinate twenty years earlier, who offered his hand to McCall who refused, saying, "Excuse me, sir. I can stand defeat but not insult."
118. Welker, 56.
119. Eckenrode & Conrad, 79.
120. Wert, *The Sword*, 114.

121. *Ibid.*, 84.
122. Eckenrode & Conrad, 75–76, argue that the Union army had already passed Glendale and Frayser's Farm much earlier in the day but Captain Oliver Wendell Holmes, 21, then with the Union army but who would someday become one of America's most distinguished justices, would vividly recall the rigors of marching through the night of the 30th.
123. *Ibid.*, 95.
124. Wert, *Longstreet*, 144.
125. *Ibid.*, 144–45.
126. Wert, *The Sword*, 116.
127. Buell, 84.
128. Rafuse, 227.
129. Alexander, Edward Porter. *Fighting for the Confederacy: The Personal Recollections of Edward Porter Alexander*, Edited by Gary C. Gallagher (1989) Chapel Hill: The University of North Carolina Press, 110.
130. Freeman, *Lee Biography Vol. II*, 199.
131. Rafuse, 227.
132. Wert, *The Sword*, 117.
133. Freeman, *Lee Biography Vol. II*, 202.
134. Buell, 86.
135. Eicher, *Longest Night*, 293.
136. Wert, *The Sword*, 118.
137. Eicher, *Longest Night*, 293.
138. Wert, *The Sword*, 119.
139. Stempel, 181–82; Wert, *Longstreet*, 147.
140. Eicher, *Longest Night*, 295.
141. Wert, *The Sword*, 120; Alexander, E.P., 127.
142. Wert, *Longstreet*, 148.
143. Wert, *The Sword*, 121.
144. Stempel, 184.
145. Glatthaar, 140.
146. *Ibid.*, 148–49.
147. Freeman, *Lee's Lieutenants Vol. I*, 633.
148. Alexander, B., *Lost Victories*, 115.
149. Freeman, *Lee's Lieutenants Vol. I*, 633.
150. *Ibid.*, 635.
151. Alexander, B., *Lost Victories*, 119.
152. Freeman, *Lee's Lieutenants Vol. I*, 639. In his report Stuart would take credit for driving off the Federals even though no Union report mentioned seeing Stuart's cavalry.
153. Freeman, *Lee Biography Vol. II*, 224.
154. While remaining at Harrison's Landing after Lincoln's visit McClellan continued to scheme about getting even with his enemies, especially Stanton, in the Administration. At the same time a majority of Lincoln's cabinet had concluded McClellan should be relieved of all command responsibilities, and had in fact sent a memorandum to that effect to Lincoln.
155. Halleck was accompanied by Ambrose Burnside who had just completed a series of amphibious assaults along the Carolina coast.
156. Buell, 93.
157. *Ibid.*, 91.
158. Buell, 94; Freeman, *Lee's Lieutenants Vol. I*, 630–31.
159. Buell, 94.

## Chapter 12

1. Porter Alexander said Pope's reputation in the old army was that of "blatherskite." Alexander, Edward Porter. *Fighting for the Confederacy: The Personal Recollections of Edward Porter Alexander*, Edited by Gary C. Gallagher (1989) Chapel Hill: The University of North Carolina Press, 123.
2. Patchan, Patrick C. *Second Manassas: Longstreet's Attack and the Struggle for Chinn Ridge* (2011) Washington, D.C.: Potomac Books, 4.
3. Eicher, David J. *The Longest Night: A Military History of the Civil War* (2001) New York: Simon & Schuster, 318. Pope's harsh words were consistent with the increased brutality of the war as raids increased resulting in more reprisals, assassinations and sabotage. As described by Thomas B. Buell in *The Warrior Generals: Combat Leadership in the Civil War* (1997) New York: Three Rivers Press, 98, the rhetoric by leaders on both sides tended to encourage such retaliatory measures.
4. Eicher, *Longest Night*, 318.
5. Work, David. *Lincoln's Political Generals* (2009) Urbana: University of Illinois Press, 28.
6. At this point in the war Confederacy law did not permit corps commands. Buell, 98.
7. Glatthaar, Joseph T. *General Lee's Army: From Victory to Collapse* (2008) New York: Free Press, 157.
8. Freeman, Douglas Southall, *R.E. Lee, A Biography Vol. II* (1934, 1936) New York: Scribner, 248.
9. *Ibid.*, 158; Slotkin, Richard. *The Long Road to Antietam: How the Civil War Became a Revolution* (2012) New York: Liveright Publishing, 115.
10. Patchan, *Second Manassas*, 4.
11. *Ibid.*, 322.
12. Alexander, Bevin. *Lost Victories: The Military Genius of Stonewall Jackson* (2004) New York: Hippocrene Books, 149–50.
13. To underscore the contention that it was a strategic mistake to withdraw McClellan from Harrison's Landing E. Porter Alexander would later write that the Union army "began the evacuation of the only position from which it could have forced the evacuation of Richmond. They were only to find it again after two years' fighting, and the loss of over 100,000 men; and they would find it then only by being defeated upon every other possible line of advance." Alexander, 179.
14. Alexander, *Fighting for the Confederacy*, 156–57.
15. Freeman, *Lee Biography Vol. II*, 273; Patchan, *Second Manassas*, 4–5.
16. Glatthaar, 159.
17. Buell, 100–01.
18. Alexander, *Fighting for the Confederacy*, 158–59.
19. Freeman, *Lee Biography Vol. II*, 289.
20. Buell, 101.
21. Freeman, *Lee Biography Vol. II*, 296–98.
22. *Ibid.*, 300–301.
23. Alexander, *Fighting for the Confederacy*, 161.
24. *Ibid.*, 162.
25. Buell, 101.
26. Eicher, *Longest Night*, 323; Patchan, *Second Manassas*, 5.
27. Slotkin, 116.
28. Alexander, *Fighting for the Confederacy*, 163.
29. Farwell, 400.
30. Buell, 101.
31. Alexander, *Fighting for the Confederacy*, 175; Patchan, *Second Manassas*, 6.
32. Wert, Jeffrey. *The Sword of Lincoln: The Army of the Potomac* (2005) New York: Simon & Schuster, 134.
33. *Ibid.*, 135.
34. Also called Brawner Farm.

35. Patchan, *Second Manassas*, 6.
36. Wert, Jeffry D. *General James Longstreet: The Confederacy's Most Controversial Soldier* (1993) New York: Touchstone, 166. By the end of the war the Union's Iron Brigade will have suffered a higher percentage of casualties than any other Union brigade while the Confederate's Stonewall Brigade would suffer more casualties than any Confederate brigade.
37. *Ibid.*, 166.
38. *Ibid.*, 168.
39. Slotkin, 118.
40. Eicher, *Longest Night,* 328.
41. Freeman, *Lee Biography Vol. II,* 324.
42. Wert, *Longstreet*, 171.
43. Slotkin, 122.
44. *Ibid.*, 123.
45. Freeman, *Lee Biography Vol. II,* 329.
46. Glatthaar, 162.
47. Wert, , *Longstreet*, 176.
48. Patchan, *Second Manassas*, 8–9.
49. Slotkin, 119.
50. Patchan, *Second Manassas*, 8.
51. The second day of Second Bull Run is sometimes called Groveton Heights.
52. Alexander, *Fighting for the Confederacy,* 195.
53. Eicher, *Longest Night,* 329.
54. Patchan, *Second Manassas*, 9.
55. *Ibid.*, 10.
56. Robert Schenck was an Ohio lawyer and politician who had helped deliver important votes for Lincoln in 1860. Very early in the war he led a brief reconnaissance outside the Washington defenses but had to fall back in disorder after being ambushed by Confederates near Vienna. Early in 1862 Schenck saw action under Frémont at Cross Keys.
57. Patchan, *Second Manassas*, 12.
58. *Ibid.*, 14.
59. *Ibid.*, 14–15.
60. Glatthaar, 162.
61. Henry Hill and Henry House Hill are used interchangeably.
62. Wert, *Longstreet*, 177.
63. Alexander, *Fighting for the Confederacy,* 201.
64. Patchan, *Second Manassas*, 20–22; much of my research about the fight across Chinn Ridge is derived from the intense and detailed writing of Scott Patchan, one of the few Civil War historians who has closely examined that portion of Second Manassas.
65. *Ibid.*, 23.
66. Wert, *Longstreet*, 177.
67. Patchan, *Second Manassas*, 25.
68. *Ibid.*, 30–31.
69. *Ibid.*, 37.
70. *Ibid.*, 38; see Chapter 14.
71. Patchan, *Second Manassas*, 41.
72. *Ibid.*, 4. For this attack Hood had three command responsibilities; He was the *de facto* field commander for Longstreet's counterattack; he commanded his division; and he commanded his own brigade.
73. Patchan, *Second Manassas*, 43.
74. *Ibid.*, 48.
75. *Ibid.*, 52.
76. *Ibid.*, 49.
77. While Schenck, a former Congressman, was recovering from his wounds, he was re-elected to Congress where he became chairman of the committee on military affairs. Col. Fletcher Webster, the last surviving son of Daniel Webster, was another Chinn Ridge casualty, being mortally wounded as his regiment was being overrun by a Mississippi regiment.
78. Patchan, *Second Manassas*, 69–70.
79. *Ibid.*, 79.
80. *Ibid.*, 79.
81. *Ibid.*, 87.
82. *Ibid.*, 86–87.
83. *Ibid.*, 90.
84. *Ibid.*, 104.
85. *Ibid.*, 104.
86. Wert, *Longstreet*, 177.
87. *Ibid.*, 104–06.
88. Slotkin, 123.
89. Wert, *Longstreet*, 178.
90. Reid, Brian Holden. *America's Civil War: The Operational Battlefield 1861–1863* (2008) New York: Prometheus Books.

## Chapter 13

1. Much of the material in this chapter is derived from two sources: Welker, David A. *Tempest at Ox Hill: The Battle of Chantilly* (2002) Cambridge: Da Capo Press, and Taylor, Paul. *He Hath Loosed the Fateful Lightning: The Battle of Ox Hill (Chantilly) September 1, 1862* (2003) Shippensburg, PA: White Mane Books, two of the few extended treatments of this battle.
2. Slotkin, Richard. *The Long Road to Antietam: How the Civil War Became a Revolution* (2012) New York: Liveright Publishing, 125.
3. Welker, 41.
4. Taylor, 17.
5. Freeman, Douglas Southall. *Lee's Lieutenants: A Study in Command Volume II Cedar Mountain to Chancellorsville* (1943) New York: Scribner, 128.
6. Welker, 125.
7. *Ibid.*, 87.
8. *Ibid.*, 87.
9. Taylor, 18–19.
10. *Ibid.*, 24–25.
11. Welker, 126.
12. Taylor, 22.
13. *Ibid.*, 22.
14. Welker, 87.
15. Taylor, 24.
16. Welker, 101–02.
17. Taylor, 30.
18. *Ibid.*, 30.
19. Welker, 103.
20. Taylor, 36.
21. *Ibid.*, 38.
22. *Ibid.*, 41.
23. Welker, 125.
24. Although appointed as a major general Reno's appointment had not yet been confirmed meaning that he was under ranked to command a corps. Additionally the 9th Corps was normally commanded by Ambrose Burnside who had been bumped up to command a wing.
25. Welker, 63.
26. *Ibid.*, 67.
27. *Ibid.*, 71.
28. Welker, 113; Slolkin, 126. It may have also been possible that many soldiers no longer had decent shoes.

29. Taylor, 45.
30. Ibid., 40.
31. Welker, 135.
32. Ibid., 136.
33. Taylor, 51.
34. Ibid., 154.
35. Welker, 149.
36. Welker, 161; Taylor, 63.
37. Welker, 169; Taylor, 58–59.
38. Taylor, 59.
39. Ibid., 74.
40. Welker, 175.
41. Welker, 178; Freeman, *Lee's Lieutenants*, 134–35.
42. Taylor, 83.
43. Ibid., 84.
44. Welker, 185–86.
45. Ibid., 189.
46. Taylor, 100.
47. Apparently Pope rode past the intersection of the Warrenton Turnpike and Ox Road without paying any attention to the fighting that almost certainly could be heard as he passed.
48. Taylor, 13.
49. Rafuse, Ethan S. *McClellan's War* (2005) Bloomington: Indiana University Press, 264.
50. Ibid., 269.
51. Ibid., 270. Strictly based upon combat command credentials and experience, Fitz-John Porter might have been the most capable candidate for appointment as army commander. However his close association with McClellan, together with questions about his commitment to assist Pope at Bull Run, removed him from any serious consideration.
52. Taylor, 121.
53. Welker, 218.
54. Freeman, *Lee's Lieutenants*, 133–34.
55. Taylor, 110.
56. Freeman, Douglas Southall, *R.E. Lee, A Biography Vol. II* (1934, 1936) New York: Scribner, 349.
57. Taylor, 108–09.
58. Welker, 209–10.
59. Ibid., 211.
60. Ibid., 212.
61. Ibid., 214.

## Chapter 14

1. McPherson, James M. *Crossroads of Freedom: Antietam* (2002) Oxford: Oxford University Press, 100.
2. Castel, Albert with Brooks D. Simpson. *Victors in Blue: How Union Generals Fought the Confederates, Battled Each Other, and Won the Civil War* (2011) Lawrence: University Press of Kansas, 113.
3. Slotkin, Richard. *The Long Road to Antietam: How the Civil War Became a Revolution* (2012) New York: Liveright Publishing, 111. Buell, Thomas B. *The Warrior Generals: Combat Leadership in the Civil War* (1997) New York: Three Rivers Press, 122, contends there was no good reason to warrant an invasion of Maryland at that time and under those circumstances.
4. Freeman, Douglas Southall, *R.E. Lee, A Biography Vol. II* (1934, 1936) New York: Scribner, 350.
5. McPherson, *Crossroads*, 89.
6. Eicher, David J. *The Longest Night: A Military History of the Civil War* (2001) New York: Simon & Schuster, 336–35.
7. McPherson, *Crossroads*, 102.
8. Alexander, Bevin. *Robert E. Lee's Civil War* (1998) Holbrook, MA: Adams Media, 83.
9. McPherson, *Crossroads*, 106.
10. Alexander, Ted. *The Battle of Antietam: The Bloodiest Day* (2011) Charleston, SC: The History Press, 21.
11. McPherson, *Crossroads*, 108.
12. Ibid., 111.
13. Most accounts say that knowledge of McClellan's possession of S.O. 191 was conveyed to Lee via Stuart but Freeman discounts these accounts because no Confederate officer mentions the discovery in an official report. See Freeman, *Lee Biography Vol. II*, fn 72, p. 369, who speculates that Lee was not aware of the Federals' discovery of S.O. 191 until after McClellan released his preliminary official report.
14. McPherson, *Crossroads*, 86–7.
15. See Chapter 11 for a brief review of Hooker's early Civil War experience.
16. Nofi, Albert A. *A Civil War Treasury: Being a Miscellany of Arms & Artillery, Facts & Figures, Legends & Lore, Muses & Minstrels, Personalities & People* (1992) Edison, NJ: Castle Books, 156.
17. Slotkin, 98.
18. Alexander, Ted, *Antietam*, 31.
19. Wittenberg, Eric J. *The Union Cavalry Comes of Age: Hartwood Church to Brandy Station, 1863* (2003) Washington, D.C.: Potomac Books, 15–16.
20. Alexander, Ted, 36.
21. Wert, Jeffry D. *The Sword of Lincoln: The Army of the Potomac* (2005) New York: Simon & Schuster, 151.
22. Wert, *The Sword*, 151.
23. Cox was a former Ohio politician who was a legitimate authority on several matters.
24. Rafuse, Ethan S. *McClellan's War* (2005) Bloomington: Indiana University Press, 296.
25. Eicher, *Longest Night*, 343.
26. Wert, *The Sword*, 152–53.
27. Alexander, Ted, *Antietam*, 22.
28. McPherson, *Crossroads*, 111.
29. Lee's first retreat since assuming command four months earlier.
30. Freeman, *Lee Biography Vol. II*, fn 72, 372.
31. McPherson, *Crossroads*, 112.
32. McPherson, *Crossroads*, 110.
33. Alexander, Ted, *Antietam*, 23.
34. Slotkin, 217; McPherson, *Crossroads*, 112.
35. McPherson, *Crossroads*, 113.
36. Rafuse, 298.
37. Ibid., 303.
38. Wert, *The Sword*, 154–155.
39. Slotkin, 222.
40. Ibid., 114.
41. Rafuse, 307.
42. Alexander, Bevin, *Lee's Civil War*, 93; see also Buell, 115.
43. Eicher, *Longest Night*, 347–48.
44. Rafuse, 308.
45. Ibid., 308.
46. McClellan's decision not to attack on the 16th remains a matter of controversy. For instance Eicher, *Longest Night*, 348, states "...lacking the initiative, McClellan abandoned a golden opportunity." Alexander, Bevin, *Lee's Civil War*, 96–97, argues that the Young Napoleon should have utilized a classic tactic of Napoleon Bonaparte by getting around to Lee's rear to cut off Lee's

retreat route to Boteler's Ford to the east. On the other hand, Buell, 116, also maintains "If McClellan had hit Lee with a full-scale coordinated attack ... the massed power would have overwhelmed and destroyed the whole of Lee's emaciated army."

47. Eicher, *Longest Night,* 349.
48. Ted Alexander, the chief historian at the Antietam National Battlefield, characterizes McClellan's battle plan as "complicated and confusing." Ted also notes that McClellan also failed to convene a council of war or to otherwise provide any meaningful coordination to his corps commanders. *Antietam,* 55,56.
49. McPherson, *Crossroads,*119.
50. Buell; see also Eicher, *Longest Night,* 349.
51. McPherson, *Crossroads,*119.
52. Oliver Wendell Holmes, Jr, future Supreme Court Justice, was one of the wounded mistakenly left to die from this battle.
53. McPherson, *Crossroads,*122.
54. Rafuse, 320. One Southern regiment was led by Col. John B. Gordon, 30, who had been wounded four times before being left for dead. His life was saved because he was bleeding from a head wound into his cap that leaked because of bullet holes. Otherwise it is likely he would have drowned in his own blood. Also while the battle of Bloody Lane raged McClellan transferred a 5th Corps brigade commander, Winfield Scott Hancock, 38, to division command in the 2nd Corps thus beginning a relationship that would eventually define the 2nd Corps.
55. McPherson, *Crossroads,*124; Rafuse, 321.
56. Rafuse, 322.
57. Wert, *The Sword,*167.
58. The 9th Corps had been augmented by the Kanawha Division from West Virginia. This division had the distinction of containing two future presidents, Rutherford B. Hayes and William McKinley. The Kanawha Division was commanded by Jacob. B. Cox. Technically Cox has succeeded Burnside as commander of the 9th Corps when the latter became wing commander for the South Mountain campaign. Burnside should have been reverted to corps commander when his wing was dissolved by placing Hooker to the north end of the Antietam battlefield but Burnside was in a snit about being so demoted and tried to act as though he was still in command of a one corps wing.
59. McPherson, *Crossroads,*125.
60. *Ibid.,* 128.
61. *Ibid.,* 116.
62. Alexander, Ted, *Antietam,* 37.
63. McPherson, *Crossroads,*116.
64. Frye, Dennis E. *Antietam Revealed: The Battle of Antietam and the Maryland Campaign as You Have Never Seen It Before* (2004) Collingswood, NJ: C.W. Historicals, 135.
65. *Ibid.,* 129.
66. Wert, *The Sword,*170.
67. Buell, 120.
68. Rafuse, 329.
69. Slotkin, 352–53.
70. Frye, 136, citing O.R. 19 (1): 620.
71. Slotkin, 353.
72. Frye, 140, citing O.R. 19 (1): 325, 333.
73. Rafuse, 329.
74. Frye, 138, citing O.R. 19 (1): 68; (2): 626–627.
75. *Ibid.,* citing O.R. 19 (1): 821; (2): 626–627.
76. Slotkin, 353.
77. Rafuse, 329.
78. Rafuse, 330; Frye, 140, citing O.R. 19 (2): 330.
79. *Ibid.,* 330.
80. Slotkin, 253.
81. Rafuse, 330.
82. Frye, 139, citing O.R. 19 (1): 982.
83. Wert, *The Sword,*171.
84. Lincoln, Stanton, and Halleck had reason to feel some progress was being made in the overall Federal effort. As noted elsewhere Rosecrans handed Van Dorn and Price a bloody repulse at Corinth while in Kentucky Buell was about to start chasing Bragg after the latter blundered into Perryville.
85. Frye, 141, citing O.R. 19 (2): 625, 626, 627.
86. *Ibid.,* 141, citing O.R. 19 (2): 633.
87. Until advised by some of his political supporters to take a more positive stance, McClellan's view of the Emancipation Proclamation was that it was "an accursed doctrine as that of servile insurrection."
88. Frye, 148, citing O.R. 19 (2): 354–355.
89. Rafuse, 338.
90. Slotkin, 358–59.
91. On the other hand McClellan's cavalry played an almost non-existent role during the battle itself. While more than 2,000 Union soldiers lost their lives that bloody single day the cavalry lost only four lives.
92. Frye, 156, citing O.R. 19 (2): 52–54.
93. *Ibid.,* 156, citing O.R. 19 (2): 52–54.
94. *Ibid.,* 156, citing O.R. 19 (2): 52–54, 415.
95. *Ibid.,* 156.
96. Rafuse, 351.
97. *Ibid.,* 352.
98. Slotkin, 388–89.
99. *Ibid.*
100. E.g., "...operate upon the enemy's communications as much as possible without exposing your own."
101. Rafuse, 354.
102. Frye, 151, citing O.R. 19 (2): 442–43.
103. Rafuse, 358.
104. Slotkin, 389–90.
105. Frye, 157–58, citing O.R. 19 (2): 485.
106. Rafuse, 360.
107. Frye, 159, citing O.R. 19 (2): 485–86.
108. The Young Napoleon still preferred to try another Peninsula campaign, which presumably could not start until the next spring.
109. McPherson, *Crossroads,*152.
110. Rafuse, 361.
111. Frye, 160, citing O.R. 19 (2): 496.
112. *Ibid.,* 160, citing O.R. 19 (2): 497.
113. Slotkin, 390.
114. Frye, 159, citing O.R. 19 (2): 685–86.
115. Slotkin, 390–91.
116. Buell, 122.
117. Eicher, *Longest Night,* 363.
118. McPherson, *Crossroads,*155; Freeman, *Lee Biography Vol. II,* Chap XXVIII, provides a extensive review of Lee's strategic and tactic decisions during the Maryland campaign.
119. Wert, *The Sword,*171.
120. Rafuse, 328.
121. *Ibid.,* 332.
122. Reid, Brian Holden. *America's Civil War: The Operational Battlefield 1861-1863* (2008) New York: Prometheus Books, 196.
123. Wert, *The Sword,*172. Albert Castel and Brooks

Simpson forcefully argue that although Antietam was "… an incomplete victory, it was one of the most, if not *the* most, decisive victories of that war." Castel with Simpson, 117. However it appears these gentlemen are using "decisive" manner than used elsewhere in this book. Specifically Castel and Simpson seem to be using decisive to mean influential or momentous.

124. Rafuse, 342.
125. This chief of staff, Thomas Keys, was no ordinary staff officer. Indeed some considerer Keys as an "evil genius" who was responsible for much of the political intrigue that permeated McClellan's staff.
126. McPherson, *Crossroads*,152.
127. A few days earlier Lincoln also fired Buell for basically the same reason of failing to vigorously march after and fight Bragg.
128. Freeman, *Lee Biography Vol. II*, 462.
129. Anders, Curt. *Injustice on Trial: Second Bull Run, General Fitz John Porter's Court-Martial, and the Schofield Board Investigation That Restored His Good Name* (2002) Zionsville, IN: Guild Press/Emmis Publishing, 82–83.
130. Taaffe, Stephen R. *Commanding the Army of the Potomac* (2006) Lawrence: University Press of Kansas, 58.
131. Anders, 408.

## Chapter 15

1. See Chapter 5.
2. Wittenberg, Eric J. *The Union Cavalry Comes of Age: Hartwood Church to Brandy Station, 1863* (2003) Washington, D.C.: Potomac Books, 7–8.
3. Guelzo, Allen C. *Gettysburg: The Last Invasion* (2013) New York: Alfred A. Knopf, 52.
4. Castel, Albert with Brooks D. Simpson. *Victors in Blue: How Union Generals Fought the Confederates, Battled Each Other, and Won the Civil War* (2011) Lawrence: University Press of Kansas, 174. See also Chapter 11.
5. Wittenberg, *Union Cavalry*, 13–14.
6. *Ibid.*, 3.
7. Dan Sickles replaced Stoneman as commander of the 3rd Corps.
8. Wert, Jeffry D. *The Sword of Lincoln: The Army of the Potomac* (2005) New York: Simon & Schuster, 223.
9. *Ibid.*, 224.
10. Wittenberg, *Union Cavalry*, 26–27.
11. *Ibid.*, 28.
12. Beattie, 9.
13. Wittenberg, *Union Cavalry*, 18.
14. *Ibid.*, 48.
15. *Ibid.*, 56.
16. *Ibid.*, 57.
17. Wert, *The Sword*, 228.
18. In approving the retaliatory raid Hooker said, "If you do [succeed] there will likely be some dead cavalrymen lying about." This statement has been misinterpreted as "Who ever saw a dead cavalryman?" *Ibid.*, 62.
19. Wittenberg, *Union Cavalry*, 71.
20. Beattie, 9.
21. *Ibid.*, 9.
22. Wittenberg, *Union Cavalry*, 96.
23. *Ibid.*, 98.
24. *Ibid.*, 99.
25. *Ibid.*, 101.
26. After the war Porter Alexander observed, "On the whole I think this plan was decidedly the best strategy conceived in any of the campaigns ever set on foot against us." *Fighting for the Confederacy: The Personal Recollections of Edward Porter Alexander,* Edited by Gary C. Gallagher (1989) Chapel Hill: The University of North Carolina Press, 195
27. Walsh, George. *"Those Damn Horse Soldiers": True Tales of the Civil War Cavalry* (2006) New York: Forge, 151.
28. *Ibid.*, 152.
29. Wittenberg, *Union Cavalry*, 178.
30. *Ibid.*, 180.
31. *Ibid.*, 184.
32. *Ibid.*, 143.
33. Castle and Simpson, 176.
34. George Meade observed that it was one thing for a subordinate to "talk very big," as Hooker had done, but "quite a different thing, acting when you are responsible" for an entire army. Wert, *The Sword*, 237.
35. Wittenberg, *Union Cavalry*, 185.
36. *Ibid.*, 185–86.
37. Castle and Simpson, 176.
38. Wittenberg, *Union Cavalry*, 187.
39. Wittenberg, *Union Cavalry*, 188; Walsh, 153. Averill was dispatched to Wheeling WV to take command of a rag tag cavalry unit that Averill rehabilitated to the point that it was able to join Sheridan's army in the Shenandoah in 1864.
40. John McIntosh, a Florida native, was the older brother of James McIntosh, a West Point graduate and Indian fighter, who was killed at Pea Ridge while fighting for the Confederacy.
41. In addition to blaming Stoneman, Hooker also made scapegoats out of O. O. Howard for the failure of his corps to hold the right flank against Jackson's flank attack and John Sedgwick for his failure to advance from Fredericksburg toward Chancellorsville. See Wert, *The Sword*, 255.
42. Castle and Simpson, 177.
43. Guelzo, 19.
44. Walsh, 153.
45. *Ibid.*, 154.
46. *Ibid.*, 159.
47. *Ibid.*, 159.
48. *Ibid.*, 256.
49. *Ibid.*, 256.
50. *Ibid.*, 159.
51. Reid, Brian Holden. *America's Civil War: The Operational Battlefield 1861–1863* (2008) New York: Prometheus Books, 268.
52. Beattie, 18.
53. *Ibid.*, 26.
54. *Ibid.*, 25.
55. Wert, *The Sword*, 260.
56. Coddington, Edwin B. *The Gettysburg Campaign: A Study in Command* (1968) New York: Touchstone, 51.
57. Not only was Culpeper County conveniently located as a staging area for a possible invasion to Northern territory it was an excellent region for Stuart to feed and fatten his horses.
58. For some reasons not very clear, Jones and Stuart had an acrimonious relationship dating back to 1861 or 1862. Upon learning that Lee had ordered his brigade be transferred to Stuart's division Jones sent a letter to Secretary of War Sedden to resign his commission

rather than to serve under Stuart. Sedden ignored Jones' letter.

59. Freeman, Robert Southall. *R.E. Lee: A Biography Volume III* (1935, 1936) New York: Scribner's Sons, 30; Beattie, 6.
60. Coddington, 56. These reviews were held on the farm or an avowed Unionist.
61. As evidence of his distain toward Stuart, Jones's brigade did not participate, Jones acting as though he was oblivious to the spectacle.
62. Coddington, 55.
63. Beattie, 20.
64. Walsh, 163.
65. Coddington, 55.
66. Beattie, 34.
67. Walsh, 164.
68. Freeman, *Lee Biography Volume III*, 32, refers to Brandy Station, also known as Fleetwood Hill, as the "greatest cavalry engagement of the entire war."
69. Walsh, 166.
70. Ibid., 168.
71. Ibid., 168.
72. Freeman, *Lee Biography Volume III*, 32.
73. Wert, *The Sword*, 262.

## *Chapter 16*

1. Lee's own appraisal of Charlottesville was that his army lost 13,000 men, failed to gain any ground, and was unable to pursue the enemy. Stackpole, Edward J. *They Met at Gettysburg 3rd Edition* (1982) Harrisburg: Stackpole Books, 1–2; See also Guelzo, Allen C. *Gettysburg: The Last Invasion* (2013) New York: Alfred A. Knopf, 19–20.
2. Bowden, Scott & Ward, Bill. *Last Chance for Victory: Robert E. Lee and the Gettysburg Campaign* (2001) Cambridge: Da Capo Press, 40–41.
3. Bowden & Ward, 41.
4. Despite the name Lee gave to his army, its majority was composed of officers and men from several other Southern states. Longstreet was from Georgia but otherwise a disproportionate number of higher ranking officers were Virginians, a situation that caused some discord among officers and governors of other states.
5. Wert, Jeffry D. *The Sword of Lincoln: The Army of the Potomac* (2005) New York: Simon & Schuster, 262.
6. Coddington, Edwin B. *The Gettysburg Campaign: A Study in Command* (1968) New York: Touchstone, 4–5; Stackpole, 14; Guelzo, Allen C. *Gettysburg: The Last Invasion* (2013) New York: Alfred A. Knopf; 20.
7. Brown, Kent Masterson. *Retreat from Gettysburg: Lee, Logistics, & the Pennsylvania Campaign* (2005) Chapel Hill: The University of North Carolina Press, 18.
8. Wert, *The Sword*, 259; Guelzo, 34.
9. Lee was also coy, if not outright deceitful, with Davis and Secretary of War Seddon about plans to move into Northern territory. It was not until Lee met with Davis and Seddon on May 14, 1863, that they quit pressuring Lee to send some of his troops to the West to reinforce Joe Johnston, presumably because Lee at last disclosed his intentions to invade Northern territory.
10. Bowden & Ward, 50.
11. Bowden & Ward, 49.
12. Cleaves, Freeman. *Meade of Gettysburg* (1960) Norman: University of Oklahoma Press, 85.
13. Kreiser, Lawrence A., Jr. *Defeating Lee: A History of the Second Corps, Army of the Potomac* (2011) Bloomington: Indiana University Press, 59.
14. Taaffe, 103–04.
15. Kreiser, 59.
16. Ibid., 61.
17. Wert, *The Sword,* 167.
18. Ibid., 180.
19. Work, David. *Lincoln's Political Generals* (2009) Urbana: University of Illinois Press, 18–19.
20. Edwin Stanton was his lead defense counsel. His victim was the son of Francis Scott Key, Philip Barton Key, whom Sickles accused of having an affair with his wife. Sickles was further, and more severely, scandalized for taking her back following his acquittal.
21. Trudeau, Noah Andre. *Gettysburg: A Testing of Courage* (2002) New York: Perennial, 109.
22. Taaffe, 85–86.
23. Wert, *The Sword,* 51.
24. See Chapter 14.
25. Taaffe, 65.
26. Castel and Simpson, 180.
27. Taaffe, 75–76.
28. Wert, *The Sword,* 251.
29. Taaffe, 75–76.
30. See Chapter 14.
31. Taaffe, 87.
32. Wert, *The Sword,* 246.
33. Ibid., 249.
34. See Chapter 14.
35. Wert, *The Sword,* 255.
36. See Chapter 13.
37. Taaffe, 89.
38. Wert, *The Sword,* 221.
39. Ibid., 239.
40. Ibid., 241.
41. Taaffe, 52.
42. Trudeau, *Gettysburg: A Testing,* 222.
43. Castel, Albert with Brooks D. Simpson. *Victors in Blue: How Union Generals Fought the Confederates, Battled Each Other, and Won the Civil War* (2011) Lawrence: University Press of Kansas, 177.
44. Coddington, 37.
45. Ibid., 45.
46. Beattie, Dan. *Brandy Station 1863: First Steps towards Gettysburg* (2008) Oxford: Osprey Publishing, 82.
47. Duffié was another example of the Peter Principle that was prevalent throughout both sides in the Civil War.
48. Beattie, 82.
49. Stackpole, 14.
50. Lincoln's characterization.
51. Wert, *The Sword,* 262; Guelzo, 62.
52. Brown, 18.
53. Guelzo, 81.
54. Beattie, 83.
55. Ibid., 84.
56. Ibid., 84.
57. Ibid., 85.
58. Bowden & Ward, 101.
59. Stackpole, 40.
60. Brown, 19.
61. Wert, *The Sword,* 264.
62. Stackpole, 45.
63. Bowden & Ward, 105.
64. Wert, Jeffry D. *Cavalryman of the Lost Cause: A*

## Notes—Chapter 16

*Biography of J.E.B. Stuart* (2008) New York: Simon & Schuster, 260.
65. Ibid., 259.
66. Bowden & Ward, 114.
67. Walsh, George. *"Those Damn Horse Soldiers": True Tales of the Civil War Cavalry* (2006) New York: Forge, 172; Brown, 19. The relationship among Stuart, Jones, and Robertson was vitriolic, to say the least. Starting in 1862 Jones had developed an intense hatred for Stuart, which Stuart reciprocated in part, while Stuart considered Robertson to the "the most troublesome man I ever had to work with." Although Jones was senior in rank to Robertson, Stuart nevertheless assigned Robertson to have overall command of these two brigades.
68. These raids being his ride around McClellan during the Peninsula campaign in the spring of 1862 and the ride around McClellan after Antietam in September 1863.
69. Walsh, 172.
70. Bowden & Ward, 119.
71. Stackpole, 52.
72. Bowden & Ward, 121.
73. However Lee's orders had been to cross the Potomac "as soon after June 24 as practicable," meaning that Stuart was already running three days late.
74. Walsh, 172–73.
75. Bowden & Ward, 122.
76. Stackpole, 54.
77. Beattie, 21.
78. Castel and Simpson, 178.
79. Stackpole, 40, speculates that Lee realized the Lincoln would never permit Washington to be exposed in the manner suggested by Hooker. Porter Alexander wrote "…the Federals were ridiculously & insanely afraid of our capturing Washn. City; … Gen. Lee appreciated their weakness, and boldly played upon it—indeed I think he must sometimes have enjoyed very hearty laughs over his successful but marvelous audacity in practicing on the enemy's fears." Alexander, Edward Porter. *Fighting for the Confederacy: The Personal Recollections of Edward Porter Alexander,* Edited by Gary C. Gallagher (1989) Chapel Hill: The University of North Carolina Press, 276–77.
80. Wert, *The Sword,* 265.
81. Trudeau, *Gettysburg: A Testing,* 93.
82. Stackpole, 41.
83. Wert, *The Sword,* 267.
84. Guelzo, 28–19.
85. Cleaves, *Meade of Gettysburg,* 123.
86. Reid, Brian Holden. *America's Civil War: The Operational Battlefield 1861–1863* (2008) New York: Prometheus Books, 279.
87. Stackpole, 43.
88. Cleaves, *Meade of Gettysburg,* 124.
89. Castel and Simpson, 180.
90. One Union officer described Meade as a "grumpy, stern, severe and admirable soldier."
91. Coddington, 210.
92. Wert, *The Sword,* 269; Coddington, 214.
93. Cleaves, *Meade of Gettysburg,* 129.
94. Ibid., 129.
95. Wert, *The Sword,* 103.
96. Taaffe, 111.
97. Ibid., 112.
98. Stackpole, 43; Cleaves, *Meade of Gettysburg,* 125.
99. Stackpole, 82.
100. Castel and Simpson, 180. This information was an example of the intelligence gathered by a network of scouts, or spies, that had been established and organized by the Federal administration.
101. Coddington, 219. Butterfield, who had risen from the enlisted ranks, had led a brigade before being wounded at Gaines' Mill where he had won the Medal of Honor. Subsequently Butterfield commanded the 5th Corps at Fredericksburg.
102. Trudeau, *Gettysburg: A Testing,* 118.
103. Coddington, 236.
104. Wert, *The Sword,* 270–71.
105. Coddington, 240.
106. Stackpole, 54–55.
107. Walsh, 174.
108. Stackpole, 56. Stackpole speculates that Stuart might have rewritten the history of Gettysburg had he tried to force his way through Kilpatrick.
109. Walsh, 176.
110. Trudeau, *Gettysburg: A Testing,* 157.
111. Alexander, *Fighting,*228.
112. Stackpole, 48–49. Stackpole also argues that it was not for want of cavalry that hampered Lee but instead it was Stuart's personal absence that handicapped Lee. It might be debatable whether the two independent brigades would have been of much use as eyes and ears to Lee since both were essentially foraging units. Some regarded one such brigade, led by Jenkins, as better horse thieves than cavalry.
113. The "scout" was a spy named Henry T. Harrison employed by Longstreet. Bowden & Ward, 142; Trudeau, *Gettysburg: A Testing,* 100, 114–15. Coddington, 181. After being married in 1863, Harrison disappeared into the Montana Territory only to reemerge in 1900 long after he had been declared dead.
114. Wert, *The Sword,* 273; Brown, 20.
115. Stackpole, 58.
116. Walsh, 176.
117. Bowden & Ward, 420.
118. Castel and Simpson, 181.
119. Brown, 23.
120. Bowden & Ward, 146.
121. Brown, 22; Bowden & Ward, 146.
122. Coddington, 206.
123. Stackpole, 24; in addition to Ewell's success in gathering badly needed supplies and foodstuffs, Imboden's cavalry was also gathering a tremendous amount of loot. Kent Brown estimates that while in Pennsylvania "Lee's army seized between 45,000 and 50,000 head of cattle, about 35,000 head of sheep, and thousands of hogs." Brown, 28. Additionally Brown reports that "Some free African Americans were seized by Lee's troops during their foraging operations in Pennsylvania." Ibid., 31. See also Guelzo, 73–74, "To have left Pennsylvania's blacks in undisturbed freedom would have been tantamount to denying the validity of the whole Confederate enterprise."
124. Coddington, 192–193.
125. Bowden & Ward, 138. This statement was remembered by Isaac Trimble, a veteran general who sometimes served as one of Lee's staff officers, a staff that was notoriously undermanned. See also Guelzo, 78–79.
126. Wert, *The Sword,* 274.
127. Walsh, 205.
128. Heth resigned as a captain in the Regular Army to be commissioned at the same rank in the Confederate

army. After serving in western Virginia and being promoted to brigadier general Heth was transferred to Bragg's army in the west where he commanded a division before Lee had him transferred back to Lee's command.

129. The story about going to Gettysburg might be more legend than factual. Edwin Coddington noted that Heth's battle report talked about "feeling the enemy" and it was not until several years later that Heth claimed he had gone "to get shoes, not to fight." Coddington, 219.

130. Trudeau, *Gettysburg: A Testing*,140–41. Although Trudeau acknowledges Hill's answer to Heth's request to go to Gettysburg, Trudeau suggests that Heth did not necessarily go to Gettysburg simply to find shoes. See also Wert, *The Sword,* 273 and Coddington, 264.

131. Alexander, *Fighting*, 231–32.

132. Wert, *The Sword,* 275.

133. Walsh, 206.

134. Wert, *The Sword,* 275.

135. Trudeau, *Gettysburg: A Testing,* 184.

136. However, General Stackpole has heaped praise upon Buford's actions, stating among other things that, "…he gave the Union army the necessary breather for Reynold's First Corps and Howard's Eleventh to reach the scene, engage the Confederates in a desperate struggle and then, falling back, to solidly occupy Cemetery Ridge, which turned out to be the keystone of the Federal defense." Stackpole, 58. In contrast, Bowden & Ward, 511–12, rank the absence of Stuart and his cavalry as the fourth most important reason for the Confederate defeat at Gettysburg.

137. Trudeau, *Gettysburg: A Testing,* 219.

138. Wert, *The Sword,* 281.

139. After a seventeen-year career in the Regular Army, Hancock was the post quartermaster in Los Angeles. Beginning in September 1861 when he was given a brigade command during the Peninsular campaign, Hancock's distinguished service propelled him through a series of increased command responsibilities until he was given command of the 2nd Corps in May 1863.

140. Trudeau, *Gettysburg: A Testing,* 244. Many of the Federal's command responsibilities and decisions of that first day are difficult to sort out. Reynolds of course had no chance to write a report but in particular Howard and Doubleday, both of whom had their own axes to grind, later wrote long, self-serving reports that are often inconsistent with the reports of others. See Coddington, 295–305.

141. Brown, 20.

142. Stackpole, 139–140.

143. Coddington, 291.

144. Trudeau, *Gettysburg: A Testing,* 248.

145. Guelzo, 216.

146. Bowden & Ward, 515; Porter Alexander, 233, had a contrary opinion stating that "I think any attack we could have made that afternoon would have failed. … Gen. Ewell thought the position too strong for assault, & Lee and Col. Long [an aide to Lee] agreed in this opinion."

147. Coddington, 280.

148. Trudeau, *Gettysburg: A Testing,* 259.

149. *Ibid.,* 247.

150. *Ibid.,* 247.

151. Guelzo, 213.

152. Stackpole, 149. There is some minor variation about this word with the other version containing the phrase "if possible,…" Trudeau, *Gettysburg: A Testing,* 247.

153. Trudeau, *Gettysburg: A Testing,* 251.

154. *Ibid.,* 252.

155. *Ibid.,* 259; Scott Bowden & Bill Ward have concluded that Ewell's failure to timely inform Lee of Culp's Hill's vulnerability and being subject to capture was the sixth largest reason for the Confederate defeat at Gettysburg.

156. *Ibid.,* 257.

157. Guelzo, 218.

158. Eicher, David J. *Gettysburg Battlefield: The Definitive Illustrated History* (2003) San Francisco: Chronicle Books, 69.

159. *Ibid.,* 69.

160. Wert, *The Sword,* 282.

161. Trudeau, *Gettysburg: A Testing,* 257.

162. Eicher, *Gettysburg Battlefield,* 71.

163. Trudeau, *Gettysburg: A Testing,* 261.

164. *Ibid.,* 261.

165. Castel and Simpson, 184.

166. Freeman, Douglas Southall, *R.E. Lee: A Biography Vol. III* (1935) New York: Scribner's, 148; while Freeman is generally considered as being the pre-eminent authority about Lee, James M. McPherson has noted that that: "Freeman portrayed a Lee almost without blemishes or warts."

167. Stackpole, 153.

168. Coddington, 321.

169. *Ibid.,* 318.

170. *Ibid.,* 321.

171. *Ibid.,* 319. Coddington opined that much of the criticism about the failure to capture Cemetery Hill is pointed at Ewell because the initial critics were Stonewall's former subordinates who contrasted Ewell with what they believe Stonewall would have done and to have criticized the lack of deployment of Hill's available units would have reflected poorly upon Lee who had been accompanying Hill.

172. Guelzo, 219–20.

173. Stackpole, 175.

174. *Ibid.,* 137.

175. Wert, *The Sword,* 206.

176. *Ibid.,* 294.

177. Taaffe, 117.

178. *Ibid.,* 117.

## Chapter 17

1. Bowden, Scott and Ward, Bill. *Last Chance for Victory: Robert E. Lee and the Gettysburg Campaign* (2001) Cambridge: Da Capo Press, 422.

2. Walsh, George. *"Those Damn Horse Soldiers": True Tales of the Civil War Cavalry* (2006) New York: Forge, 177. There are no first-hand accounts of the meeting between Stuart and Lee.

3. Freeman, Robert Southall. *R.E. Lee: A Biography Volume III* (1935, 1936) New York: Scribner's Sons, 89–92; see also Gallagher, Gary W. & Nolan, Alan T., Editors *The Myth of the Lost Cause and Civil War History* (2000) Bloomington: Indiana University Press, 40, 44.

4. Trudeau, Noah Andre. *Gettysburg: A Testing of Courage* (2002) New York: Perennial, 420.

5. Bowden & Ward, 246–47.

6. Trudeau, *Gettysburg: A Testing,* 420.

7. The legendary advance to the Confederacy's "High Tide" was led by Lewis Armistead who is portrayed

in various paintings with his hat atop the tip of his sword before being mortally wounded at the Federal lines under the command of Winfield Scott Hancock. A little more than two years earlier, when Hancock and Armistead were still posted in California, Mrs. Hancock gave a farewell dinner prior to the departures of her guests to their respective armies.

8. Bowden & Ward, 424. Although much attention has always been paid to Longstreet's delay in getting started on Day Two there were several other critical issues. For instance Freeman, *Lee Biography Volume III*, 102, declares that, "The whole of the three days' battle produced no more tragic might-have-been than [the] twilight engagement of the Confederate left," referring to the lack of support given to Early as he advanced toward East Cemetery Hill.

9. Freeman, *Lee Biography Volume III*, 103–05; Bowden & Ward, 424.

10. Brown, Kent Masterson. *Retreat from Gettysburg: Lee, Logistics, & the Pennsylvania Campaign* (2005) Chapel Hill: The University of North Carolina Press, 12–16.

11. Bowden & Ward, 427.

12. Trudeau, *Gettysburg: A Testing*, 421.

13. *Ibid.*, 430–31.

14. Wert, Jeffry D. *The Sword of Lincoln: The Army of the Potomac* (2005) New York: Simon & Schuster, 296.

15. Wert, *The Sword*, 295–96; Bowden & Ward, 428–30.

16. Wert, *The Sword*, 297–98.

17. Alexander, Edward Porter. *Fighting for the Confederacy: The Personal Recollections of Edward Porter Alexander*, Edited by Gary C. Gallagher (1989) Chapel Hill: The University of North Carolina Press, 281–82.

18. Bowden & Ward, 500; for a full account of Imboden's recollection see Alexander, *Fighting*, 279–80.

19. Alexander, *Fighting*, 283.

20. Prior to the Civil War Pickett's most notable feat was occupying an island whose ownership was disputed with Great Britain. Pickett was immediately commissioned as a Confederate colonel upon resigning as a captain in the Regular Army in June 1861. After being wounded at Gaines's Mill, Pickett returned to command a division in Longstreet's corps during the Antietam campaign.

21. Castel, Albert with Brooks D. Simpson. *Victors in Blue: How Union Generals Fought the Confederates, Battled Each Other, and Won the Civil War* (2011) Lawrence: University Press of Kansas, 187.

22. Wert, *The Sword*, 298.

23. Stackpole, Edward J. *They Met at Gettysburg* (1956) Harrisburg: Stackpole Books, 279.

24. During the attack at Brandy Station Custer's horse had panicked from all the noise and tried to take shelter next to a fence where he refused to budge. After Custer managed to pull his horse away from the fence the horse again bolted away from the battle.

25. Castel and Simpson, 186.

26. Walsh, 210. Union cavalry had been alerted by Howard's signal officers who had spotted large columns of Rebel cavalry moving to the Federal right, Trudeau, *Gettysburg: A Testing*, 456.

27. Trudeau, *Gettysburg: A Testing*, 456. Kilpatrick outranked Custer by a mere two weeks.

28. Stackpole, 282; Wert, *The Sword*, 303.

29. Walsh, 211–12.

30. *Ibid.*, 213.

31. *Ibid.*, 214; Edward Stackpole, 274, stated that Kilpatrick "was under the impression that or at least chose to believe that Meade was about to launch a major counterattack,..." Even so that does not justify Kilpatrick's order for a suicide charge against entrenched infantry.

32. Trudeau, *Gettysburg: A Testing*, 518.

33. And if ifs and buts were candies and nuts we'd all have a Merry Christmas.

34. Stackpole, 284.

35. Coddington, Edwin B. *The Gettysburg Campaign: A Study in Command* (1968) New York: Touchstone, 536.

36. *Ibid.*, 541–42.

37. Wittenberg, Eric, Pettruzzi, J. David, & Nugent, Michael F. *One Continuous Fight: The Retreat from Gettysburg and the Pursuit of Lee's Army of Northern Virginia, July 4–14, 1863* (2008) New York: Savas Beatie, 30; Brown, 108.

38. Coddington, 537.

39. Brown, 99.

40. *Ibid.*, 95–96.

41. *Ibid.*, 68.

42. Wittenberg et al., 1.

43. Brown, 84–86.

44. Coddington, 538.

45. Coddington, 538.

46. Wittenburg et al., 5.

47. Wittenburg et al., 6.

48. *Ibid.*, 9.

49. Brown, 118.

50. *Ibid.*, 69.

51. *Ibid.*, 29.

52. Among his many other attributes, Harmon was considered to be one of the most profane officers in the Confederacy.

53. Wittenburg et al., 49; Brown, 73.

54. Brown, 72.

55. *Ibid.*, 73.

56. Wittenburg et al., 51.

57. Coddington, 537–38.

58. Wittenburg et al., 54.

59. Brown, 69.

60. *Ibid.*, 126.

61. Wittenburg et al., 41.

62. *Ibid.*, 41.

63. *Ibid.*, 42.

64. Brown, 74.

65. Wert, *The Sword*, 305.

66. Coddington, 572.

67. Cleaves, Freeman. *Meade of Gettysburg* (1960) Norman: University of Oklahoma Press, 172.

68. Although only two Union division commanders were killed at Gettysburg, down the line another 300 Union officers were lost at Gettysburg.

69. Coddington, 535.

70. Brown, 47.

71. Wittenburg et al., 79.

72. Brown, 47.

73. Cleaves, *Meade of Gettysburg*, 173.

74. Coddington, 534.

75. Wittenburg et al., 35–36.

76. Coddington, 543; Wittenburg et al., 53.

77. Cleaves, *Meade of Gettysburg*, 172.

78. Wert, *The Sword*, 305.

79. Coddington, 547.

80. Many tourists came to Gettysburg to view the bat-

tlefield. Meade ordered that their carriages be impressed to transport the wounded back to Washington.

81. Wittenburg et al., 35.
82. Coddington, 541.
83. Wittenburg et al., 78.
84. *Ibid.*, 86.
85. Coddington, 542.
86. Wert, *The Sword*, 305.
87. Coddington, 544; Wittenburg et al., 46.
88. Coddington, 539.
89. Following infantry commands at the regiment and brigade levels Warren joined the staff of the Army of the Potomac in the Spring of 1863, becoming Chief of Engineers in June.
90. Brown's account differs slightly in that according to Brown Warren goes forward *after* Sedgwick has encountered the Confederates' rear guard. See Brown, 260.
91. Wert, *The Sword*, 305.
92. Wittenburg et al., 78.
93. Cleaves, *Meade of Gettysburg*, 176.
94. Coddington, 546. Haupt continued to sharply criticize his old friend long after Meade's death, inaccurately writing among other things, "Meade's army ... was less fatigued than its enemy; ... no large supply of rations was required." Wittenburg et al., 330.
95. Brown, 124.
96. *Ibid.*, 124.
97. Wittenburg et al., 54.
98. Brown, 126.
99. *Ibid.*, 131.
100. Wittenburg et al., 52.
101. *Ibid.*, 62.
102. *Ibid.*, 62.
103. Brown, 139.
104. Coddington, 548; Wittenburg et al., 62–64. Kilpatrick's troopers also captured wagons that were carrying the personal baggage belonging to several Confederate generals, including Ewell and Early.
105. However Confederate accounts either belittled or even ignored the entire encounter.
106. Wittenburg et al., 71.
107. *Ibid.*, 74.
108. Coddington, 549, opined, "In no respect did this attack cripple Lee's army or perceptibly reduce its power to fend off any major assault Meade might be able to mount."
109. Brown, 144.
110. *Ibid.*, 181.
111. Wittenburg et al., 104.
112. *Ibid.*, 104.
113. Brown, 157.
114. *Ibid.*, 167.
115. Wittenburg et al., 93.
116. Much of the confusion and chaos stemmed from the thousands of teamsters and wagoners who were part of the enormous trains.
117. Brown, 137.
118. Wittenburg et al., 93.
119. Wittenburg et al., 25, 160–62; Brown, 91.
120. Alexander, *Fighting*, 283.
121. Brown, 259.
122. Coddington, 558.
123. Cleaves, *Meade of Gettysburg*, 175.
124. Wittenburg et al., 82.
125. Brown, 190.
126. Wittenburg et al., 86.
127. Wittenburg et al., 86; Brown, 259.
128. Wittenburg et al., 86.
129. Brown, 259.
130. *Ibid.*, 259.
131. Coddington, 549.
132. Castel and Simpson, 187, offer three basic reasons why Meade did not begin his pursuit until July 6 as follows: Organizational, logistical, and prudential.
133. Lee's main army had a retreat route of 20 miles shorter than Meade's flanking route via Middletown.
134. Wittenburg et al., 107.
135. Brown, 220.
136. *Ibid.*, 219.
137. Wittenburg et al., 108.
138. Brown, 220–30.
139. Wittenburg et al., 107–18.
140. *Ibid.*, 124.
141. Brown, 237.
142. *Ibid.*, 235.
143. *Ibid.*, 246.
144. *Ibid.*, 236–47.
145. Wittenburg et al., 134.
146. Coddington, 553.
147. Brown, 250.
148. Wittenburg et al., 134–37.
149. Brown, 254.
150. Although Imboden had performed well in cobbling together an effective defense, Stuart refused to give him any credit.
151. See Wittenburg et al., 153–54.
152. Coddington, 550.
153. Coddington, 550–51; Brown, 264.
154. Brown, 265. Brown also notes that it would be days before the subsistence and quartermaster wagons would link up with the troops and animals, most of whom had not eaten for days. To compensate, Union soldiers foraged extensively while on the march.
155. Coddington, 555.
156. *Ibid.*, 556.
157. *Ibid.*, 564.
158. Brown, 290.
159. Cleaves, *Meade of Gettysburg*, 177.
160. Wert, *The Sword*, 164.
161. *Ibid.*, 307.
162. Cleaves, *Meade of Gettysburg*, 178.
163. Alexander, *Fighting*, 271–72.
164. Not to belabor the point but the retreating Rebels continued to forage all along the way with civilians reporting "the loss of horses, cows, bulls, wagons, wheat, flour, corn, and hay…" Brown, 257.
165. *Ibid.*, 285.
166. Alexander, *Fighting*, 271.
167. Wert, *The Sword*, 307.
168. Brown, 293.
169. Cleaves, *Meade of Gettysburg*, 180.
170. Brown, 320.
171. *Ibid.*, 300–03.
172. Wittenburg et al., 209–10.
173. *Ibid.*, 223.
174. *Ibid.*, 224.
175. *Ibid.*, 225.
176. Brown, 315.
177. During this period Lee's soldiers continued to plunder by taking everything they could from area residents. For instance one household near St. James College reported the loss of 2,000 bushels of wheat,

seven horses, all their cattle, and all their bacon and ham.
178. Wittenburg et al., 237.
179. *Ibid.*, 240.
180. Brown, 320-21.
181. Freeman, *Lee Biography Volume III*, 141.
182. Wittenburg et al., 244.
183. *Ibid.*, 243.
184. Coddington, 564.
185. Wittenburg et al., 215-52; Brown, 316.
186. Wittenburg et al., 258.
187. *Ibid.*, 259.
188. Wert, *The Sword*, 307.
189. Coddington, 569-70.
190. Franks, George F., III. *Battle of Falling Waters 1863: Custer, Pettigrew and the End of the Gettysburg Campaign* (2013) Published by Author, 19.
191. *Ibid.*, 28.
192. Wittenburg et al., 271.
193. Cleaves, *Meade of Gettysburg*, 183.
194. *Ibid.*, 182.
195. Franks, 35.
196. Wittenburg et al., 284.
197. *Ibid.*, 295.
198. Franks, 74. By reproducing side-by-side accounts of reports from the Falling Waters commanders, Franks also illustrates the limitations of trying to extract specific facts from the Official Records. Reading these reports can make one wonder whether the commanders were even at the same battle.
199. Wittenburg et al., 300.
200. Coddington, 570; Wittenburg et al., 301.
201. Coddington, 571; Wittenburg et al., 286, 296.
202. Cleaves, *Meade of Gettysburg*, 185-86.
203. Coddington, 565-66.
204. Wittenburg et al., 328.
205. Wittenburg et al., 302; Castel et al., 189.
206. Guelzo, Allen C. *Gettysburg: The Last Invasion* (2013) New York: Alfred A. Knopf, 432-33.
207. It is well to recall that eight months earlier at Fredericksburg Meade was still a division commander, two levels below army command. Additionally he became army commander only because Reynolds, and probably others, had refused the appointment, and because the administration presumed that Meade, as a Pennsylvanian, would fight hard to protect the soil of that state. The appointment was not made because Meade was thought to have any grand strategic vision for winning the war.
208. Meade denied they were formal councils of war but instead were mere consultations.
209. Not only did Pleasonton's failure to amass his cavalry divisions limit the horsemen's capacity to block or at least impair Lee's retreat but Meade also complained about the lack of intelligence provided by cavalry.
210. Wittenburg et al., 336.
211. *Ibid.*, 347.
212. Cleaves, *Meade of Gettysburg*, 189.
213. According to Jeffry Wert, French's 3rd Corps "veterans despised him almost to a man calling him 'the old gin barrel,' 'a perfect ignoramious and bloat,' and 'an imbcile.'" *The Sword*, 320.
214. Cleaves, *Meade of Gettysburg*, 189.
215. *Ibid.*
216. *Ibid.*
217. *Ibid.*, 195.
218. Wert, *The Sword*, 313.
219. *Ibid.*, 314-15.
220. Wert, *The Sword*, 319.
221. *Ibid.*, 324.
222. *Ibid.*, 325.
223. *Ibid.*, 325.
224. Cleaves, *Meade of Gettysburg*, 225.
225. Wert, *The Sword*, 325-26; Huntington, 231.
226. Land, Mary. *Ben Wade*, an essay found in *For the Union: Ohio Leaders in the Civil War* edited by Kenneth W. Wheeler (1998) Columbus: Ohio State University Press.
227. Trudeau, *Gettysburg: A Testing*, 546-49.
228. See Chapter 8.
229. The Committee's report was not released until May 22, 1865 but predictably was critical of Meade. Although not much attention was paid to the report since the war was over, the criticism of Meade based upon the testimony of witnesses, specifically Hooker, Doubleday, Sickles, and Pleasonton, who were collectively well-documented, amoral, life-long prevaricators. The aggregate of their self-serving, biased testimony against Meade evidentially is the genesis of the still current canard that Meade wanted to remain at Pipe Creek, wanted to retreat after Day Two but was prevented from doing so by a vote of his corps commanders, and was confused about whether his army had repulsed the Day Three attack.
230. Cleaves, *Meade of Gettysburg*, 226.

## Chapter 18

1. Castel, Albert with Brooks D. Simpson. *Victors in Blue: How Union Generals Fought the Confederates, Battled Each Other, and Won the Civil War* (2011) Lawrence: University Press of Kansas, 280-81.
2. Prior to being appointed February 17, 1864, to head the Cavalry Bureau In Washington, Wilson had served as a topographical engineer. While at the Cavalry Bureau, Wilson had tried, without complete success, to eliminate the graft that had plagued the procurement of horses. He had also worked to see that the Spencer repeating carbine was made available to more cavalry units.
3. MGen. William B. Hazen probably had the more legitimate claim to that honor. Hazen's troops apparently reached that crest well before Sheridan's and captured 18 cannons as well as many prisoners. Nevertheless, Sheridan continued to make his claim for several years.
4. This author once served with a Marine Major who would often remind him that there was only a thin red line separating initiative from insubordination.
5. Richmond was not Grant's objective *per se*. Instead he was hoping to draw Lee out into the open where Grant anticipated that Meade would have tactical advantages on the battlefield.
6. Trudeau, Noah Andre. *Bloody Roads South: The Wilderness to Cold Harbor, May-June 1864* (2000) Baton Rouge: Louisiana State University Press, 81-82.
7. While leading a flanking movement against the Federal left, Longstreet was severely wounded in his throat and shoulder. Lee chose to replace his Old War Horse with the relatively inexperienced "Dick" Anderson as the 1st Corps commander.
8. Freeman, Robert Southall. *R.E. Lee: A Biography Volume III* (1935, 1936) New York: Scribner's Sons, 298-300, 301-03.
9. Also called Spotsylvania Court House. In addition

to the loss of Longstreet as corps commander, two days later A.P.Hill became incapacitated with the sudden onset of another illness. Lee appointed Jubal Early to replace Hill as corps commander and appointed John B. Gordon to take Early's place as division commander.

10. Trudeau, *Bloody Roads*, 113–14.
11. Wittenberg, Eric J. *Little Phil: A Reassessment of the Civil War Leadership of Philip H. Sheridan* (2002) Dulles: Brassey's, 94–95.
12. Trudeau, *Bloody Roads*, 121.
13. *Ibid.*, 192.
14. Freeman, *Lee Biography Volume III*, 327.
15. Bearrs, Edwin C. *Fields of Honor: Pivotal Battles of the Civil War* (2006) Washington, D.C.: National Geographic Society, 318.
16. Wittenberg, *Little Phil*, 31, 33.
17. Grant's report of May 26, 1860, to Halleck.
18. Trudeau, *Bloody Roads*, 267.
19. By this point in the campaign many of the veterans Federal soldiers whose enlistments were about to expire were content after their first charge to "go to the ground and refuse to charge a second and third time when ordered." Bearrs, 330. Furthermore Meade's passive-aggressive attitude meant he did little to exercise what residual command authority was left to him. As a result Meade did not bother to arrange for minimal coordination among the corps commanders.
20. Castel and Simpson, 281.
21. Halleck advised Grant, "If you expect anything from [Sigel] you will be mistaken. He will do nothing but run. He never did anything else." On the other hand, Hunter might have been "…one of the most unpleasant generals to serve on either side of the Civil War" who had the nasty habit of burning homes of adversaries. Bernstein, Steven. *The Confederacy's Last Northern Offensive: Jubal Early, the Army of the Valley and the Raid on Washington* (2011) Jefferson, NC: McFarland, 17. Wert, Jeffry. *From Winchester to Cedar Creek: The Shenandoah Campaign of 1864* (1987) Carlisle: South Mountain Press, 12.
22. Castel and Simpson, 281.
23. Freeman, *Lee Biography Volume III*, 393; Trudeau, *Bloody Roads*, 309.
24. Wittenberg, Eric J. *Glory Enough for All: Sheridan's Second Raid and the Battle of Trevilian Station* (2001) Lincoln: University of Nebraska Press, xvii.
25. One of the surgeons was quickly captured, sent to Libby Prison before being transferred to Andersonville where he died from dysentery within sixty days after being captured.
26. Wittenberg, *Glory Enough*, 217.
27. Trudeau, *Bloody Roads*, 304.
28. This is the same Baldy Smith who had defied Jeb Stuart at the Carlisle Barracks and who gained Grant's friendship for planning the Cracker Line operation that helped break the Confederate siege at Chattanooga. Trudeau, *Bloody Roads*, 313.
29. Eicher, David J. *The Longest Night: A Military History of the Civil War* (2001) New York: Simon & Schuster, 687.
30. Wert, Jeffry. *The Sword of Lincoln: The Army of the Potomac* (2005) New York: Simon & Schuster, 371.
31. Wise, once described as "lacking in moderation and judgment … one of the last great individualists in Virginia history," was Meade's brother-in-law.
32. Eicher, *Longest Night*, 689.
33. Glatthaar, 378.
34. Eicher, *Longest Night*, 689.
35. Bearrs, 339.
36. Kreiser, Lawrence A., Jr. *Defeating Lee: A History of the Second Corps, Army of the Potomac* (2011) Bloomington & Indianapolis: Indiana University Press, 198.
37. Wert, *The Sword*, 372.
38. Kreister, 200.
39. Wert, *The Sword*, 371.
40. Catton, Bruce, *A Stillness at Appomattox*, 198.
41. Glatthaar, 379; One of the harshest criticisms of Lee was written by Alan T. Nolan in *Lee Considered: General Robert E. Lee and Civil War History* (1991) Chapel Hill: The University of North Carolina Press. Among other criticisms Nolan contended that Lee "…was so committed to the offensive that he suffered grievous and irreplaceable losses that progressively limited the viability of his army." Nolan also argued that Lee unnecessarily prolonged the war, and thus cost the South many lives of its soldiers, when he refused to quit upon realizing the futility of the struggle. In retrospect, and with the advantage of 20/20 hindsight, and in light of Lee's previous comment to Early about how devastating it would be if Grant crossed the James, it may be fair to speculate whether the Confederacy could have received better terms at a lower cost of lives at this point in the war.
42. *Ibid.*, 46.
43. Freeman, *Lee Biography Volume III*, 498.
44. *Ibid.*, 498.
45. Tagg, Larry. *The Generals of Gettysburg* (1998) Cambridge: Da Capo Press, 256–58.
46. Bernstein, 17.
47. Wert, Jeffry. *From Winchester to Cedar Creek: The Shenandoah Campaign of 1864* (1987) Carlisle: South Mountain Press, 7.
48. Wert, *The Sword*, 371.
49. The Spotsylvania campaign lasted from May 7 through May 20, 1864, Grant ordered various frontal assaults including a mass attack against the "mule shoe," a salient at an angle in the Confederate line. Hancock's 2nd Corps temporarily breached the Rebel defenses, capturing thousands or Southern soldiers as well as 20 guns before reinforcements could repair the breach. While Hancock's 2nd Corps scored significant gins the other Federal corps accomplished little meaning that the Spotsylvania stalemate was prolonged until Grant ordered a withdrawal and sidled further south.
50. Bernstein, 170.
51. Patchan, Patrick C. *The Last Battle of Winchester: Phil Sheridan, Jubal Early, and the Shenandoah Valley Campaign—August 7-September 19, 1864* (2013) New York: Savas Beatie, 28.
52. Castel and Simpson, 281.
53. Bernstein, 22–30.
54. Castel and Simpson, 282. After Shiloh, Wallace was criticized, perhaps wrongly, for not getting to the main battlefield in better time. As a result he was transferred to Washington where he sat on numerous boards and commissions before becoming commander of the 8th Corps, deployed west of Washington, D.C.
55. In May 1864 Wright was appointed to command the 6th Corps to succeed John Sedgwick who was killed by a sharpshooter at Spotsylvania.
56. Because there were several soldiers and officers in Lincoln's proximity it was not clear who actually ordered Lincoln to get down. Holmes himself did not claim that

honor until sixty-seven years later when he was visiting Arlington Cemetery.
57. Bernstein, 90.
58. *Ibid.*, 94.
59. Wert, *The Sword*, 357.
60. Patchan, *Winchester*, 40.
61. Bernstein, 94.
62. *Ibid.*, 94.
63. *Ibid.*, 94.
64. *Ibid.*, 94–95.
65. *Ibid.*, 95. Upon realizing he was being relieved, Hunter ordered the burning of more houses of known secessionists, including one belonging to a cousin.
66. Bernstein, 98.
67. *Ibid.*, 99.
68. *Ibid.*, 99.
69. The four departments were Susquehanna, headed by Dan Couch, headquartered in Chambersburg, Pennsylvania; West Virginia, led by George Crook; Washington, headed by Christopher Auger; and the Middle Department, commanded by Lew Wallace.
70. Castel and Simpson, 282.
71. *Ibid.*, 284.
72. Wittenberg, *Little Phil*, 52.
73. Patchan, *Winchester*, 42.
74. Wittenberg, *Little Phil*, 106.
75. Patchan, *Winchester*, 44.
76. The circumstances leading to Hooker's earlier dismissal of Averell are described in Chapter 15.
77. Castel and Simpson, 284.
78. Wert, *From Winchester*, 22.
79. Patchan, *Winchester*, 46. Patchen notes that Crook and Averell had their differences while division commanders in the Army of West Virginia, and that Hunter also had a low opinion of Averell, factors that may have influenced Grant's approval of bypassing Averell for overall cavalry command.
80. *Ibid.*, 47–48.
81. Wert, *From Winchester*, 71.
82. Also known as Opequon Creek.
83. Bernstein, 165.
84. *Ibid.*, 155.
85. While at Martinsburg, Early found copies of telegrams about Grant's visit.
86. First Winchester occurred May 25, 1862; Second Winchester occurred June 13–15, 1863, as the Confederates were advancing toward Gettysburg.
87. Bernstein, 165; Patchan, *Winchester*, 204–05.
88. Wittenberg, *Little Phil*, 63.
89. Bernstein, 167.
90. Wheelan, Joseph. *Terrible Swift Sword: The Life of General Philip H. Sheridan* (2012) Cambridge: Da Capo Press, 112.
91. Wittenberg, *Little Phil*, 64.
92. Bernstein, 168.
93. Bernstein,168; Wittenberg, *Little Phil*, 64.
94. Bernstein, 171.
95. Upton was a graduate in the May 1861 West Point class. Although he had several commands after graduation, he really made his mark at Spotsylvania where he led his brigade heading a column of regiments through a gap. When another division failed to exploit the gap created by Upton's brigade, Upton was forced to withdraw but only after capturing more than 1,000 prisoners. Wilson claimed Upton was easily the best tactical officer of either army.
96. Bernstein, 171.
97. Wittenberg, *Little Phil*, 64.
98. *Ibid.*, 66.
99. Walsh, 346.
100. Bernstein, 174.
101. Patchan, *Winchester*, 418.
102. *Ibid.*, 421.
103. *Ibid.*, 422.
104. Wheelan, 113.
105. Wert, *From Winchester*, 103. Col.George Patton, grandfather of the legendary WW II general with the same name, was mortally wounded while urging his brigade to withstand the Federal onslaught.
106. Longacre, Edward G. *Grant's Cavalrymen—The Life and History of General James H. Wilson* (2000), Paperback Edition, Mechanicsburg, PA: Stackpole Books, 150.
107. Wheelan, 114.
108. Wittenberg, *Little Phil*, 67.
109. Bernstein, 175.
110. *Ibid.*, 165.
111. *Ibid.*, 175. The constant shifting of Southern divisions between the Valley and the trenches around Petersburg and Richmond reflected Lee's necessity of robbing Peter to pay Paul. In other words manpower losses that could not be replaced meant it was almost always necessary to weaken one sector in order to maintain enough strength in another sector. Grant also shifted units between the two campaigns but the Federal commander enjoyed the advantage of doing so from a position of numerical superiority.
112. A brief description of the geography of this area is found in Chapter 10.
113. Bernstein, 176.
114. Wert, *From Winchester*, 121.
115. Wheelan, 116.
116. Wittenberg, *Little Phil*, 68.
117. Wert, *From Winchester*, 127.
118. Wheelan, 117.
119. *Ibid.*, 117; Wert, *From Winchester*, 131.
120. Bernstein, 177.
121. Wheelan, 117.
122. Eicher, *Longest Night*, 747.
123. *Ibid.*, 747.
124. Wittenberg, *Little Phil*, 116.
125. Patchan, *Winchester*, 424.
126. Wert, *From Winchester*, 73.
127. Averell had some reason for his contention that he was relieved for political reasons. For instance Wittenberg observes that "Torbert's failure was worse," yet Torbert, while criticized, was not relieved. Wittenberg speculates that Torbert's long association with the Army of the Potomac was the reason he received preferential treatment. Wittenberg, *Little Phil*, 116.
128. Bernstein, 184.
129. *Ibid.*, 184.
130. Wert, *From Winchester*, 142.
131. *Ibid.*, 43.
132. *Ibid.*, 143.
133. Eicher, *Longest Night*, 748.
134. Bernstein, 186. Rosser resigned from West Point two weeks before graduation.
135. Wittenberg, *Little Phil*, 71.
136. Bernstein, 187.
137. *Ibid.*, 188.
138. Wert, *From Winchester*, 164.
139. Eicher, *Longest Night*, 749.
140. Wittenberg, *Little Phil*, 72.

141. Glatthhaar, 432.
142. Bernstein, 188.
143. *Ibid.*, 189.
144. *Ibid.*, 190.
145. Castel and Simpson, 287.
146. Rutherford B. Hayes, the future president, barely escaped from being captured after having his horse shot dead under him.
147. Wert, *From Winchester,* 179.
148. Bernstein, 196.
149. The record is far from complete because few after action reports from Southern officers are available. Many of the contending versions were written several years later when writers such as Gordon were anxious to put themselves in the best possible light.
150. Bohannon, Keith S. "The Fatal Halt" versus "Bad Conduct," essay in *The Shenandoah Valley Campaign of 1864,* edited by Gary W. Gallagher (2006) Chapel Hill: The University of North Carolina Press, 64.
151. Freeman, Douglas Southall. *Lee's Lieutenants: A Study in Command Volume III Gettysburg to Appomattox* (1944) New York: Scribner, 605.
152. Bernstein, 197.
153. Glatthaar, 433.
154. Bohannon, 56 *et seq.* To add further confusion about Cedar Creek, it is not clear which period of inactivity, i.e., that which occurred in the morning or that occurring in the morning, was the fatal halt.
155. Wert, *From Winchester,* 234.
156. Bernstein, 198.
157. Wert, *From Winchester,* 236.
158. Wittenberg, *Little Phil,* 78.
159. Wert, *From Winchester,* 236–37.
160. Eicher, *Longest Night,* 751.
161. Bohannon, 71.
162. Wert, *From Winchester,* 249.
163. *Ibid.*, 249–50.
164. Bernstein, 200.
165. Essay by Robert E.L. Krick in *The Shenandoah Valley Campaign of 1864,* edited by Gary W. Gallagher, 186–87.
166. William C. Davis says Breckinridge was the "most capable of the lot [of Confederate secretaries of war]. ... he was in fact the first and only functioning secretary of war the Confederacy ever had..." Davis, *The Lost Cause: Myths and Realities of the Confederacy* (1996) Lawrence: University of Kansas Press, 148.
167. Castel and Simpson, 266.
168. *Ibid.*, 267.
169. Wittenberg, *Little Phil,* 135.

## Chapter 19

1. To be sure, Lincoln continued to insist upon political some considerations as shown by the appointments of Franz Siegel and Ben Butler to important command positions.
2. Varon, Elizabeth R. *Appomattox: Victory, Defeat. And Freedom at the End of the Civil War* (2014) Oxford: Oxford University Press, 8.
3. Wittenberg, Eric J., *Little Phil: A Reassessment of the Civil War Leadership of Gen. Philip H. Sheridan* (2002) Washington, D.C.: Brassey's, 98.
4. Catton, Bruce. *A Stillness at Appomattox* (1953) New York: Anchor Books, 342.
5. Wittenberg, *Little Phil,* 99.
6. *Ibid.*, 24 *et seq.*
7. Wert, Jeffry D. *From Winchester to Cedar Creek: The Shenandoah Campaign of 1864* (1987) Carlisle: South Mountain Press, 249.
8. A couple months earlier in the aftermath of the failed Hampton Roads Conference, Ord secretly met with his old friend, James Longstreet, to formulate a proposal for a "military convention" to settle the Civil War. Although Grant expressed his willingness to "leave nothing untied" he also rejected Ord's proposal because he had no authority to address political issues. Ord and Longstreet then returned to the business of fighting.
9. Jeffry Wert describes Hancock as being a "vestige" at this point in the war. *The Sword of Lincoln: The Army of the Potomac* (2005) New York: Simon & Schuster, 392.
10. Freeman, Douglas Southall, *R.E. Lee: A Biography Vol. IV* (1935, 1936) New York: Charles Scribner's Sons, 14.
11. *Ibid.*, 17.
12. *Ibid.*, 15–16.
13. Glatthaar, Joseph T., *General Lee's Army: From Victory to Collapse* (2008) New York: Free Press, 458.
14. Freeman, *Lee Biography Vol. IV,* 17.
15. *Ibid.*, 18.
16. Catton, *Stillness at Appomattox,* 337.
17. Gallagher, Gary W., *An End and a New Beginning* from *Appomattox Court House* produced by the Division of Publications, National Park Service, 36. Davis complained that Lee's order to evacuate came as a surprise but the record seems clear that Lee had given several warnings about the peril of his position and, by extension, of the capital.
18. *Ibid.*, 36–37.
19. Wittenberg, *Little Phil,* 220–21.
20. *Ibid.*, 101.
21. Freeman, *Lee Biography Vol. IV, IV* 22.
22. Catton, *Stillness at Appomattox,* 346; Wert, *The Sword,* 399.
23. Walsh, George, *"Those Damn Horse Soldiers": True Tales of the Civil War Cavalry* (2006) New York: Forge, 415; Castel, Albert with Brooks D. Simpson. *Victors in Blue: How Union Generals Fought the Confederates, Battled Each Other, and Won the Civil War* (2011) Lawrence: University Press of Kansas, 302.
24. Wert, *The Sword,* 400. Eicher, David J., *The Longest Night: A Military History of the Civil War* (2001) New York: Simon & Schuster, 808.
25. Freeman, *Lee Biography Vol. IV,* 40.
26. Castel, Albert with Brooks D. Simpson. *Victors in Blue: How Union Generals Fought the Confederates, Battled Each Other, and Won the Civil War* (2011) Lawrence: University Press of Kansas, 303.
27. Wert, *The Sword,* 402.
28. The exact reasons for Warren's abrupt dismissal remain shrouded in some mystery. Certainly Warren's personality had caused him to become unpopular with Grant and with Meade with the former authorizing Sheridan to replace Warren for cause. By almost accounts Sheridan's dismissal of Warren seemed arbitrary and capricious, and later that evening Sheridan seemed to regret his actions. Wittenberg, *Little Phil,* 106 *et seq,* offers a detailed critique of Sheridan's actions.
29. Castel and Simpson, 303, note that Warren's replacement simply continued doing what Warren had been in the process of doing.

30. Glatthaar, 459; Freeman, *Lee Biography Vol. IV*, 46–47.
31. Alexander, Bevin. *Robert E. Lee's Civil War* (1998) Holbrook: Adams Media Corporation, 301; Freeman, *Lee Biography Vol. IV*, 49–50.
32. The Black soldiers in Weitzel's U.S.C.T. regiments were largely responsible for dousing the fires.
33. Alexander, Bevin, *Lee's Civil War*, 53–54.
34. Gallagher, 44.
35. A mystery remains why so many supplies remained in the Richmond warehouses while the troops in the trenches were starving.
36. Catton, *Stillness at Appomattox*, 364.
37. Freeman, *Lee Biography Vol. IV*, 50.
38. Glatthaar, 461.
39. Small French ovens, apparently used to bake biscuits, were discarded by the hundreds.
40. Wittenberg, *Little Phil*, 150, quoting Col. George A. "Sandy" Forsyth.
41. Varon, 9.
42. Alexander, Bevin, *Lee's Civil War*, 301.
43. Freeman, *Lee Biography Vol. IV*, 66.
44. *Ibid.*, 66.
45. Walsh, 424; Wheelan, Joseph. *Terrible Swift Sword: The Life of General Philip H. Sheridan* (2012) Cambridge: Da Capo Press, 190.
46. Varon, 9.
47. Catton, *Stillness at Appomattox*, 368.
48. Alexander, Bevin, *Lee's Civil War*, 304.
49. Alexander, Bevin, *Lee's Civil War*, 304; Wheelan, 192.
50. Gallagher, 52.
51. Also known as Paine's Cross Roads.
52. Wittenberg, *Little Phil*, 151–52.
53. Also called Sayler's Creek or Sailor's Creek.
54. Varon, 12.
55. Alexander, Bevin, *Lee's Civil War*, 305.
56. Freeman, *Lee Biography Vol. IV*, 83.
57. Alexander, Bevin, *Lee's Civil War*, 306.
58. Freeman, *Lee Biography Vol. IV*, 90.
59. Wheelan, 194.
60. Varon, 14.
61. Freeman, *Lee Biography Vol. IV*, 80, called this a "dreadful day in the history of the Army of Northern Virginia."
62. Walsh, 425; Varon, 13.
63. Freeman, *Lee Biography Vol. IV*, 84.
64. Buell, Thomas B., *The Warrior Generals: Combat Leadership in the Civil War* (1997) New York: Three Rivers Press, 417.
65. Gallagher, 56.
66. Varon, 15.
67. Wittenberg, *Little Phil*, 153.
68. Walsh, 427.
69. Freeman, *Lee Biography Vol. IV*, 111; Varon, 24.
70. Glatthaar, 462.
71. Catton, *Stillness at Appomattox*, 372.
72. Alexander, E. Porter, *Fighitng for the Confederacy: The Personal Recollections of General Edward Alexander*, Edited by Gary W. Gallagher (1889) Chapel Hill: The University of North Carolina Press, 510.
73. *Ibid.*, 309.
74. Freeman, *Lee Biography Vol. IV*, 100.
75. *Ibid.*, 104.
76. *Ibid.*, 105.
77. *Ibid.*, 113.
78. Wheelan, 198.
79. Gallagher, 65.
80. Wheelan, 198.
81. Freeman, *Lee Biography Vol. IV*, 114–15.
82. Varon, 94.
83. Alexander, Bevin, *Lee's Civil War*, 311.
84. Freeman, *Lee Biography Vol. IV*, 124.
85. *Ibid.*, 139.
86. *Ibid.*, 140. Actually these rations were those confiscated from the Rebel train carrying Confederate rations that Union cavalry had recently captured.
87. Varon, 69.
88. Lee's Farewell Address, especially the phrase about being "compelled to yield to overwhelming numbers," or a common variant that "the odds against us were too great," quickly was reiterated by countless Southern speakers and commentators to the point that it became part of Southern creed for decades, becoming an integral part of the Myth of the Lost Cause. On the other hand, other historians have concluded the North won because the government in Washington, D.C., was much more unified than was its counterpart in Richmond. This point has been made by David J. Eicher in *Dixie Betrayed: How the South Really Lost the Civil War* (2006) New York Boston: Little, Brown and Company and by David Williams in *Bitterly Divided: The South's Inner Civil War* (2008) New York: The New Press. Several other reasons for the South's defeat are discussed in Berimger, Robert E.; Hattaway, Herman; Jones, Archer; & Still, William N, Jr. *Why the South Lost the Civil War* (1986) Athens: University of Georgia Press. Lee's lament also ignored other factors such as the lack of food because planters grew too much cotton and tobacco. Closer to Lee's complaint, he also ignored problems of desertion and draft dodging as well as the half million Southerners, Blacks and Whites, who served in the Union military. See Williams.
89. Freeman, *Lee Biography Vol. IV*, 164.
90. Goss, Thomas J. *The War Within the Union High Command: Politics and Generalship During the Civil War* (2003) Lawrence: University Press of Kansas, 202.

## Chapter 20

1. Griffith, Paddy. *Battle Tactics of the Civil War* (1989) New Haven: Yale University Press, 191. In his own discourse about the lack of decisive battles Earl J. Hess also takes note of Griffith's discussion while adding further perspectives. See *Civil War Infantry Tactics Training, Combat, and Small-Unit Effectiveness* (2015) Baton Rouge: Louisiana University Press.
2. Freeman, Douglas Southall. *R.E. Lee, A Biography Vol. II* (1934, 1936) New York: Scribner, 225.
3. Reid, Brian Holden. *America's Civil War: The Operational Battlefield 1861–1863* (2008) New York: Prometheus Books, 361.
4. Varney, Frank P. *General Grant and the Rewriting of History: How the Destruction of William S. Rosecrans Influenced Our Understanding of the Civil War* (2013) El Dorado Hills: Savas Beatie, 116.
5. Einolf, Christopher J., *George Thomas: Virginian for the Union* (2007) Norman: University of Oklahoma Press, 286–87.
6. Wheelan, Joseph. *Terrible Swift Sword: The Life of General Philip H. Sheridan* (2012) Cambridge: Da Capo Press, 195.

# Bibliography

Alexander, Bevin. *How Great Generals Win* (2002) New York: W.W. Norton & Company.

———. *How Wars Are Won: The 13 Rules of War from Ancient Greece to the War on Terror* (2002) New York: Three Rivers Press.

———. *Lost Victories: The Military Genius of Stonewall Jackson* (2004) New York: Hippocrene Books.

———. *Robert E. Lee's Civil War* (1998) Holbrook, MA: Adams Media.

Alexander, Edward Porter. *Fighting for the Confederacy: The Personal Recollections of Edward Porter Alexander*. Edited by Gary C. Gallagher (1989) Chapel Hill: The University of North Carolina Press.

Alexander, Ted. *The Battle of Antietam: The Bloodiest Day* (2011) Charleston, SC: The History Press.

Anders, Curt. *Injustice on Trial: Second Bull Run, General Fitz John Porter's Court-Martial, and the Schofield Board Investigation That Restored His Good Name* (2002) Zionsville, IN: Guild Press/Emmis Publishing.

Arnold, James R. *Jeff Davis's Own: Cavalry, Comanches, and the Battle for the Texas Frontier* (2007) Edison: Castle Books.

Axelrod, Alan. *Generals South, Generals North: The Commanders of the Civil War Reconsidered* (2011) Guilford, CT: Lyons Press.

Bailey, Anne J. *The Chessboard of War: Sherman and Hood in the Autumn Campaigns of 1864* (2000) Lincoln: University of Nebraska Press.

Bearrs, Edwin C. *Fields of Honor: Pivotal Battles of the Civil War* (2006) Washington, D.C.: National Geographic Society.

Beattie, Dan. *Brandy Station 1863: First Steps towards Gettysburg* (2008) Oxford: Osprey Publishing.

Berimger, Robert E.; Hattaway, Herman; Jones, Archer; & Still, William N., Jr. *Why the South Lost the Civil War* (1986) Athens: University of Georgia Press.

Bernstein, Steven. *The Confederacy's Last Northern Offensive: Jubal Early, the Army of the Valley and the Raid on Washington* (2011) Jefferson, NC: McFarland.

Blount, Roy, Jr. *Robert E. Lee: A Life* (2003) New York: Penguin Books.

Boatner, Mark M. III. *The Civil War Dictionary, Revised Edition* (1988) New York: Vintage Books.

Bobrick, Benson. *Master of War: The Life of General George H. Thomas* (2009) New York: Simon & Schuster.

Boynton, Henry V. *The Battles of Chickamauga and Chattanooga and The Organizations Engaged* (1902) Washington, D.C.: Government Printing Office.

Bowden, Scott, and Ward, Bill. *Last Chance for Victory: Robert E. Lee and the Gettysburg Campaign* (2001) Cambridge: Da Capo Press.

Bowers, John. *Chickamauga and Chattanooga: The Battles that Doomed the Confederacy* (1994) New York: Post Road Press.

Brewer, James D. *Tom Worthington's Civil War: Shiloh, Sherman, and the Search for Vindication* (2001) Jefferson, NC: McFarland.

Brown, Kent Masterson. *Retreat, from Gettysburg: Lee, Logistics, & the Pennsylvania Campaign* (2005) Chapel Hill: The University of North Carolina Press.

Buell, Thomas B. *The Warrior Generals: Combat Leadership in the Civil War* (1997) New York: Three Rivers Press.

Carmichael, Peter S. Editor, *Audacity Personified: The Generalship of Robert E. Lee* (2004) Baton Rouge: Louisiana State University Press.

Cannon, John. *War in the West: Shiloh to Vicksburg, 1862–1863* (1990) New York: Gallery Books.

Castel, Albert. *Decision in the West: The Atlanta Campaign of 1864* (1992) Lawrence: University Press of Kansas.

Castel, Albert, with Brooks D. Simpson. *Victors in Blue: How Union Generals Fought the Confederates, Battled Each Other, and Won the Civil War* (2011) Lawrence: University Press of Kansas.

Catton, Bruce. *Grant Moves South: 1861–1863* (1960) Boston: Little, Brown and Company.

———. *Never Call Retreat* (1965) London: Phoenix Press.

———. *Terrible Swift Sword* (1963) London: Phoenix Press.

Chadwick, Bruce. *1858: Abraham Lincoln, Jefferson Davis, Robert E. Lee, Ulysses S. Grant and the War They Failed to See* (2008) Naperville: Sourcebooks.

Clausewitz, Carl von. The Essential Clausewitz: Selections from *On War*; edited by Joseph I. Greene (2003) Mineola, NY: Dover.

Cleaves, Freeman. *Meade of Gettysburg* (1960) Norman: University of Oklahoma Press.

\_\_\_\_\_. *Rock of Chickamauga: The Life of General George H. Thomas* (1948) Norman: University of Oklahoma Press.

Coco, Gregory A. *A Concise Guide to the Artillery at Gettysburg* (2009) Gettysburg: Thomas Publications.

Coddington, Edwin B. *The Gettysburg Campaign: A Study in Command* (1968) New York: Touchstone.

Connelly, Donald B. *John M Schofield and the Politics of Generalship* (2006) Chapel Hill: The University of North Carolina Press.

Cozzens, Peter. *The Darkest Days of the War: The Battles of Iuka & Corinth* (1997) Chapel Hill: The University of North Carolina Press.

\_\_\_\_\_. *This Terrible Sound: The Battle of Chickamauga* (1996) Urbana: University of Illinois Press.

Cozzens, Peter, and Girardi, Robert I., Editors. *The New Annals of the Civil War* (2004) Mechanicsburg, PA: Stackpole Books.

Cunningham, O. Edward. *Shiloh and the Western Campaign of 1862* Edited by Gary D. Joiner and Timothy B. Smith (2007) New York: Savas Beatie.

Daniel, Larry J. *Days of Glory: The Army of the Cumberland, 1861–1865* (2004) Baton Rouge: Louisiana State University Press.

Davis, Kenneth C. *Don't Know Much About History: Everything You Need to Know About the America's Greatest Conflict but Never Learned* (1996) Perennial.

Davis, Stephen. *Atlanta Will Fall: Sherman, Joe Johnston and the Yankee Heavy Battalions* (2001) Wilmington, DE: Scholarly Resources.

Davis, William C. *The Cause Lost: Myths and Realities of the Confederacy* (1996) Lawrence: University Press of Kansas.

Detzer, David. *Donnybrook: The Battle of Bull Run, 1862* (2004) Orlando: Harcourt Books.

Dougherty, Kevin J. *Great Commanders of the Civil War: The Battles of the Civil War* (2008) San Diego: Thunder Bay Press.

Dowdey, Clifford. *The Seven Days: The Emergence of Robert E. Lee* (1964) New York: Skyhorse Publishing.

Dugard, Martin. *The Training Ground: Grant, Lee, Sherman, and Davis in the Mexican War, 1836–1848* (2008) New York: Little, Brown and Company.

Ecelbarger, Gary. *The Day Atlanta Died: The Battle of Atlanta* (2010) New York: St. Martin's Press.

Eckenrode, H.J. & Conrad, Bryan. *James Longstreet: Lee's War Horse* (1936, 1986) Chapel Hill: The University of North Carolina Press.

Eicher, David J. *Gettysburg Battlefield: The Definitive Illustrated History* (2003) San Francisco: Chronicle Books.

\_\_\_\_\_. *The Longest Night: A Military History of the Civil War* (2001) New York: Simon & Schuster.

Einolf, Christopher J. *George Thomas: Virginian for the Union* (2007) Norman: University of Oklahoma Press.

Ellis, John. *Cavalry: The History of Mounted Warfare* (1978, 2004) Barnsley, South Yorkshire: Pen & Sword Military Classics.

Esposito. Vincent J. BGen, Chief Editor, *The West Point Atlas of War: The Civil War* (1995) New York: Tess Press.

Farwell, Byron. *Stonewall: A Biography of General Thomas J. Jackson* (1993) New York: W.W. Norton & Company.

Field, Ron. *Confederate Ironclad vs Union Ironclad: Hampton Roads 1862* (2008) Oxford: Osprey Publishing.

Flood, Charles Bracelen. *Grant and Sherman: The Friendship that Won the War* (2005) New York: Harper Perennial.

Foote, Shelby. *The Civil War, a Narrative: Fort Sumter to Perryville* (1958) New York: Vintage.

Franks, George F., III. *Battle of Falling Waters 1863: Custer, Pettigrew and the end of the Gettysburg Campaign* (2013) Published by Author.

Freeman, Douglas Southall. *Lee's Lieutenants: A Study in Command. Volume I: Manassas to Malvern Hill* (1942) New York: Scribner.

\_\_\_\_\_. *Lee's Lieutenants: A Study in Command. Volume II: Cedar Mountain to Chancellorsville* (1943) New York: Scribner.

\_\_\_\_\_. *Lee's Lieutenants: A Study in Command. Volume III: Gettysburg to Appomattox* (1944) New York: Scribner.

\_\_\_\_\_. *R.E. Lee: A Biography Vol. III* (1935) New York: Scribner.

Gallagher, Gary W., Editor. *The Shenandoah Valley Campaign of 1864* (2006) Chapel Hill: The University of North Carolina Press.

Gallagher, Gary W., and Nolan, Alan T., Editors. *The Myth of the Lost Cause and Civil War History* (2000) Bloomington: Indiana University Press.

Garrison, Webb, Jr. *Strange Battles of the Civil War* (2001) Nashville: Cumberland House.

Garrity, John A. and Carnes, Mark C. General Editors. *American National Biography* (1999) New York: Oxford University Press.

Glatthaar, Joseph T. *General Lee's Army: From Victory to Collapse* (2008) New York: Free Press.

Goodwin, Doris Kearns. *Team of Rivals: The Political Genius of Abraham Lincoln* (2005) New York: Simon & Schuster.

Goss, Thomas J. *The War Within the Union High Command: Politics and Generalship During the Civil War* (2003) Lawrence, Kansas: University Press of Kansas.

Griffith, Paddy, *Battle Tactics of the Civil War* (1989) New Haven: Yale University Press.

Grimsley, Mark & Woodworth, Steven E. *Shiloh: A Battlefield Guide* (2006) Lincoln: University of Nebraska Press.

Groom, Winston. *Vicksburg, 1863* (2009) New York: Alfred A. Knopf.

Guelzo, Allen C. *Gettysburg: The Last Invasion* (2013) New York: Alfred A. Knopf.

Hagerman, Edward. *The American Civil War and The Origins of Modern Warfare: Ideas, Organizations and Field Command* (1992) Bloomington: Indiana University Press.

Huntington, Tom. *Searching for George Gordon Meade: The Forgotten Victor of Gettysburg* (2013) Mechanicsburg, PA: Stackpole Books.

Hess, Earl J. *Banners to the Breeze: The Kentucky Campaign, Corinth & Stones River* (2000) Lincoln: The University of Nebraska Press.

_____. *The Civil War in the West: Victory and Defeat from the Appalachians to the Mississippi* (2012) Chapel Hill: The University of North Carolina Press.

_____. *Civil War Infantry Tactics Training, Combat, and Small-Unit Effectiveness* (2015) Baton Rouge: Louisiana University Press.

_____. *The Rifle Musket in Civil War Combat: Reality and Myth* (2008) Lawrence: University Press of Kansas.

Horn, Stanley F. *The Decisive Battle of Nashville* (1991) Baton Rouge: Louisiana State University Press.

Hsieh, Wayne Wei-Siang. *West Pointers and the Civil War: The Old Army in War and Peace* (2009) Chapel Hill: The University of North Carolina Press.

Jomini, Antoine-Henri. *The Art of War.* Translated by Capt. G.H. Mendall and Lt. W.P. Craighill (2007) Mineola, NY: Dover Publications.

Jones, Archer. *Civil War Command & Strategy: The Process of Victory and Defeat* (1992) New York: The Free Press.

Katcher, Philip. *Great Gambles of the Civil War* (2003) Edison, NJ: Castle Books.

_____. *Union Cavalry, 1861–65* (1995) Osprey.

Kegel, James A. *North with Lee and Jackson: The Lost Story of Gettysburg* (1996) Mechanicsburg, PA: Stackpole Books.

Kelly, Joseph. *America's Longest Siege: Charleston, Slavery, and the Slow March Toward Civil War* (2013) New York: Overlook Press.

Kennedy, Frances H. Editor. *The Civil War Battlefield Guide* (1990) Houghton Mifflin Company.

Kennett, Lee. *Sherman: A Soldier's Life* (2001) Perennial.

Kreiser, Lawrence A., Jr. *Defeating Lee: A History of the Second Corps, Army of the Potomac* (2011) Bloomington: Indiana University Press.

Longacre, Edward G. *Grant's Cavalrymen: The Life and History of General James H. Wilson* (2000), Paperback Edition, Mechanicsburg, PA: Stackpole Books.

_____. *Lincoln's Cavalrymen: A History of the Mounted Forces of the Army of the Potomac* (2000) Mechanicsburg, PA.: Stackpole Books.

_____. *The Man Behind the Guns: A Military Biography of General Henry Hunt, Chief of Artillery, Army of the Potomac* (2003) Paperback Edition, Cambridge: Da Capo Press.

_____. *Worthy Opponents: William T. Sherman & Joseph E. Johnston—Antagonists in War, Friends in Peace* (2006) Nashville: Rutland Hill Press.

Lyman, Theodore. *Meade's Army: The Private Notebooks of Lt. Col. Theodore Lyman*/Edited by David W. Lowe (2007) Kent, OH: The Kent State University Press.

Marszalek, John F. *Commander of All Lincoln's Armies: The Life of Henry W. Halleck* (2004) Cambridge, MA: The Belknap Press of Harvard University Press.

McDonough, James Lee. *Nashville: The Western Confederacy's Final Gamble* (2004) Knoxville: The University of Tennessee Press.

McKnight, Brian D. *Contested Borderland: The Civil War in Appalachian Kentucky and Virginia* (2006) Lexington: The University Press of Kentucky.

McPherson, James M., Editor. *The Atlas of the Civil War* (2005) Courage Books.

_____. *The Battle Cry of Freedom: The Civil War Era* (1988) Oxford University Press.

_____. *Crossroads of Freedom: Antietam* (2002) Oxford: Oxford University Press.

_____. *Tried by War: Abraham Lincoln as Commander in Chief* (2008) New York: Penguin.

Miller, William Lee. *President Lincoln: The Duty of a Statesman* (2008) New York: Alfred A. Knopf.

Morris, Roy, Jr. *Sheridan: The Life & Wars of General Phil Sheridan* (Paperback Edition) (1992) New York: Vintage.

Nofi, Albert A. *A Civil War Treasury: Being a Miscellany of Arms & Artillery, Facts & Figures, Legends & Lore, Muses & Minstrels, Personalities & People* (1992) Edison, NJ: Castle Books.

Nolan, Alan T. *Lee Considered: General Robert E. Lee & Civil War History* (1991) Chapel Hill: University of North Carolina Press.

Patchan, Patrick C. *The Last Battle of Winchester: Phil Sheridan, Jubal Early, and the Shenandoah Valley Campaig, August 7–September 19, 1864* (2013) New York: Savas Beatie.

_____. *Second Manassas: Longstreet's Attack and the Struggle for Chinn Ridge* (2011) Washington, D.C.: Potomac Books.

Perret, Geoffrey. *The Untold Story of America's Greatest President as Commander in Chief* (2004) New York: Random House.

Powell, David A. *Failure in the Saddle: Nathan Bedford Forrest, Joseph Wheeler, and the Confederate Cavalry in the Chickamauga Campaign* (2010) New York: Savas Beatie.

Rafuse, Ethan S. *McClellan's War* (2005) Bloomington: Indiana University Press.

Reardon, Carol. *With a Sword in One Hand & Jomini in the Other: The Problem of Military Thought in the Civil War North* (2012) Chapel Hill: University of North Carolina Press.

Reid, Brian Holden. *The American Civil War* (1999) London: Cassell & Co.

_____. *America's Civil War: The Operational Battlefield, 1861–1863* (2008) New York: Prometheus Books.

Schultz, Duane. *The Most Glorious Fourth: Vicksburg and Gettysburg, July 4th, 1863* (2002) New York: W.W. Norton & Company.

Sifakis, Stewart. *Who Was Who in the Confederacy* (1988) New York: Facts on File.

_____. *Who Was Who in the Union* (1988) New York: Facts on File.

Slotkin, Richard. *The Long Road to Antietam: How the Civil War Became a Revolution* (2012) New York: Liveright Publishing.

Smith, Derek. *In the Lion's Mouth: Hood's Tragic Retreat from Nashville, 1864* (2011) Mechanicsburg, PA: Stackpole Books.

Smith, Graham. *Warman's Civil War Weapons* (2005) Iola, IA: KP Books.

Stackpole, Edward J. *They Met at Gettysburg* (1956) Harrisburg, PA: Stackpole Books.

Stempel, Jim. *The Battle of Glendale: The Day the South Nearly Won the War* (2011) Jefferson, NC: McFarland.

Stephens, John Richard. *Commanding the Storm: Civil War Battles in the Words of the Generals Who Fought Them* (2012) Guilford, CT: Lyons Press.

Sword, Wiley. *The Confederates' Last Hurrah: Spring Hill, Franklin, & Nashville* Paperback Edition, first published as *Embrace an Angry Wind* (1992) Lawrence: University of Kansas Press.

Symonds, Craig L. *Stonewall of the West: Patrick Cleburne & The Civil War* (1997) Lawrence: University Press of Kansas.

Taaffe, Stephen R. *Commanding the Army of the Potomac* (2006) Lawrence: University Press of Kansas.

Tagg, Larry. *The Generals of Gettysburg* (1998) Cambridge: Da Capo Press.

Tanner, Robert G. *Retreat to Victory: Confederate Strategy Reconsidered* (2001) Wilmington: Scholarly Resources.

Taylor, Paul. *He Hath Loosed the Fateful Lightning: The Battle of Ox Hill (Chantilly) September 1, 1862* (2003) Shippensburg, PA: White Mane Books.

Trout, Robert J. *After Gettysburg: Cavalry Operations in the Eastern Theater July 14, 1863 to December 31, 1863* (2011) Hamilton, MT: Eagle Editions.

Trudeau, Noah Andre. *Bloody Roads South: The Wilderness to Cold Harbor, May–June 1864* (2000) Baton Rouge: Louisiana State University Press.

_____. *Gettysburg: A Testing of Courage* (2002) New York: Perennial.

Varney, Frank P. *General Grant and the Rewriting of History: How the Destruction of William S. Rosecrans Influenced Our Understanding of the Civil War* (2013) El Dorado Hills: Savas Beatie.

Varon, Elizabeth R. *Appomattox: Victory, Defeat. And Freedom at the End of the Civil War* (2014) Oxford: Oxford University Press.

Walsh, George. *"Those Damn Horse Soldiers": True Tales of the Civil War Cavalry* (2006) New York: Forge.

Welker, David A. *Tempest at Ox Hill: The Battle of Chantilly* (2002) Cambridge: Da Capo Press.

Welch, Richard F. *The Boy General: The Life and Careers of Francis Channing Barlow* (2003) Kent, OH: The Kent State University Press.

Wert, Jeffry D. *Cavalryman of the Lost Cause: A Biography of J.E.B Stuart* (2008) New York: Simon & Schuster.

_____. *From Winchester to Cedar Creek: The Shenandoah Campaign of 1864* (1987) Carlisle: South Mountain Press.

_____. *General James Longstreet: The Confederacy's Most Controversial Soldier* (1993) New York: Touchstone.

_____. *The Sword of Lincoln: The Army of the Potomac* (2005) New York: Simon & Schuster.

Wheelan, Joseph. *Terrible Swift Sword: The Life of General Philip H. Sheridan* (2012) Cambridge: Da Capo Press.

Williams, T. Harry. *Lincoln and His Generals* (1952) New York: Dorset Press.

Wills, Brian Steel. *The South's Greatest Cavalryman: Nathan Bedford Forrest* (1992) Lawrence: University of Kansas Press.

Wittenberg, Eric J. *Glory Enough for All: Sheridan's Second Raid and the Battle of Trevilian Station* (2001) Lincoln: University of Nebraska Press.

_____. *Little Phil: A Reassessment of the Civil War Leadership of Philip H. Sheridan* (2002) Dulles: Brassey's.

_____. *The Union Cavalry Comes of Age: Hartwood Church to Brandy Station, 1863* (2003) Washington, D.C.: Potomac Books.

Wittenberg, Eric, Pettruzzi, J. David, & Nugent, Michael F. *One Continuous Fight: The Retreat from Gettysburg and the Pursuit of Lee's Army of Northern Virginia, July 4–14, 1863* (2008) New York: Savas Beatie.

Wolseley, Viscount, Field Marshal. *The American Civil War: An English View.* Edited by James A. Rawley (2002) Mechanicsburg, PA: Stackpole Books.

Woodworth, Steven E. *Nothing but Victory: The Army of the Tennessee, 1861–1865* (2005) New York: Alfred A. Knopf.

_____. *Six Armies in Tennessee: The Chickamauga and Chattanooga Campaigns* (1998) Lincoln: University of Nebraska Press.

Work, David. *Lincoln's Political Generals* (2009) Urbana & Chicago: University of Illinois Press.

Young, Bennett. *Confederate Wizards of the Saddle* (1914) Boston: Chapple Publishing Company.

# Index

acoustic shadowing 36, 47
Alexander, Bevin, cited 7, 152, 201, 340
Alexander, E. Porter 150, 151, 342, 343; cited 14, 153, 187, 189, 262, 285, 290, 340
Alexandria, VA 197, 198, 199, 207
Allatoona, GA 101, 120
Alpine, GA 67, 68, 100
Amelia Courthouse, VA 333, 336–338, 342
Anaconda strategy 24, 328, 350
Anderson, Richard 330, 337, 339
Anderson, Robert 18
Antietam battle 2, 42, 54, 78, 95, 215, 222–225, 252, 253, 260, 278, 307, 354
Appomattox Court House, VA 2, 147, 342
Appomattox Station 339, 341, 343
Armistead, Lewis 190
Army of Northern Virginia 63, 191, 198, 203, 209, 218, 228, 231, 233, 237, 245, 275, 276, 300, 309, 324, 329, 332, 341, 354
Army of Tennessee 64, 65, 69, 76, 80, 119, 144, 148, 300, 331, 351, 355, 356; Atlanta campaign 94, 107–118
Army of the Cumberland 58, 61, 63, 65, 67, 72, 76, 82, 87, 102, 141, 300, 351; Atlanta campaign 92–118
Army of the James 96, 300, 303, 304, 326, 330, 336
Army of the Ohio 57, 65, 93
Army of the Potomac 83, 86, 93, 104, 122, 157, 180, 184, 195, 211, 215, 229, 232, 236, 241, 249, 251, 253, 259, 260, 278, 286, 294, 297, 299, 300, 301, 313, 326, 328, 331, 336, 354
Army of the Shenandoah 313
Army of the Tennessee 56; Atlanta campaign 93, 109, 114
Army of the Valley 317
Army of Virginia 194, 196, 199, 216, 219, 254
Army of West Virginia 313, 315
Ashby, Turner 161
Atlanta, GA 79
Atlanta Battle 108–110, 111, 119
Atlanta Campaign 92–118, 325, 328, 351, 354

Averill, William Woods 237; Chancellorsville 239–243; Shenandoah 64 314, 315, 317–319

B & O Railroad 310, 314–315, 319
Bald Hill, GA 108, 109, 111, 119
Ball's Bluff battle 203
Banks, Nathaniel P. 96, 219, 220, 254; 2nd Bull Run 196; Shenandoah Valley 159, 160, 161, 164, 165, 169, 171
Bardstown, KY 32–33
Barlow, Francis 280
Barnard, John G. 195
The Barricades, battle 136, 137
Bate, William B. 139
Battle Above the Clouds 86–87
Battle of Axes 186
Battle of Corinth II 69, 93, 117, 351
Battle of Iuka, MS 36, 45–48
Battle of Mill Springs, KY 17, 19, 28, 39
Battle of Trevilian Station 304–305, 308, 309, 313, 356
Bearrs, Edwin C., cited 25, 303
Beauregard, Pierre T.G. 20, 21, 22, 24, 25, 28, 119, 148, 207, 297, 346–347, 1st Bull Run 149, 151–153; Overland 306–308
Beaver Creek Dam battle 177–178, 196
Bee, Barnard Eliot 151
*Ben Hur: A Tale of the Christ* 327
Benton, Thomas Hart 159
Bernstein, Steven, cited 312, 324
Berra, Lawrence ("Yogi"), cited 128
Bierce, Ambrose, cited 102
Blair, Francis P., Jr. 103, 114
Blair, Frank, Sr. 92, 175
Bloody Lane 224
Booneville, MS 25, 26
Boonsboro, MD 284
Booth, John Wilkes 343, 344
Bowden, Scott, cited 266
Boy Wonders 244, 256, 300
Boydton Plank Road 332, 333
Bragg, Braxton 21, 26, 28, 30, 37–41, 44, 54, 59, 77, 78, 79, 90, 94, 96, 119, 296; background 28; Chattanooga I 65–70; Chattanooga II 83–89, 351; Chickamauga 70–76; Stones River 59–61; Tullahoma 63–64
Brandy Station 244–248, 249, 251, 256, 273, 301, 313
Brannon, John M. 73, 76
Breckinridge, John C. 22, 59, 60, 73, 77, 95, 304, 310, 317, 325
Bridgeport, GA 66, 78, 83
Brown, John C. 43, 126
Brown, Kent Masterson, cited 276, 285
Brown's Ferry 84, 86
Buchanan, James 159, 325
Buckner, Simon B. 29, 42, 56, 65–66, 68, 79, 80, 84
Buell, Don Carlos 1, 2, 4, 18, 19, 21, 23, 28, 30–34, 37, 38–41, 44, 55, 57, 59, 66; background 28
Buell, Thomas B., cited 111, 117, 187, 188, 195, 224, 225, 339, 349
Buford, John 150, 200, 236, 237, 240, 243, 297; Brandy Station 246–248; Gettysburg 256, 264–165, 273, 313; post-Gettysburg 280, 283, 284, 286, 292–294
Bull Run Chantilly 210–216; 1st battle 9, 18, 20, 150–154, 155, 159, 160, 184, 189, 202, 203, 206, 212, 266, 309; 2nd battle 76, 95, 196–205, 209, 229, 233, 234, 251, 251, 352, 354
The Burning 320, 323
Burns, Ken, cited 135
Burnside, Ambrose 65, 67, 82, 83, 84, 88–89, 92, 150, 157, 215, 233, 236, 253, 261, 270, 308, 331; Antietam 219, 224, 225, 228, 352
Butler, Benjamin 2, 4, 26, 95, 103, 252, 300, 326, 330–331, 354; Overland 303, 306, 307
Butterfield, Daniel 253, 255, 261, 279, 285, 286, 297, 335; Gettysburg 253

Cameron, Simon 157
Carlisle Barracks 262, 263
Cashtown Pass, PA 263, 276
Cassville, GA 101
Castel, Albert, cited 117
Castel & Simpson, cited 54, 55, 313
Catton, Bruce, cited 22, 41, 59–60
Cavalry Bureau 93, 244, 255, 300

397

# Index

Cedar Creek battle 141, 321–323, 324, 325, 327, 328
Cedar Mountain, VA 197
Cemetery Hill 266, 267, 269, 270, 271, 275
Cemetery Ridge 271–273
Centreville, VA 150, 173, 199, 205, 209, 217
Chalmers, James R. 136, 258
Chambersburg, PA 228, 251, 258, 262
Chambersburg Pike 263, 265
Chancellorsville 86, 110, 184, 239–243, 250, 253, 254, 301, 310, 313, 318, 319
Chandler, Zachariah 234
Chantilly battle 210–216, 218, 352, 354
Charleston, SC 119
Chase, Salmon 40, 62, 196
Chattanooga, TN 59, 64, 65, 70, 75, 77, 78, 92, 133, 297, 351
Cheatham, Benjamin Franklin 35, 106, 110, 111; Nashville campaign 124, 126, 127
Chestnut, Mary, cited 90
Chewalla, MS 49, 50, 52, 55
Chickamauga battle 57, 70–76, 77, 78, 79, 80, 85, 88, 95, 131, 296, 351, 353
Chickamauga Creek 70, 71
Chinn Ridge battle 201–205, 206
City Point, VA 120, 311, 329
*Civil War Dictionary*, cited 168
Cleaves, Freeman, cited 281
Cleburne, Patrick R. 30, 35, 38–39, 58, 64, 68, 73, 77; Atlanta campaign 98, 102, 105, 109, 113, 114; Chattanooga II 86–89; Nashville campaign 125, 127, 131
Cleveland, Grover 56
Cobb, Howell 147
Coddingham, Edwin, cited 255, 261, 268
Cold Harbor 103, 178, 307, 308, 309, 317, 326
Columbia, TN 123, 124, 125
Columbia Pike 138, 139
Columbus, GA 147
Connor, Z.T. 170–171
Cooper, Samuel 20, 26, 155
Corinth, MS 20
Couch, Darius 252, 255
Cox, Jacob D. 221
Cozzens, Peter, cited 53
Cracker Line 84
Crampton Gap 220, 221
Crimean War 158
Crittenden, John J. 32, 40
Crittenden, Thomas 32, 34–37, 38, 40, 58, 63, 66, 67, 80; Chickamauga 70–75
Crook, George 312–317, 319, 326; war's end 332
Cross Keys, VA 169–170, 172
Croxton, John T. 71
Culpeper, VA 197, 230, 239, 240, 256
Culp's Hill 266, 267, 272, 275, 352

Cumberland Gap 37, 38–39
Cunningham, O. Edward, cited 23
Custer, George Armstrong 185, 249, 261, 273, 274, 303, 345; post-Gettysburg 283, 292; Shenandoah 64, 319, 322; war's end 332, 334, 339, 341

Dabney, Robert L. 182
Dahlgren, Ulric 249, 287, 298
Dallas, GA 102, 104
Dalton battle 79, 92, 97–99, 133, 354
Dana, Charles Anderson 80–81, 82
Daniel, Larry J., cited 25, 31, 60
Danville, VA 334, 336, 358
Davies, Henry 337
Davis, Jefferson 3, 17, 20, 26, 28, 29, 41, 42, 44, 48, 56, 79–80, 90, 94, 103, 106–107, 119, 120, 148, 152, 155, 160, 164, 170, 174, 188, 197, 226, 245, 298, 346, 350; war's end 332, 343, 344
Davis, Jefferson C. 75, 110, 114
Davis Bridge, MS 51–52
Decatur, GA 106, 107, 108, 144
Detzer, David, cited 153
Devil's Den 75, 271
Devin, Thomas 264, 332
Dinwiddie Courthouse, VA 332
Dodge, Granville 25, 97, 109, 110, 118
Dogan Hill, VA 201–203
Doubleday, Abner 270, 282, 298
Dowdey, Clifford, cited 186
Downstown, MD 290–292, 294
Drewry's Bluff, VA 26, 306
Duffié, Alfred Napoleon 246, 247, 256, 312
Dug Gap battle 98
Dug Spring battle 92

Early, Jubal 56, 150, 266–268, 329, 335; background 309; Shenandoah 64, 309–325, 328
Eicher, David, cited 178
1864 election 325, 354
Einolf, Christopher J, cited 2, 4, 145, 356
Elk River 61–65
Elliot, Washington 97
Emack, George M. 282
Emancipation Proclamation 54, 60, 227, 230, 234
Emory, William H. 313, 315, 316
Enfield rifles 182
Evans, Nathan George ("Shanks") 150, 151, 203
Ewell, Richard S. ("Dick") 9, 150, 164, 166, 168, 170, 199, 309, 347; Gettysburg 272, 275; post-Gettysburg 277, 283, 286, 292, 294; pre-Gettysburg 250, 251, 256, 259, 262–264, 266–269; war's end 333, 335, 338, 339
Ezra Church battle 111, 113

Fair Oaks battle 95, 168, 174, 182, 254
Fairfax, VA 210, 214, 217

Fairfield Gap 277, 285, 288, 294
Falling Timbers, TN 23
Falling Waters, MD 290–293
Falmouth, VA 197, 238
Farmville, VA 340–341, 343
Farnsworth, Elon J. 261, 274
Farragut, David G. 24, 157
Farwell, Byron, cited 154
The fatal halt 321–322
Fisher's Hill battle 317–320, 321, 324, 356
Five Forks battle 332–336
Fleetwood Hill 244–248
Floyd, John B. 29
Foote, Andrew H. 325
Foote, Shelby, cited 36, 53, 147
Ford Theater 343
Forrest, Nathan Bedford 16, 23, 45, 58, 65, 68, 71, 78, 80, 112, 120, 146, 333; Nashville campaign 123, 124, 125, 128, 130, 133, 137, 139–144
Fort Bragg, NC 90
Fort Donelson, TN 19, 27, 29, 42, 93, 157
Fort Fisher, NC 90, 330
Fort Henry, TN 19, 27, 93, 157
Fort Hood 148
Fort Monroe, VA 158, 173, 181, 192, 199
Fort Stedman 331–333
Fort Stevens, MD 311
Fort Sumter, SC 20, 92, 134, 175, 334, 343
Frankford, KY 31, 32–33, 35, 55
Franklin, William B. 180, 183, 185, 199, 200, 205, 211, 252, 253; Antietam 220, 221, 224, 225
Franklin, VA 163
Franklin battle 127–131
Franklin Pike 136–137
Frederick, MD 218, 257, 258, 280, 289, 310
Fredericksburg, VA 83, 196, 230, 233, 239, 251, 254, 270, 302, 307
Freeman, Douglas Southall, cited 174, 186, 189, 268, 322, 332, 333, 338, 353
Frémont, John Charles 1, 27, 196; Shenandoah '62, 159, 160, 163, 164, 167–170, 353
French, William H. 282, 289, 296, 335
Front Royal 156, 164–165, 167, 170, 172, 250, 296, 317, 318

Gaines' Mill 172, 178–180, 182, 187, 191, 252, 304
USS *Galena* 187
Gallagher, Gary, cited 337
Gamble, William 264
Garfield, James 62, 74, 75, 76, 80, 82
Garnett, Richard B. 161, 172, 234
Garnett's and Golding's Farms battle 180–181
Georgia Railroad 108
German Military Academy 196
Gettysburg, PA 2, 256, 273, 274; Day One battle 110, 275, 280, 283,

285, 313, 352; Day Three battle 107, 172, 274, 277, 279, 299, 352; Day Two battle 271, 272, 273, 282; post–Gettysburg 280
Gibbon, John 221, 266, 331, 342, 343, 345
Gilbert, Charles C. 30, 31–32, 34–37, 39, 58
Gilgel Church battle 103, 104
Glatthaar, Joseph, cited 320, 322, 331, 339
Glendale battle 183–189, 192, 195, 253
Gordon, George H. 165
Gordon, John 284, 328, 347; Shenandoah 64, 310, 315, 317, 318, 321, 323; war's end 330, 331–332, 337–340, 342, 344
Granger, Gordon 43, 47, 76, 82, 87–89, 90
Grant, Ulysses Simpson ("Sam") 2, 8, 19, 21, 22, 24, 27, 55, 57, 61, 80, 92, 102, 113, 115, 117, 118, 157, 174, 195, 251, 278, 299, 300, 326, 344–345, 346, 351, 353, 355–357; background 18; Chattanooga II 84; Corinth II 48–53; Iuka 43, 45–48; Nashville campaign 120, 122, 124, 130–134, 141; Overland 301, 303, 306, 308; Shenandoah 64, 309–312, 318, 319, 321; war's end 328–343
Gregg, David McM. 237, 246–248, 301, 314
Grierson, Benjamin H. 141–142
Griffin, Charles 333, 336, 341, 342
Griffith, Paddy, cited 348–349, 350
Groom, Winston, cited 130
Groveton, VA 199, 209
Guelzo, Allen, cited 236, 266, 268

Hagerstown, MD 261, 276, 277, 286–290, 292, 352
Halleck, Henry W. 19, 24, 25, 26, 27, 39, 43, 45, 53, 54, 58, 59, 61, 70, 82, 83, 85, 92, 93, 102, 115, 132, 133, 141, 173, 223, 227, 259; background 17–18; Chantilly 210, 215, 214, 215; post–Gettysburg 281, 289, 291, 294; 2nd Bull Run 194, 196, 197, 200; Shenandoah 64, 311, 312, 321
Hampton, Wade 150, 245, 249, 258, 274, 276, 305, 306, 308
Hancock, Winfield Scott 81, 296, 331, 335; Gettysburg 273, 279–281, 285, 295, 354; Overland 307; pre–Gettysburg 252, 255–258, 266, 268, 269
hard war 8
Hardee, William J. 29, 33, 34–36, 58, 63, 66, 118, 119, 124; Atlanta campaign 106, 107, 108, 109, 111, 113, 115, 116
Harmon, John A. 277, 291
Harpers Ferry 43, 150, 156, 157, 166, 251, 260, 282, 284, 296, 304, 310; Antietam 218, 219, 221, 222, 224, 226, 229

*Harper's Weekly* 293, 327
Harrison's Landing, VA 177, 179, 183, 191, 192, 194, 196, 219, 232–233, 306
Harrodsburg, KY 37–38
Hartwood Church 238
Haupt, Herman 282
Hayes, Rutherford B. 316
Heintzelman, Samuel 180, 183, 184, 185; Antietam 220
Henry House Hill 151, 201–205, 206, 352
Hess, Earl, cited 36
Heth, Henry 39, 264, 292, 293
High Tide 42, 273
Hill, Ambrose Powell ("A.P.") 176, 177, 179, 182, 187, 210, 213, 309; Antietam 216, 224, 225, 226, 227; Gettysburg 250, 258, 259, 263, 266–267, 275; post–Gettysburg 276, 277; war's end 330, 333
Hill, Daniel Harvey 66, 72, 79–80, 84, 176, 178, 184, 190, 191, 194, 195, 250; Antietam 221, 222, 224
Hindman, Thomas C. 69
Holly Springs, MS 51, 53, 56
Holmes, Oliver Wendell, Jr. 311
Holmes, Theophilus 176, 180, 184, 187, 188, 195
Hood, John Bell 70, 79, 118, 119, 120, 148, 179, 336, 350; Atlanta campaign 95, 101, 102, 104, 106–118; Nashville campaign 120–144, 328, 340, 355, 356; 2nd Bull Run 202, 203
Hooker, Joseph 63, 83, 84, 88, 118, 238, 297, 298; Antietam 219, 221–224; Atlanta campaign 92, 96, 101, 104, 115; Chantilly 211, 212; Command of Army of the Potomac 233, 236–261, 281, 314, 318; Seven Days 184, 188
Horn, Stanley, cited 137
Horseshoe Ridge 75, 77, 351
Houston, Sam 20
Howard, Oliver Otis 83, 123, 240, 241, 252, 254; Atlanta campaign 96, 99, 102, 109, 111, 115; background 254; Gettysburg 256, 265–266, 269, 292, 293
Huger, Benjamin 176, 184, 186, 187, 188, 195
Humphreys, Andrew A. 289, 292, 283, 296; war's end 331, 332, 336, 339, 341, 343, 357
Hunt, Henry J. 188, 331
Hunter, David ("Black Dave") 300, 305, 309–313, 326
Hurlbut, Stephen A. 45, 51–53, 55

Illinois Central Railroad 219, 250
Imboden, John D. 263, 275, 284, 287, 303

Jackson, Andrew 44
Jackson, Thomas ("Stonewall") 46, 172, 173, 196, 234, 241, 242, 243, 250, 251, 265, 268, 309, 312, 334, 339, 344; Antietam 218, 222, 225;

background 159–160; Chantilly 210–212, 214, 216; 1st Bull Run 150, 151; 2nd Bull Run 197–205, 206; Seven Days 176, 177, 182, 184, 186, 190, 194, 354; Shenandoah '62, 156–170, 171, 312, 351, 353
Jackson, William H. ("Red") 99
Jay's Mill, GA 71
Jenkins, Albert G. 245
Jenkins, Micah 187
Jermantown, VA 210, 212–214, 216
Jetersville, VA 336, 337
Johnson, Andrew 133, 148, 344, 345
Johnson, Bushrod 339
Johnson, Edward ("Allegheny") 162, 266–268
Johnston, Albert Sidney 19, 21, 24, 29, 155; background 20; Shiloh
Johnston, Joseph E. 90, 119, 148, 155, 159, 168, 173, 177, 346; Atlanta campaign 94–106, 354, 1st Bull Run 150–153; war's end 332, 336, 344
Joint Committee for the Conduct of the War 118, 253, 255, 298
Jomini, Antonie-Henri, cited 7, 10, 12, 228, 276, 354
Jones, William E. ("Grumble") 150, 245, 246, 249, 296, 305; Gettysburg 258; post–Gettysburg 277, 283, 284
Jonesboro battle 112–115, 116, 117, 354

Kautz, August V. 307
Kearny, Phillip 217; background 184–185; Chantilly 213–214, 216; Seven Days 184, 187, 190
Kelly's Ford 239
Kennesaw Mountain battle 103–106
Kennon, L.W.V., cited 324
Kentucky's importance 27
Kernstown 160–162, 166, 172, 323
Kershaw, Joseph B. 314, 315, 320, 339
Key, John 232
Keyes, Erasmus 180, 199
Kilpatrick, H. Judson ("Kilcavalry") 55, 96, 122, 249, 296, 297, 299, 300; Gettysburg 256, 259, 262, 273; post–Gettysburg 282–284, 286, 292–295
Kilpatrick-Dalgram raid 298, 313
Knoxville, TN 65, 67, 80, 85, 88, 89, 233, 297
Ku Klux Klan 147, 347

La Fayette, GA 68–70
Lancaster, OH 19
Lay's Ferry battle 100
Lee, Custis 334, 339
Lee, Fitzhugh ("Fitz") 212, 238, 256, 258, 259, 314; post–Gettysburg 276, 287, 292, 302; war's end 330, 333, 334, 342
Lee, Henry ("Light Horse") 174
Lee, Robert E. 1, 2, 8, 20, 41, 43, 63,

69, 71, 85, 86, 95, 99, 101, 106, 108, 119, 155, 164, 169, 170, 209, 211, 233, 240, 245, 200, 309, 328, 346, 353; Antietam 218, 221, 222, 223, 225, 226, 352; background 174–175; Chantilly 210, 216; Gettysburg 271–275; Overland 304; post–Gettysburg 276–296, 352; pre–Gettysburg 250–269; 2nd Bull Run 196, 199, 206, 208; Seven Days 173–194, 195; Shenandoah 64, 310, 311, 320, 321, 323, 325; war's end 329–343
Lee, Stephen D. 111, 112, 116, 201, 234; Nashville campaign 124, 127, 129, 135
Lee, William Henry Fitzhugh ("Rooney") 245, 249, 258
Lee & Gordon's Mill 69, 70
Leggett, Mortimer D. 108
Libby Prison 195
Lilley, Eli 66
Lincoln, Abraham 1, 3, 8, 27, 39, 61, 82, 83, 88, 95, 96, 117, 134, 154, 155, 174, 189, 194, 214, 218, 228–229, 244, 259, 297, 298, 301, 311, 325, 326, 328, 349; McClellan 41, 54, 255, 354; post–Gettysburg 278, 281, 289, 293, 294, 295; Shenandoah '62 156, 159, 164, 167, 353; war's end 329, 331, 341, 343
Little Round Top battle 75, 271
Logan, John A 97, 109, 110, 113, 118, 134
Long, Armistead 310
Longacre, Edward, cited 144
Longstreet, James ("Pete") 67, 70, 77, 79, 84, 85, 90, 174, 196, 233, 251, 285, 296, 325, 328, 346; Antietam 222, 225, 226; Chantilly 212, 214; at Chickamauga 72–76, 351; post–Gettysburg 271, 286, 290–291, 292; pre–Gettysburg 250, 257, 258, 269; 2nd Bull Run 197, 198, 200, 202–205, 206, 352; Seven Days 176, 181, 182, 184, 187, 188, 190, 194; war's end 330, 337–342
Lookout Mountain, GA 64, 67, 78, 83, 86–88, 118
Louisiana Military Seminary 18
Louisiana Tigers 151, 164, 165, 170, 172, 178, 344
Louisville, KY 30–31, 131, 148
Louisville & Nashville RR 30
Louisville Courier 80
Lovejoy's Station, GA 113, 114, 115, 116, 120
Luray Valley, VA 156, 296, 317, 318
Lyman, Theodore 118
Lynchburg, VA 96

MacArthur, Arthur 91
MacArthur, Douglas 91
Macon & Western RR 111, 112
Magruder, John B. 165, 182, 183, 184, 187, 188, 190, 195
Mahone, William ("Little Billy") 186–187, 205, 339, 340

Malvern Hill battle 107, 183, 187, 189–191, 193, 194, 195, 206
Manassas Junction, VA 149, 198, 199, 209, 256
Mansfield, Joseph 220, 223–224, 254
Marietta, GA 103, 106
Massanutten Mountain 156, 161, 162, 164, 169, 317, 318, 321
Maury, Dabney H. 50, 52, 56, 140
McArthur, John 51, 52, 54, 135
McCall, George 180, 185, 187, 195
McClellan, George B. 1, 2, 4, 19, 26, 27, 40, 41, 43, 54, 57, 95, 117, 131, 152, 157, 158, 161, 162, 164, 170, 175, 196, 233–234, 236, 237, 241, 248, 250, 255, 260, 279, 281, 282, 300, 325, 328, 349, 354; Antietam 218, 222–224, 229, 352; background 157–158; Chantilly 211, 214, 215; 2nd Bull Run 196, 197, 199, 200; Seven Days 173, 176–194, 306
McClellan, Henry 246, 247
McClernand, John A. 21
McCook, Alexander McD. 31, 34–36, 37, 58, 80, 82; Chattanooga I 67; Chickamauga 72–76; Stones River 59–61
McCook, Daniel 105
McCulloch, Ben 44
McCullum, David L. 83
McDonough, James Lee, cited 25, 133
McDowell, Irvin 149, 151, 152, 153, 160, 175, 211, 217, 219, 252, 266; 2nd Bull Run 196, 199, 200–205; Shenandoah '62, 157, 158, 164, 167, 168, 170
McDowell, VA 162–163, 171
McIntosh, John B. 241, 274
McKean, Thomas J. 52–53
McLaws, LaFayette 221, 285
McLean, C.H. 201–204
McLean, Nathaniel 162, 342
McPherson, James B. 51, 52–54, 55, 56; Atlanta Campaign 93, 101, 103, 104, 106, 107, 108, 109, 354
McPherson, James M., cited 36, 168–169
Meade, George G. 1, 2, 102, 110, 118, 195, 205, 223, 252, 301, 312, 326, 345, 349; Antietam battle 223; background 253, 260–261; Gettysburg 272, 275, 354; Overland 302; post–Gettysburg 278–296, 352; pre–Gettysburg 253, 256, 269, 270; war's end 330, 332, 336, 337, 342
Memphis, TN 26
Memphis & Charleston RR 48
Meridian raid 79, 90, 92, 122
USS Merrimack 173
Merritt, Wesley 225, 249, 261, 314, 315, 318, 323
Mexican War veterans 3, 9, 79, 82, 83, 150, 152, 159, 161, 175, 184, 185, 189, 203, 211, 219, 220, 252, 261, 333

Milroy, Robert Huston 162, 202, 205
minié ball 9, 15, 174, 349
Minty, Robert 63, 66, 70
Missionary Ridge battle 67, 77, 86–88, 300, 349, 351
Mobile, AL 325, 328
Mobile & Ohio RR 25, 143
Mobile Bay 17
Monterey Pass 276, 277, 282–283, 285–286, 294, 296
Montgomery Atlanta & Western RR 111, 112
Morgan, John Hunt 45, 58, 233, 250
Morris, Roy, Jr., cited 25
Mosby, John 344
Mud March 236
Mumford, Thomas 256
Murfreesboro, TN 59, 60, 61, 133, 137, 144
Myth of the Lost Cause 24, 56, 174, 271, 325, 346, 347

Nashville, TN 19, 77, 84, 120, 121, 123, 131
Nashville & Chattanooga RR 59, 60
Nashville battle 131–135
Nashville campaign 120–135, 328
National Zouaves 202
Negley, James S. 68, 73, 76, 80
New Hope Church battle 102, 104, 110
New Orleans, LA 17, 24, 150, 157, 163
New York City riots 296
New York Stock Exchange 185
*New York World* 231, 234
Newton, John 105, 270
Norfolk, VA 177
Norwich Military Academy 162

Oak Grove battle 176–177, 192
Old Cold Harbor 303–304
Orange & Alexandria RR 197, 230, 240, 245
Ord, Edward O.C. 43, 48–53, 55; war's end 330, 331, 334, 336, 341
Overland Campaign 301–309, 313, 328, 333, 355
Ox Hill battle 208, 268

Palmer, John McA. 85, 96, 105, 110, 118
Palmetto, GA 120
Parke, John G. 331
Parkhurst, John 75
Patchen, Scott, cited 202
Patrick, Marsena 285
Patterson, Robert 150, 154, 159
Pea Ridge battle 19, 44–45, 49, 50, 157
Peachtree Creek battle 107–108
Pender, William Dorsey 216
Pendleton, William N. 190, 227
Peninsula campaign 95, 158, 173, 184, 222, 252
Perryville battle 2, 33–40, 80, 351, 353
Peters, George 125

Peters, Jessie 125, 127
Petersburg, VA 147, 306–307, 309, 310, 319, 323, 325, 326, 329, 332–334, 340, 355
Petersburg & Weldon RR 330
Pettigrew, James 264, 293
Pickett, George E. 263, 273, 277, 333, 339
Pickett's Charge 78, 130, 193, 270, 272, 279, 281, 352
Pickett's Mill battle 102
Pierce, Franklin 211
Pillow, Gideon J. 29
Pinkerton's spies 222, 225
Pittsburg Landing, TN 19, 20
Pleasonton, Alfred 122, 236, 237, 242, 243, 297, 298, 300; Antietam 220, 225–228, 229; Brandy Station 245–248; Gettysburg 255–257, 261, 273; post–Gettysburg 280, 285, 288, 289, 295
Polk, James 159
Polk, Leonidas 29, 33, 34, 63, 72–76, 77, 79, 96, 99, 103
Pope, John 24, 25, 43, 194, 209, 219, 234, 254; Chantilly 210–212, 214, 215, 216; 2nd Bull Run 195–206, 208, 354
Port Republic, VA 156, 169–170
Port Royal, SC 157
Porter, Fitz-John 215, 231, 234, 253; Antietam 220, 222, 225, 227; 2nd Bull Run 197, 200; Seven Days 175, 177, 178, 179, 180, 191, 199
post–Antietam 225–227
post–Gettysburg 275–293, 301, 334
post–Nashville 135–144, 349, 356
post–Shiloh 22–24, 141
Powell, William H. 319
Prentiss, Benjamin 21
Price, Sterling 44–48, 56, 122
Pulaski, TN 122, 123, 141–143

Radical Republicans 196, 216, 222, 234, 255
Rafuse, Ethan S., cited 188, 231
Ramseur, Stephen D. 310, 322
Reconstruction 148
Reid, Brian Holder, cited 13, 26, 150, 171, 207, 231, 243, 353
Reno, Jesse 205, 211, 220, 221
Resaca battle 97–99, 100–101, 110, 120
Reynolds, John F. 201, 202, 205, 279, 295, 296; pre–Gettysburg 252, 255, 256, 261, 265–266, 270
Reynolds, Joseph J. 73, 81
Rhea, Gordon C., cited 303
Richmond, KY 30
Richmond, VA 7, 79, 92, 119, 147, 149, 157, 158, 173, 184, 191, 193, 230, 306, 319, 333, 334, 343, 350, 355
Richmond & Danville RR 334, 336
Richmond & York River RR 182
Ringgold Gap, GA 70, 89, 98
Robertson, Beverly 245, 258, 283, 297
Rockville, MD 258, 261

Rocky Face Ridge 97, 98, 102
Rodes, Robert 267, 310, 315
Rome, GA 98, 100, 101
Rosecrans, William S. 26, 41, 57, 90, 131, 159, 298; background 43; Chattanooga I 65–70; Chattanooga II 82–84; Chickamauga 70–76, 351; Corinth II 48–54, 55, 351; Iuka 44–48; Stones River 59–61; Tullahoma 61–65
Rosser, Thomas Lafayette 320
Rossville, GA 75, 77, 78
Rousseau, Lovell H. 35
Rude's Hill, VA 161, 162
Russell, David 316

Sailor's Creek battle 337–340, 343, 357
Savage's Station battle 181–183, 185
Savannah, GA 141, 145
Savannah, TN 20
Saxton, Rufus 167
Schenck, Robert 201, 204
Schofield, John M. 146; Atlanta campaign 92, 103, 104, 106, 107, 108, 112, 113, 114, 116; Nashville campaign 122, 123, 125, 128–132
Schurz, Carl 254
Scott, Winfield 7, 9, 12, 17, 20, 28, 149, 152, 154, 155, 157, 175, 185, 203, 211
Sears, Stephen W., cited 188
Secessionville battle 203
2nd U.S. Cavalry 148
Sedden, James Alexander 79, 325
Sedgwick, John 185, 224, 231, 252, 299, 335; Gettysburg 253, 255; post–Gettysburg 285–286, 288, 291, 294, 295
Selma, AL 146, 147, 333
Seminary Ridge 277, 278
Seminole War 43, 56
Seven Days campaign 95, 173–194, 197, 198, 207, 218, 229, 268, 306, 353, 354
Seven Pines battle 168, 173
Shenandoah Valley, VA 96; Campaign of 1864 309–325; Campaign of 1862 156–170, 171, 351, 353
Sheridan, Philip H. 2, 4, 16, 25, 26, 32, 35, 41, 58, 59, 61, 64, 74, 88, 122, 123, 132, 141, 278, 298, 300, 345, 345, 353, 355; background 25, 301; Overland 302–309; Shenandoah 64, 309–325; war's end 329–343, 357
Sherman, John 18
Sherman, William T. ("Cump") 8, 21, 24, 34, 45, 53, 54, 90, 118, 150, 278, 299, 300, 324, 345, 354; Atlanta Campaign 92–118; background 18, at Chattanooga II 83; Nashville campaign 120, 121, 122, 132, 140, 145; war's end 329–343, 355
Sherman's Grand Army 93, 94, 96, 97, 101, 107, 115
*Sherman's Memoirs* 118

Shields, James 161, 167, 169, 171
Shiloh battle 2, 20–22, 27, 93, 179, 191, 351, 353
Sickles, Daniel 252, 256, 269, 271, 279, 289, 298, 335
Sigel, Franz 96, 196, 201, 205, 219, 254, 300, 304
Sill, Joshua W. 32, 41
Slocum, Henry W. 83, 110, 112, 115, 120, 121, 123, 179; Gettysburg 255–256, 260, 269; post–Gettysburg 278
Slotkin, Richard, cited 222, 232
Smith, Andrew J. 122, 123, 124, 129, 132
Smith, E. Kirby 29, 31, 34, 37, 41, 56, 147, 148, 150, 195, 325, 344
Smith, William F. ("Baldy") 253, 263, 304, 306, 326, 328; Chattanooga II 83
Snake Creek Gap battle 97–99, 117, 354
Snodgrass Hill 75, 77, 108, 351
soft war 2, 8, 155, 222, 227, 234, 335, 350, 353
South Mountain 220–222, 276, 280, 285, 288, 290
Southern Historical Society 56
Southside Railroad 332, 334, 336, 337, 339, 349
Special Order 191 30, 219
Spencer repeating carbine 249
Spotsylvania battle 101, 172, 302, 303, 306, 310, 317, 333, 337
Spring Hill, TN 56, 124–128, 129, 139, 347
Springfield rifles 192
Stackpole, Edward J., cited 268
Stanley, David S. 43, 47, 52, 588061, 80–81, 85, 118; Atlanta campaign 110, 113, 114, 115, 116; Nashville campaign 122, 123, 125, 131, 134
Stanton, Edwin 9, 24, 27, 40, 61, 64, 82, 156, 157, 179, 196, 200, 214, 222, 227, 228, 260, 297, 300, 321, 343, 344, 345; Nashville campaign 121, 122, 132–134, 141, 152; Shenandoah '62, 159, 164
Staunton, VA 167, 276, 296, 300, 304, 305, 319, 320
Steedman, James 76, 131, 134, 135, 144, 146
Steuart, George H. 165–166, 172
Stevens, Isaac I. 211–213, 216, 217
Stevenson, William G. 22
Stewart, Alexander P. 110, 113, 114, 124, 126
Stone Bridge, VA 202, 206, 207, 208, 354
Stoneman, George 93, 237, 238–243, 244, 252, 254
Stoneman's Raid 239–243, 313
Stones River battle 2, 41, 57, 72, 80, 351, 353
Strasburg, VA 156, 164, 167, 169, 317, 351
Stuart, James Ewell Brown ("Jeb") 16, 43, 150, 197, 237, 249, 296, 303, 308, 314, 334, 335, 355; Anti-

etam 219, 225, 226, 228, 229–232; Brandy Station 245–248; Chancellorsville 240–241, 243; Chantilly 210, 211, 216; Gettysburg 271, 272, 274; post-Gettysburg 280, 283, 286, 290, 295; pre-Gettysburg 257, 262, 265, 270; Seven Days 174, 175, 180, 181, 192, 193–194
Sudley Spring 199
Sullivan, Jeremiah C. 312
Sumner, Edwin V. ("Bull") 180, 183, 199, 211, 252; Antietam 220, 224
Sweeny, Thomas W. 100, 118
Sykes, George 261

Taaffee, Stephen, cited 261, 270
Taylor, Richard 147, 148, 165, 172, 178, 344
Taylor, Zachary 20, 172
Tennyson, Alfred 274
Texas Rangers 28
Thomas, George H. 8, 24, 28, 30, 31, 34, 36, 57, 78, 145, 147–148, 278, 336, 353, 354; Atlanta campaign 112, 113, 115, 116, 117; Chattanooga I 67–69; Chattanooga II 84; Chickamauga 70–76; Nashville campaign 120–145; Stones River 59–61; Tullahoma 62–63
Thompson, Absolum mansion 126, 128
Tom's Brook 320, 324
Torbert, Alfred T.A. 301, 305, 314, 315, 318, 320, 321
Tower, Zeolous Bates 203, 204
Trimble, Isaac 199
Trudeau, Noah Andre, cited 255, 271, 272
Tullahoma battle 61–65
Tunnel Hill 86, 87, 89, 997
Tupelo, MS 44, 142, 143, 146, 148, 328
Turner's Gap battle 220, 221, 288
Twiggs, David 28

University of Arkansas 80
Upton, Emory 316
U.S.C.T. 331, 342, 344

Van Cleve, Horatio Phillips 75
Van Dorn, Earl ("Buck") 19, 29, 44–48, 48–54, 56, 125, 351
Van Horne, Thomas, cited 2
Varney, Frank, cited 23, 356
Varon, Elizabeth, cited 329
Vicksburg, MS 41, 53, 251
Vicksburg Campaign 56, 61, 89, 94
CSS *Virginia* 173, 177
Virginia Central RR 312, 319
Virginia Military Institute 150, 160, 169, 304, 309
von Clausewitz, Carl, cited 9–10, 12, 190, 227, 276
von Moltke, Helmuth, cited 13, 40, 154

Wade, Ben 298
Walden Ridge Road 83, 84
Wallace, Lewis 20, 310, 326
Walthall, Edward C. 130, 140, 143
Ward, Bill, cited 266
Warren, Gouverneur K. 202, 282, 285–286, 306, 308, 346–346; war's end 331, 332, 333
Washington University 92
Watkins, Sam, cited 135, 136
Weitzel, Godfrey 331
Wells, Gideon 9
Wells, William 334
Wert, Jeffry D., cited 188, 224, 231, 254, 297, 306, 308, 319, 324, 330
West Point 2, 8–9, 29, 44, 84, 110, 118, 134, 149, 150, 157, 159, 174, 190, 195, 196, 203, 237, 238, 250, 253, 256, 261, 270, 273, 313, 346, 349, 350, 353

Western & Atlantic RR 89, 97, 99, 100, 102, 103
Wheat, Chatham ("Rob") 172
Wheelan, Joseph, cited 357
Wheeler, Joseph 38, 59, 60, 62, 66, 80, 84, 97, 108, 110, 123
White House landing 175, 177, 179, 180, 181, 182, 192, 306, 308
White Oak Swamp or Creek 179, 182, 183, 186
Widow Glenn 72, 74
Widow Kolb 104
Wilder, John T. 62, 63, 66, 71, 355
The Wilderness 90, 101, 133, 172, 302, 317, 333
Williams, Alpheus 224, 255, 268
Williamsport, MD 286–287, 290, 291, 296, 305, 352
Wilmington, NC 328, 329
Wilson, James Henry ("Harry") 16, 244, 249, 300, 333, 344, 346, 355, 356; Nashville campaign 122–145, 146; Overland 301, 305, 306; Shenandoah 64, 314, 315, 317, 319
Wilson's Creek battle 44, 92
Winchester, VA 150, 156, 158, 160; 1st battle 161, 165–166, 352; 3rd battle 314–317, 324, 325, 326, 356
Wise, Henry 307
Wittenberg, Eric, cited 239, 295, 313, 327
Wood, Thomas J. 73, 75, 76, 88, 101, 131, 134, 139
Woodworth, Steve, cited 24, 50, 63, 89
Wright, Horatio G. 304; Shenandoah 64, 310, 312, 315, 316, 321, 322, 326, 327; war's end 329, 331, 336, 338, 343

Yellow Tavern, VA 303, 314, 335

www.ingramcontent.com/pod-product-compliance
Lightning Source LLC
Chambersburg PA
CBHW081533300426
44116CB00015B/2613